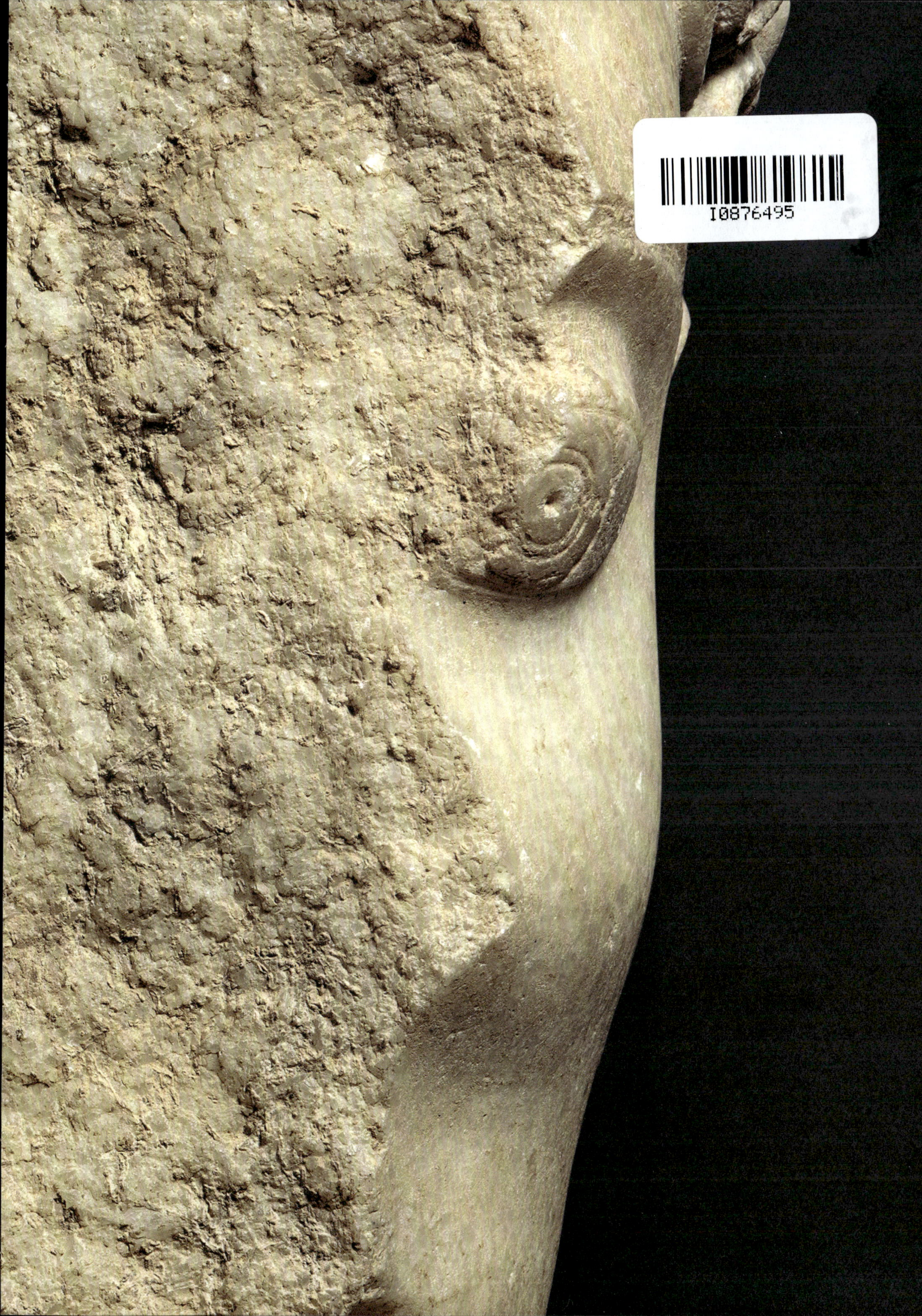

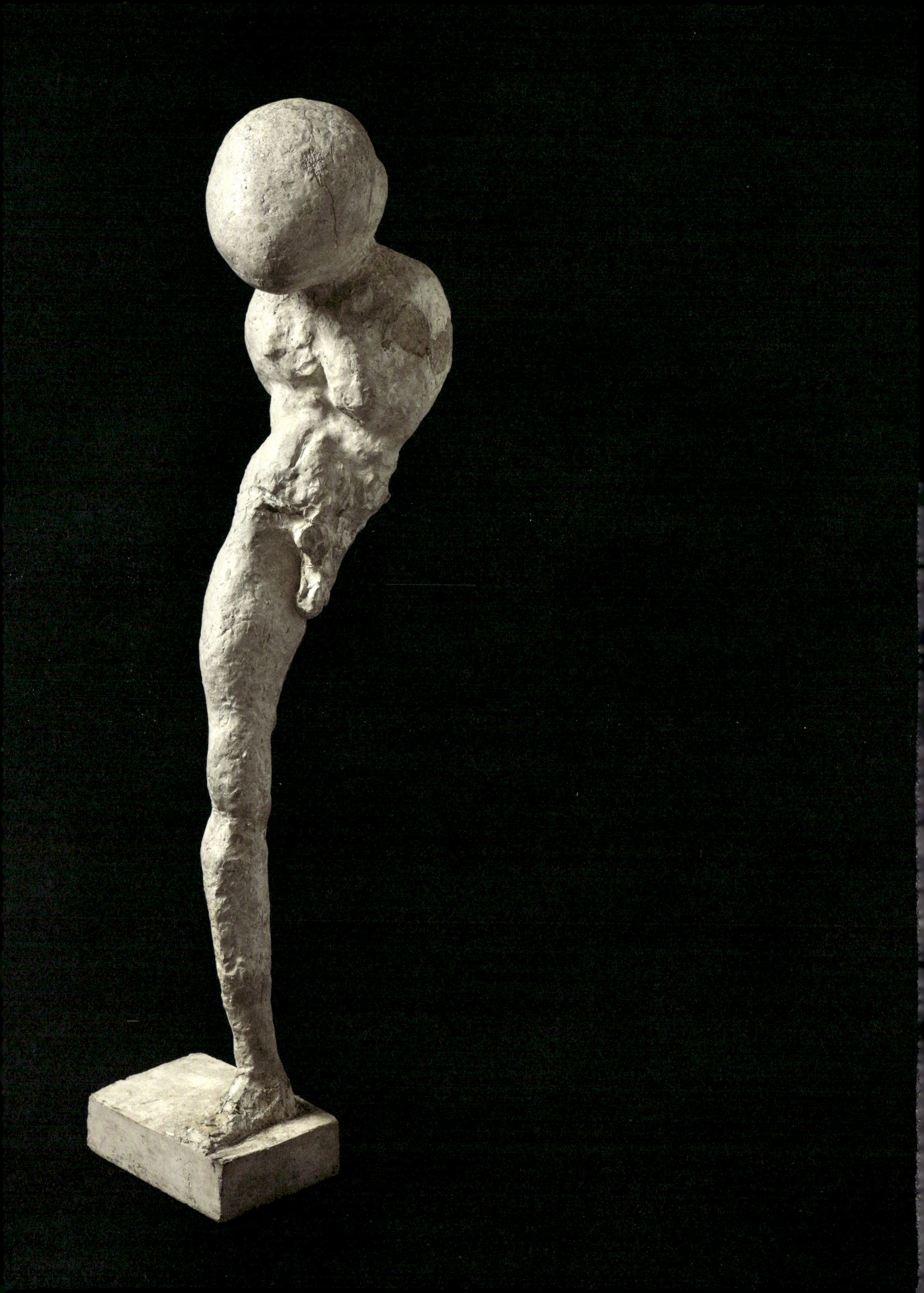

BROKEN

EDITED BY
C. D. Dickerson III and Andrew Sears

National Gallery of Art,
Washington

The University of Chicago Press,
Chicago and London

CONTRIBUTORS
Stanley Abe
Kaywin Feldman
Joanna Fiduccia
David Freedberg
Rosemarie Garland-Thomson
Dakota Hoska
Cannupa Hanska Luger
Timothy Morton
Miriam K. Said
A. E. Stallings
George Wheeler

BROKEN

THE POWER OF THE FRAGMENT IN SCULPTURE

CONTENTS

FOREWORD

Sculptures have been broken for as long as they have been made. We are intrigued by fragmented sculptures for a mix of psychological, aesthetic, and cultural reasons. What looks "broken" often feels strangely complete to us, and sometimes a broken sculpture is even more potent than it was when it was intact. Fragments compel us to consider the varied forces responsible for their making. Perhaps most familiar to us are fragments wrought by the inevitable passage of time, but many fragments document human behavior—for better or worse. Acts of breakage are integral to artistic practice, religious devotion, and societal renewal. Fragments also result from violence, whether through targeted attacks of iconoclasm or through the broader devastations of war, vandalism, and colonialism. *Broken: The Power of the Fragment in Sculpture* explores these tensions and more.

Fragments prompt responses that may seem contradictory at first: allure and awe alongside pity and empathy. Understanding brokenness's many facets requires engaging with a wide range of approaches. This volume reflects that mandate, bringing together perspectives from art history, conservation, philosophy, anthropology, social history, disability studies, ecocriticism, neuroscience, and poetry. As the lessons from these varied frameworks merge in our minds, they help us navigate the divisions of today's world by revealing surprising connections and paths to mutual understanding. Among the other ways fragments exert their influence is by inviting us to consider a world where breakage is embraced as a starting point for renewal and optimism.

The exhibition that this volume accompanies brings together more than ninety works spanning the third millennium BCE to the present, each possessing a distinct aesthetic force that bears witness to the damage it has sustained. It also emerged within a contemporary climate marked by the destruction, contestation, and removal of public monuments. These events have brought renewed international attention to the role of images in shaping collective memory and the responsibility of cultural institutions to engage with complex and sometimes contested historical legacies. *Broken* is the result of the fruitful collaboration and shared vision of the National Gallery of Art and the Fondazione Palazzo Strozzi. The exhibition unfolds across two venues, in Florence and in Washington. These are not identical repetitions, but two distinct installations calibrated to the architectural specificities and cultural contexts of each institution.

International collaborations like this exhibition are a key part of how our world can improve its current fractured state. The exhibition would not have been possible without the extraordinary generosity of public collections across the world, including in Cambodia, France, Germany, Greece, Italy, and Mexico. More than fifty institutions have entrusted us with the care of some of their most treasured objects, while also opening their storerooms and allowing us to borrow works that are lesser known, but whose stories are equally powerful. While museums are rightly understood as sites of preservation, they are also repositories of beautiful brokenness. What is more, many of the fragments have contested histories and meanings. By recognizing breakage as both a shared condition and an opportunity for healing (or at least reinterpretation), our exhibition proposes a new way of using museum collections to forge institutional partnerships.

Our sincere thanks go to C. D. Dickerson III, dean of the Center for Advanced Study in the Visual Arts and originator of the exhibition project, and to Andrew Sears, associate curator of northern European paintings, both at the National Gallery of Art, who have developed a broad and rigorous vision capable of offering new perspectives on our relationship with sculpture and the human figure. We also extend our gratitude to Laura and John Arnold, the Buffy and William Cafritz Family Fund, the Richard C. von Hess Foundation, and the Annenberg Fund for the International Exchange of Art, as well as the Comune di Firenze, Regione Toscana, Camera di Commercio and Città Metropolitana di Firenze, Fondazione CR Firenze, Intesa Sanpaolo, Fondazione Hillary Merkus Recordati, and the Committee of Partners of Palazzo Strozzi. Their generosity has made the two installations of this exhibition possible.

A final thanks is owed to the contemporary artists who have participated in this project. Many selected their own sculptures for the show or created new works for it. Their commitment to interrogating loss, erasure, and power resonates with a particular urgency today.

Kaywin Feldman
Director
National Gallery of Art

Arturo Galansino
Director General
Fondazione Palazzo Strozzi

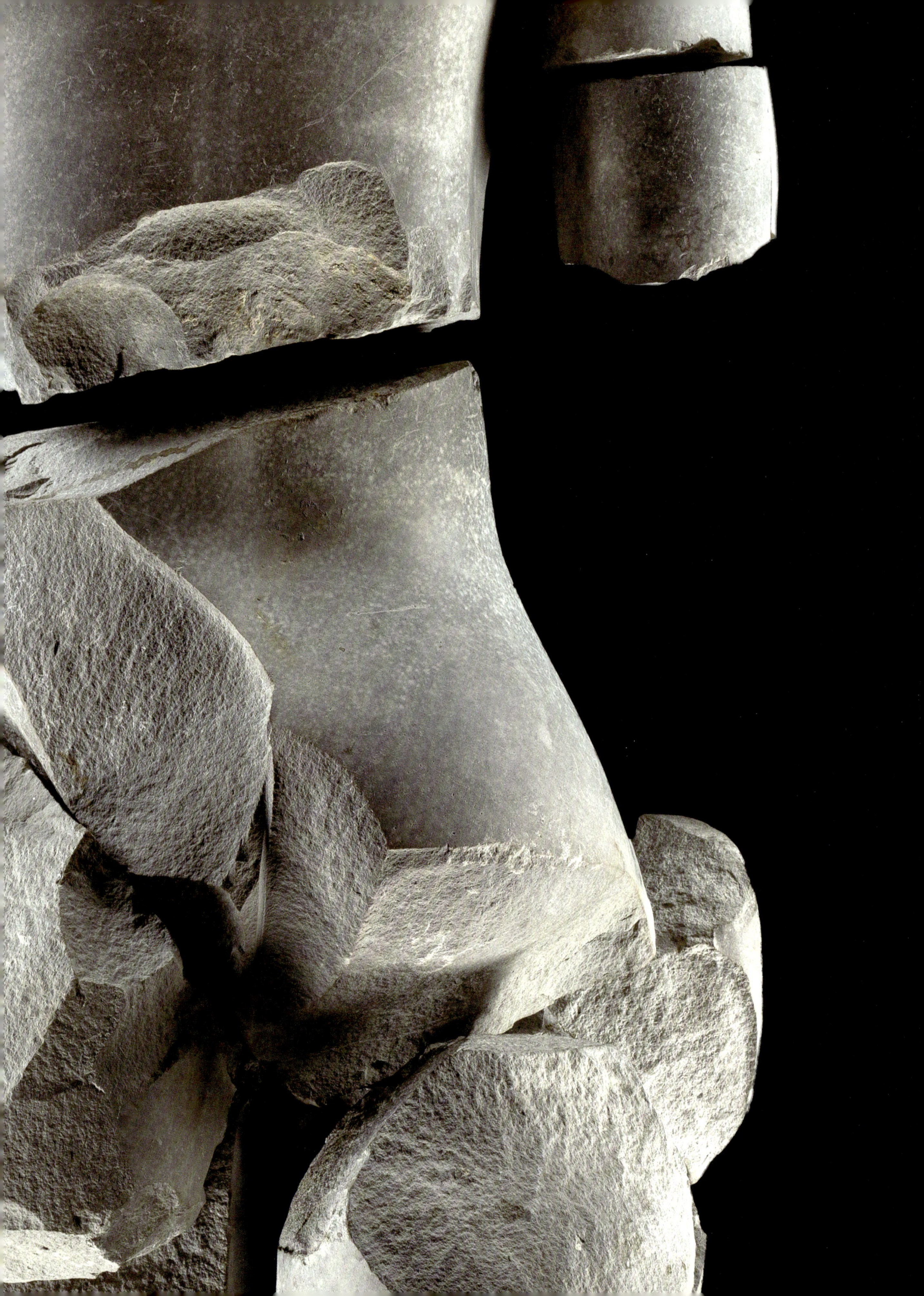

WHAT IS IT ABOUT THE FRAGMENT?

Detail, p. 211 (reverse)

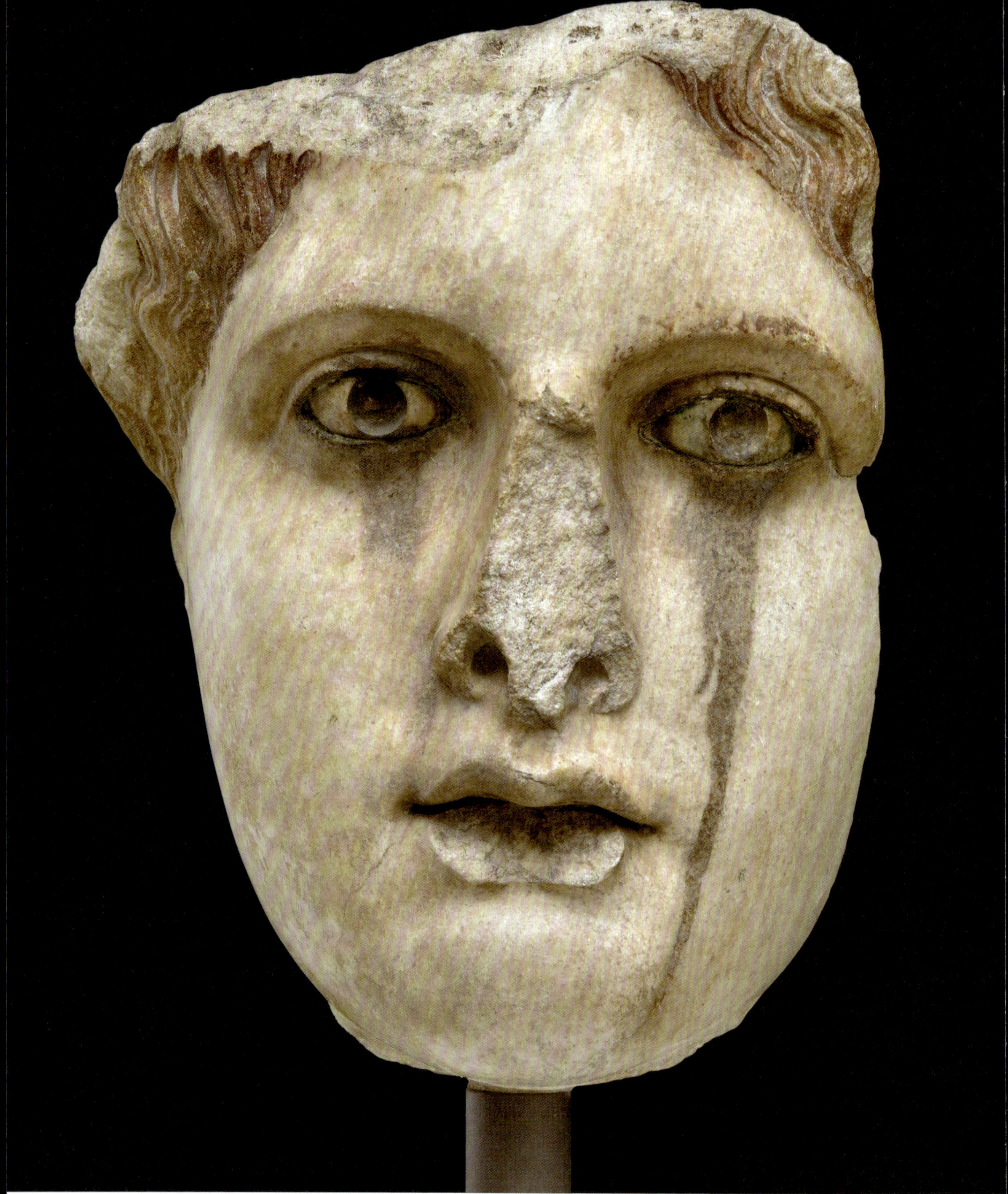

Roman (Athens), *Head of a Goddess Statue (probably Aphrodite)*, 2nd century CE, marble
Acropolis Museum, Athens, EAM 177
Cat. 26

BROKEN HEAD OF A WOMAN

A. E. Stallings

"You must change your life," the torso said—
With its blank chest, grim navel, pubic star.
But what about this woman's broken head
        That stares beyond us far

And long into the future, or the past.
She's seen some things. She stoppeth one of three
As though the lone survivor of a vast
        Storm-wracked catastrophe,

Or earthquake. And not just the stare, the stain
That runs like cheap mascara down her cheeks—
An alcoholic actress and her pain.
        It's of abuse she speaks:

A nose scarred by a splash of acid—lips
Bitten away with violence—the rape
Of war, oppression's crush, the dig that rips
        From the earth's womb. Let's drape

A veil of modesty—civilization—
Over this goddess—as she no doubt once
Was venerated: call it oxidation
        From eyelashes of bronze

(Plucked out and looted long ago) that smears
Her cheeks with verdigris. Isn't it strange,
Though, how we can't but read those streaks as tears
        For lives we cannot change?

FRAMING THE FRAGMENT

C. D. Dickerson III

For various periods between around 230 BCE and 670 CE, visitors coming to the Greek island of Rhodes were treated to an extraordinary sight on the beach fronting the principal harbor: the broken remains of a larger-than-life-size statue in bronze of the sun god Helios—the famed *Colossus of Rhodes*.[1] One person who was awestruck by the spectacle, probably around 70 CE, is the Roman historian and natural philosopher Pliny the Elder. After noting that an earthquake caused the statue to break and topple, he writes that "even lying on the ground, it is a miracle."[2] His brief description of what he saw—of the fragments strewn on the beach—cuts to the heart of this volume. As Pliny intimates, breakage is not necessarily a force of ruin. In the fragments it creates, it holds the power to transmit its own kind of spell. Looking at a statue in its broken state can be as electrifying as seeing it intact.

This volume and the exhibition it accompanies take it on faith that there is something about fragments that has always affected humans powerfully. The written record is replete with examples, while other evidence dates from prehistoric times. Furthermore, recent tools offered by the science of cognitive perception also allow an understanding of why fragments deserve to be treated as a distinct category of sculpture. But before pursuing those threads, it is first essential to establish that Pliny's fragment veneration was by no means an isolated case. His sense of wonder at seeing the *Colossus of Rhodes* in pieces on the ground would have been broadly understood during his own day.[3] By the end of the sixteenth century, it had become codified in the language of the Italian Renaissance, a mandatory first stop for any book concerned with situating the fragment in the history of sculpture and thus my primary focus here.

ROME AS CRADLE OF FRAGMENTS

Almost a full millennium separates Pliny from the next individual who is known to have written about fragments as a special case, the French theologian and clergyman Hildebert of Lavardin. During a trip to Rome in 1100 or 1123, he heaped praise on the city precisely because of the fragments he saw there: "Nothing is equal to you, Rome; although you are almost entirely a ruin. Broken, you teach how much you were worth when you were whole."[4] The passage interrelates several vital points. First, in centering Rome, it foreshadows the dominant position the city would come to occupy in the promotion of the fragment to cultlike status—a story told over the following pages.

Second, Hildebert touches on one of the most frequent ways that fragments have been acknowledged as working their magic: They provide a means of appreciating a lost totality.[5] If a fragment communicates a grandeur in its own right, or if a mass of fragments combines to convey an unthinkable sort of splendor, then we are left to assume that what's missing is many times more fabulous than what remains. Simultaneously, our estimation of the civilization responsible for creating what has disappeared soars, and we cling to the hope that through the fragments, we can retrieve an understanding (of sorts) of what's been lost.

An excellent demonstration—albeit one unknown to Hildebert—are the so-called *Giants of Mont'e Prama*, a group of colossal statues carved in sandstone that was discovered in thousands of pieces during the late 1970s in Sardinia. Among the earliest anthropomorphic figures found in Europe, they can be attributed to a people who flourished on the island between the eleventh and eighth centuries BCE. The ambitions of the sculptures, with boldly abstract faces and daringly projecting elements such as the shield held by a warrior, leave many questions about who these people were 〈 *fig.* 1 〉. On the basis of the fragments alone, we cannot help but think that the sculptures were the product of a civilization on the precipice of rivaling any in their world. As we try to fill in the pieces—both literally and figuratively—we are transported to prehistoric Sardinia and given a tantalizing glimpse of what once was.

The third point raised by Hildebert's passage concerns his use of the word "ruins." He applies it in a general way to indicate that Rome's built environment has fallen into a decrepit state. While a ruin is a part of a whole and thus technically a fragment, the word covers many different types of broken things, not only sculpture. Most often, it is used to describe a crumbled or fallen building. Admittedly, in a place like Rome, where ancient sculptures were abundant, broken columns, pediments, and vaults tended to blur in the imagination with broken heads, legs, and torsos. Nevertheless, this book draws a hard line between ruins in the architectural sense and the fragments of bodily sculptures that are its focus. This is not to discount that architectural ruins act a lot like sculptural fragments in how they move us—especially in mediating between past and present and making visible the ineluctable march of time.[6] But as the essays in this book collectively argue, when the broken object resembles a part of a human body, there is the potential for us to feel something radically different and more intensely personal. This distinction was already present in Italian thought by the early 1500s. While the idea of ruins moved in one direction, becoming a popular literary convention—how Renaissance humanists positioned themselves relative to the ancient world—it was not lost on some (especially artists) that special powers attained to fragmented statues, of which Rome had plenty.[7]

The story of the fragment's rise in Renaissance Italy begins during the thirteenth century with the earliest known description of a specific fragment locatable to Rome: the remains of a colossal statue in bronze of an emperor (likely Constantine)—a left hand, a head, and an orb (now part of the collections of the Musei Capitolini, Rome).[8] These are not to be confused with the marble fragments of an even larger statue of Constantine from the Basilica of Maxentius, including the giant hand with a pointed finger that has sat in the courtyard of the Palazzo dei Conservatori on the Capitoline Hill since the late fifteenth century ⟨ *fig.* 2 ⟩. Unlike those fragments of Constantine, however, the bronze ones cannot be identified with a specific statue or location. By the middle of the thirteenth century, they had come to be placed on columns in front of the Lateran Palace in Rome. This is how an Englishman known as Master Gregorius described seeing them during a visit to Rome around 1250 (or maybe earlier), and his reaction is revealing. He begins by emphasizing their enormous size, which he describes as "horrific," as though admitting that their presence struck a subconscious nerve.[9] He then pivots to a more reasoned assessment, extolling their beauty and the skill with which they were executed. The important part is Master Gregorius's brief moment of introspection, when he acknowledges that fragmented statues are different from whole statues in the kinds of emotions they engage.

In spite of examples like Pliny the Elder and Master Gregorius—for whom fragments were endowed with unique qualities that enabled them to engender special feelings—there was no shortage of discourse throughout the fifteenth century on how beauty was the primary measure by which fragments should be judged. Manuel Chrysoloras, a writer from Byzantium who visited Rome between 1410 and 1413, is a case in point. In his book on the differences between ancient and modern Rome, he considers the appeal of such fragments, noting that broken statues "seem beautiful even in their dismembered state."[10] Over and over we hear that

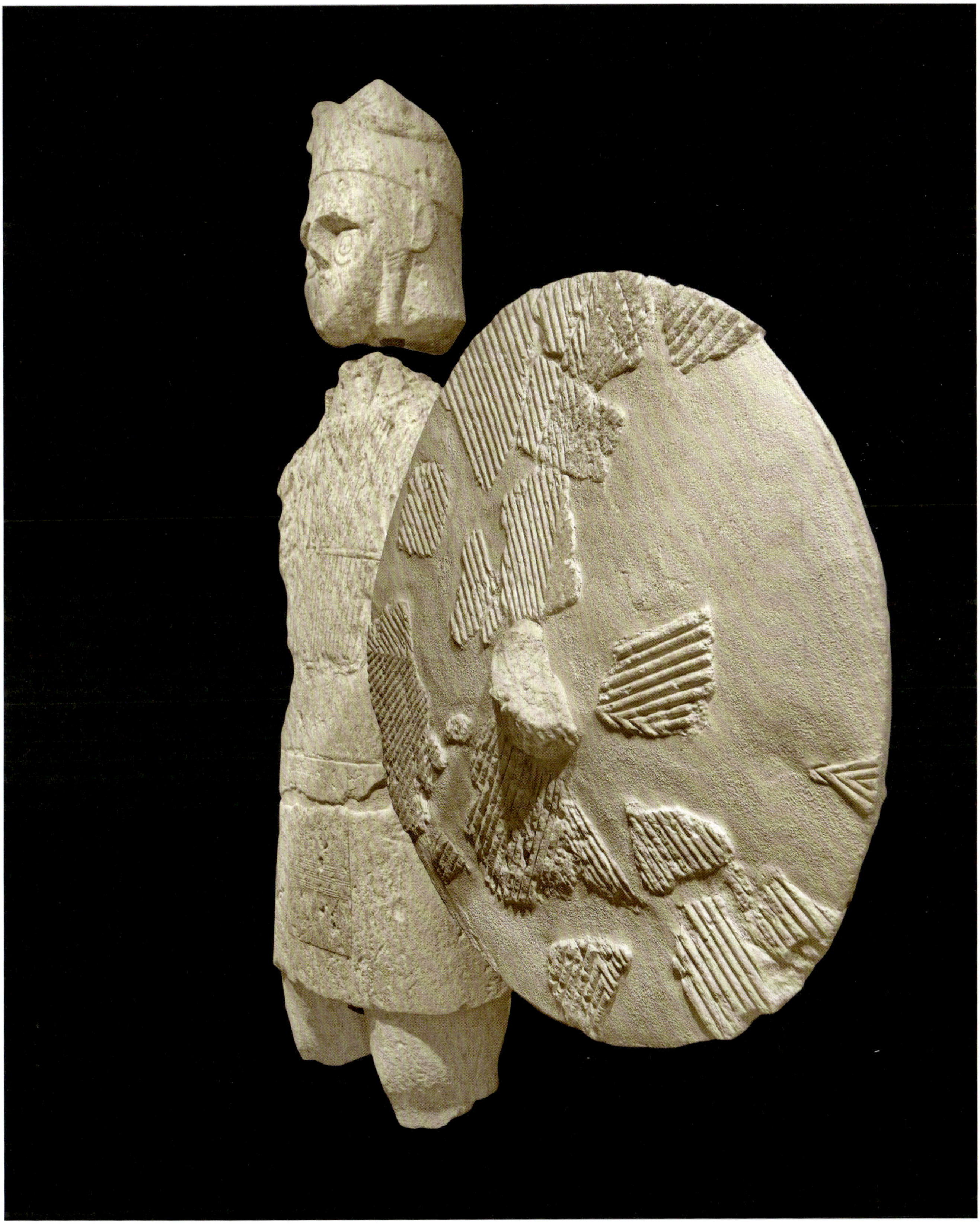

Fig. 1 Nuragic (Mont'e Prama), *Warrior with Shield,* c. 900–700 BCE, micritic limestone
Fondazione Mont'e Prama—Museo G. Marongiu, Cabras, 201879, 201881
Cat. 7

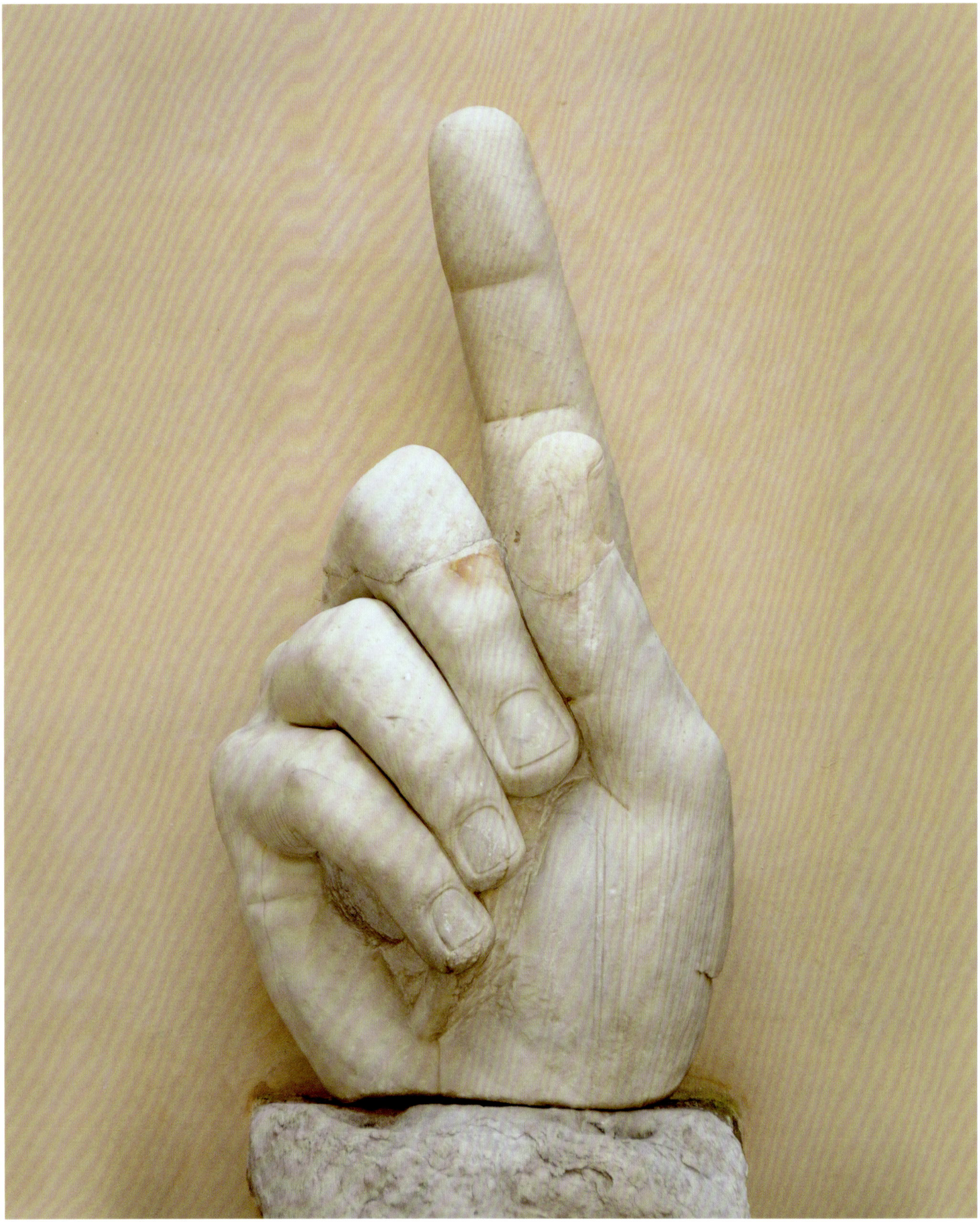

Fig. 2 Roman (Rome), *Right Hand of the Colossal Statue of Constantine*, c. 313–324 CE, Luni marble
Sovrintendenza Capitolina ai Beni Culturali, Musei Capitolini, Rome, MC S 786
Cat. 33

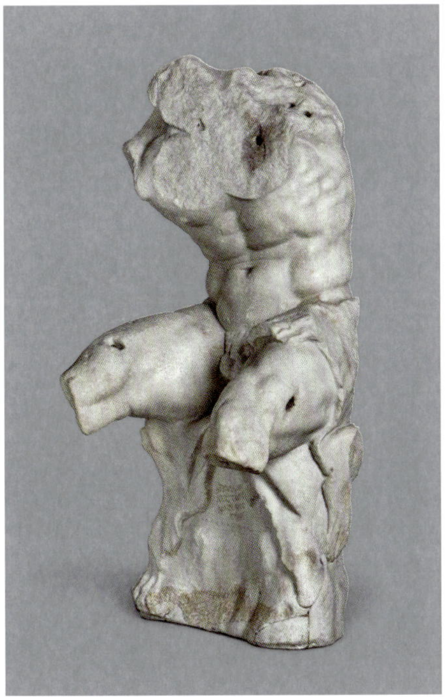

F *i g*. 3 Apollonios, *Torso Belvedere*,
1st century BCE, marble
Musei Vaticani, Vatican City, MV.1192.0.0

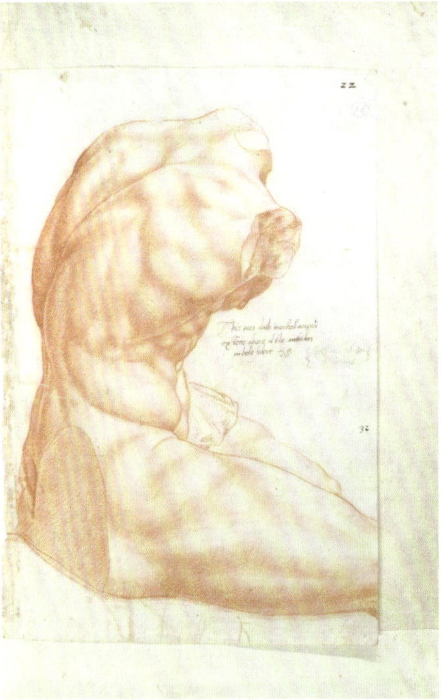

F *i g*. 4 Unknown artist, drawing after the *Torso Belvedere*, mid-1500s, red chalk
Trinity College, Cambridge, MS.R.17.3, fol. 22

there is something about fragments that simply pleases the eye, although we would be remiss to assume that we could know what beauty meant for Chrysoloras other than it likely had some basis in classical idealism. Surely, however, he did not see fragments as beautiful only because they retained some part of their classical identity. What else was he seeing? This book offers speculation, suggesting the range of sources from which fragments seem to derive their aesthetic power.

MICHELANGELO AND THE SANCTITY OF FRAGMENTS

By the end of the fifteenth century, the groundwork was solidly laid for the extraordinary reverence paid to the most famous fragment ever to turn up in Rome: the *Torso Belvedere*, which is first recorded in a collection on the Quirinal Hill in 1432 ⟨ *f i g*. 3 ⟩.[11] By around 1500 it had come into the possession of the sculptor Andrea Bregno. Here the first clues to its eventual fame emerge, as with this mention by an artist from Milan who visited Rome during the late 1490s: "Then in the house of a certain Master Andrea there is a nude torso without arms or neck the equal of which I have never seen in stone."[12]

From basically that moment forward, the *Torso* exerted a magnetic pull over artists, as demonstrated by the number of times it was drawn during the sixteenth century.[13] These drawings are particularly notable for how they celebrate the work's fragmentariness, with the *Torso* frequently shown at angles that draw attention to its fracture planes, which are often rendered with a pronounced meticulousness. A good example from around 1550, which is probably about twenty-five years after the *Torso* had moved to the statue court of the Belvedere at the Vatican Palace, is a drawing in red chalk in the collection of Trinity College, Cambridge 〈 *fig.* 4 〉.[14] The view is of the *Torso*'s back right side, which is presented with unsparing objectivity—no blurring of the break at the shoulder or concealing of the semicircular cut where the rest of the buttocks originally was. Although the draftsman is unknown, he was probably from England (or maybe Flanders), as attested by the caption on the drawing. The caption is more important for something else. It draws a direct line between the *Torso*'s fame and Michelangelo: "This pees doth michelangel exstem above all the anttickes in belle fidere."

Without Michelangelo, the *Torso Belvedere* would probably never have become the icon it is today, as the scholar Leonard Barkan has eloquently argued.[15] It was the artist's principal muse. He turned to it repeatedly throughout his career in ways both large and small. It offered a paradigm of heroic musculature and figurative tension that he could not ignore in his quest to surpass the ancients. Michelangelo must have seen its fragmentariness as a special asset here. The nature of the incompletion—no arms, no lower legs, no head—offered a vast range of possibilities for how he might reinvent the statue and thereby assert his place as the rightful heir to Apollonios of Athens, the *Torso*'s sculptor.

The *Torso Belvedere*'s fragmentariness may have inspired Michelangelo in another way: to appreciate how breakage, or incompleteness, could be an aesthetic end in itself. The artist's prolonged engagement with the *Torso* required a reckoning with its broken state. This surely helps explain, as Barkan convincingly notes, certain tendencies he developed as a sculptor, including his custom of leaving works unfinished (such as his acclaimed series of statues known as the *Slaves*) and earlier practice of breaking parts of his sculptures (such as the *Bacchus*) so that they resembled authentic antiquities newly pulled from the ground.[16]

Another manifestation can be added to the list thanks to a recent observation by the conservator Anthony Sigel. This relates to a terracotta model of a standing female in the Casa Buonarroti, Florence 〈 *fig.* 5 〉.[17] An unquestioned work by Michelangelo, it exists in a fragmentary state, most obviously lacking its arms. While the figure's left arm has definitely broken at the point we now see it, there are good reasons to think that the other arm was never any longer. The edges do not show the

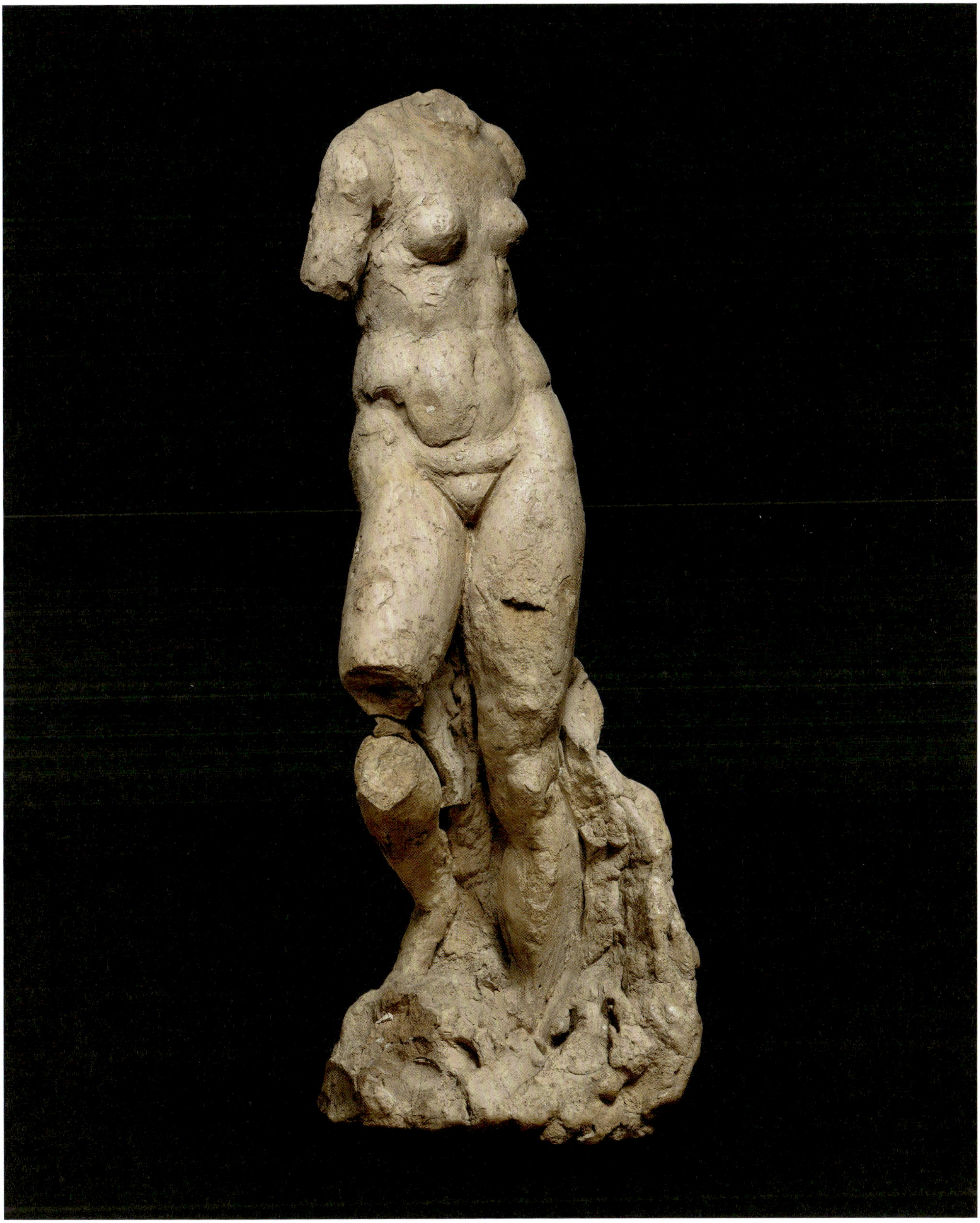

F*ig*. 5 Michelangelo Buonarroti, *Model of a Nude Woman*, c. 1533, terracotta
Casa Buonarroti, Florence, 193
Cat. 55

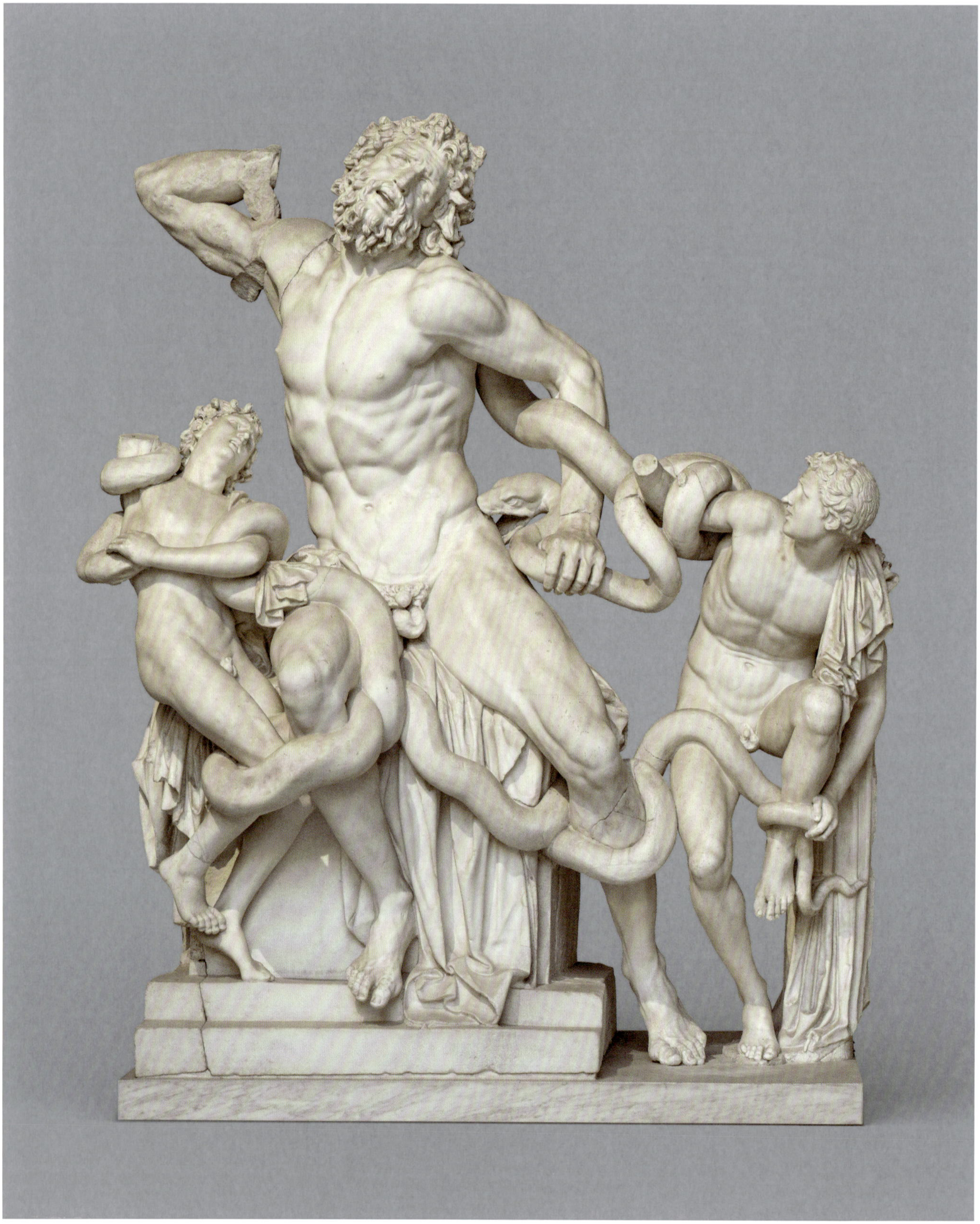

Fig. 6 Roman (Rome), *Laocoön*, c. 40–20 BCE or later, Parian marble
Musei Vaticani, Vatican City, MV.1059.0.0

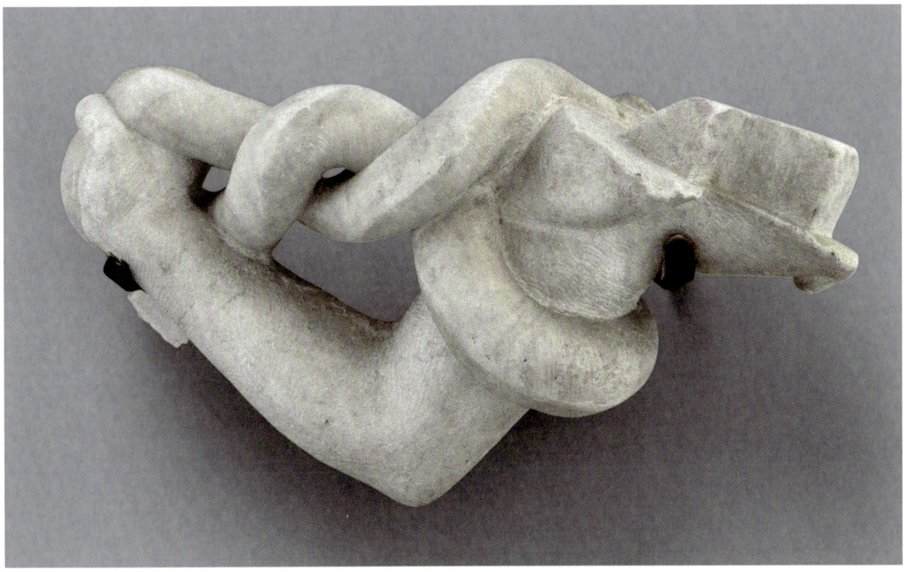

Fig. 7 Italian, *Restored Right Arm of the Laocoön*, 1540s or 1600s (before 1722), marble
Musei Vaticani, Vatican City, inv. 1067
Cat. 56

characteristic jaggedness of breakage but instead reveal the rounded contours of smoothing, where fingers have pushed the clay under the edges as part of a deliberate process of modeling. The finished statue, with its purposefully truncated arm, seems therefore to have been conceived as a fragment. Michelangelo's motives remain mysterious here but must be grounded in his understanding that fragments project an aura capable of enthralling viewers in positive (or at least in powerful) ways. Joanna Fiduccia, in her essay in this volume, considers where Michelangelo's innovation led: After having had hardly any effect on the history of sculpture for more than three centuries, it gave birth, in Auguste Rodin's hands in the late 1800s, to modern sculpture. The impulse to create sculptures that deliberately evoke fragments—an impulse that is both global and transhistorical—is also treated in essays by Kaywin Feldman and Andrew Sears.

MAKING FRAGMENTS TO REPAIR FRAGMENTS

Why was the *Torso Belvedere* never restored, while almost every other fragmented statue discovered during the Renaissance was? The answer highlights a tension between completeness and incompleteness, between modern and ancient, that was never fully resolved until Rodin. The *Torso* resisted restoration largely thanks to the protected status Michelangelo afforded it. The belief in its influence on his art also had a sanctifying effect. This is not to mean that Michelangelo was necessarily opposed to restoration. He authorized—if not actively contributed to—various restorations, including for the *Laocoön*, which he was among the first to inspect after its discovery in Rome in 1506 ⟨ *fig.* 6 ⟩.[18] In 1532 he was approached about restoring the statue but deferred, recommending that the job go to one of his favorite pupils, Giovanni Montorsoli, who ended up fashioning a new right arm for it.[19] There has been speculation that the arm was subsequently found wanting and that Michelangelo was called back in 1540, at which point he may have actually committed to the restoration.[20] A candidate for his contribution is an arm now displayed at the Musei Vaticani behind the *Laocoön* ⟨ *fig.* 7 ⟩. Rough in its manner of carving, it could date to well after Michelangelo's lifetime, in spite of an eighteenth-century tradition that it represents his direct intervention.[21]

If Michelangelo was prepared to vacillate on the subject of restoration, his average Italian contemporary was not, including those princes of the church and other wealthy individuals who were responsible for forming the major collections of ancient sculpture in Florence and Rome. Exceedingly rare were the broken statues left as they were found and proudly displayed as such. These tended to be other limbless and headless torsos like the *Torso Belvedere* and include a bronze example discovered near Livorno during the first half of the sixteenth century that became a prized possession of the first Grand Duke of Tuscany, Cosimo I de'Medici ⟨ *fig.* 8 ⟩.

The obsession with restoring sculptures was decades in the making but firmly entrenched by the middle of the sixteenth century, when it is possible to begin speaking about restoration as an industry.[22] The work wasn't all rote, however—even if many restorers may have seen themselves as factory workers of a sort, carving replacement part after replacement part and plugging them into place. There were also restorers who took a more enlightened view of their profession, appreciating how the art of fixing fragments was also an art of creating fragments. This would seem to describe the person who carved the first replacement head for the famed statue of the reclining *Ariadne*, one of the treasures acquired by Ferdinando I de'Medici, the third Grand Duke of Tuscany, during the late 1500s for his villa in Rome ⟨ *fig.* 9 ⟩. Seen by itself, which is how the head is now displayed in the Museo Archeologico Nazionale di Firenze, it presents as an authentic fragment of great visual allure, complete with a believable fracture plane where it would have mated with the original figure.

A fascinating text from 1539 validates the intrinsic worth of fragments while also looking ahead to the eighteenth century, when the pros and cons of restoration were still being debated. The author, Pietro Andrea Mattioli, takes umbrage at those who have leveled criticism against a cycle of frescoes in the Castello del Buonconsiglio in Trent ⟨ *fig.* 10 ⟩.[23]

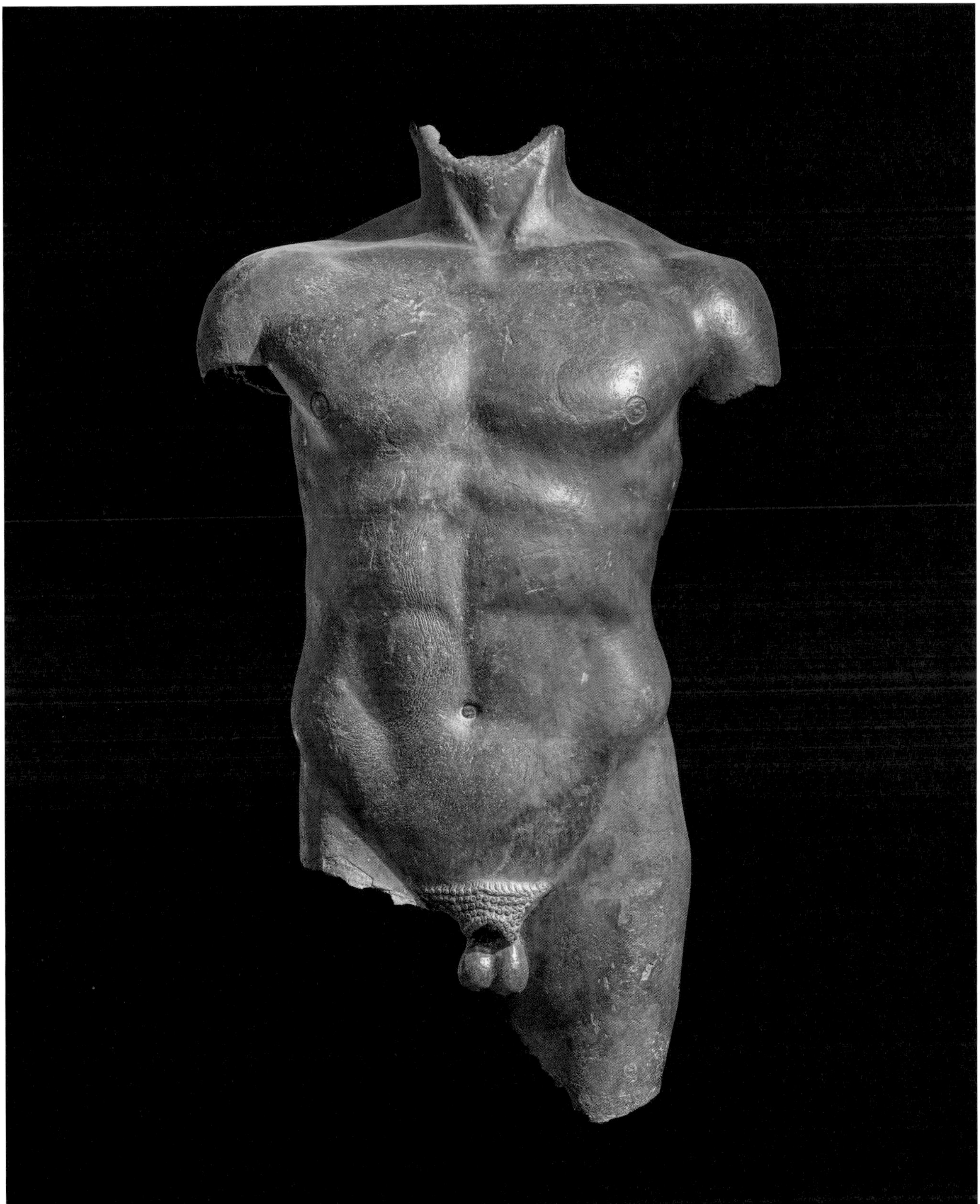

Fig. 8 Roman (Livorno), *Livorno Torso*, 1st century BCE, bronze
Museo Archeologico Nazionale di Firenze, inv. 1638
Cat. 19

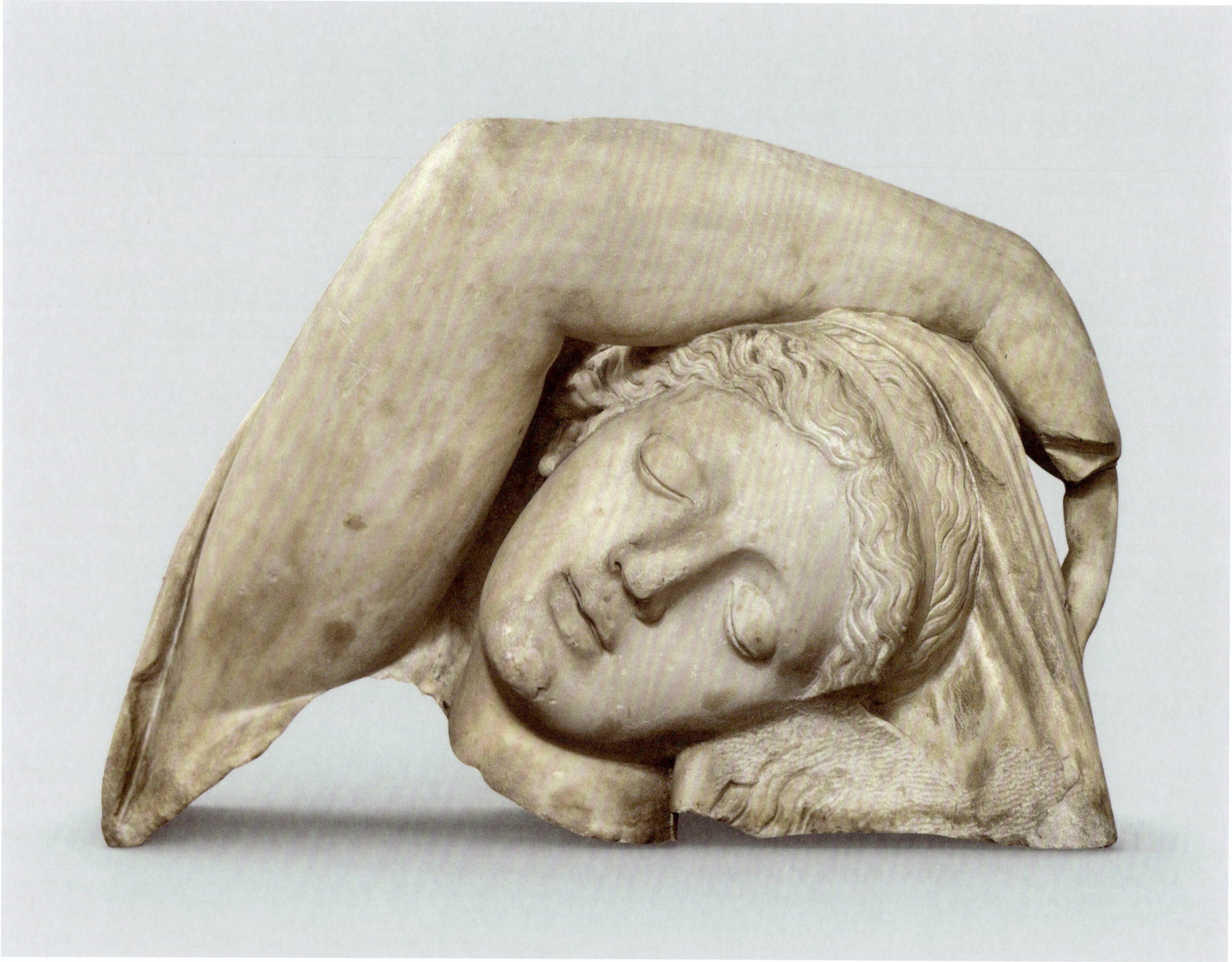

Fig. 9 Italian, *Restored Head and Right Arm of Sleeping Ariadne*, 1540s–1580s, Docimian marble
Museo Archeologico Nazionale di Firenze, inv. 13727
Cat. 57

The issue at stake was that the subject of the frescoes is a bunch of unrestored statues. Mattioli derides the critics as being "ignorant, or stupid, . . . because in their opinion the remains of an imperfect thing do not delight the eye."[24] The reader is later reminded that the condition of fragmentariness was also a condition of beauty, especially since breakage is synonymous with antiquity, which has no rival.

Jumping ahead centuries to Antonio Canova, the dominant sculptor working in Europe between the 1770s and his death in 1822, we can be certain that he would have appreciated Mattioli's directive, especially in 1815, when he was asked to recommend a plan of restoration for the group of ancient marbles from the Acropolis that Lord Elgin had brought

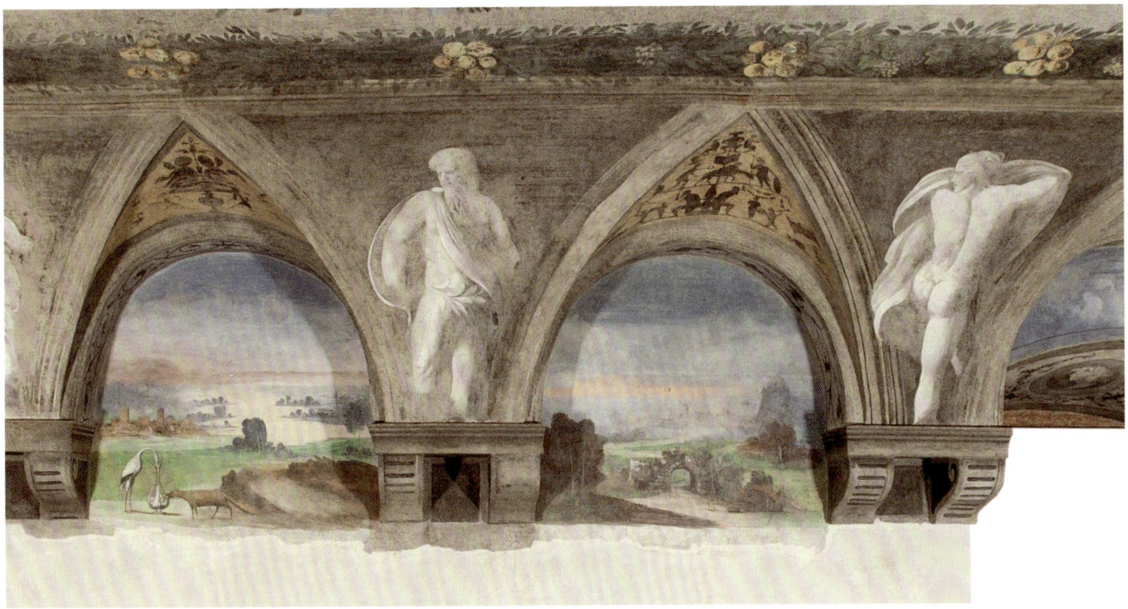

Fig. 10 Dosso Dossi, *Fables and Ruins* (detail), 1531, fresco
Stua de la Famea, Castello del Buonconsiglio, Trent

to London between 1801 and 1812. Canova flatly refused on the grounds that no one could ever improve on how the statues looked in their mutilated state.[25] For as prominent a figure as Canova to come down against restoration in a case as closely watched as the Elgin Marbles represented an inflection point for the fragment, whose autonomy as a category of art was about to be firmly sealed.[26]

As the news settled, however, Bertel Thorvaldsen, Canova's closest rival in sculpture, was busy with one of the most invasive restoration projects ever undertaken: the pediment sculptures from a temple on the Greek island of Aegina.[27] Although positively received when they were unveiled in 1830 in the new Glyptothek in Munich, they quickly lost their luster, as archaeologists decried the gross liberties that Thorvaldsen had taken with his restorations.[28] With an eye to Canova and the Elgin Marbles, successive directors of the Glyptothek began calling for their derestoration, which finally happened in the 1960s. By then it was universally recognized that the fragmentariness of fragments was a quality to be championed, as it represented the ultimate mark of authenticity.[29] This set the stage for the normalization of breakage in archaeological museums (at least in Western societies). The major effect on us is that we have become largely inured to the power of the fragment. We walk through museums of ancient sculpture, passing broken statue after broken statue, and rarely stop to reflect on the breakage: What does it mean?

THE QUALITIES OF GREAT FRAGMENTS

As the foregoing analysis has been focused on establishing, there is a lengthy tradition in Western culture of assigning special meaning to breakage—at least the kind of breakage responsible for turning whole sculptures of bodies into fragments. We have seen how broken sculptures have been admired for their beauty; for their power to astound, even to engender fear; for their capacity to hark back to a lost time (such as ancient Rome); for their ability to inspire new possibilities in art (as with Michelangelo); and for their appeal to our sense of authenticity. Certain fragments have come to be invested with extraordinary powers—the *Torso Belvedere* above all—and accordingly fetishized.

This book aims to widen our perspective on fragments in multiple ways. First it acknowledges that we must look beyond the decidedly Eurocentric lens through which the subject has traditionally been seen. Stanley Abe, in his contribution to this volume, questions what a fragment even is from the perspective of Buddhist cultures of East Asia. Focusing on the manifold problems with applying Western concepts of sculpture to Asian images, he asks us to embrace a more expansive way of seeing and understanding sculpture, especially outside of the West. Essays by Feldman and Sears further position the fragment globally, with consideration of several cultures from across millennia and the world that have centered the breaking of statues in their belief systems. What becomes evident is that the very definition of "fragment" and our responses to such objects are culturally relative. A perfectly intact crest mask made by a Bamiléké artist in central Africa, for example, is not the discrete work of art it may appear to be when displayed in a museum vitrine; it is actually a fragment, something prized from a whole, from the full costume meant to have been worn with the mask ⟨ *fig.* 11 ⟩. While not all regions of the world, including Africa, are the focus of their own essays here, it is hoped that the methodological seeds strewn across the book's contents will inspire future studies that can be more narrowly determined by culture.

Another direction in which the book moves is in admitting that it is insufficient to say that fragments belong to their own distinct category of art because they provoke special feelings. The preceding pages have attempted to tease out some of these feelings based on a reading of historical sources—mainly Italian. But what truly are those feelings, and why do they exist? A clearer understanding of them and the cognitive processes they engage comes through consideration of the qualities that seem to make certain fragments more affecting than others.

Few are more visually arresting than *Colossal Head of a Youth* ⟨ *fig.* 12 ⟩. How so gigantic a piece of marble could fracture so cleanly

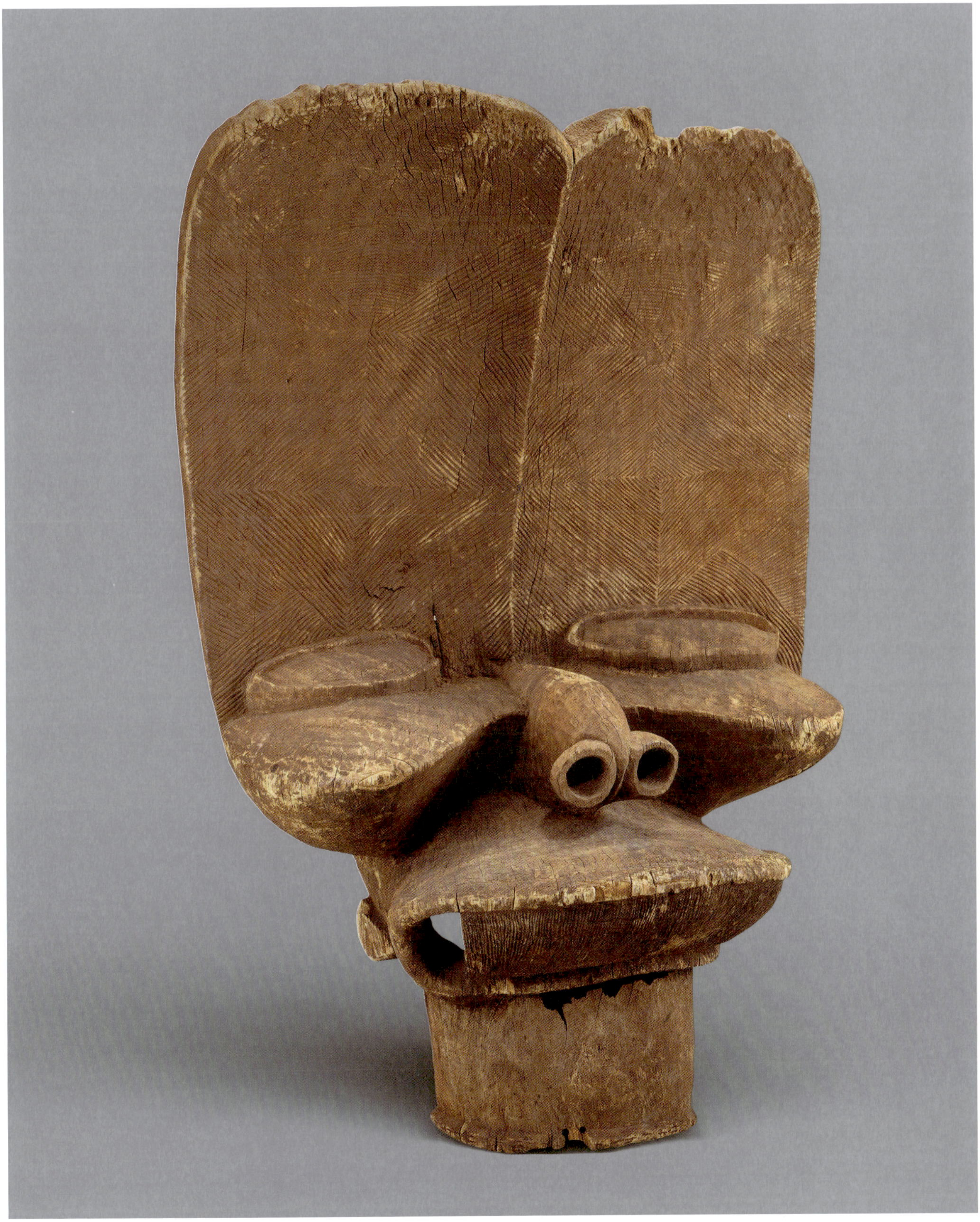

Fig. 11 Bamiléké (Bana, Cameroon), *Crest Mask (Tsesah)*, late 1800s, wood
National Museum of African Art, Smithsonian Institution, Gift of Walt Disney World Co., a subsidiary of The Walt Disney Company, 2005-6-5
Cat. 66

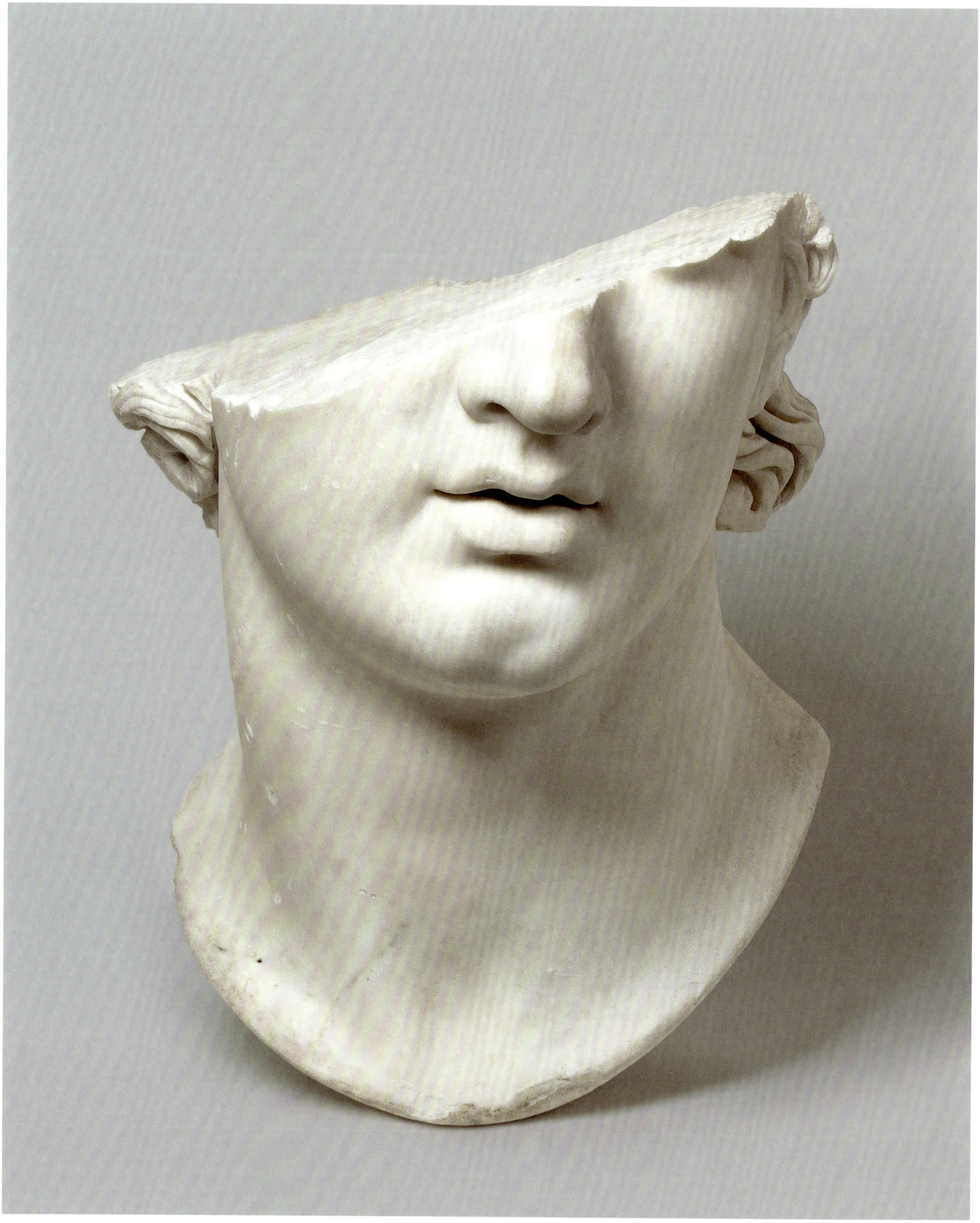

Fig. 12 Greek (Pergamon), *Colossal Head of a Youth*, c. 200–100 BCE, marble
Antikensammlung, Staatliche Museen zu Berlin, inv. AvP VII 283
Cat. 15

across the middle of the face defies normal expectations of how materials behave. Through various cognitive processes, including pattern recognition, perceptual processing, and mental modeling, the mind is able to look at the break, distinguish the material, and reconstruct the violent forces required to create the fragment.[30] In this form of embodied cognition, we feel what we perceive. A break that happens to look especially dramatic can therefore stimulate the brain to act as though it is responding to real drama and release stress hormones, which provoke those "special feelings"—that pitter-patter of the heart. This underscores why sculptures made of hard materials tend to produce "better" fragments: They are more susceptible to producing the kinds of fractures that our brains associate with a violent act of breakage. George Wheeler presents a case study of one material, red quartzite, in his essay in this volume.

Colossal Head of a Youth engages our cognitive and sensory systems in another way. As explained by David Freedberg in his essay, this engagement involves mirror neurons, which are responsible for causing our brain to simulate actions or sensations that we observe in other people. We watch someone touch a sharp object, and we feel the sting in our own finger. With *Colossal Head of a Youth*, we flinch in pain at the thought of what it is like for someone's head to be split in two across the eyes—or for someone's face to be erased, as with Adriaen de Vries's terracotta model of a satyr, a victim of an apparent fall ⟨ see Freedberg *fig.* 6 ⟩. There is even an area of the brain that activates when we are engaged in facial recognition (the fusiform face area), which could explain why we seem to flinch more strongly at the sight of a damaged or absent face as compared with any other body part (see pages 49–50). That being so, fragments with severed limbs, such as *Torso of Christ* ⟨ see Freedberg *fig.* 10 ⟩, or that exist solely as limbs, such as *Left Arm of a Boxer* ⟨ *fig.* 13 ⟩, are also effective at triggering pain as a mirror response. That pain can be transcended, however, as Rosemarie Garland-Thomson attests in her contribution to this book. Drawing on the methodologies of disability studies, she demonstrates how fragments demand compassion more than pity—a response that allows them to be understood as persistent wholes.

The brain is wired to move in other directions when looking at fragments. Among the reasons Michelangelo was attracted to the *Torso Belvedere* was the enjoyment he took in restoring it in his mind's eye. According to the neural dynamics of modal and amodal completion, we are programmed to fill in the missing parts of a three-dimensional object, a process that activates reward neurons—hence our feelings of satisfaction (see pages 54–57). An early acknowledgment of the phenomenon can be credited to the esteemed eighteenth-century archaeologist Johann Joachim Winckelmann. In his lengthy description of the *Torso*

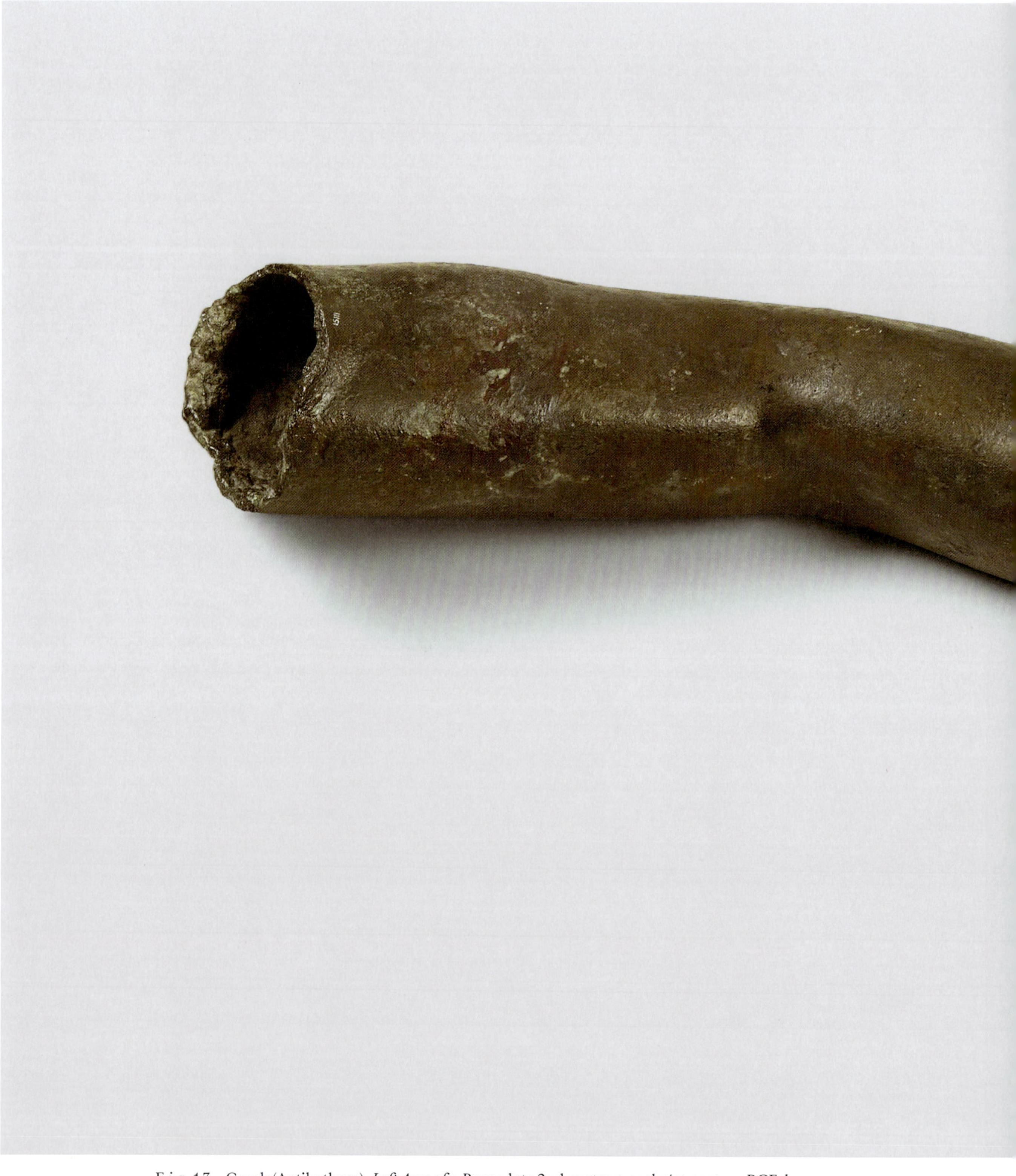

Fig. 13 Greek (Antikythera), *Left Arm of a Boxer*, late 2nd century–early 1st century BCE, bronze
Hellenic National Archeological Museum, Athens, HNAM X 15111
Cat. 18

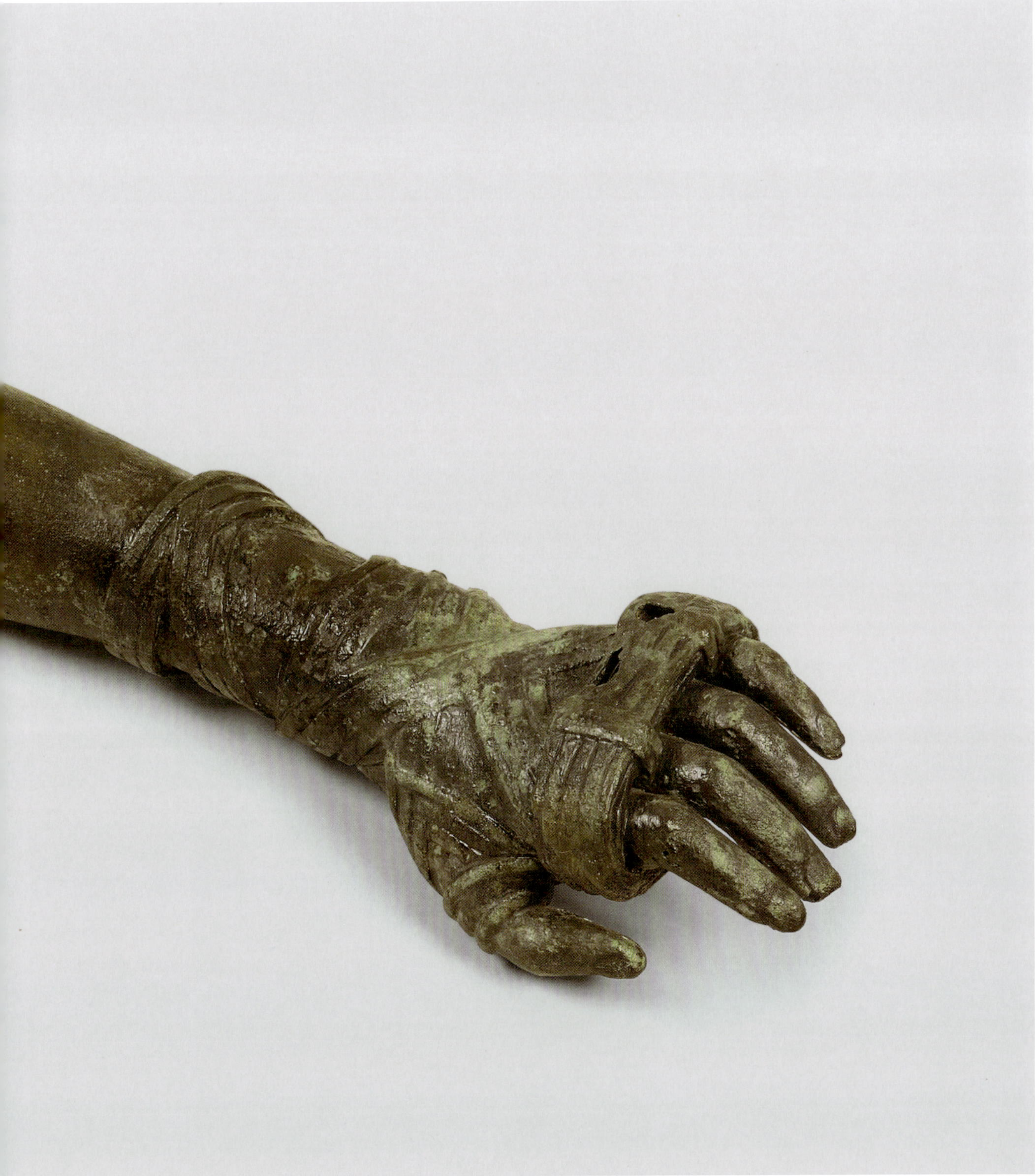

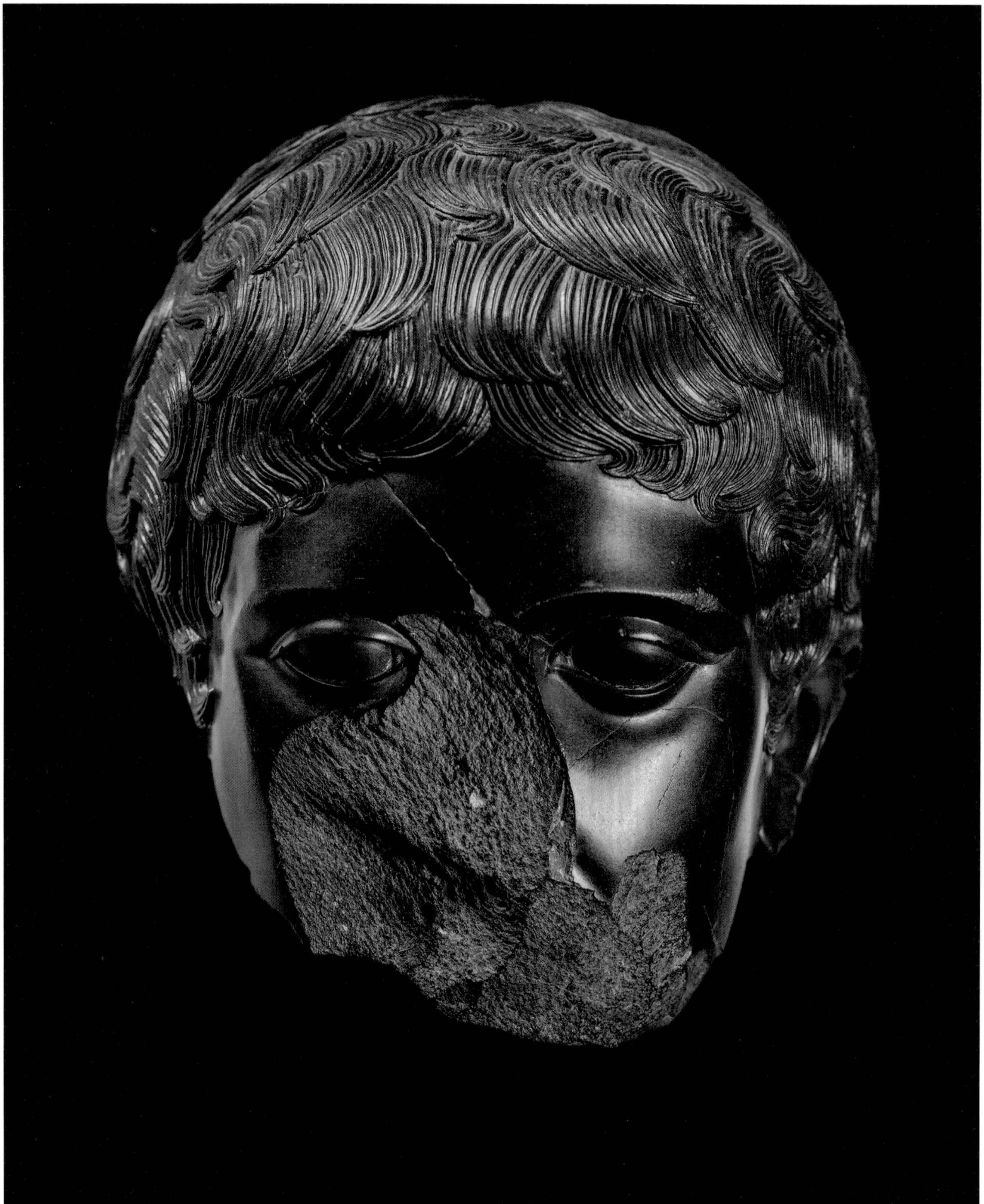

Fig. 14 Roman, *Head of a Youth (Ephebe)*, late 1st century BCE–early 1st century CE, basanite
Musei Vaticani, Vatican City, inv. 10134
Cat. 21

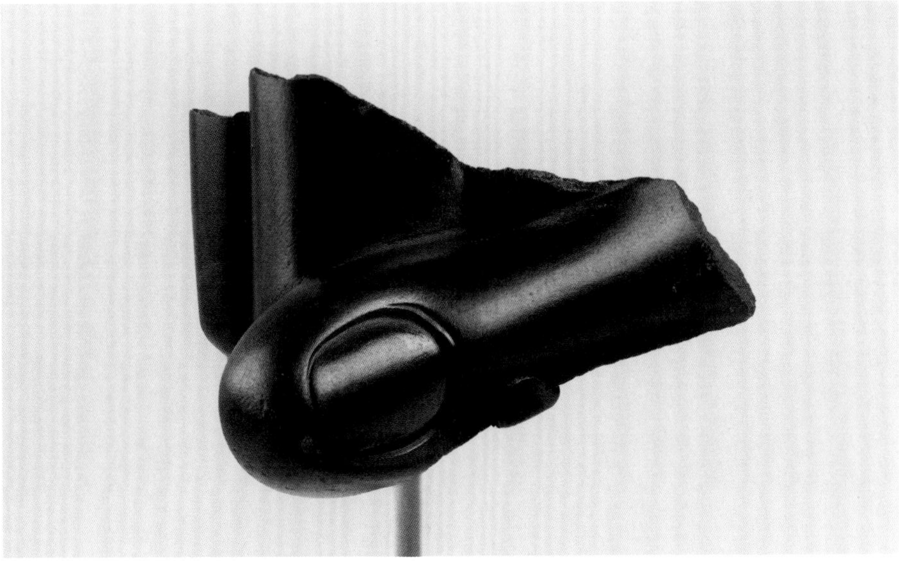

Fig. 15 Egyptian, *Fragment of a Hand from a Colossal Statue*, c. 664–630 BCE, basalt
Brooklyn Museum, Charles Edwin Wilbour Fund, 37.264E
Cat. 9

Belvedere, he recounts enthusiastically how whenever he contemplated the fragment, the missing parts would rise in his eyes and become part of the joy the statue brought him.[31]

Assumedly Winckelmann was also accustomed to letting his mind "heal" the breakage of one of the most stunning fragments he owned: *Head of a Youth (Ephebe)*, sculpted in basanite around the end of the first century BCE ⟨ *fig.* 14 ⟩. The work introduces yet another pleasure of looking at fragments. We are made to concentrate on details we might otherwise overlook, as with the exquisitely carved hair of the young man, which gains a new focus in the absence of the full face. Another example is *Fragment of a Hand from a Colossal Statue* ⟨ *fig.* 15 ⟩. It is made of basalt, an extremely hard stone similar to basanite that also takes sharp cuts from metal. The material lends itself to producing precisely the kinds of sumptuously carved details we enjoy scrutinizing as though they were their own sculptures. Who would think to pay reverence to this regal thumb were it still affixed to its colossal body?

A comprehensive picture of the various qualities of fragments and the types of feelings they may evoke takes shape over the course of this book. In their essay, Miriam K. Said and Andrew Sears invite us to consider how our response to fragments might change on learning that the breakage was caused by humans. While principally focused on iconoclasm, their essay also acknowledges that breakage could be for a host of reasons directly tied to human activity, including war, which has taken an indiscriminate toll on so much sculpture from antiquity to the present.

Breakage could also be more highly intentional, as with *Head of Bishop Andrea de' Mozzi*, a work by the Florentine sculptor Arnolfo di Cambio from around 1300 ⟨ *fig.* 16 ⟩. Originally belonging to a full-length effigy as part of a tomb, the head was deliberately cut away. The discussion of violence against sculptures over time also puts into perspective how fragmentation can be about positive change in society. From recent history, an obvious example is the many Confederate monuments dismantled or broken up from 2020 to 2022.

Timothy Morton's essay in this book, by contrast, considers the least discriminate of forces: nature. Morton meditates on how statues made into fragments through natural causes can raise ecological consciousness. Regardless of whether these fragments hold a capacity to moralize, there is an undeniable beauty in the strange accidents of form that result from wind and rain playing over the surface of a wood sculpture for decades or longer, as happened to this *hampatong* (ancestor figure) in the forests of Borneo ⟨ *fig.* 17 ⟩. Here erosion is accepted as a form of breakage because it renders whole sculptures incomplete, turning them into parts of their former selves—thus fragments. We acknowledge that in some cases (as perhaps here) makers may have intended their works to erode, which highlights the fine line that can exist between nature as sculptor and human as sculptor. The tension is also present in another work at Yale: a figure carved in wood by an artist from the Jarai culture of central Vietnam ⟨ *fig.* 18 ⟩. The sculpture would have been installed at a tomb on the occasion of a solemn send-off ceremony, then left to decay alongside the buried body that it guarded.[32]

Pliny the Elder, in his response to the *Colossus of Rhodes*, touches on an emotion that threads its way through the entire book: awe. He calls the fragments a "miracle," which suggests that there was something about them that he could not explain and that beckoned to a higher power. As he goes on to write, he was confounded by their immensity—how normal people couldn't even wrap their arms around the thumb. And when he went to look inside them, he confronted "vast caverns seen yawning," as though he couldn't fathom that he was standing witness to an incredible feat of mere mortals.[33] A mysterious force within him was clearly awakened. While there is unquestionably a neurological basis for some of what he felt, there is a lot that cannot be explained and is perhaps best captured by awe and its close cousin, wonder.[34] (Awe is a visceral response, whereas wonder is disengaged from emotion, a rational exploration of why.) This volume offers another glimpse at awe in a poem by A. E. Stallings inspired by a specific fragment. Her words express this sensation at the same time that they provoke it in the reader—not dissimilar to how the *Torso Belvedere* shook Michelangelo, fueling him to create works that leave us awestruck in their turn.

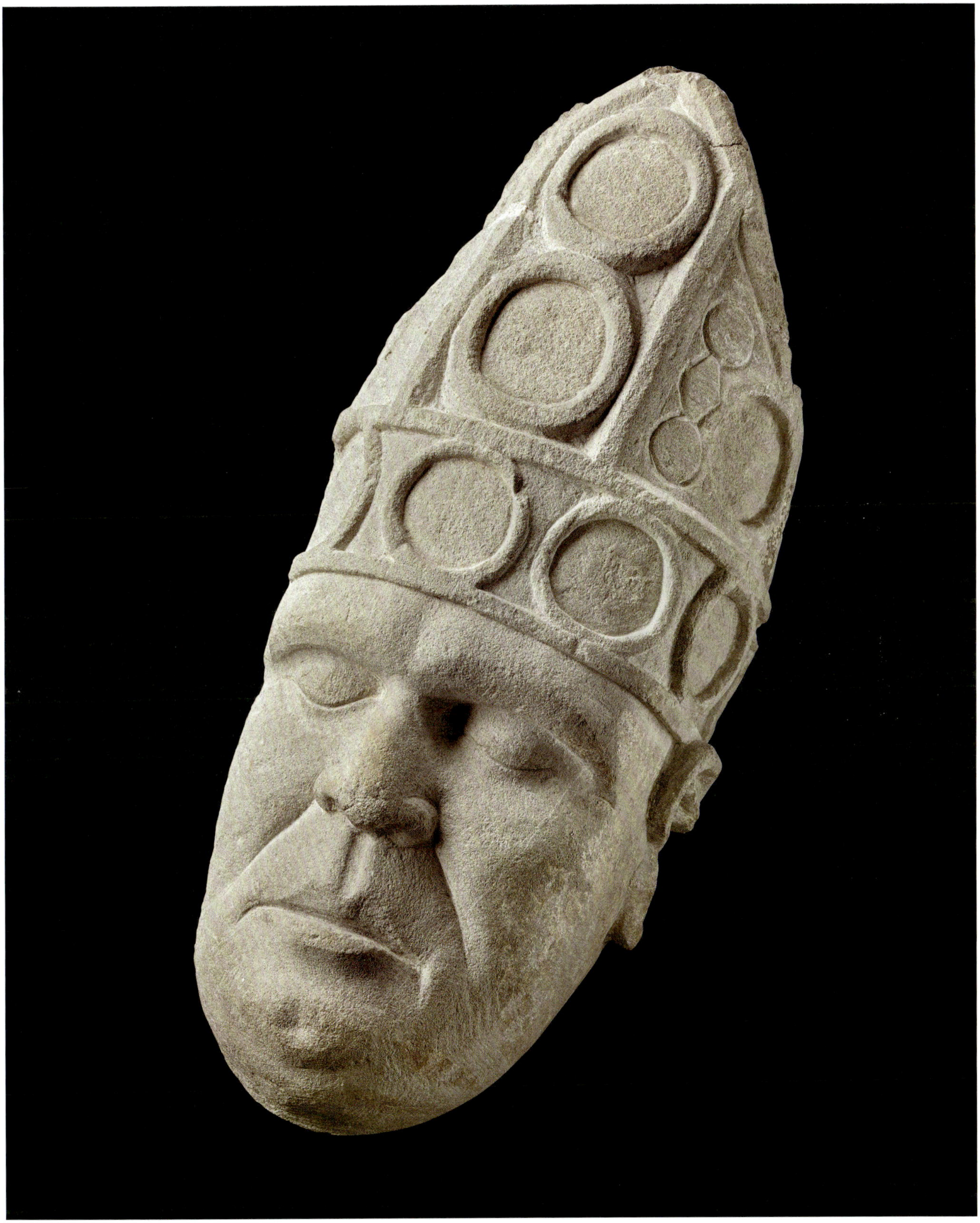

Fig. 16 Arnolfo di Cambio, *Head of Bishop Andrea de' Mozzi*, c. 1296–1300, pietra serena with traces of pigment
Private collection
Cat. 42

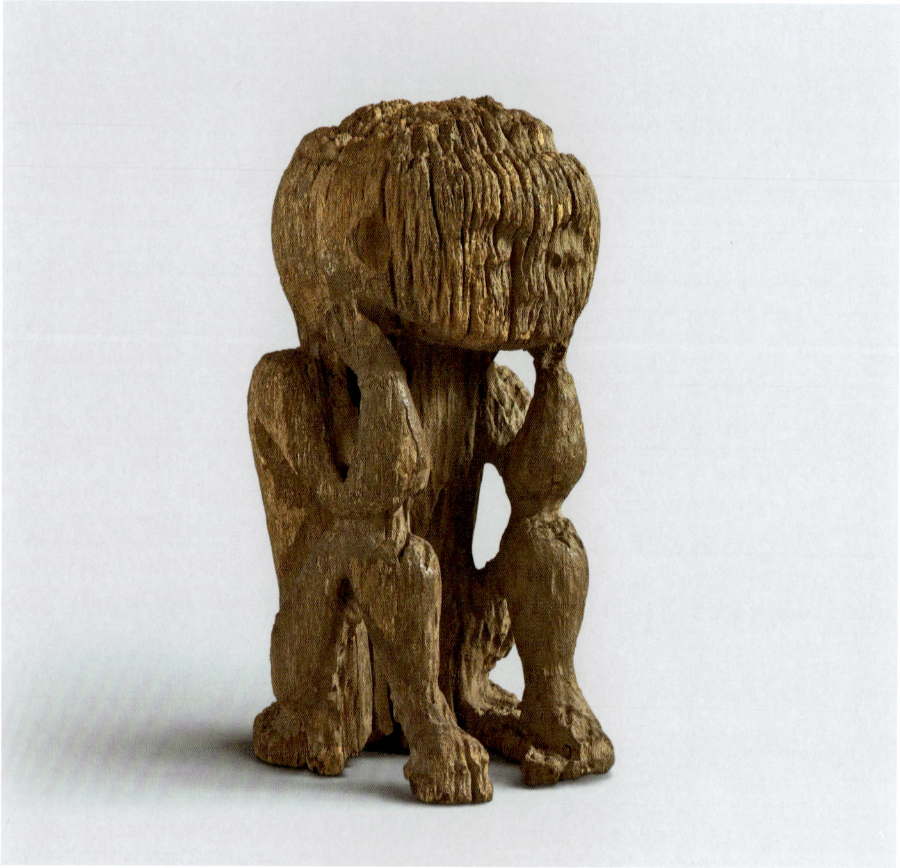

Fig. 17 Ngaju (Borneo), *Ancestor Figure (Hampatong)*, late 1600s–1800s, wood
Yale University Art Gallery, promised gift of Thomas Jaffe, B.A. 1971
Cat. 60

Fragments are unusually effective at triggering such responses because they are bound up with so many transcendental subjects, including the vastness of time and why humans are moved to break that which is intrinsically beautiful. Cannupa Hanska Luger is among the many sculptors today whose work plies in the aesthetic of fragmented bodies (including animal, human, and mythical). As he discusses in the conversation moderated by Dakota Hoska that concludes this book, Luger is drawn to the forms left by breakage for many reasons, but most especially because of their ability to underscore why breakage is an essential component of how cultures, societies, and people regenerate themselves—a different sort of provocation that leaves the viewer not in awe so much as prepared to confront the challenges of the present. To frame the fragment is ultimately to reinforce the boundless ways that fragments communicate their power and tie us together in our exploration of what it means to be human and thus better people.

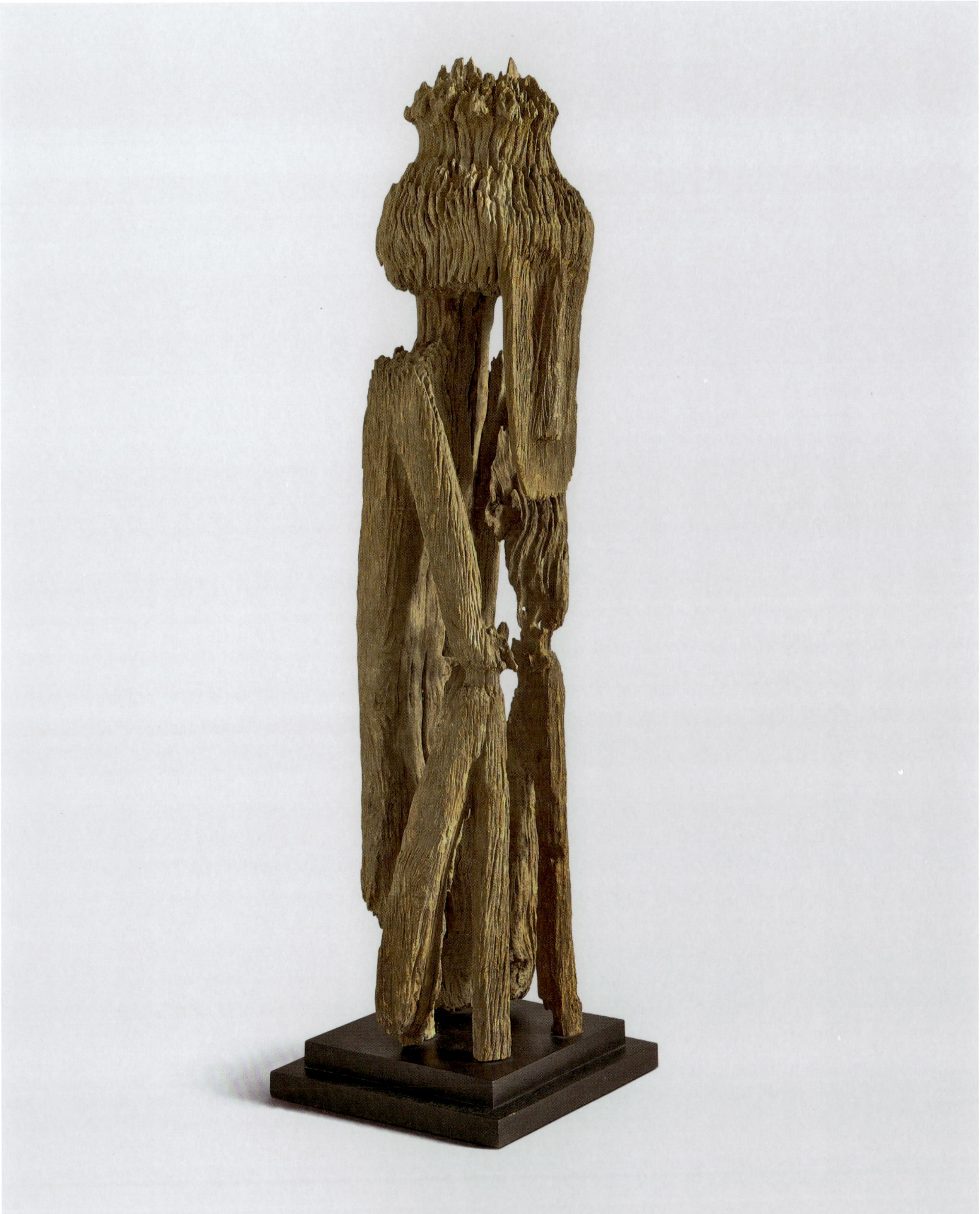

F*ig.* 18 Jarai (Central Highlands, Vietnam), *Figure Wearing a Mask*, late 1600s–1700s, wood
Yale University Art Gallery, promised gift of Thomas Jaffe, B.A. 1971
Cat. 59

ENERGIES OF THE FRAGMENT

David Freedberg

Most writers, when they speak of fragments, speak of melancholy. I will speak of their energies.

In the opening section of his great compendium of theological knowledge the *Summa Theologiae*, written between 1266 and his death in 1274, Saint Thomas Aquinas asserts the following: "Three things are required for beauty: first of all, integrity or wholeness, since *things that are lessened are by that very fact ugly*; second, due proportion or harmony; third, the clarity whereby things that have radiant colors are beautiful."[1] Most readers of this book are unlikely to agree with the first part of this tripartite claim. Of course, many fragments are indeed ugly; others testify to little more than the irreparable rupture of beauty and the vicissitudes of history, accident, and injustice. Countless pages have been dedicated to them. From the Bible to that great and moving writer on art, history, and conflict, Walter Benjamin, there is no shortage of writings about the tragedies that fragments embody. But who could look at most of the fragments illustrated in these pages without thinking them not just beautiful, but very beautiful indeed—despite (or perhaps even because of) the fact that they are *not* whole?

There are many arguments for this position not only in the West but in other cultures across the globe as well. The Japanese concept of *wabi sabi*, for example, where beauty is found in what is broken and incomplete, is the very opposite of Aquinas's view. It is a reminder that the impermanent also matters, both in nature and in art. The height of the aesthetic expression of this attitude is represented by *kintsugi*, the practice of using gold to outline or fill in the cracks and the parts of objects that are broken, as if to make clear the innate beauty and value of what is broken. It is a technique of repair that makes the incomplete even more precious than before. Although these terms do not apply specifically to sculpture, it is worth recalling such notions from other shores as we consider the works illustrated in this book.

BEAUTY WITHAL

The Greek *Colossal Head of a Youth* from the Pergamon Museum in Berlin ⟨ see Dickerson *fig.* 12 ⟩ has often been identified, not implausibly, as an idealized head of the young Alexander. It's certainly broken, but few viewers would deny its allure; even the diagonal slice across the head seems beautiful in itself. The mouth and the soft cleft of the chin are chiseled with such delicacy and sensitivity to light and shade that they seem nothing short of miraculous. One might even think the head was "not made by human hand,"[2] as Early Christians said of images of Christ that had such exceptional aesthetic and miracle-working effects that they could only be of divine origin.

Now consider a completely different kind of fragment, in terms of both scale and context. The tiny Egyptian fragment of a statue of Akhenaten of almost eleven hundred years earlier ⟨ *fig.* 1 ⟩ shows only the lips and nose of its subject—a mere sliver in comparison with *Colossal Head of a Youth.* But what a sliver! Akhenaten's features are endowed with a lush smoothness and sensuality that convey a sense of flesh that is even more convincing than in the Greek work. It's as if the sculptor of this small fragment of polished limestone had an almost supernatural command of how light passes over the gentle undulations of flesh.

In both these works, the substantial assault on their wholeness does not detract from the powerful sense of beauty they convey. Our attention to the works and our wonderment at their forms are first aroused by precisely the losses they have suffered. They are decidedly not a diminution of the beauty of the works. If anything, they enhance them.

THE EFFICACY OF THE INCOMPLETE

Friedrich Nietzsche made an important argument in favor of fragments in his great book of aphorisms *Human, All Too Human: A Book for Free Spirits* (1878). In it he claims that "just as figures in relief produce so strong an impression on the imagination (*die Phantasie*) because they are as it were on the point of stepping out of the wall but have suddenly been brought to a halt, so the relief-like, incomplete presentation of an idea, of a whole philosophy, is sometimes more effective than its exhaustive realization: *more is left for the beholder to do*, he is impelled to continue working on that which appears before him so strongly etched in light and shadow, to think it through to the end, and to overcome even that constraint which has hitherto prevented it from stepping forth fully formed."[3] It would be hard to find a clearer statement of the particular relevance of fragments to our understanding of art, not just for the

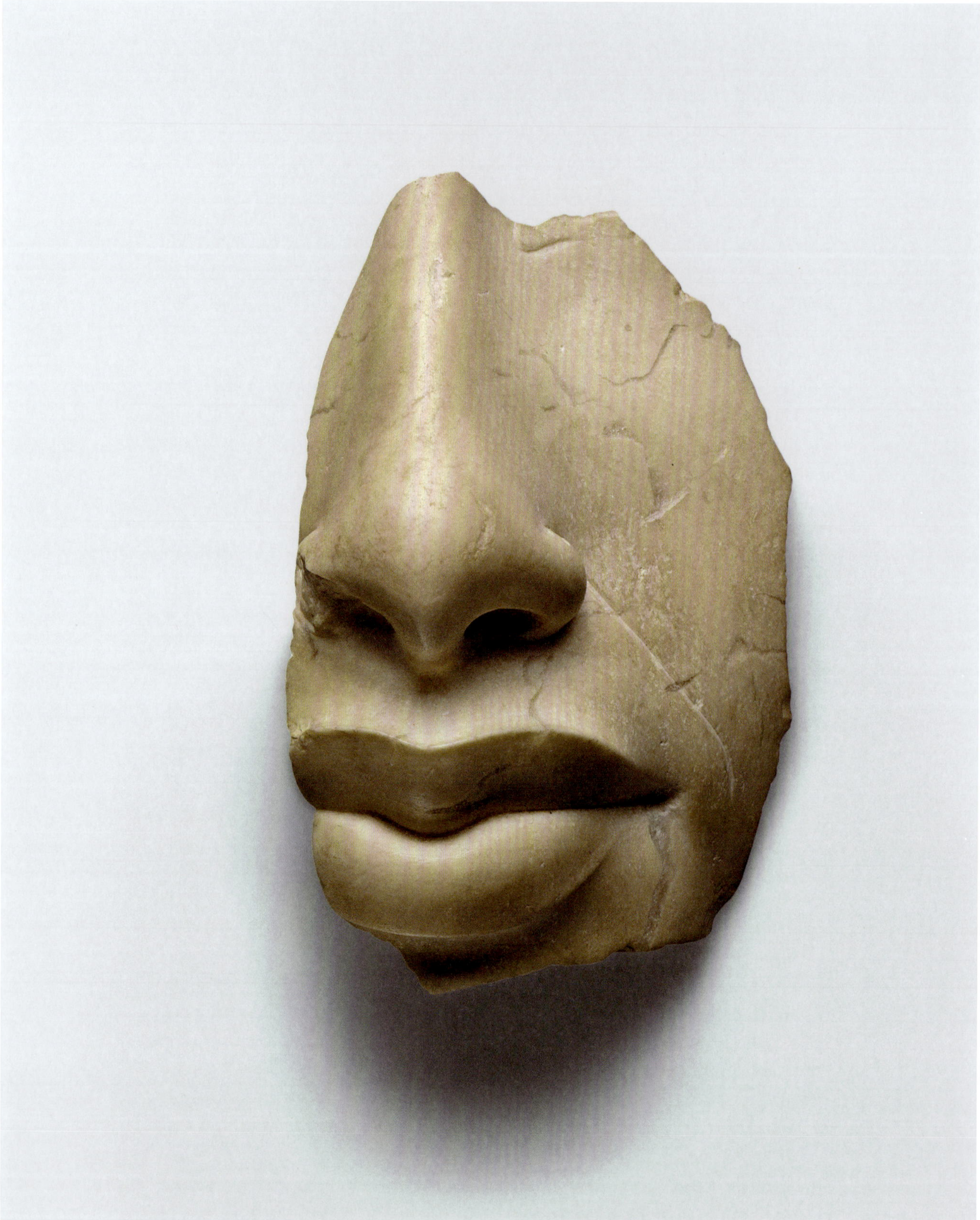

Fig. 1 Egyptian (Akhetaten [Amarna]), *Nose and Lips of Akhenaten*, c. 1353–1336 BCE, indurated limestone
Lent by The Metropolitan Museum of Art, Purchase, Edward S. Harkness Gift, 1926 (26.7.1395)
Cat. 4

emphasis on how much the effects of light and shade count in our perception of sculptural fragments, but even more, perhaps, for its suggestion of how we complete the fragment in our own minds and the role of mental imagery and imagination itself.

We will return to this subject.

SEEING AS FEELING

How is it that we have so palpable a sense of the broken features on these fragments? How are we to account for the fact that objects made of wood and stone not only give the impression of being of the same substantiality as ourselves but also acquire and convey so vivid a sense of life and emotion? At the same time we also find that we feel within our own bodies what those objects seem to feel too. How, we may also wonder, is it that the sense of sight turns so easily into a sense of touch?[4] Above all, we want to know how it comes about that apparently dead images move us so deeply in the first place.

This is a topic favored by theologians and their followers from Early Christianity through Martin Luther and on to our own time in their many arguments against images. It embodies a fear that underlies countless assaults that leave images broken.[5] But the question of how inanimate images acquire and express so vivid a sense of life and feeling is one that extends beyond the level of theological controversy. By taking into account what happens in our brains and our bodies when we look at fragments, we begin to understand that what is at stake is not only the sense we have of their beauty but also the emotions that appear to inform their expressions and their movements. We have only to look at them, even if they are immobile, trapped in their material matrix, to have similar feelings of both movement and emotion embodied within ourselves.

SUFFERING ON FRAGMENTS

Take the early sixteenth-century *Head of a Female Saint* now in the Louvre 〈 *fig.* 2 〉. What sadness on her face! Some viewers may think her mouth indicates fear too, but the downward expression of the eyes and eyelids, and above all the carved indications of tears that issue from her lower lids, convey extreme grief, enhanced, by pure chance, by the abrasions on her right eye and lips. We recognize these feelings right away, even if we do not know the story that lies behind them.

Who could look at this mouth and these saddest of eyes without seeming to feel their own face rumpled with the same quivering, almost

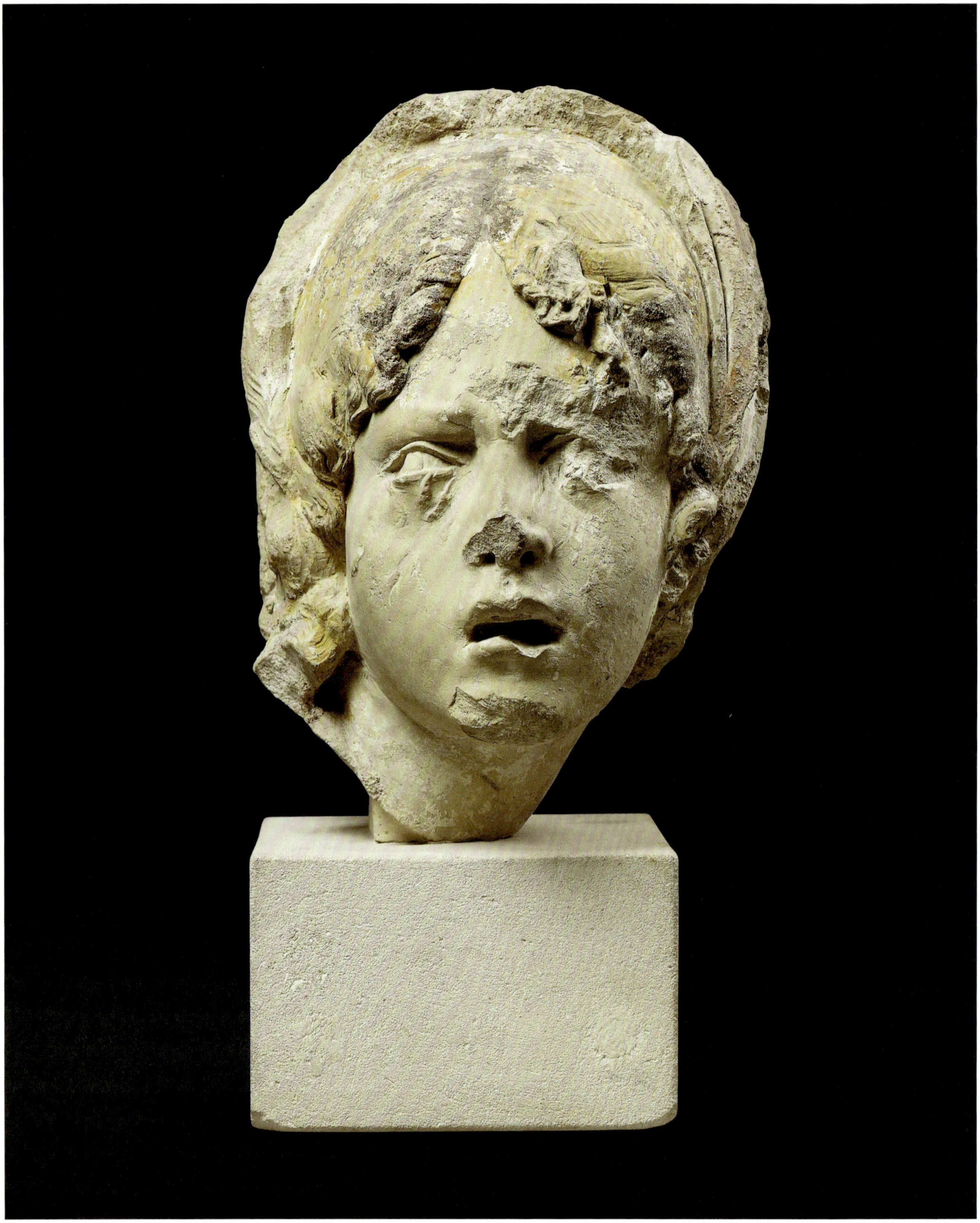

F*ig*. 2 French (Nevers), *Head of a Female Saint*, c. 1500–1515, stone with traces of pigment
Musée du Louvre, Département des Sculptures, Paris, RF 882
Cat. 54

uncontrollable feature that so powerfully suggests helplessness? Some might claim that this is a mere projection of my own responses to this image. But the fact is that we now have sufficient techniques—ranging from ever-more sophisticated forms of transcranial magnetic stimulation (TMS) to positron emission technology (PET) and functional magnetic resonance imaging (fMRI)—to provide evidence of the cortical and subcortical substrates of what we feel within our own bodies of the movements, sufferings, torments, and joys of others. These technologies bring us closer to an understanding of the basic forms of response that are prior to cultural modulation but that join humanity across all boundaries. What we learn from fragments and the sufferings of works of art themselves even further expands what we learn about ourselves.

MIRROR NEURONS

In the late 1980s and early 1990s a group of neuroscientists in Parma, Italy, working under Giacomo Rizzolatti and alongside Vittorio Gallese, made a discovery that revolutionized our understanding of the relationship between sight, movement, and emotion. Its potential was immediately apparent, but so too was the skepticism it aroused. Whatever the criticism, both initially and later, the discovery is relevant to the questions about fragments that we are addressing here. It added a fundamental new dimension to the ways in which artists, art historians, and the art-loving public think about imitation, both of other people and of works of art. Imitation became a matter not only of how artists copy what they see but also of how our own movements, both large and small, often seem to imitate or simulate the movements of others, whether in art or in life. All these forms of imitative bodily feeling and muscular activation have direct neural correlates; so do the movements they express or entail. These reactions are not merely what many might still call purely subjective feelings of the physical actions of others (and of the representation of others); they are, in fact, capable of empirical determination.

In 1988 the Parma team published their observation of neurons in the premotor cortex of monkeys that fired during the execution of distal goal-directed actions.[6] At the time, they concentrated specifically on movements of the hand such as reaching for food or a cup, grasping a tool, and reaching to touch the cheek of another monkey. But then they moved on to other parts of the body. In 1992 they found that many of the same class of visuomotor neurons they had already identified in that area of the premotor cortex and adjacent regions in the parietal cortex that fired when a monkey performed an action also fired in the brain of an observing monkey—*even if it did not actually execute the same action itself.*[7] These neurons Rizzolatti and his team called mirror neurons, which they differentiated from what they termed canonical neurons. The latter, still relatively undiscussed, respond largely to the shape and size of three-dimensional objects that code for grasping and the kinds of specific motor actions such objects might imply or require.[8] Both classes of responses, according to the Parma group, require no conceptual or conscious evaluation. They allow us to directly understand the meaning of the actions and emotions of others by internally replicating ("simulating") them without any explicit reflective mediation, as Gallese and his colleagues put it in 2004.[9] They occurred, as we would say, automatically.

A flood of articles followed. Despite the subsequent discovery of mirror neurons in humans as well,[10] the skeptics remained.[11] But the implications for the sense we so often have of seeming to imitate the actions of others are clear. There are mirror mechanisms in our brains that respond to sight of the actions of others, whether in reality or representation, *as if* we were actually moving in the same way too.[12] And what this entails, as I and many others have argued, is not only that our movements express the emotions we feel but also that the forms of embodied simulation underwritten by mirror neurons help us comprehend what others are feeling as well.[13] They do so because of our apparently automatic simulation of the movements, and even the implied movements, that express both emotion and intention.[14]

These are all matters that merit further exploration.

MOTION BEFORE EMOTION

Sight of a buccal movement (a smile, for example) activates not only corresponding motor circuits in the viewer but also the relevant somatosensory areas of the brain, in addition to emotional centers such as the amygdala (also activated in the case of fear responses), the cingulate cortex (which is involved in emotional regulation), and finally hormonal expression and inhibition deep in the brain's basal ganglia.[15] To set out even the basic networks involved in such responses would require vastly more space than this essay allows, and might seem to raise the specter of an almost phrenological approach to what neuroscientists call regional areas of interest. But it does serve to remind readers that the complexity of cortical and subcortical processing goes far beyond the mere identification of particular areas of neuronal activity.

At this point one might well ask what all these neural processes mean for fragments in particular, rather than visual images more generally. But perhaps the question should be posed differently. Perhaps it should be about what the fragment brings to our understanding of art, to imagination, and to creativity, thus still further enhancing our understanding of the role of vision and its multimodal sensory correlates in these fundamental aspects of our lives.

IMPLIED MOTION

It turns out that even the merest hint of an expression or a movement can engage viewers in a direct understanding of what the able maker of an image or a work of art wishes to convey, and it does so with a maximum of aesthetic efficiency.

We now have abundant evidence for the activation of both premotor and motor cortices at the sight not only of actual movement but also of implied movement. This relates directly to what Aby Warburg called the "most difficult problem of all for the visual arts, that of capturing images of life in motion."[16] But it's not just a matter of making still images seem to move. What we now know is that even if we see the still representation of an action that only *implies* its conclusion, our motor cortices respond as if that movement has been carried through to completion.[17]

But there is more. It has been shown for some time (as many readers of this book may long have felt) that the mere sight of the impact of an action—such as the cuts in a painting by Lucio Fontana ⟨ *fig.* 3 ⟩ or the visible signs of an iconoclastic blow in the face of Germanicus ⟨ *fig.* 4 ⟩—arouses the same cortical circuits involved in actually making the movements that produced these marks,[18] or even (in the case of blows or other injuries to the objects themselves) in feeling them.[19] This has been repeatedly demonstrated by TMS and electroencephalogram (EEG) experiments that make clear the neural substrates of what Gallese has influentially called our embodied simulation of the seen movements of others, or of the bodily effects of their impact, whether, once again, in reality or representation.[20]

The experiments with mirror neurons offered an account of the motor and sensorimotor circuits involved in our responses to the sight not only of expressions of sadness and distress but also of the movements involved in striking or otherwise wounding others, as well as the warding-off gestures we so frequently see in paintings and sculptures from ancient times to today. Such evidence illuminates the power of fragments. It may require a leap from clearly unconscious processes to their realization in our consciousness, but the fact is that often we only need to see a portion of an action (or representation of an action) in order to grasp both its intentions and its consequences or to feel the emotions it involves.[21] Even with the mere simulation of an action, there are multifold ways in which we have a sense of bodily engagement with the actual effects of such actions.

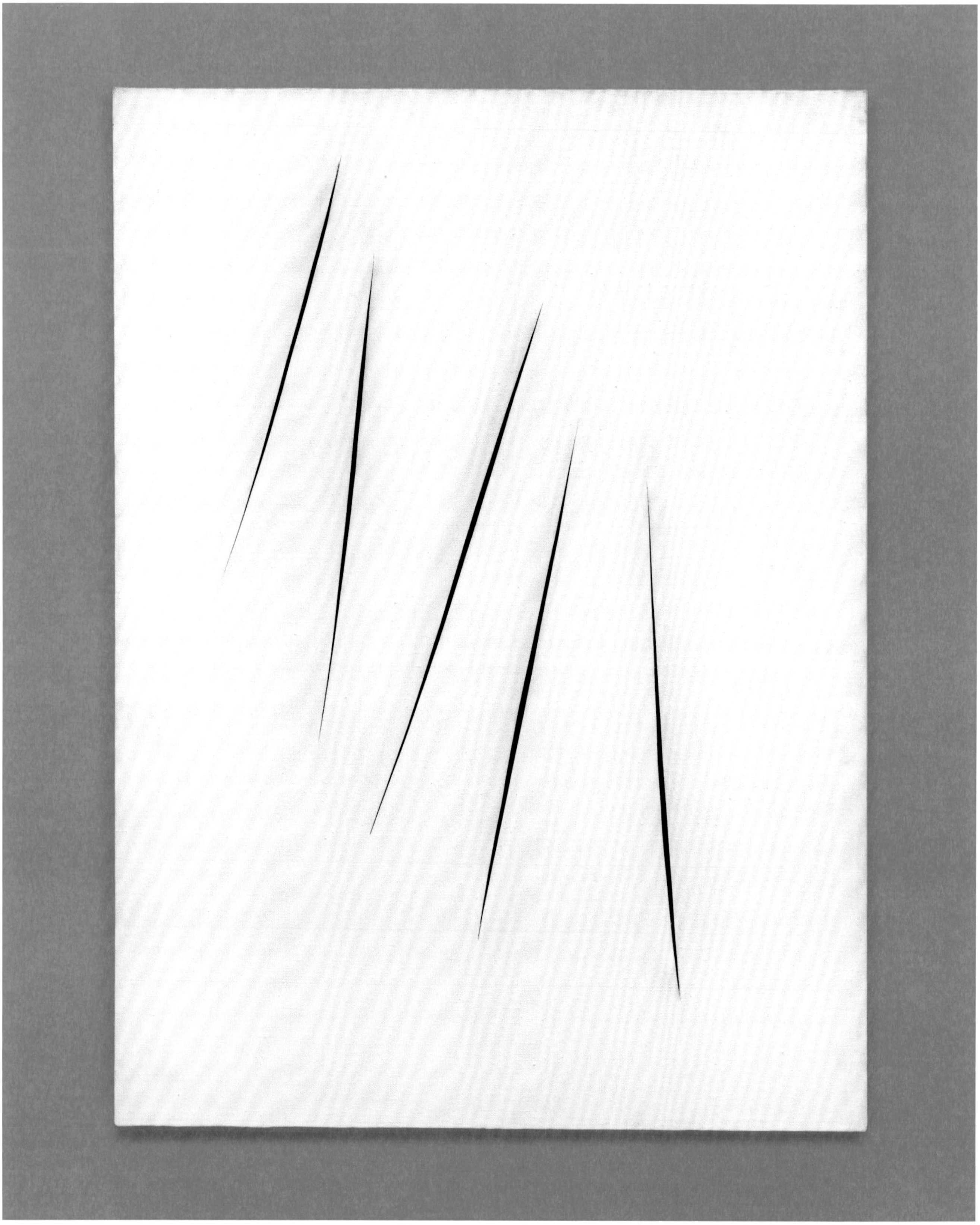

F *i g*. 3 Lucio Fontana, *Concetto spaziale, Attese*, 1965, water-based paint on canvas Guggenheim, New York, The Solomon R. Guggenheim Foundation Gift, Fondazione Lucio Fontana, 1988, 88.3590

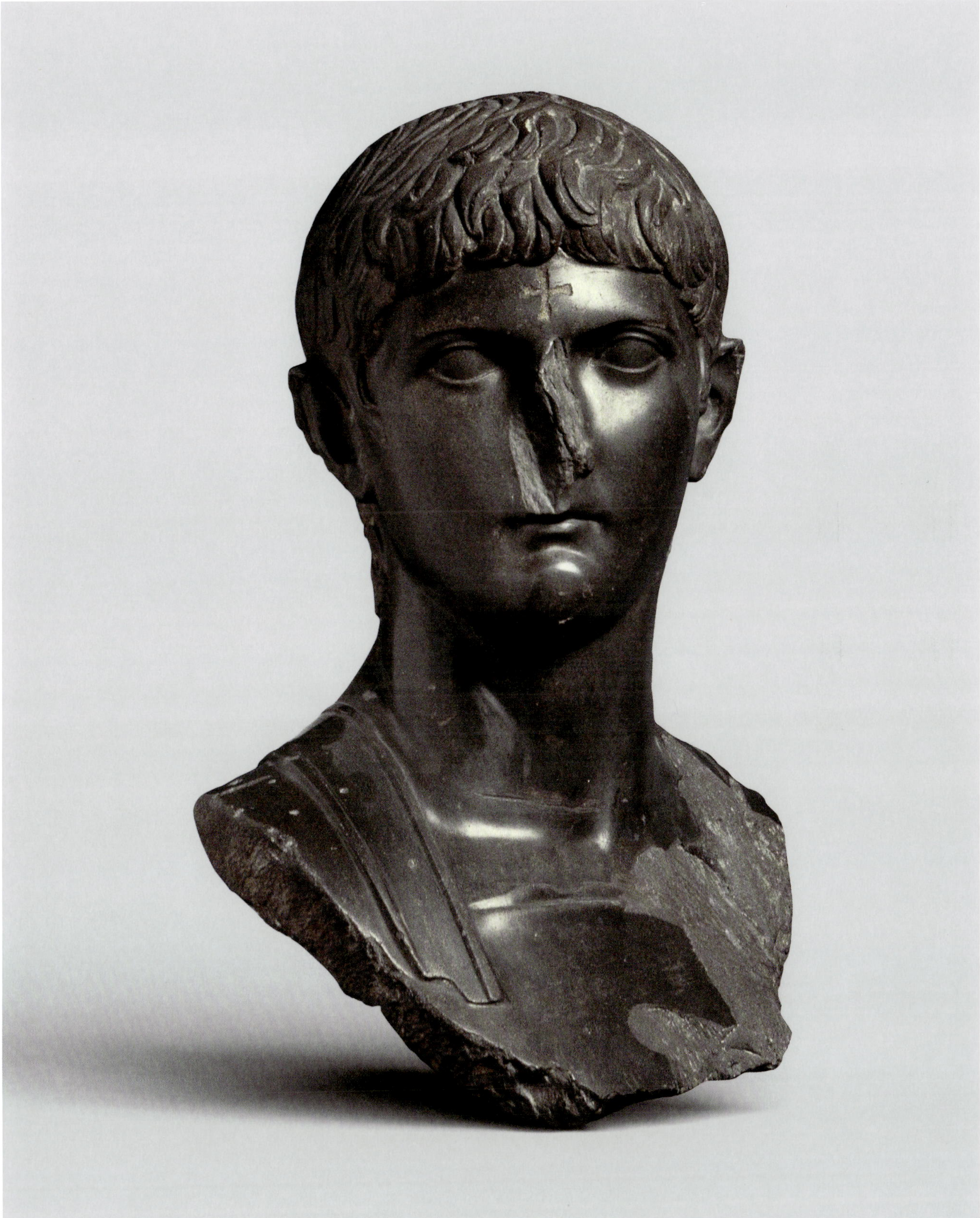

F *i g*. 4 Roman (Egypt), *Bust of Germanicus Caesar*, c. 14–20 CE, basanite
The Trustees of the British Museum, 1872,0605.1
Cat. 23

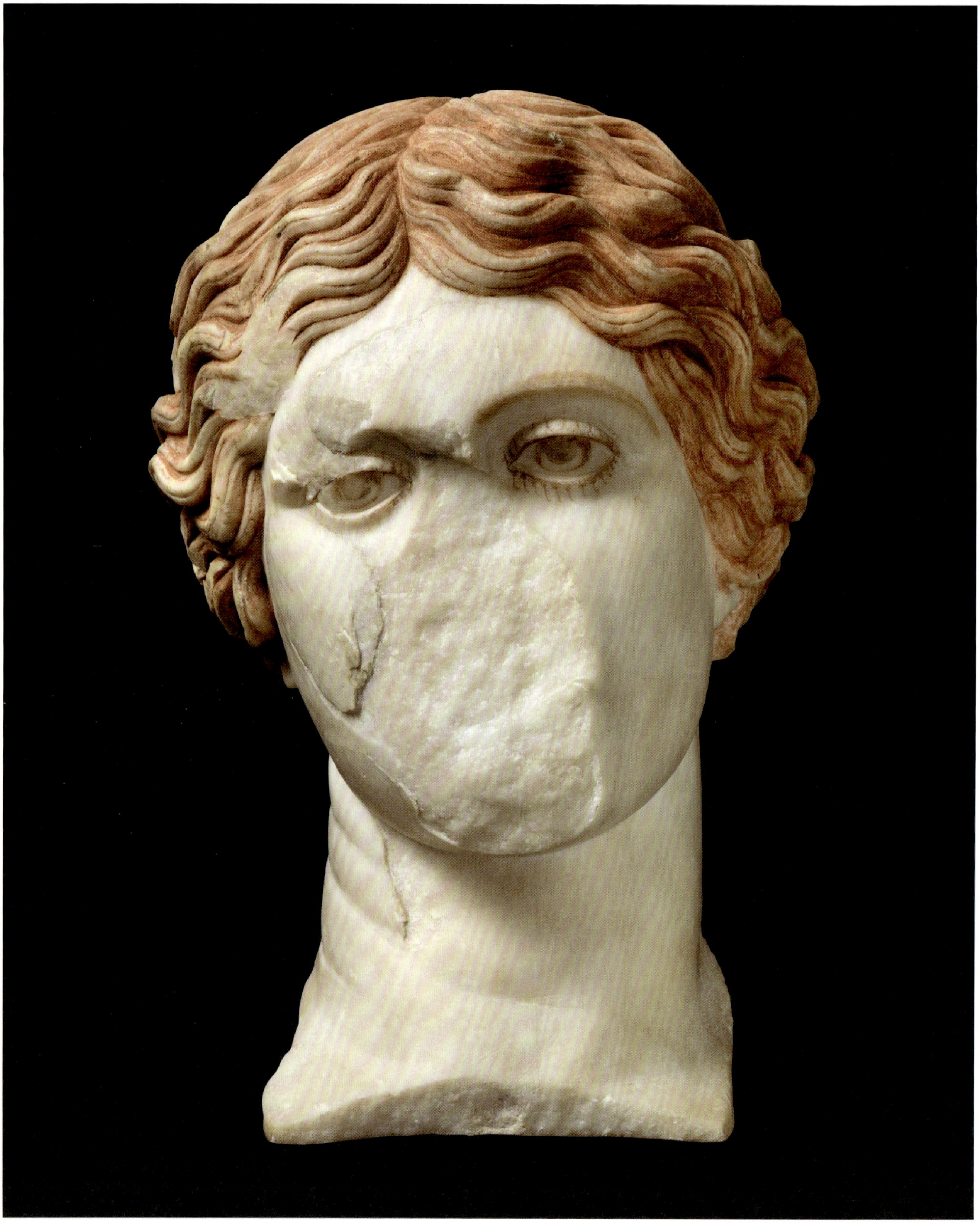

Fig. 5 Roman (Herculaneum), *Head of an Amazon (?)*, 1st century CE,
Pentelic marble with pigment
Parco Archeologico di Ercolano, Herculaneum, 87021
Cat. 22

Looking at *Head of an Amazon* ⟨ *fig.* 5 ⟩, we ask ourselves: What happened to that face? Did it fall flat on its nose, or was it smashed with a hammer? Was it a victim of God or man, of earthquake and collapse or iconoclasm? We find such pieces difficult to look at; we seem to feel a shudder ricochet throughout our own body. The instant we see this object, our own premotor cortex is activated, and it's as if we begin to take evasive action from within our bodies to protect our own face. The relevant parts of the sensorimotor areas in the brain (what neuroscientists sometimes wryly call the somatosensory homunculus) is triggered, and a feeling of prophylactic action is initiated. Such is the power of the many fragments that appear to result from an act of violence wrought against them.

In Adriaen de Vries's terracotta model *Satyr* ⟨ *fig.* 6 ⟩, the entire face and most of the left arm of the figure have been lost—probably from an accidental fall. But the face has the effect of having been blasted out, revealing the hollow core of the model. It is that empty space that draws our attention before anything else, even before we become aware of the beauty of the modeling of the satyr's anatomy: the chest, the tendons in the neck, the musculature of shoulders, biceps, triceps, and forearms. Indeed, in a case such as the De Vries or *Head of an Amazon*, we may well begin to feel that perhaps Aquinas was to some extent right after all: These fragments would have been better without their mutilated heads, so painful are they to gaze upon.

While looking at such damaged or absent faces, the anticipatory movement within our own muscles that we may feel is not to be regarded as simply the subjective feelings of a sensitive viewer. These are forms of muscular activation that are clearly revealed by TMS and EEG recordings of the relevant motor and somatosensory cortices in the brain.[22]

FACES AND BODIES

There is more to be said about how the brain responds to the sight of human bodies, body parts, and faces—and not only to their movements. Several areas in the temporal cortex respond selectively to the outward appearance of faces and bodies. When it comes to the former, the so-called fusiform face area is probably the most telling in the present context, since it responds more sensitively than the others to the least amount of information provided.[23] In other words, it responds most effectively to the contours of a face supplied even with a minimum of relevant features and cues.[24]

Nancy Kanwisher, one of the great pioneers of neural responses to the sight of faces, noted that the fusiform face area showed "a significantly larger response to stimuli with face configurations, regardless of whether face parts were present" compared with other face-responsive areas in the brain, and that even when fine-grain details of the internal facial features are missing, coarse information of external features helps to detect faces among objects.[25]

Well before this, Ernst Gombrich, perhaps the most scientifically aware of the distinguished art historians of his generation, commented on how the brain fills in plain ovoid shapes, such as that of the face, and suggested that this may well lie at the basis of many viewers' responses to figures whose facial features are damaged.[26] Even when we are supplied with a minimum of cues, imagination takes over to supply the lacking physiognomic detail.

Indeed, even where the face is entirely missing—as with the De Vries and that archetype of ancient fragments the *Torso Belvedere* 〈 see Dickerson *fig.* 3 〉—we can be sure that these works will evoke responses in the nearby temporal area known as the extrastriate body area, which responds to the body and body parts just as the fusiform face area does with faces.[27]

All such responses are subconscious, of course. But how does it come about that just seeing a foot or a hand can make us have an instant awareness of our own? The work of the neuroscientist V. S. Ramachandran with phantom-limb patients happens to provide an illustration in this regard.[28] Individuals who have lost a leg or an arm by amputation or deafferentation not only continue to have feeling in their phantom limb but also are liable to suffer excruciating pain there too. Ramachandran devised a simple device that provides immediate relief from their pain: an open-topped box divided by a one-sided mirror, on either side of which is a hole large enough for a patient to insert their hand and wrist. When they place their remaining hand through the hole on the side of the box facing the mirror and allow the site of their amputation to approach the adjacent hole, they look down and see their hand reflected in the mirror in such a way that they seem to have their missing hand and wrist restored. The mind is tricked into imagining that the lost limb is back again.[29]

However poignant an irony it may seem, what more suggestive an example could one find for how the sight of the upward-pointing finger of the *Right Hand of the Colossal Statue of Constantine* 〈 see Dickerson *fig.* 2 〉 might give us an enhanced sense of our own hand, and how it is likely to entail mirror responses to the sight of the action that the gesture entails. All such responses to body-related signals in the temporal cortex, motor areas in the frontal cortex, and body-sensitive areas of the somatosensory cortex illuminate some of the many ways in which the sight of fragments that are broken or wounded can be significantly embodied within ourselves.

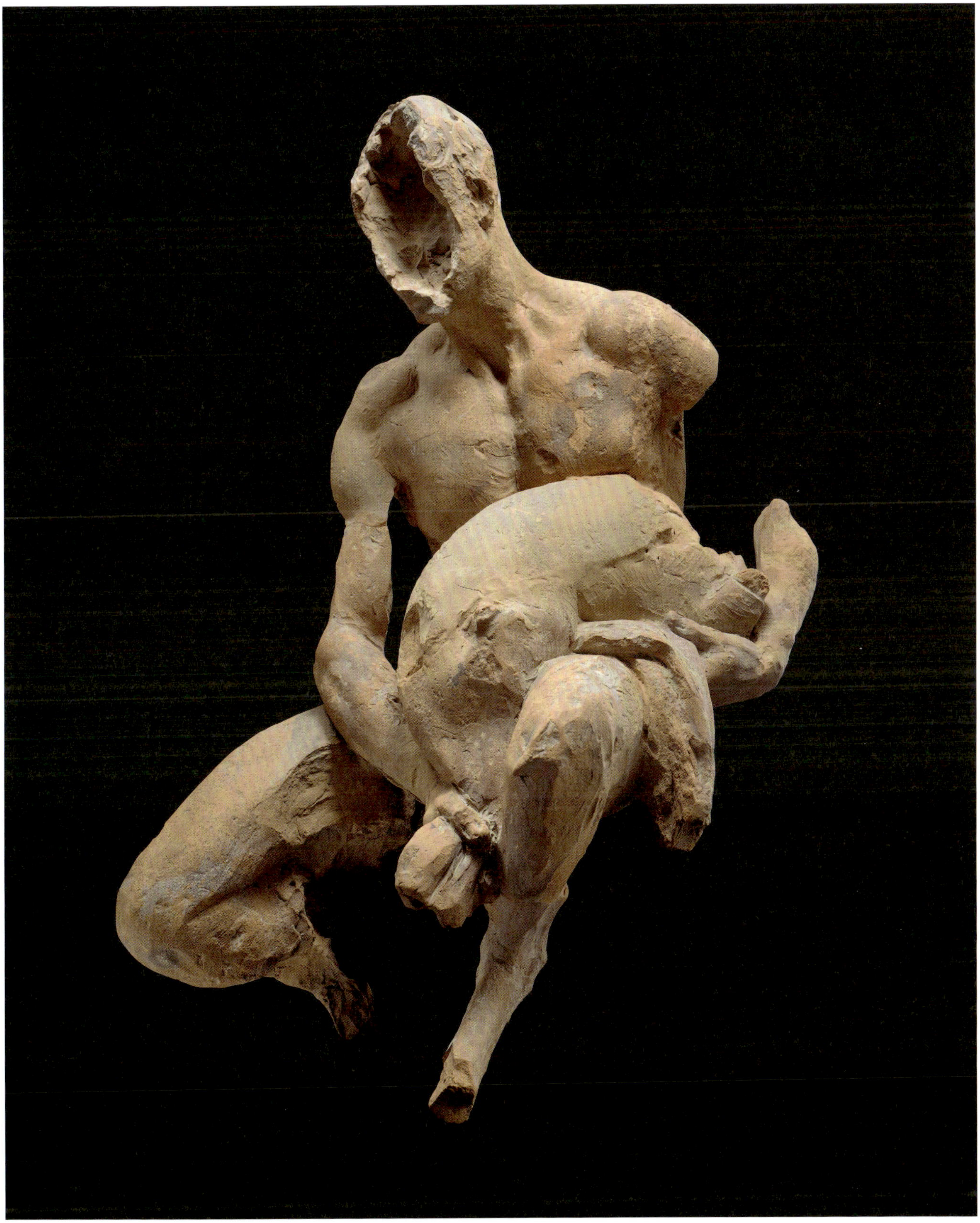

F*ig.* 6 Adriaen de Vries, *Satyr*, c. 1580–1585, terracotta
Private collection, courtesy of McClain Gallery
Cat. 58

As revealed throughout this volume, much comes down to our bodily perceptions of what we see before us and to the transference via sight of the movements and feelings—both physical and psychological—of the bodies of others to ourselves.

EMPATHY

Nothing could be more crucial to the understanding of what we broadly call empathy (from the Greek *empathein* for "feeling" or "suffering in") than the relationship between sight of the bodily movements of others and the emotions they entail. It is a relationship that is constitutive of empathy—but not of sympathy—for the suffering and sorrows of others.[30] Sympathy (from the Greek *sumpathein* for "feeling with") remains a purely psychological understanding, often predicated on one's own experience of sorrow, loss, or defeat. But empathy is always predicated on a sense of bodily engagement with the joys and particularly the pains of others.[31] It is worth noting here that even blind people, even those who completely lack their visual cortex, are able to perceive emotional expressions in the condition known as affective blindsight.[32]

The matter of empathy is not only psychological but also physical. In fact, I believe it to be essentially so. When we say, "I feel for you," do we not also feel within our own bodies that we are suffering similarly? When we see the dramatic instances of toppled and wounded statues, smashed, hammered, and drilled in body and eyes by iconoclasts, do we not feel, however weakly, many of the wounds and cicatrices in our own flesh as well, just as we do when we see the countless ways in which torture and martyrdom are visited upon others? If we seem to feel in our own bodies the twisted posture of *Crouching Venus* ⟨ *fig.* 7 ⟩, then how much more intensely are we likely to have a sense of bodily rupture within ourselves upon sight of the single arm of a Greek boxer ⟨ see Dickerson *fig.* 13 ⟩. First, we feel the action of the hand at one end of the arm—transcranial direct current magnetic stimulation would reveal the activation of the fingers and wrist in the same way as they are shown in that wrist.[33] Then we notice how the arm has been wrenched from its socket. The very signs of the ways in which this arm has been physically detached from the body to which it once was attached—the rough metal edges, the remains of solder (or whatever)—instantly turn it into flesh and bone as if it were our own. We see remnants of violence in paintings and sculptures and automatically perceive them as the effects of violence on and within the very substance of the human body itself.

The mirror theorists have written eloquently about how both primary and secondary somatosensory cortices are activated by the sight of wounds to bodies such as we often see in iconoclasm's fragments,[34]

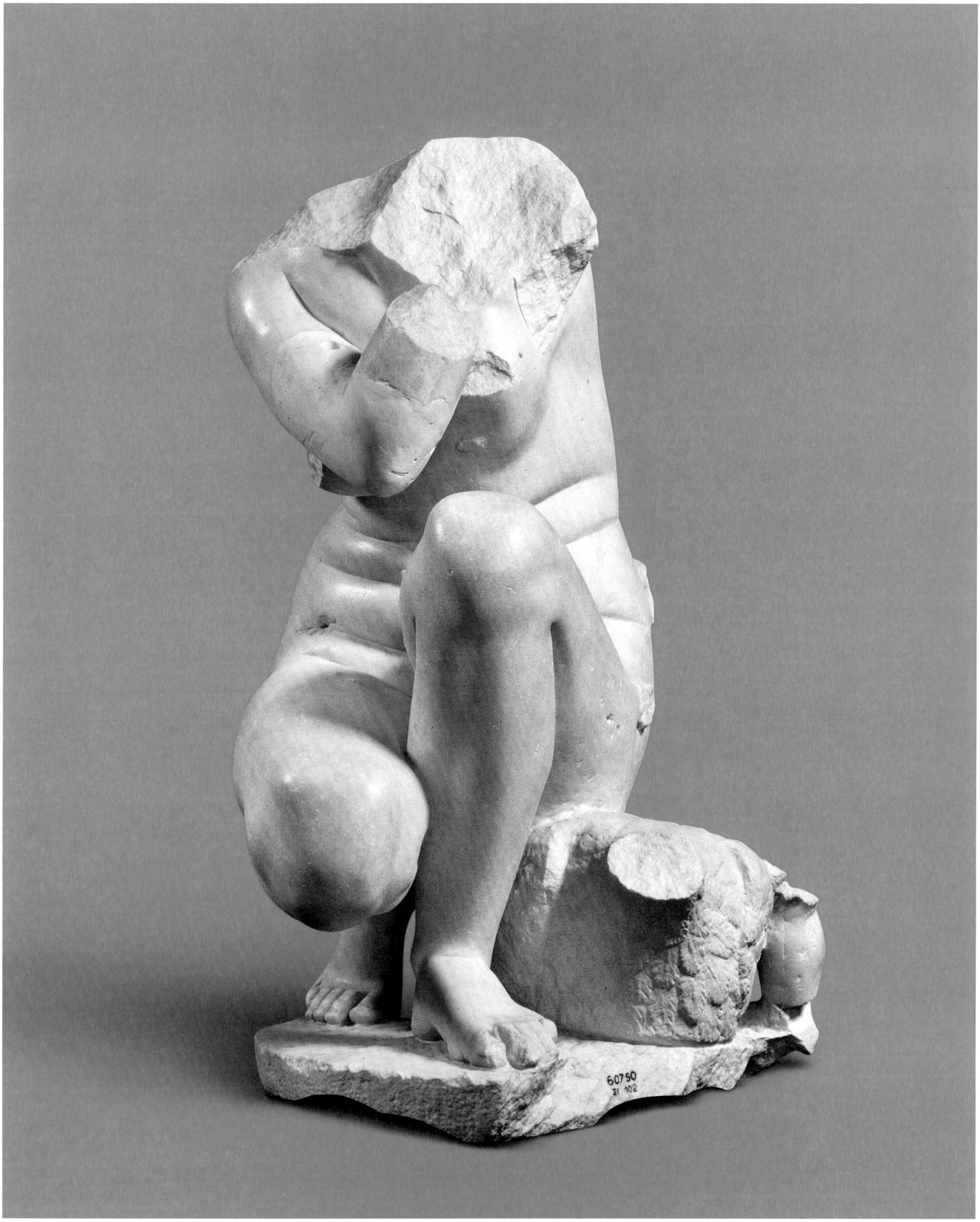

Fig. 7 Roman (Rome), *Crouching Venus*, mid-2nd century CE, marble
Museo Nazionale Romano—Palazzo Massimo, Rome, 60750
Cat. 28

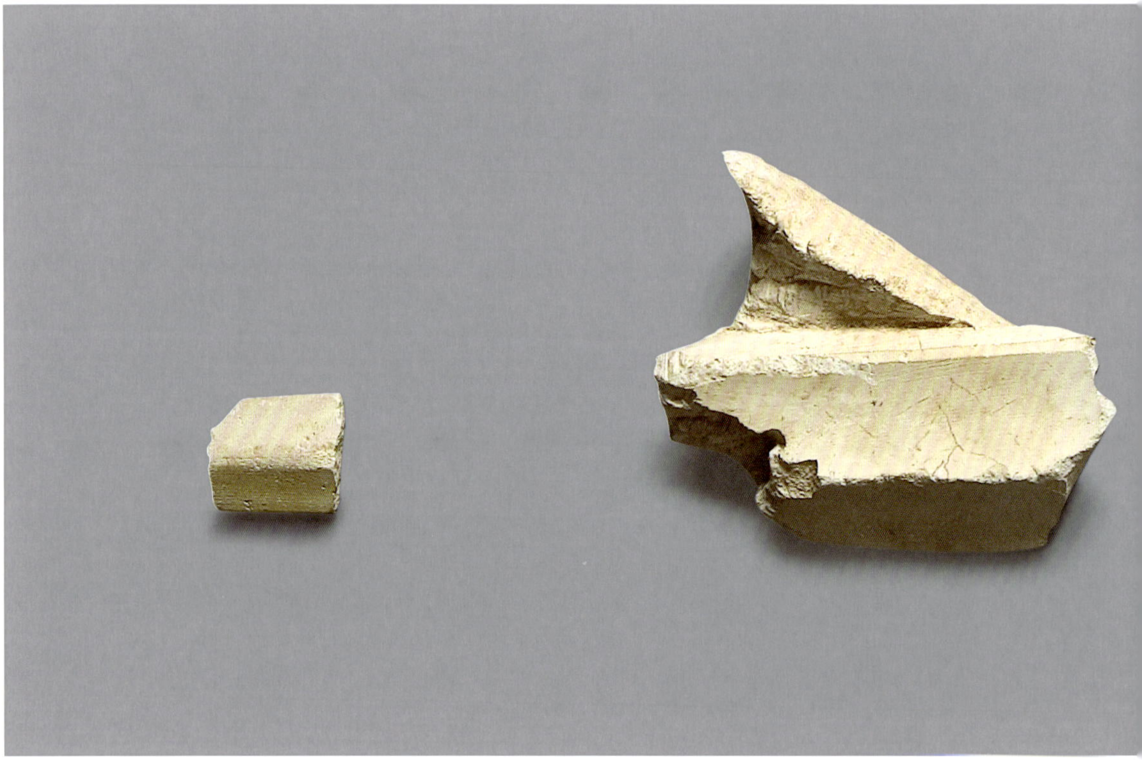

while stabbed eyes are often signs of the iconoclast's desire to deprive the image of life.[35] We wince or shudder at the sight of the damage to once beautiful objects, not only because of the damage to art but also because of the sense of loss and pain that often seems to be visited upon the human or divine prototypes of what they represent (see Said and Sears pages 117–121). We wince in pain as we look at them. We feel the movement with which the instruments of destruction are wielded or must have been wielded, and anger rises in our bones.[36]

IMAGINING THE WHOLE, COMPLETING THE FRAGMENT

Let's take a more precise look at what happens when we seek to make the fragment whole again, if not with our own hands, then at least in our heads. For some time now, cognitive scientists have distinguished between two forms of completion: the modal and the amodal. The first applies to the ways in which we imagine filling in gaps, extending broken lines, completing the broken contours of objects, and filling in absent

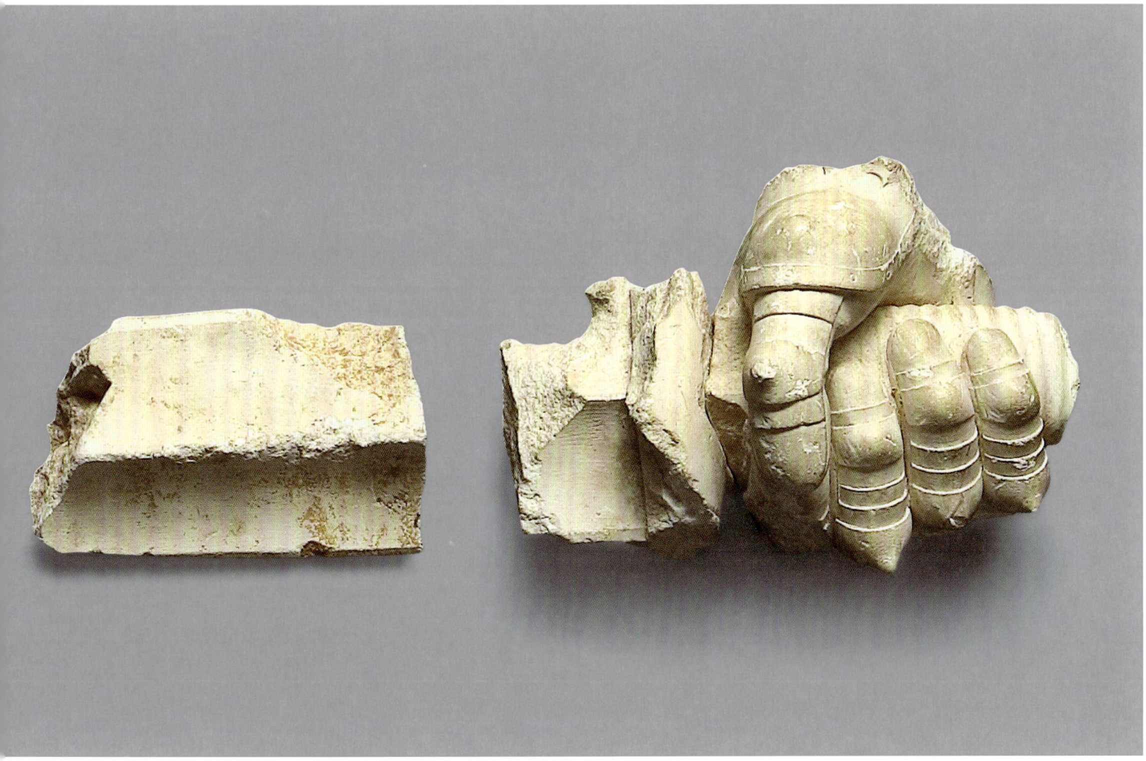

Fig. 8 Claus Sluter, *Fragments of a Statue of Saint George (Iron-Gloved Hand and Sword)*, c. 1393, limestone
Musée des Beaux-Arts, Dijon, inv. 4159/1-8

colors, textures, levels of brightness, and movement, all on the basis of adjacent sensory clues.[37]

Consider the hand and sword that are the remains of a statue of Saint George by the fourteenth-century Burgundian sculptor Claus Sluter ⟨ *fig.* 8 ⟩. In seeing the objects as they are photographed, with small gaps between the surviving pieces, we automatically read the hand and the sword as a single continuous object. It is no special feat for our minds to extend what is there across what is not. Of course, we do not actually see any of these missing lines. They are all illusory effects, just as in the case of the Kanizsa triangle, which has no actual borders ⟨ *fig.* 9 ⟩. They are entirely the products of internal brain mechanisms rather than of existing external stimuli arriving at the retina and then moving to the back of the brain to be processed in the primary visual cortex (also called the striate cortex) and adjacent visual areas in the occipital cortex and extending into the posterior temporal lobe. Further processing is constantly modified by additional contextual information supplied by top-down inputs not just from the retina but also from both long- and short-term memory and shifts in visual attention.

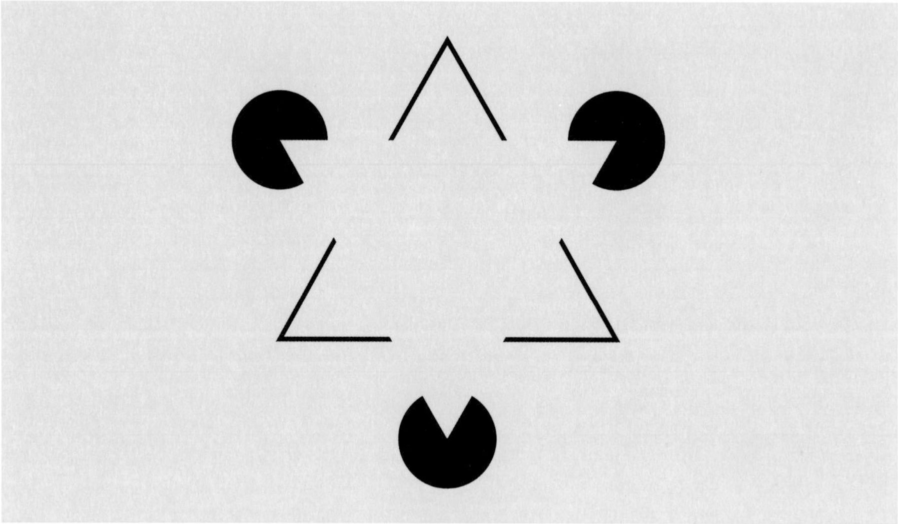

Fig. 9 A Kanizsa triangle is a visual illusion that gives the impression of a triangle superimposed on the outline of another triangle and three circles. The contours of the first triangle are altogether absent, while those of the second are only partial. The illusion illustrates how the brain can form illusory contours to complete what is wholly or partially absent.

The other process, amodal completion, is possibly even more important for the question of filling in. Probably the most famous illusions used to illustrate this form of completion are those of a cat whose body is largely occluded by a picket fence and a dog whose nose emerges from behind a solid wall at one end and its tail at the other. In other words, this form of completion has to do with what we might call our imaginary perception of something hidden below the visible surface, where there are minimal or no sensory clues to its overall form. In the examples above, our perceptual system represents those parts of the animal occluded by the fence or wall. We imagine forms that are present in our imagination and that, despite the absence of sensory clues behind the obscuring element, actually stimulate significant portions of our visual cortex.[38]

The material gathered here provides evidence that our primary visual cortex, or V1, is activated not only by external stimuli but also—although to a lesser extent—by how we imagine the look of things in our mind. That is to say, it appears that V1 is involved not only in perception but also in mental imagery and therefore imagination as well.[39] The same goes for the successive zones in the extrastriate cortex that are responsible for further neuronal tuning and adjustment—so not only in V1 but also in V2, V3, and V4 for contour, texture, depth, and color and in V5 for motion, with V4 also playing a role in visual attention as well.

While it may seem that amodal forms of filling in and completion are even more relevant for imagination than modal ones, the latter may be more applicable to the problem of how we complete fragments in our minds. It is precisely the concrete fragment that triggers the filling-in or repair-to-completion process, which in turn may be supplemented by further top-down sensory input, even in the case of the most fragmentary of forms and surfaces available to sight itself.

The importance of all this for our understanding of how we perceive and complete fragments is clear enough. But there is more. What is at stake is the light all these matters cast on that central feature of human existence, the imagination, and how we see images "in our minds," as we tend to say, or what we mean by "mental images" and "the mind's eye." In short, it turns out that by most current neuroscientific accounts, the visual imagination depends on exactly the same principal organs in the visual cortex that are critical for our ability to see all objects in the world, even though often at a lesser degree of intensity.[40]

PREDICTION AND ERROR CORRECTION

For some time now, neuroscientists—both those whose work is largely predicated on biological factors and those who are involved in the computational dimensions of neuroscientific research—have argued that the brain is basically an error-correcting machine, that its core function is to minimize prediction errors.[41] We see, or we think we see, an object in our imagination, and then the brain proceeds to adjust what it makes of the image by a complex process of error correction. It is thus constantly involved in predicting what best corresponds to the available evidence it has or is supplied by the stimuli the retina receives before passing through the lateral geniculate and on to processing in the visual cortices. Much research in this domain has its genesis in developing mathematical models for both error correction and what has come to be called predictive coding.[42]

Self-evidently, this is a gross simplification of a set of complex processes in which top-down information from memory, circumstance, and emotion modulates the basic processing of visual signals in the primary visual cortex as they move forward for further processing. At every stage they are subject to predictive coding models that allow or disallow the adjustments that arise from error correction. Both processes can now be calculated in terms of precise mathematical formulas derived from the empirical evidence provided by fMRI. We may forgo the technical details of these calculations here, but the conclusions about how the mind's eye works and how it offers up internal mental imagery for making sense of fragments could not be clearer.

In the case of *Torso of Christ*, a French sculpture from the late twelfth century ⟨ *fig.* 10 ⟩, most viewers are likely to make sense of this headless and limbless body by filling in what they imagine its missing parts to look

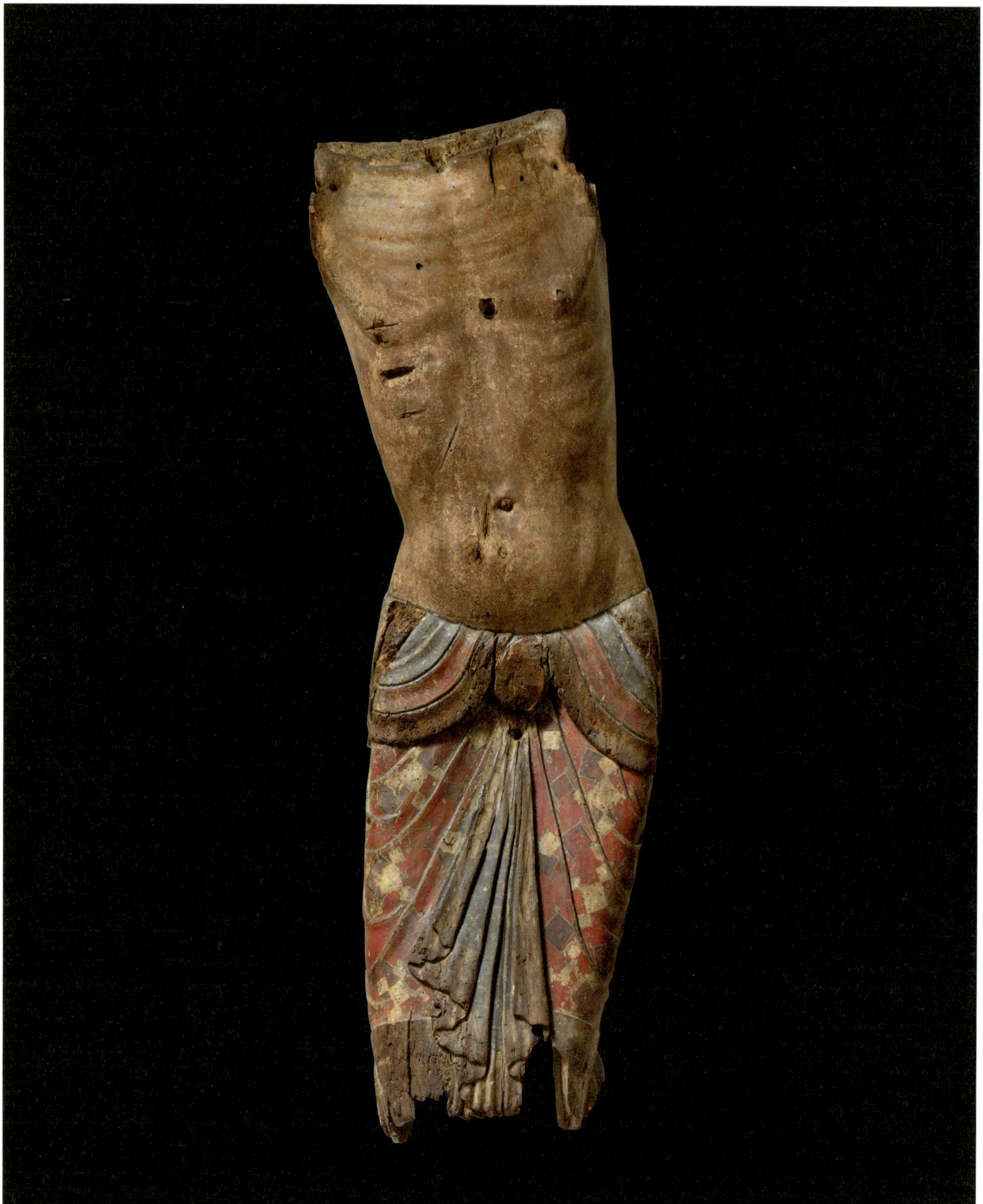

Fig. 10 French (Lavaudieu), *Torso of Christ*, late 1100s, poplar, gesso, paint, and metal leaf
Lent by The Metropolitan Museum of Art, The Cloisters Collection, 1925 (25.120.221)
Cat. 40

like. This inward reconstitution of the fragmented body may of course produce different results, depending on the individual viewer and their experiences and contexts. It is precisely this issue that the prediction and error correction models allow for. A person familiar with Christian iconography and the history of European sculpture may well see a completed Christ on the cross, with arms outstretched, head slumped, and feet overlapping, but those who are not familiar with these traditions will naturally complete it differently. What is at stake in this essay, however, is not any claim for uniformity of experience or of internal imagery, but rather an acknowledgment of the ways in which our experiences are processed in the brain and how they make themselves available for aesthetic judgment and appreciation.

Accordingly, while almost all mental imagery of the kind that fragments trigger casts substantial light on how we imagine we might complete them, in almost all cases this form of imagination begins with the sensory stimuli provoked by the actual visual evidence, however fragmentary, before us. But what happens when we remain awake and close our eyes (as we have to do when we want to imagine something), when our mind wanders, or when we are simply not focused on the external environment at all? We continue to see images in our mind. Mental imagery continues richly, abundantly, and independently of any external input via our eyes. Our brain does not shut down at all. It simply reverts to a kind of baseline resting state.

RESTING STATE, THE DEFAULT MODE NETWORK, AND IMAGINATION

In 2001 the neuroscientist Marcus Raichle was able to establish that there is an organized mode of brain function that is present as a baseline when the brain is not engaged in a goal-directed activity. This paved the way for the naming of the default mode network (DMN), which describes various regions of the brain that become active when the mind is at rest, as when it is engaged in dreaming, mind-wandering, reflection, or memory.[43]

Since then—but even more in the last decade—studies of the DMN have multiplied, making clear how the imagination works independently of directly perceived objects. The DMN engages a large network of multiple regions. These include both frontal and midbrain areas in which decisions are made relating to oneself and one's emotions, the medial temporal zone for scenes based on memory and associations, and a complex set of connections between all these areas (and the anterior cingulate cortex too) in the case of future-oriented planning on the basis of past experiences and navigating social interaction.[44]

Most interestingly, recent research has shown direct linkages between the DMN and the primary visual cortex.[45] When it comes to our perception of fragments, this now helps us to further understand the relationship between amodal completion and what Immanuel Kant called the "free play" of the imagination that emerges as a result of the link between the primary visual cortex and the DMN.[46] We thus now have much additional evidence for the connections between creativity and the imaginative life, which is animated by the energies that are released as we look at the fragments before us.

This has been an essay full of hypotheses, both silent and explicit. Completion itself consists of a series of hypothetical reconstructions or reimaginings of what might be missing. Error correction and predictive coding are self-evidently hypothetical procedures too, particularly given the ways in which probability models feature in the calculations that underlie them. This has also been an essay about how people may or may not respond to particular fragments, about what they may or may not regard as beautiful, and about how we fill in gaps. In order to understand these issues, we must also make tentative hypotheses and then adjust them as we discover new corroborative or contrary evidence. Some of these hypotheses have now been proven; others remain unfalsified—in other words, they have not yet been tested in the laboratory and subjected to tests that enable falsification.

We see a fragment, the breaks in the fragment, and our imagination is immediately unleashed. We make a hypothesis of what it might look like if it were not broken. We reconstruct a whole, and then we correct, often over and over again. This leads to a release of a creative energy that is either free or constrained by what can be retrieved as guidelines. That energy is either based on fantasy and inspiration, and the basic elements of the DMN overlap as our mind wanders and our attention sways from the determinative aspects of the reconstructive project, or it's freely creative. But both projects are clearly restorative—whether in the literal or in the therapeutic sense. Either they liberate our pleasure in the free play of the imagination and open us up to further aesthetic possibilities, or they offer us a type of mobility that we might not otherwise have. They loosen the constraints on one sense, but cross-modality may supervene to engage another one: sound, tactility, even smell.[47]

As with reconstruction in the real world, we hypothesize the rest of a fragment with our own unconstrained imagination, adding and correcting as we move along. What energies are then communicated to us when we look at these fragmented works! Sight of a fragment is always the ultimate challenge to the making of a hypothesis. We hypothesize, and we imagine as a hypothesis. And then we realize that creation itself is a hypothesis and that creation of these mental images, which we then may try to realize in more concrete form, constitutes the basis of all aesthetic theory, for both maker and responder. The rewards come from the making of the hypotheses that fill in the fragment, whether in life or in the course of looking at the objects in this volume. The satisfactions they provide come once we have found a solution to our reconstitutive efforts, and once we have rejected those things that made us stumble on the way.

In this manner we grasp even more clearly the evidence of a critical and fundamental set of elements in our understanding of the relationship between imagination, creativity, and art making and of the pleasures to be had even from our own more pedestrian and unacclaimed creativities. Perhaps sometimes fragments help us better comprehend the ways in which our own responses to works of art mirror, even if only weakly, the processes by which artistic creativity is capable of evoking in us the highest pleasures afforded by the work of the imagination.

Finally, then, we have come to a new approach to all these issues. They relate to a view of scientific discovery (and also to how we actually construe the world we see) that saves the day for fragments, not as something to make us excited for the testimony of triumph and victory they might offer, nor for the poignancy of their destruction and how they activate the sorrowful empathy for both the objects and the humans who made them, as Walter Benjamin so powerfully described.[48] This is an empathy that arises at an early stage within our embodied sense of their suffering, whether physical or emotional or both. All these factors constitute the melancholy of so many writings on this subject. But to think about the fragments we see and to continuously adjust our hypotheses and preconceptions of what needs to be there in order to make the object carry its due freight of beauty is to engage in the most life-enhancing form of creativity available to us in these fractured times.

DISMEMBERING AND REMEMBERING BODIES

Kaywin Feldman

From prehistory to today, humans have purposely fragmented the human body, both literally and symbolically. This long-standing practice invites reflection on the nature of the body and its role in human experience, a topic explored by thinkers such as the twentieth-century French philosopher Maurice Merleau-Ponty. In his pioneering book *Phenomenology of Perception*, Merleau-Ponty asserts that the body is the primary site of knowing and experiencing the world. Earlier philosophers, such as René Descartes, had argued that the mind, or the "thinking self," is separate from the physical body, creating a mind-body dualism. In contrast, Merleau-Ponty posited that the body is entwined with consciousness and shapes our perception of the world. Accordingly, we do not *have* bodies or minds; we *are* bodies and minds. As he writes, "Through perception, the body is always called upon to engage, to choose, to focus the world before any verbal reflection comes into play, and sets the scene for whatever we go on to reflectively think and say and do."[1]

If we follow Merleau-Ponty's argument that the body is the primary means through which our minds perceive and understand the world, it makes sense that humans have frequently manipulated the human body directly and symbolically as a form of ontological expression, conveying their understanding of what it means to exist. Examining the tension between embodied unity and corporeal fragmentation across time reveals insights into how humans make meaning of the body—especially in art, memory, and ritual. By considering the early history of corporeal fragmentation and the complex emotions around broken bodies that we continue to feel today, we can explore such fragmentation as it relates to perceptions of the body, the self, and our relationship to others.

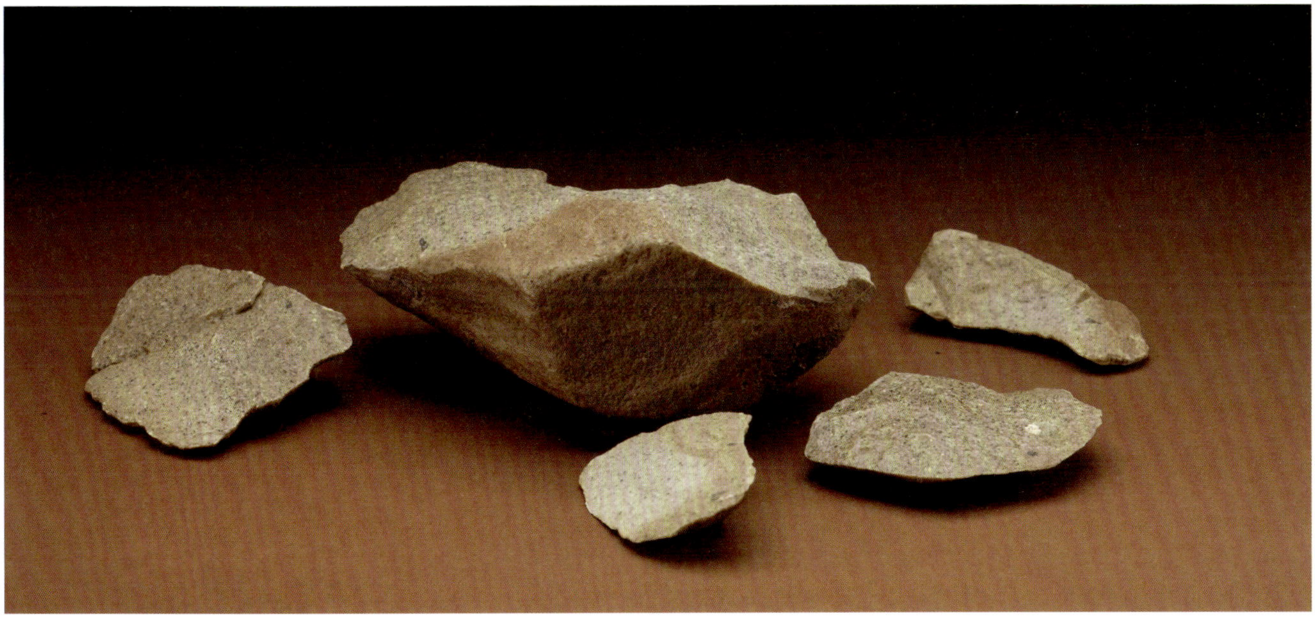

Fig. 1 Oldowan, stone core and flakes from Lokalalei, Kenya, about 2.3 million years old
Smithsonian Institution

MATERIAL CULTURE AND FRAGMENTATION

Our ancestors from the Paleolithic period (c. 2.5 million years ago–c. 10,000 BCE) were nomadic hunter-gatherers who lived in small groups and migrated out of Africa across most continents. They emerged from apelike creatures with limited cultural and technical abilities to become fully modern *Homo sapiens* with increasingly complex behaviors, including sophisticated tool production.

Human material culture evolved simultaneously with human brains and bodies. To make tools for hunting and butchering, early humans practiced flint knapping, a complex stone tool-making technology. The process requires an understanding of the properties of stone and controlled percussion, as the maker uses a hammerstone to split the stone (the core) into multiple knifelike flakes and tools. In the end, the entire rock is transformed into many useful fragments, with the core becoming the principal tool. A good example of such tools is a 2.3-million-year-old stone core with flakes found in Lokalalei, Kenya 〈 *fig.* 1 〉.

The theoretical physicist David Bohm writes in *Wholeness and the Implicate Order* that starting from the Paleolithic, humans began to break the world into segments cognitively. Fragmentary thinking is a way to simplify and organize a multifaceted world and our experience of it. We solve practical and functional challenges through fragmentation and are thereby encouraged to see the world through a fractured lens.

As Bohm argues, "Our fragmentary way of thinking, looking, and acting evidently has implications in every aspect of human life. That is to say, by a rather interesting sort of irony, fragmentation seems to be the one thing in our way of life which is universal, which works through the whole without boundary or limit . . . because the roots of fragmentation are very deep and persuasive."[2]

Despite our apparent natural disposition for fragmentation, Bohm suggests that what we desire is actually "wholeness—mental, physical, social, individual."[3] He argues that wholeness is reality and fragmentation is a sometimes-useful construct that alters our notion of reality because the parts become meaningful independent entities of their own. In turn, we begin to see the world as fragmented, which leads to a fragmented cognitive process and fractured human relationships. Bohm believes that our journey away from wholeness started millions of years ago when we began to identify as a single self or ego that is "absolutely separate and different from others."[4]

We find the earliest evidence for the impulse toward fragmentation of bodies and objects in the archaeological record from the late Paleolithic period through the Neolithic (c. 10,000–2200 BCE). For the historian of ancient Mesoamerican art Julia Guernsey, what unites all archaeological fragmentation "is an understanding of the human body as inherently partible."[5] Archaeologists have excavated burial sites from many ancient cultures across Europe, Asia, and South America containing deliberately dismembered bodies. While this funerary practice was not universal and likely signified different things across cultures, there are many commonalities. After death, the skeletons of the deceased were defleshed (either through excarnation or manual cutting) and disarticulated. In most cases, the remains were buried, often with the disarticulated bones of others. Pits were frequently reused for successive generations. The cranium and long bones were overwhelmingly preferred for disarticulation and burial. Setting aside the gruesome aspect of these burials, they enforce Bohm's argument that humans conceptually manage complexity by dividing and breaking wholeness. The burials indicate an early practice of fragmentation at the most personal level—involving one's family, social group, or perhaps enemies.

Like the practice of flinting to make stone tools, dismembering a body is a reductive process. Bones were deliberately removed from the skeleton and thereby likely acquired new meaning and significance to the survivors. Without a written record, we cannot know why prehistoric people fragmented bodies. The fragments may have represented the deceased as a kind of pars pro toto, whereby the bone fragment was representative of the entire deceased person. In accordance with Merleau-Ponty's theory of embodied experience, broken bodies linked ancestors with specific

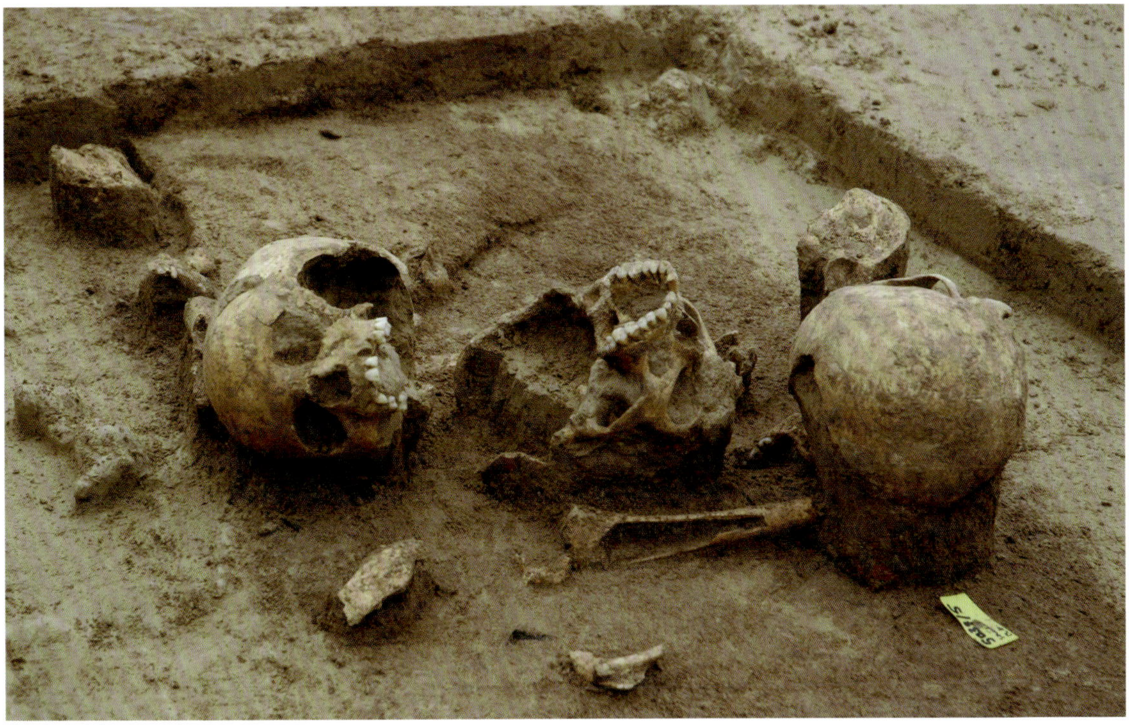

Fig. 2 Human skulls found in Herxheim, Germany, c. 5300–4950 BCE

places and people. As noted by the archaeologists Anna Sörman, Astrid A. Noterman, and Markus Fjellström, "They [body parts] can serve to activate, manipulate, or eradicate memory; to relate and make claims on ancestry, history or terrain; to be extracted for reuse—magically, religiously, medically, scientifically or for propagandistic purposes."[6]

At the Neolithic site of Herxheim in Germany (c. 5300–4950 BCE), archaeologists have excavated many disarticulated crania and long bones ⟨ *fig.* 2 ⟩. The anthropologist Jason Rasmussen hypothesized that the site functioned as a place to centralize the caching of the dead "as some form of collective identity," noting that fragmentation was part of honoring the individual in the midst of the collective.[7] The bones from Herxheim were buried not individually but rather with the remains of other people. This collective treatment of remains suggests a view of the individual not as an isolated entity but as inherently connected to a social group—a notion reflected in the anthropological concept of the "dividual." Anthropologists use the term to refer to cultures that define a person's identity only in relation to others. Some archaeologists have adopted dividual to suggest that prehistoric people may not have shared today's emphasis on the autonomous individual but rather valued people for their relationship to a group. Their identity was tied to being a fragment of the collective, a form of "fractal personhood."[8]

FRACTAL PERSONHOOD AND THE BREAKING OF SYMBOLIC BODIES

Prehistoric people broke objects, both accidentally and deliberately. The resulting fragments were long considered to be discarded trash until the archaeologist John Chapman revolutionized the study of prehistory by recognizing them to be the products of an intentional process. His research revealed that across Eurasia and over thousands of years, fragments of broken objects were sometimes shared with others, occasionally over a long distance. Objects might have been broken and buried as a kind of "ritual killing" or to promote fertility or symbolize a relationship with a people or a place.[9] Given the surfeit of mass-produced expendable goods in today's consumer culture, one must keep in mind the paucity of objects in prehistory, with each one made by human hands and embodying the maker.

Chapman believes that these fragmented objects symbolized the relationship between people, which he describes as "enchainment": "*Enchainment* refers to the varied ways in which persons created and maintained social relations with others by material means. . . . A fragment standing for the complete object in one place presences the persons and places of the object's origins and later biography in other places."[10]

Perhaps the most interesting of prehistoric broken archaeological finds include human figures made of clay or stone. Chapman and the archaeologist Bisserka Gaydarska note that these deliberately broken figurines were reused and gained new meaning after they were broken, often demonstrating an important relationship to place, symbolic meaning, and enchainment.[11]

Among the earliest examples of broken clay figures are those from Franchthi Cave and several small Neolithic caves in southern Greece. The finds include nearly twenty similar broken fragments of painted female right and left legs, some with buttocks and pubic triangles, made around 5000 BCE. Similar broken single legs were found in each of the five sites. They were deliberately designed so that each leg could easily be separated and reattached to its mate. Considering that it would have taken between half a day and several days to walk from one site to another, across difficult terrain, it is striking that the same type of broken legs were found across all these sites. Broken bodies clearly served some kind of metaphorical organizing purpose. The archaeologist Lauren Talalay has argued that the figures, after being intentionally broken, may have been used as a form of social action or contractual device, in exchange for food or marriage or symbolizing a relationship.[12]

At the Preclassic Maya site of La Blanca in Guatemala (c. 900–600 BCE), five thousand broken figurines have been excavated ⟨ *fig.* 3 ⟩. Guernsey describes their fragmentation as part of a complex social matrix. In her

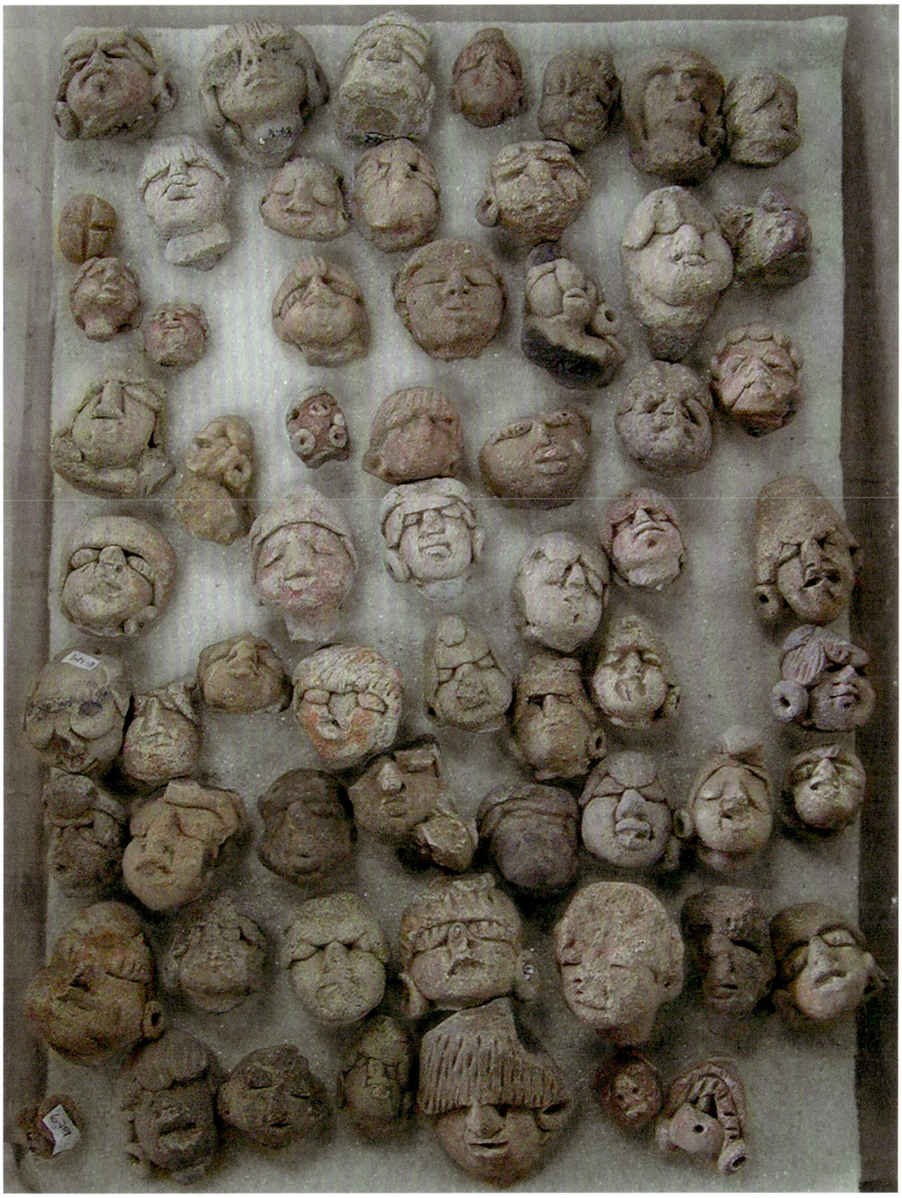

Fig. 3 Broken figurine heads from the archaeological site of La Blanca, Guatemala, c. 900–600 BCE
Shook Collection Archive, Department of Archaeology, Universidad del Valle, Guatemala

view, "Fragmentation was a social tool whose success hinged, in part, on its participatory nature, which required acts of remembering and interpreting on the part of individuals who were . . . compelled—for their well-being and that of the community—to 'connect the dots.'"[13]

More familiar to the art-loving public are Cycladic figurines from Bronze Age Greece (c. 3000–1000 BCE). Carved from marble, these stylized statues were made throughout the island archipelago of the Cyclades between 3200 BCE and 2000 BCE. Canonical Cycladic figures, called

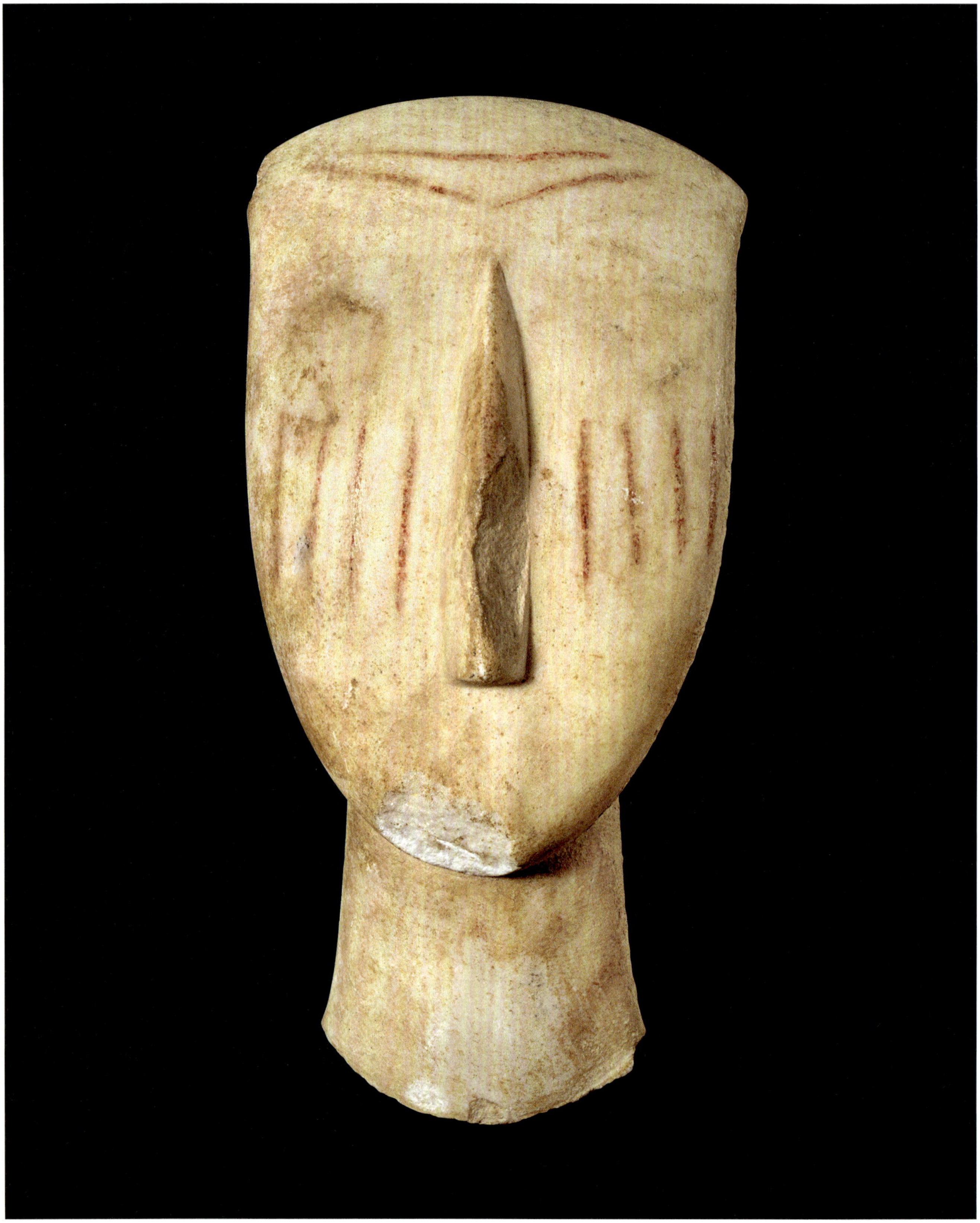

Fig. 4 Cycladic, *Head of a Figure*, c. 2700–2300 BCE, marble with black and red pigment
The National Museum of Denmark, 4697

"folded arm figures," have long been valued for their beauty and simplicity. Most of them are gendered female and share similar traits, such as an elongated form, arms folded across the abdomen, heads tilted back, and feet pointed down. Many have breasts and incised pubic triangles, and some appear to be pregnant. The heads are quite similar, with a long nose but rarely any other features. Most figures adhere to the same measurable proportions, even though they originally came from many islands.

Archaeologists have found a small number of excavated Cycladic figures, both complete and broken, in single burials. They have also discovered pits filled only with broken figurines. The sculptures were clearly valued, since people repaired some of the objects before burial and repainted some at least once. Continuing the behavior seen earlier in prehistory, almost all the figures were deliberately broken at the ankles, knees, waist, chest, and neck before burial.

Sadly, we know little about these figures due to widespread looting and lack of archaeological context. Only a tiny percentage of the thousands of Cycladic figures known today were found through professional excavation. It is therefore difficult to ascertain their function and meaning. Scholars have proposed a variety of roles for them: servants in the afterlife, apotropaic figures, guides into the underworld, and symbolic deities. Whatever their functions, they likely reflect social and economic relationships in some fashion.

A recent excavation by Colin Renfrew on the Greek island of Keros uncovered thousands of broken objects buried in deposits. Not only were the Cycladic figures broken into pieces, but the archaeological evidence indicates that they had all been deliberately broken elsewhere, perhaps as part of a public ritual, and then transported across the sea to be deposited with other broken material at the uninhabited sanctuary. None of the fragments appear to join together. Renfrew refers to Keros as a "symbolic attractor" for rituals among an affiliation of islands he calls "the Confederacy of Keros."[14]

The archaeologist Alexander Aston suggests that Cycladic figures "shaped the dynamics of social cognition in ways that supported the emergence of novel social complexity on Keros."[15] He argues that the role of these Cycladic figures was to create, perform, and sustain the understanding of relatedness, or "kinshipping."[16] Because marble is so plentiful across the Cyclades, the value was likely not in the material but in the objects' function in family, society, and material exchange, or enchainment.

The head of a Cycladic figure in the National Museum of Denmark would have belonged to one of the largest Cycladic figures known ⟨ *fig.* 4; see also cat. 1 ⟩. The detachment of the head from its body is unlikely to have been for ritualistic reasons, as there is no evidence of intentional breakage with Cycladic figures of this size. Nevertheless, the head speaks to the way these figures were bound up with ritual, as indicated by the paint found on the sculpture. Four vertical lines were painted with red pigment on each cheek, and there are indications for eyes and hair and a mark on the nose. There are several possible interpretations of the red stripes, including a relationship to clan, scarring, body decoration, an indication of age, or perhaps a motif of mourning.[17] We do not know the location of the original find, so we are unable to expand our understanding by considering associated objects or site information. The materials scientist Elizabeth A. Hendrix suggests that the painted motifs could have functioned to ensure that cultural memories were maintained across time and place, enacting a process of "being Cycladic."[18] Many of the figures were likely painted, perhaps multiple times, but little remains visible today. Some graves contained marble bowls with traces of red and blue pigments, perhaps suggesting that paint was used for cosmetic purposes in daily life.[19]

Equally mysterious are the ancient Japanese *dogū* ("earthen idols") sculptures, which were also deliberately broken before burial. Dating to the Jōmon period (c. 10,000–300 BCE), these small, fired-clay figurines depict stylized humanoid creatures. They have been found across most of Japan but were not produced after the end of the Jōmon. Because of the geographic and chronological breadth of their distribution, there is a lot of variability in the look of the figures. Most of the figures appear to be gendered female, as they often have small waists and breast-like forms and some appear pregnant. But there is debate about gender; they may in fact be asexual.

From the collection of John C. Weber, a superlative example of a dogū from the Final Jōmon period (c. 1000–300 BCE) is modeled with large, bisected eyes, often referred to as "coffee bean" eyes ⟨ *fig.* 5 ⟩. Its body is marked with patterns, lines, and designs, which may signify clothes or perhaps tattoos and body paint. Some dogū have the appearance of wearing masks and sport elaborate hairdos and headgear. The limbs are often short and stylized.

We do not know whether dogū were dolls, fertility/childbirth idols, objects used in a ceremony or ritual, or talismans to cure certain diseases. It is also possible that they depict deities to help at times of natural disasters, or that they represent supernatural beings, mother goddesses, or fetishes. Likely an animist society, the Jōmon people would have distinguished between the everyday and a shadow world. They may have broken the dogū to send the embodied figures into a kind of spirit world.[20]

Almost all dogū figures have been found in fragments, having been deliberately broken before burial ⟨ *fig.* 6 ⟩. (The dogū in figure 5 has been partially restored, but it, too, was found in fragments.) Archaeologists

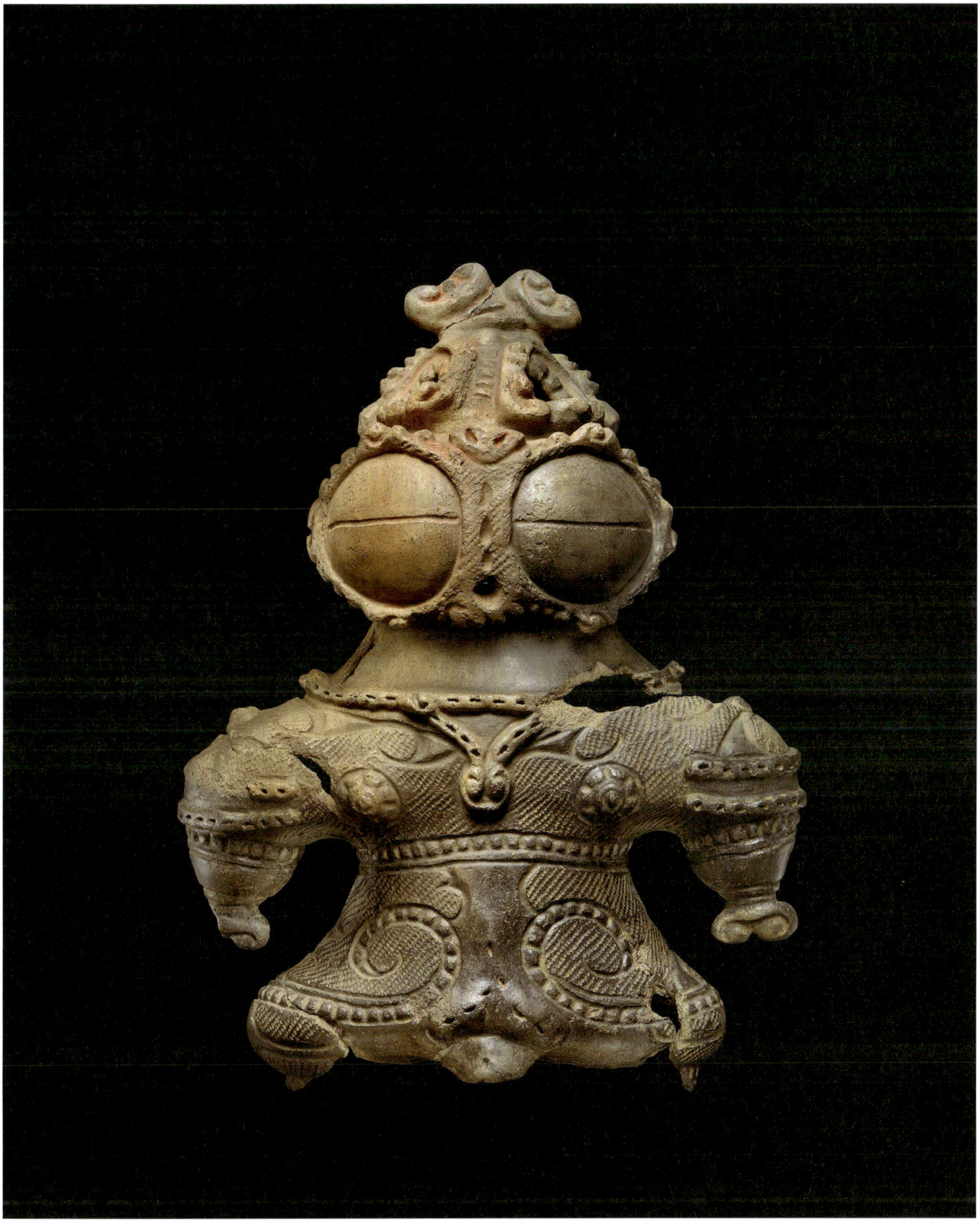

Fig. 5 Jōmon (northern Japan), *Dogū (Earthen Figure)*, c. 1000–300 BCE, earthenware
John C. Weber Collection
Cat. 6

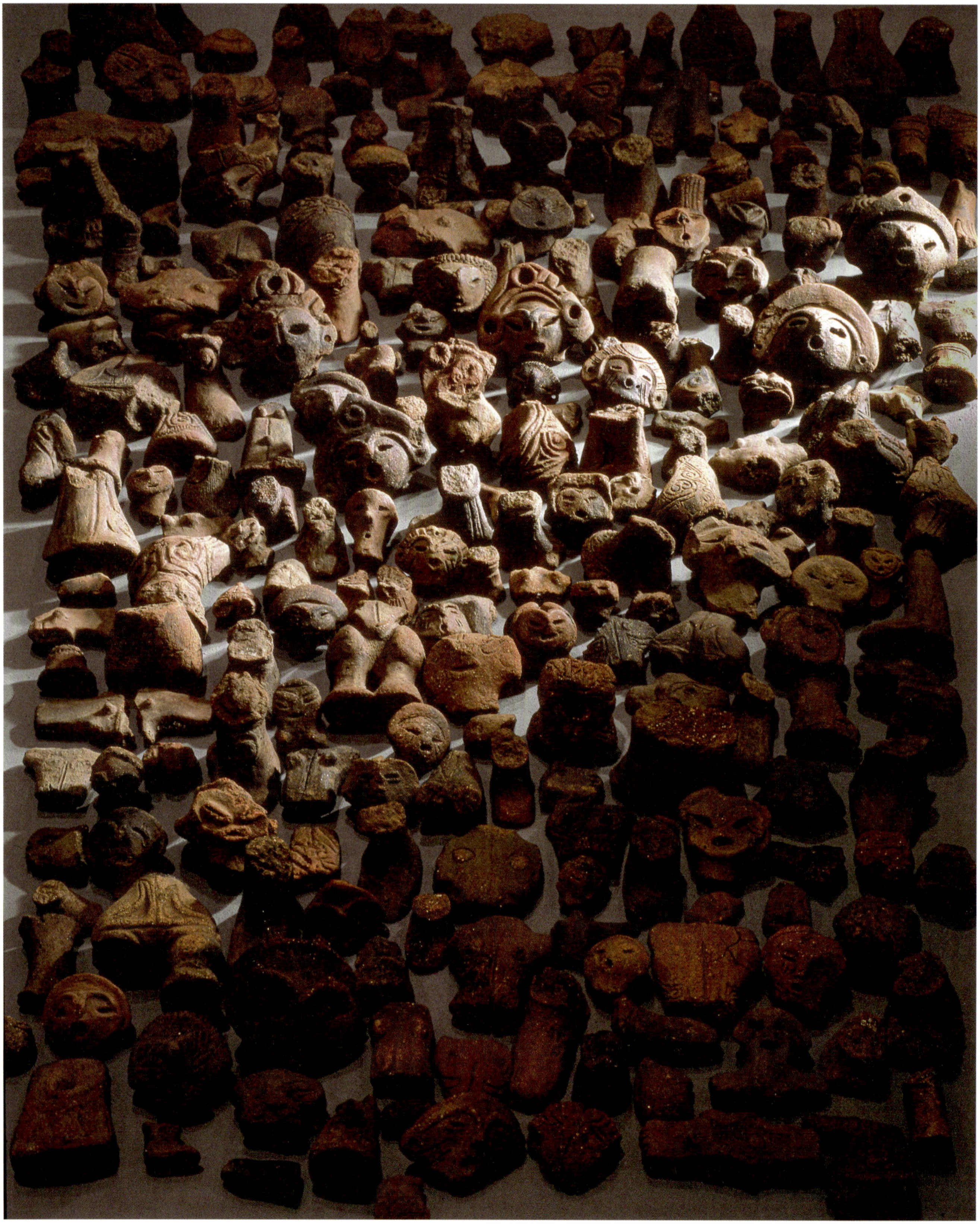

Fig. 6 Clay figurines (dogū) from the Shakado site in Yamanashi, Japan
Shakado Museum of Jōmon Culture, Fuefuki

have discovered such figures in house pits, burial sites, and middens, and scattered across sites. At the site of Shakado in Yamanashi prefecture, archaeologists excavated 1,116 individual dogū fragments (only one figure was complete). A number of the fragments could be put back together with fragments found at other sites, some from as far away as 230 meters.[21] Dogū might also have been broken as part of a ceremonial gift exchange, with the relationship between two parties being symbolized by the parts. Ilona Bausch, a scholar of prehistoric archaeology of Japan, has noted that, different from commodities, symbolic objects would retain subjective and symbolic value, even when broken.[22]

THE ONTOLOGY OF BROKEN BODIES TODAY

When we look at broken archaeological objects through contemporary eyes, we respond to them with emotions and preconceptions particular to our time. These prehistoric objects possess what the archaeologist Cornelius Holtorf refers to as "pastness."[23] Two of Holtorf's criteria for pastness are that the object correspond with what the viewer expects to see, according to their own assumptions of how the past appears, and that a plausible narrative links its "past origin and contemporary presence."[24] Holtorf echoes the Austrian art historian Alois Riegl, who referred to "age-value" (*Alterswert*), the visual traces of age—like breakage—that evoke an aura of the past and appeal to our emotions. This emotional response elicits a sense of the passage of time and the cyclical nature of life. For Riegl, the emotional and aesthetic impact of the object was equal to its historical importance.[25] The head of a goddess figure from Athens ⟨ *fig.* 7 ⟩ offers an excellent example of both pastness and age-value. There is breakage at the top and back of the head, but the face is complete enough to make a direct contemporary connection. Dating from the second century CE and possibly depicting the goddess Aphrodite, the head compels an emotional and intellectual response: The inlaid ivory eyes stare directly at the viewer, while the stain of the oxidized eyelashes suggests tears. This head is simultaneously broken *and* complete enough to evoke the idea of time's passage and cause recognition of our own future passing.

Building on emotional resonance, theoretical approaches such as Walter Benjamin's "nowness" (*Jetztzeit*) and Laurent Olivier's concept of archaeological memory shift the focus from fixed meanings to the evolving and overlapping interpretations of the past. Benjamin's articulation of nowness refers to a moment in which we are conscious of the past as politically and ethically potent, and thereby relevant to today. Olivier believes that Benjamin's goal was to "liberate historical time,"

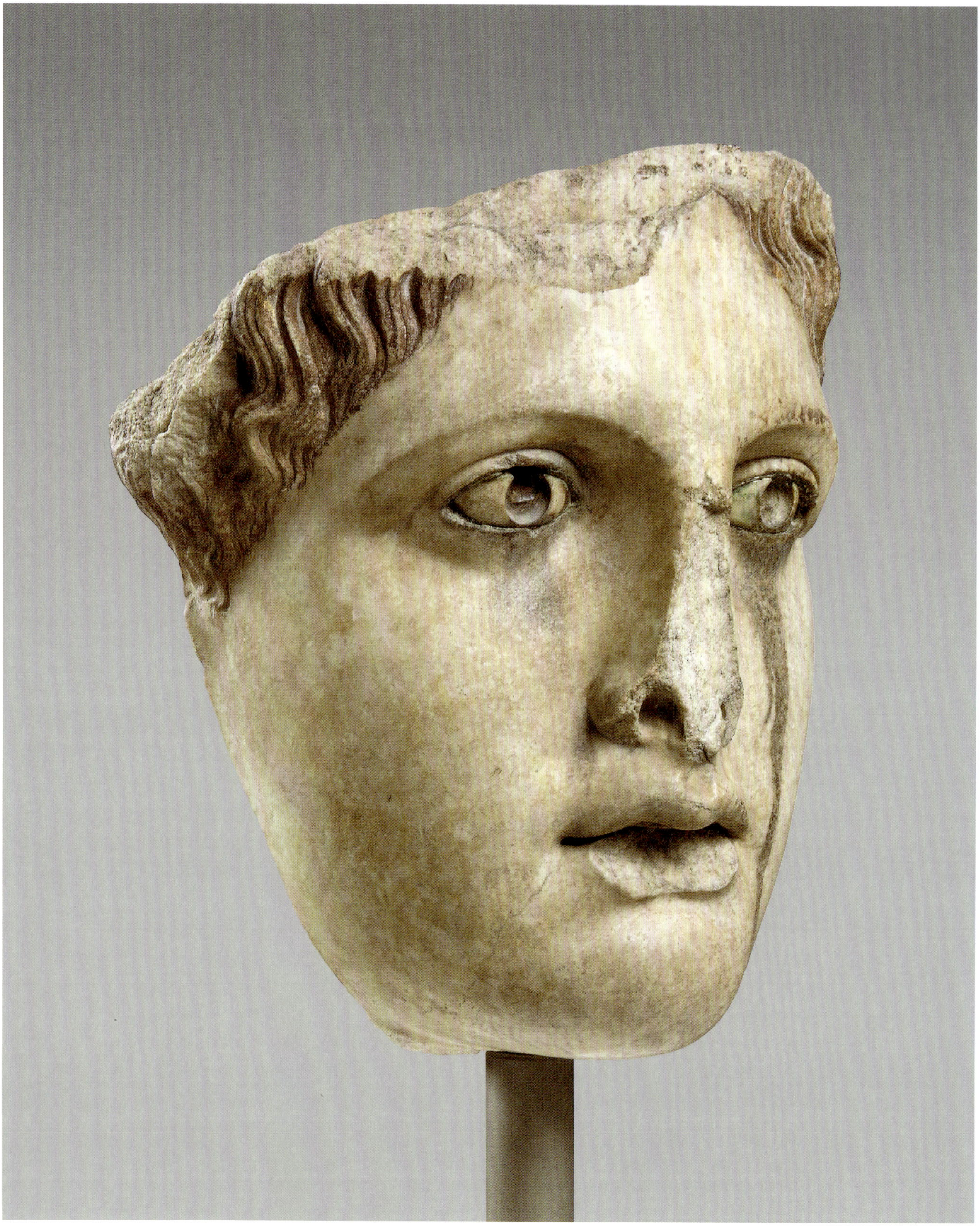

Fig. 7 Roman (Athens), *Head of a Goddess Statue (probably Aphrodite)*, 2nd century CE, marble
Acropolis Museum, Athens, EAM 177
Cat. 26

noting that "if the future is open to innumerable possibilities because it is production, then the past is as well, because it is memory."[26] Ever since the earliest excavations of prehistoric sites, archaeologists have suggested a variety of hypotheses around the meaning of these broken bodies. Interpretations have changed over time, reflecting not only the discovery of new information and the bias of the author but also the contemporary mindset of the viewer. Olivier describes archaeological objects in terms of "a palimpsest, the layered accumulation of memory."[27]

With the deliberate fragmentation of tools, corpses, Cycladic figurines, and humanoid dogū, our ancestors fashioned material layers of history and connectedness even when the layers of memory no longer remain. Given that bodily fragmentation began with the very origin of human culture and cognition, it makes sense that artists today continue to craft new palimpsests through the depiction of broken bodies. How might we look at these artists' fragmented objects to understand their motivations and connections to the distant past? What do the broken clay legs from Franchthi Cave, made seven thousand years ago, have to do with sculpted legs made by contemporary artists?

Louise Bourgeois's *Foot* ⟨ see Fiduccia *fig.* 14 ⟩ immediately evokes the trauma of a broken appendage. Like many of her sculptures, it communicates a whiff of pastness, looking like something one might come upon in a dusty bric-a-brac shop, pricking at a repressed memory. Bourgeois often depicted body parts—legs, arms, torsos—in isolation, thus highlighting moments of trauma and their physical and psychic manifestations. These bodily sculptures are metaphors for vulnerability, fragmentation, and confinement. In *Foot*, the brace attached to the leg further heightens our feeling of breakage and healing. This is not prehistory's "dividual" connected to a community but a kind of alienated and fractured self. Bourgeois's frequent use of her own fabric was a reference to her past, in part connected to memories of her mother, who was a tapestry restorer. Like the prehistoric body parts, Bourgeois's leg is a locus of memory, a palimpsest.

Robert Gober's sculptures of legs projecting from walls surprise and discomfort the viewer ⟨ *fig.* 8 ⟩. These appendages exemplify nowness, which liberates us from consideration of the past. Modeled on the artist's own legs, their wax skin, complete with human hair and actual clothes, makes them appear disturbingly real. Their context and position on the floor, against a wall, however, indicate that they are artificial. Gober's inanimate leg looks realistic, but also awkwardly strange. The viewer is disturbed by the manipulation of the familiar into something that is simultaneously aberrant and natural. Gober's numerous variations on the single detached leg all cause the viewer to experience feelings of the uncanny.

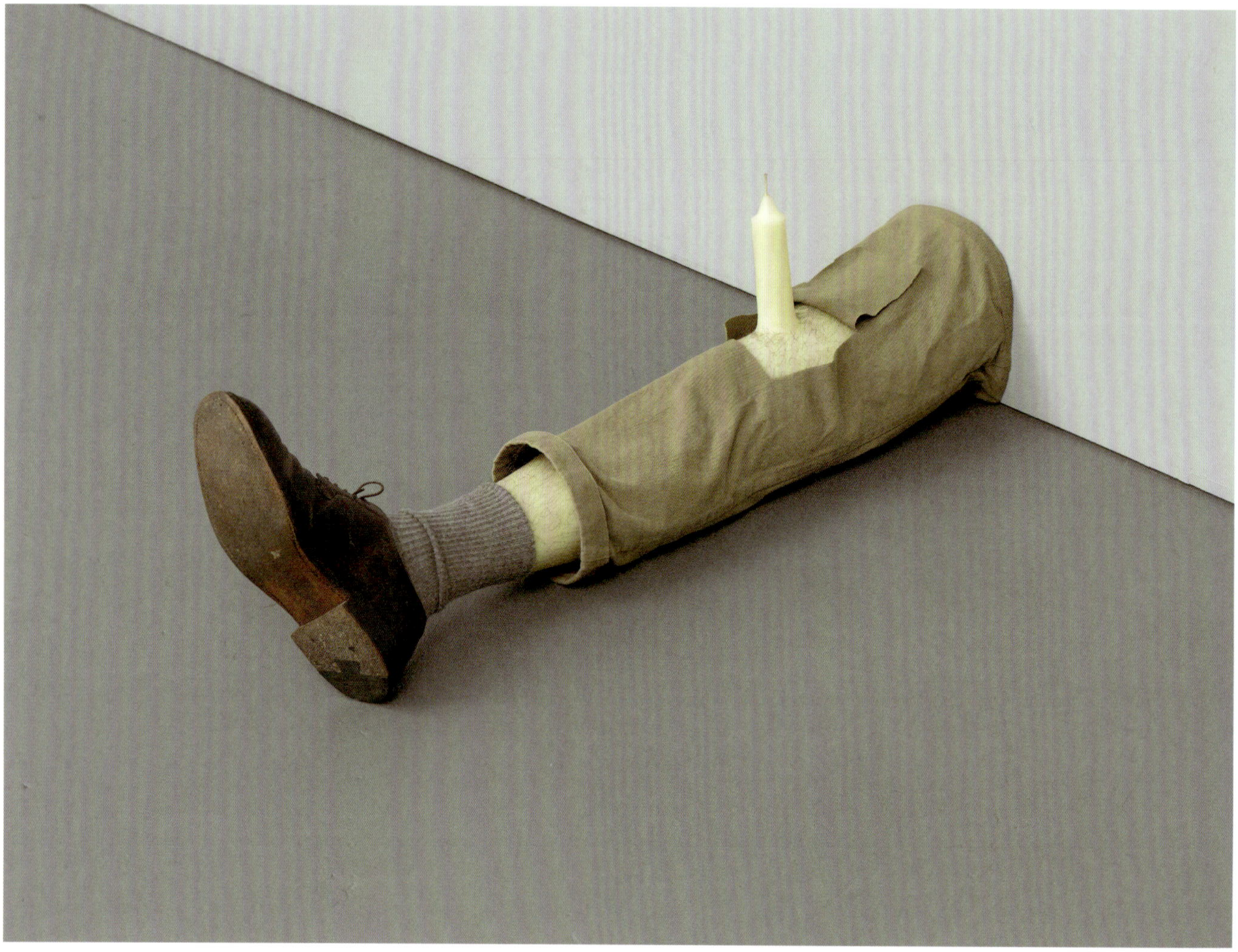

Fig. 8 Robert Gober, *Untitled*, 1991, wax, cloth, wood, leather, and human hair
Whitney Museum of American Art, New York; Purchase, with funds from Robert W. Wilson, 92.6
Cat. 79

The psychiatrist Sigmund Freud, an avid collector of classical antiquities (many of them broken), wrote about the duality of an experience that causes both fear and pleasure in his 1919 essay "Das Unheimliche" (The Uncanny). Freud defined the uncanny as something familiar but long forgotten that returns in a distorted form. It is an experience or object that causes fear not because it is alien but because it is disturbingly familiar—but not quite right, or, as the philosopher Lucy Huskinson describes, "without the memory of its original content."[28] The uncanny challenges the boundaries between self and other, real and imagined. In looking at what remains of fragmented figures, we are keenly aware of what is missing.

As with earlier objects, Gober and Bourgeois use fragments as pars pro toto. Isolated legs cause us to think about the full human body and what is missing, while also subverting categories since the sculptures were created to be fragments—they are, in fact, simultaneously complete and incomplete. Gober's leg with the projecting candle-phallus reminds the viewer that it was always intended as a complete fragment. The sculptures are melancholy and disturbing; they exude dislocation and alienation. These fragmented bodies express the fearsome duality of existence: life/death, past/future, presence/absence, allure/threat. We are simultaneously attracted to and repelled by their presence. The South Korean artist Geumhyung Jeong drags us from the prehistoric fragmented body to the alienated body of the Anthropocene ⟨ *fig.* 9; see also cat. 92 ⟩. Her works vary from static assemblages of ready-made plastic body parts to performances involving robots constructed from found objects and DIY electrical components, which she activates in relation to her own body. Whereas Merleau-Ponty used the analogy of the flesh to describe a world in balance, Jeong manipulates plastic bones, cables, and motors to depict a techno-capitalist world out of balance. In Jeong's work we move from the fragmented body that connects and memorializes us to other humans to a world without memory or connection to others.

The transition from Neolithic burials featuring fragmented human figures to contemporary artistic practices highlights a deep-seated fascination with the fractured body as a site of symbolic meaning. In prehistoric contexts, the intentional breaking and dispersal of figurines may have symbolized spiritual transformation, enchainment to others, memory, or the permeability of life and death. These early gestures of fragmentation, both physical and symbolic, resonate with the strategies employed by contemporary artists who also dismantle the human form to evoke memory, relationships, and psychological dislocation. While the Neolithic impulse may have been ritualistic, today's fragmented bodies often interrogate identity, memory, and embodiment in an increasingly fragmented world. In both eras, the broken figure becomes a palimpsest—once for transcendent belief and connection, now for critical reflection.

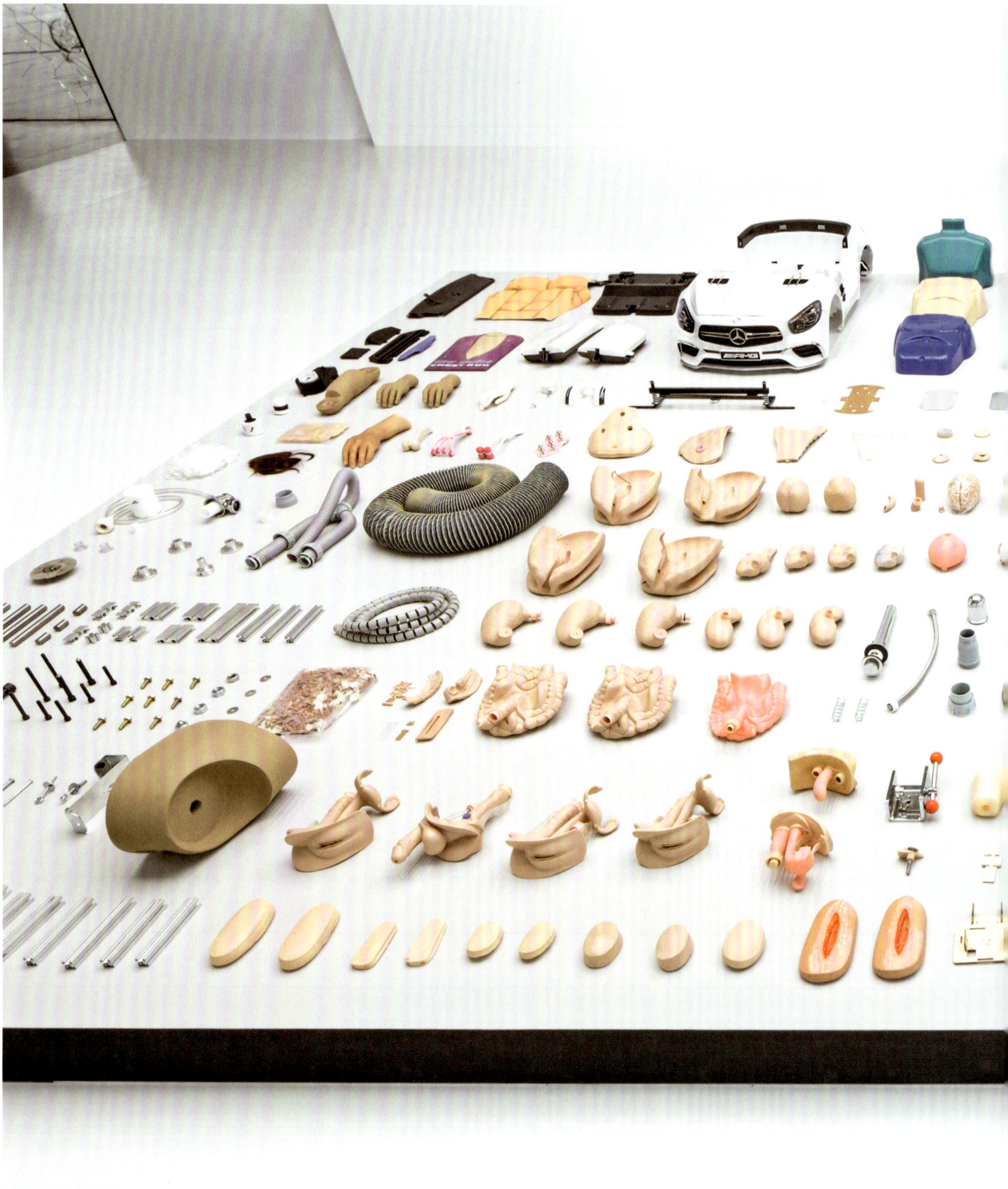

F*ig*. 9 Geumhyung Jeong, *Removed Parts*, mixed media, installation view from *Human, 7 questions*, October 8, 2021–January 2, 2022, Leeum Museum of Art, Seoul

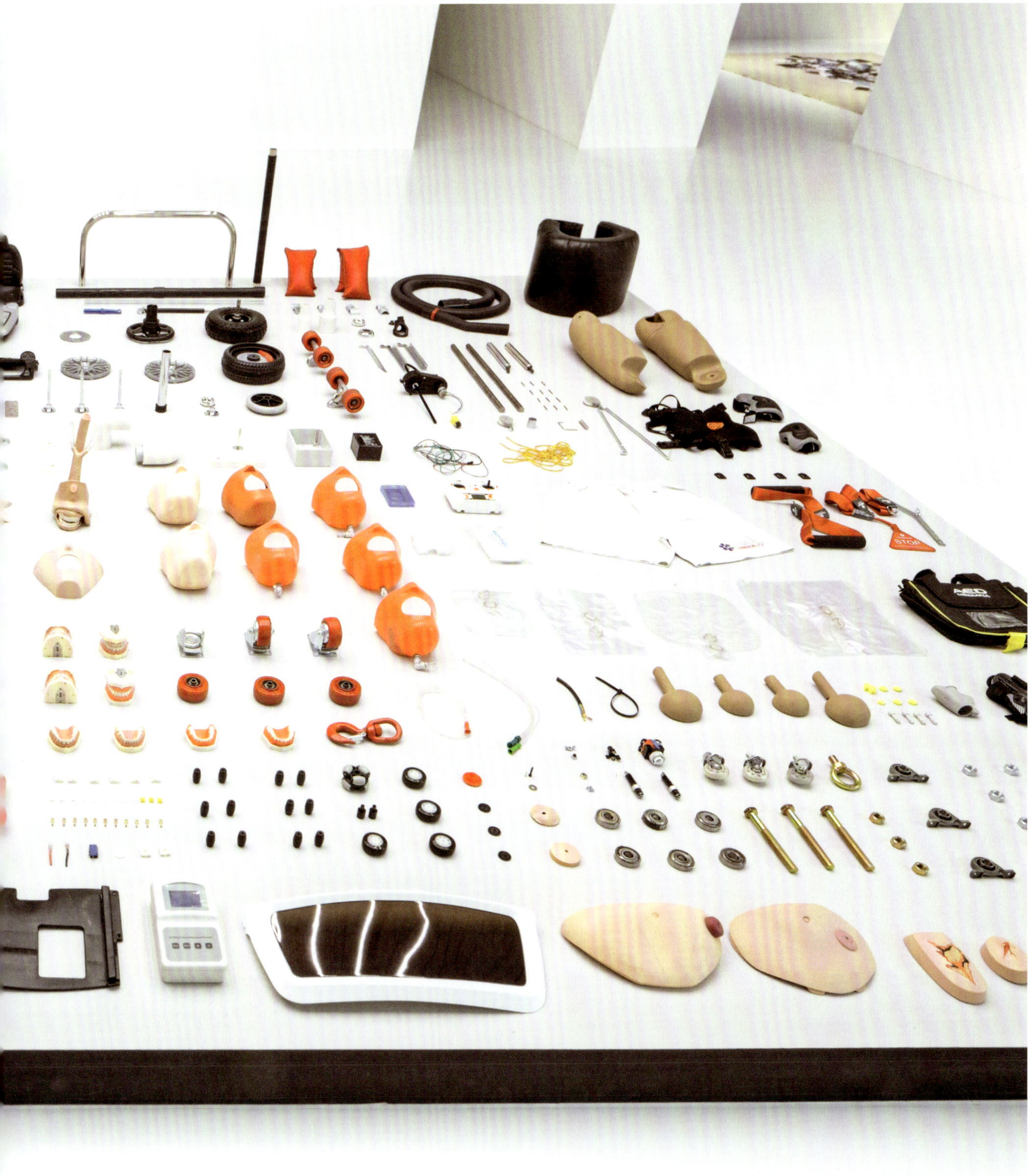
STOP

WHAT THE FRAGMENT WANTS

Rosemarie Garland-Thomson

Unlike our fellow persons, sculptural fragments do not see us, even as we see them. The experience of seeing a fragment may therefore seem to be a one-way conduit of knowledge. The visual culture theorist W. J. T. Mitchell offers us a perceptual understanding of how we see artworks that enlivens the visual interchange by speculatively endowing the work of art with visual agency. Mitchell's provocative question "What do pictures *really* want?"—the title of his article from 1996—invites the viewer of an artwork to suspend her disbelief by personifying the inanimate museum object and treating it as a visual interlocutor.[1] Following Mitchell, let us grant that sculptures, perhaps more strongly than pictures, are "things that have been marked with all the stigmata of personhood," as Mitchell explains. Sculptures, like pictures, "speak to us." A museum exhibition renders sculptures as "subjectivized" objects who haunt us with their "uncanny personhood."[2] The sculpted human figure calls to us with its distinctive presence. Our response fuses this moment with the ghosts of every other face-to-face encounter between that enlivened statue and the long-lost thousands of fellow humans who have stood before it across the time and place of its long tenure in the world. The sculpted human figure calls to us with its distinctive presence. What a sculpture wants, then, is to elicit from us what the literary scholar Wai Chee Dimock calls "resonance," for us to welcome the "echo of what it was and of what it might become" that the work radiates upon us.[3]

Sculptural fragments have something to tell us. They call to us with the eloquent authority of a cultural object that has persisted in the world and stands before us ready to speak its story. Fragments beckon to us with varying tones—many commanding, some defiant, still others furtive. An especially elusive example is the fourteenth-century *Heads of Mary and Christ from a Pietà*, now in Berlin. This fragment offers us only the two curiously serene faces, shorn from one another, silently imploring us to restore their lost embrace 〈 *figs.* 1–2 〉. This stone duet composed of two small heads, each less than a foot across, is the remnant of a statue of the Virgin Mary gazing down at her dead son, Jesus, cradled in her lap. The vanished bodies, once intimately entwined in the *Pietà*'s familiar gesture of loss, lament, and revelation, are ghosts to us now. Like so many of the sculptural fragments in the pages of this book, these two faces suspended before us present an opportunity for imaginative restoration. Each sculptural fragment puts forward an aesthetic puzzle, a distinctive invitation to bring our individual archives of cultural knowledge to repair in our own way the sculpture's wholeness that time and world have shattered. The visual culture scholar Georgina Kleege reminds us that our understanding of art

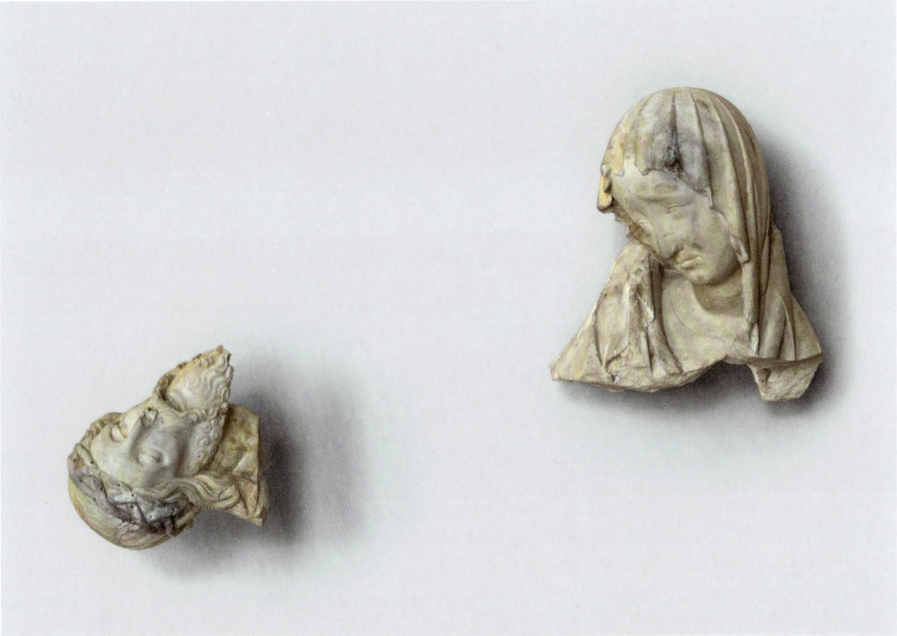

Fig. 1 Prague (Baden bei Wien), *Heads of Mary and Christ from a Pietà*, c. 1380–1400, limestone
Skulpturensammlung und Museum für Byzantinische Kunst, Staatliche Museen zu Berlin, inv. 2743
Cat. 49

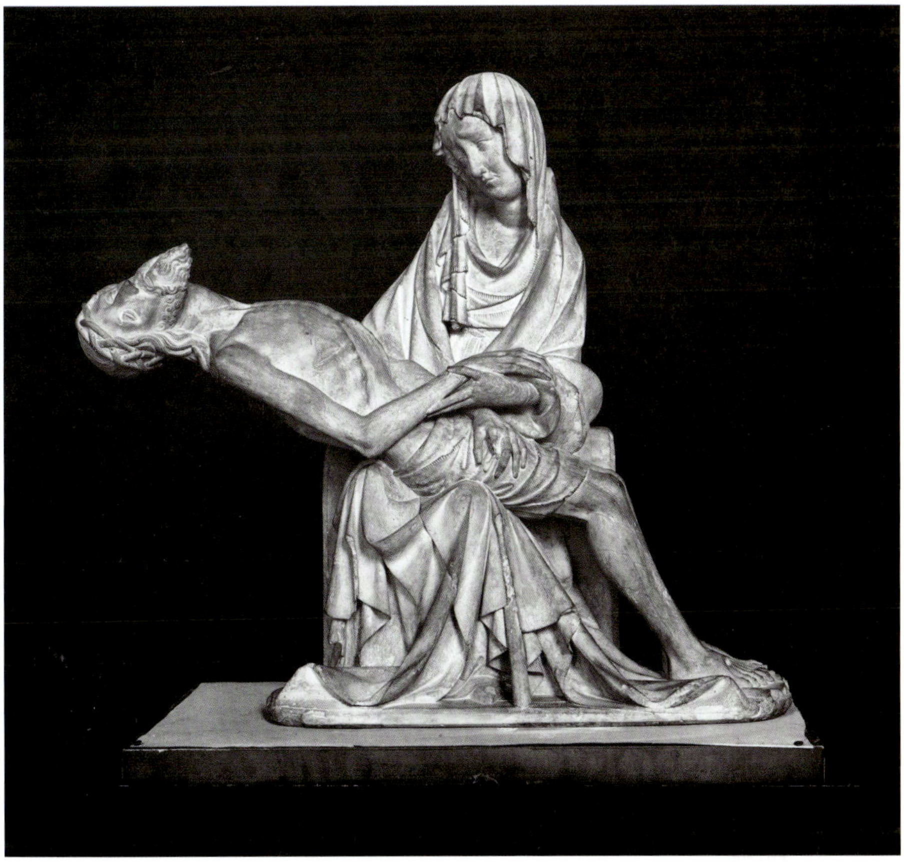

Fig. 2 Photograph of *fig.* 1 taken before 1940

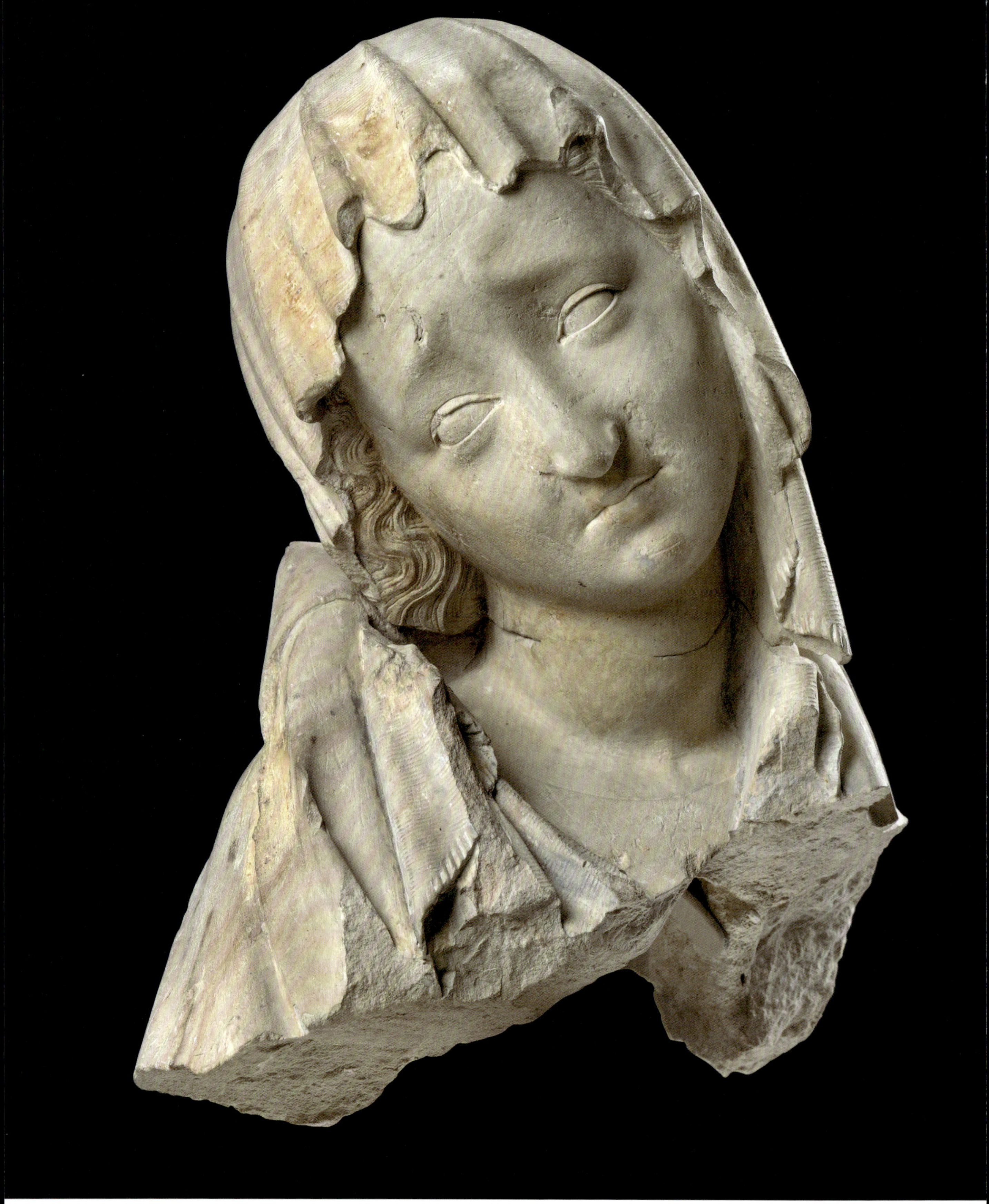

Detail, p. 81

comes more from what we have learned about art than from our direct, unmediated experience of any work of art.[4] The task of inventive restitution that the *Pietà* requests of us, then, is smoothed for most of us with the resonance of familiar meanings.

If we follow Mitchell's conceit that a work of art wants something from us and speaks to us of what it wants, we can recall the personification of sculpture offered by the Victorian art critic John Ruskin, who declared at Oxford in 1870 that the essence of sculpture is a "pleasant bossiness." Considering that, for Ruskin, the representational pleasures of a sculpture lie in its "roundness of surface," how differently might a fragment affect the viewer compared with her response to a complete, unbroken sculpture?[5] In the case of most fragments, the "pleasant bossiness" of the smooth, rounded surface has given way to a disconcertingly jagged edge, a gashed face, a severed limb. Bossy these fragments may be, but pleasant they are not. These broken sculptures command us in the service of truth more than beauty. They speak a severe truth about what time and world do to objects, both of flesh and of stone. Their unpleasant truths support Ruskin's preference for a sculpture revealing its own brokenness, as he argues in "The Lamp of Memory," his 1849 vehement defense of preservation rather than restoration.[6] The fragment bespeaks the evanescence of all enterprises.

THE FRAGMENT'S STORY

Sculptural fragments want to tell us their stories. They bear witness to the truths of persistence in the face of inevitable vanishing. They attest to the human enterprise of making things of stone that endure beyond our fragile flesh. Even so, time and world have had their way with these works of art. The naked display of the wounds that divine and human acts have imposed upon them gives urgency to their self-presentation. The fragments illustrated here garishly present us with what seem to be the amputated stumps we often hide from one another in everyday life. The usual serenity of the hushed museum accosts us instead with a smashed stone head the size of a car; limbs amputated by time, neglect, or calamity; noseless monarchs; and colossal feet and hands severed now from the vigorous wholeness they once displayed. Just as our disabled fellow humans must forever respond to the demand to account for their wounds or deformities, the sculptural fragment requests our recognition in exchange for displaying its broken body to our curious eyes.

Time and world break both flesh and stone. Like the human body, a statue begins to disintegrate from the moment of its completion, testifying to its own intransigent temporality. As we move from embryo to corpse, world imprints itself on flesh.

Sculpture bowdlerizes broken bodies, tidying up flesh's embarrassing messes. Time has worn away the realism of blood and the faces of suffering on the broken sculptures we now behold. Most of the artworks in this volume were once whole in both form and content. Indeed, the intended representational work of these sculptures honored wholeness—its beauty, power, influence. These now-broken statues, pummeled by time, are memento mori, entreating us to remember them. Whether evoking caution or celebration, a room of fragments offers viewers a contemplative encounter with the stark truths of mortality. We are witnesses to human evanescence, lining up to view in turn the open caskets of our human aspiration, to allay our vanishing by pondering flesh secured in stone. We follow an ancient and urgent impulse to grasp the fact of death by touching what remains: the final kiss of the cold lips in the coffin, the grasping at the rumpled shirt for the scent of our beloved, the fingering of the quotidian object that laid against the lost flesh stolen now from our touch. Beholding fragments is a communal ritual of witnessing the rude or tender truths of flesh, bone, and blood.

Putting a fragment in the context of a museum exhibition transforms an object crafted long ago and far away by human hands now themselves reduced to dust into a work of art vibrantly present to its viewers. We are pilgrims seeking meaning in contemplating a remnant, a material object once ordinary in its wholeness but now extraordinary in its partiality. This alchemy of exhibition turns rubble into relics: discarded and forgotten junk transformed into sacred objects offering us the opportunity to ponder in tranquility what it means that our fellow humans craft things that carry messages to us across time and place. These now-still objects are messages in bottles, floating before our eyes, alluring and inscrutable, urgent in their stolid persistence and mystery.

The young English poet John Keats, himself steadily vanishing from the consumption that took so many of us over millennia, once stood in the British Museum contemplating the broken Parthenon sculptures and the ancient Grecian urns. This witnessing compelled Keats to a poetic meditation on the terrible distinctions between his evanescent flesh and the enduring broken stones and fragile clay before him. In his 1819 lyric poem about viewing the ancient fragments, "Ode on a Grecian Urn," Keats fashioned a testimony to the artisans' hands, lost to us now, steadily pounding their message into the unyielding stone or shaping the supple clay to tell him something of what they were and how they lived. The figures on Keats's urn avow the elegiac wisdom that "Beauty is truth, truth beauty,—that is all / Ye know on earth, and all ye need to know."[7]

The English Romantic poet Percy Bysshe Shelley's 1818 sonnet "Ozymandias," an enduring elegy to the transience of glory and a testimony to human arrogance, gives us the story to go with many of the fragments shown in this volume.[8] A weary traveler tells the tale of a colossal fragment, a forgotten ruin buried in an abandoned desert. Inscribed resolutely on the crumbling pedestal is the name "Ozymandias, King of Kings." No vestiges of the eternal glory the inscription claims remain but the "lone and level sands" stretching into the distance. Many sculptural fragments are in stone what Shelley's "Ozymandias" is in verse: odes to the inescapable vanity of human ambition.

BROKEN EMBRACE: *PIETÀ*

The fragment speaks to us of what it has endured, igniting our curiosity about its original form. The shape of a body, both in life and representation, determines the story we tell about it. Form follows function, as the modernists insisted. The sculptural fragment offers viewers the opportunity to restore in their imaginations the lost wholeness that time and world have effaced from the broken sculpture. As we have considered, the sculpture's journey from origin to ruin is analogous to the human journey from our entry into the world as a fresh being to our inevitable exit as a withered corpse. As the poet William Butler Yeats reminds us in "Sailing to Byzantium," we are a vivid consciousness "fastened to a dying animal."[9] Imagining what has been shorn from a sculpture is a resurrection of the original.

This book gathers the remains of the once monumental, now dormant: a strapping muscled torso; the gigantic hands of a Buddha and a Roman emperor; the noble bust of a now misremembered Caesar. In quiet contrast, the Berlin *Pietà*, resurrected from the wreckage of a bunker fire in 1945, is a modest and somewhat perplexing fragment that differs from its fellow sculptures in scale, shape, and sensibility. The two enigmatic faces invite us to bring our experience and knowledge to interpret those fragments and complete the scene choreographed before us. The image of mother and son entwined in a sacred embrace is imprinted for many of us somewhere in our shared cultural memory. The ancient choreography of the *Pietà* is recognizable to viewers as a familiar narrative of bereavement and the promise of restoration that has been told in story and image for millennia, perhaps most vividly in Michelangelo's marble *Pietà* in Saint Peter's Basilica at the Vatican ⟨ *fig.* 3 ⟩.

The perplexing fragments resolve into the known story. The worn, solitary faces speak to us about vanishing aesthetic enterprises but also of our transitory human relationships. The small

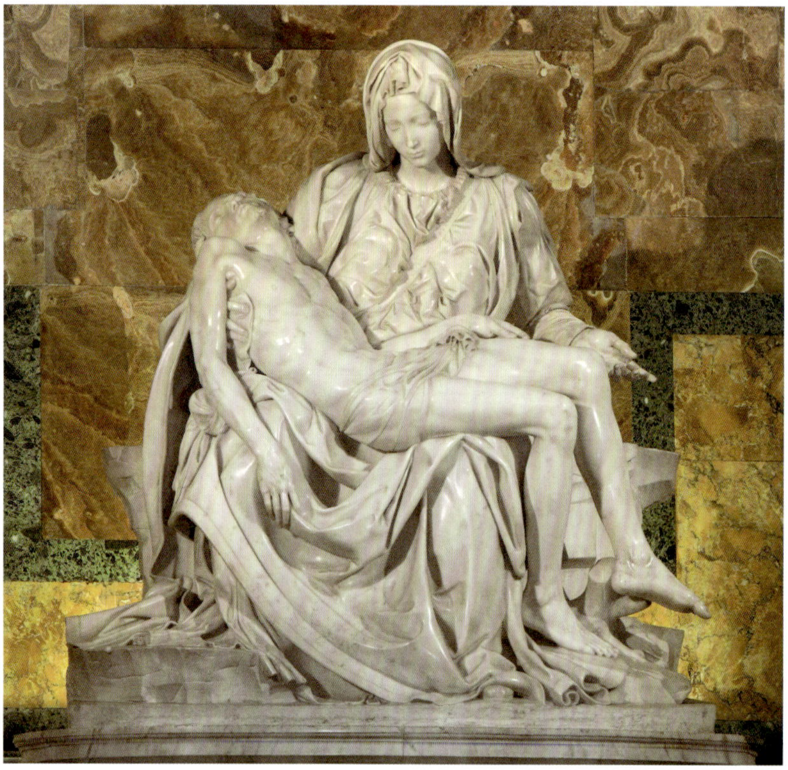

Fig. 3 Michelangelo Buonarroti, *Pietà*, 1498–1499, marble
Saint Peter's Basilica, Vatican City

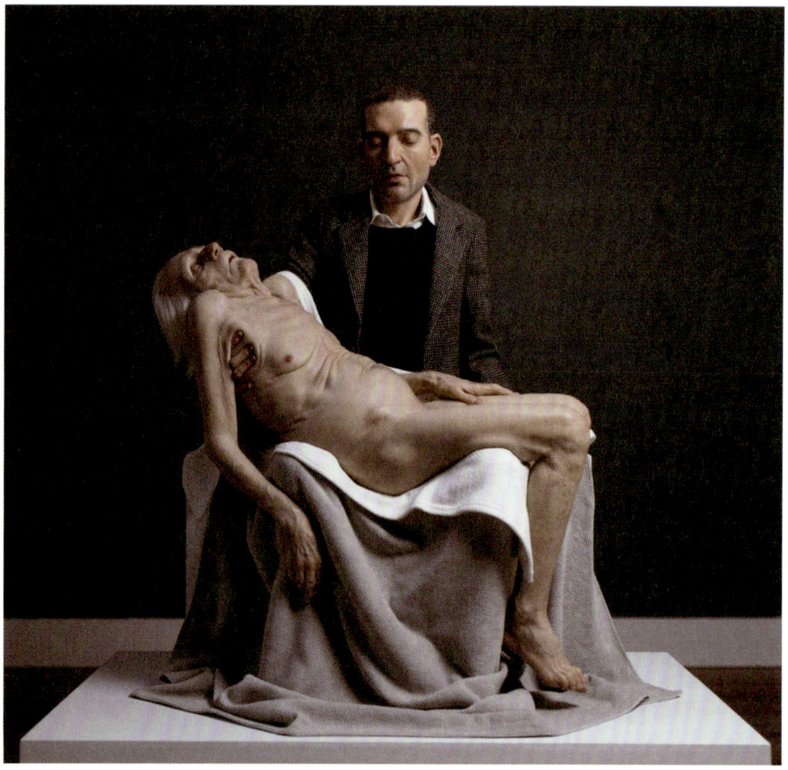

Fig. 4 Sam Jinks, *Still Life (Pieta)*, 2007, silicone, human hair, acrylic, nylon, polyurethane foam, and timber

stone faces beckon to us, quietly inviting us to contemplate their lost wholeness. They softly implore us to reestablish the embrace of mother and son that careless violence has severed, leaving us only the suppliant visages floating ghostlike, abandoned by the bodies that had coupled them for centuries. Our task in beholding this tender scene of mourning is to imaginatively reestablish the broken encirclement of the mother's lost arms and lap that cradled her beloved son's lifeless body. Their shattered faces summon us in a whisper rather than the shout of their colossal Ozymandian peers strewn through the pages of this book. This stone mother and son are gentle afterlife voices testifying to war's wreckage, mouths agape with suffering but without the command or horror of their fellow broken fragments. They whisper of our evanescent flesh and the consolation of tender, enfolding attachment. Theirs is a duet of sorrow and hope, a soft chant echoing the persistent grief of women attending to bodies they have made and loved over lifetimes.

As witnesses to the *Pietà*'s scene of attachment broken by violence, we are called by the faces to re-create the embrace lingering in our memories, however vague, of the array of Pietàs that people the cultural landscape through which we move. "Who we consider holy changes over the centuries; what we want from them has not," notes the writer Kathryn Harrison in her wonderful commentary on the meaning we bestow upon remnants.[10] As with Mitchell's yearning pictures, these stone faces beseech us to make them whole again. The challenge has been taken up across genres by artists who have perpetually recomposed that mournful scene to fit their own moment and place. In recent years, as one example, we have a modern everyman gazing down impassively at the figure of an ancient naked ancestor draped lifelessly across his knees ⟨ *fig.* 4 ⟩. These contemporary Pietàs are laments that demand our engagement, shouting rather than whispering about the troubles of our own times.

BROKEN ATTACHMENTS RESTORED: ALISON LAPPER AS PIETÀ

The social discomfort that viewers of sculptural fragments may experience was roused by a 13-ton, 12-foot-tall marble statue of a woman sculpted by Marc Quinn that was displayed on the famous fourth plinth of London's Trafalgar Square from 2005 to 2007 ⟨ *fig.* 5 ⟩. A marble statue of a nude woman on a pedestal, however enormous, might have been unremarkable now, considering its placement in a public square where grand statuary documenting famous men has been routine for centuries. This monumental representation was, however, neither the classical mythological goddess nor the honorary, properly presented female dignitary that we might expect. Quinn's imposing and unsettling statue portrayed an actual living woman, the English writer Alison Lapper, whom Quinn presents in stark realism as Lapper existed at the moment of the statue's creation: nude, heavily pregnant, and congenitally armless and partially legless.[11] Conversation and controversy piled on to this provocative public artwork that displayed a conventional marble nude figure inflected by the scandalous convergence of pregnancy and disability.[12]

We might consider Quinn's straightforwardly titled sculpture *Alison Lapper Pregnant* as an intentional sculptural fragment, the image of a body broken in its biology but whole in its humanity. At the same time, it is a wondrous irony that Lapper's disabled body—so often considered incomplete, broken by disability—finds completeness through aesthetic representation. Quinn's statue invites responses different from what the dynamic sociologist Erving Goffman identified when a viewer perceives the "bodily signs of physical disorder," such as wounding, amputation, illness, or disability. Goffman cast physical disabilities as social stigmata in unnerving 1960s vocabulary in which the "normals" confront "deviants" who bear the "abominations of the body" or bodily "imperfections" that signal moral "blemishes."[13] For anyone living with an obvious physical disability, Goffman's account of the everyday ableism that disabled people put up with in social interactions with strangers in modern life tells a tedious truth we all recognize. Encounters between flesh and world sculpt our bodies in unusual ways, transforming many of us into living fragments. Quinn's sculpture probes how unusually shaped, reshaped, or disabled bodies unsettle their visual interlocutors.

Alison Lapper Pregnant is a postmodern Ozymandias-in-the-City or a seated *Venus de Milo* that fuses neoclassical sculptural conventions with the contemporary sensationalism of Andres Serrano's *Piss Christ* (1987), the painted grotesques of Lucian Freud, the public commentary art of Banksy, or Ai Weiwei's performative dropping and breaking of a two-thousand-year-old urn. A disconcerting mash-up of the familiar and the strange, Quinn's sculpture pairs with the heroic Vice Admiral Lord Nelson, her fellow amputee, towering above her on his colossal marble Corinthian column erected a century and a half before Lapper joined him. Together, Nelson and Lapper brought disability to London's famous site of public tribute and dispute. *Alison Lapper Pregnant* provoked both productive and regressive conversations about reproductive ethics, eugenics, disability, feminism, parenting, public health, art, history, and more.

The statue of Lapper was viewed by many as a provocation that quite literally put in our faces

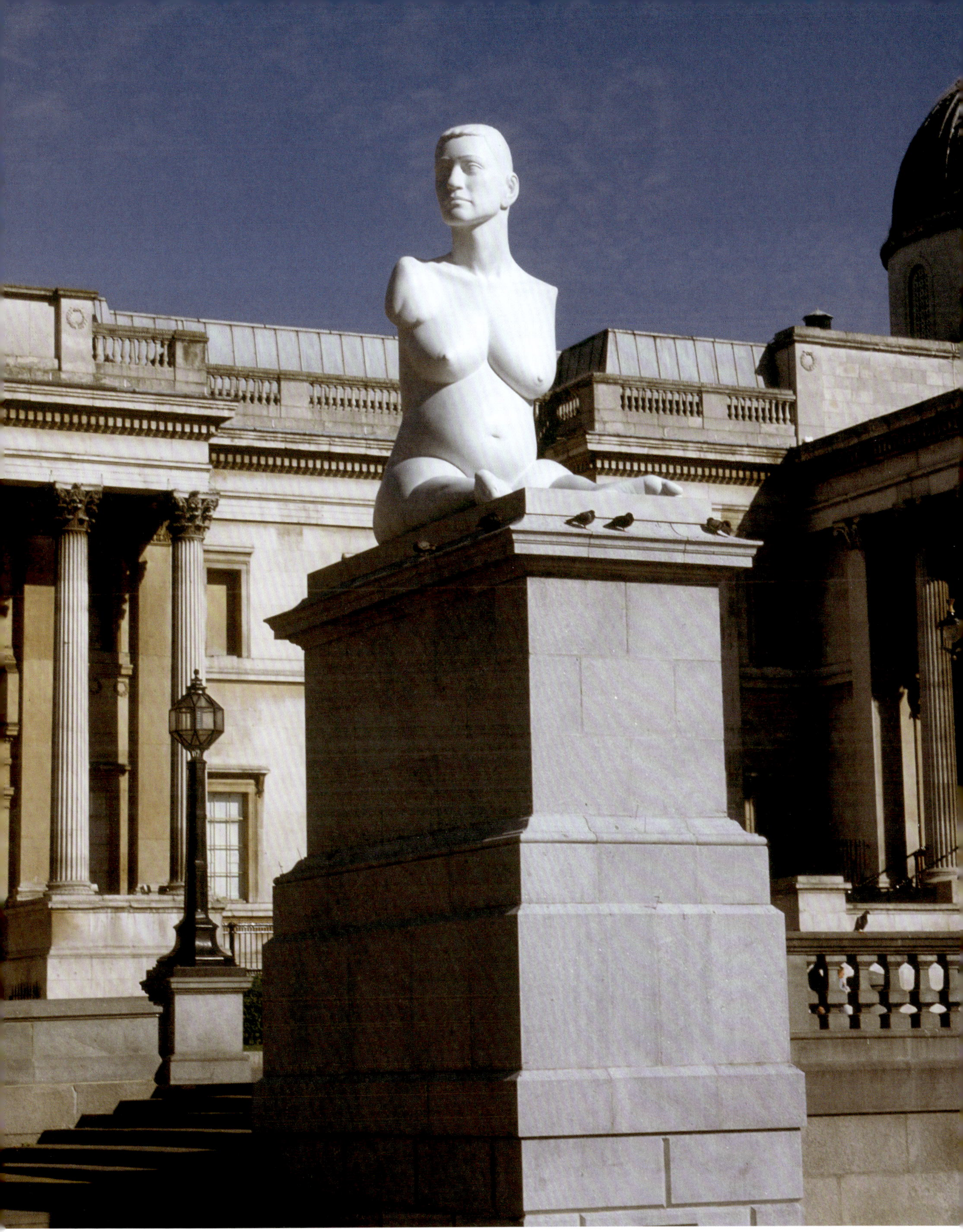

Fig. 5 Marc Quinn, *Alison Lapper Pregnant*, 2005, marble

the moral controversies raised by the modern eugenics movement of the early twentieth century. That version of genetic science aimed to prevent supposedly unfit and disabled people from reproducing and to encourage the supposedly fit and healthy to reproduce. Many point out that eugenic science has continued into the twenty-first century with reproductive practices that identify risk for producing people with disabilities. The statue of a pregnant disabled woman forced public and private discussions about the fitness for motherhood of a significantly congenitally disabled woman, setting into conflict the ethical principles of reproductive liberty, the preservation of human diversity, and the scientific medical goal of creating a healthy population.

We can interpret *Alison Lapper Pregnant* as a Pietà of celebration that reunites the maternal embrace of the broken *Pietà* in Berlin. The word *pietà* means both "pity" and "compassion" in Italian. Pity is a small emotion with narrow affect and blunted potential, whereas compassion is a more capacious gesture that extends beyond the individual sufferer into the greater world. Charged with the Christian narrative of death redeemed, the *Pietà* elicits pity for the grieving mother and compassion for all of grieving humanity. The *Pietà* wants compassion more than pity. The *Alison Lapper Pregnant* Pietà offers that compassion.

The *Pietà* in Berlin recounts the double sorrow of violence: the image of the grieving mother and the dead son parted by death and a sculptural embrace shattered by war's brutality. The mother and child in Quinn's Pietà are, in contrast, irrevocably entwined in a natal union that cannot be broken. While the traditional Pietà endlessly iterated in our aesthetic archive bespeaks maternal sorrow and untimely death, the maternal duet represented in *Alison Lapper Pregnant* suggests an innovative restoration of the attachment between mother and child. Whereas Mary gazes mournfully at the dead son she cradles in her lap—even as she solemnly anticipates his promised restoration—Lapper looks impassively outward toward the world, sphinxlike, alert and poised to bring her stone bulk to defend the child she has made and carries within her. Lapper's form is without the traditional tools of defense that ordinary mothers call upon—arms, hands, legs, and feet. Nonetheless, she is quietly fierce as her bounteous breasts hover over her ample belly, protecting the curled infant within her body from the hostile world that aims its violence at her beloved offspring or at their shared violation of modernity's reverence for normalcy.

The two Pietàs differ in time, place, and scale but converge in meaning and in their appeals to onlookers. Each sculpture implores us to recognize truths of human attachment, transience, and mortality. We might consider Quinn's *Alison Lapper Pregnant* as a bold response to the Berlin *Pietà*'s muted call to imagine the lost embrace between mother and child. As the sacred scene transforms over time, the lachrymose downward gaze of the Madonna changes into the impassive vitality of Lapper's gently challenging outward gaze that meets the perplexed eyes of her curious spectators.

Alison Lapper Pregnant restores the sundered *Pietà*, with its recognition of death and violence, by reuniting mother and child in a life-giving embrace. The Lapper Pietà rises out of the metaphorical ashes of the broken rubble of a thousand smashed scenes of human endeavor. The delicate faces of mother and son in their vanished embrace of sacred maternity are overrun by Quinn's gigantic Madonna, gazing out atop her enormous pedestal in Trafalgar Square. She is a womanly Ozymandias of our time, announcing her solidity and authority in stone and scale. This Madonna and Child is no lamentation; rather, it boldly asserts a narrative of persistent attachment that at once honors and presages the uncertainties of human enfleshment.

There's an alchemy at work between the elegant sculptural choreographies of mother and child in these two tender scenes of nested procreative incarnation. Their public display renders them sacred relics, one miniature and one gigantic, talismans calling to us with their rough certainties. As such, they do the cultural meaning-making work of relics, transforming us into witnesses of objects worthy of our veneration. The sculptures offer us a duet: *Alison Lapper Pregnant* responds with stolid ferocity to the *Pietà*'s gentle beckoning from broken faces. Theirs is a sculptural pas de deux affirming truths through the solidity of what remains when human flesh has vanished. Sculptural fragments are Sirens calling to us about the endurance of things across time and world. Their stony wisdom insists on what the poet Laurie Clements Lambeth reminds us: "All creatures who persist are whole."[14]

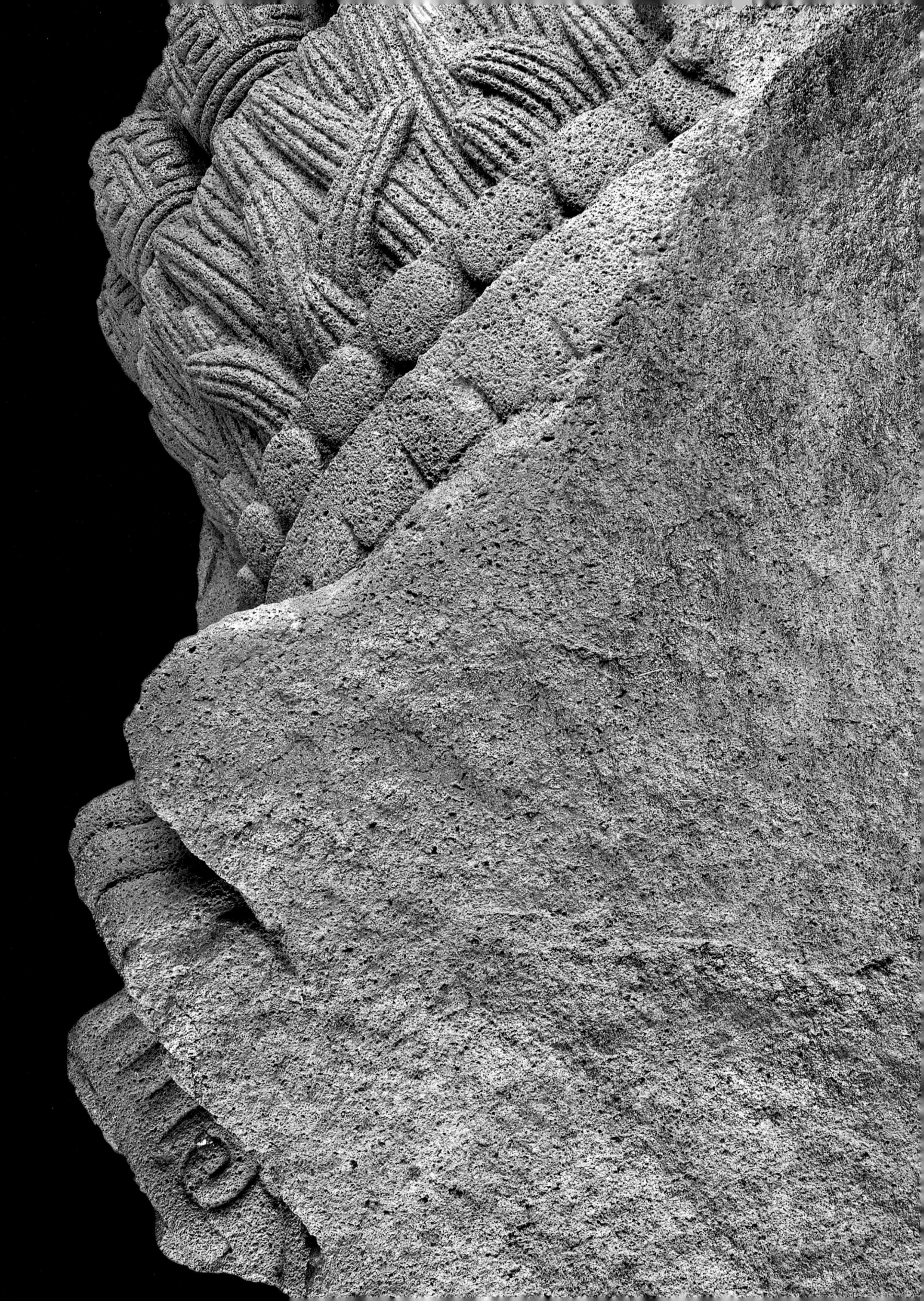

FORCES OF BREAKAGE

Detail, p. 105

PATTERNS OF DESTRUCTION

EPISODES IN THE HISTORY OF ATTACKING SCULPTURE

Miriam K. Said and Andrew Sears

A sculptural relief in the British Museum in London depicts what initially seems to be an idyllic scene of repose set within a lush garden ⟨ *fig.* 1 ⟩. King Ashurbanipal of Assyria has laid his weapons on the table at far right and reclines on a chaise longue underneath a grapevine. Opposite him, Queen Libbali-šarrat sits upright in a richly appointed chair, her feet resting on a matching stool. The royal couple has just been served refreshments by their courtly servants and raise shallow bowls to their lips, at which point the banquet's tranquility starts to unravel. The queen cannot drink from her bowl because her mouth has been chiseled away. The king's bowl and face alike have been violently and deliberately hacked out of existence. Mere decades after this sculpture was carved to commemorate Ashurbanipal's military prowess and the peace he claimed to have secured for his realm, it was attacked by a coalition of Babylonians and Medes. In 612 BCE, they sacked the city of Nineveh, defaced public images of its rulers in the North Palace, including this one, and brought an end to both Ashurbanipal's reign and the Neo-Assyrian Empire.[1]

The insurgents appear to have carefully examined the relief before picking up their chisels, and their choices reveal much about the logic underlying iconoclasm and the destruction of images more broadly. The king and queen were the principal targets because their representation was believed to possess a certain vitality that needed to be killed. In contrast, the head of the Elamite king Teumann, which hangs from a tree on the left, remains untouched—despite being an enemy of both Ashurbanipal and the attackers—because he was already shown as dead. Also targeted were the royal couple's closest courtly attendants, many of whose noses were chipped away. Perhaps less a "killing" than a harsh retribution, these acts of disfigurement served as an admonition for any viewers who might think to remain loyal to the previous regime. The intentions of destruction extended well beyond the depicted individuals or their immediate viewers. To deface a sculpture required significant labor and persistence. The objective was not necessarily to destroy images but rather to gradually chip away in the hope of destabilizing and eventually dismantling the social and political structures that erected them. Erasure is rarely an aim of iconoclasms, since the final goal of attacking sociopolitical systems requires some kind of spectacle in order to visualize a cause. Iconoclasm, in other words, paradoxically depends on images to be successful. Acts of violence against artworks are never singular events, carrying instead layered intentions that yield enduring consequences. As we will see, destruction is a process that affects the object itself, the person it represents, the communities that surround it, the institutions that raised and dismantled it, and the centuries—or millennia—of viewers who have confronted its broken surfaces.

KILLING

Throughout history, images have inspired strong feelings—awe, terror, admiration, arousal, joy, or disgust—which in turn have provoked visceral reactions such as crying, stroking, praying, kissing, or smashing and slashing. For many cultures of the premodern world, sculptures elicited these types of embodied responses because they were believed to be more than mere representations; instead, they were seen to be alive, materially manifesting the depicted subject. Some sculptures were even ritually given breath to animate them, after which they required daily provisions of food, drink, and clothing.[2] Others required continued attention and veneration in order to grant wishes and perform miracles.[3] Ruler portraits were seen to be extensions of the sovereign's body: They were inaugurated in celebration, were placed to survey his or her political domain, or were forced upon defeated people as a reminder of conquest.[4] For all these reasons and more, individuals, religious and cultural groups, and nation-states have always been—and likely will always be—motivated to deprive sculpture of its life force.[5]

In the late third millennium BCE, the landscape of ancient West Asia was peppered with the sculptural forms of Akkadian kings. Sargon of Akkad and his successors built an empire and consolidated what had previously been independent city-states in what is today Iraq.[6] They commemorated their victories and imperial aspirations by installing statues of themselves, their soldiers, and their defeated enemies in strategic locations: from temples, to distant peripheries of the state, to places they hoped to bring under the purview of Akkadian rule.[7] Within each image, or *ṣalmu*, was the active essence of the ruler, completely indistinct from his living body; as such, only the most valuable materials were used in the execution of

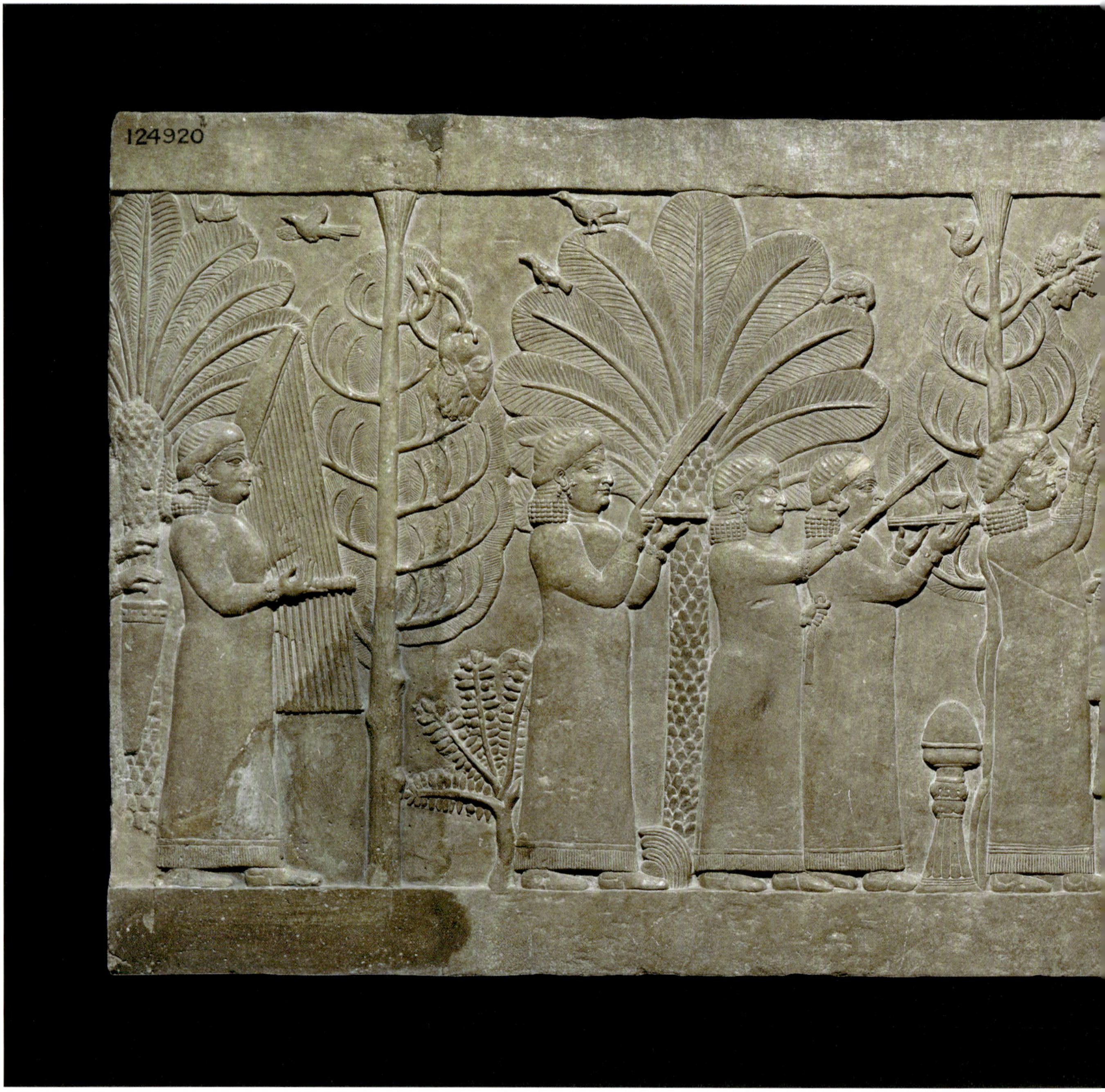

Fig. 1 Neo-Assyrian, *Banquet Scene Relief from the North Palace of Nineveh*, 645–635 BCE, gypsum
British Museum, London, 1856,0909.53

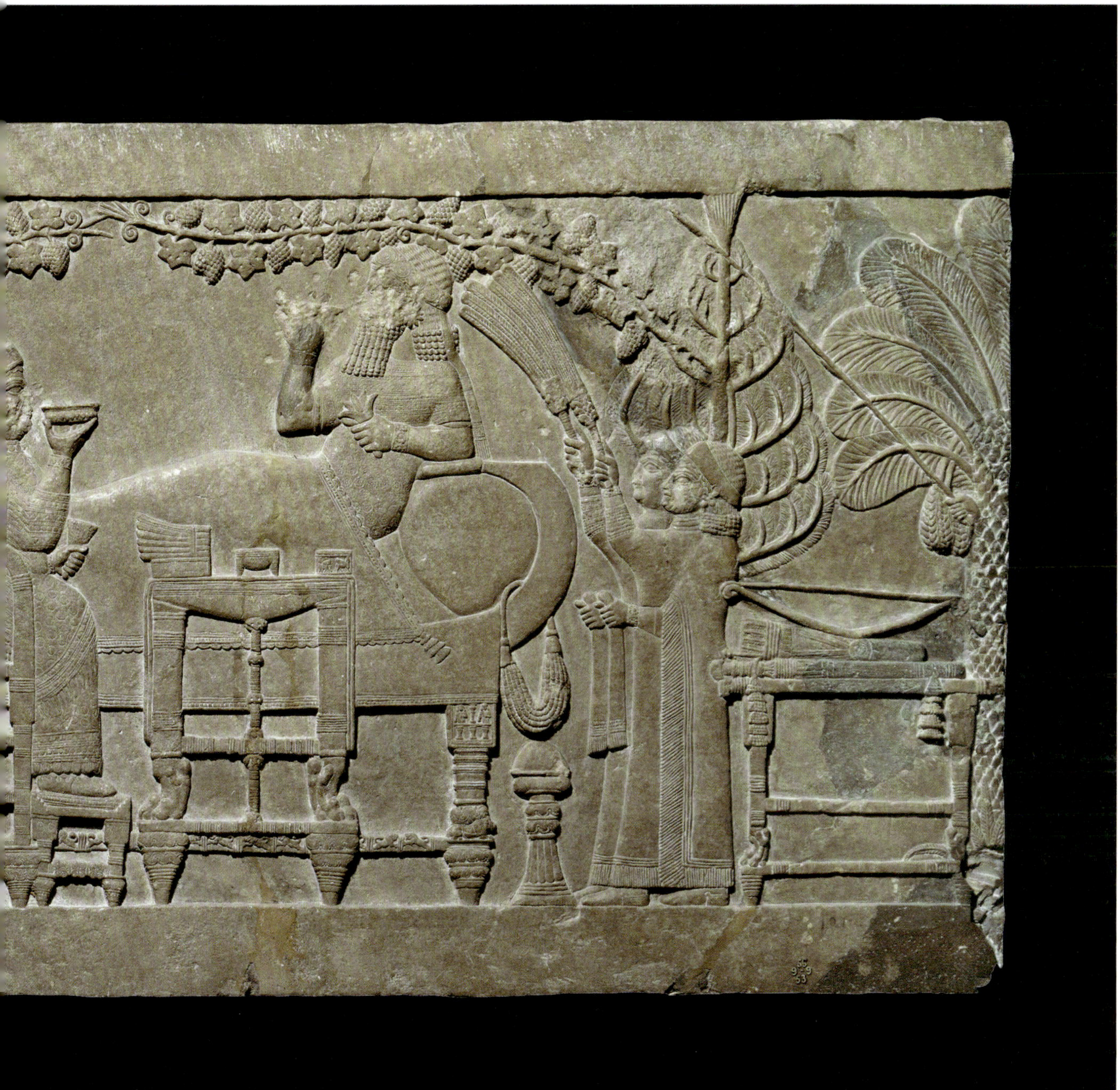

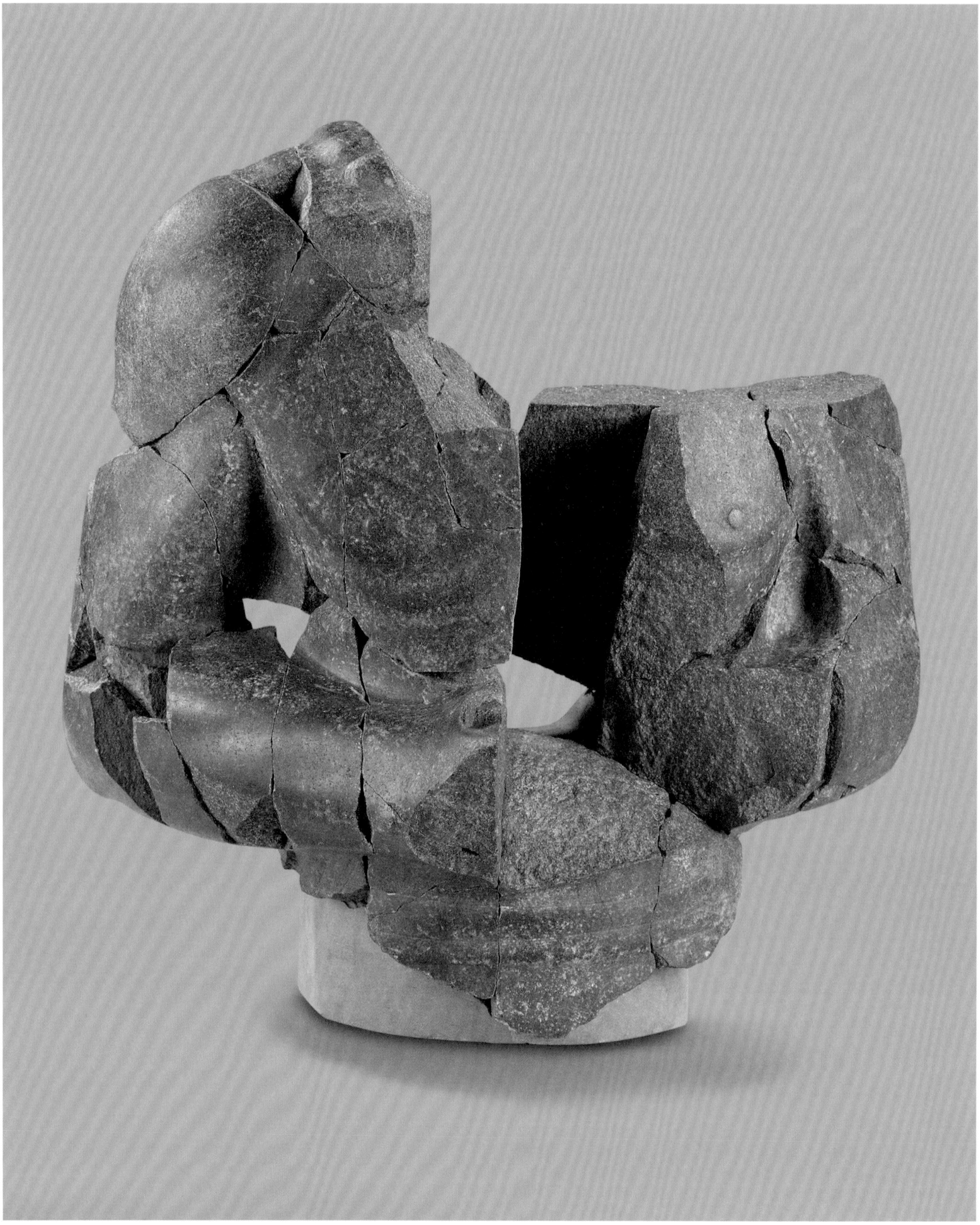

Fig. 2 Akkadian (Aššur), *Torso of a Ruler*, c. 2300–2250 BCE, gabbro
Staatliche Museen zu Berlin–Vorderasiatisches Museum, VA 17312
Cat. 2

these statues. *Torso of a Ruler*, which currently survives in approximately two hundred fragments, was sculpted from gabbro, favored for large-scale royal statuary beginning under Sargon's son, Maništušu 〈 *fig.* 2 〉. A dark stone that is exceptionally hard and can be polished to a high luster, it was especially suited to showing off Akkadian feats of naturalism and technical mastery.[8] This particular sculpture was excavated in 1908 from the vicinity of two temples, and it remains unclear when and how it came to be so broken.[9] Similar to the image of Ashurbanipal and his queen that opened this essay, it may have been targeted by a coalition of Babylonians and Medes in the late seventh century BCE, as the form of Akkadian rulers was highly recognizable and thus an obvious target for iconoclasts. Alternatively, given the value of the stone, its durability, and its distant origins, the sculpture may have been repurposed as building material and used to reinforce the fourteenth-century BCE street under which it was found. Regardless of whether the sculpture was attacked or recycled, its status as rubble reveals the extent to which rulers, their images, and their memories were destroyed after they had fallen from favor.

Across the ancient world, and especially in Egypt, such killing was often motivated by the fear of the subject's agency lingering within the image. *Face and Shoulder from an Anthropoid Sarcophagus*, made during the Ptolemaic period (c. 332–330 BCE), was probably initially broken by ancient tomb looters looking for gold amulets and other precious adornments with which mummies were often interred 〈 *fig.* 3 〉. Scared that the deceased tomb owner might seek vengeance through the image, the vandals subsequently chipped its nose to deprive it of any life force.[10] Such anxieties about the power of images continued into late antique Egypt, especially after it became a province of the Roman Empire and adopted Christianity in the third century CE. In the process of conversion, Christians across the region began to reuse, recycle, or destroy artifacts of Egypt's pagan past.[11] A bust identified as representing Germanicus, heir to the Roman emperor Tiberius, was deliberately targeted by Christians, who likely considered the sculpture's existence an affront to their belief in the one true God 〈 see Freedberg *fig.* 4 〉. Germanicus visited Egypt shortly before his death in Antioch in 19 CE, so the creation of the bust likely dates to that visit. Roman emperors, beginning with Augustus, were deified, and there was likely some fear that the statue was or could become animate. To mitigate its liveliness, Germanicus's nose was hacked off, and his upper earlobes were cut.[12] The faint saw marks at the base of the throat attest to attempts to remove the head from its neck; alas, the basanite rock was too durable for severing.

In addition to the sculpture being deprived of its sensory organs, it has a cross carved in the center of its forehead.[13] The intended purpose of this secondary carving is not definitively known. It has been suggested that carving the cross on the forehead was a form of Christian appropriation of imperial imagery, with the act of carving akin to baptism.[14] Others have suggested that carving the cross was reminiscent of the ancient practice of marking enslaved persons with tattoos, thus making Germanicus a "slave of god." Alternatively, this could also attest to the supremacy of Christians over pagan forerunners, a violation of Germanicus's impotent likeness, or a way of releasing the "demon" locked within the image so that no harm could befall Christian viewers.[15] All these potential motivations demonstrate a desire to mark, control, and thus regulate the embodied power of sculpture.

HARMING

Centuries later, the policing of images within a Christian worldview continued and came especially to the fore during the Protestant Reformation. Across sixteenth-century northern Europe, and especially in southern Germany and Switzerland, cities began convening public debates to deliberate whether images fostered improper devotion. The primary concern for Protestant reformers was not, however, that images had unruly power that needed to be feared. Instead, they questioned whether images had any agency to begin with beyond enticing believers to place undue confidence in material forms. Numerous publications of the time, stemming from Martin Luther's writings around 1520, describe the absurdity of performing daily superstitions in front of blocks of wood or stone.[16]

In the iconoclastic waves that followed, the primary goal was to deter people from endowing images with an unnecessary degree of power. Destruction extended far beyond acute attacks on altarpieces or supposed idols and encompassed the wholesale stripping of church interiors, thus discouraging Catholics from investing in any kind of image, whether monetarily or spiritually. Among the most extensive campaigns were those spearheaded by the authorities of Bern.[17] Following the city council's order that the Catholic Mass be abolished and its churches cleared, the Bernese expanded their efforts by invading the neighboring Pays de Vaud. In 1537 they began taking down sculptures, destroying altars, whitewashing wall paintings, and demolishing tombs at a variety of churches—from the Cathedral of Lausanne to the famed Cluniac Abbey of Romainmôtier.

Among the casualties at Romainmôtier was a nearly life-size sculpture of a kneeling prior, believed to represent Guillaume de Montricher ⟨ *fig. 4* ⟩. It was discovered in 1986 alongside a figure of a kneeling knight, perhaps Guillaume's father, Jacques. Originally adorning a

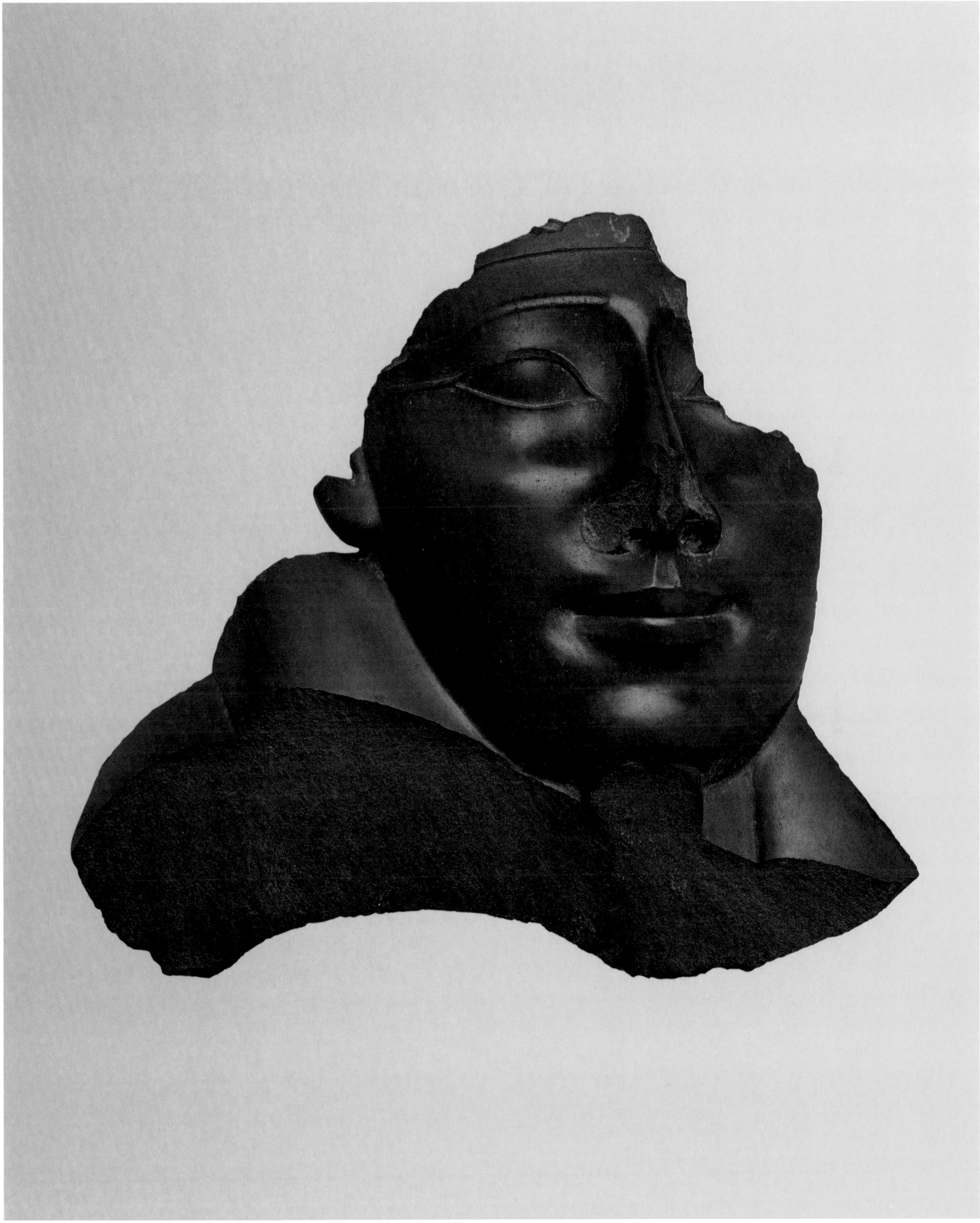

Fig. 3 Egyptian, *Face and Shoulder from an Anthropoid Sarcophagus*, c. 332–330 BCE, graywacke
Brooklyn Museum, Charles Edwin Wilbour Fund, 37.1516E
Cat. 12

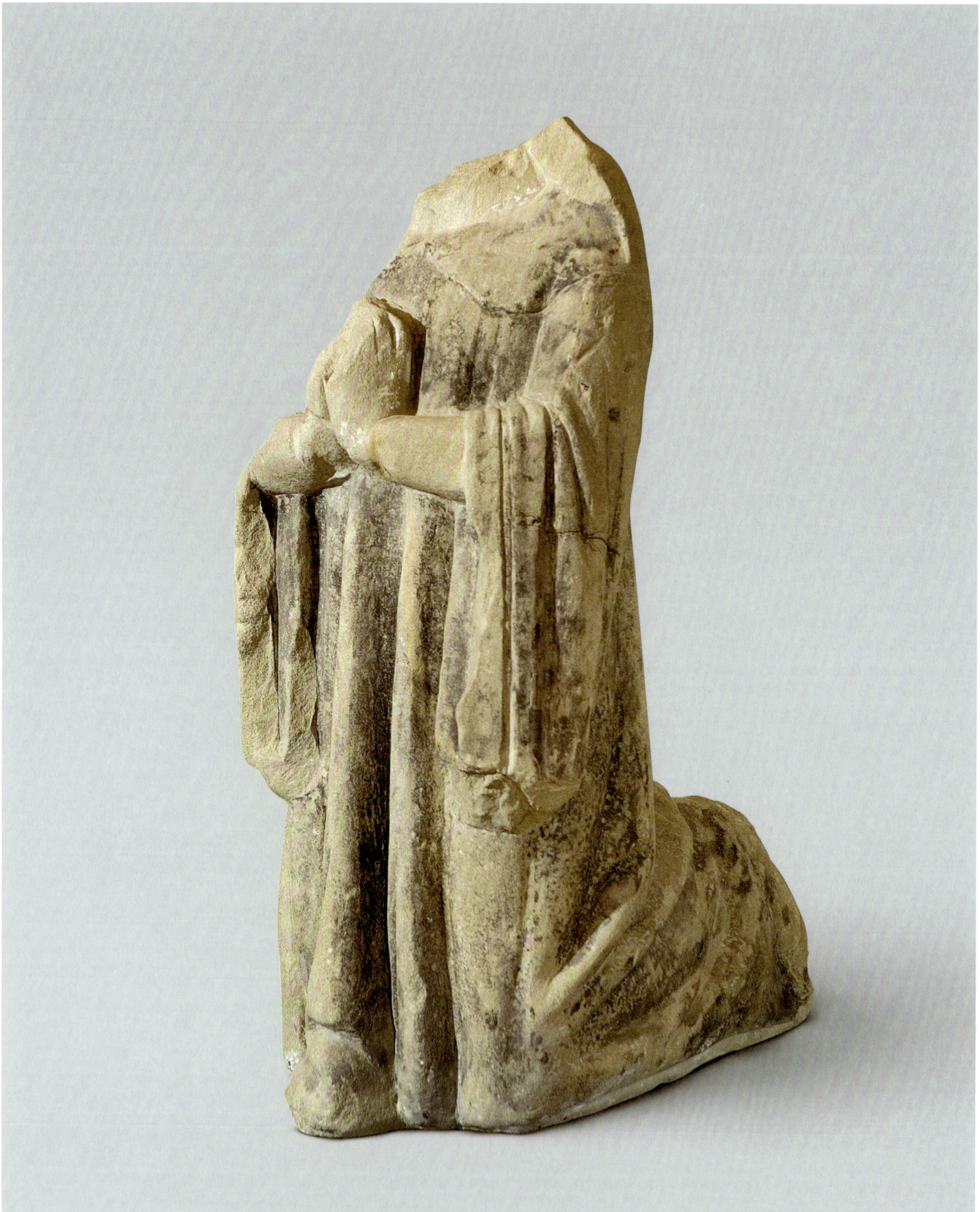

F *i g.* 4 Pays de Vaud Workshop? (Romainmôtier), *Kneeling Cluniac Prior (Guillaume de Montricher?)*, c. 1330–1336, molasse sandstone and pigment
Collection of the Musée Cantonal d'Archéologie et d'Histoire, Lausanne, RO86/17279
Cat. 46

monumental tomb, the works were obvious targets for the iconoclasts.[18] Depicted in perpetual prayer, the figures modeled the type of devotion that reformers were trying to discourage. Moreover, the union between members of the secular elite and the Catholic Church on an extravagant tomb must have been perceived as especially egregious, embodying networks of privilege while also suggesting the degree to which images had come to facilitate self-promotion more than devotion.[19] For the reformers, such works needed to be destroyed to pave the way for a new social order.

A similar tactic of using image destruction to exert control over communities was deployed by Europeans across the globe in the sixteenth century, most dramatically in the context of the Spanish colonization of the Americas. Writing to the Holy Roman Emperor Charles V in 1519–1520, the Spanish conquistador Hernán Cortés recounted how, after arriving at the Mexica capital of Tenochtitlan, he destroyed an array of "idols" at the Templo Mayor by having them thrown down the stairs of the temple pyramid. According to Cortés, the aim was to instruct the Indigenous population about what he believed to be the irrationalities of their belief system: "I made them understand through interpreters how deceived they had been in believing in those idols which were made by their own hands from unclean things, and that they had to understand that there was only one universal God, lord of all, who had created the heaven and earth and all things."[20] This program of extirpation continued for decades, as inquisitorial procedures sought to identify and eradicate idolatry throughout New Spain.[21]

Two sculptures that may have been damaged in this context are a defaced representation of the goddess Chalchiuhtlicue and a remnant of a monumental statue of Coatlicue 〈 *figs.* 5–6 〉.[22] Chalchiuhtlicue has been brutally disfigured—her face attacked by a sharp instrument and her arms cut off—though her defining attributes remain intact: her skirt and cape encrusted with representations of precious greenstones (*chalchihuitl*).[23] The once-towering monolith of Coatlicue has effectively been reduced to rubble, though this surviving fragment preserves several rattlesnake rattles that once formed the fringe of her skirt and served as the basis of her name: *coatl* meaning "snake" and *icue*, "her skirt."[24]

It is possible that such acts of disfigurement were undertaken by the Mexica themselves, who periodically destroyed their own statuary, most notably during the New Fire ceremony. Occurring every fifty-two years, the ceremony entailed the breaking or disposal of household wares as well as images of gods in order to renew the sun and avert the end of the world. Yet given the scale and sustained nature of colonial iconoclasm across sixteenth-century Mesoamerica, destruction was more likely directed by the Spanish, some of whom observed a New Fire ceremony, recorded and studied it through Nahua informants, and seemingly

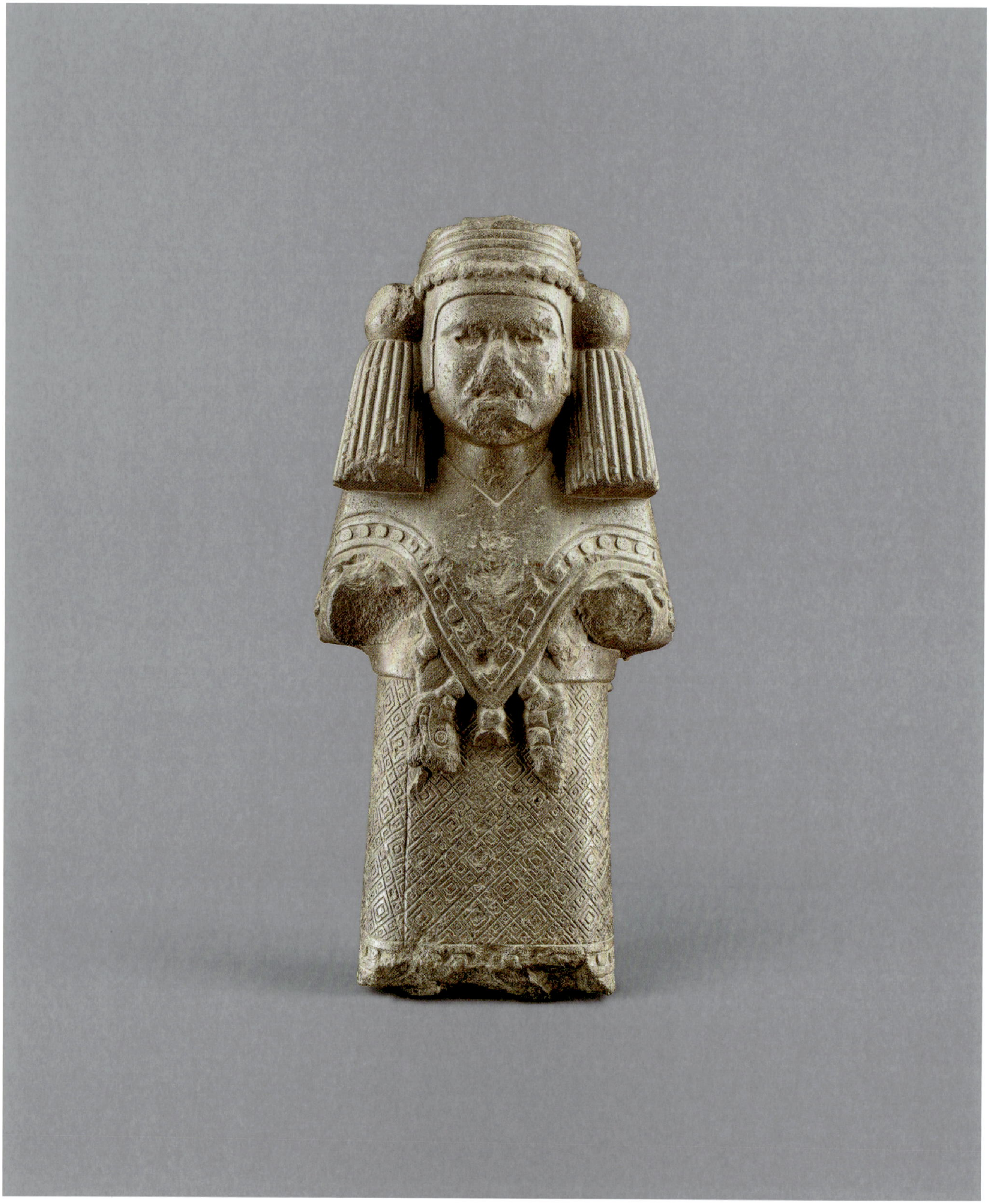

Fig. 5 Mexica (Tenochtitlan [Mexico City]), *Statue of Chalchiuhtlicue*, c. 1325–1521, diorite
Museo Nacional de Antropología, Mexico City, Secretaría de Cultura—Instituto Nacional de Antropología e Historia, 10-82215
Cat. 45

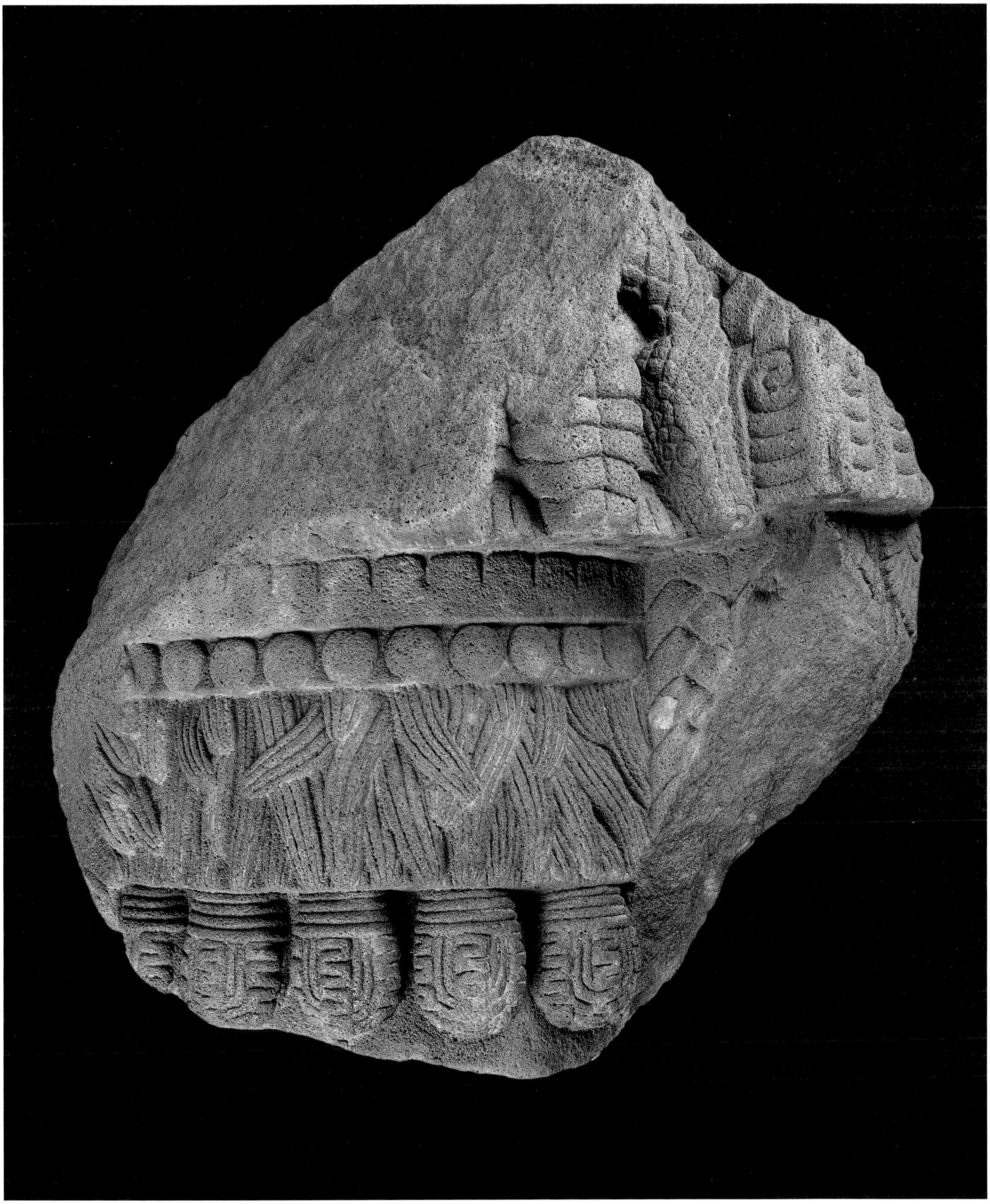

Fig. 6 Mexica (Tenochtitlan [Mexico City]), *Fragment of a Serpent Skirt of Coatlicue*, c. 1400–1500, basalt
Museo Nacional de Antropología, Mexico City, Secretaría de Cultura—Instituto Nacional de Antropología e Historia, 10-393493
Cat. 51

appropriated the dialectic of destruction and generation as a means of consolidating control over the Indigenous population.[25] Relying mainly on brute force—colonialism's own version of ritual violence—the Spanish sought to damage Mexica "idols" so extensively as to create a void that could be filled with an immediate solution, Christianity. Cortés himself reported to Charles V that once sculptural decoration had been removed from the Templo Mayor and its various chapels had been emptied and whitewashed, he erected images of the Virgin Mary and other Christian saints in their place.[26] As swiftly as sculptures were destroyed, so too were Indigenous belief systems and solidarity, which were then reformulated and reconstituted to advance the dominant power's interests.[27]

DISMANTLING

One of the key motivations for damaging sculptures and harming communities was to dismantle and rebuild new structures. When the Achaemenid Persians attacked Athens in 480 BCE as part of their second incursion into Greece, they left a massive amount of destruction in their wake. The Acropolis was only loosely guarded and easily overrun by Persian soldiers, who burned Athens's most sacred structures and destroyed or pillaged much of the sculpture on the mound. Particularly grievous to the Athenians was the destruction of the Late Archaic temple to Athena Polias, which housed in its inner sanctum an olive-wood statue of the goddess so old that the residents believed it had fallen to earth from heaven.[28] During their retreat from the city, the Persians also burned homes and toppled the many funerary monuments erected by the city's elite that decorated its landscape, especially freestanding sculptures of idealized men and women—*kouroi* and *kourai*—and tall stele decorated with individuals carved in relief. The scope of such destruction suggests the target was not images or people so much as the larger sociopolitical context within which they operated.

Head of a Kouros can be described as a victim of the Persian Wars, but perhaps not in the way one might initially think ⟨ *fig.* 7 ⟩. While a significant portion of the kouros's youthful face has been lost, the one remaining eye is visibly intact. As already shown with the fragments in the first section, acts of purposeful destruction are typically indicated through targeted attacks of sensory organs. In the case of much of the statuary believed to be destroyed by the Persians, heads are decapitated, throats are sliced, arms and legs are broken, and eyes and mouths are chiseled away, as seen in the features of the boy carved on a Greek grave marker from about 525 BCE ⟨ *fig.* 8 ⟩.[29] *Head of a Kouros* may have been purposefully destroyed, but by the Athenians themselves. In the decades

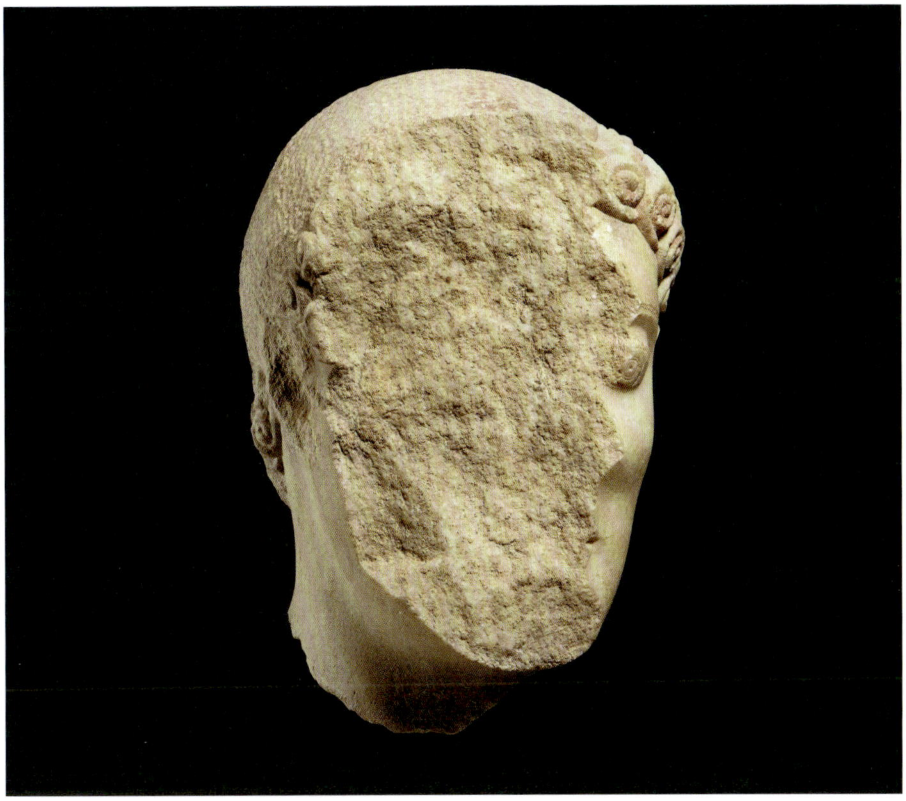

F i g. 7 Greek (Athens), *Head of a Kouros*, c. 530–515 BCE, marble
Museum of Fine Arts, Boston, Bartlett Collection—Museum purchase with funds from the Francis Bartlett Donation of 1912, 34.169
Cat. 10

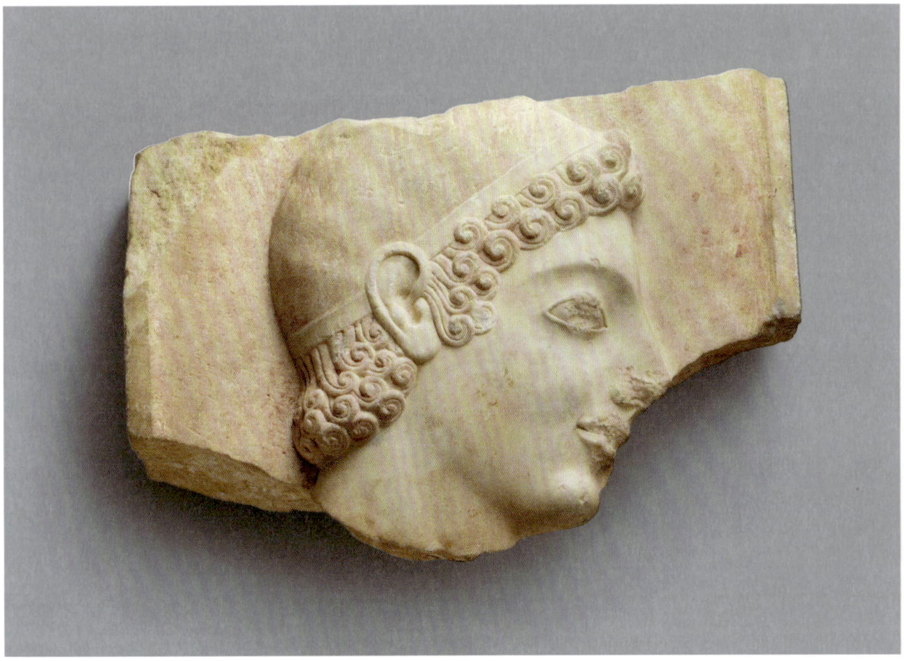

F i g. 8 Greek, *Head of a Youth from a Marble Stele (Grave Marker)*, c. 525 BCE, Parian marble
The Metropolitan Museum of Art, New York, Rogers Fund, 1942, 42.11.36

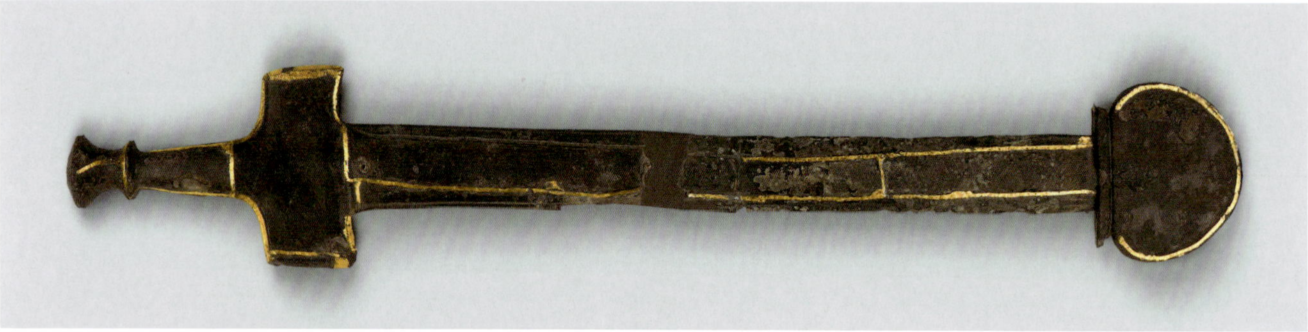

Fig. 9 Greek (Athens), *Sword from an Equestrian Statue (King Demetrios Poliorketes?)*, c. 320–270 BCE, bronze with traces of gilding
The Museum of the Ancient Agora, Athens, B1382
Cat. 13

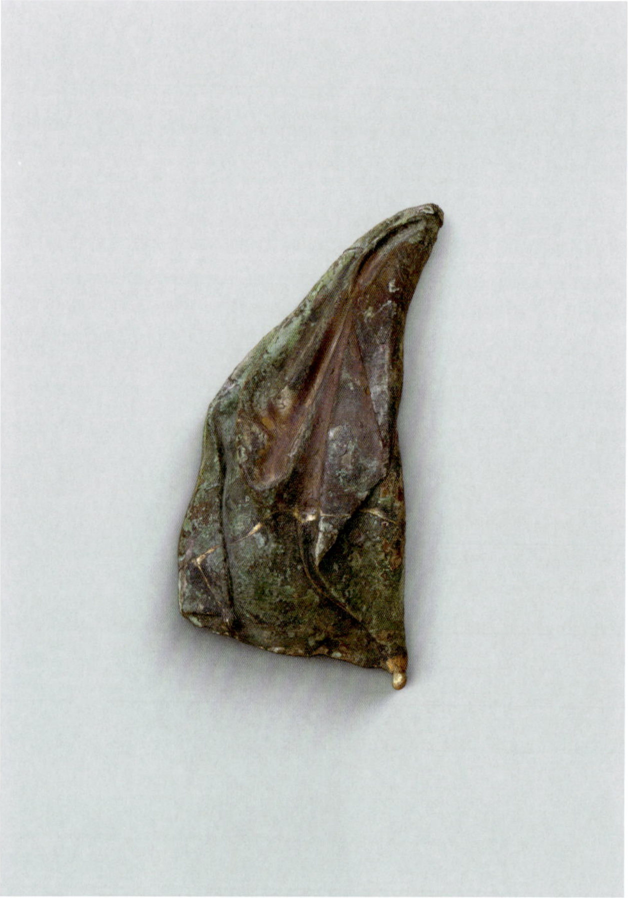

Fig. 10 Greek (Athens), *Drapery from an Equestrian Statue (King Demetrios Poliorketes?)*, c. 320–270 BCE, bronze with traces of gilding
The Museum of the Ancient Agora, Athens, B1383
Cat. 13

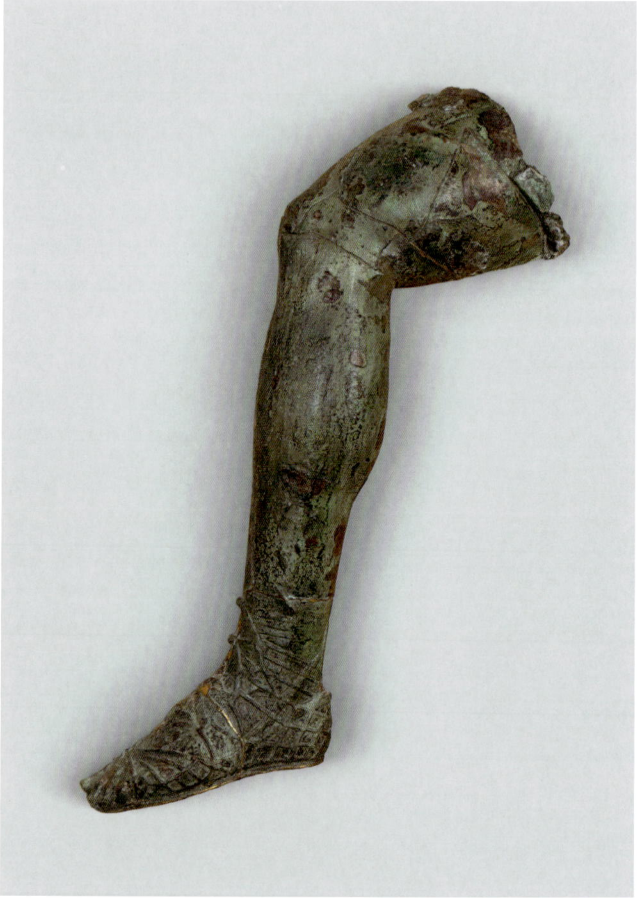

Fig. 11 Greek (Athens), *Leg from an Equestrian Statue (King Demetrios Poliorketes?)*, c. 320–270 BCE, bronze with traces of gilding
The Museum of the Ancient Agora, Athens, B1384
Cat. 13

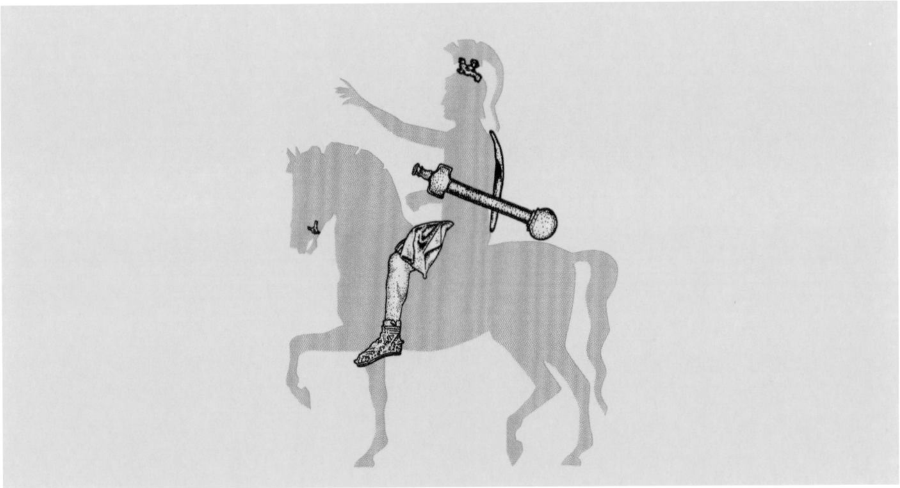

Fig. 12 Reconstruction drawing of the equestrian monument fragments found at the Athenian Agora
From Caroline Houser, "Alexander's Influence on Greek Sculpture: As Seen in a Portrait in Athens," *Studies in the History of Art* 10 (1982): 232

after the war, haunted by the memory of pillaging, the destruction of their city, and the dismantling of its monuments, the Athenians destroyed and repurposed their own sculptures into building materials for new city walls. Ritual votives to deities or images of the honored dead were hacked, carved, and sheared off their bases to complete their transformation into architectural spolia.[30] The life and afterlife of this kouros is at once a symbol of grief and mourning—of individuals lost, religious piety violated, and an Athens sullied by war—as well as an index of Athenian resilience, integrated into the newly reformed city walls that presaged Athenian hegemony in the Aegean during the fifth century BCE. Knowing that the Persians had striven to destroy their city, they used that rubble to try to rebuild it.

Such a cycle of attacking, dismantling, and rebuilding continued amid ongoing efforts among dueling parties to control Athens. In the following century, after the Macedonian king Alexander the Great conquered large swaths of the known Mediterranean and western Asian worlds, Athens (and nearly all of Greece) came under the control of Alexander's successors, Antigonus I Monophthalmos and his son, Demetrios Poliorketes. In 306 BCE, after helping the Athenians cast out the invading army of Alexander's rival Cassander, Demetrios and his father declared themselves kings over Greece and were warmly welcomed in Athens.[31] Around 303–302 BCE, Demetrios was gifted a bronze equestrian portrait that was installed in the Agora; a group of fragments discovered there in 1971 are believed to come from this statue ⟨ *figs.* 9–12 ⟩. The placement of this imposing sculpture of a single ruler in what was the heart of the

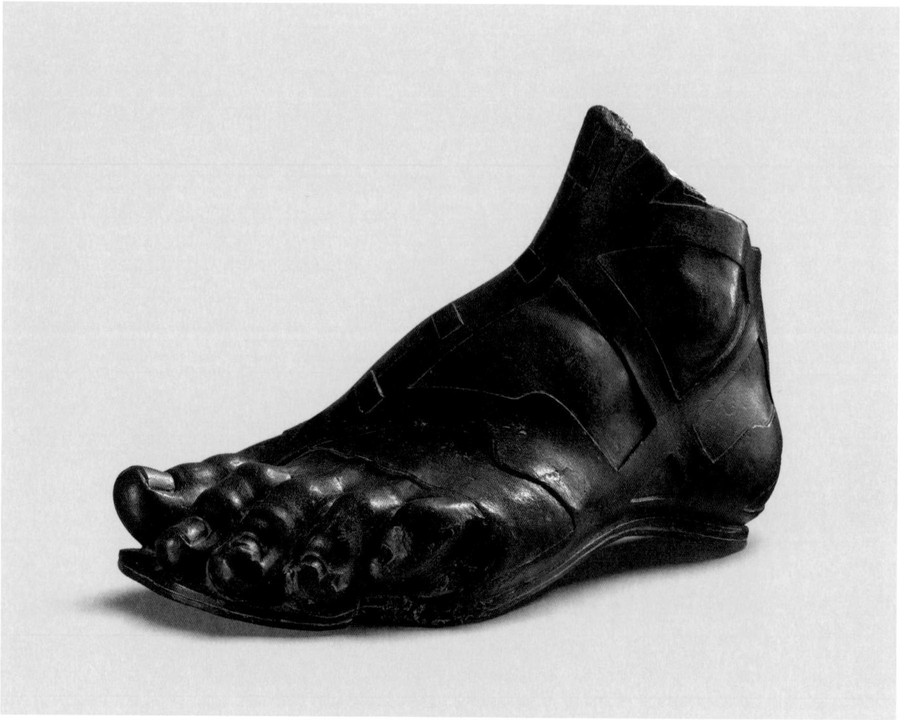

Fig. 13 François Girardon (designer) and Jean Balthazar Keller (caster), *Left Foot from the Equestrian Statue of King Louis XIV*, 1692–1694 (cast and finished), bronze
Musée du Louvre, Département des Sculptures, Paris, MR3448. On long-term loan to the Musée Carnavalet—Histoire de Paris
Cat. 61

city's democratic politics—a site intended to function as a beacon of equality among men, or at least citizens—attests to the seismic geopolitical and social shifts that took place in the decades following the death of Alexander.

Despite the monument's fragmentary nature, it clearly portrays a strong yet relaxed rider, the artist seemingly styling the youthful and popular Demetrios as the successor to Alexander, a similarly victorious commander in chief. As pointed out by the art historian Caroline Houser, the artful arrangement of the surviving drapery is stylistically similar to that of the Parthenon figures, while the sword is distinctly Macedonian, perhaps a melding of Demetrios's heritage and his new status as Athenian king.[32] Additionally, the sculpture was plated in gold, a technique typically restricted to images of the gods, indexing the moment when cults of deified kingship emerged across the Hellenistic world. Unfortunately for Demetrios, the monument was destroyed nearly a century later in retaliation for attacks against the Athenians perpetrated by his great-grandson, Philip V. In an act of *damnatio memoriae* (condemnation of memory), the Athenians destroyed all written and artistic memory of the Antigonid

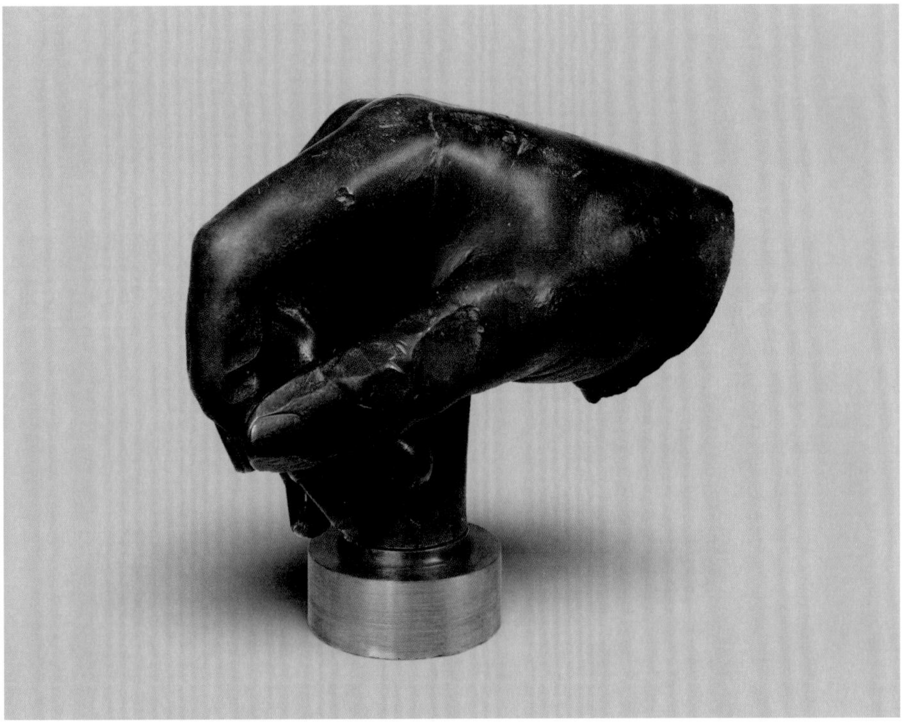

F*ig.* 14 Edme Bouchardon, *Right Hand from the Equestrian Statue of King Louis XV*, 1758 (cast), bronze
Musée du Louvre, Département des Sculptures, Paris, RF94. On long-term loan to the Musée Carnavalet—Histoire de Paris
Cat. 62

dynasty in 200 BCE.[33] The equestrian bronze was taken apart, stripped of its gold, and tossed down a well in the Agora, signaling the end of the dynasty.[34] Despite its ignominious fate, this equestrian statue still remains the earliest life-size example of this artistic form—one that would go on to become the standardized image of rulership in the West for the next two thousand years, and a type of public image that was dismantled as often as it was erected.

As a symbol of royal power, the equestrian statue served as a natural focal point of concentrated political attention by faithful subjects as well as by political rivals and rebellious forces. Like the statue of Demetrios, two later monuments further demonstrate how the dissolution and destruction of this form was akin to the dismantling of broader political and social structures. These are the equestrian monuments of the French kings Louis XIV and Louis XV, which were both toppled during the French Revolution and are often recognized as a turning point within larger histories of iconoclasm and image destruction—and in the history of recognizing that these destroyed images also constituted a new kind of art ⟨ *figs.* 13–14 ⟩.[35] Although the revolutionaries also attacked

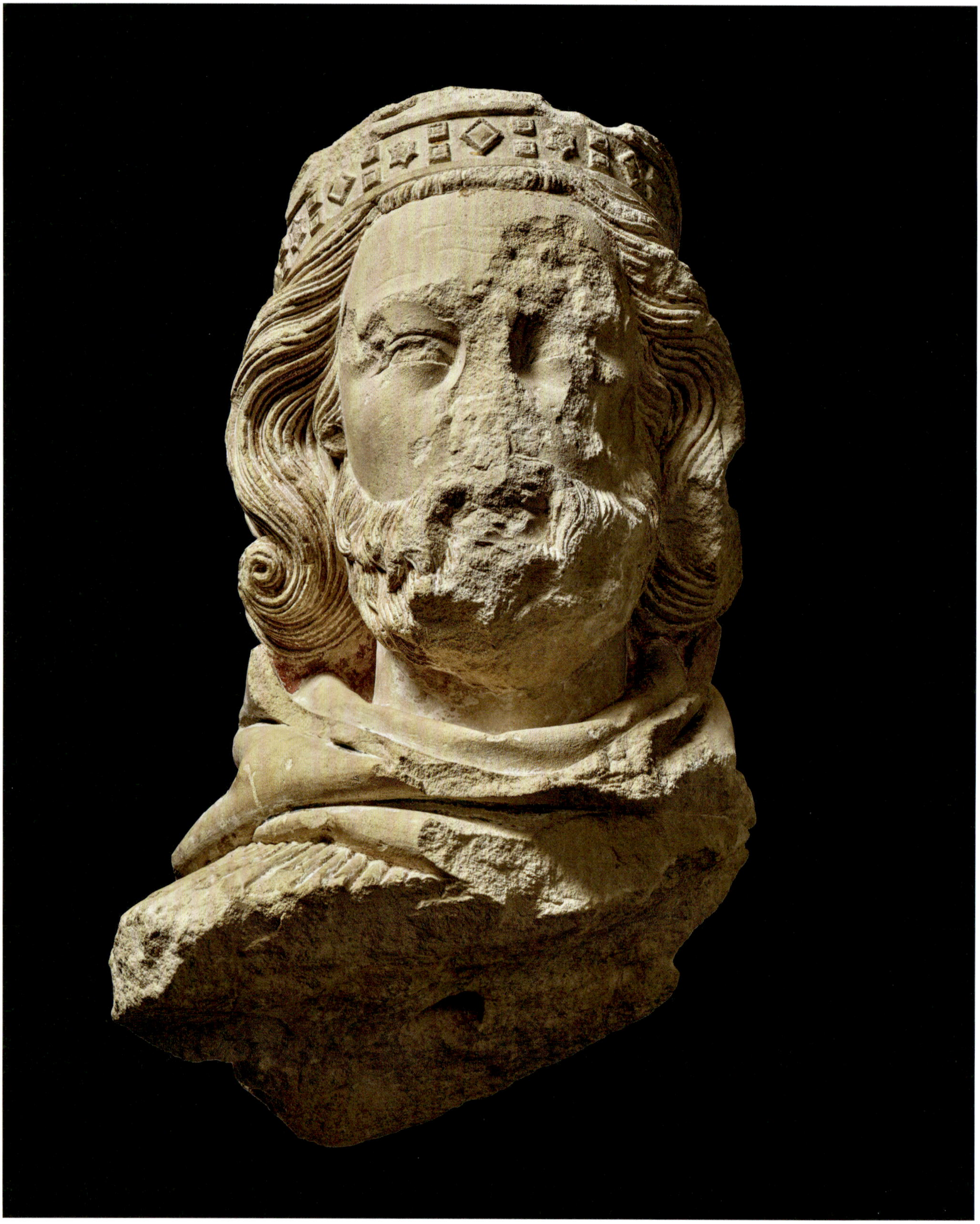

Fig. 15 Workshop of Jean de Chelles?, *Head of a Magus*, 1250–1258, lutetian limestone with traces of pigment
Musée de Cluny–Musée National du Moyen Âge, Paris, Cl. 23127
Cat. 41

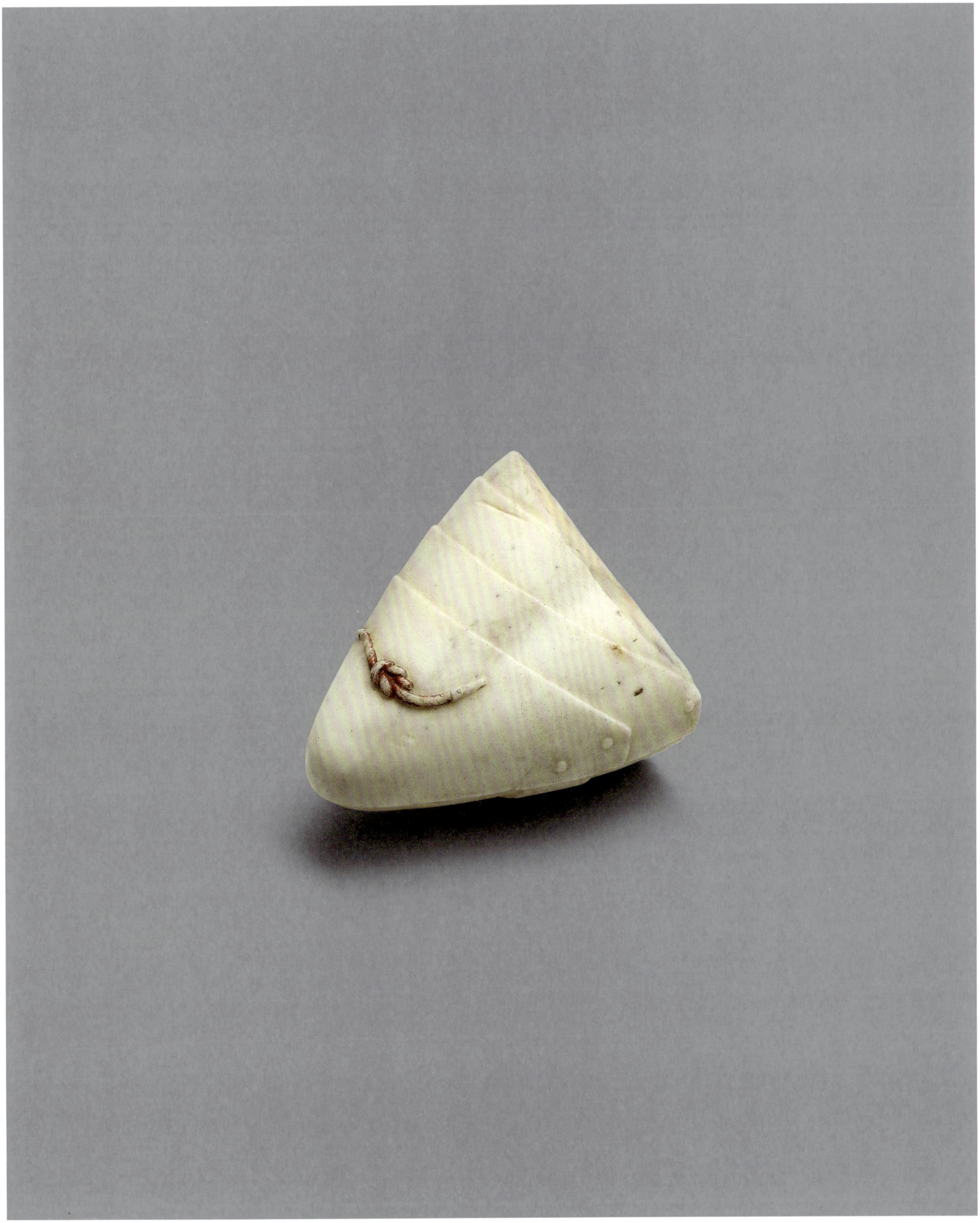

Fig. 16 Claus de Werve, *Left Foot of the Tomb Effigy of Philip the Bold*, c. 1406–1410, marble with traces of pigment
Musée des Beaux-Arts, Dijon, inv. 1096/1

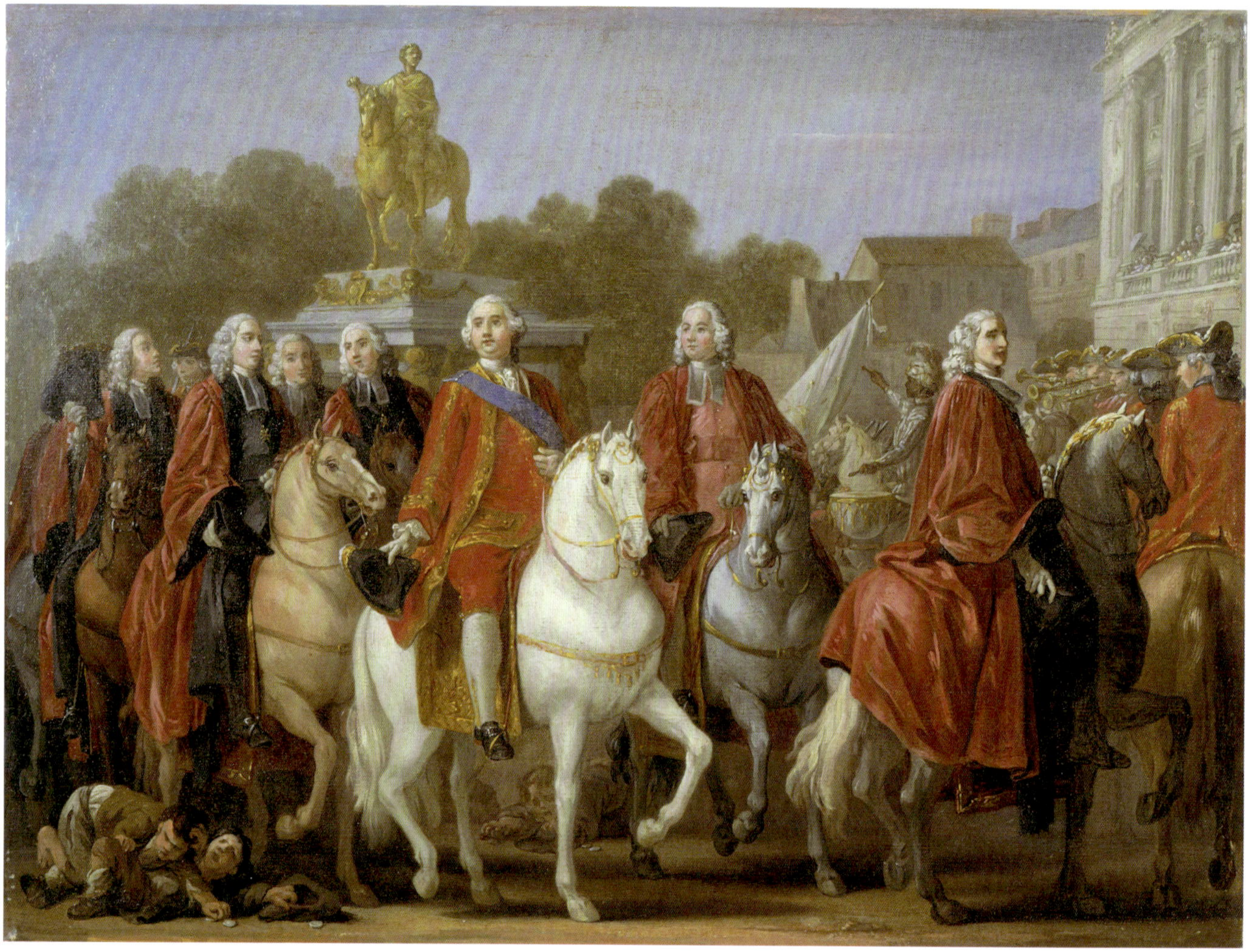

F*ig.* 17 Joseph-Marie Vien, *Inauguration of the Statue of Louis XV at the Square of the Same Name, by the Municipal Council of the City of Paris, June 20, 1763*, c. 1763, oil on canvas
Musée Carnavalet—Histoire de Paris, P2085

religious sculptures perceived to embody the *longue durée* of church and state's entanglements in France—such as the *Head of a Magus* from the north-transept portal of Notre-Dame in Paris 〈 *fig.* 15 〉 or the tomb effigy of the Burgundian duke Philip the Bold, of which only his hands and the tip of his armor-clad foot remain 〈 *fig.* 16 〉—their principal focus was sites and symbols that most directly enacted the political agenda of the absolutist ancien régime.

The two equestrian monuments—that of Louis XIV created by François Girardon and erected in what is today the Place Vendôme in 1699 and that of Louis XV by Edme Bouchardon—were ripe targets for what we might term political assassination. Not merely symbolic of royal rule, the statues were physical substitutions for the king's body, installed in sites of public festivities often overseen by the monarch. While the festivals were finite in their duration, the statues and by proxy the king himself surpassed such ephemerality and permanently marked the urban fabric with royal presence.[36] In a painting from around 1763 by Joseph-Marie Vien commemorating the inauguration of Louis XV's monument, the monarch and his statue are shown as doubles that together overtake public space—an imposing presence that would have been immediately apparent to Parisians visiting the purpose-built square, which was named Place Louis XV ⟨ *fig.* 17 ⟩. This synergy between image, person, and place became anathema to the revolutionaries and had to be destroyed through a variety of means: The statue was dismantled, a guillotine was installed to facilitate public executions, and the square was renamed Place de la Concorde.[37]

Later sources specifically refer to the destruction of Louis XIV's effigy as an "execution" that took place on July 13, 1792. Curious onlookers saved the left foot and sent it to be housed in the Louvre.[38] Similarly, Bouchardon's right hand of Louis XV was not destroyed but gifted to the writer Jean-Henri Masers de Latude, who had been imprisoned in the Bastille by order of Madame de Pompadour, the long-standing mistress of the king.[39] The boundary between art and life was even more indistinct when one newspaper commenting on the fragment published this description: "It was this hand that . . . signed the *lettre de cachet* which put this unfortunate victim of despotism in irons for more than thirty years."[40] Both fragments were necessary to commemorate the dissolution of the king's body—and the body politic—for who would recall such an amazing feat without evidence of the sculptures' existence? In their persistent state of violation, these fragments acted as reminders for the people that a new phase of French life was on the horizon and that the age of absolutism had ended.

PUBLICIZING

Attacked artworks have complicated afterlives. Many were removed from view and forgotten: *Head of a Magus* for centuries, the Akkadian *Torso of a Ruler* for millennia. In some cases, artworks suffered more from subsequent neglect than from the original attack. As shown by the fragment of an altarpiece from the Oude Kerk in Soest (near Utrecht), forgetfulness was its own kind of violence ⟨ *fig.* 18 ⟩. The altar was dismantled and hidden in the church tower before it could be destroyed by sixteenth-century Protestant reformers and remained there until it was discovered in 1905 in a derelict state.[41] Other examples exist of attacked artworks that were given a new life and repurposed. The first equestrian monument erected

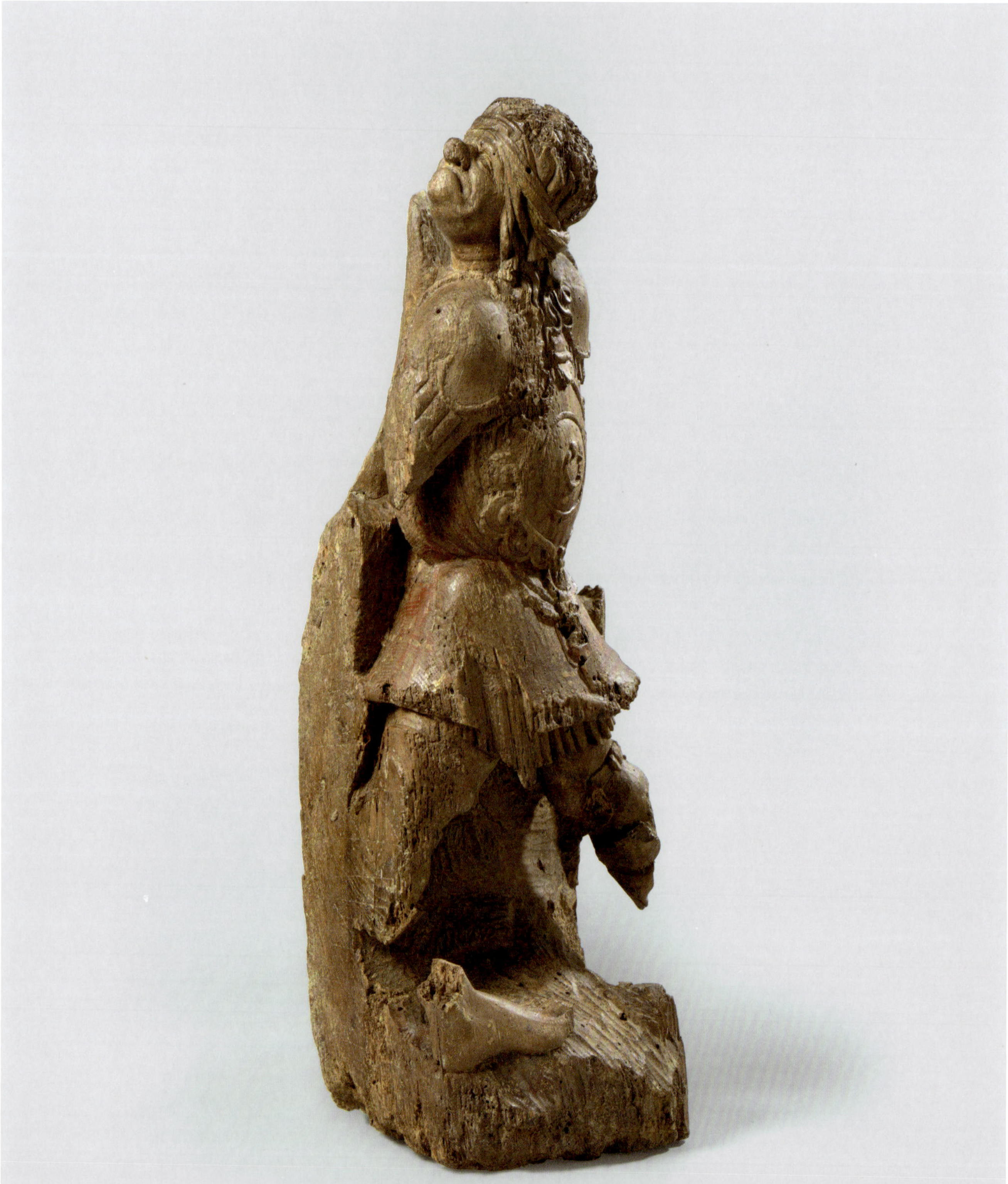

Fig. 18 Master of the Soest Altarpiece, *Soldier from Christ Carrying the Cross*, c. 1475–1500, oak with traces of pigment and gilding
Loan from the Rijksmuseum, BK-NM-12006-15-B
Cat. 53

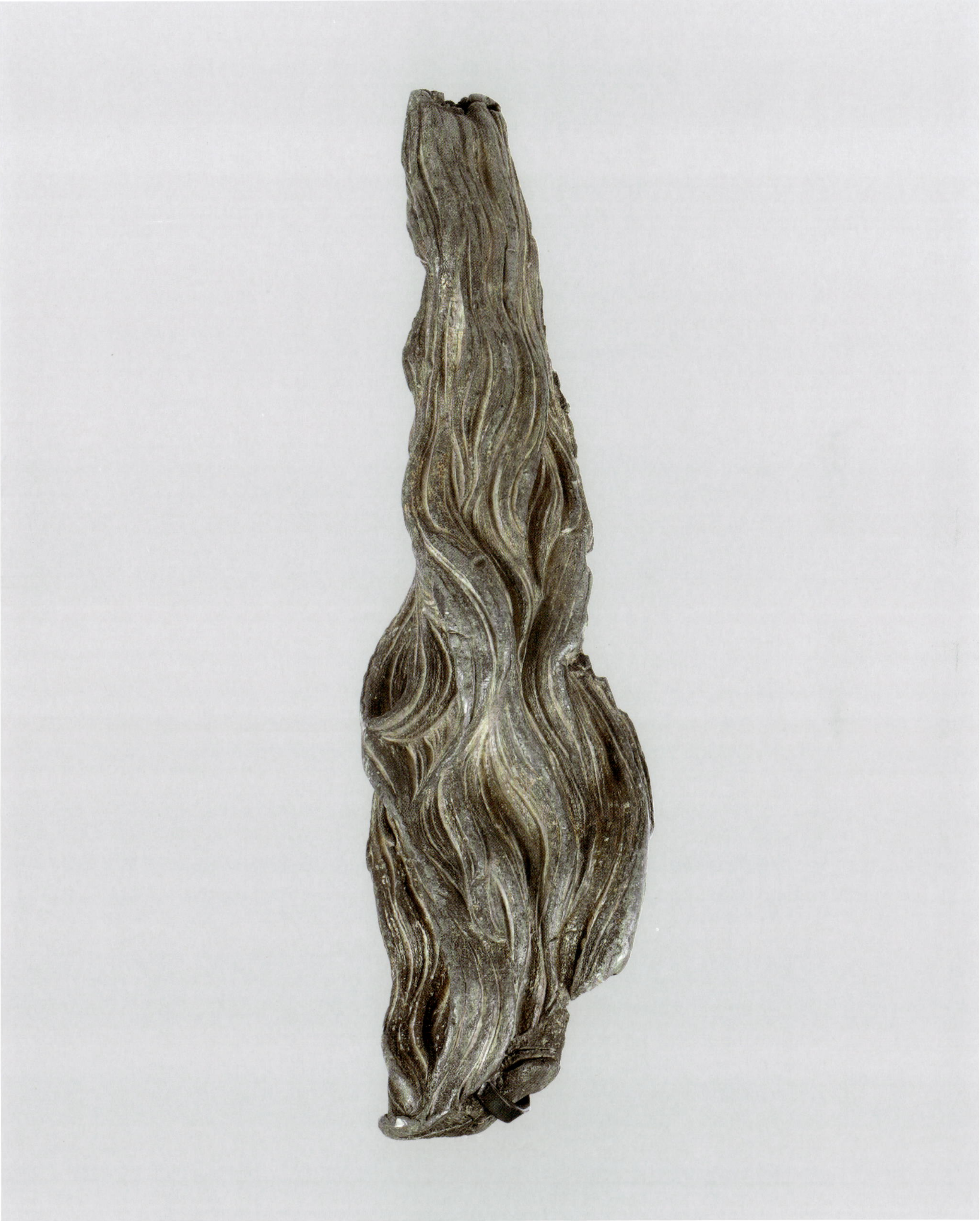

Fig. 19 Joseph Wilton, *Tail from the Equestrian Statue of King George III*, 1770–1776, gilded lead
The New York Historical, Purchase, 1878.6
Cat. 63

in the United States, depicting King George III of England, was dismantled at the onset of the American Revolution, melted down, and turned into musket balls for fighting the war. Only a few small pieces escaped that fate, including the horse's tail, which soon disappeared and was discovered in a swamp in Wilton, Connecticut, in 1871 ⟨ *fig.* 19 ⟩.[42]

Yet for most of the sculptures included in this essay and many in this volume, their broken or fragmented condition became a public spectacle and a means of publicizing a larger cause—whether by the victorious or the defeated. Destruction and violence have a particular aesthetic that commands visibility, attention, and action. For that reason, the aesthetics of violence and its pervasive influence in shaping social order are among the few cultural principles shared across time and place. To return to the ancient Mesopotamian context with which this essay started, as early as the second millennium BCE, when the Sumerian myth *Enki and the World Order* was composed, war and art were defined as central and inseparable tenets of civilization.[43] As the art historian Zainab Bahrani has argued, this notion has persisted into modernity; in arguably the first modern philosophical treatise on war, Carl von Clausewitz's *Vom Kriege* (*On War*), written in 1832 in the wake of the Napoleonic Wars, the author describes how war depended on art, together with science, as the instruments through which violence legitimizes itself and justifies its role in politics and society more broadly.[44]

Today, the aesthetics of war and violence have evolved to become increasingly complicated, influencing societies and minds in paradoxical ways. On the one hand, in an age of mass media and endlessly circulating images, violence is more visible than ever. Destruction truly has become a shared global aesthetic.[45] On the other hand, according to the philosopher José Fernández Vega, we also see and experience such images in increasingly uneven ways. For much of the world, violence is more than seen; it is lived and embodied. In much of the West, however, it is mediated and habituated through digital representations and is thus almost beyond understanding. To quote Vega, violence is "incomprehensible to those who demand 'security' only for themselves."[46] This tension raises an important question about the status of the artworks illustrated in this volume: Does the publishing and publicizing of sundered sculptures help foster greater awareness of and constructive reflection on the histories of violence, or does it risk aestheticizing violence within Western cultural institutions largely insulated from the very traumas these objects index? Is there an appropriate way to present violence, and if so, what, if anything, results beyond stirring trauma, fear, or sympathy?

Two final examples might help us to think through the implications of publicizing and publishing violence. The first is a monumental grave figure excavated from Tell Halaf in northeastern Syria that was destroyed

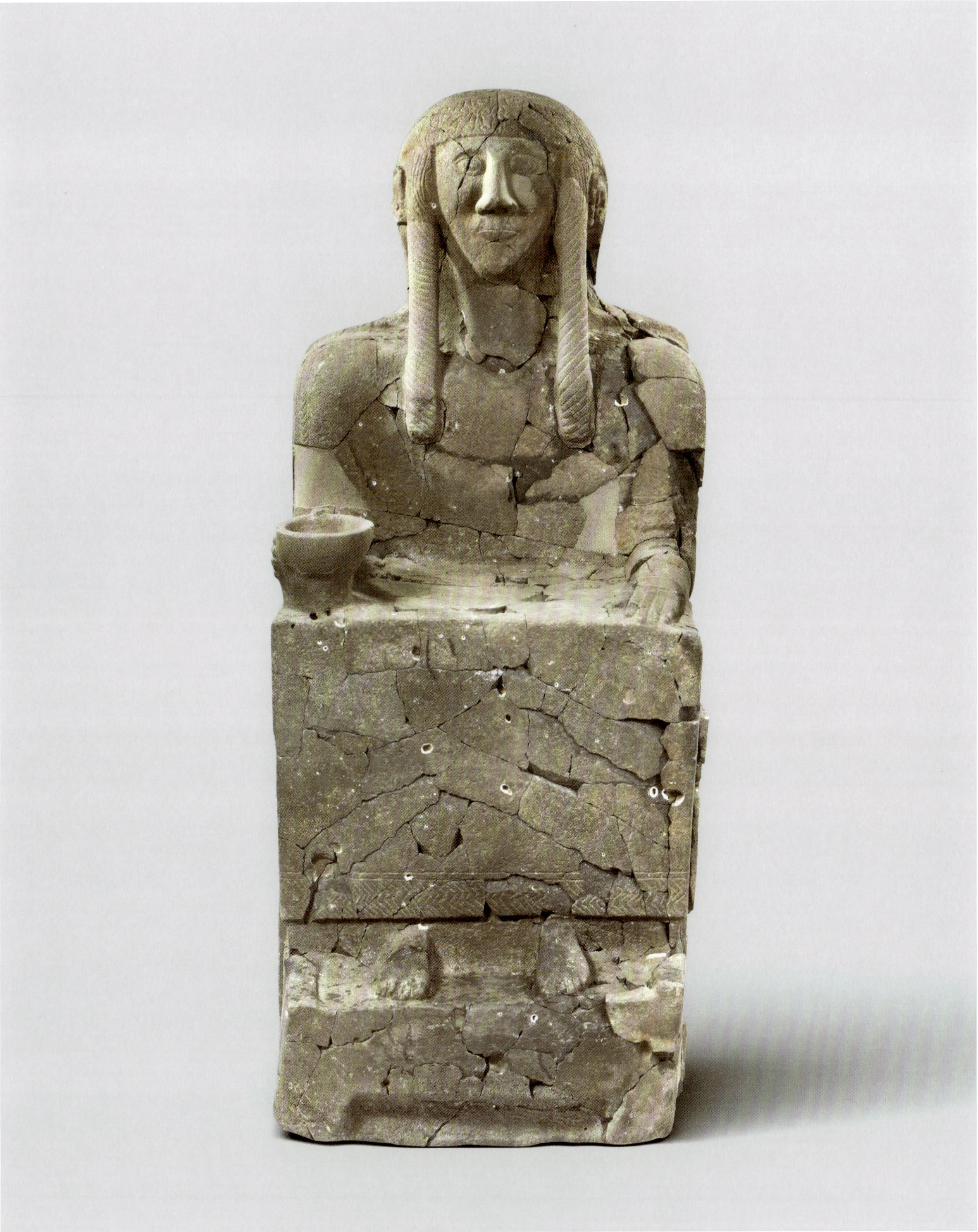

F*ig*. 20 Neo-Hittite (Guzana [Tell Halaf]), *Seated Grave Figure*, c. 1000–800 BCE, basalt
Max Freiherr von Oppenheim Foundation, Cologne, TH B 0001
Cat. 5

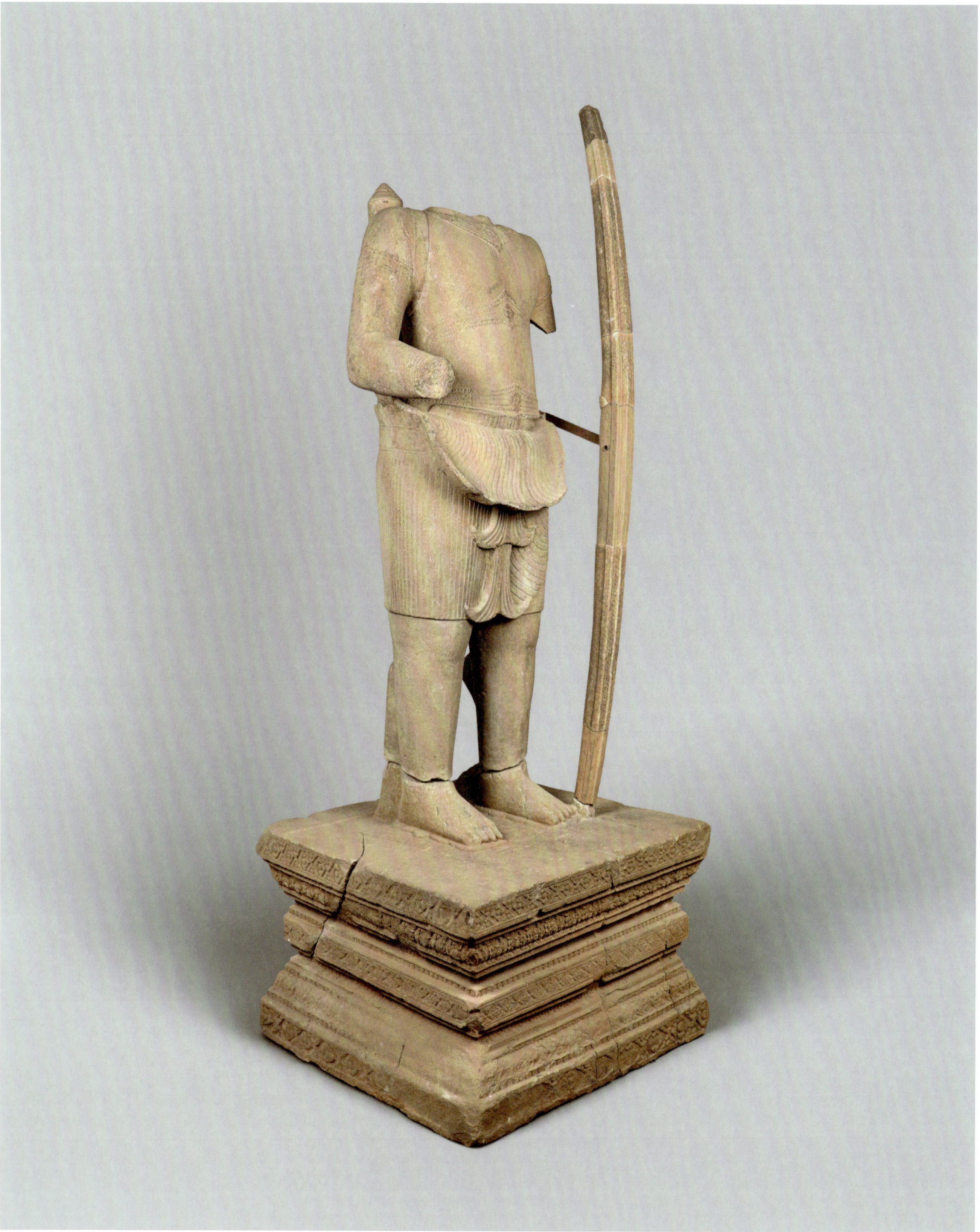

Fig. 21 Khmer (Koh Ker), *Statue of Rama*, 900s CE, sandstone
Royal Government of Cambodia, National Museum of Cambodia, Phnom Penh, NMC.277
Cat. 37

during World War II when Allied bombs hit the Tell Halaf Museum in Berlin on the night of November 23, 1943 ⟨ *fig.* 20 ⟩.[47] One of the few restored artworks illustrated in this volume, the sculpture simultaneously bears witness to its own ruin and repair. Perhaps the most effective way to narrate histories of violence without inadvertently valorizing them is by highlighting acts of reparation, such as conservation. The same logic might apply to the *Statue of Rama* from the Prasat Chen temple in Koh Ker in northern Cambodia. The figure was sawn from its base either during the Cambodian civil war (1970–1975) or in the extreme political volatility that followed until the surrender of the Khmer Rouge in 1998 ⟨ *fig.* 21 ⟩.[48] The sculpture, which eventually made its way into the Denver Art Museum in 1986, was returned to Cambodia in 2016. The widely circulated photographs of the restitution ceremony and the sculpture's reunion with its original pedestal counteract past violence by illustrating breakage as a basis for remediation.[49]

Yet, at least for the *Statue of Rama*, these ostensibly encouraging images come with certain risks, namely because they gloss over the fact that the sculpture is still a fragment and is missing its head and arms. It may never be fully restored—or at least not in the foreseeable future—because its smaller missing pieces have been lost to a broader context of violence and looting whose immense scale continues to unfold. It is estimated that in the 1980s and 1990s, more than half of Cambodia's art was plundered, much of it entering the global market through complex networks of local aides, looting syndicates, and Western antiquarian dealers who obfuscated or fabricated provenances.[50] These networks are only gradually being reconstructed through archival research, fieldwork, and oral histories conducted with residents of Koh Ker.[51] This particular sculpture, perpetually caught between fragmentation and restoration, resists categorization and confronts us again with the question of how to respond to its continued state of half-broken.

For many of the sculptures discussed here, images of their damaged conditions prompt a desire to know more: about the moment of destruction, its human and political consequences, and the potential of brokenness to guide us toward a more critical understanding of how past violence shapes the present. Images can be a means through which viewers might emotionally and intellectually decipher the inherent "power of the fragment." At the same time, we may be so accustomed to analyzing such images that we fail to recognize an important tension: The power of the images themselves does not necessarily translate to the fragments they depict. Broken sculptures like the *Statue of Rama* cannot advocate for themselves. Attending to this disjunction between potent images and vulnerable fragments is vital, as it hopefully encourages responses beyond the emotional or intellectual and leads to material and political forms of redress.

FROM FRAGMENT TO FRAGMENT

THE VIOLENT LIFE OF *SENWOSRET III*

George Wheeler

Breakage tells us things. Critically, it can provide a means for reconstructing how a fragment came to be in the most literal sense. What follows is my technical reading of how *Face of Senwosret III* ⟨ *fig.* 1 ⟩, part of an Egyptian sculpture of the king from the early second millennium BCE, ended up broken. Multiple chapters of the story can be discerned. As we see the object today—a fragment of red quartzite—it is the product of successive, violent actions: the quarrying of the block, the chiseling of the face, the damage from vandalism, and the forceful removal from some unknown context, probably either a bust or a larger sculpture of a seated or standing figure. Even before becoming a sculpture, it endured a form of breakage. The quarrying of the stone was by necessity a violent act. The red quartzite from which the head was fashioned was likely taken from the large mass of silicified sandstone on Gebel-el-Ahmar (Red Mountain or Red Hill), just northeast of Cairo.[1]

There is benefit in describing the stone and its geological genesis in detail, as that information contributes to speculating on the object's history. Silicified sandstone—also called orthoquartzite—begins as a terrestrial sandstone, thus as the debris of existing rocks that has collected as a sediment, which is subsequently lithified by an overburden of a further collection of rock debris.[2] These sandstones, which are relatively porous and easily carved, were used extensively in ancient Egypt. They range in color from a neutral gray to tan, orange-red, and red. The colorations derive from grains of iron oxides deposited between the matrix of quartz that makes up most of the stone: yellowish hydrated iron oxides such as limonite and goethite, the deep red of hematite, and mixtures thereof that can produce anything from brown to orange-red. These terrestrial sandstones are transformed into orthoquartzite when, over millions of years, silica-bearing fluids percolate through the existing rock mass and deposit more silica onto the resident grains of quartz and into the intergranular spaces. The result is a tough, indurated rock with low porosity and high strength: the rock mass seen at Gebel-el-Ahmar. The intergranular hematite imparts the red color to the stone and the name to the site.

How was the violent act of quarrying the stone for the statue of Senwosret III executed? Whatever the actual size of the original sculpture, an oversize block of stone would have been taken from the quarry. There is no definitive consensus on quarrying (or carving) techniques in Pharaonic Egypt, but several hypotheses have been articulated. The most likely process was the use of hard stone hammers, possibly in conjunction with large balls of hard stones, to apply percussive forces to pulverize the stone in the existing rock mass along a defined line.

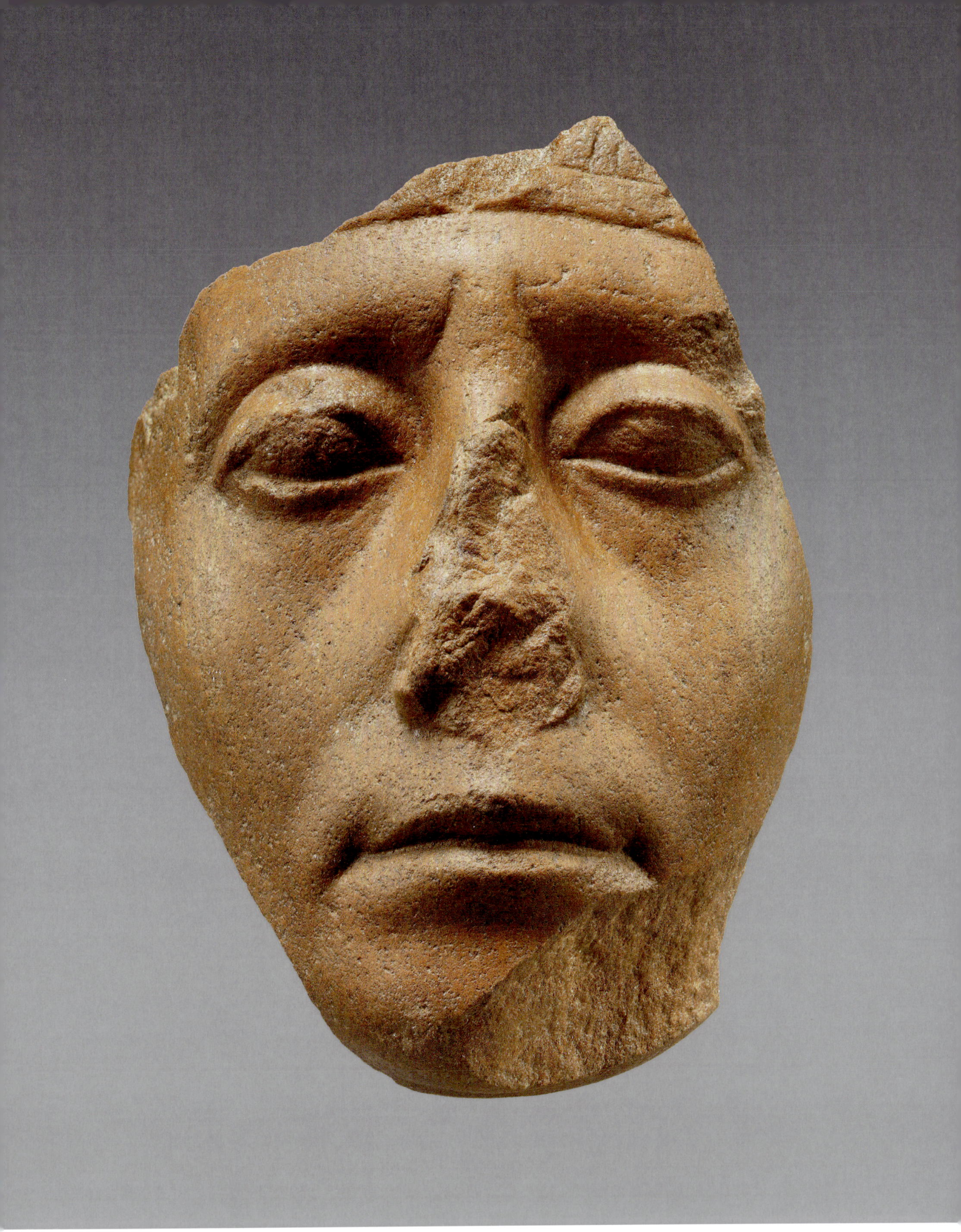

Fig. 1 Egyptian, *Face of Senwosret III*, c. 1878–1840 BCE, red quartzite
Lent by The Metropolitan Museum of Art, Purchase, Edward S. Harkness Gift, 1926 (26.7.1394)
Cat. 3

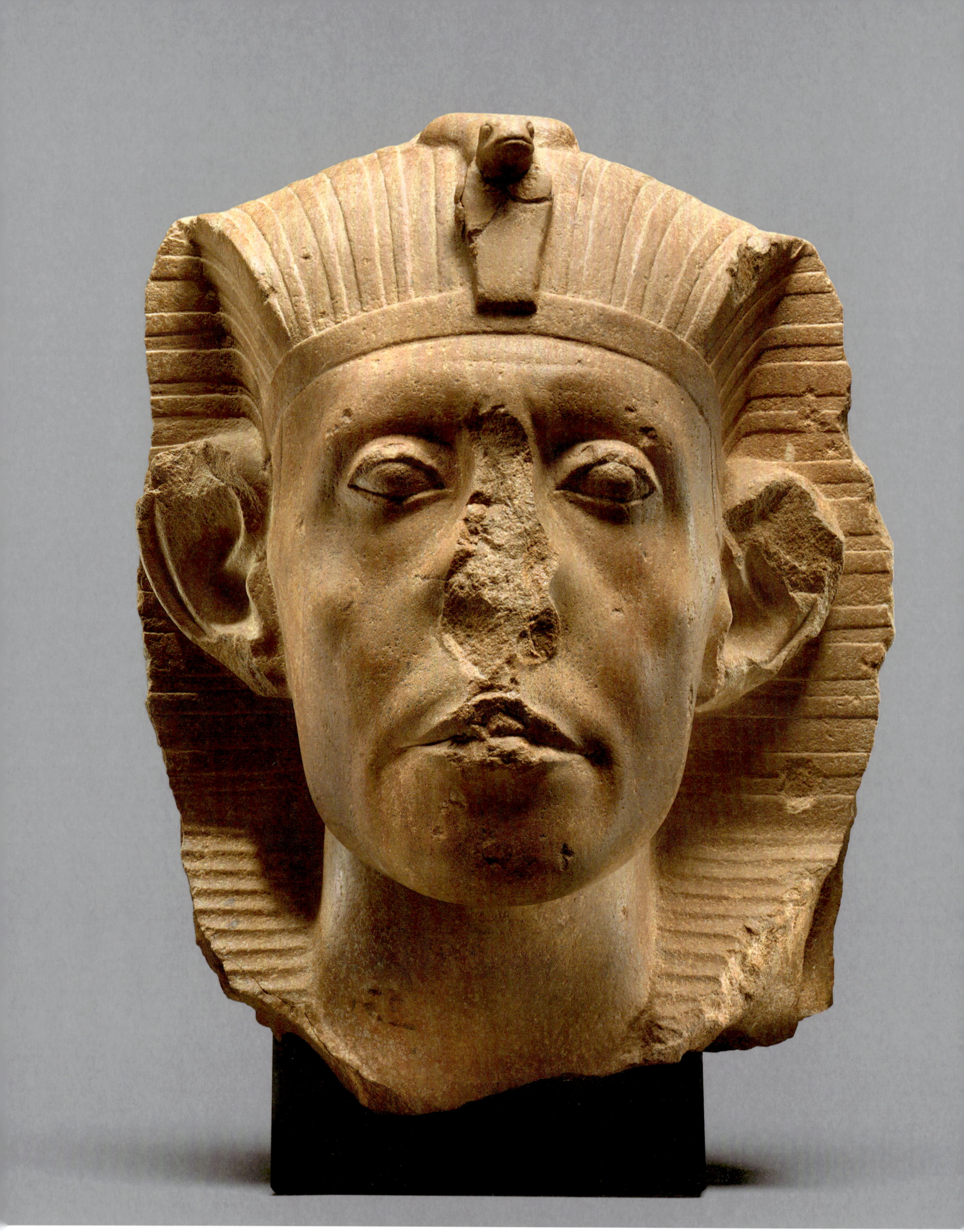

F*ig.* 2 Egyptian, *Head of Sen-useret III*, c. 1874–1855 BCE, yellow quartzite
Nelson-Atkins Museum of Art, Purchase: William Rockhill Nelson Trust, 62-11

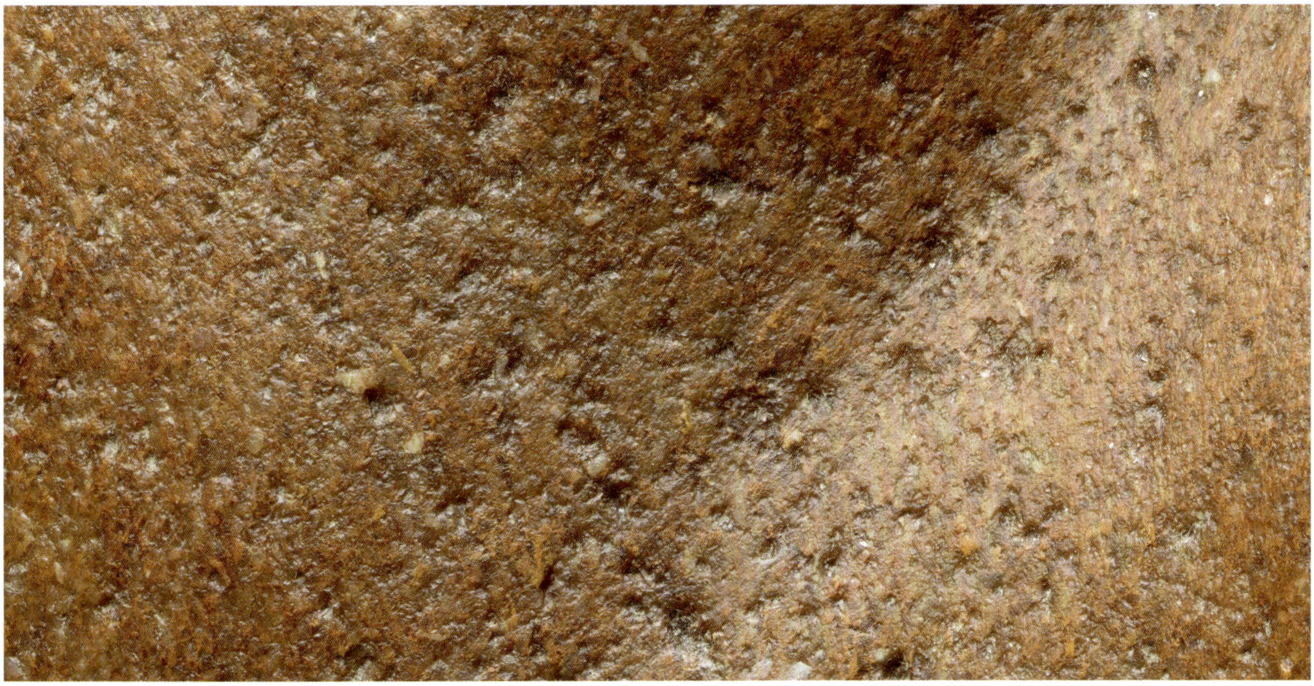

Fig. 3 Detail of *fig.* 1 showing the pitting and abundant spots of yellow limonite on the carved surface

Resulting debris would be swept away, and the hammering would continue until a deep channel was formed. This laborious process would take place on a sufficient number of planes to extract a block.[3]

While the sculpture's original overall form is unknown, it may have been similar to another quartzite head of Senwosret III in the Nelson-Atkins Museum of Art ⟨ *fig.* 2 ⟩.[4] The carving of *Face of Senwosret III* is likely to have involved less violent actions than the quarrying. Some additional percussive forces were probably employed with hard stone hammers for rough shaping, but the production of the shape of the face and finer features—cheeks, eyes, nose, and lips—was likely done with scrapers and chisels of chert or flint.[5] The smoothing of surfaces was then likely achieved with abrasives of hard minerals such as quartz.[6]

A close examination of the carved surface helps formulate a story of some of its later life. The detail illustrated here demonstrates several notable features ⟨ *fig.* 3 ⟩: the overall red-brown coloration of the stone imparted by the intergranular hematite; the pitted surface from losses of quartz grains; and the small yellow-orange spots representing the in situ hydration of red hematite, Fe_2O_3, to yellow limonite, FeO(OH). Some limonite would certainly have been present in the freshly quarried quartzite, but the abundance on the carved surfaces indicates slow conversion of one iron oxide form to another over a long period of exposure to the elements.

A similarly close examination of the fractured surface of the nose reveals the same flecks of limonite seen on the carved surfaces ⟨ *fig.* 4 ⟩. This surface shows visible wear but lacks the pitted grain loss seen on the carved surfaces, so is not likely to have experienced the same conditions (or time) of exposure as the carved surfaces, which is to be expected if it were broken at some point after the work had been carved. While the breakage could

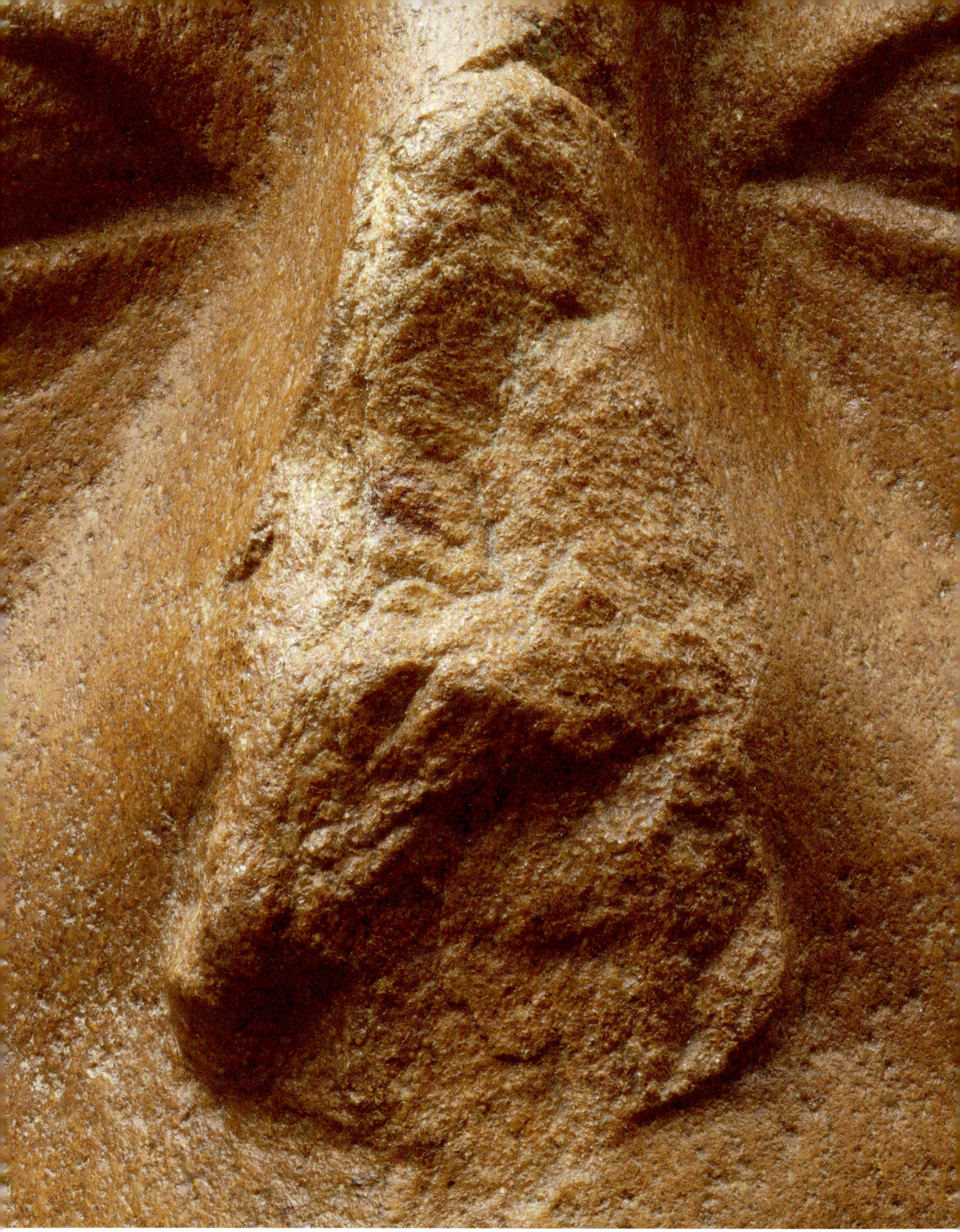

F *i g*. 4 Detail of *f i g*. 1 showing the fractured surface where the nose once existed. Flecks of limonite are visible in this surface. The area exhibits visible wear but lacks the pitted grain losses seen on the carved surfaces.

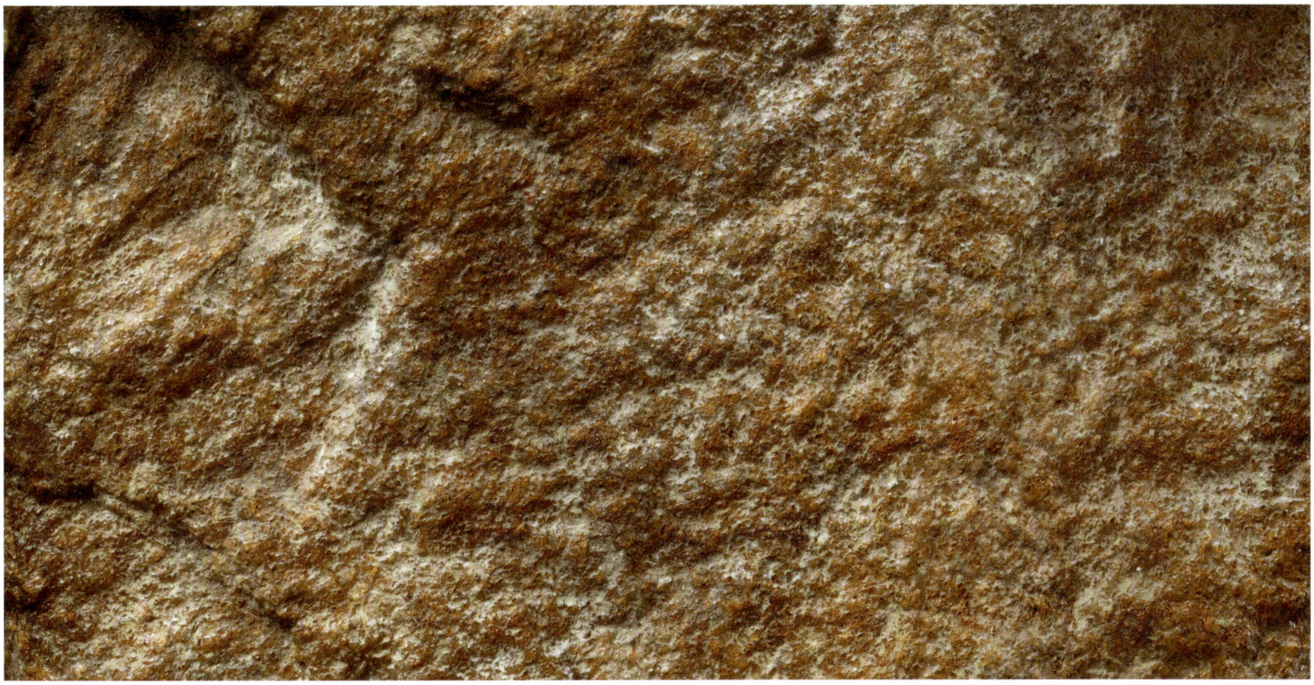

Fig. 5 Detail of *fig.* 1 showing the fractured surface created by removing the fragment from its last context. The surface shows some wear but no pitting and no flecks of limonite. In addition, many fine (and highly reflective) grains of what appears to be quartz are found in recesses.

reflect an incident of vandalism that occurred during ancient times, the damage to the nose (and similarly in the proper right eye), though clearly very old, cannot be dated with certainty.[7]

The final act of violence to *Face of Senwosret III* came with separation from its original context. To shear this fragment from the rest of the stone would have required formidable force. Returning to the Nelson-Atkins head, one can understand how a deftly administered chisel at the juncture where the smooth part of the cheek meets the plane of the background decoration would communicate a force along that plane. Chiseling applied at several such points could result in the shearing of the face from its context. The existing fractured surfaces in *Face of Senwosret III* show features quite different from the carved surfaces and the damaged area of the nose 〈 *fig.* 5 〉. These surfaces show some wear but no pitting and no flecks of limonite. In addition, many fine (and highly reflective) grains of what appears to be quartz are found in recesses, perhaps left from the rupture of the stone during removal of the fragment. It can be argued that this removal is somewhere on the line between clever and careless, as the fragment leaves no hints as to its original or final context.[8] What can be said about context, however, is that at some point in its history, the sculpture was exposed to the elements—thus left outdoors—as the weathered surfaces could not have resulted from a lifetime indoors. It should also be noted that this weathered surface is in sharp contrast to the well-preserved surface seen on the head in Kansas City.

The *Senwosret III* that we see before us began its life in the arduous separation of a block of stone from a quarry; it was then subjected to the somewhat gentler actions of creating the sensitive face and finally the more violent acts of vandalism and separation.

FRAGMENTS AND POWER

BREAKING SCULPTURE IN ASIA

Stanley Abe

Damaged sculptures and fragments have long been appreciated in the West as great works of art as well as inspiration for great works of art. But what about fragments of sculpture from other places? I was asked, as a specialist in ancient Chinese Buddhist sculpture, to discuss Asian and Buddhist attitudes toward broken sculpture and fragments. That task seems straightforward but is not. Sculpture as we know it in the West—as represented in places like the Palazzo Strozzi or the National Gallery of Art—did not exist in most of the world until the nineteenth century. It was only when Western institutions, such as art museums, art academies, and schools of art, were replicated in the European colonies and beyond that the idea of sculpture in its modern global form was established.[1]

Western sculpture—its definition, unique characteristics, and history—shapes our modern understanding of sculpture throughout the world. It serves as our point of reference.[2] Sculpture from Asia may be similar or different, but the Western concept of sculpture is the norm. But sculpture is really a local idea that dreams it is universal.[3]

In China or Japan or Java there was no comparable idea of sculpture until the modern era. And even then, there was no single category of Asian art or Buddhist sculpture. Similarly, there is neither a single religion called Buddhism nor a single definition of Buddhist beliefs or practices. To discuss Buddhist sculptural fragments writ large, we are required to take up the subject across Asia in various specific historical moments. The reader is thus asked to follow a broken story, one with many unanswered questions, and to consider the examples below together with those provided elsewhere in this volume as a very preliminary discussion of a difficult question: How do we compare the incommensurable?[4]

DEFINING SCULPTURE

In most Asian cultures, statues, stele, and carved and molded figures—what we in the West consider to be sculpture—were historically viewed as religious objects. Produced in large numbers and with enviable skill, these objects were the work of craftspeople, not artists. In China, for example, painting and calligraphy were seen as the paramount forms of artistic expression. Educated male elites were schooled in the arts of the brush, historical and antiquarian scholarship, and the appreciation of archaic bronze vessels, ceramics, and jades.[5] The study of inscriptions was also highly valued, especially those carved on ancient stone stele and texts preserved only in ink rubbings. The most prized art objects were those created for the imperial court and powerful literati officials who served in the civil bureaucracy.

Three-dimensional works mainly consisted of stone, bronze, clay, and wood religious figures, as well as fired and unfired earthenware tomb objects produced by teams of largely uneducated craftsmen. We find only a few names of image makers in the historical records and even fewer honored with individual recognition in the inscriptions on extant objects.[6] There was no lineage of famous named sculptors or artists, as there was for Chinese painting.[7]

In Chinese the three-dimensional figure is a *xiang* 像, or image. A *fo-xiang* 佛像 is a Buddha image, and an image stele is a *zaoxiangbei* 造像碑. These terms are used in premodern texts about Buddhist images and as terms of self-identification in ancient inscriptions found on such images. The same terms continue to be used into the present for Buddhist figural images. The modern terms for sculpture—*diaoke* 雕刻 (carving) or *diaosu* 雕塑 (modeling)—and fine art (*meishu* 美術) were adapted into the Chinese language only in the latter part of the nineteenth century, when foreign art forms like sculpture were part of the expansion of Western power and authority in Asia and many other parts of the world. In short, the Western system of renowned sculptors and sculpture, patrons and commissions, connoisseurs and art markets, arrived late in Asia. Sculpture as a form of fine art is a largely Western concept and institution. What does this mean for how we define non-Western objects as sculpture or fragments? How should we consider fragments of Buddhist sculpture in China and beyond?

BURIED ARTIFACTS

In China ancient stone Buddhist images are most often discovered as chance finds broken and scattered just below the surface of the ground.[8] Other fragments have been found in wells or used in building foundations.

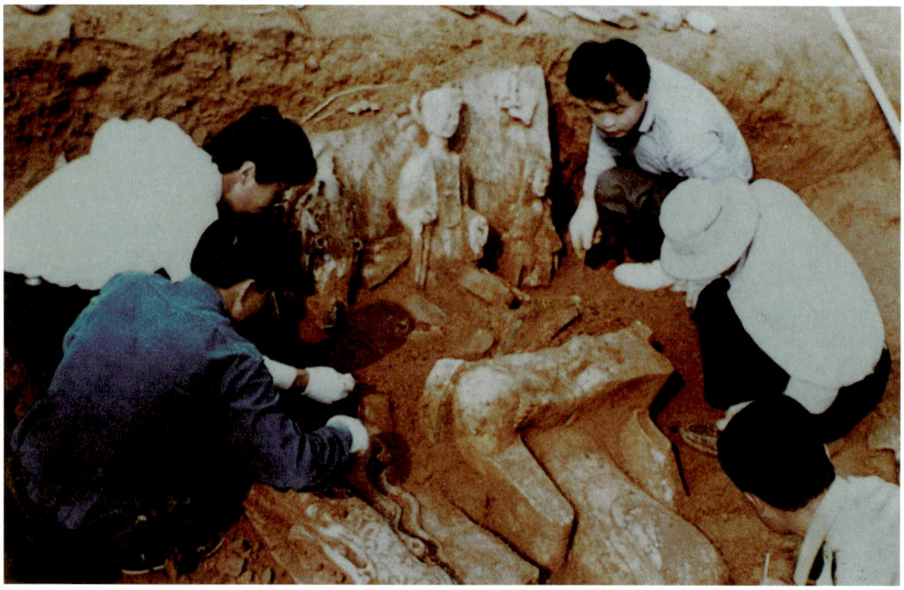

Fig. 1 Buried cache of stele and statue fragments, Qingzhou, Shandong province
From Lukas Nickel, ed., *Return of the Buddha: Buddhist Sculptures of the 6th Century from Qingzhou, China* (Zurich: Museum Rietberg, 2002), fig. 21

In general it does not seem that damaged statues and stele were treated as sacred or powerful fragments. In 1996, however, workers at a primary school in Qingzhou, Shandong province, uncovered a pit 8.7 by 6.8 meters and 2 meters in depth holding the fragments of more than three hundred stone figures and stele 〈 *fig.* 1 〉.[9] These were found carefully arranged, with reed mats placed between layers and coins sprinkled over them as offerings. All the images were broken. A few had previously been repaired and some showed smoke and fire damage. Only a few works could be restored completely from their fragments. Much material had been lost.

The large pit was dug close to the no-longer extant Longxing temple. The objects are all made from the local limestone, and the carving is in the local sixth-century style.[10] The earliest inscribed regnal date on a buried work is the equivalent of 529; the latest is 1026. A porcelain bowl of the Northern Song dynasty (960–1127) was found under the layers of stone figures in the pit. Some fragments have weathered unevenly, which suggests that some pieces were long exposed to the elements in separate locations. In sum, the evidence indicates that these Buddhist images were broken during anti-Buddhist violence in the sixth century.[11] These stone fragments were likely scattered in the ground for some five centuries before they were gathered and carefully interred in the eleventh century. An inscription dated to 1004 from the nearby Mingdao temple records the similar efforts of two traveling monks who sponsored the interment of broken Buddhist images beneath a pagoda.[12]

It is common practice to repair Buddhist images and return them to their place in a temple. The large number of discarded images in the Longxing temple pit underscores that, in the sixth century, repair was not an option. Buddhism, along with its temples and images, had been thoroughly destroyed and would not regain a foothold in the region for many years. The treatment of the broken Buddhist statues and stele at the Longxing temple is deeply respectful of the religious value of each image. But unlike fragments in the West, broken Chinese Buddhist images were venerated as images, not as powerful relics of a holy saint or remnants of sculptural masterpieces created by great individual artists for their wealthy patrons.

After some 1,500 years, the fragments from the pit emerged anew, not as broken pieces of once-revered Buddhist deities but as valuable ancient works of sculpture and rare art in a radically different modern global context. Highlighting this change, the excavators rightly feared that criminals might attempt to steal the new cultural treasures. Sculptures in the Qingzhou style were soon available on the global art market. It is unclear whether these works originally came from the Longxing pit, were discovered separately, or were newly fashioned forgeries.[13]

Other examples from across Asia suggest that the breaking and burial of stone Buddhist statues was a widely shared practice. The burial of broken images shows respect and veneration, but it does not seem that special powers were attributed to the fragment.[14]

FORGOTTEN TREASURES

Kōfukuji (*ji* means temple, so Kōfuku temple), one of the oldest Buddhist temples in Japan, has suffered damage to its wooden structures many times from political unrest, natural disasters, and fires.[15] In 1937 a worship hall that had last been rebuilt in 1047 was dismantled for conservation. The conservationists removed a wall behind the main Buddha image, which had been damaged by fire in 1411, and opened the base of the image. To their surprise, they discovered a long-forgotten bronze Buddha head securely packed inside the base 〈 *fig.* 2 〉. The large head, 98.3 centimeters high, had toppled during an intense conflagration, crushing the left side and ear. Scholars believe the head was originally part of the image damaged in the 1411 fire.

Research has established that the full Buddha image was initially cast in 685 for Yamadera Temple. After parts of the nearby Kōfukuji were destroyed in 1181, the priests from Kōfukuji took the Yamadera image to their temple and installed it as their own.[16] Bronze images were difficult to repair, so broken works were usually melted down for the materials

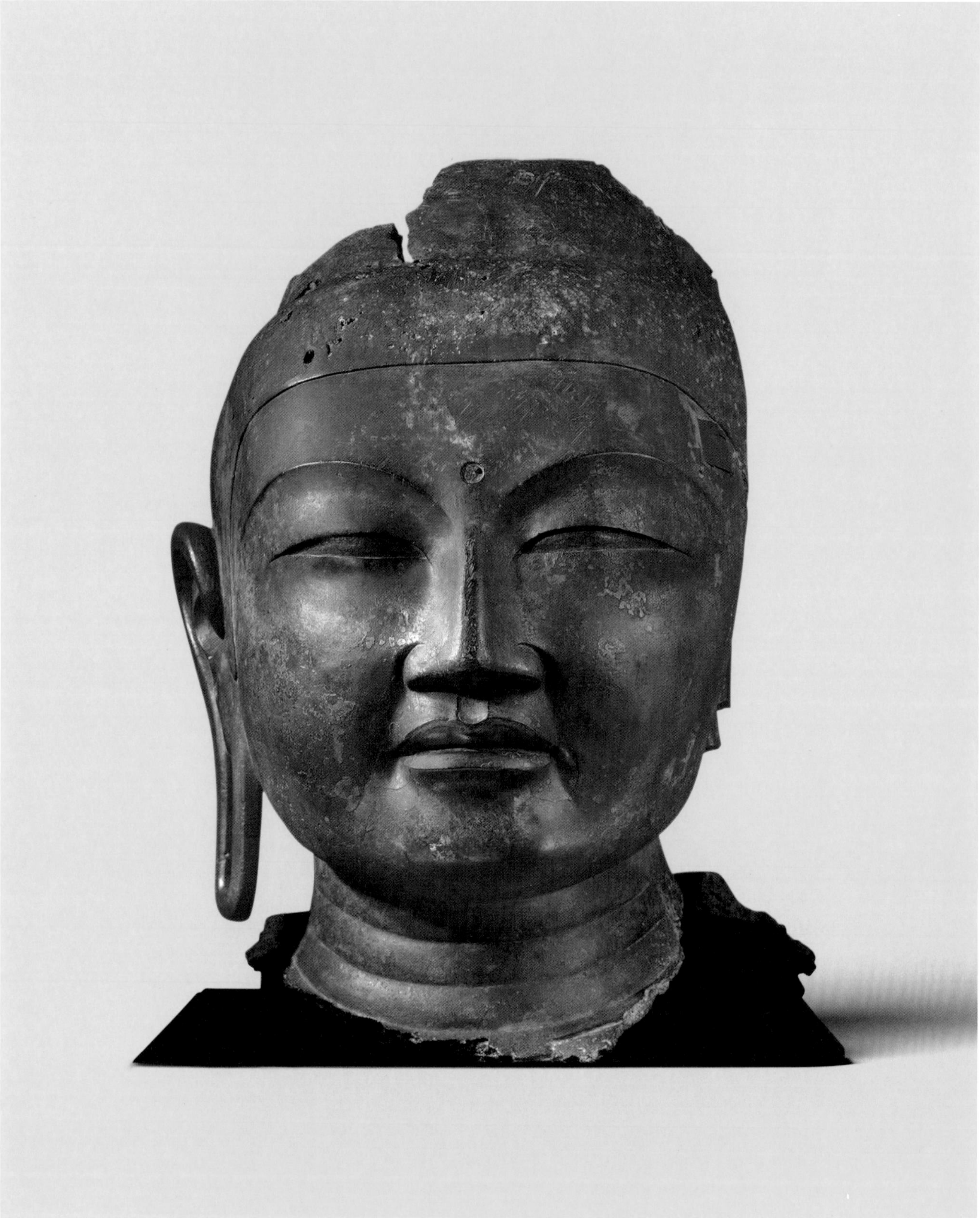

Fig. 2 Japanese, *Former East Golden Hall Main Image* (旧東金堂本尊), 685 CE, bronze
Kōfukuji, Nara

required to cast a replacement. Why was the Kōfukuji bronze head hidden and forgotten instead? We may never know.[17]

Soon after its rediscovery, the Buddha head was designated a *kokuho,* or national treasure. The designation, which formally protects ancient Buddhist temples and Shinto shrines, as well as the most important works of ancient cultural property, was part of a response to violent attacks on Buddhist institutions in the 1870s and 1880s.[18] The indiscriminate destruction of Buddhist images was of special concern. Government legislation required temples and shrines to protect national treasures and share responsibility for their conservation. In a stroke the law transformed a religious object like the Buddha head—even one badly damaged—into a work of art in a museum, a new, modern register of economic and cultural value. The Buddha head is now empowered as a representative of the nation-state.

SOUVENIRS

On the island of Java stands Borobudur, an imposing eighth- and ninth-century Buddhist monument constructed out of some 1.5 million volcanic stone blocks ⟨ *fig.* 3 ⟩. The seven terraces in the shape of a stepped pyramid feature more than a thousand relief carvings and some five hundred seated-Buddha images. There is a massive and deeply considered spiritual program expressed in the plan of Borobudur, but to this day experts disagree. Is Borobudur a stupa? A mandala? The narrative of a spiritual quest?[19]

Java is known for its stone Buddhist and Hindu temples constructed before the population was converted to Islam in the sixteenth century. Since then there have been few Buddhists or Hindus to appreciate the achievements of their ancestors.[20] But local residents long knew about Borobudur. They understood that the colossal temple was dedicated to the Buddha and that the many carved scenes illustrated his teachings. Although not followers of the Buddha, islanders often brought flowers and offerings to the temple.[21] Borobudur and other ancient temples were powerful reminders of the glory of their Hindu-Buddhist cultural heritage.[22]

In 1814 Borobudur was "rediscovered" by the British administrator, scholar, and soldier Stamford Raffles (1781–1826).[23] Raffles saw sublime ruins and ordered the overgrown site to be cleared.[24] It is said that Raffles gathered fallen heads from the ruins.[25] The next year he included three stone Buddha heads from Borobudur in a shipment of objects sent home to London ⟨ *fig.* 4 ⟩.[26] For Raffles, the stone heads were a familiar type of sculpture displayed in places like the British Museum.[27] They were souvenirs, objects that, as poet and literary critic Susan Stewart has said, "serve as traces of authentic experience."[28]

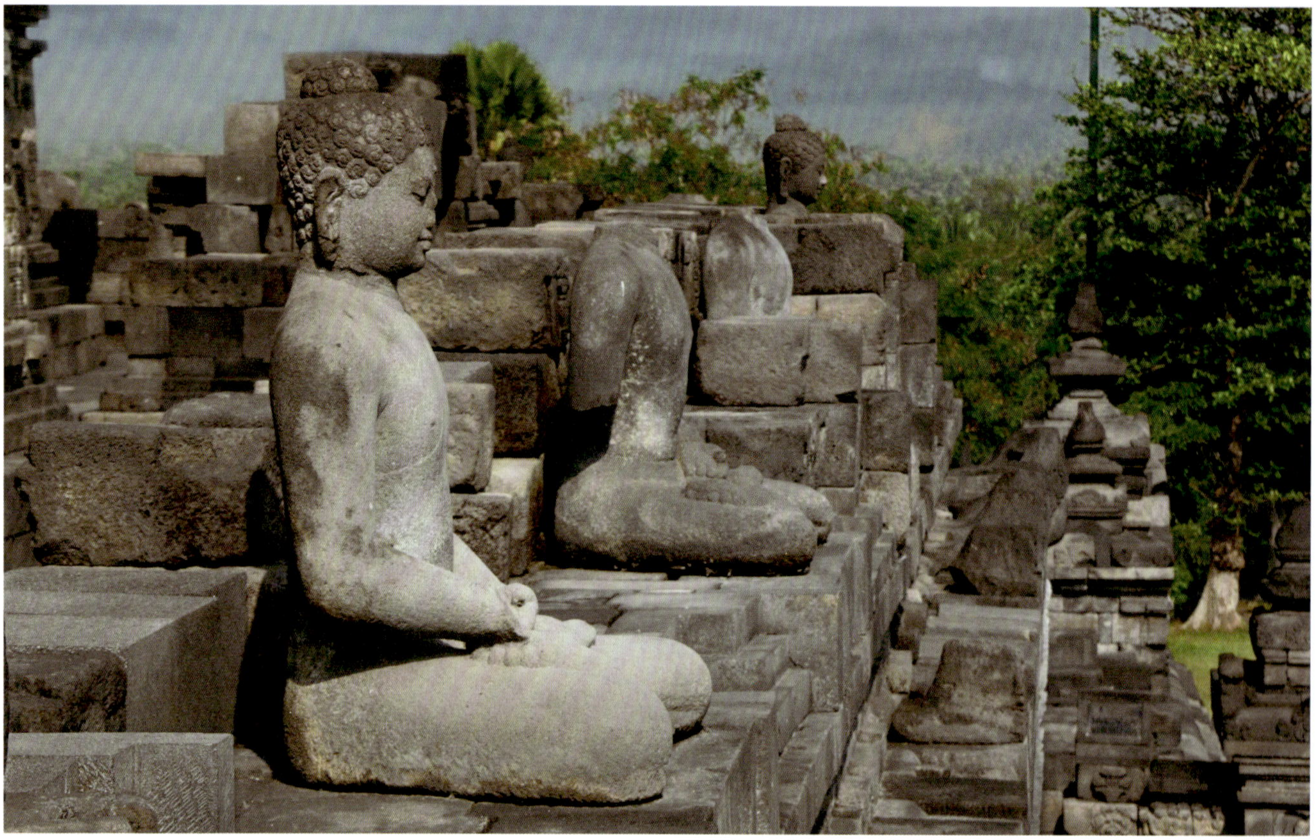

Fig. 3 Borobudur Temple, Java, 770s–850s CE

On Java, stone was thought to have a special quality. Life forces were believed to flow through rocks. Large pieces of stone were often moved to direct and store energy, and old carved blocks were regularly shifted around to channel the flow of energy.[29] Locals also found fragments of sculpture useful as materials for new building projects. And colonial officials were enthusiastic collectors of the odd but intriguing old Hindu-Buddhist stone deities.[30] They joined in the enthusiasm for relocating huge stones by moving some onto the grounds of their residences. Locals may have understood the colonists to be managing the vital forces coursing through ancient stone just as they did. Raffles taking three stone Buddha heads away may have appeared to be an attempt to add the power of stone to the British Empire. They would not have considered the possibility that the artistic value of a stone head separated from its body might be enhanced, as in Western sculpture.

In 1894 the Buddhist King of Siam, Chulalongkorn, visited Borobudur. He was familiar with ancient Buddhist architecture and imagery across Southeast Asia. Climbing the terraces, the king carefully inspected the monument and offered prayers to the Buddha. At the end of his visit, with

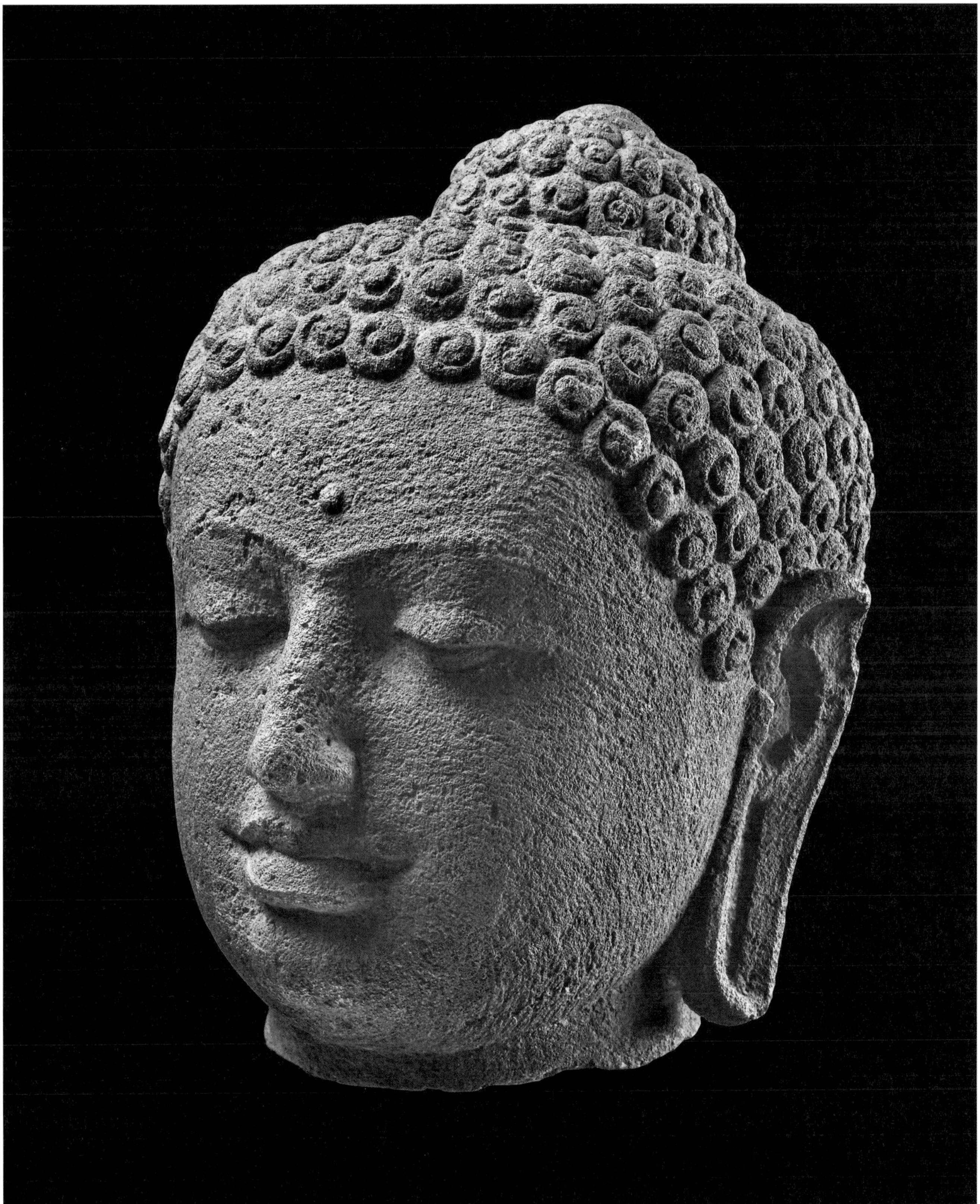

Fig. 4 Javanese (Borobudur), *Head of a Buddha*, late 700s CE, volcanic stone
The Trustees of the British Museum, 1859,1228.177
Cat. 36

the consent of the Dutch colonial authorities, he selected stone carvings from Borobudur to take home with him. Included were fragments of relief carving and five complete Buddha statues.[31] King Chulalongkorn did not choose to remove any heads, because he would not have considered them valuable as independent works of art.

MARKETABLE ANTIQUITIES

On a crisp spring day in 1909, a young Chinese man strides purposefully across the green expanse of the Parc Monceau in Paris's Eighth Arrondissement. His destination appears to be the Avenue Vélasquez, a single tree-lined block of imposing mansions. Passing out of the park and under the iron arch of the gate, he pauses in front of the first house to his right—number 7. His gaze slowly rises to take in the grand three-story stone facade, imposing and grim like a church or a bank. High above, flanking the arched glass doors above the entrance, his eyes pause on a pair of mosaic busts in round medallions—Michelangelo on the left and Plato on the right.

The young man is twenty-nine-year-old Ching-Tsai Loo (Lu Qinzhai 盧芹齋, 1880–1957). The house is the former residence of Henri Cernuschi (1821–1896), Italian émigré banker and wealthy Republican, and it is filled with objects he acquired in Japan and China in 1872. The house and collection had been left to the city of Paris upon Cernuschi's passing in 1896 and opened as a public museum in 1898. Loo arrived from Shanghai two years later and used connections with Qing dynasty officials in Paris to establish himself as an independent trader in Chinese objects, primarily the ornate porcelains favored by wealthy collectors. Now he hopes to make a sale to the fledgling museum of Asian art.

Loo is led up the wide staircase to the office of Henri d'Ardenne de Tizac (1877–1932), the young curator appointed only four years prior. Loo is given a tour of the galleries, then they sit down to discuss the objects he has to offer. Ardenne de Tizac slides a photograph across his desk of an elegant stone head of a bodhisattva ⟨ *fig.* 5 ⟩. The curator is not interested in porcelains or bronze figurines. Loo can see that the museum is well-stocked with these, the types of objects collected by Cernuschi. No, Ardenne de Tizac tells Loo, he would like old and rare stone sculpture—real Chinese sculpture.

Loo had never considered selling stone sculpture. Chinese collectors had no interest in sculpture, and, thus far, neither had the wealthy Parisians whose tastes he gauged as a matter of course. Loo later wrote that "this fine stone immediately awakened in me a desire to develop a new line in Chinese art."[32] Intrigued, he promises Ardenne de Tizac that he will inquire with his "partners" in China about the stone head and

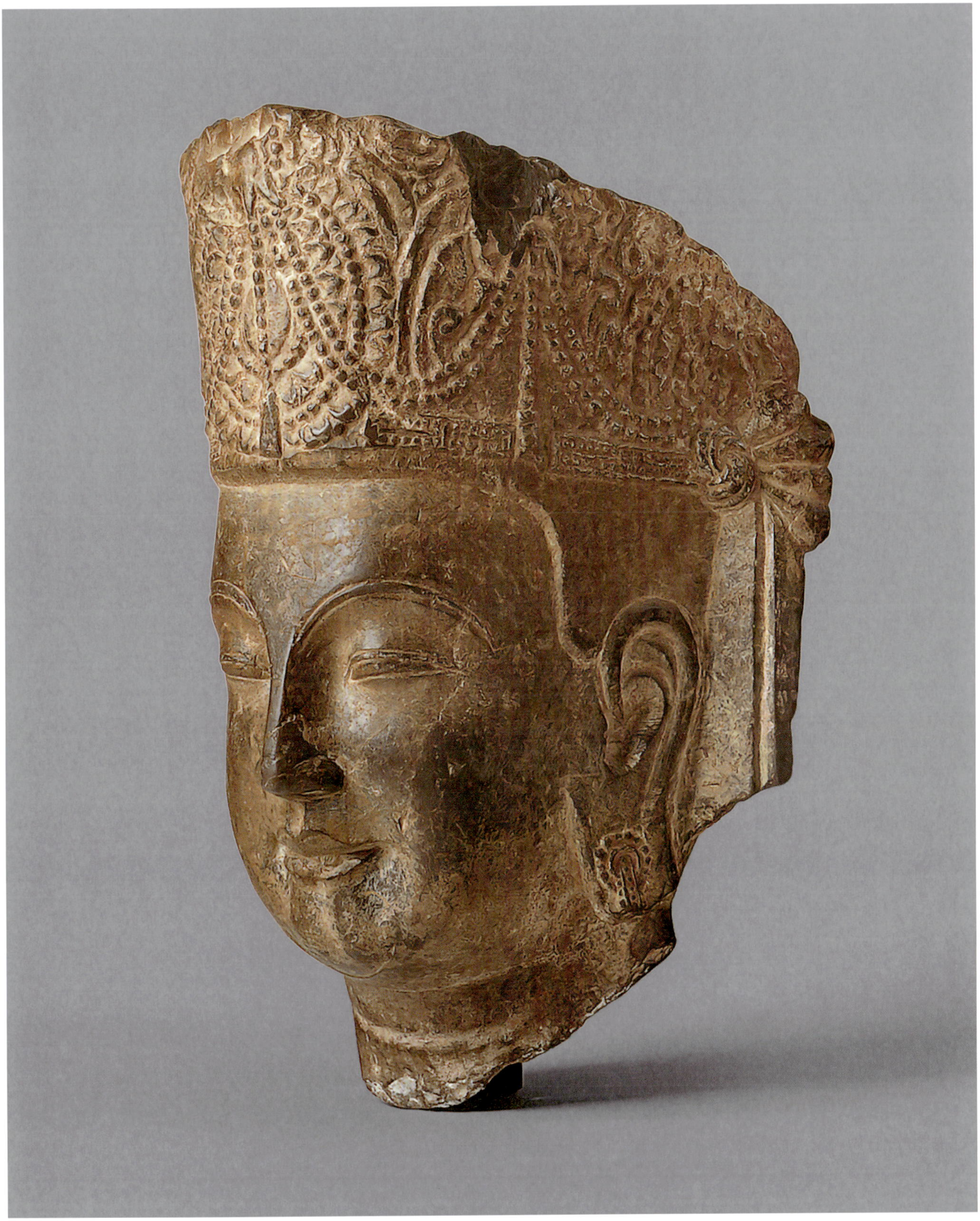

Fig. 5 Chinese, *Head of a Bodhisattva*, 581–618, stone
From *Chinese Works of Art from the Stoclet Collection* (London: Eskenazi, 2003), 40, no. 11

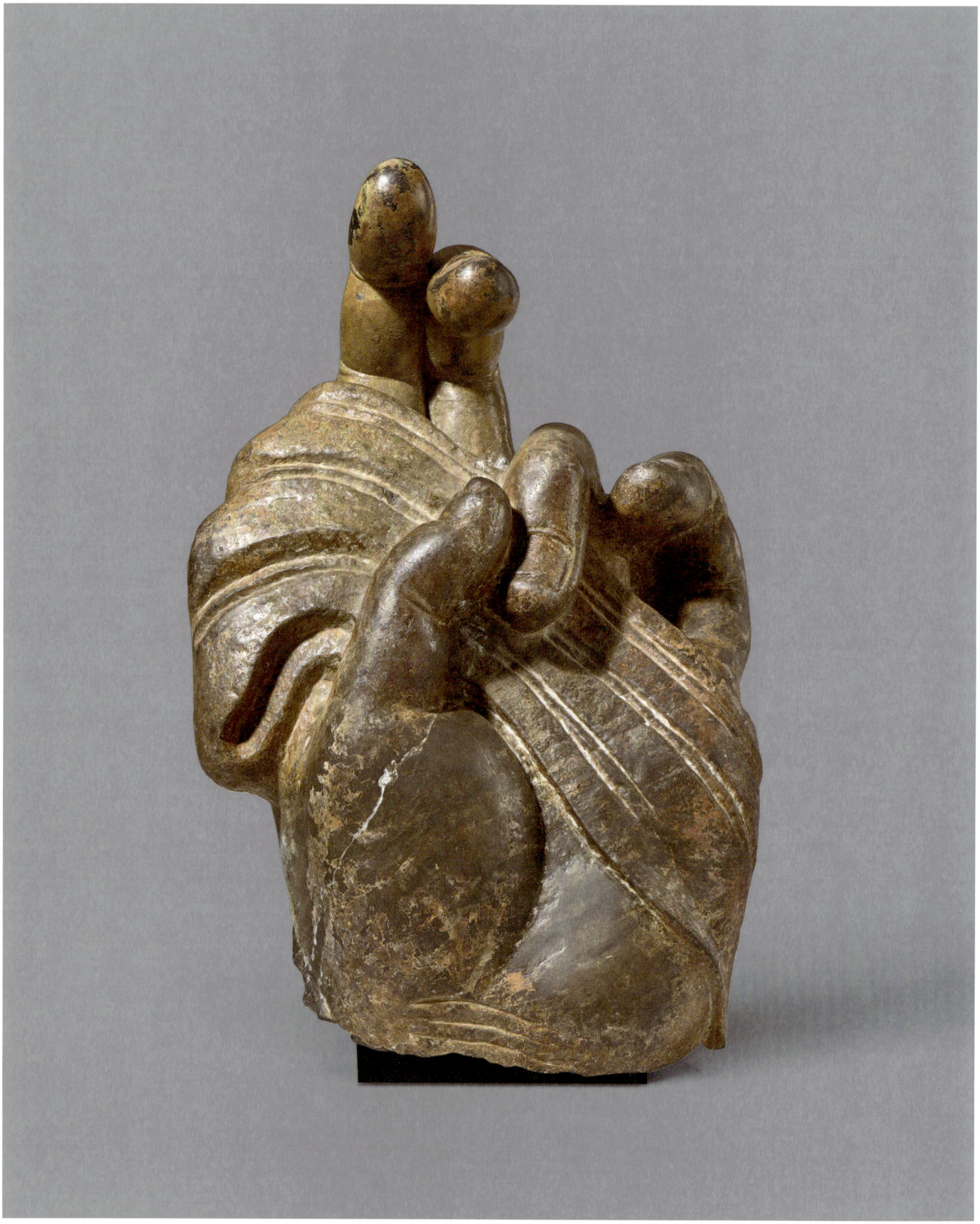

F i g. 6 Chinese, *Left Hand of Maitreya, Buddha of the Future*, c. 550–560 CE, limestone
Asian Art Museum of San Francisco, Transfer from the Fine Arts Museums of San Francisco, Gift of the M. H. de Young Endowment Fund, B69S37
Cat. 34

departs Parc Monceau with the photograph tucked into his valise. Loo would soon learn that the head had already been acquired in China by another French dealer, Marcel Bing.[33]

Loo would indeed go on to develop a new line as one of the most successful dealers of Chinese sculpture in the West. But it was difficult to acquire and transport bulky stone sculpture and then successfully market the works to a limited clientele.[34] So Loo was willing to try a wide range of objects. In his own Paris *pagode*, constructed in 1924, intricate wooden South Asian architectural fragments framed Chinese tomb figurines and Buddhist paintings.[35] Besides heads, Loo trafficked in hands. Two were cut from a large, seated Buddha statue at the extensively looted cave temple site of North Xiangtangshan and now reside in two separate museum collections.[36] The raised right hand with palm out, *abhaya mudra*, signifies "no fear," the gesture of reassurance. The hand is repaired across the palm, and the tip of the middle finger has been replaced.[37] Loo gave the hand to the Metropolitan Museum of Art in 1930. The left hand of the same Buddha, now in the Asian Art Museum of San Francisco, grasps the end of his robe ⟨ *fig.* 6 ⟩. Two fingers have broken off, and there is a crack across the palm. The hand was in the collection of Hagop Kevorkian in New York in 1934 and is said to have been acquired by the de Young Museum soon after.[38]

Today many stone Buddhist images have had their protruding hands inadvertently or purposefully broken off. Limbs were often removed as a precaution before attempting to move an entire statue. In the case of these hands, the brutal cuts at the wrist appear deliberate. Perhaps the hands were cut off because it was deemed impossible to remove the whole Xiangtangshan Buddha figure from its niche.

CREATING BUSTS

While limbs, hands, or heads of statues were admired as sculptures in the West, the body parts of a Buddhist deity in Asia were not collected or displayed as objects of devotion or works of art.[39] To purposefully cut the head or hands from the body of a Buddha was an act of destruction, and the resulting incomplete image of the Buddha would have been considered pointless ⟨ *fig.* 7 ⟩. But in the West, heads have been a familiar mode of sculpture from Classical antiquity to the present. The bust is a venerable form of portraiture largely limited to Western art. The result is the matter-of-fact display of Buddhist heads in museums as works of sculpture not qualified by the terms "broken" or "fragment."

In 1909 Victor Segalen (1878–1919) and Auguste Gilbert de Voisins (1877–1939) embarked on an expedition across northern China.[40] Their

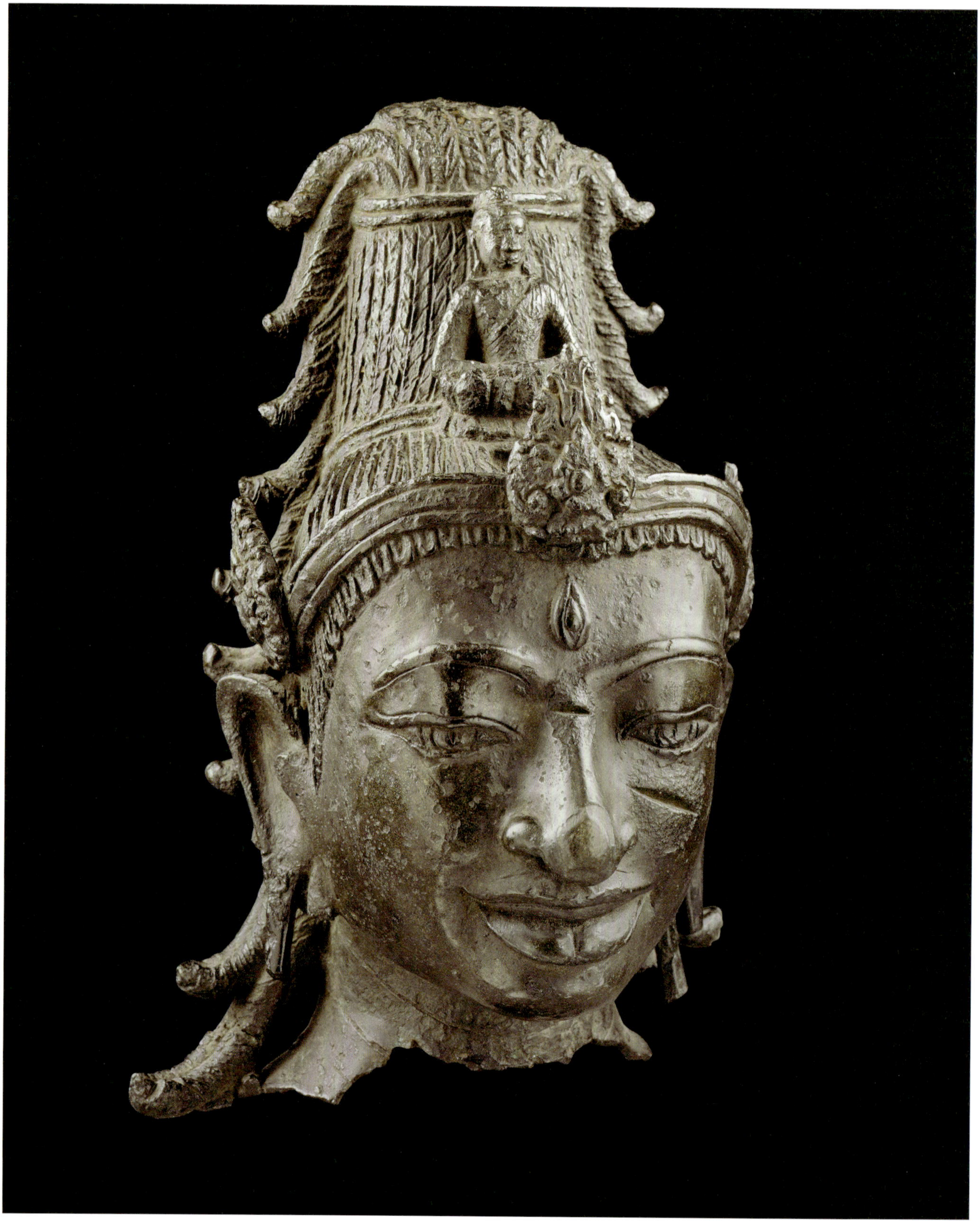

Fig. 7 Cham (Quang Nam Province, central Vietnam), *Head of Bodhisattva Avalokiteśhvara*, c. 700–800 CE, copper alloy
Guimet—Musée National des Arts Asiatiques, Paris, MA7067
Cat. 35

charge was to explore and photograph largely unknown territory and report on conditions in China. Segalen was a French naval officer, physician, poet, critic, and essayist who traveled in China from 1909 to 1914 and again in 1917. He learned the Chinese language and published widely on Chinese literature, archaeology, and sculpture.[41] Voisins was a close friend and writer who documented their journey through China.

On August 29, 1909, in Shanxi province south of Taiyuan, Voisins recorded their encounter with a Buddha image.[42] Stopping to explore a dilapidated pagoda by the roadside, Segalen and Voisins came upon a splendid wooden statue.

> Despite its missing two arms and a torso that seemed to be in poor shape, this life-size statue is still alive: its profile has retained its nobility, its eyes their gaze, the smile of its mouth its generous sweetness and a kind of irony. This statue, we must have it! We won't leave it as if it were a mere bronze vase! We will not leave without it! With chosen words that bind us, we make a pledge. This is all very well, but how should we proceed? Take it? Steal it? It would be impossible for us even to lift that piece of wood! Very well then! We will cut its head!
>
> Immediately, fetching an axe from our luggage, we undertake the sacrilegious work. With all my strength, I strike the first blow on the golden neck, but I hardly make a mark on this age-old wood. We struggle in vain. Segalen strikes with all his strength, without any more success. This lasts for about half an hour, when just as we are about to give up . . . two peasants who were passing on the road, attracted by the noise, enter suddenly. We feel quite embarrassed, our cynicism has its limits. . . . To pollute a temple by debasing the statue of its god is an act for which there is hardly any excuse. But the newcomers, far from showing any anger or indignation, behave, on the contrary, in a way that stupefies us: they offer to help us!

In his posthumously published book on Chinese sculpture, *Chine: La grand statuaire*, Segalen criticized the negative impact of foreign styles of Buddhist sculpture adopted in China. He was convinced that an older, native approach to stone sculpture used for mortuary figures and commemorative stele was superior in conception and technique but had been unhappily overwhelmed by an inferior foreign strain of Buddhist sculpture.[43] But on this occasion, he hoped to abscond with a foreign Buddha head.

> First, they make us understand that it is pointless to try to behead this Buddha, which is too heavy, while standing. They lay it down on its face, with its head on a block, put wedges under its sides, fix it with straw plugs, and finally, laughing at our clumsiness, take the axe from our hands. With a few well-directed strokes, crackles, an atrocious tear, it is done; the beheading is perpetrated. In the chest

> we find some cash, which we leave to our accomplices, and papers, which I keep. Our horses are now stamping in the mud. We jump into the saddle without further delay and ride away.

How will Segalen and Voisins convince us that their actions were defensible, or even enlightened? With a story—a good story.

> On the way back, Segalen imagines the plot of a nice story, based on our action today. He is so ashamed of this sacrilege that he wants to justify himself to posterity. In particular, he is so ashamed of our impunity that he heaps a thousand calamities, each more atrocious than the other, on the main character of his story. In this way, he believes that he can to some extent avoid them himself. Only when he laid out the conclusion of his story, which I may add is perfectly horrible, did he perhaps feel relieved and find his peace of mind again.

When Segalen, Loo, and others were collecting sculpture from China in the early twentieth century, Chinese Buddhism and China itself were at a very low point. The ruling Qing dynasty was collapsing. Colonial powers—foremost England, France, Germany, Russia, Japan, and the United States—forcibly pressed for concessions in trade and territory. Ancient Chinese sculpture, not prized in China, was available for a pittance if not for the taking.

Voisins's record of their destruction of a Buddha image—and creation of a Buddha bust—is a surprisingly frank account of pillage. He and Segalen, with their Western understanding of sculpture, viewed both the Buddha image they found (already damaged and abandoned) and the bust they created as works of art. In their account they express remorse for their "sacrilege," but local residents seem not to have attributed great value—religious or artistic—to the already broken image. Voisins portrays their helpers as accomplices to plunder. We are witness to the emergence of a new commodity in the Chinese market: old Buddhist statues, stele, and figures, once whole images, now broken sculpture. These are the heads, torsos, hands, and limbs that became powerful treasures on the global art market.

The stories presented in this essay offer a few of the varied ways in which broken Buddhist sculpture and fragments were viewed in Asia. These objects seem not to have been treated with the awe and respect given to broken sculpture in the Western tradition. In retrospect, this seems logical. The status of broken sculpture in the West is a very special characteristic of Western sculpture and is not widely shared in other parts of the world. There is a gap separating the treatment of Buddhist images and Western sculpture, and this difference is significant.

Rather than absorbing the East into Western art history—as so often happens—it is crucial that we consider Western and Asian art with an understanding of all their historical differences. Everything from the language of this essay to the way we are trained to look at art is unavoidably determined by a Western art historical framework. In a volume presenting sculpture fragments from across the globe, it is vital to reflect on the defining terms and values of our comparative approaches.

WEATHERING PAGANISM

A CHRISTIAN-ECOLOGICAL MEDITATION

Timothy Morton

Can thinking about ecology interact with thinking about "broken" art? Yes. But the ways in which one can do this may surprise you. I am going to argue, perhaps perversely, that ecological thinking has more in common with Christianity than you might suspect. This has nothing to do with contrasting religion and science, but rather with contrasting *two different kinds of religion*: Christian and Etruscan.

Let's look at two pieces: an Etruscan lion's paw resting on the head of a bearded man from about 150 BCE ⟨ *fig.* 1 ⟩ and a statue of Jesus from around 1400 in Florence ⟨ *fig.* 2 ⟩.

"Paw-Head" is made of nenfro, a kind of tufa. Carbonate minerals precipitate from water to create this very, very soft volcanic stone. With or without human intervention, tufa is highly susceptible to sculpting. Looking at this piece, I am faced with some inspiring challenges to do with the role of nonhuman beings. When we drop some rather unnecessary concepts regarding acting versus behaving—a series of binaries that have to do with rigid and untenable distinctions between human beings and everything else—what is called "weathering" is simply another kind of sculpting. There is evidence that we are not averse to such things in our regular lives. We talk in everyday speech about how the water has "carved" the gigantic channels that comprise the Grand Canyon, for instance. When it comes to tufa, I am looking at a substance that to my human eyes easily appears to have been shaped by water and wind. I can find smooth, flattened steps of tufa in China, pyramid-like tufa domes in Nevada, and weathered columns of tufa in Mono Lake, California. I have to reach for human architectural and sculptural terms to describe them. I wonder what it would be like to do the reverse: to reach for watery, windy ways of describing what humans make from stone.

"Broken Jesus" now resides in the Museo di San Marco in Florence. In 1966 the river Arno burst its banks in a flood that killed thirty-five people and broke the sculpture. The flood got uninhibited access to precious books, manuscripts, and artworks inside the city's churches, including a crucifix by Cimabue from Santa Croce and Broken Jesus, whose original location remains unknown. The flood acted like iconoclasts bursting into a basilica and smashing the icons. How strangely like the rapid and fervid history of Jesus himself is this? Meanwhile, trillions of undying hands with the tiniest fingers have been slowly and rhythmically stroking Paw-Head for centuries.

What are the differences between human sculpting and nonhuman sculpting? Is it to do with unconscious versus conscious, with accidental versus deliberate? It is notoriously difficult to figure out whether an artistic decision by a human being was deliberate or not, and it is difficult in itself to express what we mean by "deliberate." Conscious

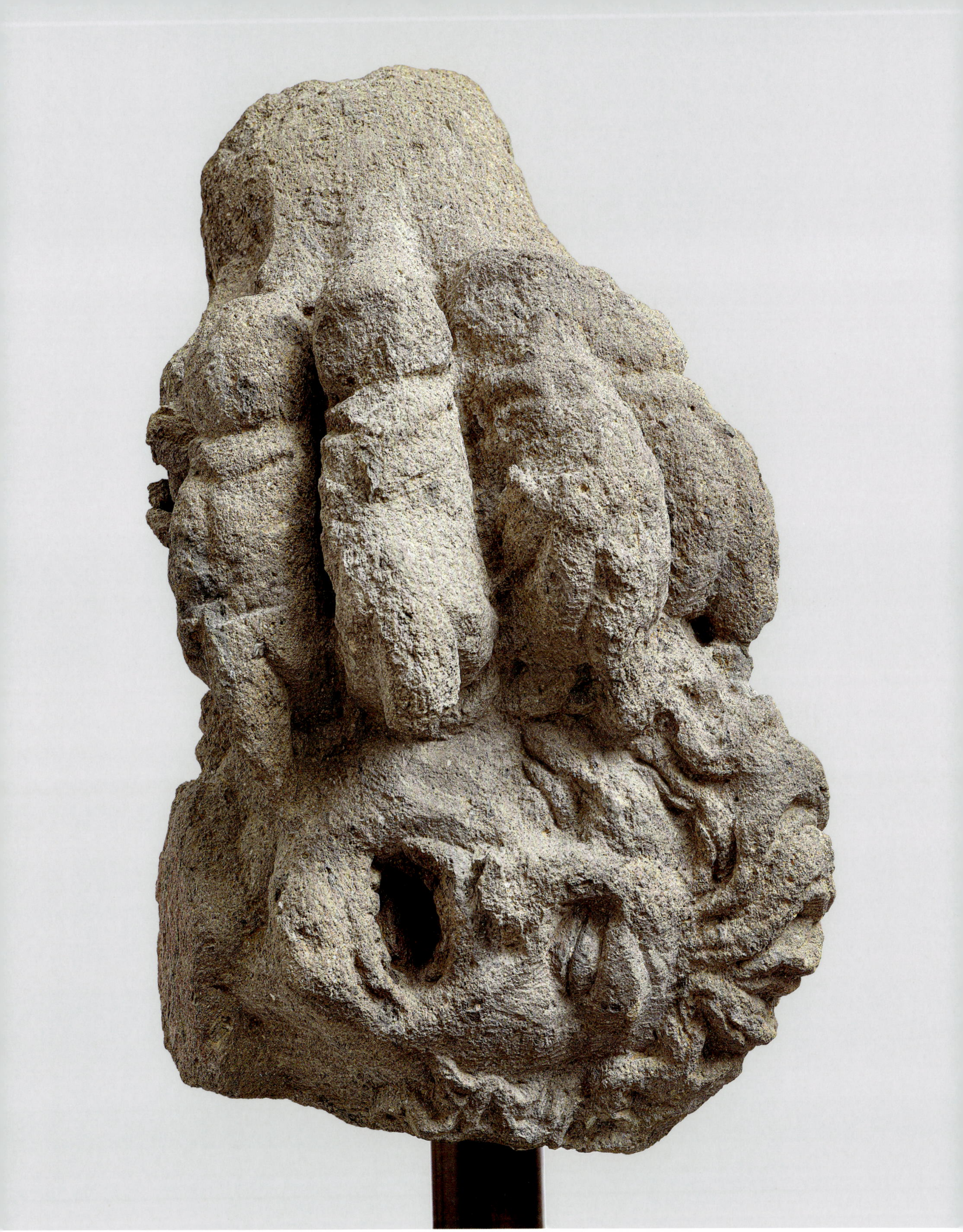

F *i g.* 1 Etruscan, *Lion's Paw on a Severed Human Head*,
c. 150 BCE, nenfro
Ny Carlsberg Glyptotek, Copenhagen, HIN 0250
Cat. 17

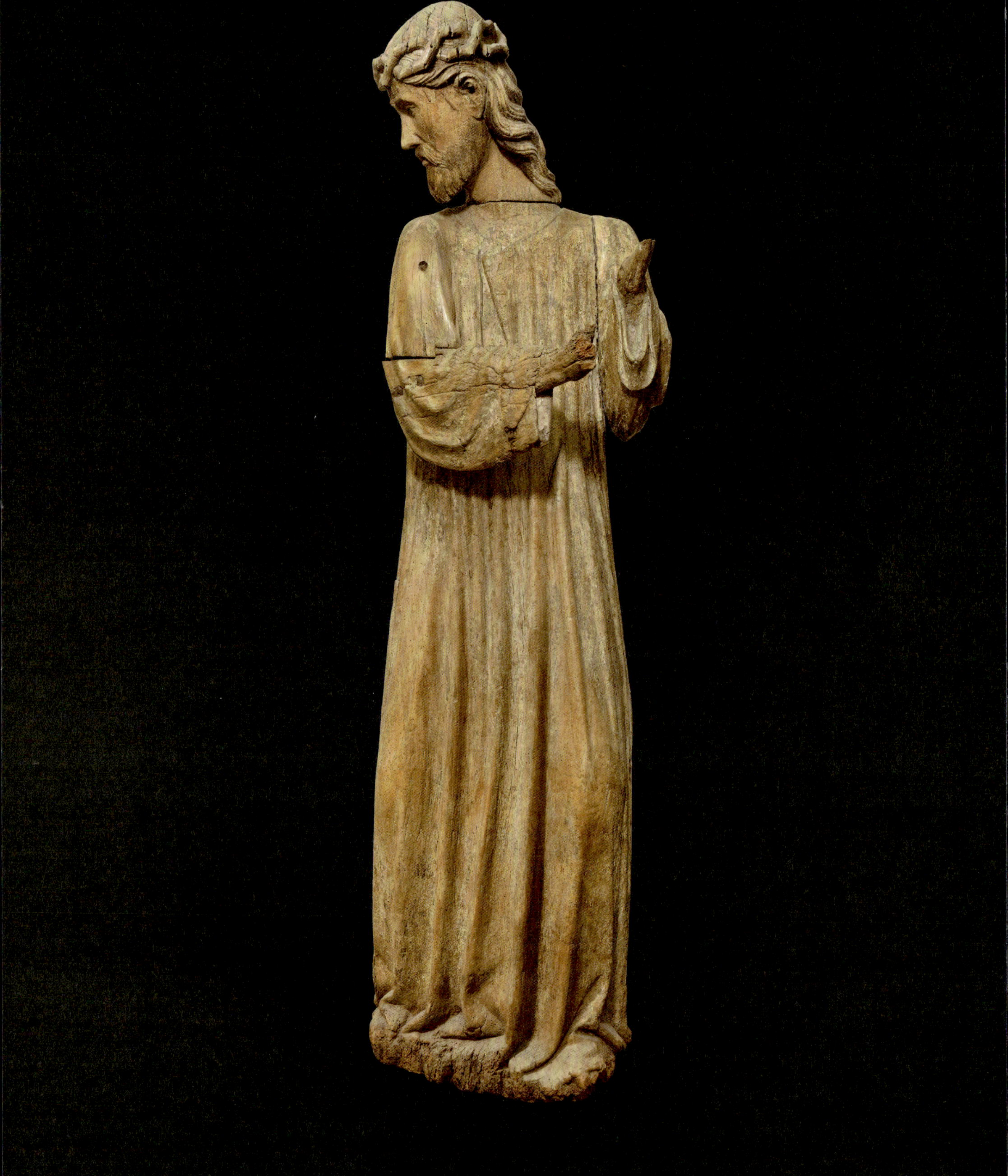

F*ig.* 2 Tuscan, *Christ Carrying the Cross*, late 14th–early 15th century, poplar wood with traces of pigment and gilding
Museo di San Marco, Florence
Cat. 50

will looks like an illusion when we take neuroscience into account. By the time I have decided to pick up a cup, I have already started doing it.[1] What if the rigid binary between deliberate and accidental were spurious? There is plenty of art that values dropping or loosening "intention." Keith Rowe of the music group AMM talks about the role of "un-intention" in his work.[2] But fancy terms, theories, and propositions aside, artists drop intentionality all the time. Michaelangelo famously felt as if he was stripping the stone away to reveal a figure trapped within it.

When determining what "nature" did and what human sculptors did, perhaps I shouldn't use words like "deliberate" and "accidental," "conscious" and "unconscious," "intended" and "unintended." When I use such terms, it is almost as if I want to tame these broken pieces. Not only are these sculptures broken, these sculptures *break the very idea of sculpture* as such. They break my prejudices.

What we are dealing with—the whole assemblage of humans, artworks, the sculptural forces of nonhuman entities, considered as a colossal whole stretched out over time—is what I have called a hyperobject: something so massively distributed in time and space that it is impossible to see all at once, though perfectly possible to understand.[3] When we think of Paw-Head and Broken Jesus as visible parts of a hyperobject, we realize how and why their presence is so thought-provoking.

Perhaps the intensity of art as such is always about breaking my prejudices, even when I behold something conventionally beautiful. I think it has to do with talk of "the neighbor" in Judaism, Islam, and Christianity. The idea of the neighbor, despite its domestication in the phrase "next door," pertains to anyone, actually fleshy anyone with whom I find myself proximate: not physically, but *phenomenologically*. When I think of a hypothetical alien living millions of light-years away, they are my neighbor in this sense. Much philosophy has devoted itself to exploring the neighbor, who never fits the sorting algorithms that divide "self" and "other." Emmanuel Levinas's thinking about the intrinsically disturbing "face" of the neighbor; Slavoj Žižek's meditations on the neighbor as abject; and indeed Christian theology, which radically revised Roman and Greek thought about those to whom I owe a moral or physical debt to include the "untouchable," abject class known to Greek civilization as *ptochoi*, to whom philanthropy traditionally owed nothing at all.[4] "Love thy neighbor as thyself" is radical. It is even more radical when we consider the Greek for "as" (*hos*), a highly surfactant adverb that melts the self into the neighbor—the only way I love *myself* is in the key of loving the neighbor.

The word "neighbor" stems from Old English and German words that roughly mean "the guy nearby" ("boor" is a casual term for a person, as in "boorish," and "nigh" means near).[5] The neighbor is a living being, not an idea like "the other." The neighbor is the one next to whom we just happen to find ourselves: someone in the lunch queue, the guy across the street, a homeless person at a traffic light. The neighbor is therefore a powerful and disturbing category; it disrupts the habitual sense that ethics ("good habits") lines up with morality (right and wrong).

The proximity of the neighbor does not mean tape-measure closeness. I can be thinking about Paw-Head sitting at my computer in Houston, Texas. Broken Jesus can haunt me without me having to visit it in person. The neighborliness of these artworks won't vanish or even diminish, no matter how far away or close I am. In addition, this volume (and the exhibition it accompanies) has removed them from their contexts, and this makes me want to recontextualize them. Art can disrupt the familiar worlds in which I carelessly glide. Every artwork is perhaps a broken fragment of a whole that I imagine might pacify its threat. But how I recontextualize them also begins to become weird. The very idea of context has been ripped out of its context. The contexts that explain *these* particular works must include the nonhuman beings that I normally ignore when I look at a work in an art gallery. The very way in which they are "not artistic" because they have been fragmented and weathered is what in the end is most artistic about them!

Paw-Head and Broken Jesus talk to one another in very strange ways. That would include the differences between "pagan" worlds and Christian ones, and how these worlds persist today. I refer to the worlds of Rome, Greece, Babylon, Etruria, Mesopotamia . . . worlds whose agricultural and architectural (and political and . . .) procedures many nations might still be following. Christianity itself spread in large part thanks to its incorporation into the Roman Empire, and European colonialism was enabled by the church in all kinds of ways too numerous to spell out here.

These Mesopotamian-style societies are well-organized, orderly, hierarchical, caste-based, rigidly determined. They are worlds of empire and tribute; worlds in which there are distinct and intimidating rulers; worlds of mastery and of slavery; worlds that may well have seemed infinite in their oppressive sameness to those who dwelt in them. Naturally I include what we could call Christendom within this description. In Mesopotamian-style realms, power requires constant maintenance in the form of propitiation, "making examples" of people, and obedience. In Mesopotamian-style worlds concepts such as fate and luck play powerful roles. I think many people still feel this way about the environment. People "live" hurricanes and fires like this: The "natural" world seems to impinge on "civilization" from the outside. Erosion and flooding seem like external forces.

When I look at Paw-Head, immediately I think of the metaphorical paw of a tyrant on the head of a regular person such as myself. Actual lions and other animals might have gotten a raw deal in some parts of imperial space, but they often symbolized the power of the monarch. It is likely that in this case, because Paw-Head is Etruscan, the monarch we are talking about might be Death, the fateful ruler of all life. A regular person such as myself would have experienced the Mesopotamian-style world as one where the forces of the monarchy seemed as inevitable as death or the ocean or sand. Nature and civilization exert the same kind of power over me, despite how different they seem.

I think about the image of the severed head in Gerald Scarfe's film created to accompany the live performance of Pink Floyd's "Welcome to the Machine." It lies on its side, its mouth agape, slowly weathering into the surrounding desert.[6] These are frozen moments of suffering human life. Imagine a paw, stamping on a human face—forever.[7] That face might be that of an enslaved person, and the face is at any rate subjugated by the paw; the open mouth, the grotesque stare, remind me of slave masks in classical drama, the Mesopotamian-style equivalent of blackface.[8] Under a real paw, a mouth would only scream for a few seconds. The weathering of the tufa only adds to this uncanny effect, as in the petrified victims of Vesuvius. I think about the impulse, driven by a sense of rigid hierarchy and the sadistic feelings that such hierarchies train humans to enjoy, to depict the scream, to set it in stone like that . . . I think about my impulse to imagine the wind and the rain's lavish licking of that face for over two thousand years; how the grotesqueness of erosion weirdly overlaps with the grotesqueness of a sculptor's—and a culture's—desire to depict a face crushed by a paw in the first place. I might even think, "Well, this artifact is getting its just desserts." As in Percy Shelley's "Ozymandias," I see the ruin of empires in Paw-Head.

Broken Jesus, on the other hand, is strangely "less damaged." Jesus was *already "broken."* What is special to Christianity is the idea that God let himself become a slave, even let himself be killed, in the name of nation and empire. (Philippians 2:7 uses the Greek term *doulos*, which definitively means "slave" and not "servant.")[9] Missing part of his left arm and having his head severed resembles what human beings had already done to Jesus. What becomes visible is a sharp difference between *Christianity* and *Christendom*, between a hyperobject and people. Water and the shrapnel that moves around in water have not done anything very different than what human beings do to condemned, scapegoated people. Now Paw-Head is also already broken, since it depicts a dead individual on a tomb. And it also kind of represents just what happens to victims of force, death, and so on. But viewers in the culture from which it comes would surely see this not as shocking, but just as the kind of thing that happens to people—as fate, not as a determinate political action affecting a specific person.

I am arriving at an astonishing suggestion. Might Abrahamic religions, despite their appropriations by territorial forces, be *more in sync* with ecological awareness than the cultural logics of the Mesopotamian-style worlds from which Abrahamic religions emerged? Even more weirdly, might this resonance pertain to the very *discontinuity* between "humanity" on the one hand, and a naturalized "civilization" on the other? "Pagan" means "of the countryside," yet what is named in this term is not the nonhuman world per se. That belongs to the far more problematic term "savage," meaning "of the forest." "Pagan" names a hyperobject: that vast, regularized, standardized, cyclic, repetitive, mass-production mode we call agriculture.[10] Before server farms, before plantations, there were *fields*, endlessly plowed and sown and reaped in farmer-centric societies based on "propitiating" an algorithm, a recipe for success: "It worked well last year, so we should do it again."[11]

Farmer-centricity and its repetitive procedures have persisted. Paw-Head comes from a distant empire, but Paw-Head could not be more contemporary: it represents an "agrilogistical" culture where strict sets of codes required constant adherence, maintenance, and propitiation. Yet, my way of beholding it is conditioned by Christianity, the world that created Broken Jesus. It is this strange oscillation between distance and proximity that generates in me an uneasy feeling when I look at Paw-Head, the kind I was describing in the passage on the aesthetics and ethics of the neighbor. At a time when the actual planet on which you are reading this is being pushed beyond its limits by the very forces that generated Paw-Head, I face the equally uncanny possibility that *Christianity* (despite *Christendom*) might permit me to see the human and the nonhuman world on a *nonhierarchical continuum*. What I see in Broken Jesus is . . . broken Jesus. A set of beliefs and cultures that speak about a radical *transcendence* of this world are, if I can endure my own logic here, ways of realizing my *immanence* to that world. Even weirder, this happens despite the very ways in which Christendom (Europe and America) trafficked in transcendence while leaving the worlds of empire and agriculture all too intact, fanning the flames that generated "secular" formats in which nation-states competed for two centuries over who could be the cruelest of them all to their citizens, to other humans, and to the life-forms that comprise our biosphere.

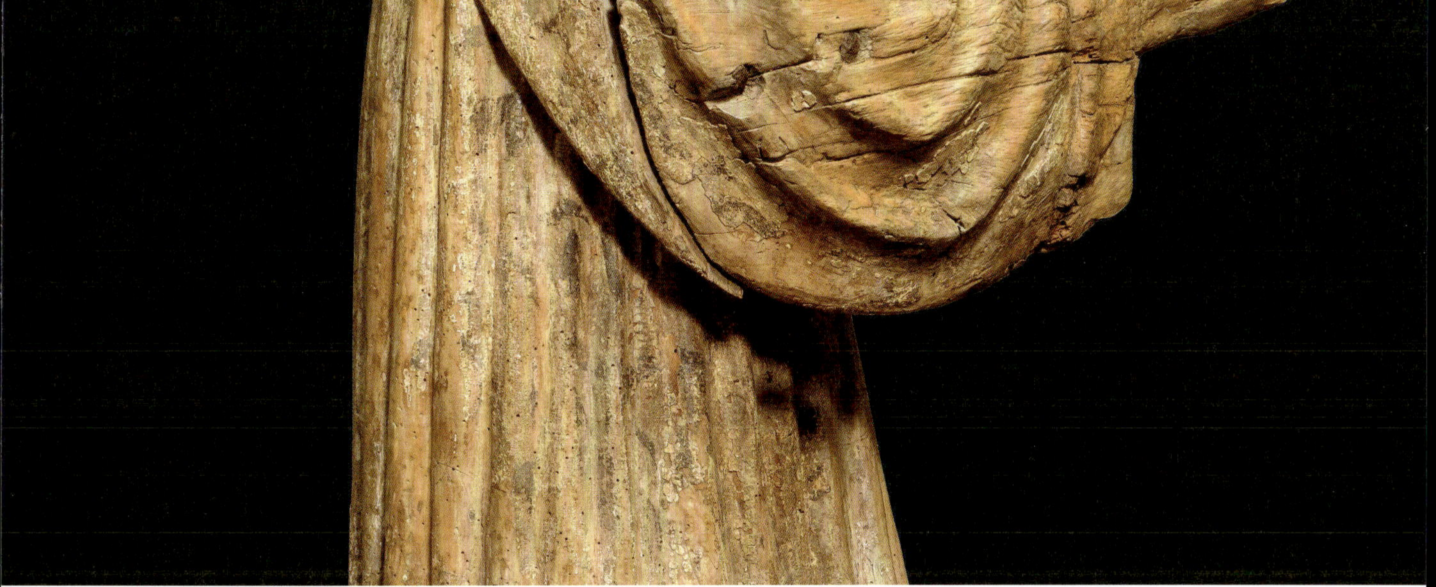

Detail, p. 146

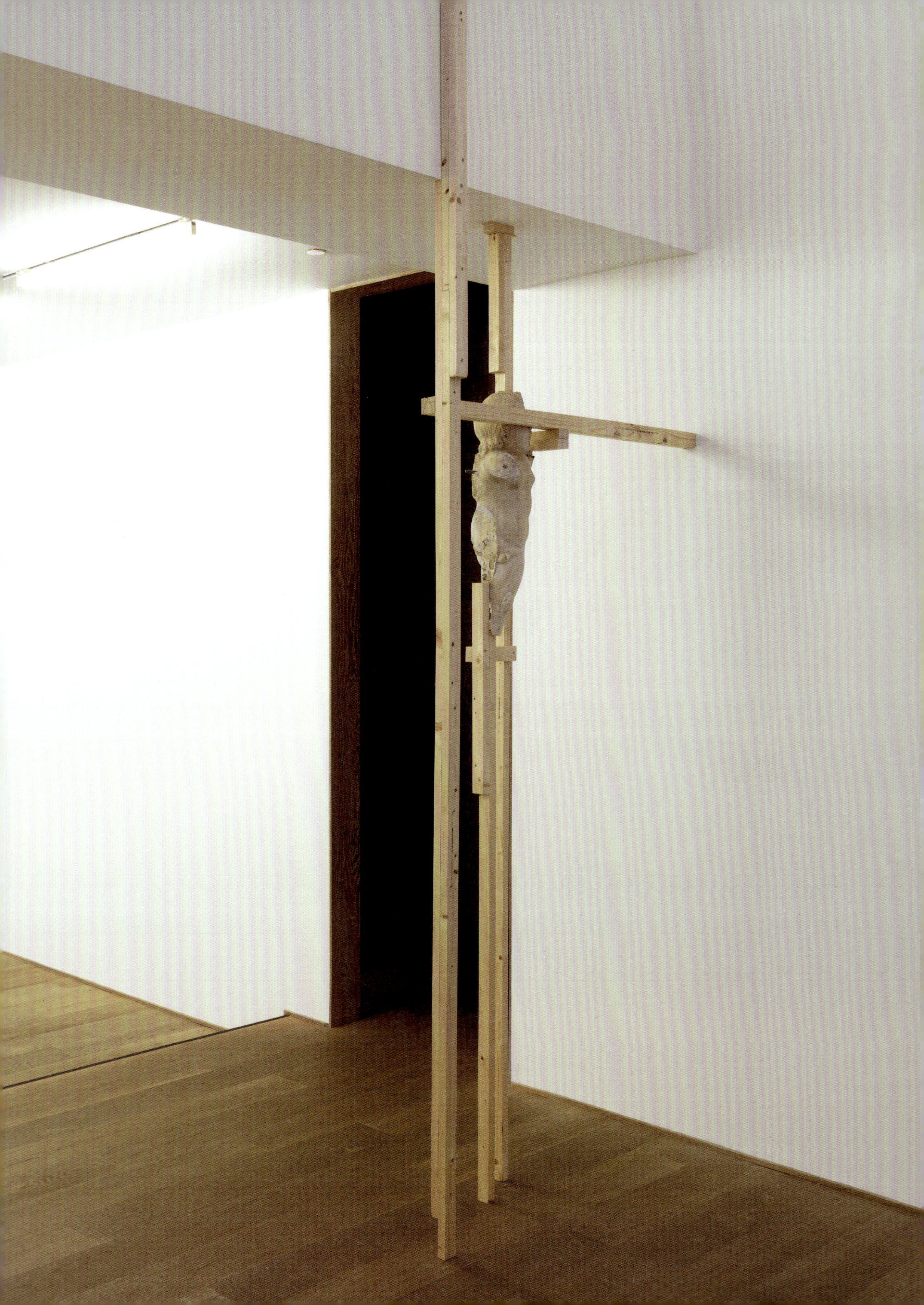

THE ART OF THE FRAGMENT

Installation view, p. 180

BROKEN TO COMPLETION

Andrew Sears

Around 1400, the Mexica of Tenochtitlan (present-day Mexico City) were in the middle of an extensive campaign to renovate the sacred precinct at the city's center, a large double pyramid now known as the Templo Mayor (*Huey Teocalli* in Nahuatl).[1] One of the most notable additions was a brightly painted sculpture carved from volcanic stone that was placed at the north pyramid's summit before the entrance to the shrine of the rain god Tlaloc ⟨ *fig.* 1 ⟩. This *chacmool*—showing a recumbent figure turning its head and holding a vessel in its lap—belongs to a common sculptural type found across Mesoamerican temples. Although it remains unknown whom exactly such works were meant to depict—perhaps a priest, an ancestor, or a captive awaiting sacrifice—the containers they hold suggest they served as receptacles for offerings.[2]

Like many acts of refurbishment, the installation of this chacmool spoke as much to the present as to the past. The sculpture's archaizing style was meant to evoke the much older ones erected by the Toltecs at Tula, a site that had been abandoned around 1150 and by the fifteenth century survived only in ruins. The Mexica were conscious of the fact that they were a rather young society, having begun as a seminomadic group who settled in their capital of Tenochtitlan only in 1325. To legitimize their emergent power, they looked to venerable past civilizations whose architectural and artistic remains surrounded them in the Valley of Mexico. Toltec art was especially important for Mexica self-fashioning because the first Mexica king, Acamapichtli, was believed to have descended from Tula's royal lineage.[3] Throughout the fifteenth and early sixteenth centuries, before the arrival of the Spanish in 1519, the Mexica traveled regularly to Tula to explore and excavate. While many of their findings served as sources of artistic inspiration, others were believed to index Toltec power and were subsequently transported back to Tenochtitlan to endow their new constructions with material potency. These ranged from small, portable objects, like pieces of

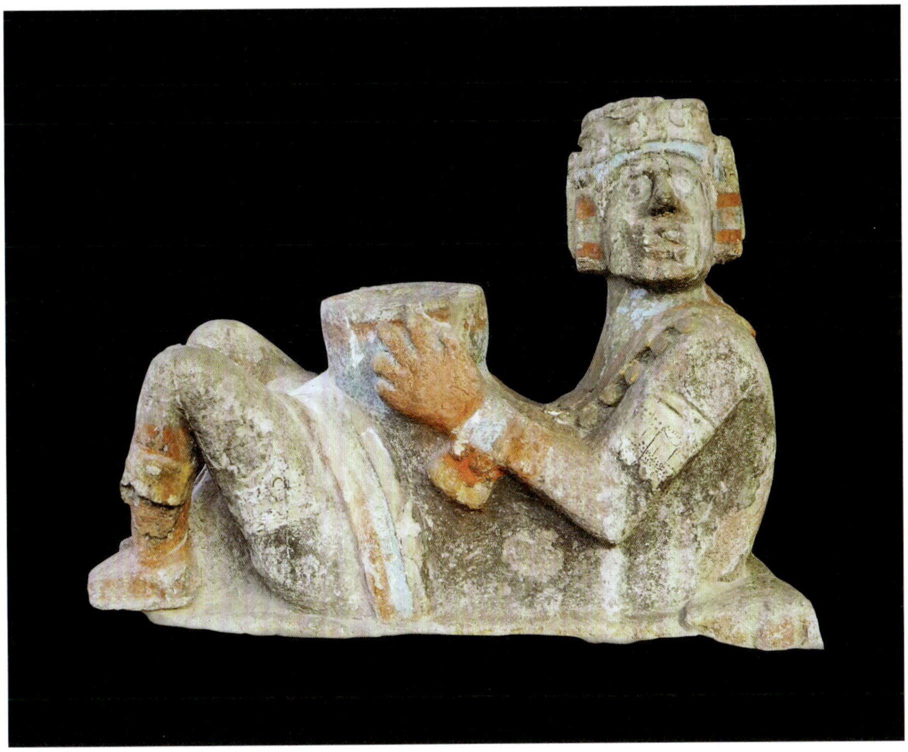

Fig. 1 Mexica, *Chacmool* at the Stage II Tlaloc Shrine of the Templo Mayor, c. 1375–1427 CE, pink andesite, stucco, and pigment
Museo del Templo Mayor, Mexico City, Secretaría de Cultura—Instituto Nacional de Antropología e Historia

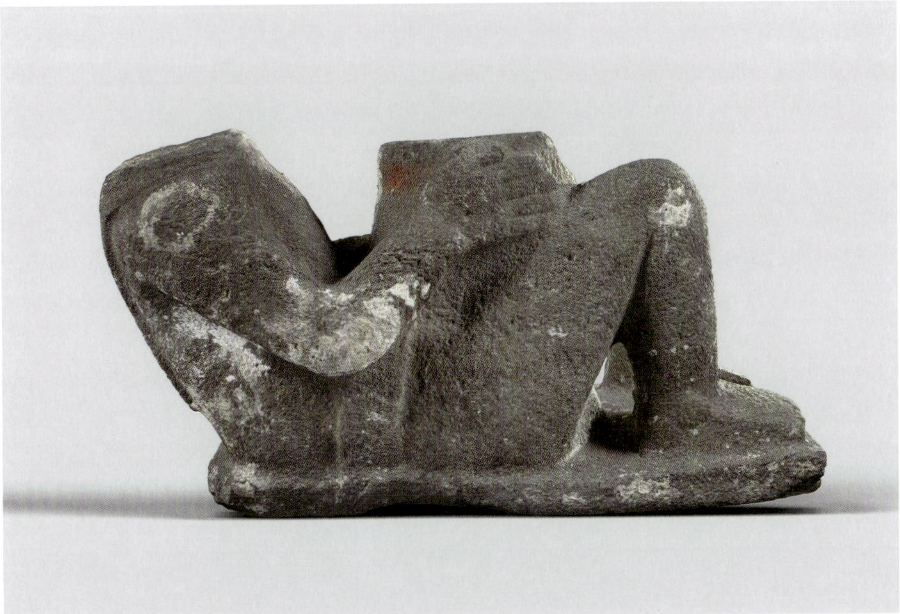

Fig. 2 Mexica (Tenochtitlan [Mexico City]), *Chacmool*, c. 1350–1450, volcanic rock and stucco
Museo del Templo Mayor, Mexico City, Secretaría de Cultura—Instituto Nacional de Antropología e Historia, 10-262479
Cat. 48

jade and obsidian, to monumental sculptures and monoliths, including a Toltec chacmool weighing 1.5 tons that was carried over fifty miles.[4]

Many fifteenth-century cultures shared this impulse toward antiquarian self-fashioning. As C. D. Dickerson discusses in his essay in this volume, Italians in the same period were also undertaking frenzied excavations, unearthing ancient sculptures, and mobilizing a past civilization—the Roman Empire—to engender a cultural "rebirth" (*rinascita*) that today we call the Renaissance. Yet these two cultures diverged in their artistic and conceptual approaches to the remains they encountered. In Italy, the convention was to repair fragments of the Roman past through conservation and restoration—acts motivated by the belief that the past needed to be "completed" in order to be efficacious.[5] In contrast, the Mexica seem to have understood completion to be wholly unattainable and thus modeled their approach to rebuilding and reclaiming the past on the ruinous state of their surroundings. Confronted with innumerable fallen and broken sculptures across their landscape, the Mexica perhaps saw their future as being just as inevitably fragmented as their past. As the scholar of ancient Mesoamerican art Claudia Brittenham describes, they built in a way that already anticipated what would eventually be "broken, turned upside down, ignominiously exposed."[6]

Across the Templo Mayor, acts of breakage, fragmentation, and displacement were integral to renovation, as evidenced by the degree to which new construction was continually counterbalanced with deposits of fractured sculptures, remains of humans and fauna, and offerings divorced and decontextualized from their original locations.[7] Before the installation of the chacmool at the shrine of Tlaloc, for example, a substantial cache of precious greenstone and obsidian offerings of unknown origins was interred beneath it, and caches nearby contained similar objects that were intentionally broken.[8] In other instances, chacmools themselves appear to have been broken and turned into offerings; twelve examples have been found across the site, many of them cleanly decapitated, which suggests some kind of ritual transformation was carried out before they were deposited into new building fabric ⟨ *fig.* 2 ⟩.[9]

Breaking and creating were inseparable, if not synonymous, and within this context it becomes increasingly difficult to distinguish between the two. Indeed, the painted chacmool atop the Tlaloc shrine and the decapitated example deposited in the ground may have been understood as not all that different, since both were part of the same dialectical processes that endowed the site with potency. The fragmented chacmool—a work that might appear "broken" to modern eyes but in its original context was considered to be fully realized—indicates just one of the many ways in which artists since premodernity have engaged in and conceptualized acts of breakage and fragmentation as generative modes of creation.

BREAKING AND MAKING

For many ancient and premodern cultures, breakage heightened the potency of sculptures and arguably made them more "complete." As Kaywin Feldman discusses in her essay in this volume, among the earliest works bearing traces of deliberate breakage are the *dogū* figures of Jōmon Japan ⟨ see Feldman *fig.* 5 ⟩. Known for their minute surface decorations achieved by pressing cord into wet clay, these sculptures are the basis for the term *Jōmon* itself, meaning "cord-patterned." Produced as early as the fourth millennium BCE, they became increasingly embellished and plastically modeled by the Final Jōmon period (c. 1000–300 BCE), when this example was made: a type known as a *shakōki dogū* for the "light-blocking device" protecting its eyes like snow goggles.[10] The genre remains enigmatic, for its long production history is paralleled by an equally prolonged history of breakage. Indeed, it seems that the sculptures were even designed specifically to be handled this way. Composed of balls of clay that were added to a torso, the figurines possessed many seams that, although being covered at the very end of production with a thin layer of slip, were known to their users. According to the Jōmon scholar and archaeologist Kobayashi Tatsuo, these deliberately engineered weak points presented options for fracturing according to one's wishes.[11]

In one of the first qualitative studies of dogū figurines, the historian Taniguchi Yasuhiro examined 677 examples across six sites and found that only three figures, or 0.4 percent of the total group, were intact. The majority of the findings, 70.1 percent, were buried without an adjoining piece, a sign of just how methodically breakage and dispersal were carried out.[12] Some dogū fragments were deposited as offerings in groups alongside other ceramics, and countless others were found scattered across settlements. Such a vast but heterogeneous pattern of distribution suggests that breakage was a constant cultural practice. Because most dogū are gendered female, it has been suggested that they were perhaps regularly broken in an act of petition for human or agricultural fertility. Alternatively, their parts may have been customarily exchanged as a means for forging social bonds.[13] As Feldman illuminates in her essay, whatever role these sculptures may have had in connecting individuals to one another or mediating relationships with a deity, they achieved the power to do so by being broken.[14]

Tracing these generative histories of breakage is not always straightforward, especially for sculptures that have a less extensive archaeological record. In the case of the *Fragment of a Kneeling Figure*, made by a Jenné-Jeno workshop in medieval Mali, the sculpture's fractured surface is the main evidence that exists, making it difficult to determine whether its condition resulted from time, ritual, or conflict ⟨ *fig.* 3 ⟩.[15] Perhaps owing to

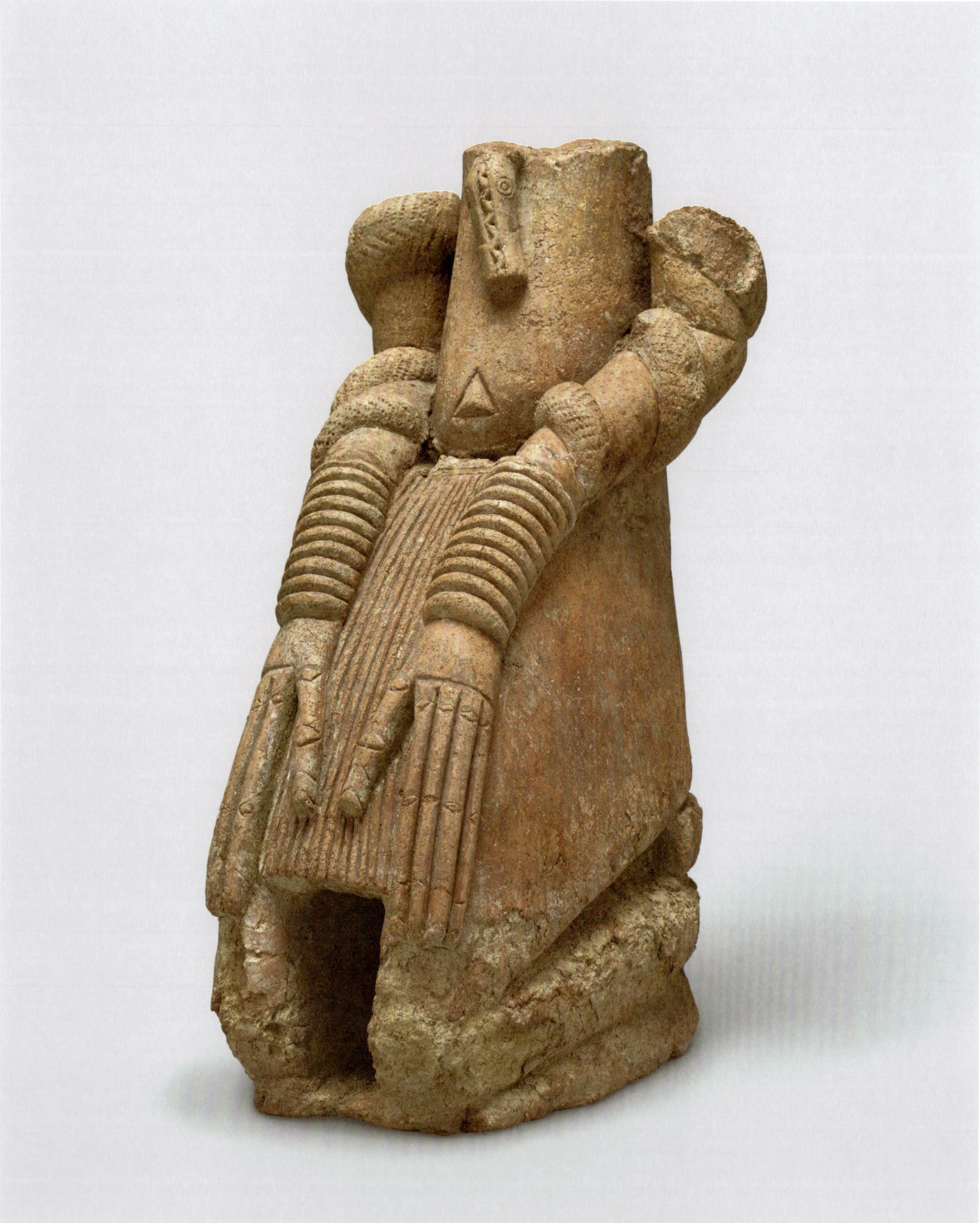

Fig. 3 Inland Niger Delta (Jenné-Jeno), *Fragment of a Kneeling Figure*, c. 1000–1400, terracotta
The Art Institute of Chicago, Maurice D. Galleher, Ada Turnbull Hertle, and Laura R. Magnuson funds, 1983.917
Cat. 39

modern habituation to images of violence, iconoclasm is often assumed to have been the cause of many premodern fragments.[16] The prevalence of broken terracottas from the Inland Niger Delta, for example, has frequently been (mis)attributed to the spread of Islam in the thirteenth and fourteenth centuries. Although a regional shift toward an aniconic religion may have occasioned breakage, it is vital to consider such acts as measured and methodical more than violent or destructive. Conversion was a gradual process of adopting and adapting new religious practices, and communities modified their ritual objects accordingly.[17]

It is also possible that the *Kneeling Figure* may have been fragmented independently of the spread of Islam. Excavations of other terracottas at Jenné-Jeno reveal evidence of ritualized and customary breakage both before and after the region's conversion. Similar to the context of the Templo Mayor, the dialectic of breaking and making appears to have been a widespread cultural practice that was integral to the splendor of the city's built environment. At Jenné-Jeno, certain kneeling figures have been found buried within the foundations of residences; their ritual pose, associated with acts of offering, was perhaps seen to serve a fortifying function. Other examples were interred alongside ritual objects like ceramics inside small, purpose-built structures that were then intentionally toppled, the resulting rubble subsequently used as the ground for further building.[18] The many possible religious or ritual practices through which the *Kneeling Figure* achieved its current state reveal just how inadequate the term "broken" is—a word that overlooks the agency of those who thoughtfully reworked the sculpture to engender transformation, whether in the form of confessional change or civic expansion.

So elided were destruction and creation that even clearly violent acts of breakage might be characterized as modes of reverence. The greenstone *Standing Figure* from Teotihuacan, for example, was likely attacked shortly before or during the city's fall around 700 CE—a time of political turmoil that appears to have motivated the breaking of ritual objects to engender change ⟨ *fig.* 4 ⟩.[19] Believed to have been carved between 150 and 250 CE and probably placed in a secluded shrine for an elite audience, the figure belongs to a group of twelve examples all thought to have been destroyed around the same time. All bear similar losses of heads and limbs, and several bear fractures consistent with strikes from chisels and other sharp instruments, thus indicating deliberate and systematic efforts to sever the exceptionally hard and dense greenstone. It is possible these blows resulted from some kind of ritual "killing" conducted in conjunction with the sacrifice of a live prisoner, but they might also have taken place during Teotihuacan's destruction, when a group of insurgents annihilated the city, attacked its people, and destroyed its ritual objects. These two scenarios may not be as distinct as they initially seem, since the archaeological evidence suggests that the same level of precision and care was given to the sculptures' destruction as to their interment.[20] Whoever broke them clearly acknowledged their potency, dispersing the fragments widely to preclude any possibility that their power reconstitute and reemerge.

Certain objects provide motifs or iconographies that help us better understand how the relationship between destruction and creation was conceived in their original contexts. Such is the case for the so-called *Birger Figurine*, sculpted from flint-clay by a Mississippian artist working in the twelfth century near Cahokia, then the most populous city in the Western Hemisphere north of the Valley of Mexico. In accordance with the wishes and authority of the descendant tribes of Cahokia, an image of this sculpture is not shown in this volume, nor was the figure included in the related exhibition. It is discussed, however, because of the importance of remembering that Indigenous people of North America remain present and contributed to the exhibition's conversations around breakage and fragmentation.[21]

The *Birger Figurine* bears many layers of fragmentation, some of which predate its rediscovery nearly fifty years ago.[22] In 1979, during excavations at the BBB Motor Site in preparation for the construction of Interstate 270, the sculpture was unearthed when the back of its head was severed by a paddle-wheel scraper. After it was removed from the ground and began to dry out, preexisting cracks became evident, suggesting that the figure had already been intentionally broken and loosely reassembled by the Cahokian people: The head had been separated from the torso, and the right hand had likewise been detached.[23] The fact that the sculpture had been deposited in a special place after being broken suggests it had been ritually disarticulated and then buried. The site where it was found was an important location during Cahokia's existence for preparing bodies for burial, so it is posited that the sculpture was connected to and subjected to the same cycle of life, death, and renewal as one or more of the individuals interred nearby.[24]

A description of the sculpture offers a deeper understanding of the meaning of this cycle and of breakage more broadly. The depicted individual, believed to be the Old Woman Who Never Dies—a Mississippian adaptation of an Earth Mother figure regarded as the spirit world's most powerful female inhabitant—is shown as a cultivator working the land.[25] She kneels before a crescent-shaped plot of earth, digs with a tool in her right hand, and carries on her back the fruits of her labor, shown by a cluster of gourds still attached to their vines. Yet the earth that encircles her has a head and reveals itself to be a serpent of the underworld; the vines and gourds that wrap around the Old Woman are its tail. Bounty comes from death, an inevitable tension that perhaps explains the Earth

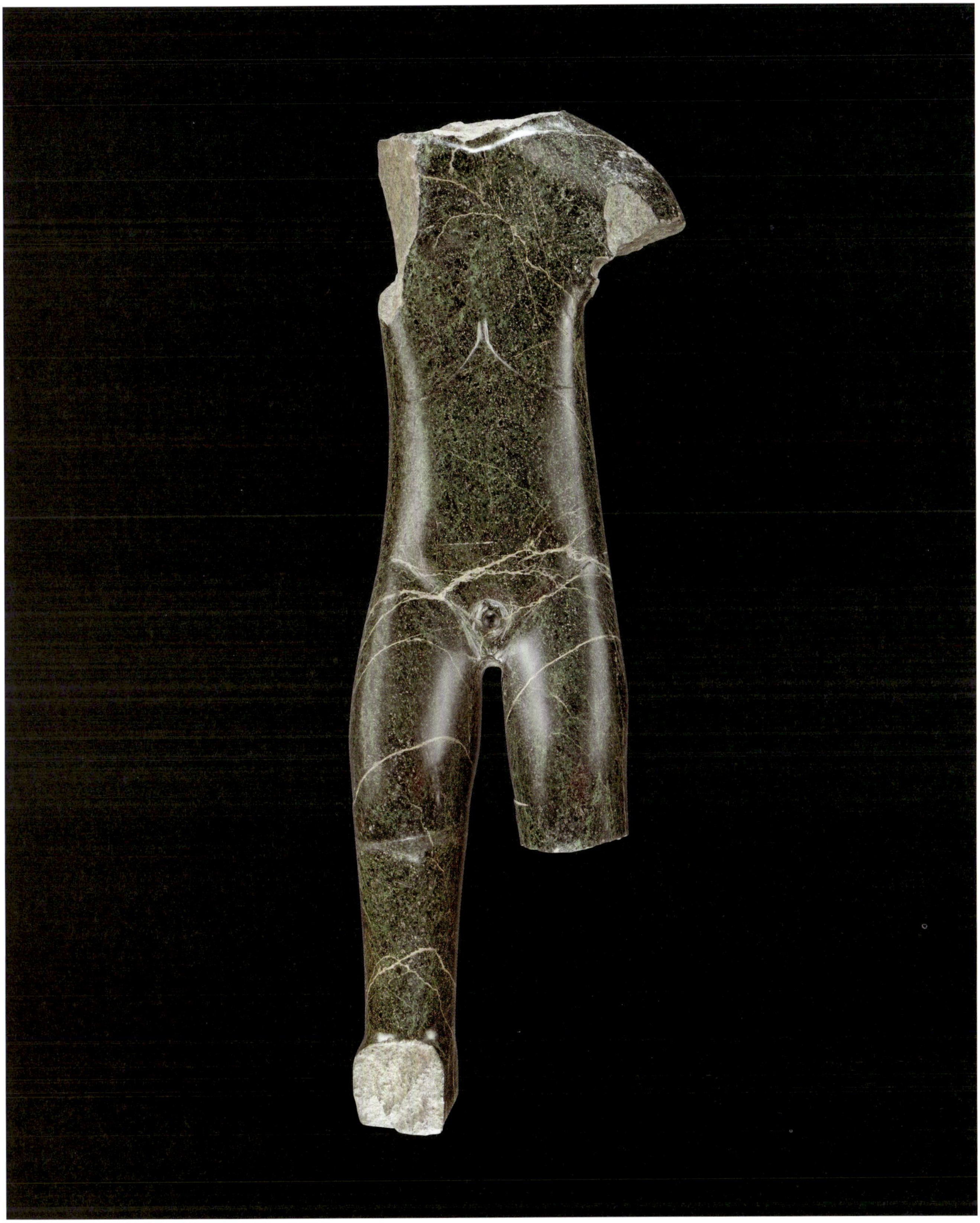

F*ig.* 4 Teotihuacan, *Standing Figure*, c. 150–250 CE, greenstone (serpentine)
Museo Nacional de Antropología, Mexico City, Secretaría de Cultura—Instituto Nacional de Antropología e Historia, 10-81806
Cat. 27

Mother's grimace as she works between these two forces. The sculpture seems to comment on the cycle of destruction and generation to which it belongs. Such forces are inextricable from one another, and in that regard, there is perhaps not that much that separates creating and breaking.

MORE THAN A FRAGMENT

Many premodern artists strove for fragmentation when first conceptualizing their creations and before taking up their tools. Reducing, abbreviating, or isolating figural forms allowed sculptors to explore the possibilities and potentials of what bodies are and can be when freed from the constraints of normativity. Despite the sophistication with which their makers approached their practice, many of these sculptures have been mischaracterized as somehow missing something. Such was the case of the bronze arm that once decorated one of the famed Nemi ships constructed under the Roman emperor Caligula in the first century CE ⟨ *fig.* 5 ⟩. For centuries, antiquarians, archaeologists, and architects attempted to recover the two legendary ships sunk at the bottom of Lake Nemi, some twenty miles south of Rome. These efforts yielded a profusion of fragments, some immediately celebrated and others, like the arm, regarded as mysterious and only an isolated piece of an elusive whole.[26]

When the antiquarian dealer Eliseo Borghi discovered the arm in his excavation campaign of 1895, he described it only cursorily: as a rudder decoration that probably represented Averruncus, the god of averting harm.[27] The invocation of the apotropaic was a common trope in nineteenth-century discourses and was regularly applied to artifacts that resisted prevailing art historical expectations of completeness or legibility.[28] Though an enigmatic piece of the ship to which it once belonged, the sculpture is also a discrete artwork in its own right: a single piece of bronze cast as an autonomous fragment. In its original context, it was mounted at the end of an outrigging beam that supported one of the ship's rudders, broadcasting the vessel's directional movement with an authoritative gesture of an outstretched hand.[29] From just this one example, we begin to see how premodern artists experimented with modes of isolating bodily forms in order to capture and intensify the fragments' expressive power to act both through and beyond themselves.

A similar logic appears to have guided the maker of a jade pendant ⟨ *fig.* 6 ⟩ carved from an Olmec mask originally produced between 900 and 600 BCE along the southern Gulf Coast of Mexico ⟨ see *fig.* 7, as an example ⟩.[30] It is not known when or where this reworking occurred, or whether the mask was intact or broken, but the sculptor clearly saw its state as an opportunity for further reduction and transformation.

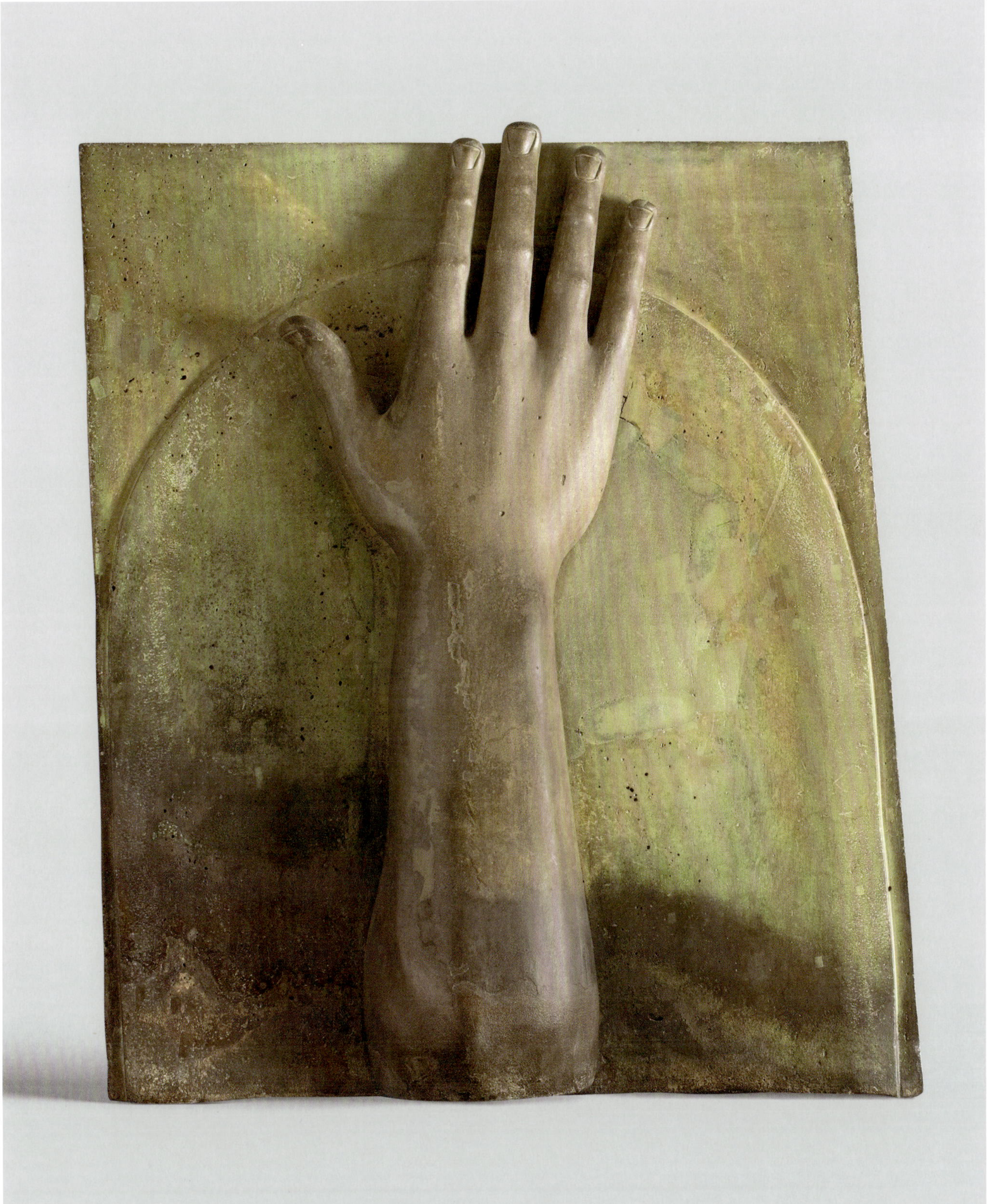

Fig. 5 Roman (Lago di Nemi), *Figured Crossbeam Head with Hand and Forearm from Second Nemi Ship*, c. 37–41 CE, bronze
Museo Nazionale Romano—Palazzo Massimo, Rome, inv. 33788
Cat. 24

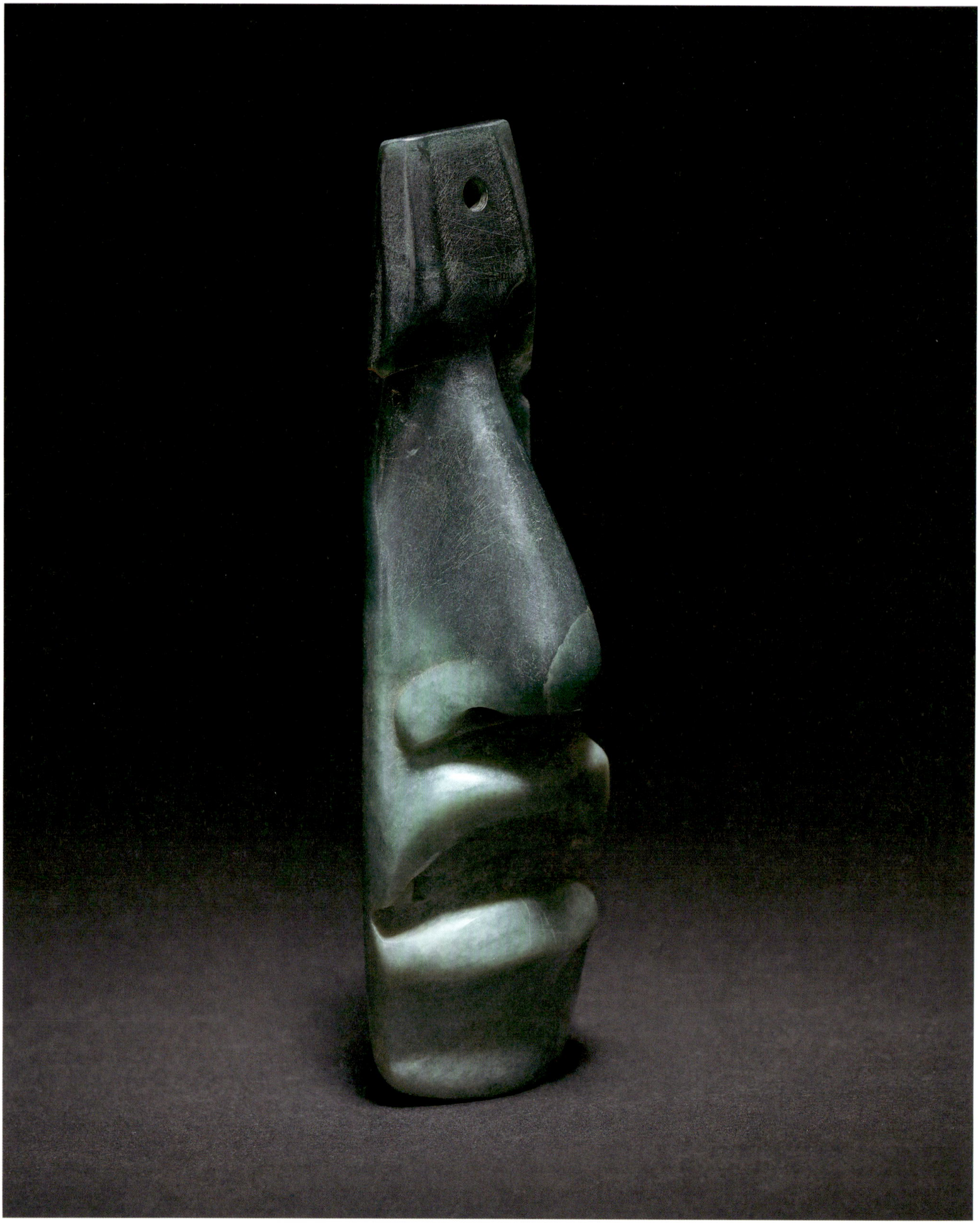

Fig. 6 Olmec (Costa Rica), *Mask Fragment Pendant*, c. 900–600 BCE, jade
The Al Thani Collection, ATC1029
Cat. 8

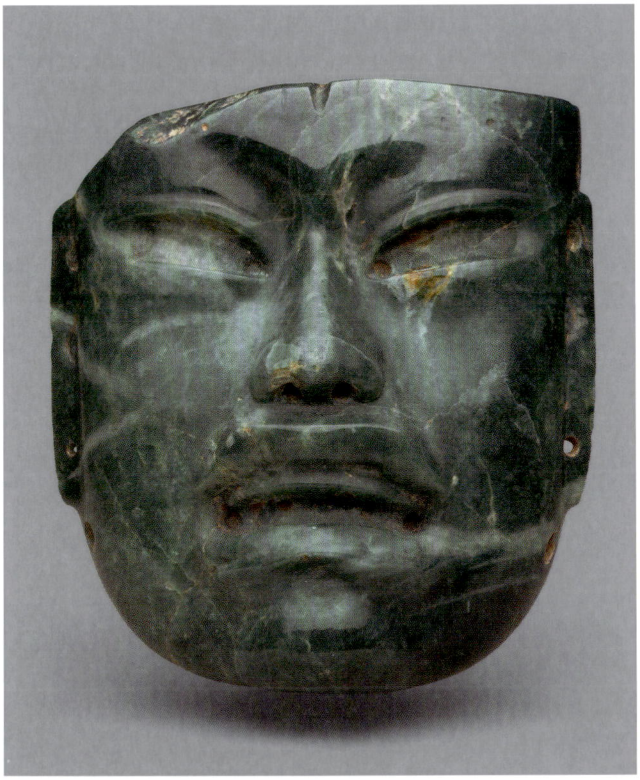

Fig. 7 Olmec, *Mask*, 900–400 BCE, jadeite
The Metropolitan Museum of Art, New York, Bequest of Alice K. Bache, 1977, 1977.187.33

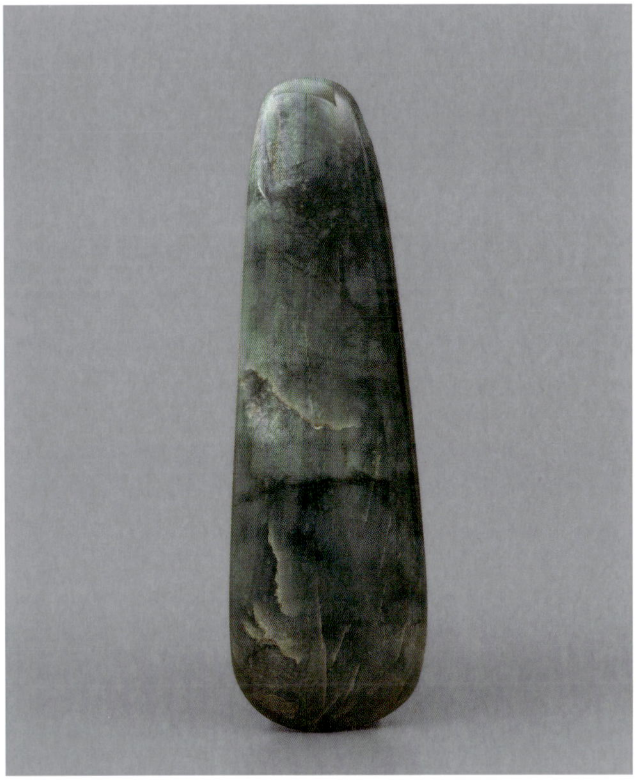

Fig. 8 Olmec, *Celt*, 900–300 BCE, jadeite
Dumbarton Oaks Research Library and Collection, Washington, DC, PC.B.028

By reshaping the mask into a narrow, teardrop shape, the artist produced a new kind of object charged with an array of material and formal associations. Its new silhouette echoed that of jadeite axes, or celts 〈 *fig.* 8 〉. As the Mesoamericanist Karl Taube has argued, celts and celt-shaped pendants were highly evocative forms whose formal restraint opened them up to a wide range of symbolic associations. Heavily ground down, smoothed, and polished, such reductions allowed jadeite's materiality to project itself: The most expensive raw material in ancient Mesoamerica, jadeite was prized for its radiant blue-green hue and believed to be charged with the powers of life-giving waters and agricultural abundance.[31] The organic shape of the celt also echoed that of an ear of maize, a plant first domesticated in Mexico in the third millennium BCE and widely cultivated during the periods when the mask was made and eventually repurposed.[32] Within an emerging agrarian economy of which maize was the staple crop, maize-shaped celts and pendants were emblems of success and surplus.[33] So effective was the artist in distilling form that this pendant came to operate within a world of signs and symbols beyond the figural or human.

Freed from the constraints of completion or notions of bodily normativity, sculpted fragments were often made as tools for facilitating communication with a divine sphere that existed beyond these limits. Such was the function of the terracotta Etruscan and Roman votives of the late first millennium BCE ⟨ *fig.* 9 ⟩.[34] Ranging from heads, torsos, and limbs to internal organs and viscera, these bodily pieces were mass-produced with molds and purchased by individuals to present as offerings at temples. They were sometimes given as petitions or as thanks for bodily restoration—that is, a devotee would offer a sculpture of the body part in need of care or that a deity had just healed—but were often used to establish a dialogue with the deity. Gifts of body parts might express a hope for being endowed with amorphous, intangible, or suprahuman conditions such as vitality and strength. In some cases, the offerings may not have referred to the donor's body at all and instead functioned as signs or gestures indicating the nature of communication sought with the deity. Ears, for example, might express a desire to be heard, and eyes a plea for divine attention.[35]

The most sanctified images in the premodern world were often composed as fragments: an admission that human understanding of the world was piecemeal. In medieval Europe, it was commonly believed that the terrestrial realm was just an illusion of a divine sphere that lay beyond full comprehension. Relics—fragmented, bodily remains of holy individuals like saints—were considered to be especially alluring, since their grotesquely shriveled appearance belied the heavenly power they were believed to possess.[36] They were a constant reminder of the limits of perception. Medieval Europeans often encased saintly remains in sumptuous containers like the *Arm Reliquary of Saint Babylas*, which gave devotees an approximate—though fragmentary—glimpse at an eternal heavenly body ⟨ *fig.* 10; see also cat. 43 ⟩. Here, the power of the bones housed behind the grille have been given the form of an energetic arm raised in a legible gesture of divine benediction.[37] The precious gold, silver, and gemstones composing the reliquary were especially vital for conveying the saint's palpable but otherworldly nature. Valued for their unique ability to reflect and refract light, these materials were seen to evade visual apprehension and were deemed the closest earthly approximations of what the divine sphere looked like. Medieval Christian theologians frequently described how the celestial capital, Heavenly Jerusalem, was built entirely from precious metals and stones.[38]

The enduring and incorruptible nature of such sumptuous fragments also prompted rulers and elite individuals to appropriate that potency for their own bodily remains. On the North Coast of Peru, a Lambayeque artist around the turn of the first millennium fashioned a similarly opulent golden arm, adorned with silver fingernails and inlaid turquoise, which

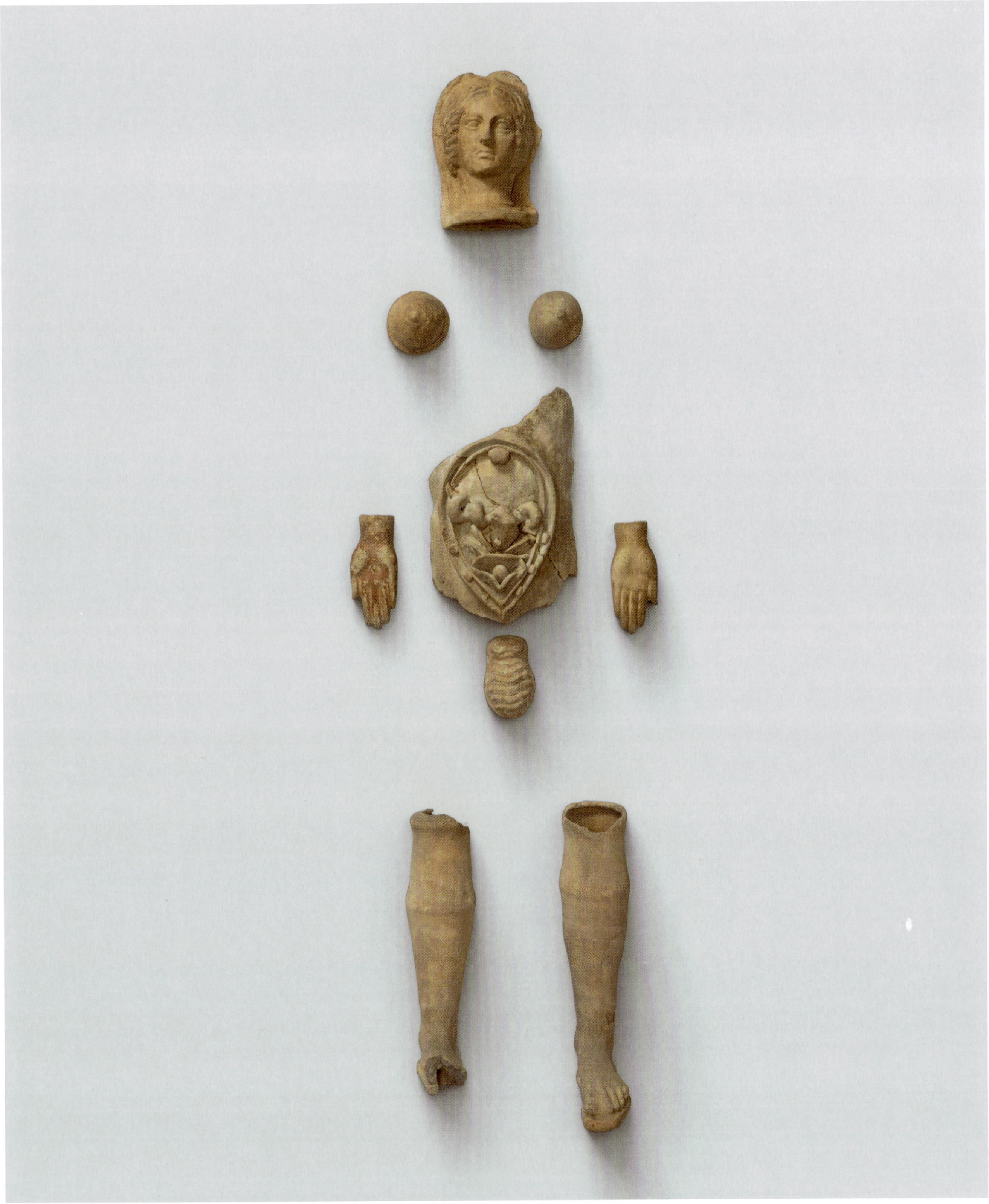

Fig. 9 Roman, *Anatomical Votives: Head, Breasts, Hands, Polyvisceral Torso, Uterus, Legs with Feet*, c. 300–100 BCE, terracotta
Museo Nazionale Romano—Terme di Diocleziano, Rome, inv. 115308/1, 14599, 14602, 14609, 14383, 14393, 14695, 47222/4, 47222
Cat. 14

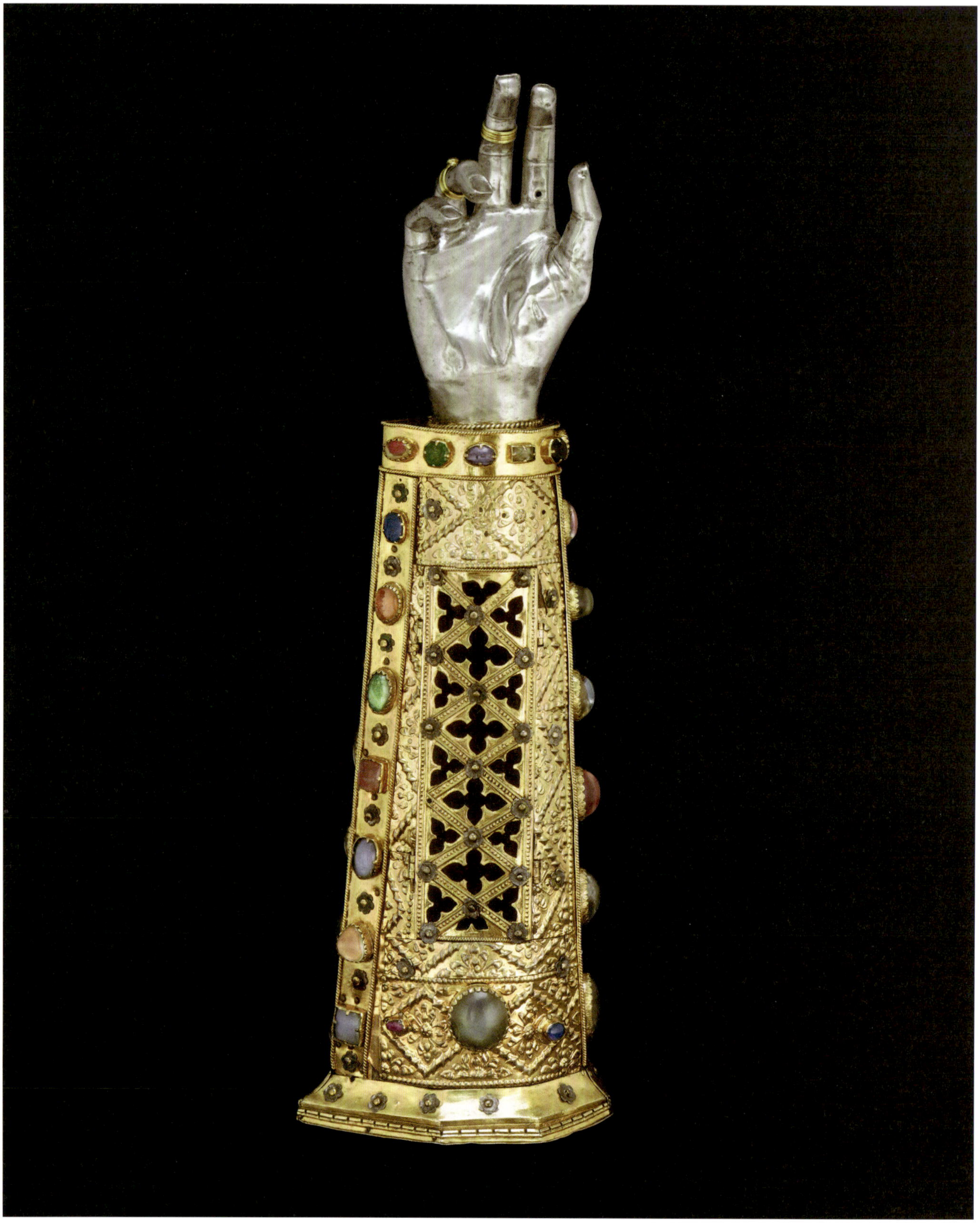

Fig. 10 German (Braunschweig), *Arm Reliquary of Saint Babylas*, 1467,
silver, gilded silver, enamel, glass paste stones, rock crystals, and one amethyst on an oak core
Philadelphia Museum of Art, Purchased with Museum funds, 1951, 1951-12-1
Cat. 52

was likely placed in an elite tomb alongside the body of the deceased ⟨ *fig.* 11 ⟩.[39] Such arms were frequently accompanied by golden beakers (*keros*) ⟨ *fig.* 12 ⟩ depicting in relief an elite figure grasping at a ceremonial object like a beaker or knife (*tumi*): a complex orchestration of gestures that extended the deceased's agency into the afterlife not unlike the European saint's hand perpetually frozen in the act of benediction.[40] More than mere fragments, these sculptures, through their expressive gestures and material excess, transformed even the most finite-seeming kind of destruction—death—into something enlivened and enduring.

RELATIVE POWER

Sculpted fragments suspend a persistent and unsettling kind of tension. Fragmentation may be generative, but in the process, creation starts to look increasingly melancholic. Many of the artworks considered thus far were made expressly to embrace these contradictions and were produced in transitional moments when such forces remained unresolved: funerary contexts, processes of religious conversion, political and regime shifts, or periods when divine intervention was needed. The capacity of fragmented sculptures to negotiate the complexities of change persisted well beyond premodernity and became especially important in the decades around 1900—a period marked globally by immense uncertainty about the ways in which modernity was being born from destructive forces such as industrialism and colonialism. The dialectic of breaking and making, therefore, came to have a function beyond discrete, culturally specific contexts and reflected global concerns and anxieties about the risks of so-called progress.

As Joanna Fiduccia observes in the essay that follows, around the turn of the twentieth century, artists used the fragment to give form to the fraught societal shifts that coined their historical moment. For Camille Claudel, as for many of her peers, fragmentation offered a means of foregrounding the inherent contradictions of modernity. Her *Torso of a Crouching Woman* collapses the forces of destruction and creation into a single object ⟨ see Fiduccia *fig.* 8 ⟩. She began by creating a plaster figure inspired by ancient precedents—namely, a crouching Aphrodite that had been acquired by the Musée du Louvre in 1878—and after slicing off parts of the model, she deemed her sculpture finished and had it cast in bronze. The resulting work seems to twist and contort both because of and against its fragmentation; it at once displays its breakage and is bound by it. Claudel crafted a modern creation that captures power, vulnerability, and uncertainty. As Fiduccia observes, it seems "ready to spring into new and undefined action."[41]

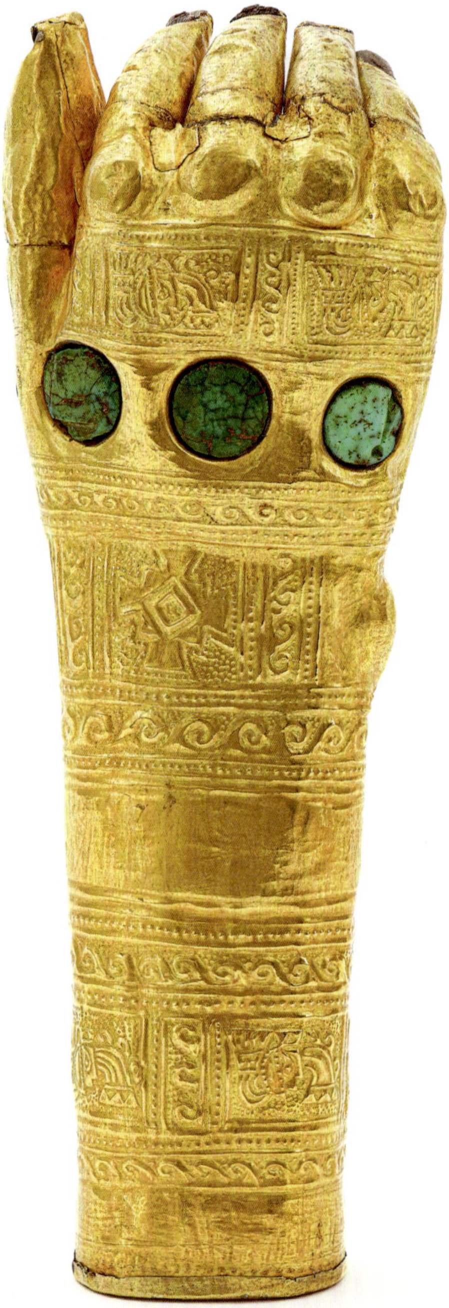

Fig. 11 Lambayeque (North Coast, Peru), *Hand and Forearm*, c. 900–1100 CE, gold, silver, and turquoise
Dumbarton Oaks Research Library and Collection, Pre-Columbian Collection, Washington, DC, PC.B.463
Cat. 38

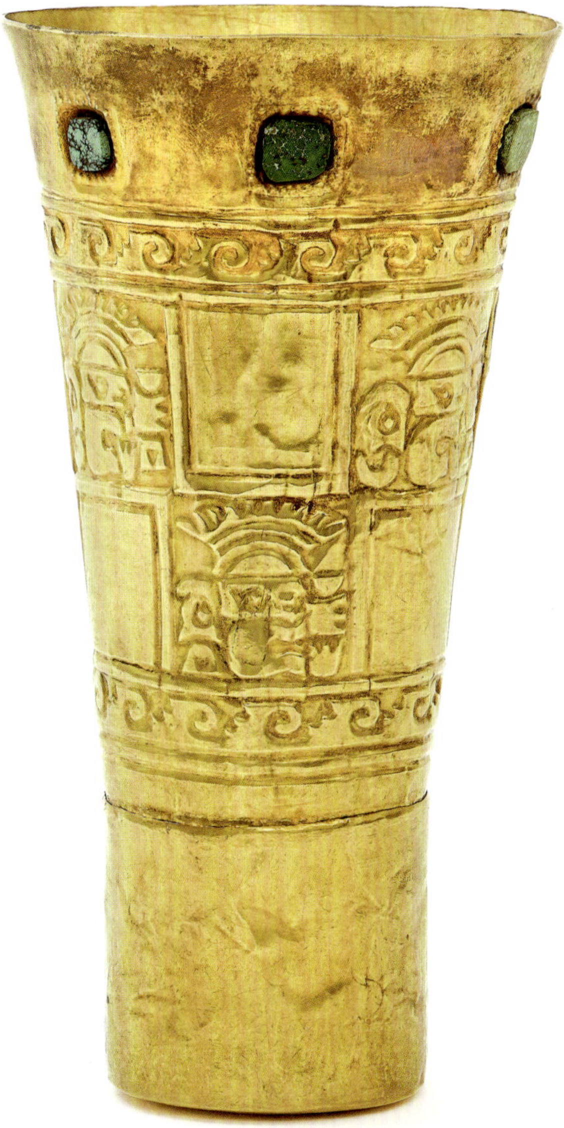

F*ig*. 12 Lambayeque, *Kero*, 900–1100, gold and turquoise
Dumbarton Oaks Research Library and Collection, Pre-Columbian Collection, Washington, DC, PC.B.464

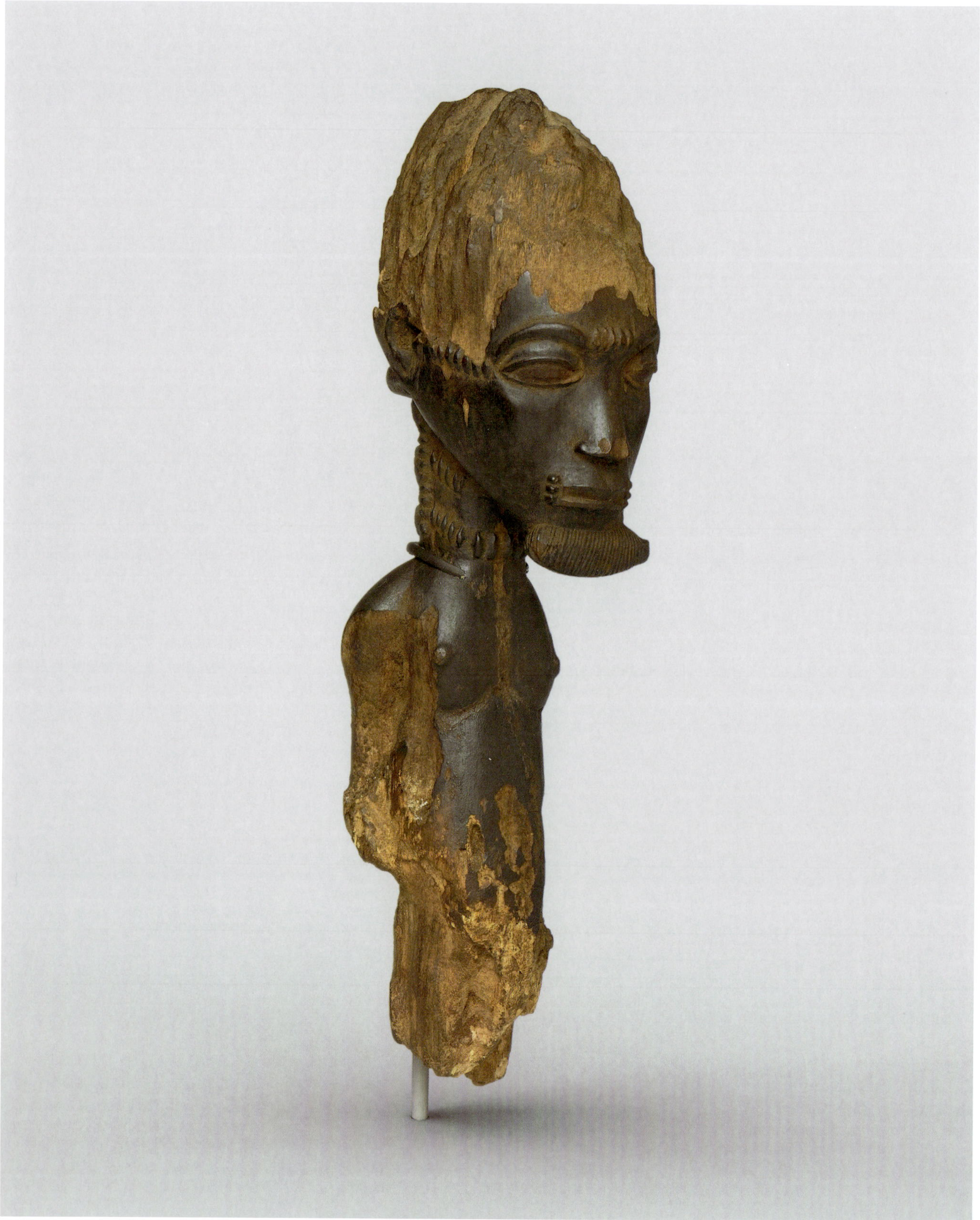

Fig. 13 Baule (Lacs, N'zi Comoe, or Valle du Bandama region, Côte d'Ivoire), *Male Figure (Waka Sran)*, c. 1900, wood
Brooklyn Museum, Frank L. Babbott Fund, 61.3
Cat. 69

Not all fragments produced in this period were granted the same opportunity to speak to the concerns of their time. Sculptures like the *Male Figure (Waka Sran)*, made by a Baule artist of Côte d'Ivoire around 1900, were often misinterpreted as far older than they actually were ⟨ *fig.* 13 ⟩.[42] Oily patinas and signs of abrasion were systematically misread by European dealers and collectors as evidence of great age—even medieval origin—despite the fact that these additions and transformations were intentionally and methodically carried out on sculptures that were only decades old.[43] At a historical moment when fragmentation in European art signified the avant-garde, these same qualities were mobilized to "primitivize" contemporary sculptures from other cultures and situate them as counterpoints to the purported advancements brought by empire.[44] While Europeans saw their own fragments as deliberately created, they perceived others as merely broken.

The Baule artist, rather than aspiring to make a fragment that captured tension in absolute form, produced a sculpture that explores how fragmentation is a relational and relative concept, contingent upon the position and priorities of the viewer. Known as a *waka sran*, which roughly translates to "person in wood," the sculpture was originally carved to completion in order to embody an individual's "spirit spouse": a partner that among the Baule every person was believed to have had before birth and that one could conjure through tactile interaction with the sculpture's finely wrought surface. Such objects were carefully tended to, and the owner of this spirit husband must have rubbed it repeatedly with palm oil to build a luminous patina. After the owner's death, the heirs probably deposited the figure in the forest, where its palm oil–saturated surface attracted insects and rats, thus beginning a process of material transformation.[45]

Encounters with the sculpture's continuing deterioration would have elicited manifold perspectives that were dependent on the viewer's personal relationship to the deceased and the spirit husband. For some family members, decay may have registered as a sign of loss. For the widower, however, the transformation may have been seen as gratifying. According to the curator Susan Vogel, a living spouse often felt a rivalry with their partner's spirit spouse, and when this sculpture was in use, the aging husband might have come to resent its eternally youthful and beautiful image.[46] One can easily imagine, as the art historian Zoë Strother has suggested, the smile on the widower's face in seeing his sculptural nemesis's deterioration.[47] Able to provoke such an array of responses, the fragment demonstrates how its tension is neither encapsulated by its form nor ever resolved; its dialectical meaning continually unfolds depending on who is looking and how one looks.

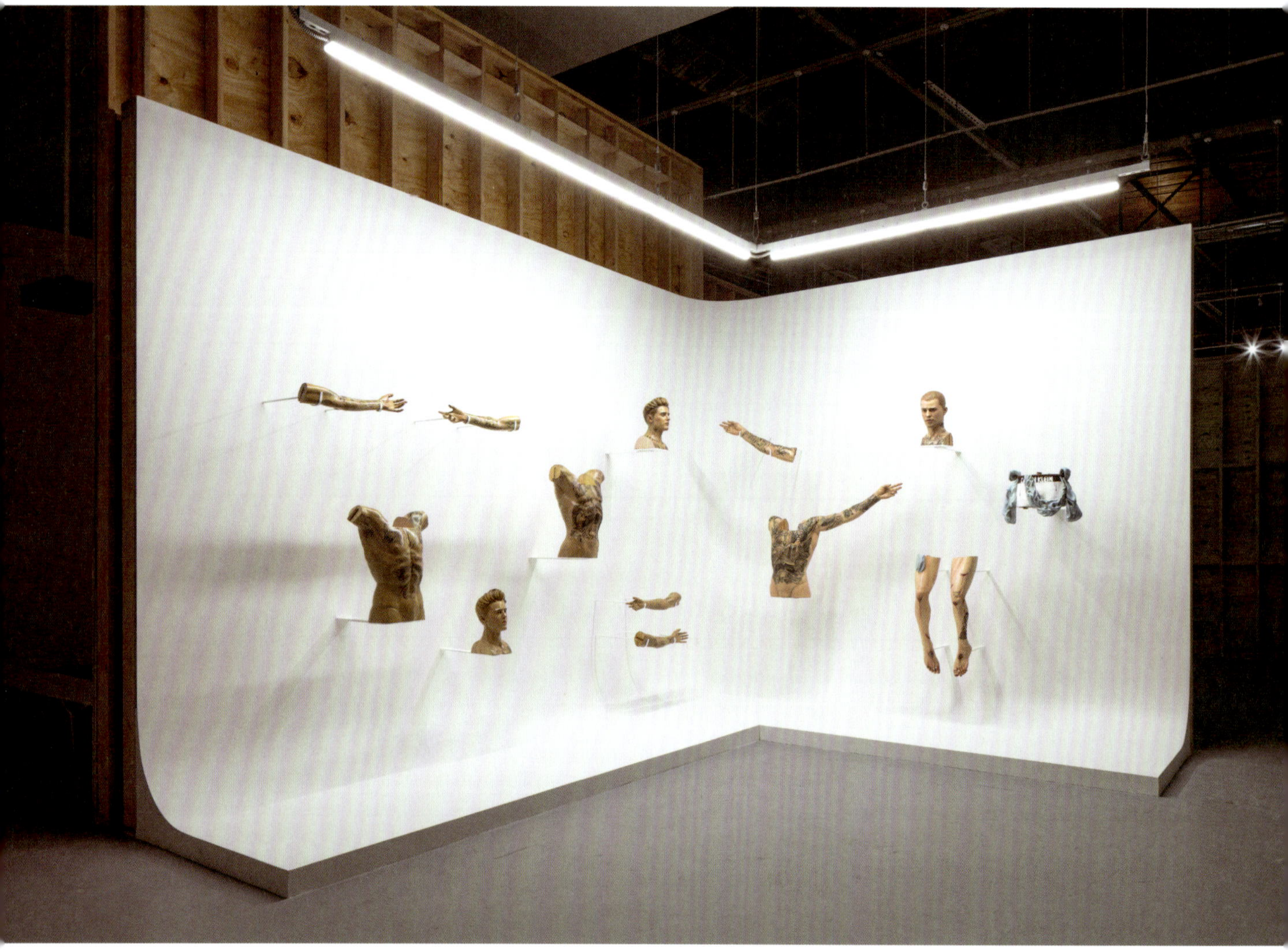

Fig. 14 *Paul Pfeiffer: Prologue to the Story of the Birth of Freedom*, installation view, November 12, 2023–June 16, 2024, Geffen Contemporary at MOCA, Los Angeles

By inviting a more expansive view of the fragment and its many meanings, the *waka sran* seems to challenge the notion of the absolute fragment. Fragmentation inherently resists fixity; its power does not reside intrinsically within the object or its form but instead emerges relationally based on what one brings to the object. What appears as generative to some may register as breakage to others, a disparity that exposes just how arbitrary and highly relative the Western gaze was at the turn of the twentieth century. In their pursuit of absolute, "modern" fragments, Europeans failed to acknowledge their own positionality and the impossibility of achieving the objectivity they presumed to have. The very framework through which this object's effacement was inculcated—a subjective and circumstantial way of seeing—becomes the means through which this fragment gains its power.[48]

Such relativity of perception is a notion that many contemporary artists continue to explore. Paul Pfeiffer's ongoing series *Incarnator* (2018–present) probes reflection on one's own positionality and the multiple meanings produced by fracture ⟨ *fig.* 14; see also cat. 83 ⟩. On the one hand, the series seems to be composed of a monstrous Western fragment: the disjointed body of Justin Bieber, recognizable by his tattoos, whose parts are spread across a wall and seem to reproduce and metamorphose in a way that would make them impossible to ever coalesce into a whole. On the other hand, the installation reveals itself to be a constellation of discrete artworks produced by sculptors working in cities across the former Spanish Empire: Paete, Pampanga, Seville, and Tlaxcala. Complete in their own right, these sculptures are unburdened by any imperative to adjoin, precisely because they were never conceived to do so. The work urges us to hold these seemingly contradictory perspectives simultaneously: The body is made more than whole by being fragmented, much like Western imperialism is completed by being dismantled. Seen this way, the logic of Pfeiffer's *Incarnator* recalls historical examples, like the chacmools that opened this essay, and extends into our present public sphere, where Confederate and other contested monuments are sculpted anew through the creative acts of decommissioning and dismantling. Taken together, these works invite viewers to find solace in states of (dis)assembly, for new and more generative structures emerge not through preserving the past but through breaking it apart.

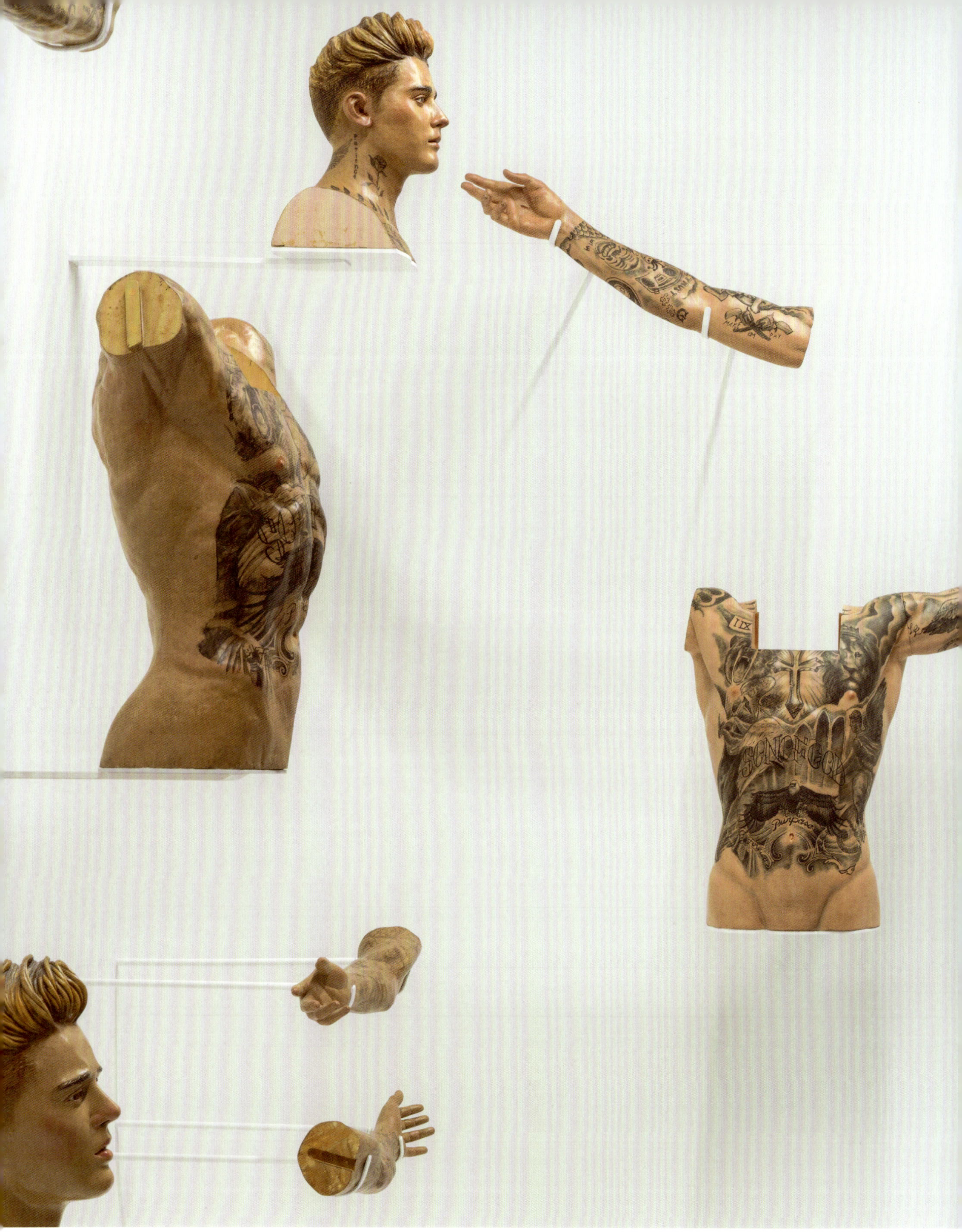
SON OF GOD
Purpose

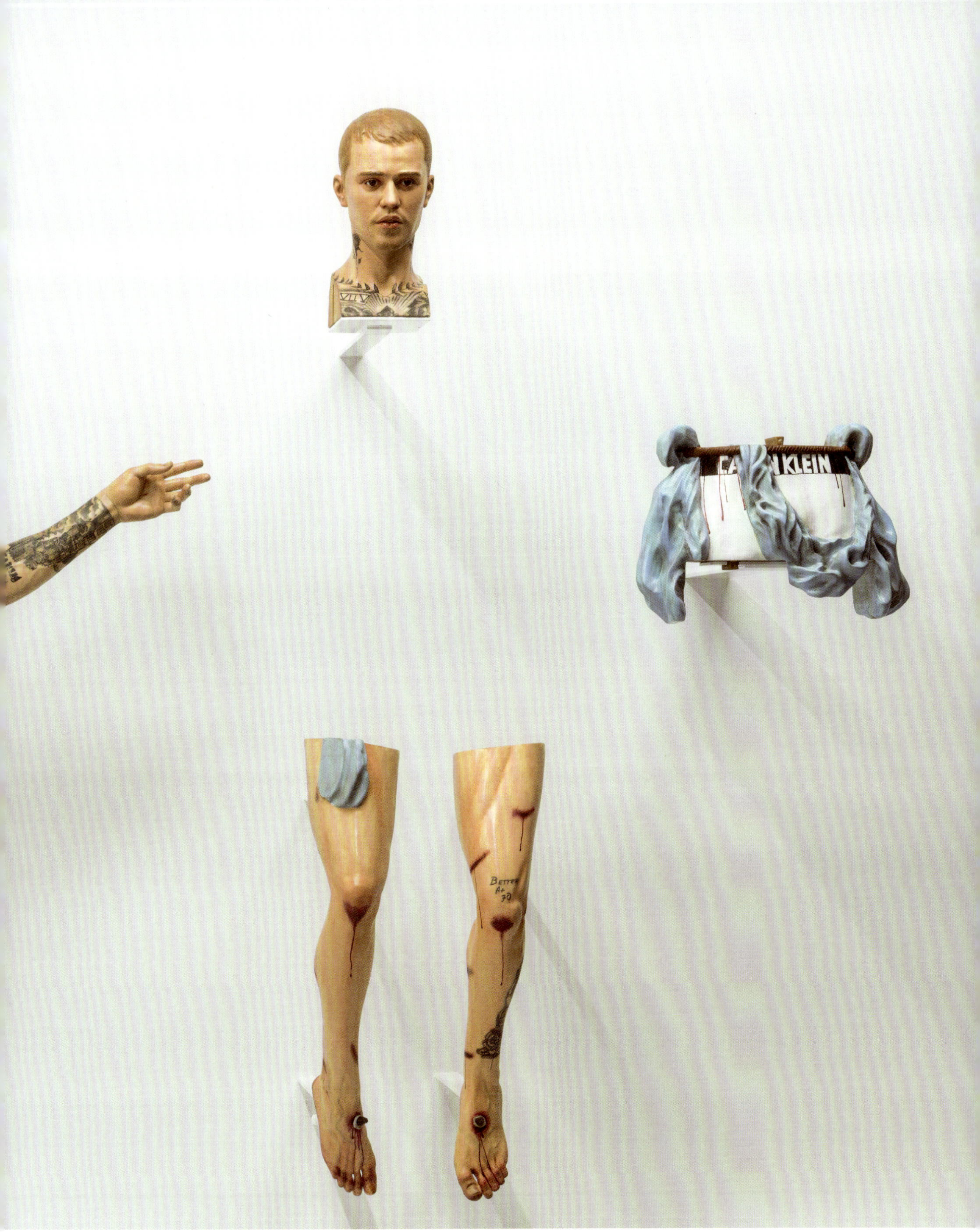

Detail, p. 174

SCULPTING THE FRAGMENT

Joanna Fiduccia

A carry-on suitcase stands on end, slightly parted, so that if you were to stand to one side of it, you could glimpse its contents: three severed limbs and a feathered wing. The disarticulated cupid of Danh Vo's *meat cables* has been fixed in place by two-by-fours whose plainness seems to visit yet another indignity upon the softly mottled, touchingly plump marble body ⟨ *figs.* 1–3 ⟩. Although less grisly than the series to which it pays homage—the fleshy wax nuggets that Paul Thek strung on metal cables in the late 1960s ⟨ *fig.* 4 ⟩—Vo's work still has one foot in the genre of body horror: the spectacle of the freshly dead corpse, sawn and stuffed into a duffel bag. Of course, there is nothing fresh or dead about the god. A confusion of early modern and second-century parts, it recalls the kind of object that is often transported in cases from the archaeological dig to the museum and, generally speaking, from the south to the north, where its brokenness will only confer upon it added age-value.[1] Yet the hard-shell case at hand, from the luxury brand Rimowa, has the peculiar effect of desublimating that value, plunking it into the midst of familiar signifiers of privilege and autonomy. There, wealth and the freedom to move easily across borders unite with the assurance that antiquity can be a possession, one's own special and unburdensome baggage.[2] And yet the horror lingers, and with it a sense that Vo has wedged together the transport of two quite different bodies: the imported sculptural fragment, carried across frontiers for centuries as part of European nation-building projects; and the traffic in enslaved or smuggled people, moving through both legal and unauthorized channels. The sculptural fragment, as *meat cables* suggests, comes down to us today through modern systems of value whose effort to hold apart the prized bodies from the abject ones betrays their status as fellow travelers.

Modernity and fragmentation have been entwined for so long that they have come to seem homologous. For some, to be modern is to experience

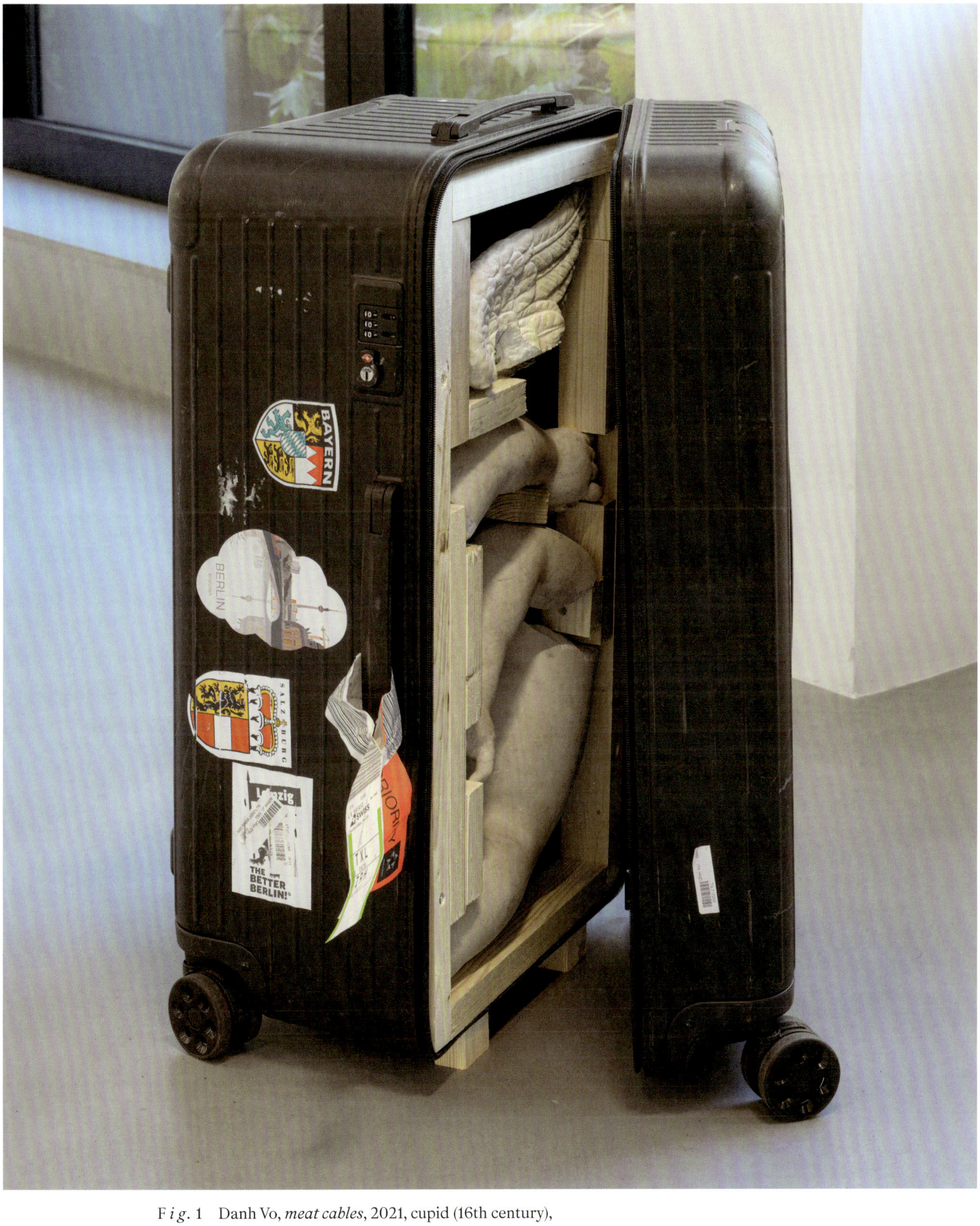

Fig. 1 Danh Vo, *meat cables*, 2021, cupid (16th century), Roman marble (1st–2nd century CE), and Rimowa luggage
Courtesy of the artist and Xavier Hufkens, Brussels
ProWinko ProArt Collection
Cat. 86

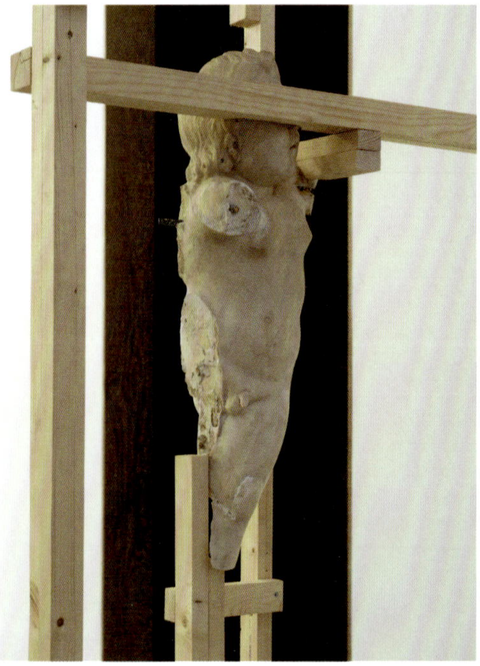

Fig. 2 Danh Vo, *meat cables* (detail), 2021, cupid (16th century), Roman marble (1st–2nd century CE), and construction wood
Courtesy of the artist and Xavier Hufkens, Brussels
Cat. 87

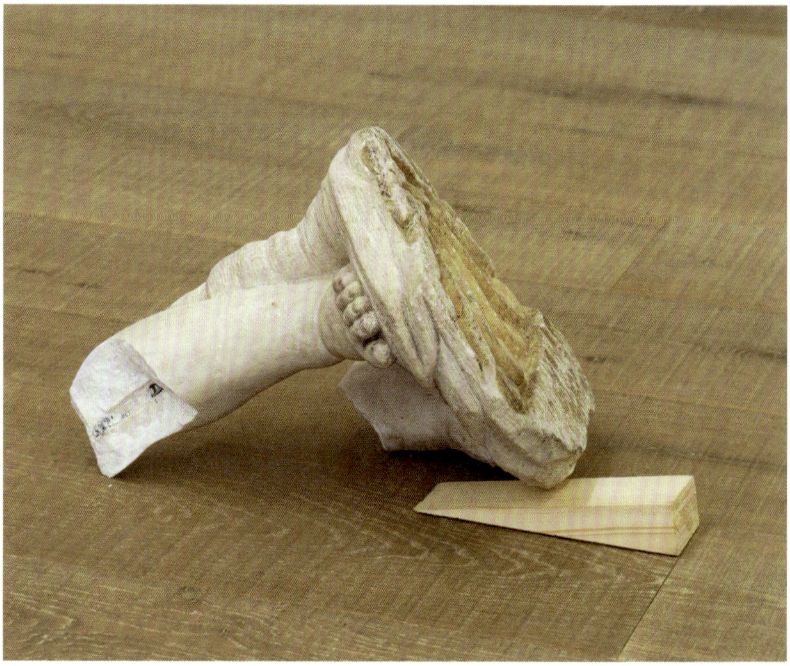

Fig. 3 Danh Vo, *meat cables*, 2021, cupid and column (16th century), Roman marble (1st–2nd century CE), and construction wood
Courtesy of the artist and Xavier Hufkens, Brussels
Private collection
Cat. 88

a broken world, while for others, it is modern experience itself that is fragmented; it can, of course, be both. To the first go such memorable images as the critic and cultural theorist Walter Benjamin's Angel of History, who surveys the past as a single, colossal, and ever-growing mountain of rubble, as well as the poet and playwright Alfred de Musset's portentous observation that the modern age "hardly has forms. . . . *We live on debris alone*, as if the end of the world were near."[3] Yet if the modern world is an apocalyptic jumble, modern experience appears fragmented as a consequence of too much order. For the Marxist philosopher György Lukács, the industrialization that segmented our once-unified labor practices produced complementary effects on our consciousness.[4] The self came to appear like something that could be parsed into objectified, alienable qualities. From this shattering of identity came social anomie and, along with it, a host of ills and madnesses that bound modernity's irrationalism to its excess rationalization.

Modern artists made their work in this doubly fragmented world. They anticipated it through privatized styles that dealt in the incomplete or broken, or they attempted to remedy it, to "overcome the disintegrative effects—social psychic, political—inscribed in the modern," writes the art historian Linda Nochlin, "by hypostatizing them within a higher unity."[5]

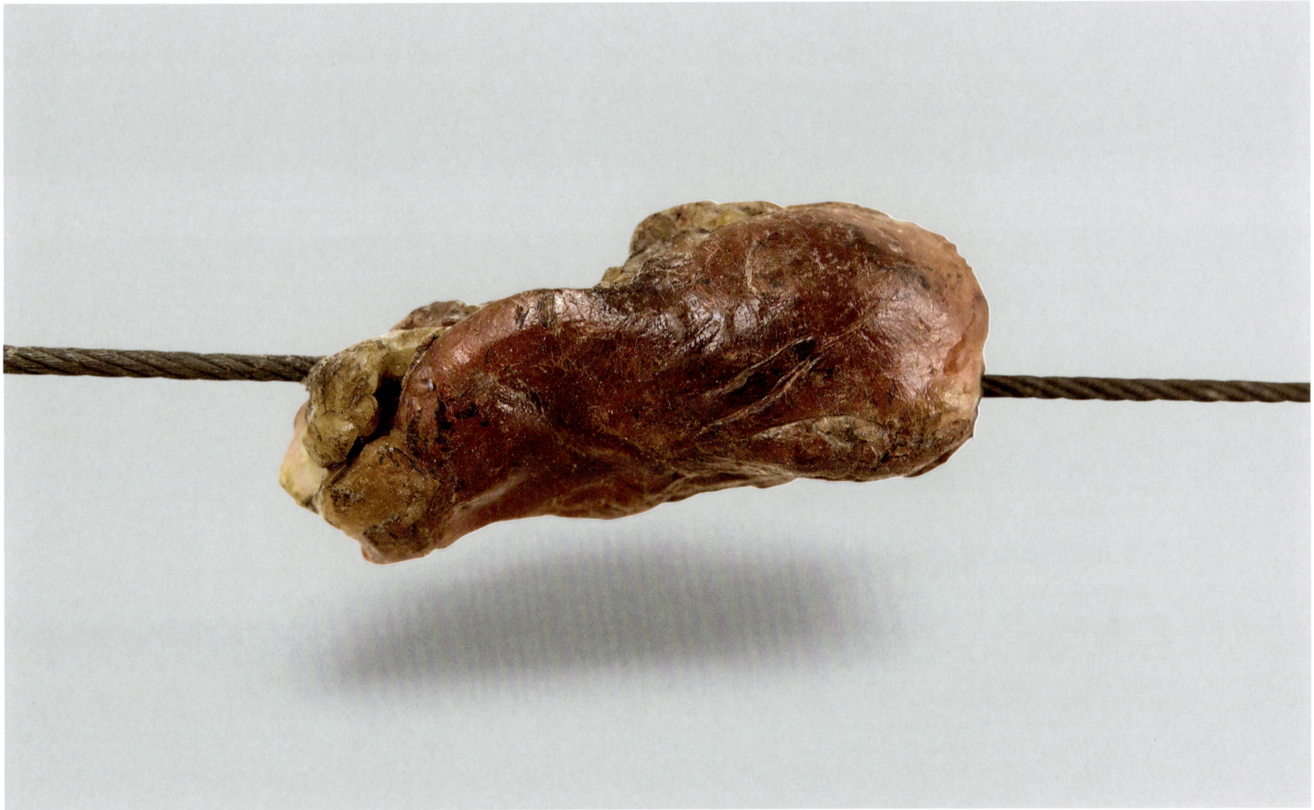

Fig. 4 Paul Thek, *Untitled (Meat Cable)* (detail), 1969, wax, paint, steel cable, and turnbuckles
Tate: Presented as part of the D. Daskalopoulos Collection Gift 2023, T16080
Cat. 77

The fragment was not new, but its synecdochic character and its totalization were. Modernism not only gives us more fragments; it gives us only fragments, by endowing even what is not literally broken off with the status of a partial expression, which seems to be the only statement capable of addressing a fractured reality. The circle of Romantic writers centered in Jena, Germany, at the turn of the nineteenth century promoted the prose fragment because its incompletion gestured toward an otherwise unrepresentable ideal. The Romantic fragment had a monadic integrity—"complete in itself like a porcupine" was the philosopher Friedrich Schlegel's peculiar image—as well as an embryonic aspect that matured in the reader's imagination into sublime excess.[6] The twentieth-century writers who followed this tradition (Ezra Pound, T. S. Eliot, Marianne Moore, and H.D., among others) also built a poetics of the fragment, but their version was alchemical rather than allusive.[7] Their poems generated meaning through a combinatorial practice of evoking the remnants of a rapidly receding preindustrial world and the castoffs of mass culture, and then organizing them within remaindered poetic forms.

These literary accounts have parallels in the modern sculptural fragment, which first celebrated the partial figure as a visionary mode of presenting an elusive aliveness, and subsequently pursued its own magical materialism. But sculpture has a particular relationship to brokenness that makes its fragments work differently. Vo's suitcase reminds us that, unlike the literary fragment, the sculptural fragment has a long history in which it was foremost not an incomplete thought but rather a disarticulated part of the human body. Fragmented sculptures—even when minimally figural, indeed even when abstract—may stir up anxieties about the body's dismemberment or incoherence, or they may transmit the erotic charge of bodily zones. At the same time, the figure they invoke is a symbolic one, exceptional like the body of the king and general like the body politic. It is the special capacity of modern sculpture to make the fragmentation of that symbolic body something we can feel: a shattering of a common world that is, at one and the same time, a figure for our shattered experience.

THE ABSOLUTE FRAGMENT

Accounts of both modern sculpture and the modern sculptural fragment tend to share a starting point: Auguste Rodin, whose tremendous influence has been affirmed and reimagined by successive generations of art historians. The artist's iconic *The Walking Man (L'Homme qui marche)* emblematized both his personal force and his approach to sculpting the human body through what the art historian Albert E. Elsen calls the "partial figure," a synecdochic tactic of making incompletion contribute to, rather than detract from, the sculpture's status as a unified representation 〈 *fig.* 5 〉.[8] By removing those body parts that are inessential to the act of walking—arms, with their ornamental swing, or the head, churning with thoughts unrelated to the stride—Rodin presents pure walking, walking as a gesture that "retain[s]," writes the art critic Leo Steinberg, "just so much of the anatomical core as that gesture needs to evolve."[9] In this pars pro toto fashion, Rodin's sculpture transfigured the apparent mutilation of the body into a means of reconciling sculptural representation with the presentation of a living body.[10] Sculptors have no choice but to abstract and immobilize what they depict, congealing it in motionless materials. Rodin's partial figure transforms this limitation into an expression of the artist's perspicuity: He selects just those portions of the body that best express its vitality and allow it to persist through imaginative suggestion. Rodin's *Walking Man* is, in fact, conspicuously immobilized. His thick feet adhere to a slab of bronze, and his legs are spread so wide that his torso sits on that stablest of geometries, an

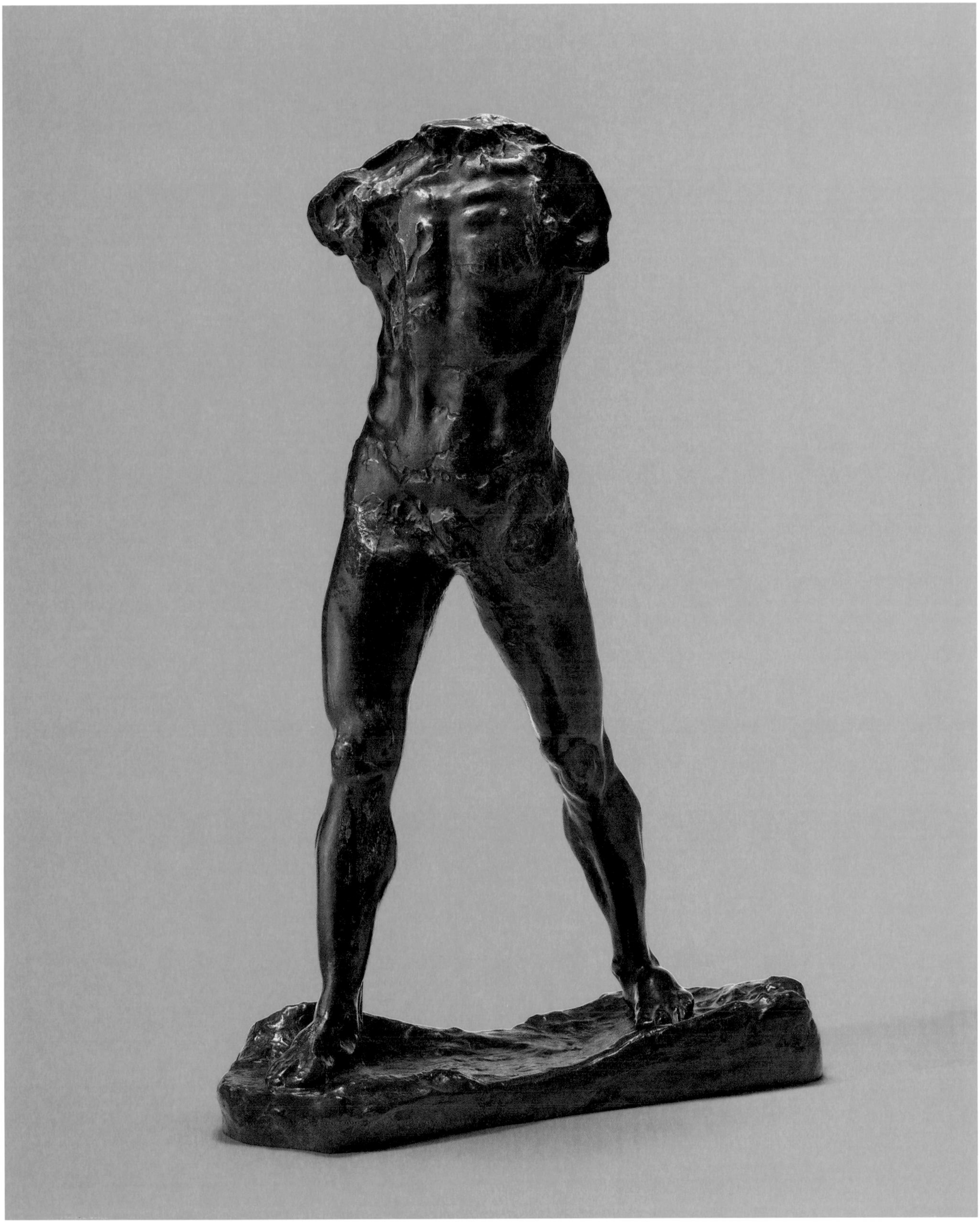

Fig. 5 Auguste Rodin, *The Walking Man (L'Homme qui marche)*, c. 1878–1900 (model); probably 1903 (cast), bronze
National Gallery of Art, Washington, Gift of Mrs. John W. Simpson, 1942.5.11
Cat. 70

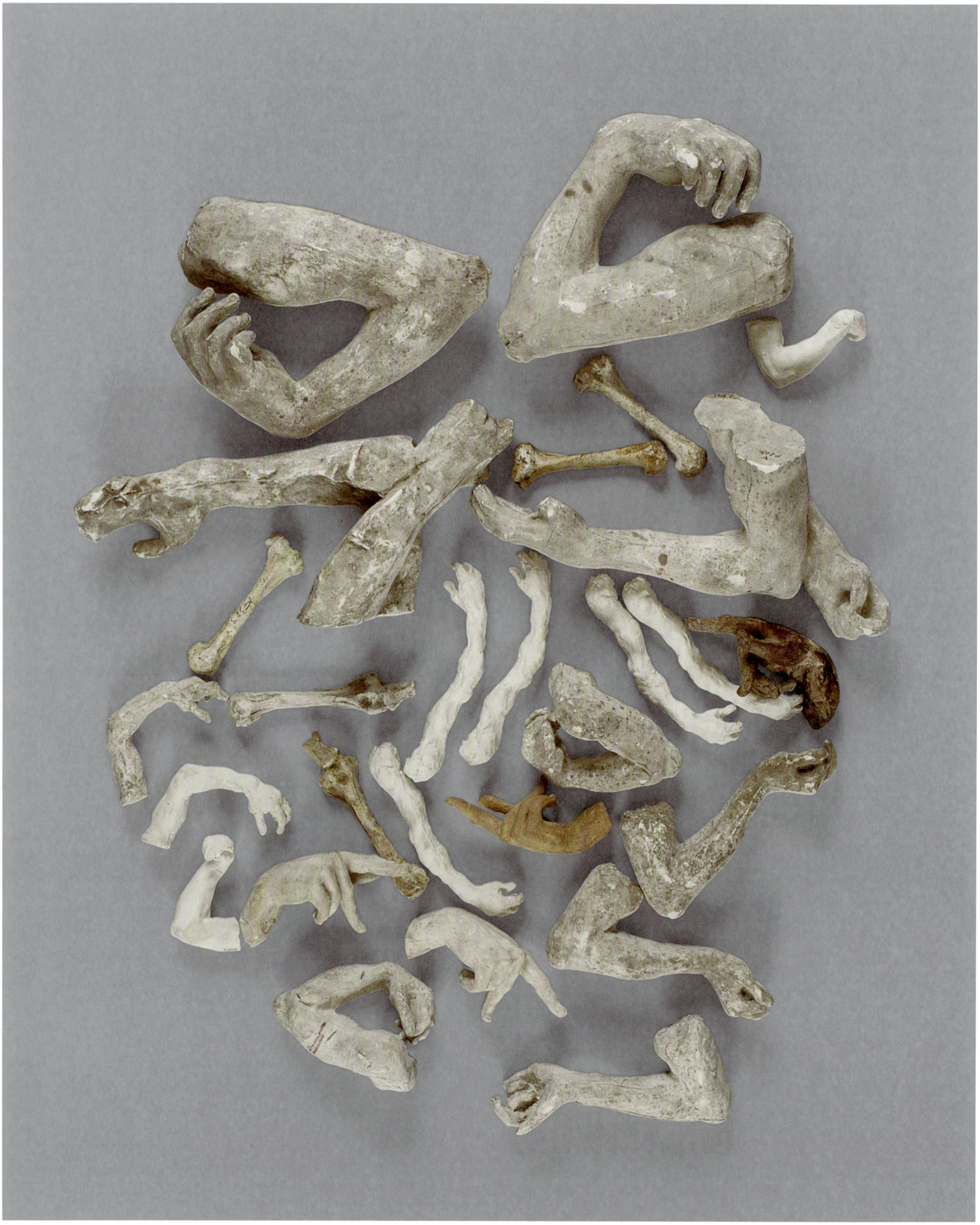

F*ig.* 6 Auguste Rodin, *Group of* Abattis *(Body Parts)*, 1880–1917, plaster
Musée Rodin, Paris, S.01266, S.01286, S.04527, S.04983, S.05074, S.05088, S.05108–110, S.05275, S.05284, S.05500, S.05523, S.05527, S.05538, S.05553, S.05569, S.06178, S.06200, S.06260, S.06374
Cat. 67

equilateral triangle. And yet movement is insinuated elsewhere: in the light that gurgles over the sculpture's surface; in its contained force; and in the very fact of its incomplete figuration, which suggests that there is still more to be elaborated or disclosed. The fragment is on the move.

Schlegel's famous line about the fragment makes its modernity a matter of its inception: "Many of the works of the ancients have become fragments. Many modern works are fragments as soon as they are written."[11] Not only was the modern fragment born that way; it distinguished itself from the remnant or ruin through its relation to something yet to come. Defined by its "progressive" feeling, the modern fragment was neither residual nor merely unfinished. Instead, its incompletion was evocative, a means to communicate projects so total and ambitious that only the dynamism of the not-yet-whole could convey them.[12] "Rather than implying some loss or lack of presence," the philosopher Rodolphe Gasché concludes, the Romantic fragment "represents the *positive* mode in which presentation of the whole occurs. More precisely, it is an index of thinking's shift to conceptualizing the very occurring, or coming into presence, of the idea."[13] For Rodin, the body was like the idea, perpetually becoming itself, and the "whole body" was less a form than total animatedness as such. Certain of Rodin's fragments thus press past the point of intelligibility, their economy no longer serving to distill a gesture but instead to multiply its possibilities. These fragments, writes Steinberg, "pass beyond any test of meaningful gesture to become almost pure sculptural energy."[14] They come down to us as precocious experiments in the atomic splitting of individuals, unleashing their charge into the field of modern art.

Rodin was a highly experimental maker of plaster fragments and truncated bronzes 〈 *fig.* 6 〉.[15] That practice was embedded in *Walking Man*, a work he produced in a series of disconnected moments and from disconnected parts. The torso was initially a terracotta study of *Saint John the Baptist* (1878–1880), which the artist rediscovered in his studio in 1887 and joined up to some studies of *Saint John*'s legs two years later. The final figure preserves the seams of this Frankensteinian maneuver alongside its casting marks. It thus telescopes two processes built on fragments: the creative compositing of the body and the technical procedure of bronze casting, which entails fragmentation and reassembly as well as the division of labor between different sites and hands. Rodin's "genius" was to make all those technical steps appear subordinate to his hand in dispersing and reunifying sculptural fragments.[16] The fragment accordingly came to enjoy the status not of the remnant of some lost whole but of the spare part awaiting recombination.

This approach to fragmentation was by no means unique to Rodin. Camille Claudel, who worked as Rodin's assistant and collaborator from 1884 to 1892, developed her own form of the fragment, which her brother

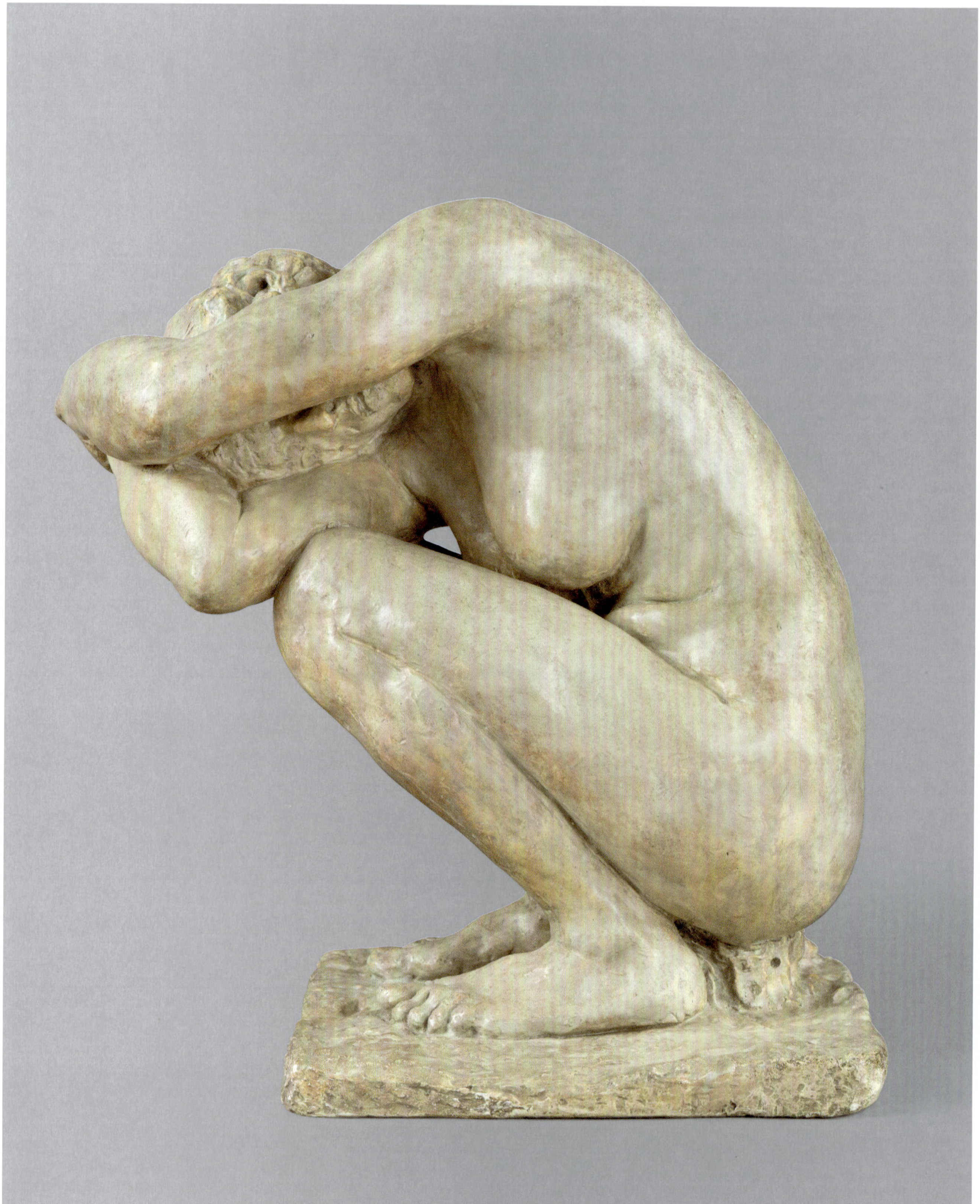

Fig. 7 Camille Claudel, *Crouching Woman*, c. 1884–1885, patinated plaster
Musée Camille Claudel, Nogent-sur-Seine, 2010.1.2

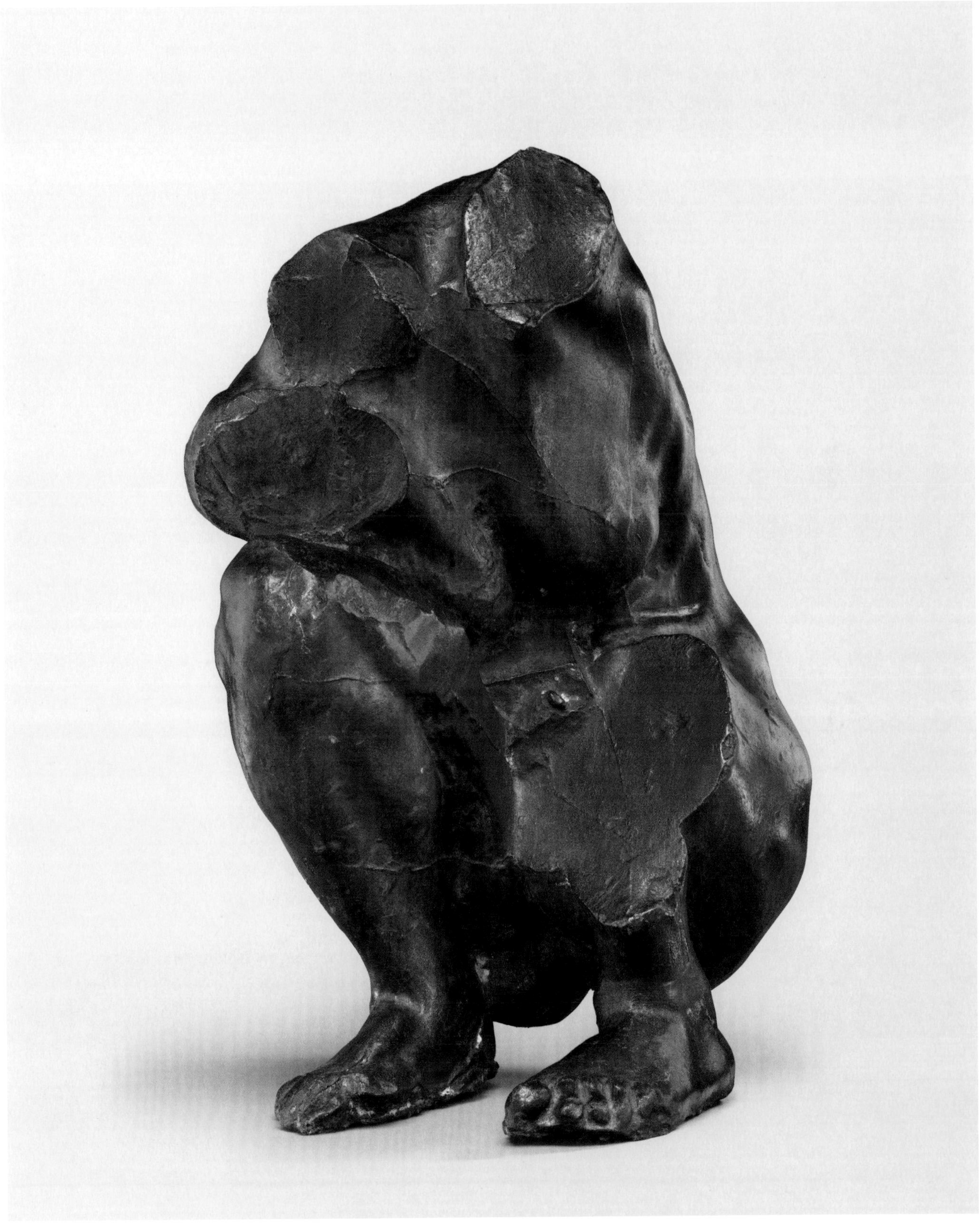

Fig. 8 Camille Claudel, *Torso of a Crouching Woman*, c. 1884–1885 (model); c. 1913 (cast), bronze
The J. Paul Getty Museum, Los Angeles, 2018.32
Cat. 72

Paul would later describe as "a kind of shared figure, a precarious and multiple being."[17] In the early 1880s, both Claudel and Rodin took up the motif of the crouching woman, most likely working from the same model. While Rodin sculpted an ecstatically contorted nude, Claudel showed the figure twisting upon herself self-protectively ⟨ *fig.* 7 ⟩. Claudel's *Torso of a Crouching Woman* is an unworking of this first sculpture that intensifies its contrast between guarded and explicit depiction ⟨ *fig.* 8 ⟩.[18] Claudel has lopped off the limbs, head, and knee of her figure, and yet there is no resulting anatomization of the female nude—no bared bits and certainly no narrative explanation for the pose that could allow us to penetrate the figure psychologically. Her *Torso* instead uses the crouch to undo the hierarchies of the body, redirecting our attention to its alternately leathery and flinty texture and abstract, bounding shape.[19] The fragmented torso becomes not more exposed but more obscure and protean, ready to spring into new and undefined action.

Claudel points the way past the Romantic fragment and toward the plastic possibilities of modernist figuration in the twentieth century. Consider Constantin Brâncuși's *Torso of a Young Man*, a forking cylinder of polished bronze, set on a stack of two carved pedestals ⟨ *fig.* 9 ⟩. Brâncuși's torso distills the body into a form that is part machine element, part synecdoche, part fetish.[20] Through abstraction, the accidental amputations of a classical torso become the means to convert a body into both pure phallus and its absence (this phallic trophy notably lacks the "young man's" organ). Alina Szapocznikow's *Filozof (Philosopher)* also depicts the male body as a fragment in order to amplify its strangeness ⟨ *fig.* 10 ⟩. A glans-like head balances on a sinewy leg, recalling Rodin's monument to male genius *Balzac* (1897). But there is something unruly and alien to Szapocznikow's symbolism of the intellectual as a conventionally masculine figure, which insists, the artist writes, on the "vague and ephemeral sensations of the body" conceived as a "total erogenous zone."[21] In these works, the male nude as a symbol of virility and coherence becomes an absurd machine component or an assemblage of sensitive parts, more ambiguous for all its simplification.

Brâncuși and Szapocznikow were both central Europeans who immigrated to France in times of political upheaval and instability. Brâncuși trekked to Paris from Romania at the beginning of the Crisis Phase in 1904; Szapocznikow arrived for the first time in 1948 as a recent survivor of Bergen-Belsen via Auschwitz. For these artists, and many other modern sculptors working through the crises of the twentieth century, Schlegel's bon mot took on a new sense. What body could aspire to wholeness in those decades? To be born a fragment was to meet the times. Few sculptors have channeled the midcentury crisis of man as absolutely as Alberto Giacometti. *La Jambe (The Leg)* looms above its viewer as though it were

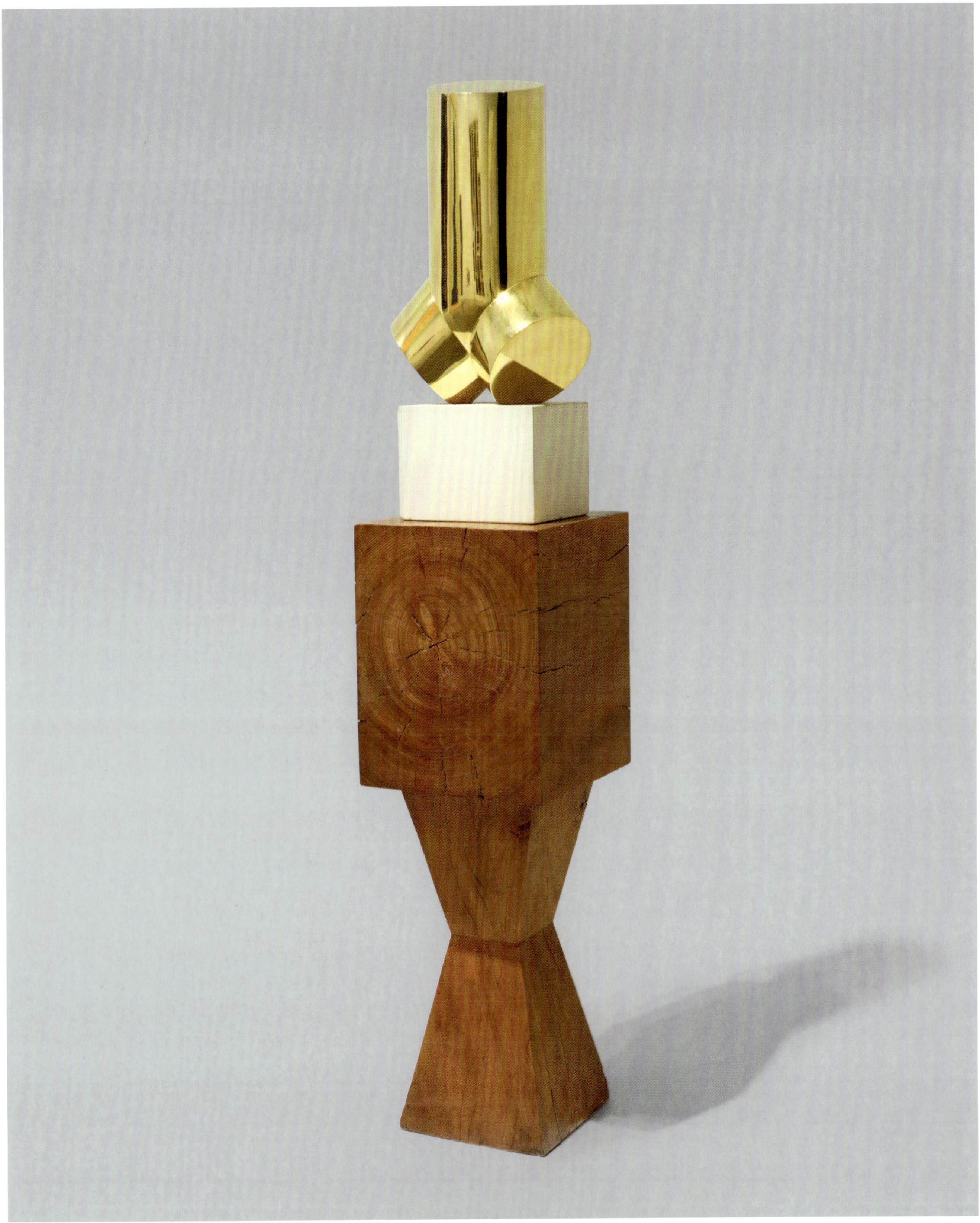

Fig. 9 Constantin Brâncuşi, *Torso of a Young Man*, 1924, brass, limestone, and wood
Hirshhorn Museum and Sculpture Garden, Smithsonian Institution, Washington, DC,
Gift of Joseph H. Hirshhorn, 1966, 66.611
Cat. 74

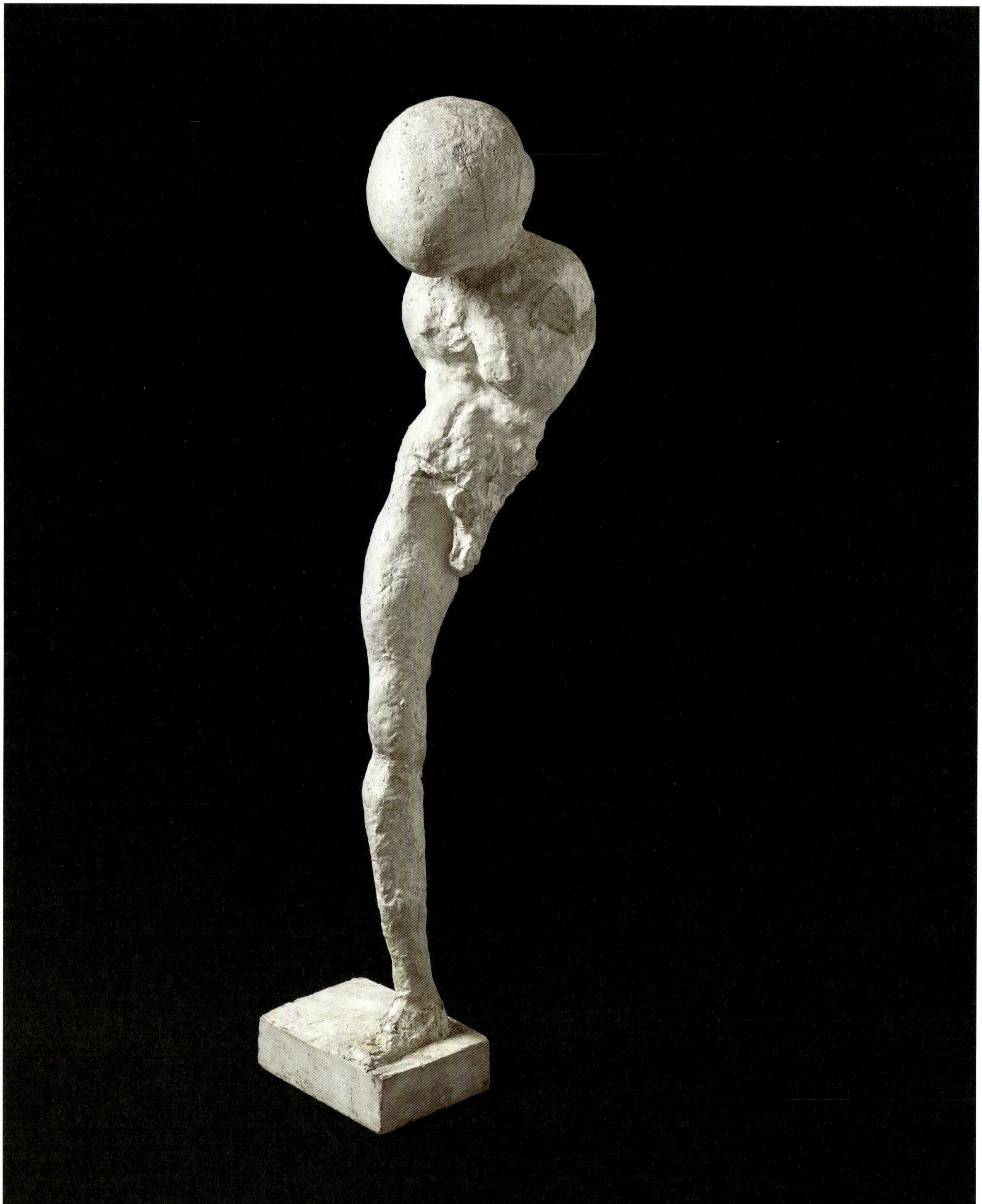

Fig. 10 Alina Szapocznikow, *Filozof (Philosopher)*, 1965, plaster
Courtesy The Estate of Alina Szapocznikow | Galerie Loevenbruck, Paris | Hauser & Wirth
Cat. 76

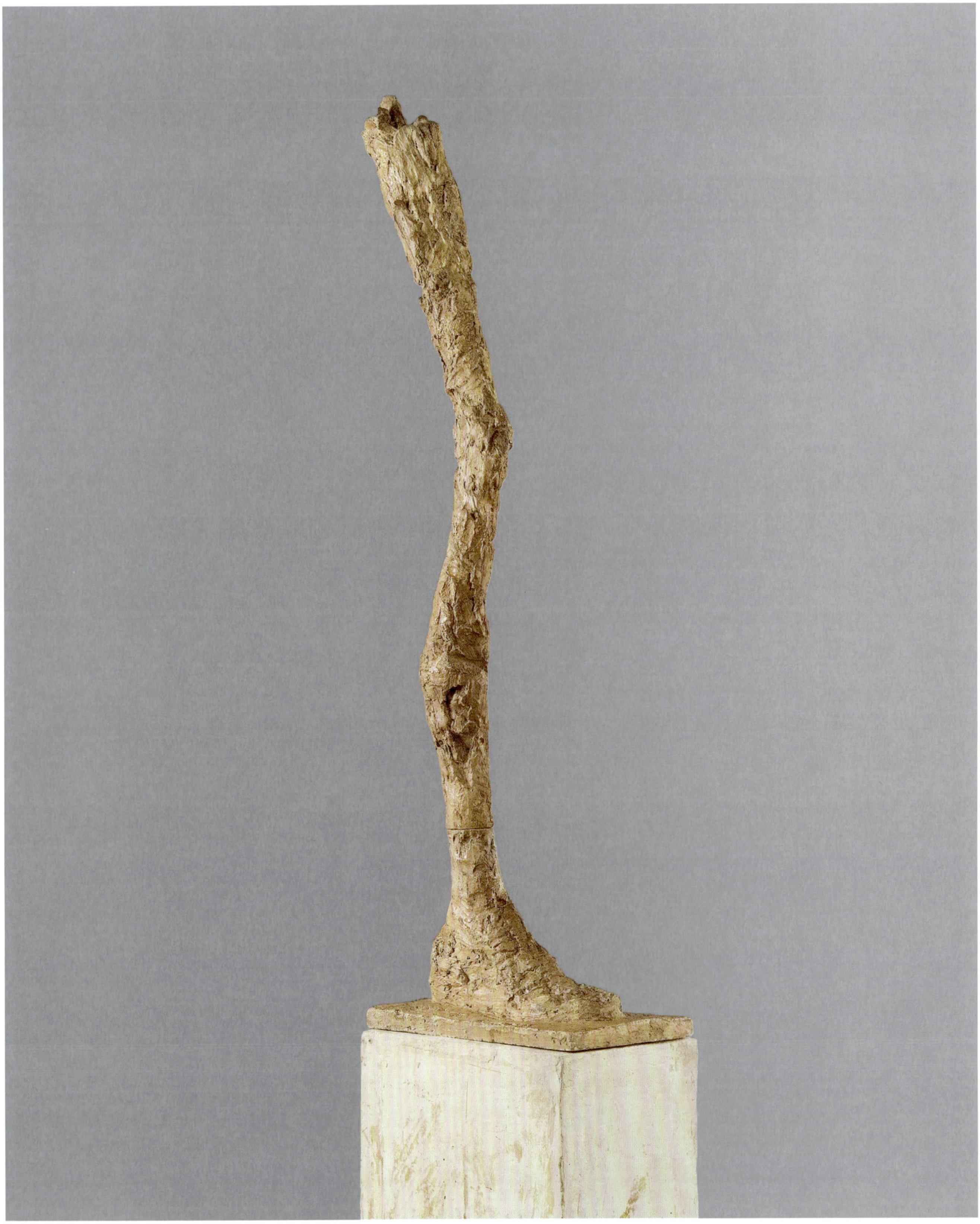

F*ig*. 11 Alberto Giacometti, *La Jambe (The Leg)*, 1958, plaster with pigment
Fondation Giacometti, 1994-0347
Cat. 75

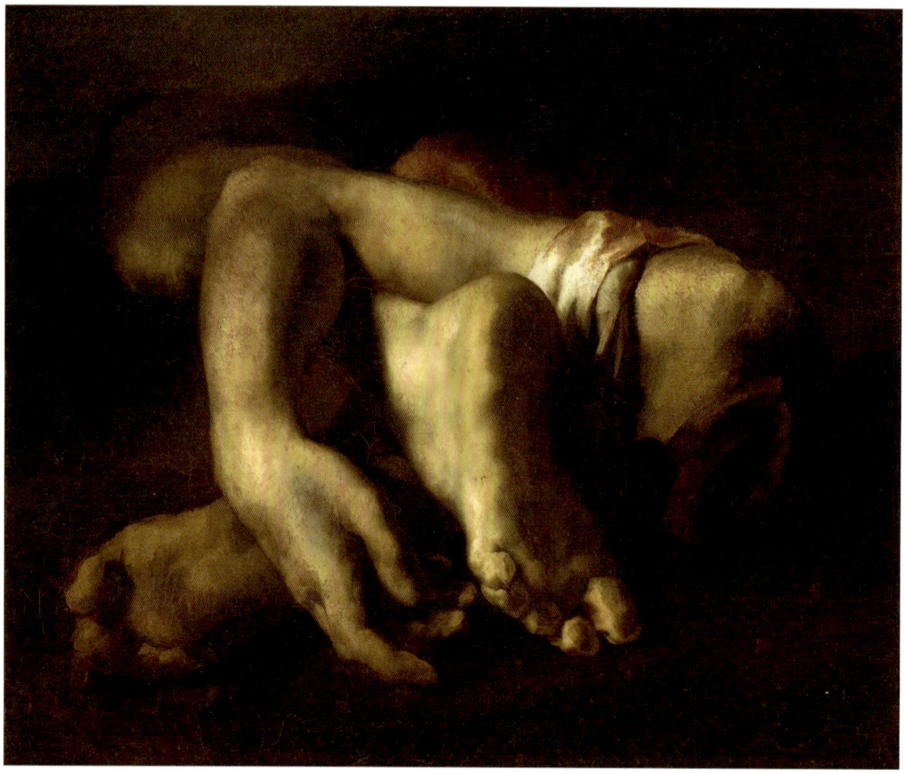

Fig. 12 Théodore Géricault, *Study of Feet and Hands*, 1818, oil on canvas
Musée Fabre, Montpellier, 876.3.38

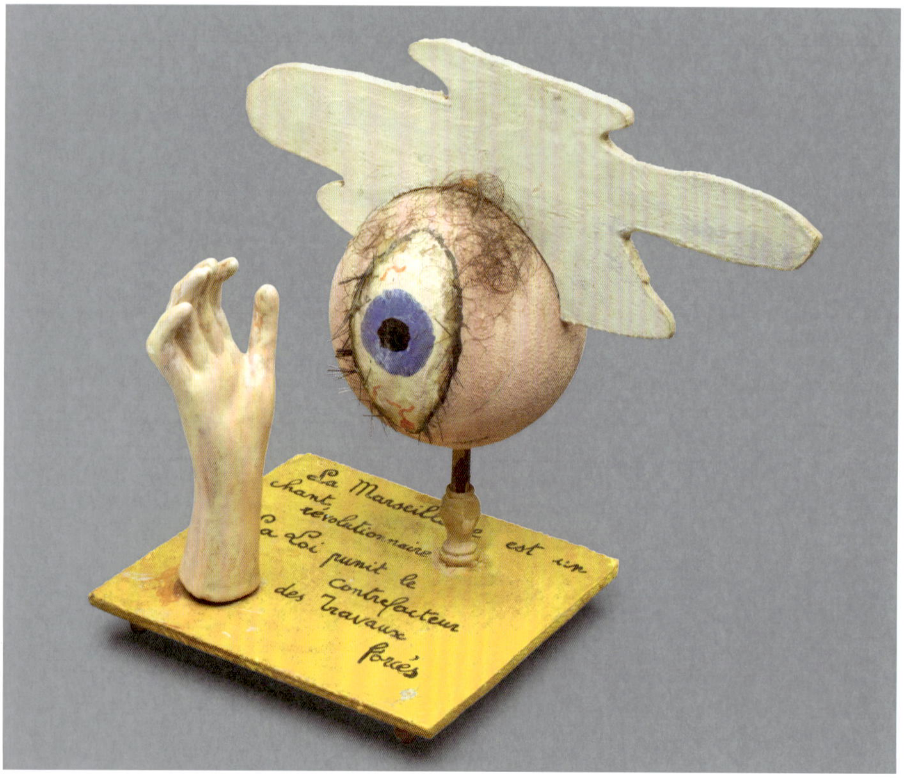

Fig. 13 Claude Cahun, *Object*, 1936, wood and paint with tennis ball, hair, and found objects
Art Institute of Chicago, Through prior gift of Mrs. Gilbert W. Chapman

the last remnant of a lesser colossus ⟨ *fig.* 11 ⟩. But the limb itself is elongated and precariously thin, and appears not broken off but rent from the hip. Because of its height—including its pedestal, the sculpture measures over seven feet tall—we cannot quite see the site of this visceral detachment; we are instead face-to-face with the mobile, rutted texture of the plaster. The tactility that enlivened Claudel's and Rodin's figures serves a different purpose here. As with the disturbing and sensuous studies of body parts made by Théodore Géricault in preparation for his painting *The Raft of the Medusa* (1818–1819), the solicitation to touch overrides the violence implicit in the fragmented body, or at least seems to render that violence momentarily unimportant ⟨ *fig.* 12 ⟩.[22] If the modern fragment is congenital, that does not mean that destruction had no hand in its creation, but rather that the breaking of bodies had become so familiar as to seem like a precondition of our intimacy with them.

THE MODERN FRACTURE TURNED INWARD

The nature of that contact became still more volatile in the final decades of the twentieth century, as sculptors turned toward a parallel modern tradition of fragmentation: the surrealist object. The broad class of existing and possible objects that interested the surrealists in the interwar period had a capacity to destabilize viewers' relationship to the external world by presenting them with items in unexpected combinations, split off from their initial purpose or value. Juxtaposition and isolation, or the bringing together and breaking off of elements, worked hand in hand to strip things of their familiar guises and so uncover both psychosexual and political latencies ⟨ *fig.* 13 ⟩. In the 1990s, artists returned to these operations with renewed vigor, plumbing the uncanny nature of the fragment not to stimulate revelation but to better enact the force of psychic drives.[23] No longer in a position to invoke an ideal and unrepresentable whole, the fragment turned inward to stoke psychic processes.

In Louise Bourgeois's *Foot*, a plush leg is encased in a plastic and metal brace that calls to mind early twentieth-century splints for the war-wounded ⟨ *fig.* 14 ⟩. But the soft body recalls something else: those nubbly stuffed animals and other comforting articles that the psychoanalyst D. W. Winnicott termed transitional objects—items that, by surviving the child's fierce affection and aggression, demonstrate the reality of an external world capable of withstanding her ambivalence.[24] That Bourgeois's leg bears its injury suggests a failure of this crucial psychic task and a corresponding triumph of subjective omnipotence. The desire for comfort and the will to destruction conjured by *Foot* mark out sculpture as a target of the drives rather than a means of negotiating

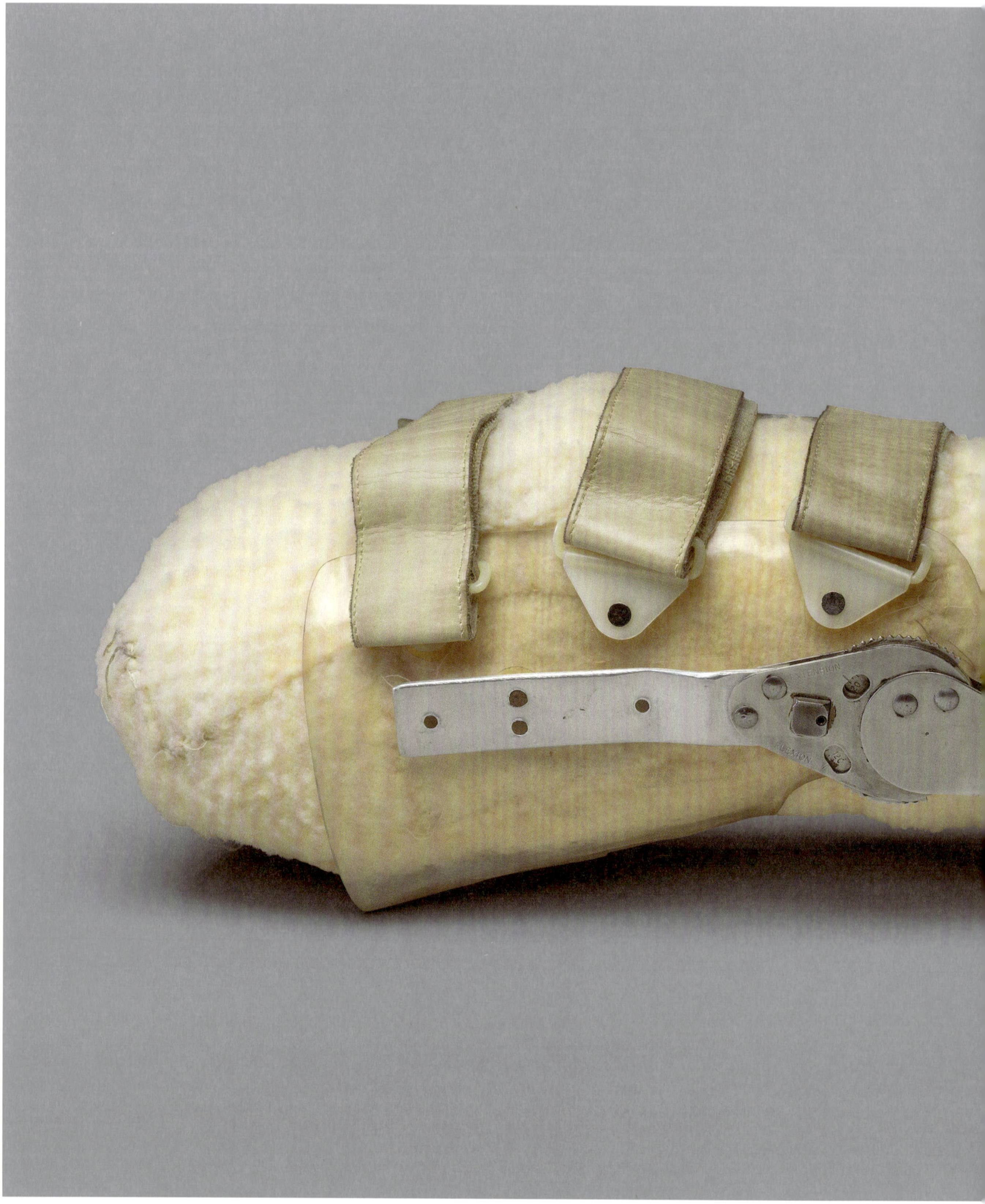

Fig. 14 Louise Bourgeois, *Foot*, 1997, fabric, metal, and plastic
Private collection, New York
Cat. 81

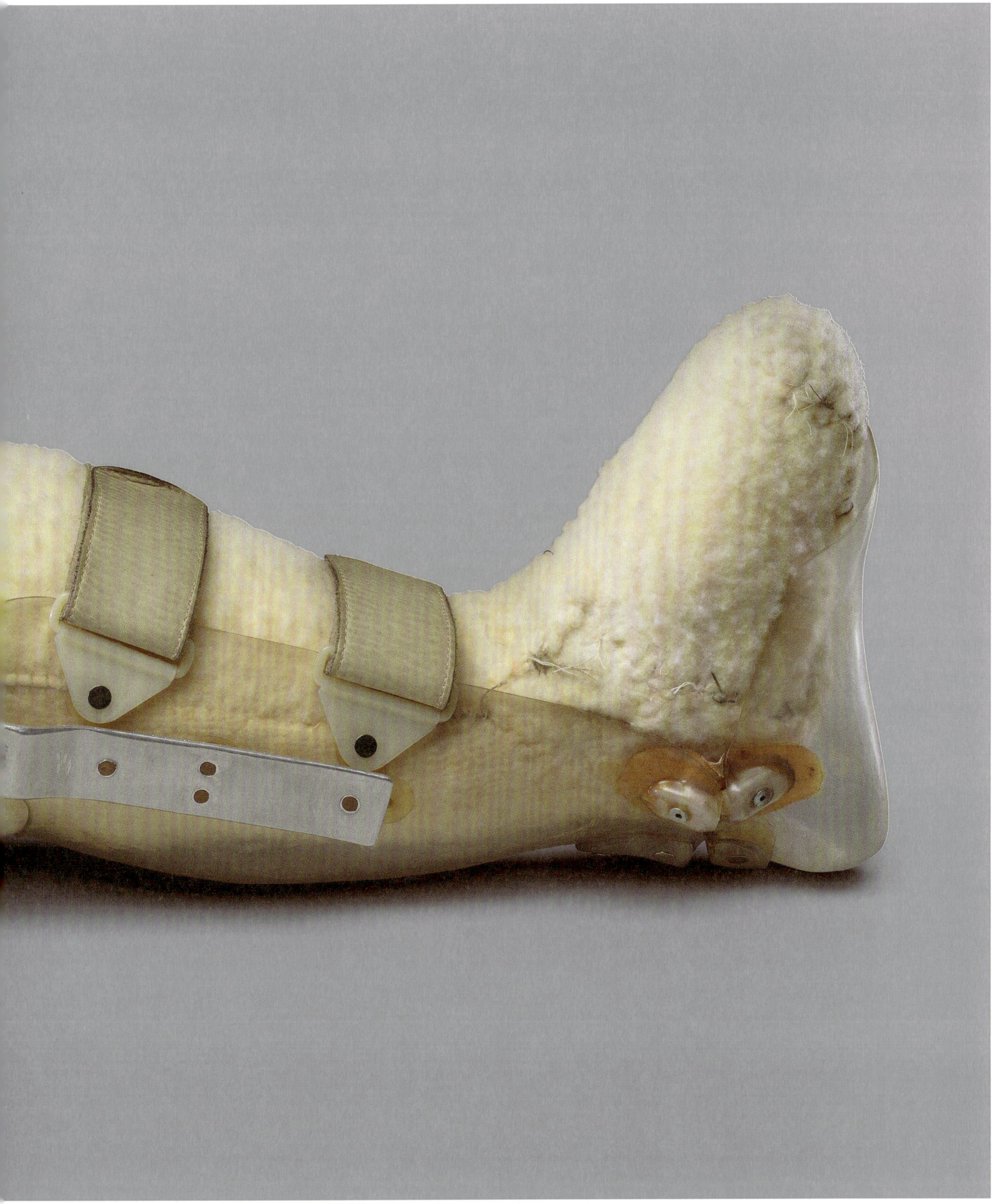

interiority and external reality.[25] Robert Gober's wax limbs similarly bring together the possibilities of pleasure and ruin. Originally cast from the artist's own leg, but shod and clothed so as to seem perfectly generic, Gober's *Untitled* projects from a wall, sprouting a candle from its thigh ⟨ see Feldman *fig.* 8 ⟩. A ritual object, a displaced erection, a memento mori: this candle offers competing erotic and sacred frames of engagement—perhaps ecstatic, perhaps desecrating—while satisfying neither.[26] The work presents as an enigma, missing an explanation much as the limb misses a body.[27] Like Bourgeois's leg, it draws upon the form of the fetish not to set up the sculptural fragment in place of a whole body but instead to emphasize what has been left incomplete, absent, lacking, *maudite*.

The range of practices collected under the rubric of assemblage forms the other pole of these postmodern returns to the avant-garde fragment. What distinguishes these works is their interest in stimulating what I earlier called a magical materialism, which fuses together fragments of the modern world—often, straightforwardly, its junk—in order to bring forth their collective charge. The series of assemblages that Fred Wilson has made over the past several decades from his personal collection of "degradaria," his coinage for the derogatory ornamental objects and bibelots sometimes called "Black collectibles," plies this principle on the material residues of racism in the United States.[28] In *Inside Story*, a blackamoor candlestick has been broken at the waist so that the figure—a generic representation of a Black servant dressed in Turkish clothing and a turban, whose orientalization of classical motifs of enslavement echoed eighteenth-century Atlantic fantasies and forms of racial conquest—appears to have lowered himself into a dramatic "Turkish drop" ⟨ *fig.* 15 ⟩.[29] Out of his hollow waist rises a ceramic figurine of a white boy reading a book. The simplicity of the assemblage gesture belies the complexity of its proposition. Is it an illustration of a racist universalism that would model the true self on an image of white innocence, or a demonstration of the dependence of that same innocence on the violence visited upon Black bodies, or a more pointed indictment of the white intelligentsia? The irresolution among these allegorical readings appears very much to the point. *Inside Story* offers a meta-reflection on assemblage as a tactic to conceal multiple meanings behind its "inescapable de-facto-ness," its ability to set in motion divergent meanings while maintaining an appearance of neutrality.[30] This strategy provides cover for the assemblage's capacity to unsettle its viewers, in part by revealing how they might identify differently with its components. Rather than unify the fractured world by constructing an intelligible and shared lesson from its remnants, the assemblage deploys art against the stable social relations that sculpture has long served to maintain.[31]

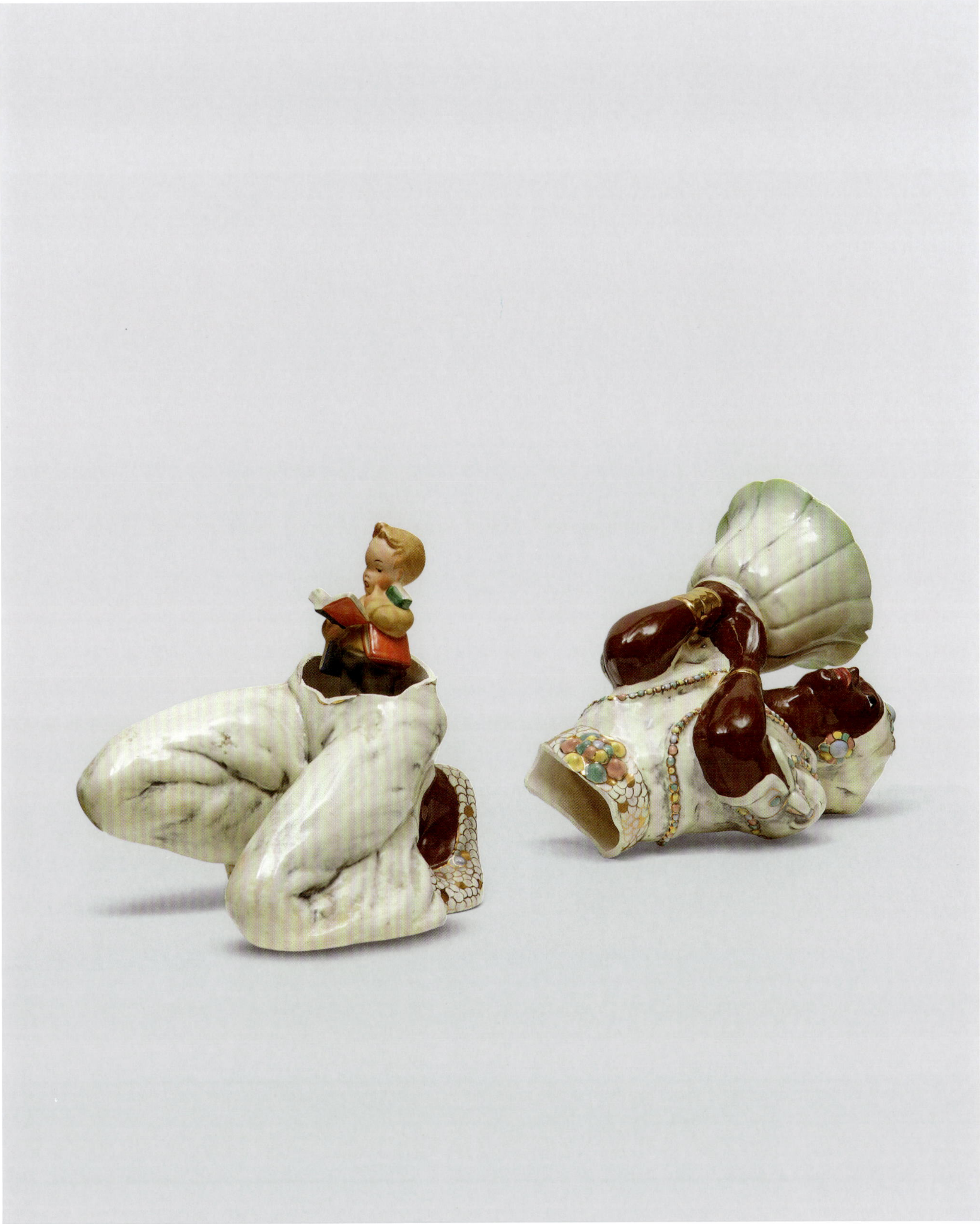

Fig. 15 Fred Wilson, *Inside Story*, 1995, glazed ceramic found objects
Courtesy of the artist and Pace Gallery
Cat. 80

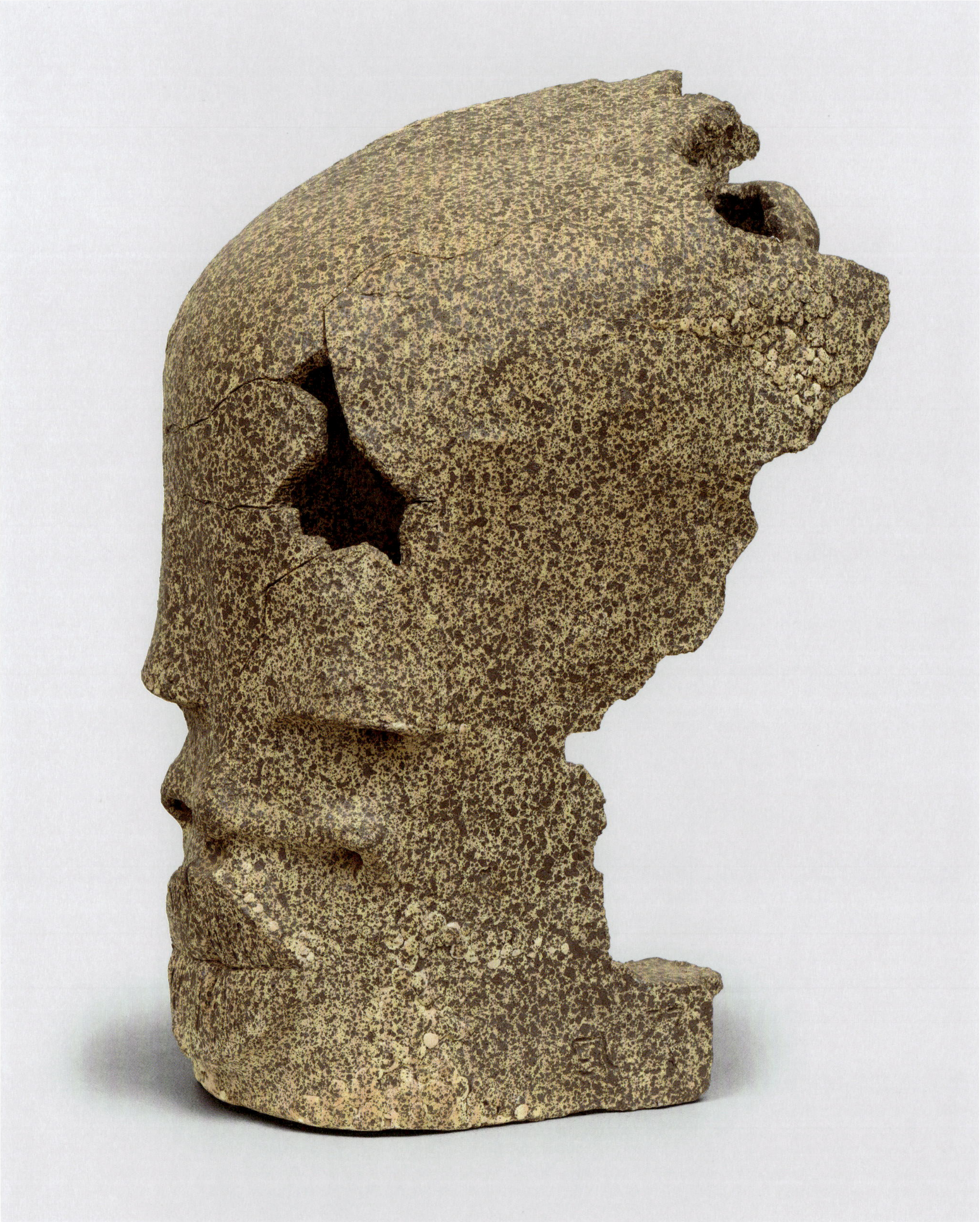

Fig. 16 El Anatsui, *Chambers of Memory*, 1977, ceramic and manganese
Courtesy of the artist and Jack Shainman Gallery, New York
Cat. 78

THE UNFINISHED STATE

As Wilson's assemblage suggests, the forms of incompletion and irresolution conveyed in the sculptural fragment extend beyond the individual psyche to the collective. A personal loss may be mapped onto a social whole, and the divergent understandings of that loss may demonstrate that the social whole is itself fractured. Both El Anatsui's and Huma Bhabha's works address the relationship of the artist to the destruction of grand historical narratives that subtend social unities. Anatsui's *Chambers of Memory* is composed from pulverized potsherds, combined with manganese to produce the coarse texture of an excavated antiquity ⟨ *fig.* 16 ⟩. The features on its face evoke the terracotta figures sculpted by the ancient Nok culture in present-day Nigeria, the earliest of which date to around 500 BCE and which were often discovered in fragments, perhaps because they were deliberately broken for ritual purposes. The reverse side of Anatsui's sculpture is honeycombed like an improvised hollow core door, whose titular chambers house a handful of clay baubles. The title references Kofi Awoonor's 1964 poem "Rediscovery," whose stanzas, like the rooms of a memory palace, retain not the residues of a historical event but rather "the new chorus of our forgotten comrades / and the halleluyahs of our second selves."[32] In Bhabha's *Untamed*, the sculpture's pocked and rusted surface endows it with such a hypertrophic sense of age and decay that it uproots the object from any fixed location in the past ⟨ *fig.* 17 ⟩. Her instant ruins—"simultaneously eternal and on the brink of collapse," reflects the critic and curator Tausif Noor—have a peculiar temporality that invokes the classical bust as well as the automaton, or something destroyed beyond recognition and something that could never receive it.[33] Corrosion eats away not just at the bust but at the cultural memory it purports to preserve, and it does so in the shortest of possible timelines.

Like the modern prose works theorized by Schlegel, *Untamed* was a fragment as soon as it was sculpted. Yet the effect is far from melancholy. Its vivid oxidation suggests a resurfacing and reshaping of old forms, a lively unruliness come to disrupt the classical genre of the bust. Schlegel's famous aphorism cited earlier is the 24th fragment, published in the *Athenaeum*, the literary journal he edited alongside his brother beginning in 1798. The 26th fragment, in a seeming departure from its aesthetic reflections, muses that "Germany is probably such a favorite subject for the general essayist because the less finished a nation is, the more it is subject for criticism and not for history."[34] The proximity of these lines appears less adventitious when held against the history of modern sculpture. When understood to reflect not merely a literal body but also a metonymic one—a body politic—the incoherence or brokenness of

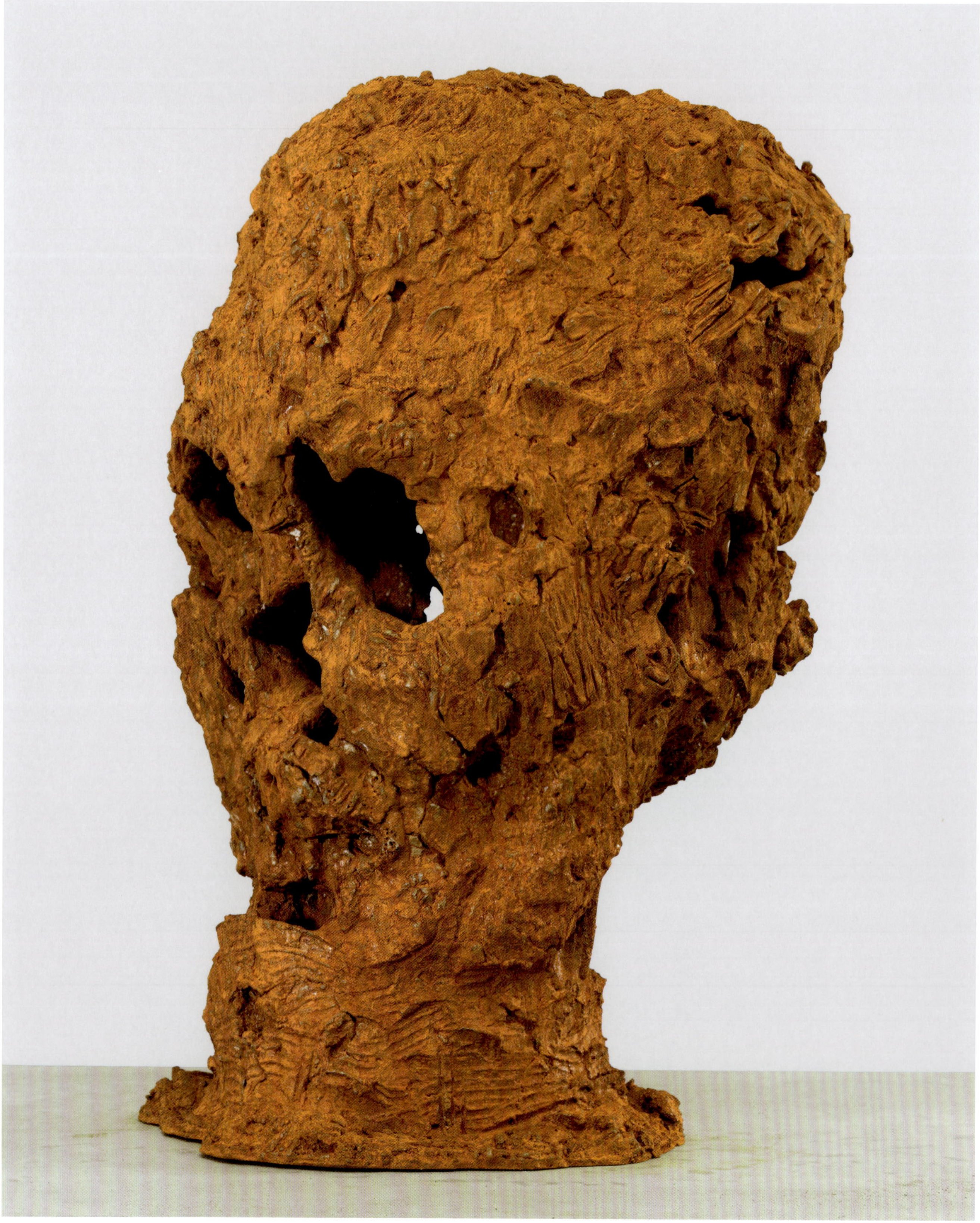

Fig. 17 Huma Bhabha, *Untamed* (detail), 2024 (edition of 3, and 1 artist's proof), cast iron and concrete (pedestal)
Courtesy the artist and David Zwirner
Cat. 91

sculpture may in fact harbor strange optimism. In the incompletion of the project of the nation lies the capacity for critiquing it; in the dismantling of a form lies the possibility of assembling it anew.

Perhaps no recent work speaks as directly to this possibility for the sculptural fragment as Danh Vo's *We the People* ⟨ *fig.* 18 ⟩, a series of repoussé copper elements that replicate segments of Frédéric-Auguste Bartholdi's *Statue of Liberty* at scale. Although the installation does not enact a straightforward scene of iconoclasm—the nature of these components as replicas is made plain by the unoxidized copper and the provisional buttresses that suggest a worksite rather than a junkyard—it is a work both of satire and of sacrilege. As the anthropologist Michael Taussig observes, it impugns the state's power to "enlarg[e] reality," which "passes unnoticed as a property of the might of the state and the statuesque," until one or the other is publicly disassembled.[35] But it also unleashes new energy, enlivening the collective rituals that monuments have historically displaced. The individual components of the *Statue of Liberty* can be seen as oddly vulnerable hollow forms and sensuous details: the swooping folds and puckers of a tunic, the flex and splay of fingers. Vo's shattering of a national symbol thus neither presents one of modernism's inaugurating ruptures nor somberly observes the ruins of its nation-building projects. Instead, it has a carnival air, inviting us to reenact modernity's ever-unfinished attempt to construct something from the debris.

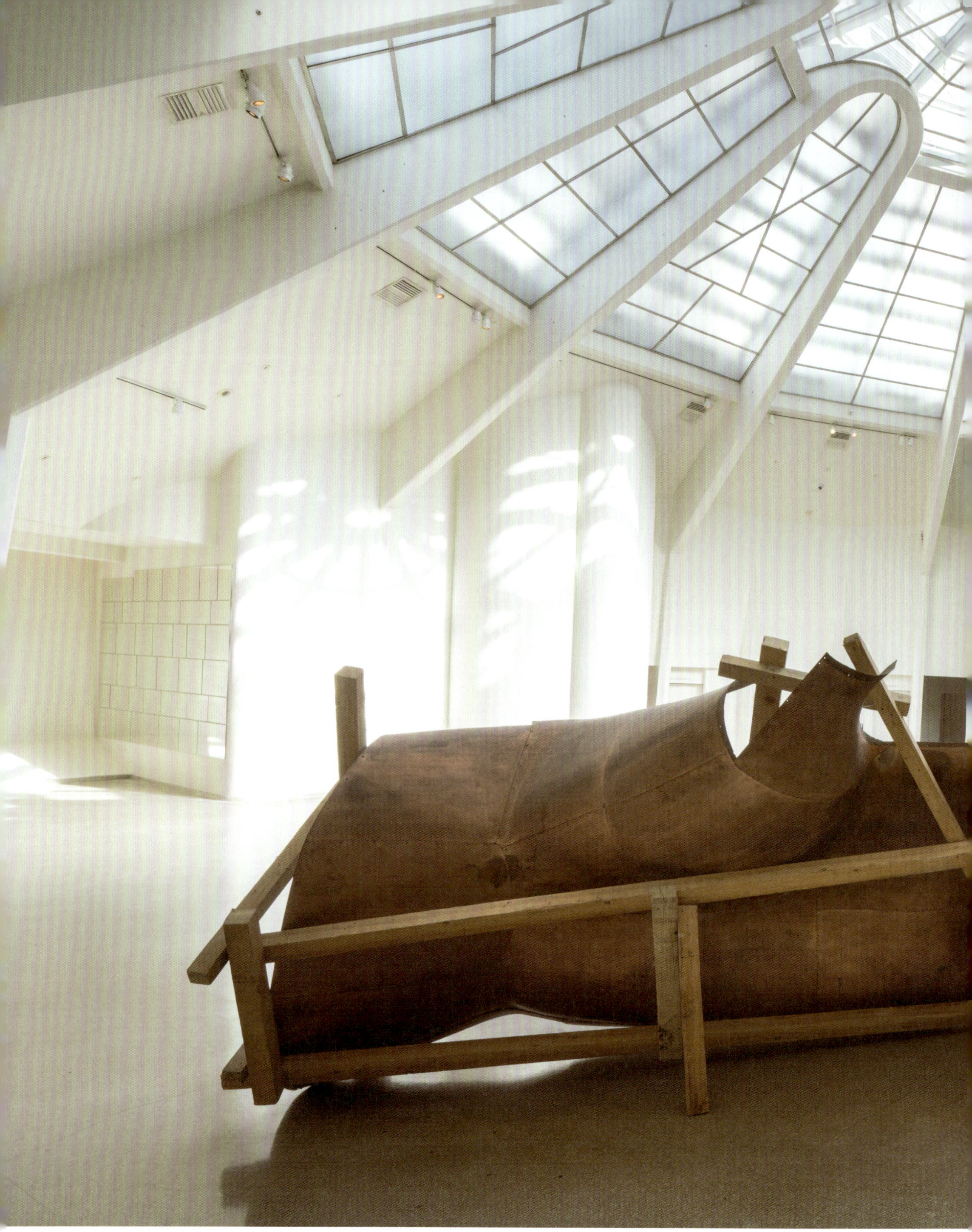

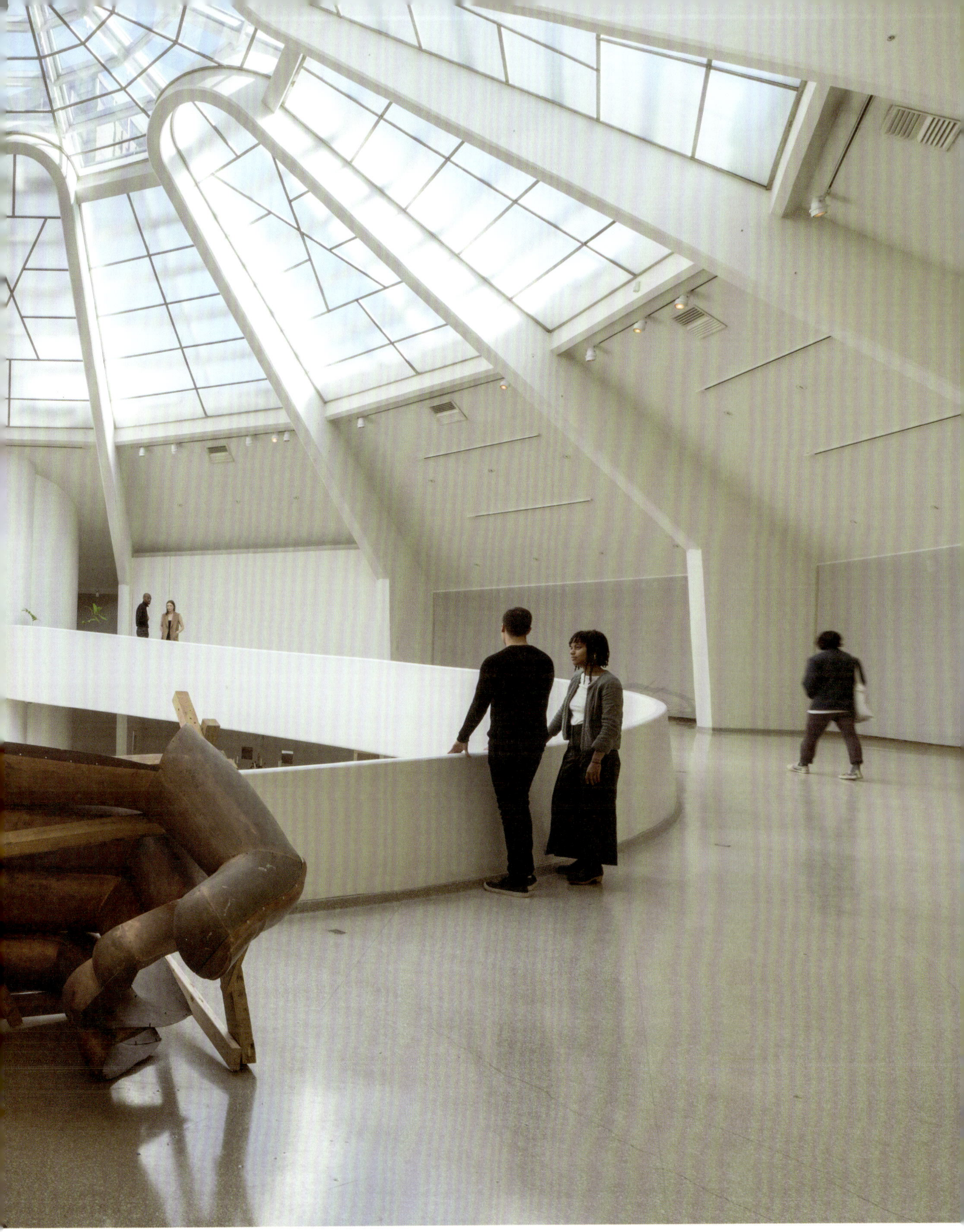

Fig. 18 Danh Vo, *We the People*, 2011–2016, copper and wood, installation view, *Danh Vo: Take My Breath Away*, February 9–May 9, 2018, Guggenheim, New York

DESTRUCTION AS CREATIVE PROCESS

Cannupa Hanska Luger in conversation with Dakota Hoska

Cannupa Hanska Luger is a multidisciplinary artist whose work Emergent ⟨*fig.* 1⟩ *appears in the exhibition accompanying this publication. Dakota Hoska, curator of Native American and global Indigenous art at the National Gallery of Art, and Luger joined in conversation to discuss historical works from the exhibition as well as the role of fragmentation in Luger's practice.*

DAKOTA HOSKA: What were your thoughts when we first approached you about contributing to this exhibition?

CANNUPA HANSKA LUGER: I've done a few works where there are pieces broken or severed or removed from the whole. And I thought that was pretty exciting. And then just looking over the overall exhibition, I thought it was fascinating, because so much of the visual language that I grew up seeing and experiencing in public school, but also just generally in life, have been these pieces without context.

And I think things being broken and presented leaves things to the imagination. And in that space, I was excited to participate. Like I said, I've made work consciously thinking about the absence of form and the challenge of communicating without context.

DH: I had that experience of going to that community-driven performance that you did in Santa Fe. You had all these people make these plates, and then you served everybody food. And then we all got in line and broke the plates. It really stuck with me for a couple of reasons. First, all the different reactions people had to breaking things. There were some that were super exuberant. And then, do you remember that little boy that just couldn't break it? You so beautifully spoke to him about how there was growth in letting things go, how much bravery it took to release something that you cherished.

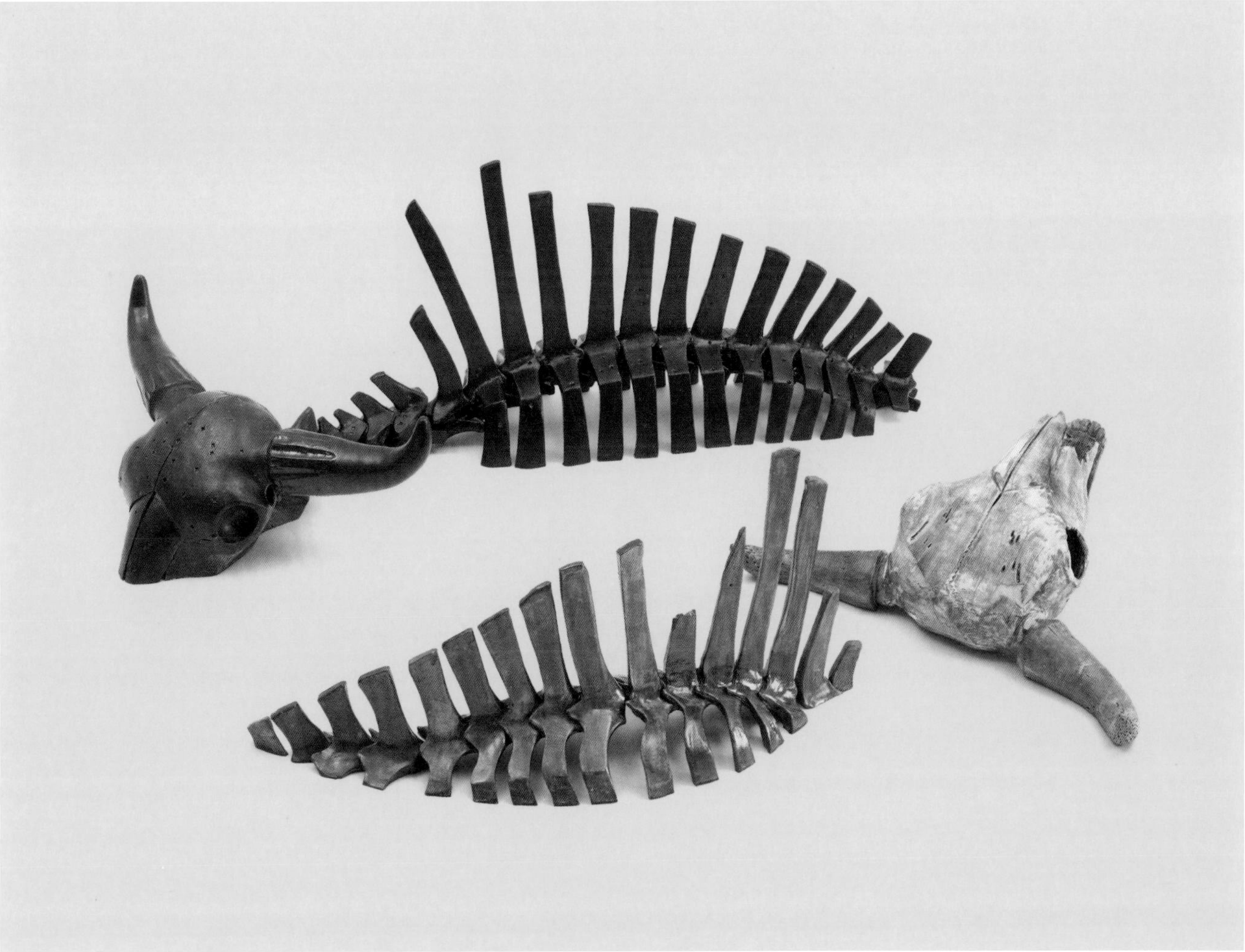

F*ig.*1 Cannupa Hanska Luger, *Emergent*, 2021, ceramic
Courtesy of the artist and Garth Greenan Gallery, New York
Cat. 85

CHL : It definitely sits in the realm of my own thoughts and beliefs that the destruction component to any creative act isn't the end of it, but instead it opens up the potential for something new to take its place. And I think it's pretty interesting, even talking about this exhibition, *Broken*, because I think about when I first did that piece that you're talking about, I was really thinking about how much of our Native people's work existed in museums in broken versions of itself, and how that presentation of it negates why they're broken.

The tendency to gather the detritus of a culture to better understand it without actually talking to the people is always fascinating to me. And I thought it was interesting to encourage people to destroy this work that didn't have that deep-time conversation, and that you were actually participating in that moment of destruction. I work with clay, and thinking about clay in the historical record, of course, things break on accident, but oftentimes things are broken on purpose. Without having that conversation around their destruction and trying to piece together the object, you disempower its destruction. Why was this destroyed in the first place? Just from a cultural context or, really, maybe even a human context, we have a hard time letting go of things.

And I think that has to do with perhaps our rituals of death and how we've perverted the natural potential of something ending by trying to perpetuate its existence, to preserve it. And I feel like destruction is part of the maintenance of a thing. This thing is destroyed so that we can create something new in its place. And I think for as long as we perpetuate the preservation of these sorts of things, it's harder to fill those spaces with something new, something that's more relevant to our present than the pieces of our past.

DH: I'm just as guilty of this as anyone. When I learned about this exhibition [*Broken*], I knew a lot of those pieces, those broken pieces. And I'm fascinated with them. And I think there's something really lovely about their brokenness. So, what do you think it is that the audiences are bringing to that piece? Are they projecting something on it? Is there a nostalgia there? What do you think gives these broken pieces their appeal to the visitors?

CHL: I think you're absolutely right. I think the appeal to a broken piece, one, you have our education system informing us about cultures from far into time. And a complete sculpture is finished in that timeline, but a broken piece, it builds all of this inquiry in the audience member.

And that becomes a space to receive projection. But I think from the audience standpoint, it creates an opportunity for them to transform the past, and maybe their own past. And maybe there's something in the human condition that excites us about observing these pieces—particularly, I would say, the human form, where there's parts that are recognizable, but the identity has been removed. And in that absence of identity, I imagine it creates a space for you to project anything onto that—yourself, maybe a loved one. You're beginning to transform your own memory and history.

Even though we are alive, we have these moments of break and fissure in our own memory and our own experience. And sometimes those objects can help us mend something in our own mind and our own history. And that is not a part of the exhibition, right? That is a part of the viewer's experience. So, by presenting prompts of broken pieces, it is also a prompt to recognize that we have agency in our own history and our own memory and our own timeline. So perhaps that's why we are attracted to these broken pieces.

DH: I just love how you're using the word "prompts" for these broken elements. I wouldn't have thought of it that way. But yeah, they really are prompts towards our imagination and prompts towards the stories. You said that a broken piece builds all of this inquiry. It's like it builds potentiality, in a way.

CHL: That's the power of art, right? Even when it's presented in its complete form, it exists as a prompt. I think the visual language, because it's not written and specific, it doesn't hold the same power that word does, because for the last couple thousand years since the written word, we've embedded our laws in language. And the word of law is significant.

But a much older component to that was the presentation of these prompts, a visual language, that encourages people to embody the lessons and rules and moral expectations in themselves, rather than it being something written. And I think that's the power of art.

And why it will always be significant is that the audience has to embody those lessons, whereas a written lawbook can be shelved. You know that you can look it up and that it's in there, if you need specificity. But then you don't have to embody it until you're penalized by it.

But I think this is why we see these sculptures. This is why we see these pots. This is why we see art as a prompt. It's an opportunity for people to embody the lessons that are being presented, or the ideas.

So, showing them broken is also something interesting. If we're talking about them as rules or social expectations, these broken versions let us know that even deep into antiquity the rules by which we agree to participate are also subject to entropy.

DH: Two pieces from the exhibition touch on something that you've been discussing. This first piece, I'm responding to what you said about entropy. Part of this sculpture was buried in the sand underwater—it sank to the bottom of the Aegean Sea after being caught in an ancient shipwreck—and part was not 〈 *fig.* 2 〉. And so then you can see how that made a difference in this sculpture's experience, or his entropy.

There is a section in the exhibition that's talking about nature as the collaborator. And I think you really lean into that in some of your works. I'm thinking specifically of *Emergent* 〈 see *fig.* 1 〉, your bison skeletons that are half in the ground, or you only see a portion of those. But can you speak to that—nature as a collaborator in your artwork?

CHL: The irony of this is, look at how well the sand and the earth preserved this piece. Whereas the part that's exposed, the parts that are weathered and worn, these were the ones that were affected by these natural forces—time, current, sand, and abrasion.

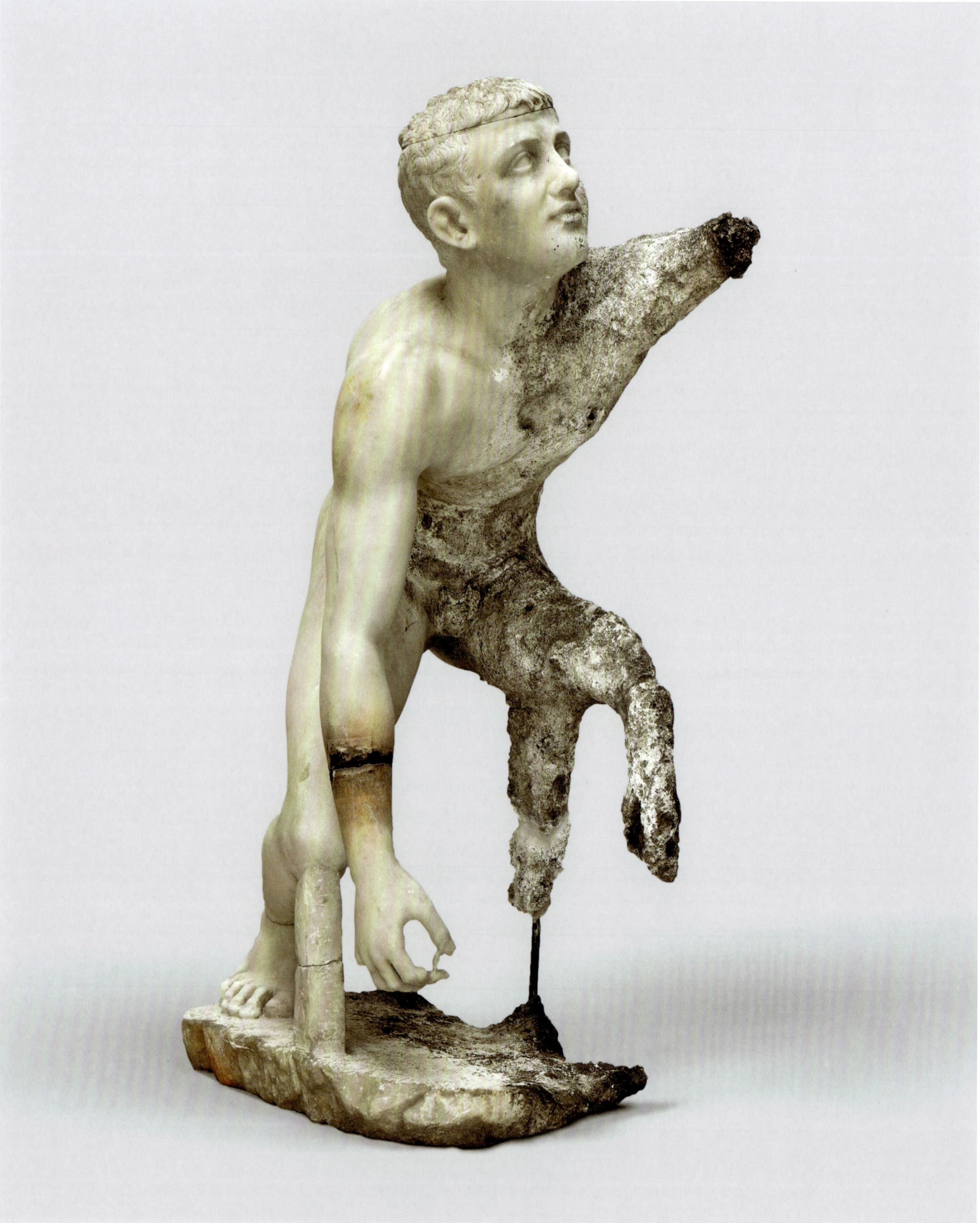

Fig. 2 Greek (Antikythera), *Crouching Boy (Wrestler?)*, early 1st century BCE, Parian marble
Hellenic National Archeological Museum, Athens, HNAM 2773
Cat. 20

DH: And on the other side that was exposed to the seawater, it's corroded, but also there's additive animal encrustations from species that eat away at and add to the constitution of the marble.

CHL: Well, now you have to take on the responsibility. For anybody who took it out of the ground, the preservation is now in your hands to maintain that. I just think it's funny—is it hubris that we can do a better job than just leaving it in the sand? And then the irony of it being a wrestler I think is interesting.

Tethering that to *Emergent*: I was interested in presenting the museum as a relatively young thing that we hold in this high prestige. How long has the museum existed? And how many museums have collapsed, have burned? How many things have we lost because of war and being on the surface? But the sand preserved that wrestler for thousands of years.

So I think that there's something interesting in this, and it's something that I've dove into as an artist as well, thinking about these buffalo skeletons being embedded in the land itself. And then that process of excavating the surface to build a museum exposes an emergent history.

This piece in particular talks to the emergent history component, because let us also consider that what nature built served a purpose. This wrestler, now abandoned at the bottom of a sea floor, becomes an anchor for new things to grow and to build a life, a total life from beginning to end. And this is how these things become encrusted with all of these different organisms. They chose to wrestle with the *Crouching Boy*, to anchor themselves to it, and to build their own lives, catching food and stuff off his exposed hand and leg. And we stopped that.

DH: There's something beautiful there about building on the ruin, or other things coming in to build on something that was left behind.

CHL: Right. And I think these sorts of pieces are going to be fascinating to consider. Once again, without context, what can you build out of an exposed arm and leg? I think it's interesting.

DH: So, on your beautiful buffalo sculptures, I love those with the grass coming through them. Do you think there will be things that come in and colonize those skeletal forms?

CHL: Definitely. In fact, I've done pieces where I've used unfired clay, making skeletal remains, but putting seed into the clay body and using them, recognizing that this too shall disintegrate. But how do you start life from the point of death? So, create a ceramic skull or bone parts, but embed seed into it and know that the environment's going to weather and wear it, and plant those seeds in its place. It's just a way to work with clay and sculpture, but recognize that there is a much deeper timeline and lineage that's also at play. Even when you fire a piece, it can last 1,000 years. It can last 10,000 years. But it will eventually become a part of place. And I think that there's something profoundly more interesting in that.

At this point in my life, I'm using the museum as a time capsule. I make this work, and I know that it will probably influence far more lives than I could totally imagine. And the audience for my work may be a century down the road. And it's using the museum as a time capsule, as a way to time travel this work into that space. But, turns out, you could also just bury it in the sand.

DH: This next object is a life-sized sculpture that scholars believe had been intentionally disarticulated by the Huastec people and then left beside a natural spring, perhaps as an offering ⟨ *fig.* 3 ⟩. There were other things like figurines, ceramics, and shells found in that same area, and scholars also believe these were deliberately broken before they were left. You were talking about how in trying to put things back together, you're almost disempowering the original intention of whoever was intentionally taking these things apart, or in its destruction.

CHL: So this was, according to what we understand, broken. But let's first say that it was *made*. The time and the effort to create this piece is energy. This is my life I am spending to create this. And even if its purpose is to be destroyed and placed in this site, it's self-sacrifice.

And throughout human history, we've seen instances where others are sacrificed. And we hold a certain disdain for that sacrificing of human life, without recognizing that if you build a sculpture, you build a pot, you do any of this sort of thing, you are putting your life into it. And in the destruction of it, you are destroying your own life, your own time, your own energy.

And there's something interesting about the thought that it's OK to remove them far after. And maybe it is. I don't know. But it's pretty wild to consider that desecrating that site is OK, especially if you know it was intentionally destroyed for that. Even with reassembly, it's still not complete. It's still destroyed. It still served its purpose. And now we're examining it.

DH: I was just fascinated, too, with what you're saying here about desecrating and thinking about: somebody took the time to intentionally destroy this and then bury it. That burial was also intentional. It wasn't an accidentally lost thing that was ever meant to resurface. So, you disrupt the agency of the ceremony, the medicine person, the community, whoever was responsible for putting it here.

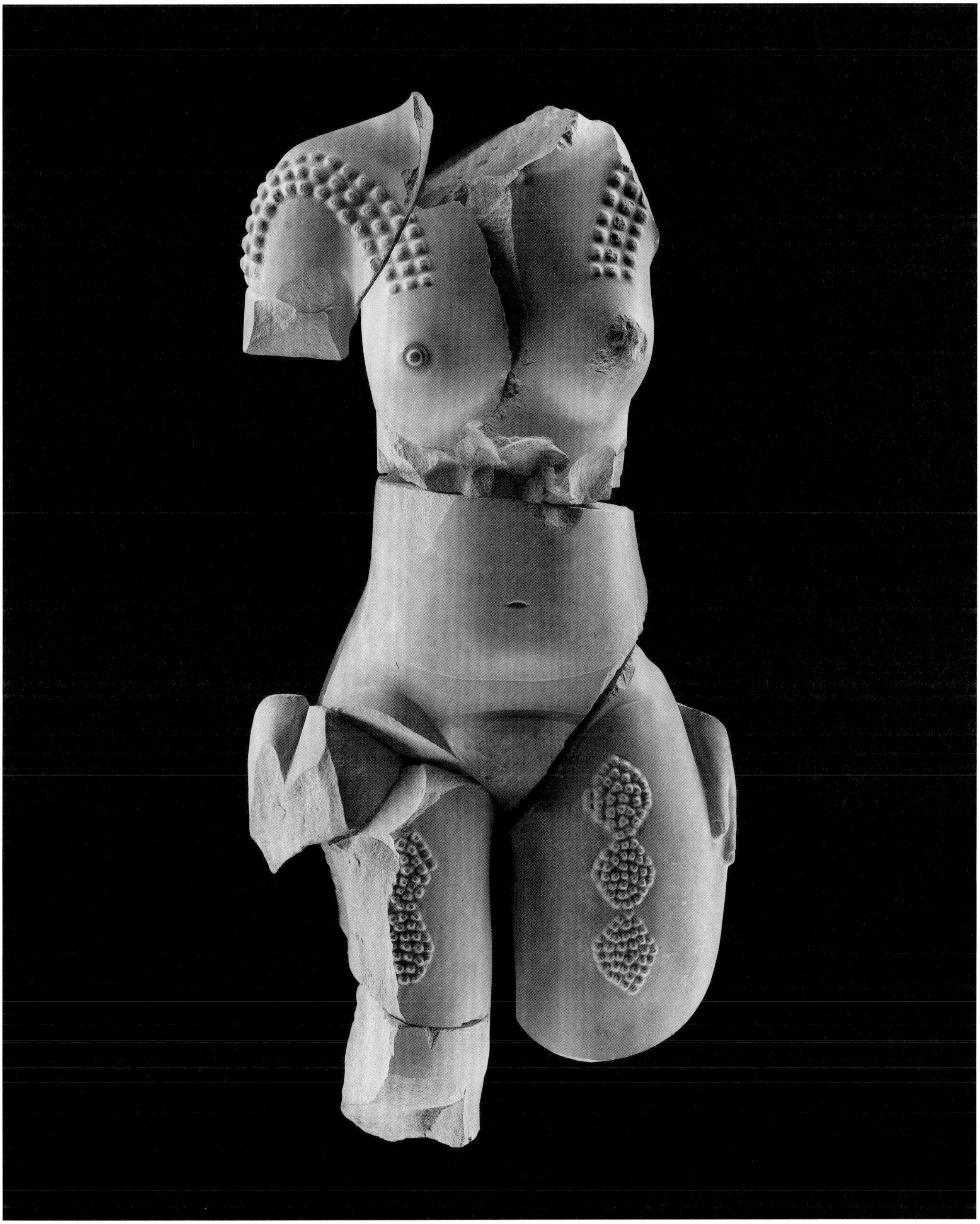

Fig. 3 Huastec (Tamtoc), *Scarified Woman*, c. 200 CE, sandstone
Zona Arqueológica de Tamtoc, San Luis Potosí, Secretaría de Cultura—Instituto Nacional de Antropología e Historia, 10-655098
Cat. 31

CHL: Well, another example of destroyed pieces that you see is when regimes change, where people in power shift and all likenesses of them are destroyed in the process so that their legacy doesn't prevail. We do that today. Now we have to destroy character on social media, because it's all just photographs of people. But all the same, there is an impulse to destroy the representation of that oppression and that conflict.

And for this object, we don't know who this person is. It could be a piece that is honoring, as you were saying, some water deities or something along those lines and building that effort and putting them back in. But in other instances where the face is purposely broken and removed, it's pretty fascinating to think about how, once again, it's the reconstruction of our history through taking things out of context, but also providing us context. Not knowing why it was destroyed, but finding broken pieces of it, or looking at walls where names were etched out.

It all, on one hand, is taken out of context, but on the other hand, provides this context. And I just don't think we'll ever completely understand or know or really even be able to embody the pain that the person experienced who was enacting the desecration of the form.

DH: I want to speak more about your practice and to respond to what you said: When you break a piece of art, you're also breaking that person's life or their time. And I just want to point out that you have now killed yourself through your performances several times—but intentionally. Was there something about that donation of time, or about relinquishing control over that thing, that was really appealing to you?

CHL: Yes. For me, the art isn't the thing that's made. It's the making. And so even if the object is broken, the knowledge that's gained through the process of creating something isn't destroyed. It's additive.

So for the creative hand, for the artist hand, for the maker's hand, the destruction of the object does not destroy the art. You've learned so much in the process of doing it. And sometimes you make things to learn. And the only good thing you can do with it is destroy it.

In my *New Myth* installation, these are severed monstrous parts left on the floor that you walk into in the wake of these two monster-slayer characters ⟨ *figs.* 4–5 ⟩. They are already disembodied. They were built whole, but they're disembodied parts.

So, these are not broken versions of the sculpture. These are to recognize that destruction is a creative process, that the monstrous inhibit our movement, and that destruction of the oppressive force is generative. And so leaving its parts on the field, like a barnacle or a bug or anything else, will make something good out of it.

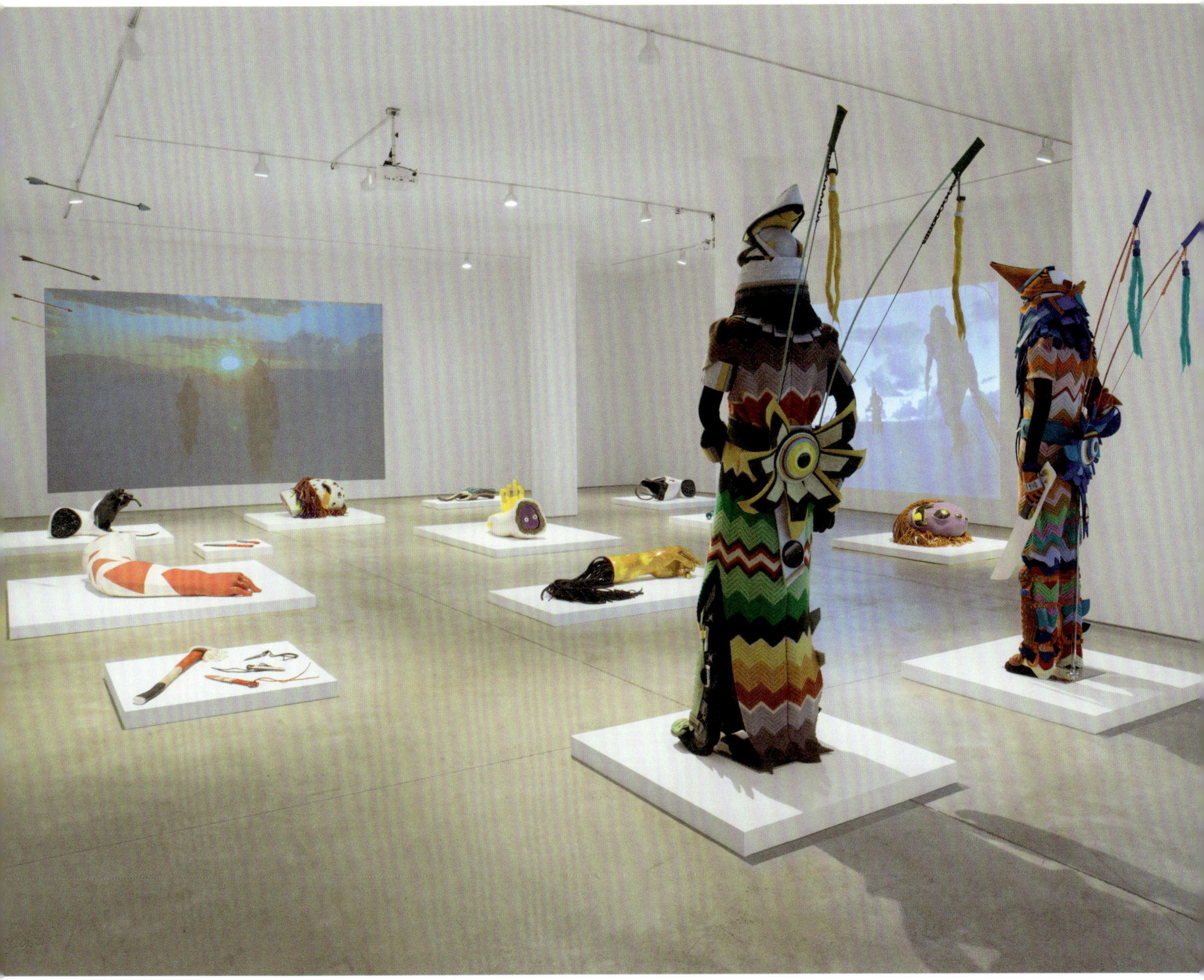

Fig. 4 *Cannupa Hanska Luger: New Myth*, installation view, September 10–October 23, 2021, Garth Greenan Gallery, New York

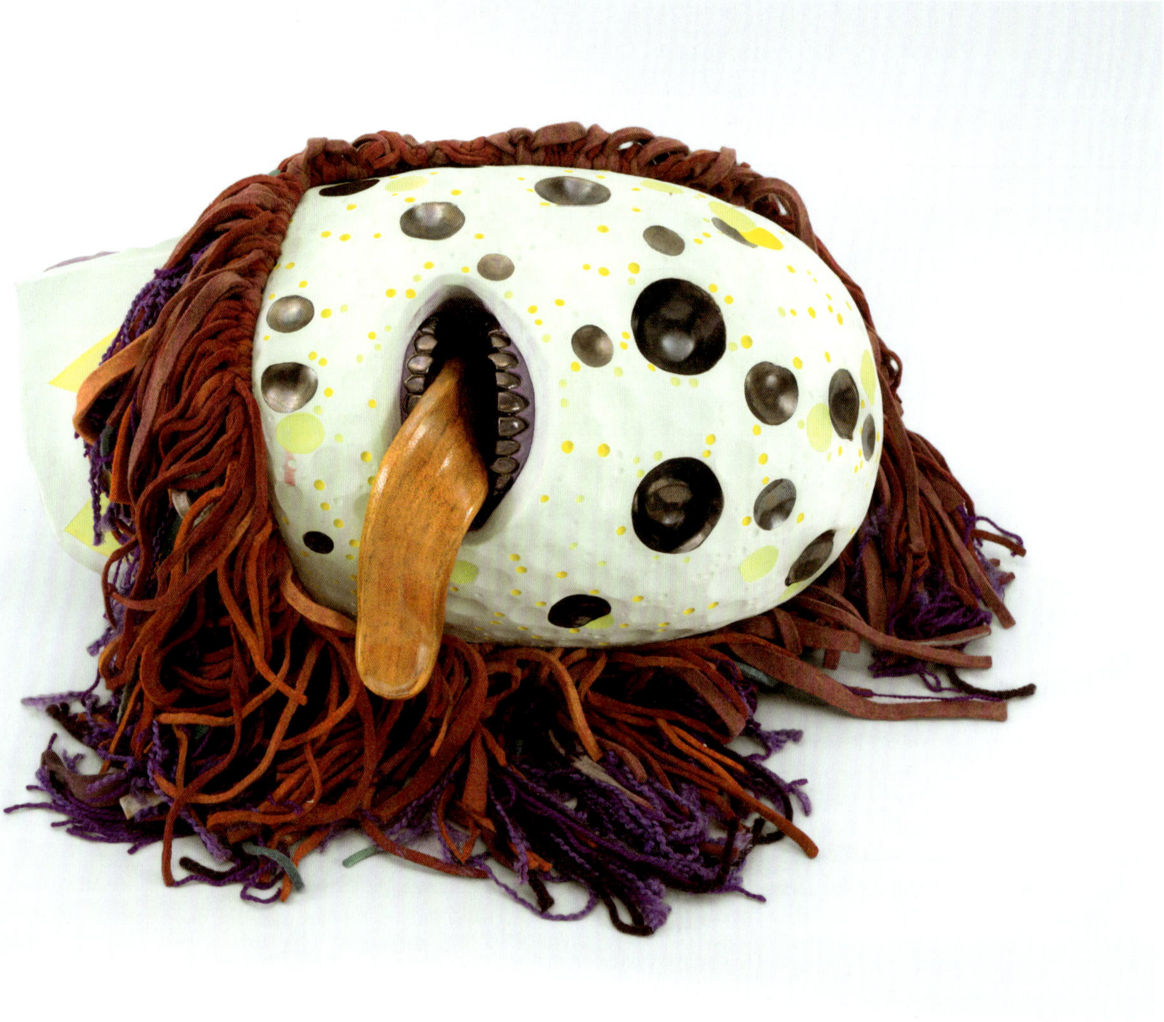

Fig. 5 Cannupa Hanska Luger, *Corruption*, 2021, ceramic and mixed media
Courtesy of the artist and Garth Greenan Gallery, New York

I have made pieces that I intentionally destroyed in the process, because there was a catharsis that was created in the process of making something. But I was afraid the object would perpetuate what it is that I'm trying to explore. So, presenting the broken version of it or destroying it was intentional.

I had done these ceramic boom boxes that were stereos, and they were all Native stereotypes. And before the exhibition was completed, I let go of them. And the idea was to play with the fact that all things are subject to entropy. But ideas live longer than things. I made them ceramic things so that I didn't even have to do much to destroy them. I simply had to let them go. And I think, thinking about stereotypes, I was learning something in that process: these are external impositions upon you. And if you embody them, they become true. But if you let them go, they fall apart. And so there was a whole process of creating the work, and then letting work go, as a model.

DH: How do you respond to this idea that something broken gives birth to something new? How do you reconcile the violence of something being broken with the romance surrounding broken objects?

CHL: I feel as though oftentimes it is our love of something that can destroy it. That we hold on to things so tightly sometimes that we crush them in our grip. And moreover, it's challenging. Sometimes when you love something so great, you lose yourself in it.

And that creates a disdain for it. I think these things go part and parcel—our romance for it, not the general and true love, but the romantic impulse, the superimposition of it being greater than what it actually is, the romantic gaze. And once that real thing shows itself wholly, you might not love it the way that you imagined you did. I think often when we're talking about cultures and the representation of gods or great people, their destruction is that they've failed to live up to the romance that we've empowered them with. Destruction follows that.

But meanwhile, we still have these broken objects that we're putting into an exhibition in a museum. And returning to an earlier point: I do think of the museum as a time capsule, because the model for it is a preservation model rather than a maintenance model.

Anything that gets absorbed into the museum gets preserved with great and continuous effort. The cotton gloves, the hermetically sealed rooms, the carbon dioxide, emergency gas. All of that stuff is fascinating. And this is a good place to put some stuff that people are going to see far into the future. I experienced that, when I came across pieces that a museum shouldn't have. I ended up seeing them.

And my first impulse is to take them and put them back where they belong. But that was me thinking of them as objects, when really what they are is a transmission. It's a transmission from our ancestors to our present. So how can you decentralize the power of the museum and recognize that this is a time capsule, and that the thing that you are seeing is not a thing, but a transmission? And can you receive the transmission? If you can, you've taken it out of the museum and put it back where it belongs.

NOTES

FRAMING THE FRAGMENT

1 For the history of the statue, including the various times it fell and was reerected, see Reynold Higgins, "The Colossus of Rhodes," in *The Seven Wonders of the Ancient World*, ed. Peter A. Clayton and Martin J. Price (London: Routledge, 1988), 124–137; and Lawrence I. Conrad, "The Arabs and the Colossus," *Journal of the Royal Asiatic Society* 6, no. 2 (1996): 165–187.

2 Pliny the Elder, *The Natural History*, bk. 34, chap. 18. My translation follows that of Harris Rackham (Loeb Classical Library, vol. 9), although I have chosen to translate *miraculo* as "miracle" rather than as "marvel."

3 Mary Beagon, "Situating Nature's Wonders in Pliny's *Natural History*," *Vigilia Est: Essays in Honour of Barbara Levick* (*Bulletin of the Institute of Classical Studies, Supplement*, no. 100) (2007): 19–40.

4 Bruce Gibson, "Hildebert of Lavardin on the Monument of Rome," in *Word and Context in Latin Poetry: Studies in Memory of David West*, ed. A. J. Woodman and Jakob Wisse (Cambridge, UK: Cambridge Philological Society, 2017), 133.

5 For a late fifteenth-century example of the sentiment, see Francesco Colonna, *Hypnerotomachia Poliphili: The Strife of Love in a Dream*, trans. Joscelyn Godwin (London: Thames & Hudson, 1999), 30–31, 59.

6 The literature on ruins is vast. See especially Rose Macaulay, *Pleasure of Ruins* (London: Weidenfeld & Nicolson, 1953); Christopher Woodward, *In Ruins* (London: Chatto & Windus, 2001); Robert Ginsberg, *The Aesthetics of Ruins* (Amsterdam: Editions Rodopi, 2004); Susan Stewart, *The Ruins Lesson: Meaning and Material in Western Culture* (Chicago: University of Chicago Press, 2020); and Prika Aleksandra, *Decay and Afterlife: Form, Time and the Textuality of Ruins, 1100 to 1900* (Chicago: University of Chicago Press, 2022).

7 On the emergence of ruins as a vital literary construct during the Renaissance, see Andrew Hui, *The Poetics of Ruins in Renaissance Literature* (New York: Fordham University Press, 2016).

8 On the bronze fragments and the identity of the colossal statue to which they originally belonged, see Serena Ensoli, "I colossi di bronzo a Roma in età tardoantica: Dal Colosso di Nerone al Colosso di Constantino; A Proposito dei tre frammenti bronzei dei Musei Capitolini," in *Aura Roma: Dalla città pagana alla città cristiana*, ed. Serena Ensoli and Eugenio La Rocca (Rome: "L'Erma" di Bretschneider, 2000), 66–90; and Giovanni Agosti and Dante Isella, eds., *Antiquarie prospetiche romane* (Parma: Ugo Granda Editore; Milan: Fondazione, Pietro Bembo, 2004), 93–94.

9 Master Gregorius, *The Marvels of Rome*, trans. John Osborne (Toronto: Pontifical Institute of Mediaeval Studies, 1987), 23, 48–53. See also Magister Gregorius, *Narracio de mirabilibus urbis Rome*, ed. R. B. C. Huygens (Leiden: E. J. Brill, 1970), 17.

10 Carolyn Smith, *Architecture in the Culture of Early Humanism: Ethics, Aesthetics, and Eloquence 1400–1470* (New York: Oxford University Press, 1992), 158.

11 For an authoritative account of the statue's history, see Francis Haskell and Nicholas Penny, *Taste and the Antique: The Lure of Classical Sculpture, 1500–1900* (Turnhout: Harvey Miller, 2024), 1:511–518.

12 Agosti and Dante Isella, *Antiquarie prospetiche romane*, 9.

13 Leonard Barkan, *Unearthing the Past: Archaeology and Aesthetics in the Making of Renaissance Culture* (New Haven, CT: Yale University Press, 1999), 192–197.

14 Maria Teresa Fiorio, entry in *The Genius of the Sculptor in Michelangelo's Work*, ed. Pierre Théberge (Montreal: Montreal Museum of Fine Arts, 1992), 122–124.

15 Barkan, *Unearthing the Past*, 197–207.

16 Barkan, *Unearthing the Past*, 201–207.

17 During a fellowship at Harvard University's Villa I Tatti in Florence in 2016, Anthony Sigel (then senior conservator of objects at the Harvard Art Museums) was able to examine the terracotta outside its vitrine and photograph it. We are grateful to Sigel for sharing his unpublished conclusion with us.

18 For a concise account of Michelangelo's potential involvement with restoring the *Laocoön*, see Haskell and Penny, *Taste and the Antique*, 3:378. See also Ludovico Rebaudo, *Il braccio mancante: I restauri del* Laocoonte *(1506–1957)* (Trieste: Editreg, 2007).

19 Giorgio Vasari, *Le Vite de' più eccellenti pittori scultori ed architettori*, ed. Gaetano Milanesi (Florence: G. C. Sansoni, Editore, 1906), 6:632–633.

20 For the idea that Michelangelo may have stepped in and offered his own restoration around 1540, see Barkan, *Unearthing the Past*, 11; Rebaudo, *Il braccio mancante*, 30–42; and Filippo Magi, "Il ripristino del *Laocoonte*," *Atti della Ponteficia Accademia Romana di Archeologia*, ser. 3, vol. 9 (1960): 46–50. We at least know that in 1540 Francesco Primaticcio removed Montorsoli's arm when making his bronze cast of the *Laocoön* for King Francis I—a potential sign of disagreement over the orientation chosen by Montorsoli.

21 Consider the statement by Jonathan Richardson, *An Account of Some of the Statues, Bas-reliefs, Drawings and Pictures in Italy, etc. with Remarks* (London: printed for J. Knapton, 1722), 277, that the arm was considered to be by Michelangelo when he saw it in 1722, which would seem to rule out that it has anything to do with restorations to the statue from the early eighteenth century. For why the arm should be discounted as a work by Michelangelo, see Alan Chong, "Copies, Restorations, and Caricatures: Montorsoli at the Vatican," in *The Sculpture of Giovan Angelo Montorsoli and His Circle: Myth and Faith in Renaissance Florence*, ed. Alan Chong and Lorenzo Principi (Manchester, NH: Currier Museum of Art, 2018), 51

22 For a general history of restoration in Renaissance Italy, see Orietta Rossi Pinelli, "Chirugia della memoria: Scultura antica e restauri storici," in *Memoria dell'antico nell'arte italiana*, vol. 3, *Dalla tradizione all'archeologia*, ed. Salvatore Settis (Turin: Giulio Einaudi Editore, 1986), 183–250.

23 Giancarlo Fiorenza, "Fables, Ruins, and the 'bell'imperfetto' in the Art of Dosso Dossi," *MLN* 119, no. 1, Italian Issue Supplement: Studia Humanitas: Essays in Honor of Salvatore Camporeale (2004): S274–S290.

24 Fiorenza, "Fables, Ruins," 286–287, quoting and translating Pietro Andrea Mattioli, *Il Magno Palazzo de Cardinale di Trento* (Venice, 1539), st. 263–265

25 As related in the anonymously written *Memorandum on the Subject of the Earl of Elgin's Pursuits in Greece* (London: William Miller, 1811), 39–40.

26 On this shift in approach, see Orietta Rossi Pinelli, "From the Need for Completion to the Cult of the Fragment: How Tastes, Scholarship, and Museum Curators' Choices Changed Our View of Ancient Sculpture," in *History of Restoration of Ancient Stone Sculptures*, ed. Janet Burnett Grossman, Jerry Podany, and Marion True (Los Angeles: J. Paul Getty Museum, 2003), 68–71.

27 On the project and Thorvaldsen's role, see Lars Olof Larsson, "Thorvaldsens Resturierung der Aegina-Skulpturen im Lichte zeitgenössischer Kunstkritik und Antikenauffassung," *Konsthistorisk tidskrift* 38 (1969): 23–46; and Raimund Wünsche, "'Perikles' sucht 'Pheidias': Ludwig I. und Thorvaldsen," in *Künstlerleben in Rom: Bertel Thorvaldsen (1770–1844); Der danische Bildhauer und seine deutschen Freunde* (Nuremberg: Germanisches Nationalmuseum, 1991), 313–317.

28 William J. Diebold, "The Politics of Derestoration: The Aegina Pediments and the German Confrontation with the Past," *Art Journal* 54, no. 2 (1995): 60–66.

29 Consider the position already staked out by Alois Riegl in 1903: Alois Riegl, "The Modern Cult of Monuments: Its Character and Its Origin," trans. Kurt W. Forster and Diane Ghirardo, *Oppositions*, no. 25 (1982): 21–51. For a source from the early 1960s, consider Cesare Brandi, who articulates an approach to valuing fragments (losses) during restoration: Cesare Brandi, *Theory of Restoration*, trans. Cynthia Rockwell (Florence: Nardini Editore, 2005). For a summary of the philosophical positions, see Steven D. Hales, "Value Pluralism in Restoration Aesthetics," *The British Journal of Aesthetics* 64, no. 3 (July 2024): 397–414.

30 For two studies that point in this direction, see Roland W. Fleming, "Material Perception," *Annual Review of Vision Science* 3 (2017): 365–388; and Bei Xiao and Chenxi Liao, "Material Perception Connects Vision, Cognition, and Action," *Nature Reviews Psychology* 4 (2025): 687–701.

31 Johann Joachim Winckelmann, *History of the Art of Antiquity*, trans. Harry Francis Mallgrave (Los Angeles: Getty Research Institute, 2006), 146. This derives from a standalone essay on the sculpture he published in 1759.

32 On this tradition, see Ho Thi Thanh Nhan, "Funeral Sculptures of the Jrai People in the Central Highlands, Vietnam," *AIP Conference Proceedings* 2406, no. 1 (2021), https://doi.org/10.1063/5.0066494; and Ho Thi Thanh Nhan, "Wooden Funeral Sculptures of the Jrai and Bahnar in the Vietnam Central Highlands: Conservation or Destruction?," in *Global Changes and Sustainable Development in Asian Emerging Market Economies*, ed. An Thinh Nguyen and Luc Hens (Cham: Springer, 2022), 2:13–33.

33 Pliny the Elder, *Natural History*, bk. 34, chap. 18.

34 A key recent source for an understanding of awe is Dacher Keltner, *Awe: The New Science of Everyday Wonder and How It Can Transform Your Life* (New York: Penguin Books, 2024). For an indication of the neurological underpinnings of awe, see Michiel van Elk, M. Andrea Arciniegas Gomez, Wietske van der Zwaag, Hein T. van Schie, and Disa Sauter, "The Neural Correlates of the Awe Experience: Reduced Default Mode Network Activity During Feelings of Awe," *Human Brain Mapping* 12, no. 40 (2019): 3561–3574.

ENERGIES OF THE FRAGMENT

The basic research for this essay was completed with the assistance of a generous grant on neuroscience and culture from the Nomis Foundation. As always, I am grateful to Vittorio Gallese, Beatrice de Gelder, Fortunato Battaglia, and Paul Linton for their advice, and to Fabio Tononi, whose PhD dissertation, "Beyond Vision: An Interdisciplinary Study of the Phenomenon of the Unfinished in the Drawing Practice of the Florentine Renaissance and a Neuroscientific Account of Responses to Incomplete Images" (Warburg Institute, University of London, 2019), was written under my supervision. The neuroscientific literature on this subject has reached vast proportions. In the following notes, I have confined myself to significant early articles on each cited topic, except in cases where the updatings seemed critical.

1 Saint Thomas Aquinas, *Summa Theologiae*, Part 1, Question 39. The emphasis here is mine. When, almost seven hundred years later, James Joyce's alter ego Stephen Daedalus cited this passage by Aquinas in chapter V of *Portrait of the Artist as a Young Man* (1916), he too emphasized the importance of wholeness, harmony, and radiance as the defining qualities of beauty (though as if wryly acknowledging the insufficiency of this claim, he noted that he was still intending to write a treatise on that sentence).

2 Directly from the Greek word *acheiropoietos*, one of the most frequently used terms for exceptional images of Christ in the Early Christian and Byzantine literature.

3 Friedrich Nietzsche, *Human, All Too Human* (1878), §178, here as excellently translated by Andrew Hui in "Nietzsche: The Fragments of the Unfinished," chap. 6 in *A Theory of the Aphorism: From Confucius to Twitter* (Princeton: Princeton University Press, 2019), 151.

4 For fundamental mirror data on the transformation of sight into feelings of touch and the activation of both primary and secondary somatosensory cortices, see C. Keysers, B. Wicker, V. Gazzola, J. L. Anton, L. Fogassi, and V. Gallese, "A Touching Sight: SII/PV Activation During the Observation and Experience of Touch," *Neuron* 42, no. 2 (April 22, 2004): 335–346. The subject of cross-modal responses such as those involving both sight and touch is critical, in terms of both two- and three-dimensional objects. A critical contribution to the study of cross-modality beginning with sight is Vittorio Gallese, "The Manifold Nature of Interpersonal Relations: The Quest for a Common Mechanism," *Philosophical Transactions of the Royal Society B, Biological Sciences* 358, no. 1431 (2003): 517–528.

5 The argument that images of wood and stone cannot be alive or have feelings, whether psychological or bodily, of the kind that humans of flesh and blood have is one of the commonest topoi in the vast anti-image literature in almost all cultures and certainly not only in Christian ones (much as the role of Christ's incarnation was used as a justification for the use of images of Him). For a discussion of this literature, especially in the Early Church Fathers and in the Protestant Reformation and after, see David Freedberg, *The Power of Images: Studies in the History and Theory of Response* (Chicago: University of Chicago Press, 1989), as well as many earlier and subsequent articles, ranging from "The Structure of Byzantine and European Iconoclasm," in *Iconoclasm*, ed. Anthony Bryer and Judith Herrin (Birmingham: Centre for Byzantine Studies, University of Birmingham, 1977), 165–177, to "The Fear of Art: How Censorship Becomes Iconoclasm," *Social Research* 83, no. 1 (2016): 67–99.

6 G. Rizzolatti, R. Camarda, L. Fogassi, M. Gentilucci, G. Luppino, and M. Matelli, "Functional Organization of Inferior Area 6 II Area F5 and the Control of Distal Movements," *Experimental Brain Research* 71 (1988): 491–507.

7 G. di Pellegrino, L. Fadiga, L. Fogassi, V. Gallese, and G. Rizzolatti, "Understanding Motor Events: A Neurophysiological Study," *Experimental Brain Research* 91 (1992): 176–180. This was followed by the two basic articles of 1996: V. Gallese, L. Fadiga, L. Fogassi, and G. Rizzolatti, "Action Recognition in the Premotor Cortex," *Brain* 119 (1996): 593–609; and L. Fadiga, V. Gallese, and L. Fogassi, "Premotor Cortex and the Recognition of Motor Actions," *Cognitive Brain Research* 3, no. 2 (1996): 131–141.

8 A. Murata, L. Fadiga, L. Fogassi, V. Gallese, V. Raos, and G. Rizzolatti, "Object Representation in the Ventral Premotor Cortex (Area F5) of the Monkey," *Journal of Neurophysiology* 78, no. 4 (1997): 2226–2230. But see also M. Jeannerod, M. A. Arbib, G. Rizzolatti, and H. Sakata, "Grasping Objects: The Cortical Mechanisms of Visuomotor Transformation," *Trends in Neuroscience*, 18, no. 7 (1995): 314–320.

9 V. Gallese, C. Keysers, and G. Rizzolatti, "A Unifying View of the Basis of Social Cognition," *Trends in Cognitive Science* 8, no. 9 (2004): 398.

10 R. Mukamel, A. D. Ekstrom, J. Kapla, M. Iacoboni, and I. Fried, "Single Neuron Responses in Humans During Execution and Observation of Actions," *Current Biology* 20 (2010): 750–756.

11 In fact, the fierce criticisms of the Rizzolatti group's assessment of the importance, significance, and functions of mirror neurons include, for example, Gregory Hickok, "Eight Problems for the Mirror Neuron Theory of Action Understanding in Monkeys and Humans," *Journal of Cognitive Neuroscience* 21, no. 7 (2009): 1229–1243. Other critics include Alfonso Caramazza at Harvard and Cecilia Heyes in Oxford, but this is not the place to enter into a refutation of their arguments or indeed those of others.

12 G. Rizzolatti, L. Fogassi, and V. Gallese, "Neurophysiological Mechanisms Underlying the Understanding and Imitation of Action," *Nature Reviews Neuroscience* 2 (2001): 661–670.

13 See not only Gallese, Keysers, and Rizzolatti, "Unifying View," but also the useful overview in Vittorio Gallese, "Embodied Simulation: From Mirror Neuron Systems to Interpersonal Relations," in *Empathy and Fairness: Novartis Foundation Symposium 278*, ed. Greg Bock and Jamie Goode (Chichester, UK: John Wiley & Sons, 2007), 3–12.

14 For a selection of the abundant literature on implied motion and its relevance to the matter of the movements that fragments so frequently imply, see note 13 above.

15 This is my summary of a much more complex process. In addition to the works cited in note 13 above, see also the important articles by Ulf Dimberg, beginning with his much-cited "Facial Reactions to Racial Expressions: Evidence for Automatic Mimicking, *Psychophysiology* 19, no. 6 (1982): 643–647, and on through Ulf Dimberg. Monika Thunberg, and Kurt Elmehed, "Unconscious Facial Reactions to Emotional Facial Expressions," *Psychological Science* 11, no. 1 (2000): 86–89.

16 Aby Warburg, *Werke in einem Band*, ed. Martin Treml, Sigrid Weigel, and Perdita Ladwig (Berlin: Suhrkamp, 2010), 107.

17 For mirror responses to implied motion, even for those implied by hidden figures, see M. A. Umiltà, E. Kohler, V. Gallese, L. Fogassi, L. Fadiga, C. Keysers, and G. Rizzolatti, "I Know What You Are Doing: A Neurophysiological Study," *Neuron* 31, no. 1 (July 19, 2001): 155–165; and M. Alessandra Umiltà, Cristina Berchio, Mariateresa Sestito, David Freedberg, and Vittorio Gallese, "Abstract Art and Cortical Motor Activation: An EEG Study," *Frontiers in Human Neuroscience* 6 (2012): 1–9. In the context of sculpture, also relevant here are Carmen Concerto, Mohamad Al Sawah, Carmenrita Infortuna, David Freedberg, Eileen Chusid, Eugenio Aguglia, and Fortunato Battaglia, "Neural Circuits Underlying Motor Facilitation During Observation of Implied Motion," *Somatosensory and Motor Research* (September 30, 2015): 1–4; and Carmen Concerto, Carmenrita Infortuna, Ludovico Mineo, Manuel Pereira, David Freedberg, Eileen Chusid, Eugenio Aguglia, and Fortunato Battaglia, "Observation of Implied Motion in a Work of Art Modulates Cortical Connectivity and Plasticity," *Journal of Exercise Rehabilitation* 12, no. 5 (2016): 417–423.

18 See David Freedberg and Vittorio Gallese, "Motion, Emotion and Empathy in Esthetic Experience," *Trends in Cognitive Science* 11, no. 5 (May 2007): 197–203.

19 Again, there is very substantial literature. Classic articles on the motor cortical and somatosensory responses one has to the mere sight of a blow visited on a rubber hand on a table before one, as well as, mutatis mutandis, to looking at a picture of attacks on either people or indeed on images are Matthew Botvinick and Jonathan Cohen, "Rubber Hands 'Feel' Touch That Eyes See," *Nature* 391, no. 6669 (February 19, 1998): 756–761; and Henrik Ehrsson, C. Spence, and Richard Passingham, "That's My Hand! Activity in Premotor Cortex Reflects Feeling of Ownership of a Limb," *Science* 305, no. 5685 (August 6, 2004): 875–877. For many examples of reactions to the sight or signs of a bodily blow, see David Freedberg, *Iconoclasm* (Chicago: University of Chicago Press, 2021). See also the references in notes 22 and 33–35 below.

20 As in Gallese et al., "A Unifying View," and his very useful summary in Gallese, "Embodied Simulation."

21 See, for example, H. H. Ehrsson, K. Wiech, N. Weiskopf, R. J. Dolan, and R. E. Passingham, "Threatening a Rubber Hand That You Feel Is Yours Elicits a Cortical Anxiety Response," *Proceedings of the National Academy of Sciences of the United States of America* 104, no. 23 (June 5, 2007): 9828–9833.

22 On all this, see the excellent study by A. Avenanti, D. Bueti, G. Galati, and S. M Aglioti, "Transcranial Magnetic Simulation Highlights the Sensorimotor Side of Empathy for Pain," *Nature Neuroscience* 8, no. 7 (July 2005): 955–960.

23 Nancy Kanwisher has done the basic research on responses to the facial fusiform area, although by now many other researchers have contributed to our understanding of this and other facial response areas in the human brain. See N. Kanwisher, J. McDermott, and M. M. Chun, "The Fusiform Face Area: A Module in Human Extrastriate Cortex Specialized for Face Perception," *Journal of Neuroscience* 17, no. 11 (June 1, 1997): 4302–4311. This was followed by a series of articles and a useful summary updating Kanwisher and her team's findings and countering criticisms (notably by Isabel Gauthier) of her modular views; see Nancy Kanwisher and Galit Yovel, "The Fusiform Face Area: A Cortical Region Specialized for the Perception of Faces," *Philosophical Transactions of the Royal Society London B, Biological Sciences* 361, no. 1476 (2006): 2109–2128.

24 On the extrastriate body area, see Beatrice de Gelder's fundamental and accessible *Emotions and the Body* (Oxford: Oxford University Press, 2016) and, for her abundant work on emotional body language, Beatrice de Gelder, "Towards the Neurobiology of Emotional Body Language," *Nature Reviews Neuroscience* 7 (2006): 242–249.

25 Jia Liu, Alison Harris, and Nancy Kanwisher, "Perception of Face Parts and Face Configurations: An fMRI Study," *Journal of Cognitive Neuroscience* 22, no. 1 (2010): 207.

26 See E. H. Gombrich, *Art and Illusion: A Study in the Psychology of Pictorial Representation* (New York: Pantheon Books, 1960), 144, 174.

27 Among the fundamental articles are P. E. Downing, Y. Jiang, M. Shuman, and N. Kanwisher, "A Cortical Area Selective for Visual Processing of the Human Body," *Science* 293, no. 5539 (2001): 2470–2473; M. V. Peelen and P. E. Downing, "The Neural Basis of Visual Body Perception," *Nature Reviews Neuroscience* 8, no. 8 (2007): 636–648; and M. V. Peelen and P. E. Downing, "Selectivity for the Human Body in the Fusiform Gyrus," *Journal of Neurophysiology* 93, no. 1 (2005): 603–608. See also Cosimo Urgesi, Giovanni Berlucchi, and Salvatore M. Aglioti, "Magnetic Stimulation of Extrastriate Body Area Impairs Visual Processing of Nonfacial Body Part," *Current Biology* 14, no. 23 (2004): 2130–2134. On the extrastriate body area as well as on the field to which she has contributed fundamental research, that of emotional body language, see De Gelder, *Emotions and the Body*.

28 V. S. Ramachandran and W. Hirstein, "The Perception of Phantom Limbs: The D. O. Hebb Lecture," *Brain* 121, no. 9 (1998): 1603–1630, remains the classic article.

29 V. S. Ramachandran, D. Rogers-Ramachandran, and S. Cobb, "Touching the Phantom Limb," *Nature* 377, no. 6549 (1995): 489–490.

30 As in David Freedberg, "From Absorption to Judgement: Empathy in Aesthetic Response," in *Empathy: Epistemic Problems and Cultural-Historical Problems of a Cross-Disciplinary Context*, ed. Vanessa Lux and Sigrid Weigel (London: Palgrave-Macmillan, 2017), 139–180. Outside my own work and that of the mirror neuron team, see the important work of Jean Decety, such as the useful summary in J. Decety and P. L. Jackson, "The Functional Architecture of Human Empathy," *Behavior and Cognitive Neuroscience Reviews* 3, no. 2 (2004): 71–100.

31 See P. L. Jackson, A. N. Meltzoff, and J. Decety, "How Do We Perceive the Pain of Others? A Window into the Neural Processes Involved in Empathy," *NeuroImage* 24 (2005): 771–779; L. Carr, M. Jacoboni, M-C Dubeau, and G. L. Lenzi, "Neural Mechanisms of Empathy in Humans: A Relay from Neural Systems for Imitation to Limbic Areas," *Proceedings of the National Academy of Sciences* 100, no. 9 (2003): 5497–5502; and S. D. Preston and F. B. De Waal, "Empathy: Its Ultimate and Proximate Bases," *Behavioral and Brain Sciences* 25, no. 1 (2002): 1–20.

32 While the initial studies of blindsight were made in 1974 by Lawrence Weiskrantz, Beatrice de Gelder has long been in the forefront of research on the phenomenon of affective blindsight, beginning with Beatrice de Gelder, Jean Vroomen, Gilles Pourtois, and Lawrence Weiskrantz, "Non-Conscious Recognition of Affect in the Absence of Striate Cortex," *NeuroReport* 10, no. 18 (1999): 3759–3763; but see also Marco Tamietto and Beatrice de Gelder, "Affective Blindsight in the Intact Brain: Neural Interhemispheric Summation for Unseen Fearful Expressions," *Neuropsychologia* 46, no. 3 (2008): 820–828.

33 As in F. Battaglia, S. Lisanby, and D. Freedberg, "Corticomotor Excitability During Observation and Imagination of a Work of Art," *Frontiers in Human Neuroscience* 5, no. 79 (2011): 1–6. Compare also the early experiments with monkey hand actions, as in T. Brochier, R. L. Spinks, M. A. Umilta, and R. N. Lemon, "Patterns of Muscle Activity Underlying Object-Specific Grasp by the Macaque Monkey," *Journal of Neurophysiology* 92, no. 3 (2004): 1770–1782, with those of humans, as in B. Sbriscia-Fioretti, C. Berchio, D. Freedberg, V. Gallese, and M. A. Umiltà, "ERP Modulation During Observation of Abstract Paintings by Franz Kline," *PloS One* 8, no. 10 (2013), 1–6.

See also the substantial literature on motor-cortex and premotor responses to sight of wounds and blows to the body. Always striking are the responses to sight of hands about to strike or hammers about to deliver blows as, for example, Ehrsson et al., "That's My Hand," and Ehrsson et al., "Threatening a Rubber Hand." Critical to the matter of self-attribution of seen blows and assaults by others is M. Tsakiris and P. Haggard, "The Rubber Hand Illusion Revisited: Visuotactile Integration and Self-Attribution," *Journal of Experimental Psychology: Human Perception and Performance* 31, no. 1 (2005): 80–91. Of course, the mirror experiments make clear not just the matter of self-attribution but also the cortical imitative firings upon sight of the movements and reactions of another, as discussed in the section on mirror neurons above. See also F. de Vignemont and P. Haggard, "Action Observation and Execution: What Is Shared?," *Social Neuroscience* 3, no. 3–4 (2008): 421–433.

34 See, for example, Keysers et al., "A Touching Sight."

35 As noted and illustrated in Freedberg, *Iconoclasm*, esp. 12–15, 77–80, although commented on in many of my earlier articles on iconoclasm (as listed in the bibliography of *Iconoclasm*) and Freedberg, *The Power of Images*, 412–415.

36 All illustrated as well in, for example, Ehrsson et al., "That's My Hand," and Tsakiris and Haggard, "Rubber Hand Illusion Revisited."

37 For a good introduction to modal and amodal vision, see Bence Nanay, "The Importance of Amodal Completion in Everyday Perception," *i-Perception* 9, no. 4 (2018): 1–16.

38 Nanay, "Importance of Amodal Completion."

39 For Stephen Kosslyn's fundamental research on this topic largely on the basis of PET experiments, see, among many others, S. M. Kosslyn, N. M. Alpert, W. L. Thompson, V. Maljkovic, S. B. Weise, C. F. Chabris, S. E. Hamilton, S. L. Rauch, and F. S. Buonanno, "Visual Mental Imagery Activates Topographically Organized Visual Cortex: PET Investigations," *Journal of Cognitive Neuroscience* 5, no. 3 (1993): 263–287; and S. M. Kosslyn, W. L. Thompson, and N. M. Alpert, "Neural Systems Shared by Visual Imagery and Visual Perception: A Positron Emission Tomography Study," *NeuroImage* 6, no. 4 (1997): 320–334. But see also the later articles, all relevant, in the following note, on the similarities and dissimilarities between the neural substrates of perception and imagery.

40 See the excellent review by Joel Pearson, "The Human Imagination: The Cognitive Neuroscience of Visual Mental Imagery," *Natures Reviews Neuroscience* 20 (2019): 624–634. Joel Pearson, T. Naselaris, E. A. Holmes, and S. M. Kosslyn, "Mental Imagery: Functional Mechanisms and Clinical Applications," *Trends in Cognitive Science* 19, no. 10 (2015): 590. For cautions about exaggerating the overlap, see Kalanit Grill-Spector and, Rafael Malach, "The Human Visual Cortex," *Annual Review of Neuroscience* 27, no. 1 (2004): 649–677; and Amir Amedi, Rafael Malach, and Alvaro Pascual-Leone, "Negative BOLD Differentiates Visual Imagery and Perception," *Neuron* 48, no. 5 (2005): 859–872.

41 Predictive coding is an influential model of cortical neural activity. It proposes that perceptual beliefs are furnished by sequentially minimizing "prediction errors—the differences between predicted and observed data." A. Tschantz, B. Millidge, A. K. Seth, and C. L. Buckley, "Hybrid Predictive Coding: Inferring, Fast and Slow," *PLoS Computational Biology* 19, no. 8 (2023): e1011280. See the now-classic Karl Friston and Stefan Kiebel, "Predictive Coding Under the Free-Energy Principle," *Philosophical Transactions of the*

Royal Society London B, Biological Sciences 364, no. 1521 (2009): 1211–1221. See also Tschantz et al., "Hybrid Predictive Coding," which contains a useful introduction prior to moving on to the computational dimensions of these issues.

42 See, for example, Hanneke E. M. den Ouden, Jean Daunizeau, Jonathan Roiser, Karl J Friston, and Klaas E. Stephan, "Striatal Prediction Error Modulates Cortical Coupling," *Journal of Neuroscience* 30, no. 9 (2010): 3210–3219.

43 R. L. Buckner, J. R. Andrews-Hanna, and D. L. Schacter, "The Brain's Default Network: Anatomy, Function, and Relevance to Disease," *Annals of the New York Academy of Sciences* 1124 (2008): 1–38. For an updated anatomical and functional account, see R. L. Buckner and L. M. DiNicola, "The Brain's Default Network: Updated Anatomy, Physiology, and Evolving Insights," *Nature Reviews Neuroscience* 20, no. 10 (2019): 593–608.

44 For a still more recent overview, see V. Menon, "20 Years of the Default Mode Network: A Review and Synthesis," *Neuron* 111, no. 16 (2023): 2469–2487.

45 Zheng Zhang, Delong Zhang, Zengjian Wang, Junchao Li, Yuting Lin, Song Chang, Ruiwang Huang, and Ming Liu, "Intrinsic Neural Linkage Between Primary Visual Area and Default Mode Network in Human Brain: Evidence from Visual Mental Imagery," *Neuroscience* 379 (2018): 13–21.

46 On this link, see also Pearson, *Human Imagination*, 624.

47 See the important article by Gallese, "Manifold Nature" (see note 4 above).

48 Few have written more eloquently on this tension than Walter Benjamin. He does so most powerfully in his skeptical reflections on empathy, which include many comments on the subject of fragments. They are directly tied to the ways in which Benjamin develops his concepts of history, cultural heritage, and the kinds of involvement one must have not just with the victors who carry off the spoils of history but also with those who made them. See Walter Benjamin, *The Arcades Project*, trans. Howard Eiland and Kevin McLaughlin (Cambridge, MA: Belknap Press of Harvard University Press, 1999), 846, and the famous section VII of his "On the Concept of History," in Walter Benjamin, *Selected Writings*, vol. 4, *1938–1940*, ed. Howard Eiland and Michael W. Jennings, trans. Edmund Jephcott (Cambridge, MA: Belknap Press of Harvard University Press, 2006), 392–396.

DISMEMBERING AND REMEMBERING BODIES

1 Maurice Merleau-Ponty, *Phenomenology of Perception*, trans. Donald A. Landes (New York: Routledge 2014), 146, 147. Originally published as *Phénoménologie de la perception* (Paris: Éditions Gallimard, 1945).

2 David Bohm, *Wholeness and the Implicate Order* (London: Routledge, 2002), 20.

3 Bohm, *Wholeness and the Implicate Order*, 3.

4 David Bohm, "Fragmentation and Wholeness in Religion and Science," *Zygon: Journal of Religion and Science* 20, no. 2 (1985): 130.

5 Julia Guernsey, *Human Figuration in Preclassic Mesoamerica: From Figurines to Sculpture* (Cambridge: Cambridge University Press, 2020), 96.

6 Anna Sörman, Astrid A. Noterman, and Markus Fjellström, "Fragmentation in Archaeological Context—Studying the Incomplete," in *Broken Bodies, Places and Objects: New Perspectives on Fragmentation in Archaeology*, ed. Anna Sörman, Astrid A. Noterman, and Markus Fjellström (London: Routledge, 2023), 9.

7 Jason Rasmussen, "Fragmented Remains: A Case for Social Memory vs. Violence," *Chronika* 8 (2018): 15–25.

8 Roy Wagner, "The Fractal Person," in *Big Men and Great Men: Personifications of Power in Melanesia*, ed. Maurice Godelier and Marilyn Strathern (Cambridge, UK: Cambridge University Press, 1991), 159–173.

9 John Chapman, *Fragmentation in Archaeology: People, Places and Broken Objects in the Prehistory of South Eastern Europe* (London: Routledge, 2000), 23.

10 John Chapman and Bisserka Gaydarska, "The Fragmentation Premise in Archaeology: From the Paleolithic to More Recent Times," in *The Fragment: An Incomplete History*, ed. William Tronzo (Los Angeles: Getty Research Institute, 2009), 132.

11 John Chapman and Bisserka Gaydarska, *Parts and Wholes: Fragmentation in Prehistoric Context* (Oxford: Oxbow Books, 2006), 8.

12 Lauren E. Talalay, "Rethinking the Function of Clay Figurine Legs from Neolithic Greece: An Argument by Analogy," *American Journal of Archaeology* 91, no. 2 (1987): 161–169.

13 Guernsey, *Human Figuration in Preclassic Mesoamerica*, 111.

14 Colin Renfrew, Michael Boyd, and Christopher Bronk Ramsey, "The Oldest Maritime Sanctuary? Dating the Sanctuary at Keros and the Cycladic Early Bronze Age," *Antiquity* 86, no. 331 (2012): 144–160.

15 Alexander Aston, "How the Cycladic Islanders Found Their Marbles: Engagement, Social Cognition and the Emergence of Keros," *Cambridge Archaeological Journal* 30, no. 4 (2020): 589.

16 Aston, "How the Cycladic Islanders Found Their Marbles," 594.

17 Elizabeth A. Hendrix, "Painted Early Cycladic Figures: An Exploration of Context and Meaning," *Hesperia: The Journal of the American School of Classical Studies at Athens* 72, no. 4 (2003): 420.

18 Hendrix, "Painted Early Cycladic Figures," 444.

19 Colin Renfrew, *The Cycladic Spirit: Masterpieces from the Nicholas P. Golandris Collection* (London: Thames & Hudson, 1991), 124.

20 Harada Masayuki, "Dogū Broken and Enshrined: Traces of a Jōmon World View," in *The Power of Dogū: Ceramic Figures from Ancient Japan*, ed. Simon Kaner (London: British Museum Press, 2009), 53.

21 Masayuki, "Dogū Broken and Enshrined," 50.

22 Ilona Bausch, "Fragmentation Practices in Central Japan: Middle Jōmon Clay Figurines at Shakado," in *Anthropomorphic and Zoomorphic Miniature Figures in Eurasia, Africa and Meso-America: Morphology, Materiality, Technology, Function and Context*, ed. Dragos Gheorghiu and Ann Cyphers (Oxford: Archaeopress, 2010), 101.

23 Cornelius Holtorf, "On Pastness: A Reconsideration of Materiality in Archaeological Object Authenticity," *Anthropological Quarterly* 86, no. 2 (2013): 431.

24 Holtorf, "On Pastness," 434.

25 Alois Riegl, "Der moderne Denkmalkultus: Sein Wesen und seine Entstehung" (Vienna: Braumüller, 1903). Republished in Alois Riegl, *Gesammelte Aufsätze*, ed. K. Swoboda and H. Sedlmayr (Vienna-Augsburg: Filser, 1929). English translation published as "The Modern Cult of Monuments: Its Character and Its Origin," trans. Kurt W. Forster and Diane Ghirardo, *Oppositions*, no. 25 (1982): 21–51.

26 Laurent Olivier, *The Dark Abyss of Time: Archaeology and Memory*, trans. Arthur Greenspan (Lanham: Rowman & Littlefield, 2011), Kindle edition, chap. 5.

27 Olivier, *Dark Abyss of Time*, chap. 4

28 Lucy Huskinson, "Uncanny Places," *The Psychologist* (published by the British Psychological Society), October 11, 2021, https://www.bps.org.uk/psychologist/uncanny-places.

WHAT THE FRAGMENT WANTS

1 W. J. T. Mitchell, "What Do Pictures *Really* Want?," *October* 77 (1996): 71–82.

2 Mitchell, "What Do Pictures *Really* Want?," 72.

3 Wai Chee Dimock, "A Theory of Resonance," *PMLA* 112, no. 5 (1997): 1197 (abstract).

4 Georgina Kleege, *More Than Meets the Eye: What Blindness Brings to Art* (New York: Oxford University Press, 2018).

5 John Ruskin, *Aratra Pentelici: Six Lectures on the Elements of Sculpture, Given Before the University of Oxford in Michelmas Term, 1870* (New York: John Wiley & Sons, 1872), 20.

6 John Ruskin, "The Lamp of Memory," chap. 6 in *The Seven Lamps of Architecture* (London: Smith, Elder, 1849).

7 John Keats, "Ode on a Grecian Urn," Poetry Foundation, https://www.poetryfoundation.org/poems/44477/ode-on-a-grecian-urn.

8 Percy Bysshe Shelley, "Ozymandias," Poetry Foundation, https://www.poetryfoundation.org/poems/46565/ozymandias.

9 William Butler Yeats, "Sailing to Byzantium," Poetry Foundation, https://www.poetryfoundation.org/poems/43291/sailing-to-byzantium.

10 Kathryn Harrison, "What Remains: The Lure of Relics in a Faithless Age," *Harper's Magazine*, December 1995, 55.

11 Marc Quinn, "Artworks: *Alison Lapper Pregnant*," http://marcquinn.com/artworks/single/alison-lapper-pregnant1.

12 Ann Millett, "Sculpting Body Ideals: *Alison Lapper Pregnant* and the Public Display of Disability," *Disability Studies Quarterly* 28, no. 3 (2008), https://doi.org/10.18061/dsq.v28i3.122. See also Maev Kennedy, "Pregnant and Proud: Statue of Artist Wins Place in Trafalgar Square," *The Guardian*, March 16, 2004, https://www.theguardian.com/uk/2004/mar/16/arts.artsnews; Hadley Freeman, "'Why shouldn't my body be art?,'" *The Guardian*, March 17, 2004, https://www.theguardian.com/artanddesign/2004/mar/17/art.fashion; and Rachel Cooke, "Bold, Brave, Beautiful," *The Guardian*, September 18, 2005, https://www.theguardian.com/artanddesign/2005/sep/18/art.

13 Erving Goffman, *Stigma: Notes on the Management of Spoiled Identity* (New York: Simon & Schuster, 1963), 4–5.

14 Laurie Clements Lambeth, "The Three-Legged Dog Who Carried Me," *New York Times*, December 7, 2016, https://www.nytimes.com/2016/12/07/opinion/the-three-legged-dog-who-carried-me.html.

PATTERNS OF DESTRUCTION

1 Carl Nylander, "Breaking the Cup of Kingship: An Elamite Coup in Nineveh?," *Iranica Antiqua* 34, no. 2 (1999): 71–93. For more on the fall of Assyria, see John MacGinnis, "The Fall of Assyria and the Aftermath of the Empire," in *I Am Ashurbanipal: King of the World, King of Assyria*, ed. Gareth Brereton (London: Thames & Hudson; in collaboration with the British Museum, 2018), 276–285.

2 Christopher Walker and Michael B. Dick, "The Induction of the Cult Image in Ancient Mesopotamia: The Mesopotamian *mīs pî* Ritual," in *Born in Heaven, Made on Earth: The Making of the Cult Image in the Ancient Near East*, ed. Michael B. Dick (Winona Lake, IN: Eisenbrauns, 1999), 55–122.

3 Hans Belting, *Likeness and Presence: A History of the Image Before the Era of Art*, trans. Edmund Jephcott (Chicago: University of Chicago Press, 1994), 1–13.

4 See, for example, the commission and installation of Neo-Assyrian monoliths such as the so-called Kurkh Monolith, which celebrated Shalmaneser III's victory at the Battle of Qarqar in 853 BCE against allied Syrio-Levantine forces (British Museum, 118884), and the Black Obelisk, depicting Shalmaneser III receiving tribute from vassal nations (British Museum, 118885).

5 David Freedberg, *Iconoclasm* (Chicago: University of Chicago Press, 2021), 1–16.

6 For a comprehensive overview of the Akkadian period, see Benjamin R. Foster, *The Age of Agade: Inventing Empire in Ancient Mesopotamia* (London: Routledge, 2016). For analysis of nineteenth- and early twentieth-century reception and designation of Akkad as imperial, see Marian H. Feldman, "Naturalism, Photography, and Empire," in *Mortals, Deities and Divine Symbols: Rethinking Ancient Imagery from the Levant to Mesopotamia; Studies Offered to Tallay Ornan* (Bicester, UK: Archaeopress, 2025), 39–48.

7 Anne Porter, "When the Subject *Is* the Object: Relational Ontologies, the Partible Person and Images of Naram-Sin," in *Critical Approaches to Ancient Near Eastern Art*, ed. Brian A. Brown and Marian H. Feldman (Berlin: De Gruyter, 2014), 597–617.

8 See Irene J. Winter, "What/When Is a Portrait? Royal Images of the Ancient Near East," *Proceedings of the American Philosophical Society* 153, no. 3 (September 2009): 254–270; and Melissa Eppihimer, "Assembling King and State: The Statues of Manishtushu and the Consolidation of Akkadian Kingship," *American Journal of Archaeology* 114 (2010): 365–380, esp. 366–372.

9 The German archaeologists working in 1908 were excavating a Middle Assyrian temple to Ištar and a Late Assyrian temple to Nabû. On the sculpture in the context of this excavation campaign, see Walter Andrae, *Das wiedererstandene Assur, 2. durchgesehene und erweiterte Auflage*, ed. Barthel Hrouda (Munich: Beck, 1997), 127–129.

10 Edward Bleiberg, "Why Are the Noses Broken on Egyptian Statues?," in Edward Bleiberg and Stephanie Weissberg, *Striking Power: Iconoclasm in Ancient Egypt* (New York: Brooklyn Museum; St. Louis: Pulitzer Arts Foundation, 2019), 27–64, esp. 48.

11 Elisabeth R. O'Connell, "Living with the Monumental Past," in *Egypt: Faith After the Pharaohs*, ed. Cäcilia Fluck, Gisela Helmecke, and Elisabeth R. O'Connell (London: British Museum Press, 2015), 92.

12 According to a passage in the Jewish *Mishna*, one is advised to nullify the power of an idol by cutting "off the tip of its ear, the tip of its nose, the tip of its finger." See Troels Myrup Kristensen, "Embodied Images: Christian Response and Destruction in Late Antique Egypt," *Journal of Late Antiquity* 2, no. 2 (2009): 224–250, esp. 231. See also Stephanie Lenk, "Iconoclasm," in *Imagining the Divine: Art and the Rise of World Religions*, ed. Jaś Elsner and Stefanie Lenk (Oxford: Ashmolean Museum, University of Oxford, 2017), 128–133.

13 It is not known if the attack on Germanicus's features and the carving of the cross were done in the same or separate attacks.

14 Kristensen, "Embodied Images," 230.

15 O'Connell, "Living with the Monumental Past," 96.

16 Keith P. F. Moxey, "Image Criticism in the Netherlands Before the Iconoclasm of 1566," *Nederlands archief voor kerkgeschiedenis* 57, no. 2 (1977): 148–162, esp. 149–150; David Freedberg, "Art and Iconoclasm, 1525–1580: The Case of the Northern Netherlands," in *Kunst voor de beeldenstorm: Noordnederlandse kunst 1525–1580*, ed. J. P. Filedt Kok, Willy Halsema-Kubes, and W. Th. Kloek (Amsterdam: Rijksmuseum, 1986), 69–84.

17 Martin Sallmann, "The Reformation in Bern," in *A Companion to the Swiss Reformation*, ed. Amy Nelson Burnett and Emidio Campi (Leiden: Brill, 2016), 127–169, esp. 143–150.

18 On the tomb and other archaeological finds at Romainmôtier, see Brigitte Pradervand and Nicolas Schätti, "Inhumations et fondations funéraires dans l'église prieurale (XIe–début du XVIe siècle)," in *Romainmôtier restaurée, 1991–2001: L'église et son décor (XIe–XXe siècle)*, Cahiers d'archéologie romande 145, ed. Brigitte Pradervand and Nicolas Schätti (Lausanne: Cahiers d'archéologie romande, 2014), 86–117, esp. 87–88; and Peter Eggenberger, "Synthèse des résultats des recherches archéologiques: L'évolution architecturale de Romainmôtier de la période gallo-romaine à la sécularisation du prieuré après la Réforme, en 1537," in *Romainmôtier: Mille ans de monachisme; Résultats des recherces archéologiques entre 1971 et 2006*, Cahiers d'archéologie romande 183, ed. Peter Eggenberger (Lausanne: Cahiers d'archéologie romande, 2020), 29–168, esp. 156–158.

19 Brigitte Pradervand, Nicholas Schätti, and Jacques Bujard, "Les tombeaux monumentaux en Suisse romande à la fin du Moyen Âge," in *Le marbre et la poussière: Le patrimoine funéraire de la Suisse romande, XIVe–XVIIIe siècles*, Cahiers d'archéologie romande 143, ed. Dave Lüthi (Lausanne: Cahiers d'archéologie romande, 2013), 35–52.

20 Byron Ellsworth Hamann, "Producing Idols," *Latin American and Latinx Visual Culture* 1, no. 1 (2019): 25.

21 Barbara E. Mundy, "Extirpation of Idolatry and Sensory Experience in Sixteenth-Century Mexico," in *Sensational Religion: Sensory Cultures in Material Practice*, ed. Sally M. Promey (New Haven, CT: Yale University Press, 2014), 515–535.

22 On the Chalchiuhtlicue and Coatlicue statues of the Templo Mayor, see Elizabeth H. Boone, "The 'Coatlicues' at the Templo Mayor," *Ancient Mesoamerica* 10, no. 2 (1999): 189–206; Leonardo López Luján and Marie-France Fauvet-Berthelot, "El último dibujo faltante de la descripción histórica y cronológica de Antonio de León y Gama," *Arqueología Mexicana* 29, no. 172 (2022): 76–85; and Leonardo López Luján, *El capitán Guillermo Dupaix y su album arqueológico de 1794* (Mexico City: Instituto Nacional de Anthropología e Historia, 2015), 158–169.

23 On the status of greenstone in images of Chalchiuhtlicue, see Danièle Dehouve, "The Rules of Construction of an Aztec Deity: Chalchiuhtlicue, the Goddess of Water," *Ancient Mesoamerica* 31, no. 1 (2020): 7–28; and Alison Caplan, entry in Joanne Pillsbury, Timothy Potts, and Kim N. Richter, eds., *Golden Kingdoms: Luxury Arts in the Ancient Americas* (Los Angeles: J. Paul Getty Museum and the Getty Research Institute, 2017), 258.

24 On the status of the relationship between Coatlicue's body and her serpent skirt, see Cecelia F. Klein, "A New Interpretation of the Aztec Statue Called Coatlicue, 'Snakes-Her-Skirt,'" *Ethnohistory* 55, no. 2 (2008): 229–250; and Ann De León, "Coatlicue or How to Write the Dismembered Body," *MLN* 125, no. 2 (2010): 259–286.

25 On the New Fire ceremony, see Emily Umberger, "Aztec Art in Provincial Places: Water Concerns, Monumental Sculptures, and Imperial Expansion," in *Altera Roma: Art and Empire from Mérida to Mexico*, ed. John. M. D. Pohl and Claire L. Lyons (Los Angeles: Cotsen Institute of Archaeology Press, 2016), 109–145; and Byron Ellsworth Hamann, "Chronological Pollution: Potsherds, Mosques, and Broken Gods Before and After the Conquest of Mexico," *Current Anthropology* 49, no. 5 (2008): 803–836.

26 Hamann, "Producing Idols," 25.

27 Serge Gruzinski, *Images at War: Mexico from Columbus to "Blade Runner" (1492–2019)*, trans. Heather MacLean (Durham, NC: Duke University Press, 2001), 30–52.

28 Rachel Kousser, *The Afterlives of Greek Sculpture: Interaction, Transformation, and Destruction* (New York: Cambridge University Press, 2017), 94.

29 Kousser, *Afterlives of Greek Sculpture*, 97. For the grave marker, see Paul Zanker, *Afterlives: Ancient Greek Funerary Monuments in the Metropolitan Museum of Art* (New York: Scala, in association with Metropolitan Museum of Art, 2022), no. 6, 38–39.

30 Seth Estrin, *Grief Made Marble: Funerary Sculpture in Classical Athens* (New Haven, CT: Yale University Press, 2023), 18.

31 Thomas C. Rose, "Demetrius the Besieger (and Fortifier) of Cities," in *Brill's Companion to Sieges in the Ancient Mediterranean*, ed. Jeremy Armstrong and Matthew Trundle (Leiden: Brill, 2019), 169–190, esp. 176.

32 Caroline Houser, "Alexander's Influence on Greek Sculpture: As Seen in a Portrait in Athens," *Studies in the History of Art* 10, Symposium Series I: Macedonia and Greece in Late Classical and Early Hellenistic Times (1982): 231.

33 Livy, *History of Rome,* 31.44.4–5.

34 For excavation history, see T. Leslie Shear Jr., "The Athenian Agora: Excavations of 1971," *Hesperia: The Journal of the American School of Classical Studies in Athens* 42, no. 2 (1973): 121–179.

35 Dario Gamboni, *The Destruction of Art: Iconoclasm and Vandalism Since the French Revolution* (New Haven, CT: Yale University Press, 1997), 31–36.

36 See Jean-Marie Apostolidès, *Le roi-machine: Spectacle et politique au temps de Louis XIV* (Paris: Éditions de Minuit, 1981), 14; Stephen Rombouts, "Art as Propaganda in Eighteenth-Century France: The Paradox of Edme Bouchardon's Louis XV," *Eighteenth-Century Studies* 27, no. 2 (1993–1994): 255–282; and Andrew McClellan, "The Life and Death of a Royal Monument: Bouchardon's Louis XV," *Oxford Art Journal* 23, no. 2 (2000): 1–27, esp. 13–16.

37 McClellan, "Life and Death of a Royal Monument," 25–27.

38 Arthur de Boislisle, "Notice historiques sur la Place des Victoires et sur la Place de Vendôme," *Mémoires de la société de l'histoire de Paris et de l'Île de France* 15 (1888): 1–272, esp. 203.

39 McClellan, "Life and Death of a Royal Monument," 25.

40 *Courier français*, August 30, 1792, 6; cited in McClellan, "Life and Death of a Royal Monument," 25.

41 Klara Broekhuijsen-Kruijer, "Het Passieretabel uit Soest," *Bulletin van het Rijksmuseum* 32, no. 1 (1984): 3–16; Bas Nederveen, "Het passieretabel van Soest: Kanttekeningen bij een reconstructie," *Bulletin van het Rijksmuseum* 52, no. 3–4 (2004): 270–281; Bram van den Hoven van Genderen, entry in Micha Leeflang and Kees van Schooten, eds., *Middeleeuwse beelden uit Utrecht, 1430–1530* (Utrecht: Museum Catharijneconvent, 2012), 218–223.

42 See A. J. Wall, "The Statues of King George III and the Honorable William Pitt Erected in New York City, 1770," *New York Historical Society Quarterly Bulletin* 4, no. 2 (1920): 4–57; Wendy Bellion, *Iconoclasm in New York: Revolution to Reenactment* (University Park: Pennsylvania State University Press, 2019), 77–82, 97–99, 109–110, 114–122; Stacy Boldrick, *Iconoclasm and the Museum* (New York: Routledge, 2020), 98–108; and Erin L. Thompson, *Smashing Statues: The Rise and Fall of America's Public Monuments* (New York: W. W. Norton, 2021), 3–12.

43 Jerrold S. Cooper, *Enki and the World Order: A Sumerian Myth* (Berlin: De Gruyter, 2025), 4–12.

44 Zainab Bahrani, *Rituals of War: The Body and Violence in Mesopotamia* (New York: Zone Books, 2008), 9–10; Carl von Clausewitz, *On War*, trans. J. J. Graham (Middlesex, England: Penguin, 1968).

45 Horst Bredekamp, *Image Acts: A Systematic Approach to Visual Agency*, trans. Elizabeth Clegg (Berlin: De Gruyter, 2018), 186–192; Freedberg, *Iconoclasm*, 19–49; Aaron Tugendhaft, *The Idols of ISIS: From Assyria to the Internet* (Chicago: University of Chicago Press, 2020), 75–96; Charlotte Klonk, *Terror: When Images Become Weapons* (Manchester: Manchester University Press, 2020), 168–197; Eugenia Roldán and Manuel Molina, "Iconoclasm as a Critique of the Digital Scopic Regime," *Studies in Visual Arts and Communication* 11, no. 1 (2024): 15–23.

46 José Fernández Vega, "War as 'Art': Aesthetics and Politics in Clausewitz's Social Thinking," in *Clausewitz in the Twenty-First Century*, ed. Hew Strachan and Andreas Herberg-Rothe (Oxford: Oxford University Press, 2007), 122–137, esp. 137.

47 For the most recent and comprehensive overview of the Tell Halaf restorations, see Nadja Cholidis and Lutz Martin, eds., *Tell Halaf V: Im Krieg zerstörte Denkmäler und ihre Restaurierung* (Berlin: De Gruyter, 2010), 1–21.

48 Chea Socheat, Muong Chanraksmey, and Louise Tythacott, "The Looting of Koh Ker and the Return of the Prasat Chen Statues," in *Returning Southeast Asia's Past: Objects, Museums, and Restitution*, ed. Louise Tythacott and Panggah Ardiyansyah (Singapore: National University of Singapore Press, 2021), 62–86, esp. 66–67; Brigitta Hauser-Schäublin, "Looted, Trafficked, Donated, and Returned: The Twisted Tracks of Cambodian Antiquities," in *Cultural Property and Contested Ownership: The Trafficking of Artefacts and the Quest for Restitution*, ed. Brigitta Hauser-Schäublin and Lyndel V. Prott (London: Routledge, 2016), 64–81, esp. 65–69.

49 Khuon Narim, "Ancient Khmer Rama Statue Officially Received by Government," *Cambodia Daily*, March 29, 2016, https://english.cambodiadaily.com/2016/03/29/ancient-khmer-rama-statue-officially-received-by-government/.

50 Masha Lafont, *Pillaging Cambodia: The Illicit Traffic in Khmer Art* (Jefferson, NC: McFarland, 2004), 67; Simon Mackenzie and Tess Davis, "Temple Looting in Cambodia: Anatomy of a Statue Trafficking Network," *British Journal of Criminology* 54, no. 5 (2014): 722–740.

51 Keiko Miura, "Destruction and Plunder of Cambodian Cultural Heritage and Their Consequences," in Hauser-Schäublin and Prott, *Cultural Property and Contested Ownership*, 23–44; Socheat, Muong, and Tythacott, "Looting of Koh Ker," 68–71.

FROM FRAGMENT TO FRAGMENT

I want to thank Anna Serotta, conservator in the Sherman Fairchild Center for Objects Conservation at the Metropolitan Museum of Art, for providing access to the object and for her generous sharing of knowledge on ancient Egyptian stone-working technologies. See Anna Serotta, "Reading Tool Marks on Egyptian Stone Sculpture," *Rivista del Museo Egizio* 7 (2023), https://doi.org/10.29353/rime.2023.5098.

1 Rosemarie Klemm and Dietrich D. Klemm, *Stones and Quarries in Ancient Egypt* (London: British Museum Press, 2008). In addition to Serotta and Klemm and Klemm, seminal work on stone Egyptian technologies has been done over many years by James Harrell. See, for example, James A. Harrell, *Archaeology and Geology of Ancient Egyptian Stone* (Oxford: Archaeopress, 2024).

2 Silicified sandstone or orthoquartzite should be distinguished from metaquartzites. While both are hard stones composed of almost only quartz, orthoquartzites are of sedimentary genesis, and *meta*quartzites are—as the name implies—generated in the high temperature and pressure environments of metamorphic activity.

3 The process that employed drilling and so-called feathers and wedges (assisted by the wetting of the wooden wedges) was thought not to have been employed until much later than the time of this figure.

4 Attempting to determine the original context of the fragment is both intriguing and frustrating. Given how little stone remains beyond the barest perimeter of the face, the fragment may have come from a sphinx, such as another *Senwosret III* at the Metropolitan Museum of Art (17.9.2), or from a standing, kneeling, or seated figure. In addition, there is no documentation related to its removal or provenance. See Simon Connor and Luc Delvaux, "Ehnasya (Heracleopolis Magna) et les colossus en quartzite de Sésostris III," *Chronique d'Egypte* 92, no. 184 (July 2017): 247–265.

5 On flint (and chert), see Michael Kobusiewicz, *The Production, Use and Importance of Flint Tools in the Archaic Period and the Old Kingdom in Egypt* (Oxford: Archaeopress, 2016).

6 Abrasives of emery (corundum) have long been postulated as the materials for shaping and polishing due to the mineral's hardness, although their employment for ancient Egyptian stone working has not been demonstrated.

7 See Edward Bleiberg and Stephanie Weissberg, *Striking Power: Iconoclasm in Ancient Egypt* (New York: Brooklyn Museum; St. Louis: Pulitzer Arts Foundation, 2019).

8 See note 4 above.

FRAGMENTS AND POWER

1 The first museums were established by colonial elites. For example, the first museum in South Asia was the Indian Museum in Kolkata, established in 1814 by William Jones and the Asiatic Society of Bengal. For an overview, see Saloni Mathur and Kavita Singh, eds., *No Touching, No Spitting, No Praying: The Museum in South Asia* (New Delhi: Routledge, 2015).

2 Shuchen Wang, "Museum Coloniality: Displaying Asian Art in the Whitened Context," *International Journal of Cultural Policy* 27, no. 6 (September 2021): 720–737. For additional viewpoints, see Stanley K. Abe et al., "Pulitzer Foundation Workshop," *Archives of Asian Art* 62 (2012): 81–103.

3 For China, see Stanley K. Abe, *Imagining Sculpture: A Short Conjectural History* (Munich: Hirmer, 2022).

4 Stanley Abe and Jaś Elsner, "Introduction: Some Stakes of Comparison," in *Comparativism in Art History*, ed. Jaś Elsner (London: Routledge, 2017), 1–15.

5 Participation by women as artists and patrons in the arts of the brush, including Buddhist painting, is a developing field of inquiry. See Soohyun Yoon, "Chinese Women Artists and New Manifestations of Guanyin, 1550–1750" (PhD diss., Duke University, 2023).

6 The earliest extant biography and evaluation of artists dates from the ninth century. See William Reynolds Beal Acker, *Some T'ang and Pre-T'ang Texts on Chinese Painting, Translated and Annotated* (Leiden: E. J. Brill, 1954, 1974).

7 Patronage for sculpture was enthusiastic and widespread. But for many of the educated classes, Buddhist or Daoist gods for a family altar or molded servant figures for a tomb were common, even superstitious, objects, not to be thought of as fine art. Ancient stone Buddha images were found by chance, dusty and dirty, hardly appropriate for display as a treasure in a refined or elegant home interior. Even when rare, such objects were intimately associated with death and the tomb. Buddhism was also associated with death, as monks have long been responsible for funerary rites in East Asia.

In Japan inscriptions on old statues do record the names of some esteemed sculptors. For example, the Kei school of the Kamakura period was led by the masters Kaikei (1185–1223) and Unkei (1151–1223). Master sculptors trained apprentices in the making of wood statues. The appearance of multiple hands suggests a sophisticated system for meeting the demands of Buddhist temples. But it should be noted that Japanese statues were meant for use only in temples. Such works were not sold or traded. See Miyeko Murase, *Bridge of Dreams: The Mary Griggs Burke Collection of Japanese Art* (New York: Metropolitan Museum of Art, 2000), 70–78 and 411.

8 See the list of deposits in Shandong province in Zhang Zong, "The Region of Qingzhou as a Center of Buddhist Art in the Sixth Century," in *Return of the Buddha: The Qingzhou Discoveries*, ed. Lukas Nickel (London: Royal Academy of Arts, 2002), 65–66.

9 Lukas Nickel, "Longxing Temple in Qingzhou and the Discovery of the Sculpture Hoard," in Nickel, *Return of the Buddha*, 34–43; Zhang Bohan and Xiao Shying, "Primary Discoveries in the Buddhist Sculpture Hoard of the Longxing Temple in Qingzhou," in *Posui yu juhe: Qingzhou Longxingsi fojiao zaoxiang* 破碎与聚合：青州龙兴寺佛教造像, ed. Fan Di'an 范迪安 and Zheng Yan 郑岩 (Shijiangzhuang 石家庄, China: Hebei Fine Arts Publishing House 河北美术出版社, 2016), 24–27; Zhonghua shijitan yishuguan 中华世纪坛艺术馆 and Qingzhou shi bowuguan 青州市博物馆, *Qingzhou beichao fojiao zaoxiang* 青州北朝佛教造像 (Beijing 北京: Beijing chubanshe 北京出版社, 2002).

10 Zhang Zong, "Region of Qingzhou," 67–68.

11 Alexander L. Mayer, "The Buddha Image in the Light of the Doctrine," in Nickel, *Return of the Buddha*, 100–101.

12 Zhang Zong, "Region of Qingzhou," 65–66.

13 Stanley K. Abe, "Review Essay of Lukas Nickel, ed., *Return of the Buddha: The Qingzhou Discoveries*," *Artibus Asiae* 62, 2 (2002): 293–299.

14 The mass burial of Buddhist statues is not limited to China. In 2001 some 274 Buddha statues were discovered carefully placed in underground pits near Angkor Vat, Cambodia. Groups of stone images appear to have been purposefully damaged, some broken in half, some with heads detached. This may be the result of iconoclasm. Excavators noted evidence of burnt ritual offerings that suggest a ceremony was held in the pit. Masako Marui and Yoshiaki Ishizawa, "La découverte de 274 sculptures et d'un caitya Bouddhique lors des campagnes de fouilles de 2000 et 2001 au Temple de Banteay Kdei à Angkor," *Arts Asiatiques* 57 (2002): 206–218.

15 Fabio Rambelli and Eric Reinders, eds., *Buddhism and Iconoclasm in East Asia: A History* (New York: Continuum International Publishing Group, 2012), 77. Thank you to C. D. Dickerson for bringing this example to the author's attention.

16 From https://www.kohfukuji.com/english/e009/ and J. Edward Kidder, *Early Buddhist Japan* (New York: Praeger, 1972), 203. Also see Hara Hiroshi 原浩史, "興福寺蔵旧山田寺仏頭再考 一当初の安置堂宇と尊名の再検討を中心に一 Reconsideration on the Head of Buddha of Kofuku-Ji Temple (Originally Belonging to Yamada-Dera Temple—Centering on Identification of the Hall Where the Buddha Was Originally Installed and Its Identification," *Bukkyo geijutsu* 佛教藝術 322 (2012): 9–31. Thank you to Ishimatsu Hinako and Sherry Fowler for the citation. See also Kataoka Naoki 片岡直樹, "Kōfukuji buttō 興福寺仏頭," in *Kōfukuji bijutsu-shi kenkyū no ayumi* 興福寺美術史研究のあゆみ (2011): 61–84. Thank you to Ishimatsu Hinako.

17 Scholar Katoaka Naoki notes that countless devotees worshipped the main Buddha image while also unknowingly praying to the damaged head. See Kataoka, "Kōfukuji buttō," 63.

18 Christine Guth, "Kokuhô: From Dynastic to Artistic Treasure," *Cahiers d'Extrême-Asie* 9 (1996–1997): 313–322.

19 Gifford Hudaya Kandahjaya, "A Study on the Origin and Significance of Borobudur" (PhD diss., Graduate Theological Union, 2004), 273–278.

20 Shelly Errington, "Making Progress on Borobudur: An Old Monument in New Order," *Visual Anthropology Review* 9, no. 2 (Fall 1993): 32–59.

21 Pauline Lunsingh Scheurleer, "Collecting Javanese Antiquities," in *Colonial Collections Revisited*, ed. Pieter ter Keurs (Leiden: CNWS Publications, 2007), 71–114.

22 Ann R. Kinney, Marijke J. Klokke, and Lydia Kieven, *Worshiping Siva and Buddha: The Temple Art of East Java* (Honolulu: University of Hawai'i Press, 2003).

23 Neil MacGregor in *A History of the World*, episode 59, "Borobudur Buddha Head," originally aired in 2010 on BBC Radio 4, https://www.bbc.co.uk/ahistoryoftheworld/about/transcripts/episode59/ (accessed October 16, 2025).

24 Sarah Tiffin, *Southeast Asia in Ruins: Art and Empire in the Early 19th Century* (Singapore: NUS Press, 2016), 82; Sarah Tiffin, "Java's Ruined Candis and the British Picturesque Ideal," *Bulletin of the School of Oriental and African Studies, University of London* 72, no. 3 (2009): 527–529.

25 MacGregor, "Borobudur Buddha Head."

26 The three stone heads from Borobudur were donated to the British Museum in 1859: British Museum 1859.1228.175, 176, and 177. Stephen A. Murphy, Naomi Wang, and Alexandra Green, eds., *Raffles in Southeast Asia: Revisiting the Scholar and Statesman* (Singapore: Asian Civilisations Museum, 2019), 31. There is no suggestion that the British cut the heads off the seated Buddha figures.

27 MacGregor, "Borobudur Buddha Head," states that the Raffles collection in the British Museum includes two stone heads from Borobudur.

28 Susan Stewart, *On Longing: Narratives of the Miniature, the Gigantic, the Souvenir, the Collection* (Durham, NC: Duke University Press, 1993), 135. Stewart continues: "Through narrative the souvenir substitutes a context of perpetual consumption for its context of origin. It represents not the lived experience of its maker but the 'secondhand' experience of its possessor/owner. Like the collection, it always displays the romance of contraband, for its scandal is its removal from its 'natural' location."

29 Monica Janowski, "Stones Alive! An Exploration of the Relationship Between Humans and Stone in Southeast Asia," *Bijdragen tot de Taal-, Land- en Volkenkunde* 176, no. 1 (2020): 105–146.

30 Pauline Lunsingh Scheurleer, "The Well-Known Javanese Statue in the Tropenmuseum, Amsterdam, and Its Place in Javanese Sculpture," *Artibus Asiae* 68, no. 2 (2008): 288.

31 Marieke Bloembergen and Martijn Eickhoff, "Exchange and the Protection of Java's Antiquities: A Transnational Approach to the Problem of Heritage in Colonial Java," *Journal of Asian Studies* 72, no. 4 (2013): 893–916.

32 The author has created the Loo narrative based on C. T. Loo & Co., *An Exhibition of Chinese Stone Sculptures* (New York: C. T. Loo & Co., 1940), preface. Also see Yiyou Wang, "The Louvre from China: A Critical Study of C. T. Loo and the Framing of Chinese Art in the United States, 1915–1950" (PhD diss., Ohio University, 2007); and Gèraldine Lenain, *Monsieur Loo, Le roman d'un marchand d'art asiatique* (Arles: Éditions Philippe Picquier, 2013).

33 Loo, *An Exhibition of Chinese Stone Sculptures*, preface.

34 Loo recounted the difficulties in selling a set of standing stone statues in 1914. For six of the works, see "Early Chinese Sculpture," *The Burlington Magazine for Connoisseurs* 25, no. 133 (April 1914): 40, 42–43.

35 Daisy Yiyou Wang, "Papa's Pagoda in Paris: The Gift of the C. T. Loo Family Photographs to the Freer and Sackler Galleries," *Orientations* 44, no. 2 (March 2013): 135–144.

36 For a photograph of the Maitreya Buddha in situ in the 1920s, see Daijo Tokiwa and Tadashi Sekino, *Buddhist Monuments in China* (Tokyo: Bukkyo-Shiseki Kenkyu-kwai, 1926), 3: pl. 91. For context in detail, see J. Keith Wilson and Daisy Yiyou Wang, "The Early Twentieth-Century 'Discovery' of the Xiangtangshan Caves," in Katherine R. Tsiang, *Echoes of the Past: The Buddhist Cave Temples of Xiangtangshan* (Chicago: Smart Museum of Art, 2010), 105–129.

37 Metropolitan Museum of Art 30.81. Denise Patry Leidy and Donna K. Strahan, *Wisdom Embodied: Chinese Buddhist and Daoist Sculpture in the Metropolitan Museum of Art* (New York: Metropolitan Museum of Art, 2010), nos. 10A and 81.

38 Originally identified as from the Longmen cave temples, the left hand was correctly determined to be from the Xiangtangshan Maitreya Buddha by Genevieve K. Benton, "Hand of a Chinese Buddha," *The Pacific Art Review* 1 (1941): 30–32.

39 William A. Southworth, "The Disembodied Human Head in Southeast Asian Art," *Aziatische Kunst* 43, no. 2 (July 2013): 27–30.

40 For their itinerary, see Vinca Baptiste, *Missions archéologiques françaises en Chine: Photographies et itinéraires, 1907–1923* (Paris: Guimet—Musée National des Arts Asiatiques, Réunion des Musées Nationaux, 2004), 192. For Segalen, see 37–40, and for Voisins, see 41–54. For photographs of China, see 77–87.

41 Yvonne Y. Hsieh, *Victor Segalen's Literary Encounter with China: Chinese Moulds, Western Thoughts* (Toronto: University of Toronto Press, 1988).

42 Bernard Faure, "The Buddhist Icon and the Modern Gaze," *Critical Inquiry* 24, 3 (Spring 1998): 776–777. Translated passages by Bernard Faure after Auguste Gilbert de Voisins, *Ecrit en Chine*, in *Le Voyage en Chine: Anthologie des voyageurs occidentaux du Moyen Âge à la chute de l'Empire chinois*, ed. Ninette Boothroyd, Muriel Detrie, and Fernand Bunel (Paris, 1992), 1053–1054.

43 Victor Segalen and Annie Joly-Segalen, *Chine: La grande statuaire* (Paris: Flammarion, 1972); translated as Victor Segalen and Annie Joly-Segalen, *The Great Statuary of China* (Chicago: University of Chicago Press, 1978). For a review, see Nick Pearce. "'In a Space of Time Past': Segalen's *The Great Statuary of China*," in *Reading Diversity = Lectures du divers*, ed. Charles Forsdick and Susan Marson (Glasgow: University of Glasgow French and German Publications, 2000), 67–88.

WEATHERING PAGANISM

1 Daniel M. Wegner and Daniel Gilbert, *The Illusion of Conscious Will* (Cambridge, MA: MIT Press, 2017).

2 Keith Rowe in David Toop, *Haunted Weather: Music, Silence and Memory* (London and New York: Serpent's Tail, 2004), 239–240.

3 Timothy Morton, *Hyperobjects: Philosophy and Ecology After the End of the World* (Minneapolis: University of Minnesota Press, 2013).

4 David Bentley Hart, "A Nomad City," *Leaves in the Wind*, Substack, January 13, 2026, accessed January 17, 2026, https://substack.com/inbox/post/183369955.

5 *Oxford English Dictionary*, "neighbor," accessed October 20, 2025, https://www.oed.com/dictionary/neighbour_n?.

6 Pink Floyd, "Welcome to the Machine," music video by Gerald Scarfe (1977).

7 To paraphrase George Orwell, *1984* (New York: Penguin, 2023), 267.

8 David Bentley Hart, *Atheist Delusions: The Christian Revolution and Its Fashionable Enemies* (New Haven, CT: Yale University Press, 2010), 168.

9 Henry George Liddell and Robert Scott, *Greek-English Lexicon*, ed. Henry Stuart Jones (Oxford: The Clarendon Press, 1996).

10 Timothy Morton, *Dark Ecology: For a Logic of Future Coexistence* (New York: Columbia University Press, 2016), 3–60.

11 David Graeber and David Wengrow, *The Dawn of Everything: A New History of Humanity* (New York: Allen Lane, 2021), 267–269.

BROKEN TO COMPLETION

1 On the renovations at the Templo Mayor, see Eduardo Matos Moctezuma, *El Templo Mayor: Excavaciones y estudios* (Mexico City: Instituto Nacional de Antropología e Historia, 1982); Miguel León-Portilla, "The Ethnohistorical Record for the Huey Teocalli of Tenochtitlan," in *The Aztec Templo Mayor*, ed. Elizabeth Hill Boone (Washington, DC: Dumbarton Oaks Research Library and Collection, 1987), 71–95; Augusto F. Molina Montes, "Templo Mayor Architecture: So What's New?," in Boone, *Aztec Templo Mayor*, 97–107; and Eduardo Matos Moctezuma, "The Templo Mayor of Tenochtitlan: History and Interpretation," in *The Great Temple of Tenochtitlan: Center and Periphery in the Aztec World*, ed. Johanna Broda, Davíd Carrasco, and Eduardo Matos Moctezuma (Berkeley: University of California Press, 1987), 15–60.

2 On the function and meaning of the *chacmool* and the relationship of this sculpture to the larger corpus, see Mary Ellen Miller, "A Re-Examination of the Mesoamerican Chacmool," *Art Bulletin* 67, no. 1 (1985): 7–17; Alfredo López Austin and Leonardo López Luján, "El *chacmool* Mexica," *Caravelle* 76–77 (2001): 59–84; and Alfredo López Austin and Leonardo López Luján, *Monte Sagrado-Templo Mayor: El cerro y la pirámide en la tradición religiosa mesoamericana* (Mexico City: Universidad Nacional Autónoma de México and Instituto de Investigaciones Antropológicas, 2009), 440–448.

3 On Mexica revivals of the past, and especially of the Toltecs, see Emily Umberger, "Antiques, Revivals, and References to the Past in Aztec Art," *Res: Anthropology and Aesthetics* 13 (1987): 62–105; Leonardo López Luján, "The Aztecs' Search for the Past," in *Aztecs*, ed. Eduardo Matos Moctezuma and Felipe Solís Olgulín (London: Royal Academy of Arts, 2002), 22–29; Leonardo López Luján and Alfredo López Austin, "The Mexica in Tula and Tula in Mexico-Tenochtitlan," in *The Art of Urbanism: How Mesoamerican Kingdoms Represented Themselves in Architecture and Imagery*, ed. William L. Fash and Leonardo López Luján (Washington, DC: Dumbarton Oaks Research Library and Collection, 2009), 384–422; and Claudia Brittenham, *Unseen Art: Making, Vision, and Power in Ancient Mesoamerica* (Austin: University of Texas Press, 2023), 107–114.

4 Leonardo López Luján, Alfredo López Austin, and José María García, "El *chacmool* tolteca de la Casa del Apartado: Imitación, reúso, y legitimidad," *Arqueología Mexicana* 22, no. 130 (2014): 22–29.

5 Leonard Barkan, "The Beholder's Tale: Ancient Sculpture, Renaissance Narratives," *Representations* 44 (1993): 133–166; Leonard Barkan, "Fragments," chap. 3 in *Unearthing the Past: Archaeology and Aesthetics in the Making of Renaissance Culture* (New Haven, CT: Yale University Press, 1999).

6 Brittenham, *Unseen Art*, 114.

7 On the offerings deposited at the Templo Mayor, see Johanna Broda, "The Provenience of the Offerings: Tribute and *Cosmovisión*," in Boone, *Aztec Templo Mayor*, 211–256; Umberger, "Antiques, Revivals, and References," 67–68, 97–98; Leonardo López Luján, *The Offerings of the Templo Mayor of Tenochtitlan*, trans. Bernard R. Ortiz de Montellano and Thelma Ortiz de Montellano (Niwot: University Press of Colorado, 1994); and Brittenham, *Unseen Art*, 114–118.

8 López Luján, *Offerings of the Templo Mayor*, 403–407; Alfredo López Austin and Leonardo López Luján, "Los Mexicas y el *chacmool*," *Arqueología Mexicana* 9, no. 49 (2001): 68–73, esp. 72; López Austin and López Luján, "El *chacmool* Mexica," 68–70; López Austin and López Luján, *Monte Sagrado-Templo Mayor*, 440–448.

9 López Austin and López Luján, "El *chacmool* Mexica," 68; López Austin and López Luján, "Los Mexicas y el *chacmool*," 72-73; López Luján and López Austin, "The Mexica in Tula," 400–403; Keith Jordan, "Crowned Not Bound: Context and Iconography of Chacmool Sculptures at Tula," *Latin American and Latinx Visual Culture* 2, no. 1 (2020): 56–77, esp. 65–68.

10 Johannes Maringer, "Clay Figurines of the Jōmon Period: A Contribution to the History of Ancient Religion in Japan," *History of Religions* 14, no. 2 (1974): 128–139, esp. 136–137; Doi Takashi, "Dogū: Representing the Body in the Jōmon Archipelago," in *The Power of Dogū: Ceramic Figures from Ancient Japan*, ed. Simon Kaner (London: British Museum Press, 2009), 40–49.

11 Kobayashi Tatsuo, *Dogū haniwa* [Ceramic figures and *haniwa*], in *Nihon tōjiki zenshū* [Corpus of Japanese ceramics] (Tokyo: Chūō Kōronsha, 1977); Harada Masayuki, "Dogū Broken and Enshrined: Traces of a Jōmon World View," in Kaner, *Power of Dogū*, 50–59.

12 Taniguchi Yasuhiro, "Dogū no kowarekata [Breakage patterns of figurines]," *Kikan kōkogaku* [Archaeology quarterly] 30 (1990): 63–67; Douglas Bailey, Andrew Cochrane, and Jean Zambelli, *Unearthed: A Comparative Study of Jōmon Dogū and Neolithic Figurines* (Norwich, UK: Sainsbury Institute for the Study of Japanese Arts and Cultures, 2010), 9.

13 Maringer, "Clay Figurines," 136–138; Harada, "Dogū Broken and Enshrined," 50–58; Ilona R. Bausch, "Fragmentation Practices in Central Japan: Middle Jōmon Clay Figurines at Shakadō," in *Anthropomorphic and Zoomorphic Miniature Figures in Eurasia, Africa and Meso-America: Morphology, Materiality, Technology, Function, and Context*, ed. Dragos Gheorghiu and Ann Cyphers (Oxford: Archaeopress, 2010), 99–112, esp. 101.

14 See Feldman's essay in the present volume, pages 70–73.

15 For further discussion of this sculpture, see Bernard de Grunne, "Ancient Sculpture of the Inland Niger Delta and Its Influence on Dogon Art," *African Arts* 21, no. 4 (1988): 50–55; Kathleen Bickford and Cherise Smith, "Art of the Western Sudan," *Art Institute of Chicago Museum Studies* 23, no. 2 (1997): 104–119, esp. 108; and Kathleen Bickford Berzock, entry in *Speaking of Objects: African Art at the Art Institute of Chicago*, ed. Constantine Petridis (Chicago: Art Institute of Chicago, 2020), 34–35.

16 See Said and Sears's essay in the present volume, pages 94–95.

17 Paulo F. de Moraes Farias, "Islam in the West African Sahel," in *Sahel: Art and Empires on the Shores of the Sahara*, ed. Alisa LaGamma (New York: Metropolitan Museum of Art, 2020), 108–137, esp. 109–111; Risham Majeed, review of *Caravans of Gold, Fragments in Time: Art, Culture, and Exchange Across Medieval Saharan Africa*, ed. Kathleen Bickford Berzock, and *Sahel: Art and Empires on the Shores of the Sahara*, ed. Alisa LaGamma, *Art Bulletin* 103, no. 1 (2021): 140–146.

18 On the meaning of the kneeling pose, see De Grunne, "Ancient Sculpture," 54–55; Bernard de Grunne, *Djenné-Jeno: 1000 Years of Terracotta Statuary in Mali* (Brussels: Mercatorfonds, 2014), 34–55. On the various findspots of kneeling figures, see Roderick J. McIntosh and Susan Keech McIntosh, "Terracotta Statuettes from Mali," *African Arts* 12, no. 2 (1979): 51–53; and Roderick J. McIntosh, "Middle Niger Terra Cottas Before the Symplegades Gateway," *African Arts* 22, no. 2 (1989): 74–83, esp. 81–82.

19 Leonardo López Luján et al., "The Destruction of Images in Teotihuacan: Anthropomorphic Sculpture, Elite Cults, and the End of a Civilization," *Res: Anthropology and Aesthetics* 49/50 (2006): 13–39, esp. 13–14; Anabel Villalonga Gordaliza, "Cuerpos de piedra en la ciudad de los dioses: Idiosincrasia de la escultura antropomorfa teotihuacana" (PhD diss., Universitat Autònoma de Barcelona, 2014), 515–549.

20 López Luján et al., "Destruction of Images in Teotihuacan," 13–39.

21 The author would like to thank Dakota Hoska and Tamira Brennan for lending their expertise to the discussion of the *Birger Figurine*.

22 For more on this sculpture, see Thomas E. Emerson, *Mississippian Stone Images in Illinois* (Urbana: Illinois Archaeological Survey, 1982), 5–8; Thomas E. Emerson and Douglas K. Jackson, eds., *The BBB Motor Site*, American Bottom Archaeology FAI-270 Site Reports Vol. 6 (Urbana: Illinois Department of Transportation and University of Illinois Press, 1984), 254–261; Guy Prentice, "An Analysis of the Symbolism Expressed by the Birger Figurine," *American Antiquity* 51, no. 2 (1986): 239–266; Thomas E. Emerson, *Cahokia and the Archaeology of Power* (Tuscaloosa: University of Alabama Press, 1997), 195–199, 209–212; Carol Diaz-Granados and James R. Duncan, "Reflections of Power, Wealth, and Sex in Missouri Rock-Art Motifs," in *The Rock-Art of Eastern North America: Capturing Images and Insight*, ed. Carol Diaz-Granados and James R. Duncan (Tuscaloosa: University of Alabama Press, 2004), 145–158, esp. 155; James R. Duncan and Carol Diaz-Granados, "Empowering the SECC: The 'Old Woman' and Oral Tradition," in Diaz-Granados and Duncan, *Rock-Art of Eastern North America*, 190–215, esp. 196–197; and Gayle J. Fritz, *Feeding Cahokia: Early Agriculture in the North American Heartland* (Tuscaloosa: University of Alabama Press, 2019), 99, 104–107, 111–112.

23 Emerson and Jackon, *BBB Motor Site*, 254–258.

24 Prentice, "Analysis of the Symbolism," 242–243, 262–263.

25 On the iconography of the Old Woman Who Never Dies, see Duncan and Diaz-Granados, "Empowering the SECC," 196–197; and Fritz, *Feeding Cahokia*, 110–112, 149–150.

26 Biondo Flavio, *Italy Illuminated, Volume 1, Books I–IV*, ed. and trans. Jeffrey A. White (Cambridge, MA: Harvard University Press, 2005), 188–193; Rodolfo Lanciani, "The Mysterious Wreck of Nemi," *North American Review* 162, no. 471 (1896): 225–234.

27 Eliseo Borghi, *La verità sulle navi romane del Lago di Nemi* (Rome: Tipografia dell'unione cooperative editrice, 1901), 29–31. See also Lanciani, "Mysterious Wreck," 234.

28 Renate Schlesier, "Apotropäisch," in *Handbuch religionswissenschaftlicher Grundbegriffe*, ed. Hubert Cancik, Burkhard Gladigow, and Matthias Laubscher (Stuttgart: Verlag W. Kohlhammer, 1990), 2: 41–45; Renate Schlesier, *Kulte, Mythen und Gelehrte: Anthropologie der Antike seit 1800* (Frankfurt am Main: Fischer Taschenbuch Verlag, 1994), 53–55.

29 On the sculpture and its relationship to the ship, see Guido Ucelli, *Le navi di Nemi* (Rome: La Libreria dello Stato, 1940), 18; Carla De Stefanis, "Le decorazioni di bordo: I bronzi di Palazzo Massimo," in *Caligola: La trasgressione al potere*, ed. Filippo Coarelli and Giuseppina Ghini (Rome: Gangemi Editore, 2013), 131–133; and Carla De Stefanis, entry in *Palazzo Massimo alle Terme: Le collezioni*, ed. Carlo Gasparri and Rita Paris (Rome: Ministero per I Beni e le Attività Culturali; Milan: Electa, 2013), 318.

30 Gerald Berjonneau, Emile Deletaille, and Jean-Louis Sonnery, eds., *Rediscovered Masterpieces of Mesoamerica* (Boulogne: Editions Arts, 1985), 42; Michael D. Coe, ed., *The Olmec World: Ritual and Rulership* (Princeton: Princeton University Press, 1995), 255; Margaret Young-Sánchez, entry in *Treasures of the Al Thani Collection at the Hôtel de la Marine*, ed. Amin Jaffer, Jasper Gaunt, and Émilie Foyer (Paris: Éditions du Patrimoine / Centre des Monuments Nationaux, 2021), 192–193.

31 Karl A. Taube, "The Symbolism of Jade in Classic Maya Religion," *Ancient Mesoamerica* 16 (2005): 23–50, esp. 23–25; Laura Filloy Nadal, "Forests of Jade: Luxury Arts and Symbols of Excellence in Ancient Mesoamerica," in *Golden Kingdoms: Luxury Arts in the Ancient Americas*, ed. Joanne Pillsbury, Timothy Potts, and Kim N. Richter (Los Angeles: J. Paul Getty Museum and Getty Research Institute, 2017), 67–77.

32 Karl Taube, "The Olmec Maize God: The Face of Corn in Formative Mesoamerica," *Res: Anthropology and Aesthetics* 29/30 (1996): 39–81, esp. 39–54; Karl Taube, "Lighting Celts and Corn Fetishes: The Formative Olmec and the Development of Maize Symbolism in Mesoamerica and the American Southwest," in *Olmec Art and Archaeology in Mesoamerica*, ed. John E. Clark and Mary E. Pye (Washington, DC: National Gallery of Art, 2000), 297–337, esp. 297–303; Richard A. Diehl, "The Olmec Legacy in Stone: A Mesoamerican Alpha and Omega," in *Olmec: Colossal Masterworks of Ancient Mexico*, ed. Kathleen Berrin and Virginia M. Fields (San Francisco: Fine Arts Museums of San Francisco; Los Angeles: Los Angeles County Museum of Art, in association with Yale University Press, 2010), 76–85, esp. 81–82.

33 Taube, "Olmec Maize God," 71; Taube, "Lighting Celts and Corn Fetishes," 300–301.

34 One of the most important findspots for Roman votives was the Temple of Diana overlooking Lake Nemi. See Jessica Hughes, "Fractured Narratives: Writing the Biography of a Votive Offering," in *Ex Voto: Votive Giving Across Cultures*, ed. Ittai Weinryb (Chicago: University of Chicago Press, 2016), 23–48. On the function and meaning of votives more generally, see Velia Boecker, *Kulte, Orte, Körperteile: Eine Neubewertung der Weihung anatomischer Votive in Latiums Heiligtümer* (Weisbaden: Reichtert Verlag, 2023), 1–10, 26–42.

35 On the ability of votives to function as both depictions and signs, see Matthias Recke, "Science as Art: Etruscan Anatomical Votives," in *The Etruscan World*, ed. Jean MacIntosh Turfa (London: Routledge, 2013), 1068–1085, esp. 1074–1077; Emma-Jayne Graham, "Hand in Hand: Rethinking Anatomical Votives as Material Things," in *Lived Religion in the Ancient Mediterranean World: Approaching Religious Transformations from Archaeology, History, and Classics*, ed. Valentino Gasparini, Maik Patzelt, Rubina Raja, Anna-Katharina Rieger, Jörg Rüpke, and Emiliano Rubens Urciuoli (Berlin: De Gruyter, 2020), 209–235, esp. 212–215.

36 Brigitte Buettner, "From Bones to Stones: Reflections on Jeweled Reliquaries," in *Reliquiare im Mittelalter*, ed. Bruno Reudenbach and Gia Toussaint (Berlin: Akademie Verlag, 2011), 43–59; Michele Ferrari, "Gold und Asche: Reliquie und Reliquiare als Medien in Thiofid von Echternachs *Flores epytaphii sanctorum*," in *Reliquiare im Mittelalter*, ed. Bruno Reudenbach and Gia Toussaint (Berlin: Akademie Verlag, 2011), 61–74.

37 Cynthia Hahn, "The Voices of the Saints: Speaking Reliquaries," *Gesta* 36, no. 1 (1997): 20–31; Cynthia Hahn, "What Do Reliquaries Do for Relics?," *Numen* 57, no. 3/4 (2010): 284–316; Cynthia Hahn, "The Spectacle of the Charismatic Body: Patrons, Artists, and Body-Part Reliquaries," in *Treasures of Heaven: Saints, Relics, and Devotion in Medieval Europe*, ed. Martina Bagnoli et al. (Cleveland: Cleveland Museum of Art; Baltimore: Walters Art Museum; London: British Museum, 2010), 163–172.

38 Bruno Reudenbach, "'Gold ist Schlam': Anmerkungen zur Materialbewertung im Mittelalter," in *Material in Kunst und Alltag*, ed. Monika Wagner and Dietmar Rübel (Berlin: Akademie Verlag, 2002), 1–12; Gia Toussaint, "Heiliges Gebein und edler Stein: Der Edelsteinschmuck von Reliquiaren im Spiegel mittelalterlicher Wahrnehmung," *Das Mittelalter* 8 (2003): 41–66; Martina Bagnoli, "The Stuff of Heaven: Materials and Craftsmanship in Medieval Reliquaries," in Bagnoli et al., *Treasures of Heaven*, 137–147.

39 On the techniques of making this hand and of Lambayeque goldsmith work more broadly, see Federico Kauffmann, "Mensaje iconográfico de la orfebrería lambayecana," in *Oro del Antiguo Peru*, ed. José Antonio de Lavalle (Lima: Banco de Credito del Perú en la Cultura, 1992), 237–264; Paloma Carcedo Muro, "Metalurgia Precolombina: Manufactura y técnicas en la orfebrería Sicán," in Lavalle, *Oro del Antiguo Peru*, 265–302; and Elizabeth Hill Boone, ed., *Andean Art at Dumbarton Oaks* (Washington, DC: Dumbarton Oaks Research Library and Collection, 1996), 195–198.

40 On the status of goldsmith works and wealth in tombs, see Joanne Pillsbury, "En la corte de Ñaimlap / At the Court of Ñaimlap," in *Ñaimlap: Memoria lambayeque y materialidad histórica / Lambayeque Memory and Historical Materiality*, ed. Carlos Wester (Lima: EY, 2021), 204–251. On Lambayeque burials, especially the important case study of Huaca Loro, see Izumi Shimada, *Cultura Sicán: Dios,*

riqueza y poder en la Costa Norte del Perú (Lima: Fundación del Banco Continental para del Fomento de la Educación y la Cultura, Edubanco, Lima, 1995), 39–126. There is also evidence that these burial objects were made in conjunction with human sacrifice; see Elizabeth P. Benson, "Why Sacrifice?," in *Ritual Sacrifice in Ancient Peru*, ed. Elizabeth P. Benson and Anita G. Cook (Austin: University of Texas Press, 2001), 1–20; and Haagen D. Klaus and Izumi Shimada, "Bodies and Blood: Middle Sicán Human Sacrifice in the Lambayeque Valley Complex (AD 900–1100)," in *Ritual Violence in the Ancient Andes: Reconstructing Sacrifice on the North Coast of Peru*, ed. Haagen D. Klaus and J. Marla Toyne (Austin: University of Texas Press, 2016), 120–149.

41 See Fiduccia's essay in the present volume, page 188.

42 For more on this sculpture, see Susan Mullin Vogel, *African Art, Western Eyes* (New Haven, CT: Yale University Press, 1997), 8; William C. Siegmann, Kevin D. Dumouchelle, and Joseph Adande, *African Art: A Century at the Brooklyn Museum* (New York: Prestel, 2009), 96–97; and Z. S. Strother, "Les iconoclasmes en Afrique: Émergence d'un sujet d'étude," *Perspective* 2 (2018): 219–246, esp. 231–232.

43 John Warne Monroe, "Surface Tensions: Empire, Parisian Modernism, and 'Authenticity' in African Sculpture, 1917–1939," *American Historical Review* 117, no. 2 (2012): 445–475, esp. 455–460.

44 Sally Price, *Primitive Art in Civilized Places* (Chicago: University of Chicago Press, 2001), 1–6, 82–99.

45 On the relationship between Baule sculpture and "spirit spouses," see Philip L. Ravenhill, "Baule Statuary Art: Meaning and Modernization," *Working Papers in the Traditional Arts* 5 (1980): 1–36; Susan M. Vogel, "Beauty in the Eyes of the Baule," *Working Papers in the Traditional Arts* 6 (1980): 1–43; Philip L. Ravenhill, *The Self and the Other: Personhood and Images Among the Baule, Côte d'Ivoire* (Los Angeles: Fowler Museum of Cultural History and University of California, Los Angeles, 1994); Strother, "Les iconoclasmes en Afrique," 231–232.

46 Vogel, *African Art*, 78–105, 240–267.

47 Strother, "Les iconoclasmes en Afrique," 231–232.

48 This phrasing is indebted to Rozsika Parker, *The Subversive Stitch: Embroidery and the Making of the Feminine* (London: Women's Press, 1984), 215.

SCULPTING THE FRAGMENT

1 I refer here to the concept elaborated by Alois Riegl, for whom "age-value," carried in the visible traces of passing years that naturally accrue on an object, was both the most universal source of our appreciation and the locus of our deepest sympathy for monuments; their decay recalls to us our own mortality. Alois Riegl, "The Modern Cult of Monuments: Its Character and Its Origin," trans. Kurt W. Forster and Diane Ghirardo, *Oppositions* 25 (Fall 1982): 20–51.

2 Vo recounts that the origin of this series of works was an encounter in an Amsterdam antiques shop with a crumbling sixteenth-century wooden statue of Saint Joseph. In order to transport the work back to his home in Berlin without paying shipping costs, Vo sawed the statue into pieces that could fit inside his carry-on luggage, and subsequently presented this luggage and its cargo as the artwork *Untitled* (2008). Luigi Fassi, "Terra Incognito: The Art of Danh Vo," *Artforum* 48, no. 6 (February 2010): 157.

3 Quoted in Alain Corbin, *Fragilitas: Le plâtre et l'histoire de France* (Paris: PLON, 2023), 48–49, from Alfred de Musset, *La confession d'un enfant du siècle* (Paris: Librairie générale française, 2003), 65 (my translation, emphasis in original).

4 György Lukács, "Preface to the New Edition" (1967), in *History and Class Consciousness: Studies in Marxist Dialectics*, trans. Rodney Livingstone (Cambridge, MA: MIT Press, 1971), xxiv.

5 Linda Nochlin, *The Body in Pieces: The Fragment as a Metaphor of Modernity* (London: Thames & Hudson, 1994), 53. For this first account of fragmentation in the twentieth century, see Fredric Jameson, "Postmodernism and Consumerist Society," in *Postmodernism and Its Discontents: Theories, Practices*, ed. E. Ann Kaplan (London: Verso, 1988), 194. For an important study of the fragment in nineteenth- and twentieth-century sculpture, see *Le corps en morceaux*, ed. Anne Pingeot (Paris: Réunion des Musées Nationaux, 1990).

6 Friedrich Schlegel, "Athenaeum Fragments," in *Philosophical Fragments*, trans. Peter Firchow (Minneapolis: University of Minnesota Press, 1991), 45; for the embryonic aspect, see 20–21. See also Philippe Lacoue-Labarthe and Jean-Luc Nancy, *The Literary Absolute: The Theory of Literature in German Romanticism*, trans. Philip Barnard and Cheryl Lester (Albany: State University of New York Press, 1988), 43; Anne Janowitz, "The Romantic Fragment," in *A Companion to Romanticism*, ed. Duncan Wu (Malden, MA: Blackwell, 1999), 479; and Sophie Thomas, *Romanticism and Visuality: Fragments, History, and Spectacle* (New York: Routledge, 2007), 25.

7 Janowitz, "Romantic Fragment," 486.

8 Albert E. Elsen, *The Partial Figure in Modern Sculpture from Rodin to 1969* (Baltimore: Baltimore Museum of Art, 1969); Albert Elsen, "Notes on the Partial Figure," *Artforum* 8, no. 3 (November 1969): 61.

9 Leo Steinberg, "Rodin," in *Other Criteria: Confrontations with Twentieth-Century Art* (Chicago: University of Chicago Press, 2007), 362. According to Albert E. Elsen, "Degas reportedly asked Rodin: 'Why did you make your *Walking Man* without head or arms?'; to which Rodin replied in a manner that explains their friendship: 'Have you ever seen a man walk on his head? As for the arms, I preferred to have him walk on his legs like ordinary mortals—like you and me.'" Albert E. Elsen, *Rodin* (New York: Museum of Modern Art, 1963), 173.

10 See Elsen, *Rodin*, 180–181.

11 Schlegel, "Athenaeum Fragments," 21.

12 Paul de Man, "Intentional Structure of the Romantic Image," in *The Rhetoric of Romanticism* (New York: Columbia University Press, 2000), 1–17.

13 Rodolphe Gasché, "Foreword: Ideality in Fragmentation," in Schlegel, *Philosophical Fragments*, xxvii–xxviii. See also Elizabeth Wanning Harries, *The Unfinished Manner: Essays on the Fragment in the Later Eighteenth Century* (Charlottesville: University of Virginia Press, 1994).

14 Steinberg, "Rodin," 369. Compare this observation with the remark made by the surrealist sculptor David Hare: "The completion of a figure makes it static while its fragmentation explodes it back into the movement of life." Quoted in Elsen, "Notes on the Partial Figure," 63.

15 Reassessments of Rodin's importance half a century ago placed new emphasis on these bronzes and plasters, rescuing him from his reputation as a maker of sentimental marbles. See in particular Rosalind Krauss, "The Originality of the Avant-Garde" and "Sincerely Yours," in *The Originality of the Avant-Garde and Other Modernist Myths* (Cambridge, MA: MIT Press, 1985), 151–157, 175–194.

16 Anne M. Wagner, "Rodin's Reputation," in *Eroticism and the Body Politic*, ed. Lynn Hunt (Baltimore: Johns Hopkins University Press, 1991), 191–242; David J. Getsy, *Rodin: Sex and the Making of Modern Sculpture* (New Haven, CT: Yale University Press, 2011).

17 Paul Claudel, "Camille Claudel, statuaire," *L'art décoratif*, no. 193 (July 1913), reprinted in *Camille Claudel: Au miroir d'un art nouveau* (Paris: Gallimard; Roubaix: La Piscine, 2015), 247.

18 The authors of Claudel's catalogue raisonné note that it is "difficult to date with precision the amputations that the artist inflicted upon the original work," concluding that they were most likely executed after 1898 but before a photograph of the work appeared in Paul Claudel's 1913 article on his sister's work. Anne Rivière, Bruno Gaudichon, and Danielle Ghanassia, *Camille Claudel: Catalogue raisonné*, 3rd ed. (Paris: Adam Biro, 2001), 72. See also Clarisse Fava-Piz, "In Rodin's Studio," in *Camille Claudel* (Los Angeles: J. Paul Getty Museum, 2023), 122–123.

19 By the removal of the extremities, Claudel reveals the likeness of the tensile curve of the figure's back to the sculptural fragment known as the "Crouching Aphrodite," or *Venus de Vienne*, which had recently been purchased by the Louvre in 1878—retroactively transforming the *Venus*'s blank back into its most salient aspect. On the crouch or squat as an "iconography of the unreadable" that "gives the body a utopian directionless," see George Baker, "The Squatter: Reconsidering Picasso's *Les Demoiselles d'Avignon*," in *Cornerstones* (Berlin: Sternberg, 2011), 19, 25.

20 On the principle of synecdoche, or the "part-for-whole," as opposed to both the partial object and the "part-by-part logic of the drives," for Brâncuși, see Mignon Nixon, *Fantastic Reality: Louise Bourgeois and a Story of Modern Art* (Cambridge, MA: MIT Press, 2005), 229; and Rosalind Krauss, *Bachelors* (Cambridge, MA: MIT Press, 1999), 54.

21 Alina Szapocznikow, "Mon oeuvre puise des racines . . . ," April 1972, typescript in the Alina Szapocznikow Archive, Museum of Modern Art in Warsaw, accessed August 7, 2025, https://archiwum.artmuseum.pl/en/archiwum/archiwum-aliny-szapocznikow/104/7322#.

22 See Darcy Grimaldo Grigsby's analysis of these studies as images of a "peace of remarkable, one might say revolutionary, reordering." Darcy Grimaldo Grigsby, *Extremities: Painting Empire in Post-Revolutionary France* (New Haven, CT: Yale University Press, 2002), 205.

23 See Mignon Nixon, "Posing the Phallus," *October* 92 (Spring 2000): 98–127.

24 D. W. Winnicott, "Transitional Objects and Transitional Phenomena," in *Playing and Reality* (London: Routledge, 1989), 1–14.

25 Mignon Nixon thus analyzes Bourgeois's sculpture through the frame of the part-object, which "marks the convergence of the libido and death drive" and which gleans its significance from its relationship to early fantasies defined, much like the transitional object, by ambivalent feelings of love and hate. Nixon, *Fantastic Reality*, 213.

26 These two modes of engaging the sculpture are mirrored in Gober's description of the dual origin of his series of wax legs: both in his recollection of the titillating sight of a businessman's bare ankle and in a story related by his mother, a nurse, who was shocked to be handed an amputated leg during the very first surgery she attended. Isabel Friedli and Simone Moser, "Catalogue of Sculptures and Installations, 1979–2007," in *Robert Gober: Sculptures and Installations, 1979–2007*, ed. Theodora Vischer (Basel: Schaulager; Göttingen: Steidl, 2007), 284.

27 On the relation of Gober's body fragments to Jean Laplanche's concept of "enigmatic signifiers," objects situated outside of us but with which we are most intimately concerned (paradigmatically, the maternal breast), see Hal Foster, *Prosthetic Gods* (Cambridge, MA: MIT Press, 2004), 330.

28 Fred Wilson, Jered Sprecher, and Amy J. Elias, "Objects and Identities: An Interview with Fred Wilson," *ASAP/Journal* 2, no. 1 (January 2017): 10.

29 On the conventions of "ornamental blackness" and the blackamoor, see Adrienne L. Childs, "Sugar Boxes and Blackamoors: Ornamental Blackness in Early Meissen Porcelain," in *The Cultural Aesthetics of Eighteenth-Century Porcelain*, ed. Alden Cavanaugh and Michael E. Yonan (Farnham, UK; Burlington, VT: Ashgate, 2010), 159–177. See also Adrienne L. Childs, *Ornamental Blackness: The Black Figure in European Decorative Arts* (New Haven, CT: Yale

University Press, 2025); and Cyra Levenson, Chi-ming Yang, and Ken Gonzales-Day, "Haptic Blackness: The Double Life of an 18th-Century Bust," in *British Art Studies* 1 (November 2015), https://britishartstudies.ac.uk/issues/01/bust-of-a-man.

30 Jonathan D. Katz, "'Committing the Perfect Crime': Sexuality, Assemblage, and the Postmodern Turn in American Art," *Art Journal* 67, no. 1 (Spring 2008): 49.

31 As Julia Kelly reflects, the antiart practice of assemblage works to "unravel the understanding of what art is *for*, becoming less an object of contemplation and poetic transfiguration than a tool for doing things." Julia Kelly, "The Anthropology of Assemblage," *Art Journal* 67, no. 1 (Spring 2008): 30.

32 Kofi Awoonor, "Rediscovery and Other Poems," in *African Writing Today*, ed. Ezekiel Mphahlele (Harmondsworth, UK: Penguin, 1967), 96.

33 Tausif Noor, "Foreigners Everywhere: Huma Bhabha's Art of Alienation," in *Huma Bhabha: Welcome . . . to the one who came* (New York: David Zwirner Books, 2025), 101. On Bhabha's "instant ruins," see Huma Bhabha, "Lecture Extracts," in *Statuesque: Pawel Althamer, Huma Bhabha, Aaron Curry, Thomas Houseago, Matthew Monahan, Rebecca Warren*, ed. Nicholas Baume (New York: Public Art Fund, 2011), 66; and Eva Raspini, "Instant Ruins," in *Huma Bhabha: They Live* (Boston: Institute of Contemporary Art, 2019), 11.

34 Schlegel, "Athenaeum Fragments," 21.

35 Michael Taussig, "Scale Is Everything," *Parkett* 93 (2013): 179.

LIST OF EXHIBITED WORKS

Note to the reader: The objects in this list are in chronological order from earliest to latest. The location in parentheses next to the culture of manufacture indicates the likely findspot or original location based on collection records. When the circumstances of breakage are known, that information is provided.

1 Cycladic, *Head of a Figure of the Early Spedos Variety*, c. 2600–2500 BCE
marble with traces of pigment, 22.8 × 8.9 × 6.4 cm (9 × 3 ½ × 2 ½ in.)
The J. Paul Getty Museum, Villa Collection, Malibu, California, 96.AA.27
Washington only

Selected references: Marit Jentoft-Nilson, entry in Marion True and Kenneth Hamma, eds., *A Passion for Antiquities: Ancient Art from the Collection of Barbara and Lawrence Fleischman* (Malibu: The J. Paul Getty Museum, 1994), 42–43; Elizabeth A. Hendrix, "Painted Early Cycladic Figures: An Exploration of Context and Meaning," *Hesperia* 72, no. 4 (2003): 418; Christos Tsirogiannis et al., "A Corrupt Cycladic Corpus of Marble Figures," *Journal of Eastern Mediterranean Archaeology and Heritage Studies* 13, no. 3 (2025): 215.

2 Akkadian (Aššur), *Torso of a Ruler*, c. 2300–2250 BCE
gabbro, 45 × 46 × 28.5 cm (17 ¹¹⁄₁₆ × 18 ⅛ × 11 ¼ in.)
Staatliche Museen zu Berlin–Vorderasiatisches Museum, VA 17312

Possibly broken and reused as building material for reinforcing the fourteenth-century BCE street under which the sculpture was found. Possibly attacked and broken by political rivals in the late seventh century BCE.

Selected references: Walter Andrae, *Das wiedererstandene Assur, 2. durchgesehene und erweiterte Auflage*, ed. Barthel Hrouda (Munich: Beck, 1977), 127–129; Melissa Eppihimer, "Assembling King and State: The Statues of Manishtushu and the Consolidation of Akkadian Kingship," *American Journal of Archaeology* 144 (2010): 371n28.

3 Egyptian, *Face of Senwosret III*, c. 1878–1840 BCE
red quartzite, 16.5 × 12.6 × 11.4 cm (6 ½ × 4 ¹⁵⁄₁₆ × 4 ½ in.)
Lent by The Metropolitan Museum of Art, Purchase, Edward S. Harkness Gift, 1926 (26.7.1394)

Selected references: Cyril Aldred, "Some Royal Portraits of the Middle Kingdom in Ancient Egypt," *Metropolitan Museum Journal* 3 (1970): 44–45; Adela Oppenheim, entry in Adela Oppenheim, Dorothea Arnold, Dieter Arnold, and Kei Yamamoto, eds., *Ancient Egypt Transformed: The Middle Kingdom* (New York: Metropolitan Museum of Art, 2015), 79, 81–83.

4 Egyptian (Akhetaten [Amarna]), *Nose and Lips of Akhenaten*, c. 1353–1336 BCE
indurated limestone, 8.1 × 6.3 × 5.5 cm (3 ³⁄₁₆ × 2 ½ × 2 ³⁄₁₆ in.)
Lent by The Metropolitan Museum of Art, Purchase, Edward S. Harkness Gift, 1926 (26.7.1395)

Selected references: Cyril Aldred, *Akhenaten & Nefertiti* (New York: Brooklyn Museum, 1973), 91; Kristin Thompson and Marsha Hill, *Statuary from Royal Buildings at Amarna: Its Creation and Contexts* (London: Egypt Exploration Society, 2024), 511–512.

5 Neo-Hittite (Guzana [Tell Halaf]), *Seated Grave Figure*, c. 1000–800 BCE
basalt, 192 × 82 × 100 cm (75 ⁹⁄₁₆ × 32 ⁵⁄₁₆ × 39 ⅜ in.)
Max Freiherr von Oppenheim Foundation, Cologne, TH B 0001

Broken into thousands of pieces by a fire caused by an Allied incendiary bomb that hit the Tell Halaf Museum in Berlin in 1943; restored between 2001 and 2010.

Selected references: Dietrich Opitz and Anton Moortgat, *Tell Halaf III: Die Bildwerke* (Berlin: De Gruyter, 1955), 7–8, 10–11, 35–36; Lutz Martin, entry in Nadja Cholidis and Lutz Martin, eds., *Tell Halaf V: Im Krieg zerstörte Denkmäler und ihre Restaurierung* (Berlin: De Gruyter, 2010), 42, 210–219; Kim Benzel, Rayyane Tabet, and Clare Davies, *Rayyane Tabet: Alien Property* (New York: Metropolitan Museum of Art, 2019), 14–15, 37–38; Vincent Blanchard, ed., *Royaumes oubliés: De l'empire Hittite aux Araméens* (Paris: Louvre Éditions, 2019).

6 Jōmon (northern Japan), *Dogū (Earthen Figure)*, c. 1000–300 BCE
earthenware, 26 × 23 × 12 cm (10 ¼ × 9 1⁄16 × 4 ¾ in.)
John C. Weber Collection

7 Nuragic (Mont'e Prama), *Warrior with Shield*, c. 900–700 BCE
micritic limestone, figure: 198 × 61 × 32 cm (77 15⁄16 × 24 × 12 ⅝ in.); shield: 65 × 65 × 16 cm (25 9⁄16 × 25 9⁄16 × 6 5⁄16 in.)
Fondazione Mont'e Prama—Museo G. Marongiu, Cabras, 201879, 201881

Selected references: Barbara Faedda and Paolo Carta, eds., *A Lost Mediterranean Culture: The Giant Statues of Sardinia's Mont'e Prama* (New York: Columbia University Press, 2023), iii, 7–8.

8 Olmec (Costa Rica), *Mask Fragment Pendant*, c. 900–600 BCE
jade, 12.7 × 3.9 × 3 cm (5 × 1 9⁄16 × 1 3⁄16 in.)
The Al Thani Collection, ATC1029

Selected references: Gerald Berjonneau, Emile Deletaille, and Jean-Louis Sonnery, eds., *Rediscovered Masterpieces of Mesoamerica* (Boulogne: Éditions Arts, 1985), 42; Michael D. Coe, *The Olmec World: Ritual and Rulership* (Princeton: Princeton University Art Museum, 1995), 255; Margaret Young-Sánchez, entry in Amin Jaffer, Jasper Gaunt, and Émilie Foyer, eds., *Treasures of the Al Thani Collection at the Hôtel de la Marine* (Paris: Éditions du Patrimoine / Centre des Monuments Nationaux, 2021), 192–193.

9 Egyptian, *Fragment of a Hand from a Colossal Statue*, c. 664–630 BCE
basalt, 4.6 × 9.2 × 11 cm (1 13⁄16 × 3 ⅝ × 4 5⁄16 in.)
Brooklyn Museum, Charles Edwin Wilbour Fund, 37.264E

10 Greek (Athens), *Head of a Kouros*, c. 530–515 BCE
marble, 25 × 18.4 × 19.1 cm (9 13⁄16 × 7 ¼ × 7 ½ in.)
Museum of Fine Arts, Boston, Bartlett Collection—Museum purchase with funds from the Francis Bartlett Donation of 1912, 34.169
Washington only

Possibly toppled or vandalized during the Persian invasion of Athens in 480 BCE; damage may also have resulted from the Athenians, who used older sculptures as building material after the siege.

Selected references: Cornelius C. Vermeule and Mary B. Comstock, *Sculpture in Stone and Bronze in the Museum of Fine Arts Boston: Additions to the Collections of Greek, Etruscan, and Roman Art, 1971–1988* (Boston: The Museum, 1988), 106.

11 Master of Apollo? (Portonaccio in Veii), *Head of Hermes (Turms)*, c. 510–500 BCE
terracotta with traces of pigment, 46 × 28 × 26 cm (18 ⅛ × 11 × 10 ¼ in.)
Museo Nazionale Etrusco di Villa Giulia, Rome, 40772
Florence only

12 Egyptian, *Face and Shoulder from an Anthropoid Sarcophagus*, c. 332–330 BCE
graywacke, 47 × 52.1 × 12.7 cm (18 ½ × 20 ½ × 5 in.)
Brooklyn Museum, Charles Edwin Wilbour Fund, 37.1516E

Likely broken in antiquity by grave robbers seeking the gold and other precious items interred with the mummy.

Selected references: Edward Bleiberg, "Why Are the Noses Broken on Egyptian Statues?," in Edward Bleiberg and Stephanie Weissberg, *Striking Power: Iconoclasm in Ancient Egypt* (New York: Brooklyn Museum; St. Louis, MO: Pulitzer Arts Foundation, 2019), 48.

13 Greek (Athens), *Sword, Drapery, and Leg from an Equestrian Statue (King Demetrios Poliorketes?)*, c. 320–270 BCE
bronze with traces of gilding, sword: 88 × 5.5 cm (34 ⅝ × 2 3⁄16 in.); drapery: 41 × 21 cm (16 ⅛ × 8 ¼ in.); leg: 87 × 23 cm (34 ¼ × 9 1⁄16 in.)
The Museum of the Ancient Agora, Athens, B1382, B1383, B1384

Dismantled and stripped of its gilding in 200 BCE by the Athenians as part of a campaign against images of Antigonid rulers following Philip V's attack on the city.

Selected references: T. Leslie Shear, "The Athenian Agora: Excavations of 1971," *Hesperia: The Journal of the American School of Classical Studies at Athens* 42, no. 2 (1973): 166–167; Caroline Houser, "Alexander's Influence on Greek Sculpture: As Seen in a Portrait in Athens," *Studies in the History of Art* 10 (1982): 228–238; Rachel Kousser, *The Afterlives of Greek Sculpture: Interaction, Transformation, and Destruction* (New York: Cambridge University Press, 2017), 208–212; Andrew Stewart, "'Memorials of All Our Noble Deeds': Politics, Power, and Representation in the Athenian Agora, 510 B.C. to A.D. 14; A Critical Review," *Hesperia* 92, no. 2 (2023): 245.

14 Roman, *Anatomical Votives: Head, Breasts, Hands, Polyvisceral Torso, Uterus, Legs with Feet*, c. 300–100 BCE
terracotta, head (inv. 115308/1): 26 × 20 × 10 cm (10 ¼ × 7 ⅞ × 3 15⁄16 in.); breast (inv. 14599): 10 cm (3 15⁄16 in.); breast (inv. 14602): 11 cm (4 5⁄16 in.); polyvisceral torso (inv. 14609): 43 × 27 × 13 cm (16 15⁄16 × 10 ⅝ × 5 ⅛ in.); hand (inv. 14383): 20 × 9 × 6 cm (7 ⅞ × 3 9⁄16 × 2 ⅜ in.); hand (inv. 14393): 20 × 9 × 5.5 cm (7 ⅞ × 3 9⁄16 × 2 3⁄16 in.); uterus (inv. 14695): 15 × 9.5 × 4 cm (5 ⅞ × 3 ¾ × 1 9⁄16 in.); leg and foot (inv. 47222/4): 46 × 13 × 15 cm (18 ⅛ × 5 ⅛ × 5 ⅞ in.); leg and foot (inv. 47222): 49 × 12.5 × 25 cm (19 5⁄16 × 4 15⁄16 × 9 13⁄16 in.)
Museo Nazionale Romano—Terme di Diocleziano, Rome, inv. 115308/1, 14599, 14602, 14609, 14383, 14393, 14695, 47222/4, 47222

Selected references: Massimo Osanna, Stéphane Verger, Maria Luisa Catoni, and Demetrios Athanasoulis, *L'istante e l'eternità: Tra noi e gli antichi* (Milan: Electa, 2023), 236.

15 Greek (Pergamon), *Colossal Head of a Youth*, c. 200–100 BCE
marble, 58 × 33 × 44 cm (22 13⁄16 × 13 × 17 5⁄16 in.)
Antikensammlung, Staatliche Museen zu Berlin, inv. AvP VII 283
Washington only

Selected references: Ralf von den Hoff, entry in Andreas Scholl, ed., *Katalog der Skulpturen in der Antikensammlung der Staatlichen Museen zu Berlin*, vol. 1, *Griechische und römische Bildnisse* (Berlin: Staatliche Museen zu Berlin; Michael Imhof Verlag, 2016), cat. 33; Ralf von den Hoff in Carlos A. Picón and Seán Hemingway, eds., *Pergamon and the Hellenistic Kingdoms of the Ancient World* (New York: Metropolitan Museum of Art, 2016), 151–152.

16 Greek/Italian, *Statuette of an African Youth*, c. 180–150 BCE (head); before 1590 (body)
bronze (head and legs), silver plate (teeth and corneas), blue glass (pupils), black and white Aquitaine marble (body), breccia with paint (base), 45.5 × 16.5 × 16 cm (17 15⁄16 × 6 ½ × 6 5⁄16 in.)
Museo Archeologico Nazionale di Firenze, inv. 2288
Florence only

Selected references: Gabriella Capecchi, entry in Barbara Arbeid and Mario Iozzo, eds., *Piccoli grandi bronzi: Capolavori greci, etruschi e romani delle collezioni mediceo-lorenesi nel Museo Archeologico Nazionale di Firenze* (Florence: Edizione Polistampa, 2015), 182–184.

17 Etruscan, *Lion's Paw on a Severed Human Head*, c. 150 BCE
nenfro, 53 × 30 × 17 cm (20 7⁄8 × 11 13⁄16 × 6 11⁄16 in.)
Ny Carlsberg Glyptotek, Copenhagen, HIN 0250
Washington only

Selected references: Mette Moltesen, "Dødens triumf," *Meddelelser fra Ny Carlsberg Glyptotek* 41 (1985): 56–61; Mette Moltesen and Marjatta Nielsen, *Etruria and Central Italy, 450–30 B.C.: Catalogue* (Copenhagen: Ny Carlsberg Glyptotek, 1996), 40–44.

18 Greek (Antikythera), *Left Arm of a Boxer*, late 2nd century–early 1st century BCE
bronze, 76 × 14.5 × 24 cm (29 15⁄16 × 5 11⁄16 × 9 7⁄16 in.)
Hellenic National Archeological Museum, Athens, HNAM X 15111

Broken as the result of a shipwreck that occurred around 70–50 BCE off the coast of the island of Antikythera.

Selected references: Elena Vlachogianni, "Sculpture: 'Gods and heroes from the depths of the sea,'" in *The Antikythera Shipwreck: The Ship, the Treasures, the Mechanism*, ed. Nikolaos Kaltsas, Elena Vlachogianni, and Polyxeni Bouyia (Athens: Kapon Editions, 2012), 88–89; Brian Martens, "A Gymnasion Assemblage Lost at Sea? The Statues from the Antikythera Shipwreck Reconsidered," *Annual of the British School at Athens* (2025): 5–8.

19 Roman (Livorno), *Livorno Torso*, 1st century BCE
bronze, 93 × 58 × 32 cm (36 5⁄8 × 22 13⁄16 × 12 5⁄8 in.)
Museo Archeologico Nazionale di Firenze, inv. 1638

Selected references: Carol C. Mattusch, "The Bronze Torso in Florence: An Exact Copy of a Fifth-Century BC Greek Original," *American Journal of Archaeology* 82 (1978): 101–104; Stefano Bruni, "Un torso di bronze, una equivoca lettura e una falsa provenienza," in *Alle origini di Livorno: L'età etrusca e romana*, ed. Stefano Bruni (Florence: Polistampa, 2009), 21–24.

20 Greek (Antikythera), *Crouching Boy (Wrestler?)*, early 1st century BCE
Parian marble, 111.5 × 45 × 66 cm (43 7⁄8 × 17 11⁄16 × 26 in.)
Hellenic National Archeological Museum, Athens, HNAM 2773

Found in 1900 partially buried on the seafloor after having sunk with a ship full of sculpture that crashed around 70–50 BCE off the coast of the island of Antikythera.

Selected references: Elena Vlachogianni, "Sculpture: 'Gods and heroes from the depths of the sea,'" in *The Antikythera Shipwreck: The Ship, the Treasures, the Mechanism*, ed. Nikolaos Kaltsas, Elena Vlachogianni, and Polyxeni Bouyia (Athens: Kapon Editions, 2012), 104–105; Brian Martens, "A Gymnasion Assemblage Lost at Sea? The Statues from the Antikythera Shipwreck Reconsidered," *Annual of the British School at Athens* (2025): 15–20.

21 Roman, *Head of a Youth (Ephebe)*, late 1st century BCE–early 1st century CE
basanite, 20 × 17 × 20 cm (7 7⁄8 × 6 11⁄16 × 7 7⁄8 in.)
Musei Vaticani, Vatican City, inv. 10134

Selected references: Jens M. Daeher, entry in Jens M. Daehner and Kenneth Lapatin, eds., *Power and Pathos: Bronze Sculpture of the Hellenistic World* (Los Angeles: J. Paul Getty Museum, 2015), 300–301.

22 Roman (Herculaneum), *Head of an Amazon (?)*, 1st century CE
Pentelic marble with pigment, 34 × 23 × 25 cm (13 3⁄8 × 9 1⁄16 × 9 13⁄16 in.)
Parco Archeologico di Ercolano, Herculaneum, 87021

Selected references: Giacomo Ciccondicola, entry in Claudio Parisi Presicce, Nadia Agnoli, Allesandra Avagliano, and Francesca De Tomasi, *Fidia* (Rome: L'Erma di Bretschneider, 2023), 223.

23 Roman (Egypt), *Bust of Germanicus Caesar*, c. 14–20 CE
basanite, 47 × 30 × 24 cm (18 ½ × 11 13⁄16 × 9 7⁄16 in.)
The Trustees of the British Museum, 1872,0605.1

Likely defaced by Early Christians in Egypt sometime after the fourth century CE.

Selected references: Troels Myrup Kristensen, "Embodied Images: Christian Response and Destruction in Late Antique Egypt," *Journal of Late Antiquity* 2, no. 2 (2009): 229–232; Elisabeth R. O'Connell, "Living with the Monumental Past," in *Egypt: Faith After the Pharaohs*, ed. Cäcilia Fluck, Gisela Helmecke, and Elisabeth R. O'Connell (London: British Museum Press, 2015), 96; Stefanie Lenk, "Iconoclasm," in *Imagining the Divine: Art and the Rise of World Religions*, ed. Jaś Elsner and Stefanie Lenk (Oxford: Ashmolean Museum, University of Oxford, 2017), 128–231.

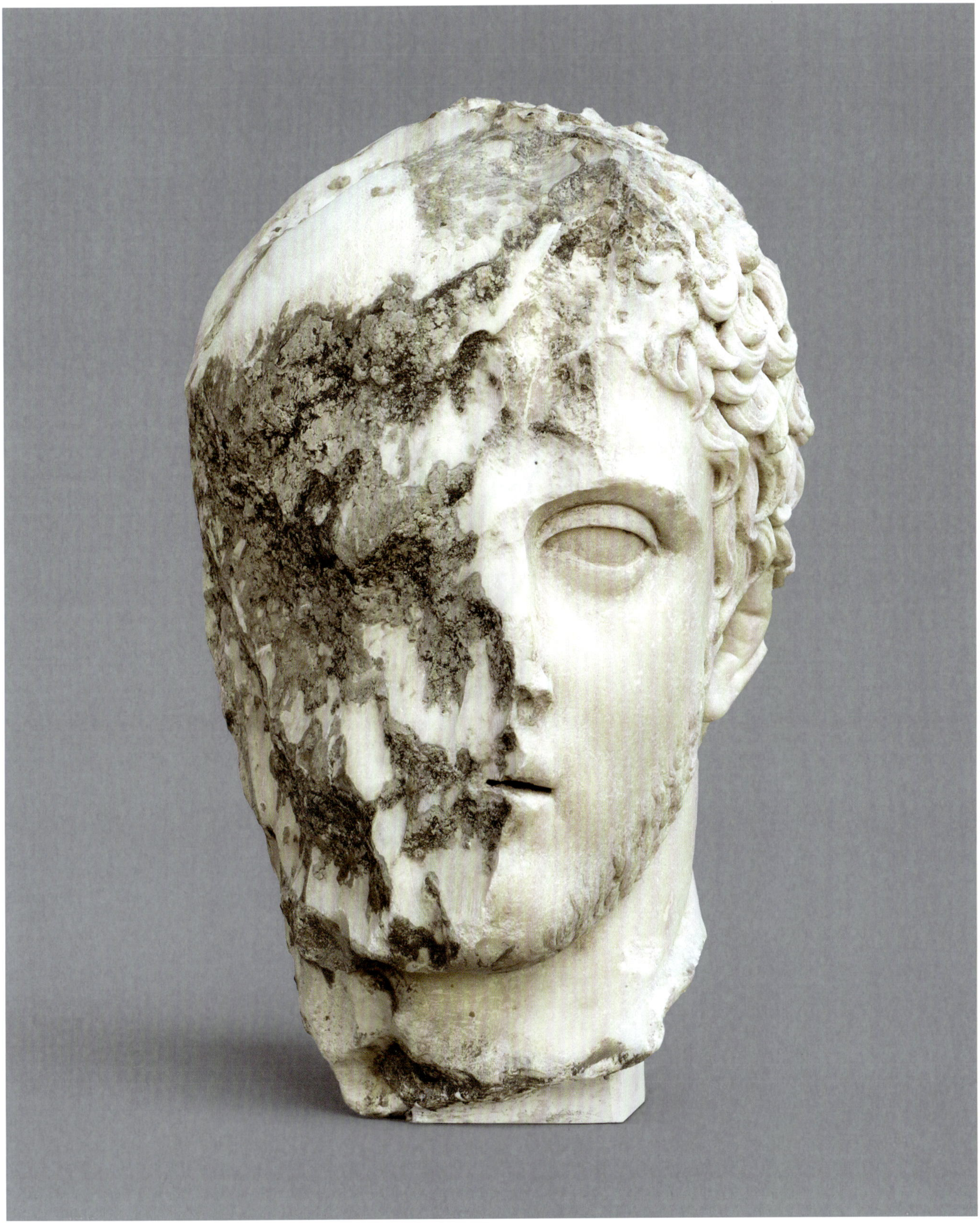

Roman (Rome), *Head of Diomedes (?)*, late 2nd century CE, marble
Museo Nazionale Romano—Terme di Diocleziano, Rome, inv. 52397
Cat. 29

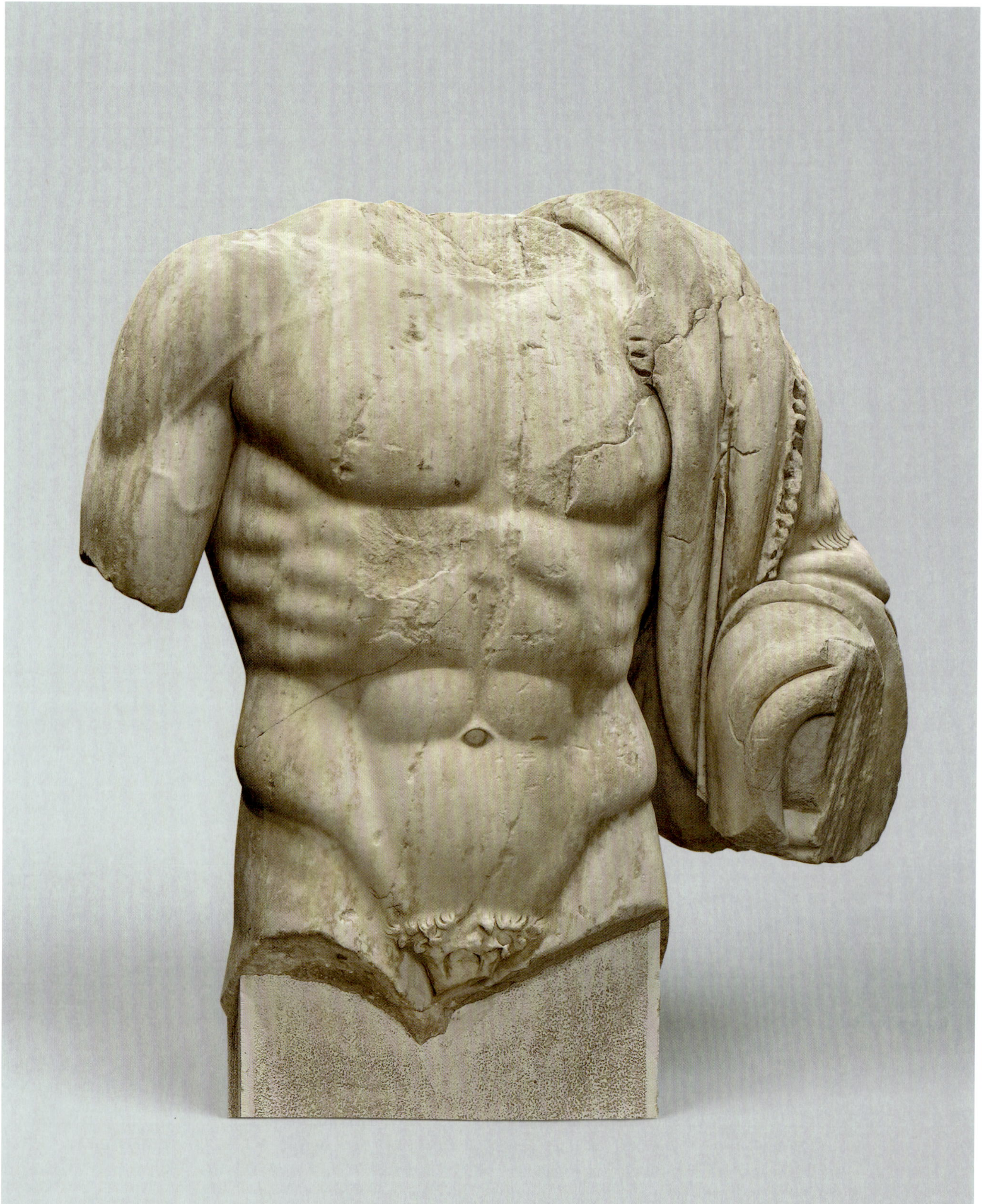

Roman (Rome), *Colossal Torso of Domitian Dressed as Hercules in Combat*,
late 2nd century CE, marble
Museo Nazionale Romano—Terme di Diocleziano, Rome, 2002932
Cat. 30

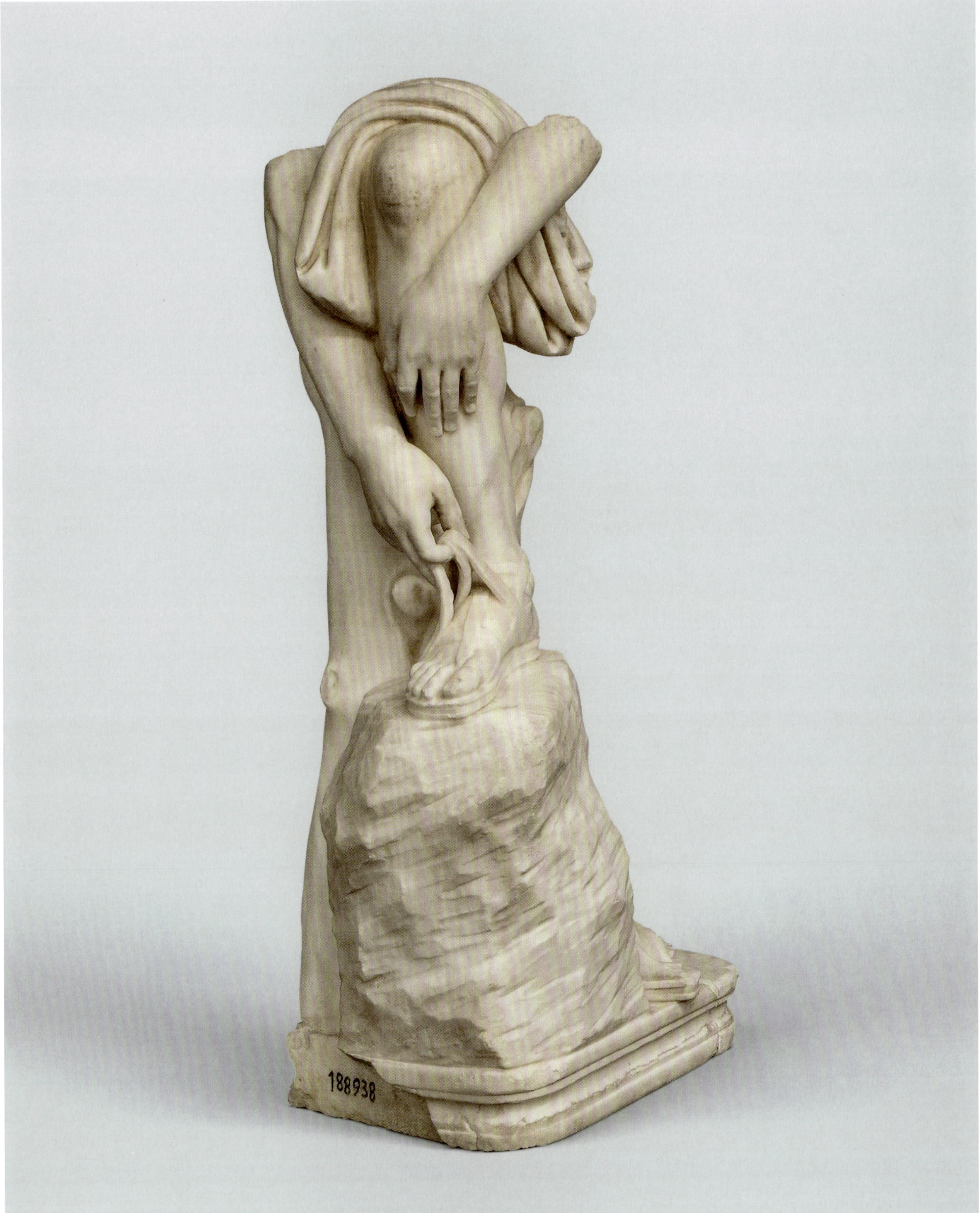

Roman (Rome), *Fragment of Hermes Tying His Sandal*, 2nd century CE, marble
Museo Nazionale Romano—Terme di Diocleziano, Rome, 188938
Cat. 25

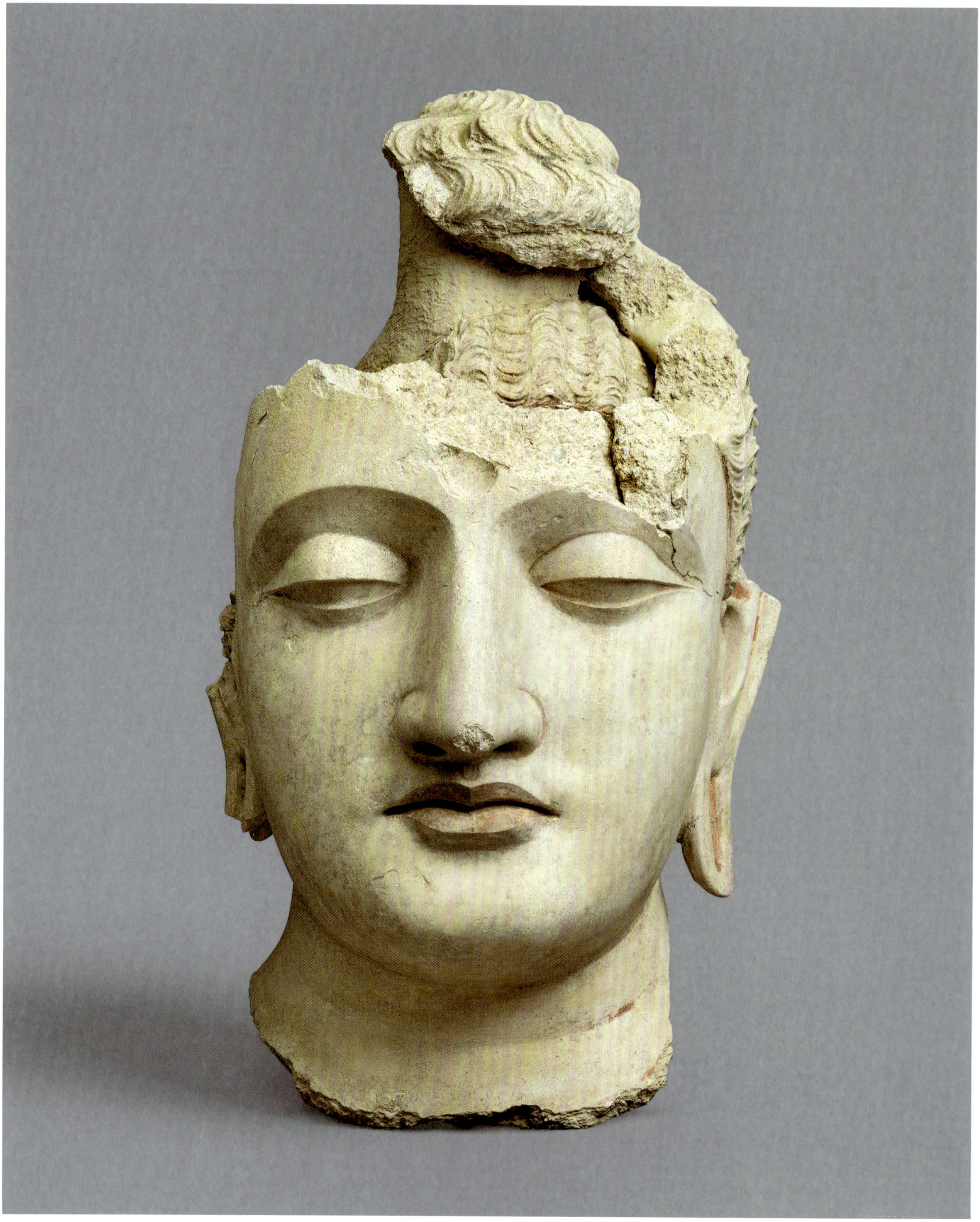

Gandharan (northwest Pakistan or Afghanistan), *Head of Buddha*, c. 300–400 CE, stucco with traces of pigment
MAO Museo d'Arte Orientale, Turin, IAs/17
Cat. 32

24 Roman (Lago di Nemi), *Figured Crossbeam Head with Hand and Forearm from Second Nemi Ship*, c. 37–41 CE
bronze, 60 × 54.5 × 31 cm (23 5⁄8 × 21 7⁄16 × 12 3⁄16 in.)
Museo Nazionale Romano Palazzo Massimo, Rome, inv. 33788

Selected references: Carla De Stefanis, "Le decorazioni di bordo: I bronzi di Palazzo Massimo," in *Caligola: La trasgressione al potere*, ed. Filippo Coarelli and Giuseppina Ghini (Rome: Gangemi Editore, 2013), 131–133; Carla De Stefanis, entry in Carlo Gasparri and Rita Paris, eds., *Palazzo Massimo alle Terme: Le collezioni* (Rome: Ministero per I Beni e le Attività Culturali; Milan: Electa, 2013), 318.

25 Roman (Rome), *Fragment of Hermes Tying His Sandal*, 2nd century CE
marble, 90 × 59 × 40 cm (35 7⁄16 × 23 1⁄4 × 15 3⁄4 in.)
Museo Nazionale Romano—Terme di Diocleziano, Rome, 188938
Florence only

Selected references: Francesco Vezzoli and Stéphane Verger, eds., *Vita Dulcis* (Rome: Quodlibet, 2023), 140–141, no. 9.

26 Roman (Athens), *Head of a Goddess Statue (probably Aphrodite)*, 2nd century CE
marble, 23.7 × 19 × 14.5 cm (9 5⁄16 × 7 1⁄2 × 5 11⁄16 in.)
Acropolis Museum, Athens, EAM 177

Selected references: Giorgos Dontas, "Ein verkanntes Meisterwerk im Nationalmuseum von Athen: Der Marmorkopf Γ. 177 und Überlegungen zum Stil Eupharnors," in Nikolaus Himmelmann, Hans-Ulrich Cain, Hanns Gabelmann, and Dieter Salzmann, eds., *Festschrift für Nikolaus Himmelmann: Beiträge zur Ikonographie und Hermeneutik* (Mainz: P. von Zabern, 1989), 143–150.

27 Teotihuacan, *Standing Figure*, c. 150–250 CE
greenstone (serpentine), 71.2 cm × 23 × 11.2 cm (28 1⁄16 × 9 1⁄16 × 4 7⁄16 in.)
Museo Nacional de Antropología, Mexico City, Secretaría de Cultura—Instituto Nacional de Antropología e Historia, 10-81806

Broken around the time of the fall of Teotihuacan in circa 700 CE, either as part of a ritual "killing" by the city's inhabitants or by iconoclasts who invaded the city.

Selected references: Clara Luzi Díaz Oyarzabal, entry in Kathleen Berrin and Esther Pasztory, eds., *Teotihuacan: Art from the City of the Gods* (San Francisco: Fine Arts Museums of San Francisco, 1993), 177; Leonardo López Luján, Laura Filloy Nadal, Barbara W. Fash, William F. Fash, and Pilar Hernández, "The Destruction of Images in Teotihuacan: Anthropomorphic Sculpture, Elite Cults, and the End of a Civilization," *Res: Anthropology and Aesthetics* 49/50 (2006): 19–28; Anabel Villalonga Gordaliza, "Cuerpos de piedra en la ciudad de los dioses: Idiosincrasia de la escultura antropomorfa Teotihuacana" (PhD diss., Universitat Autònoma de Barcelona, 2014), 1:311, 392, 464–465, 2:79–83.

28 Roman (Rome), *Crouching Venus*, mid-2nd century CE
marble, 99 × 70 × 72 cm (39 × 27 9⁄16 × 28 3⁄8 in.)
Museo Nazionale Romano—Palazzo Massimo, Rome, 60750
Florence only

Selected references: Orietta Vasori, entry in Antonio Giuliani, ed., *Museo Nazionale Romano*, vol. 1, pt. 1, *Le sculture* (Rome: De Luca, 1979), 145–147; Marina Caso, entry in Carlo Gasparri and Rita Paris, eds., *Palazzo Massimo alle Terme: Le collezioni* (Rome: Ministero per I Beni e le Attività Culturali; Milan: Electa, 2013), 215.

29 Roman (Rome), *Head of Diomedes (?)*, late 2nd century CE
marble, 29 × 20 × 22 cm (11 7⁄16 × 7 7⁄8 × 8 11⁄16 in.)
Museo Nazionale Romano—Terme di Diocleziano, Rome, inv. 52397

Selected references: Francesco Vezzoli and Stéphane Verger, eds., *Vita Dulcis* (Rome: Quodlibet, 2023), 141, no. 18.

30 Roman (Rome), *Colossal Torso of Domitian Dressed as Hercules in Combat*, late 2nd century CE
marble, 165 × 125 × 70 cm (64 15⁄16 × 49 3⁄16 × 27 9⁄16 in.)
Museo Nazionale Romano—Terme di Diocleziano, Rome, 2002932
Florence only

Selected references: Francesco Vezzoli and Stéphane Verger, eds., *Vita Dulcis* (Rome: Quodlibet, 2023), 116–117, no. 6.

31 Huastec (Tamtoc), *Scarified Woman*, c. 200 CE
sandstone, 112 × 21.5 × 44 cm (44 1⁄8 × 8 7⁄16 × 17 5⁄16 in.)
Zona Arqueológica de Tamtoc, San Luis Potosí, Secretaría de Cultura—Instituto Nacional de Antropología e Historia, 10-655098

Selected references: Guillermo Córdova Tello, Estala Martínez Mora, and Patricia Olga Hernández Espinoza, eds., *Tamtoc: Esbozo de una antigua sociedad urbana* (Mexico City: Instituto Nacional de Antropología e Historia, 2012), 26–27, 288–289; Amalia Attolini Lecón, ed., *Golfo: Mosaico ancestral* (Mexico City: Instituto Nacional de Antropolgía e Historia, 2019), 2–15, 238–239; Dominique Michelet, ed., *Les Olmèques et les cultures du golfe du Mexique* (Paris: Musée du Quai Branly–Jacques Chirac, 2020), 242–243.

32 Gandharan (northwest Pakistan or Afghanistan), *Head of Buddha*, c. 300–400 CE
stucco with traces of pigment, 84.5 × 51 × 56 cm (33 1⁄4 × 20 1⁄16 × 22 1⁄16 in.)
MAO Museo d'Arte Orientale, Turin, IAs/17
Florence only

33 Roman (Rome), *Right Hand of the Colossal Statue of Constantine*, c. 313–324 CE
Luni marble, 166 × 90 × 65 cm (65 3⁄8 × 35 7⁄16 × 25 9⁄16 in.)
Sovrintendenza Capitolina ai Beni Culturali, Musei Capitolini, Rome, MC S 786

Selected references: Claudio Parisi Presicce, "Constantino come Giove: Proposta di ricostruzione grafica del colosso acrolitico dalla Basilica Costantiniana," *Bullettino della*

Commissione Archeological Comunale di Roma 107 (2006): 127–139; Claudio Parisi Presicce, "From Jupiter to Constantine: A Marble Colossus Reused, Dismembered, 'Reconstructed,'" in *Recycling Beauty*, ed. Salvatore Settis (Milan: Fondazione Prada, 2022).

34 Chinese (Xiangtangshan), *Left Hand of Maitreya, Buddha of the Future*, c. 550–560 CE
limestone, 69.5 × 41.3 × 29.5 cm (27 ⅜ × 16 ¼ × 11 ⅝ in.)
Asian Art Museum of San Francisco, Transfer from the Fine Arts Museums of San Francisco, Gift of the M. H. de Young Endowment Fund, B69S37
Washington only

Sometime after 1922, chiseled away from a statue of the Buddha of the Future located in the North Cave at Northern Xiangtangshan.

Selected references: Genevieve Benton, "Hand of a Chinese Buddha," *Pacific Art Review* 1 (1941): 30–32; Katherine R. Tsiang, *Echoes of the Past: The Buddhist Cave Temples of Xiangtangshan* (Chicago: Smart Museum of Art, University of Chicago Press, 2010), 122, 163.

35 Cham (Quang Nam Province, central Vietnam), *Head of Bodhisattva Avalokiteśhvara*, c. 700–800 CE
copper alloy, 23 × 23 × 12 cm (9 1/16 × 9 1/16 × 4 ¾ in.)
Guimet—Musée National des Arts Asiatiques, Paris, MA7067

Selected references: Pierre Baptiste, entry in Pierre Baptiste and Thierry Zéphir, eds., *Tresors d'art du Vietnam: La sculpture du Champa, Ve–XVe siècles* (Paris: Guimet—Musée des Arts Asiatiques, Réunion des Musées Nationaux, 2005), 202–203; John Guy, entry in John Guy, ed., *Lost Kingdoms: Hindu-Buddhist Sculpture of Early Southeast Asia* (New York: Metropolitan Museum of Art, 2014), 261–262.

36 Javanese (Borobudur), *Head of a Buddha*, late 700s CE
volcanic stone, 33 × 26 × 29 cm (13 × 10 ¼ × 11 7/16 in.)
The Trustees of the British Museum, 1859,1228.177

Originally attached to one of the 504 sculptures of the seated Buddha decorating Borobudur Temple in central Java. Taken from the site in 1814 by Sir Thomas Stamford Raffles (lieutenant-governor of the Dutch East Indies), who either found the head already detached or forcibly removed it.

Selected references: Alexandra Green, entry in Stephen A. Murphey, Naomi Wang, and Alexandra Green, eds., *Raffles in Southeast Asia: Revisiting the Scholar and Statesman* (Singapore: Asian Civilisations Museum, 2019), 162.

37 Khmer (Koh Ker), *Statue of Rama*, 900s CE
sandstone, torso: 154 × 68 × 46 cm (60 ⅝ × 26 ¾ × 18 ⅛ in.); pedestal: 84 × 103 × 103 cm (33 1/16 × 40 9/16 × 40 9/16 in.)
Royal Government of Cambodia, National Museum of Cambodia, Phnom Penh, NMC.277

Originally located at the Prasat Chen temple; sawn from its pedestal during the Cambodian civil war (1970–1975) or amid the political volatility of the decades that followed and subsequently trafficked for sale on the art market.

Selected references: Éric Bourdonneau, "Nouvelles recherches sur Koh Ker (*Chok Gargyar*): Jayavarman IV et la maîtrise des mondes," *Monuments et mémoires de la Fondation Eugène Piot* 90 (2011): 122; Brigitta Hauser-Schäublin, "Looted, Trafficked, Donated, and Returned: The Twisted Tracks of Cambodian Antiquities," in *Cultural Property and Contested Ownership: The Trafficking of Artefacts and the Quest for Restitution*, ed. Brigitta Hauser-Schäublin and Lyndel V. Prott (London: Routledge, 2016), 66–68; Vireak Kong, "Cambodia: The Koh Ker Restitution Cases," *World Heritage* 87 (2018): 21; Chea Socheat, Muong Chanraksmey, and Louise Tythacott, "The Looting of Koh Ker and the Return of the Prasat Chen Statues," in *Returning Southeast Asia's Past: Objects, Museums, and Restitution*, ed. Louise Tythacott and Panggah Ardiyansyah (Singapore: National University of Singapore Press, 2021), 76–77.

38 Lambayeque (North Coast, Peru), *Hand and Forearm*, c. 900–1100 CE
gold, silver, and turquoise, 20.2 × 7.4 × 4.4 cm (7 15/16 × 2 15/16 × 1 ¾ in.)
Dumbarton Oaks Research Library and Collection, Pre-Columbian Collection, Washington, DC, PC.B.463

Selected references: Paloma Carcedo Muro, "Metalurgia Precolombina: Manufactura y técnicas en la orfebrería Sicán," in *Oro del Antiguo Peru*, ed. José Antonio de Lavalle (Lima: Banco de Credito del Perú en la Cultura, 1992), 270–271; Alana Cordy-Collins, "Lambayeque," in *Andean Art at Dumbarton Oaks*, ed. Elizabeth Hill Boone (Washington, DC: Dumbarton Oaks Research Library and Collection, 1996), 195–198; Elizabeth P. Benson, "Why Sacrifice?," in *Ritual Sacrifice in Ancient Peru*, ed. Elizabeth P. Benson and Anita G. Cook (Austin: University of Texas Press, 2001), 9.

39 Inland Niger Delta (Jenné-Jeno), *Fragment of a Kneeling Figure*, c. 1000–1400
terracotta, 48 × 23 × 26 cm (18 15/16 × 9 1/16 × 10 ¼ in.)
The Art Institute of Chicago, Maurice D. Galleher, Ada Turnbull Hertle, and Laura R. Magnuson funds, 1983.917

Possibly broken as the population around Jenné-Jeno began converting to Islam during the thirteenth and fourteenth centuries; also possible that breakage resulted from a tradition of commemorating the start of a new building by shattering a sculpture and burying the remains in the foundation.

Selected references: Bernard de Grunne, "Ancient Sculpture of the Inland Niger Delta and Its Influence on Dogon Art," *African Arts* 21, no. 4 (1988): 54–55; Kathleen Bickford and Cherise Smith, "Art of the Western Sudan," *Art Institute of Chicago Museum Studies* 23, no. 2 (1997): 108; Kathleen Bickford Berzock, entry in Constantine Petridis, ed., *Speaking of Objects: African Art at the Art Institute of Chicago* (Chicago: Art Institute of Chicago, 2020), 34–35.

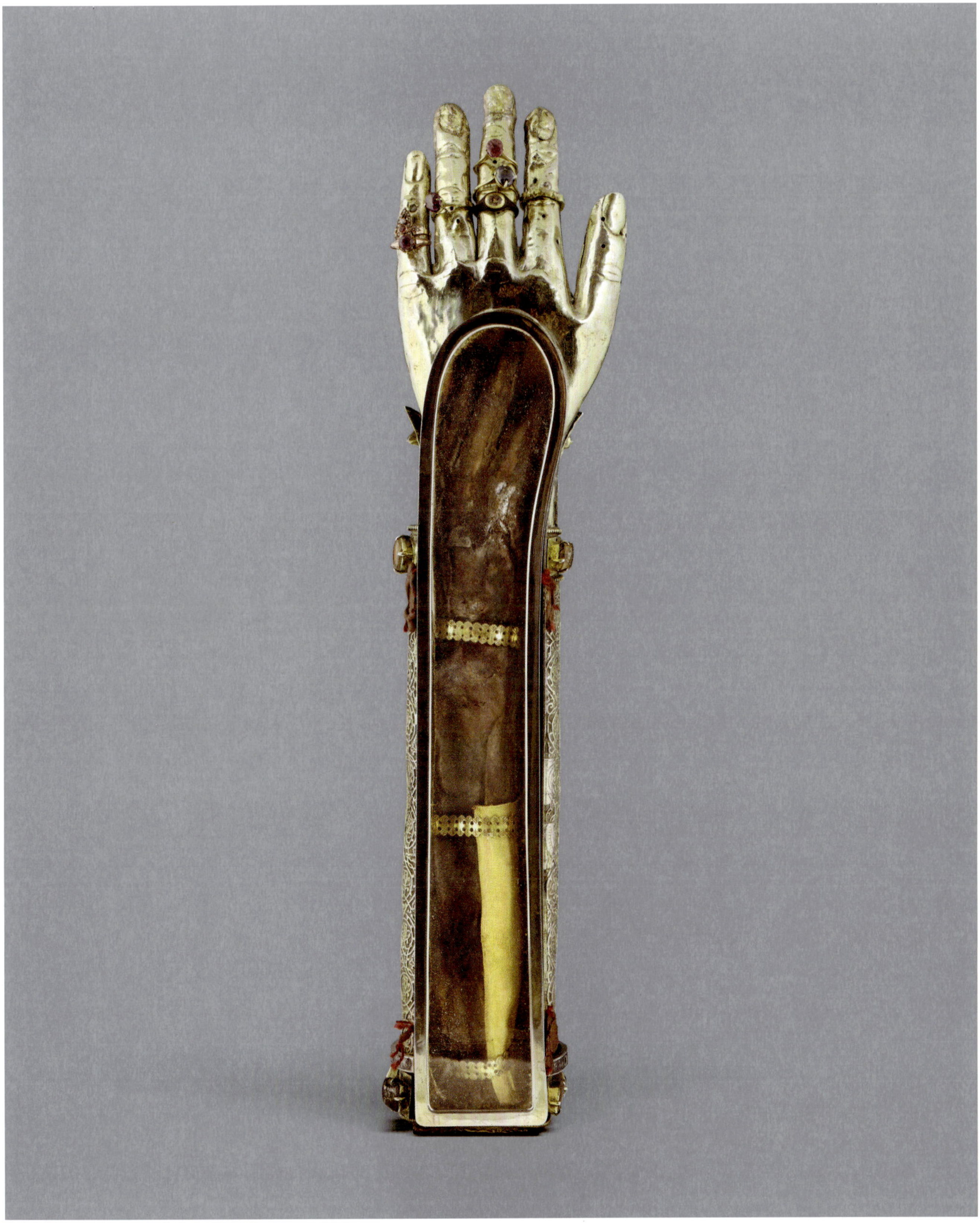

Byzantine, *Arm Reliquary of Saint Anna*, 1300s, gilded silver, gold, gems, and semiprecious stones
Museo del Tesoro di San Lorenzo, Genoa
Cat. 43

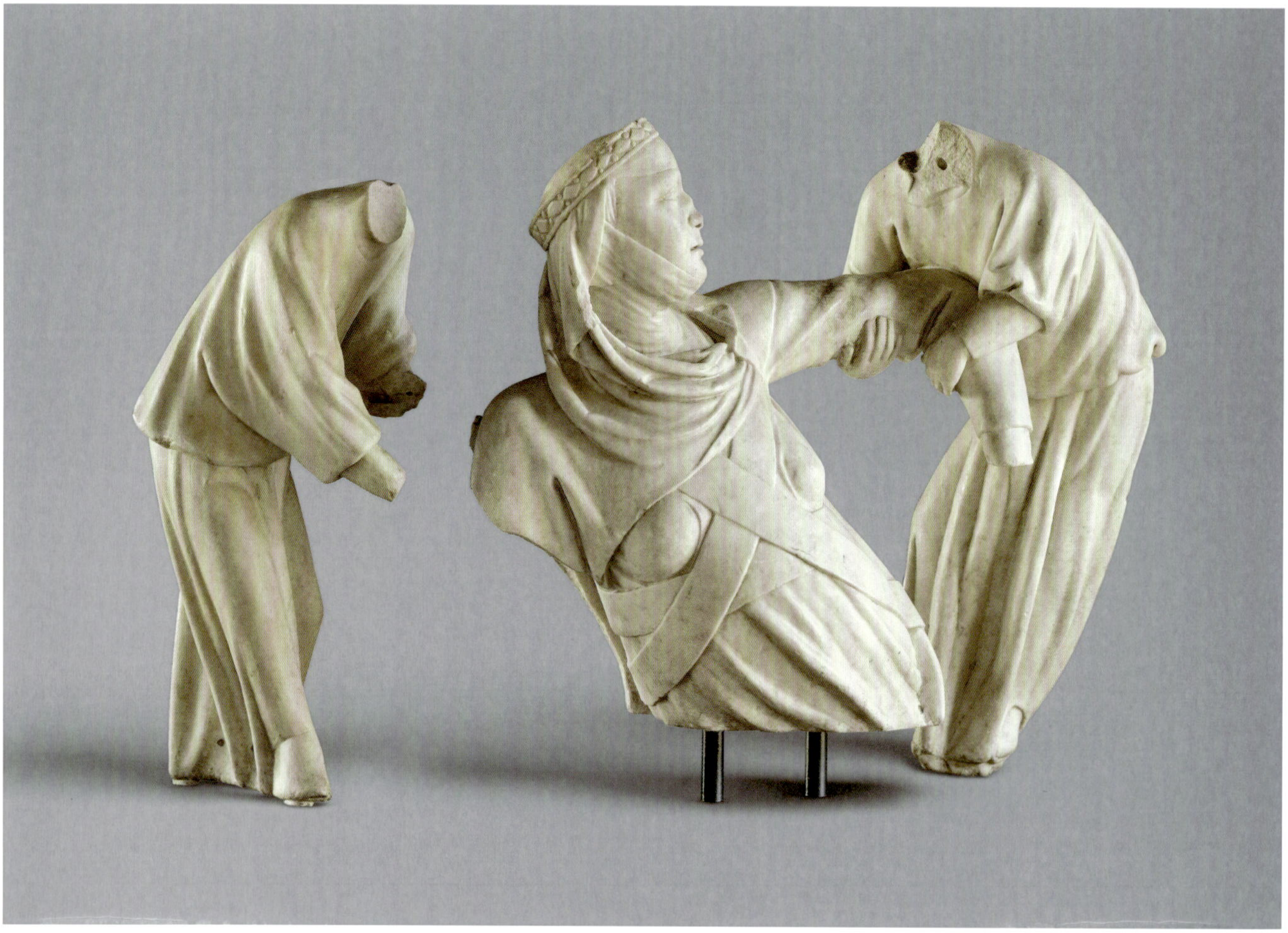

Giovanni Pisano, *Fragments of the Funerary Monument of Margaret of Brabant (Elevatio animae)*, c. 1312–1314, Apuan marble
Museo di Sant'Agostino, Genoa, MSA 258
Cat. 44

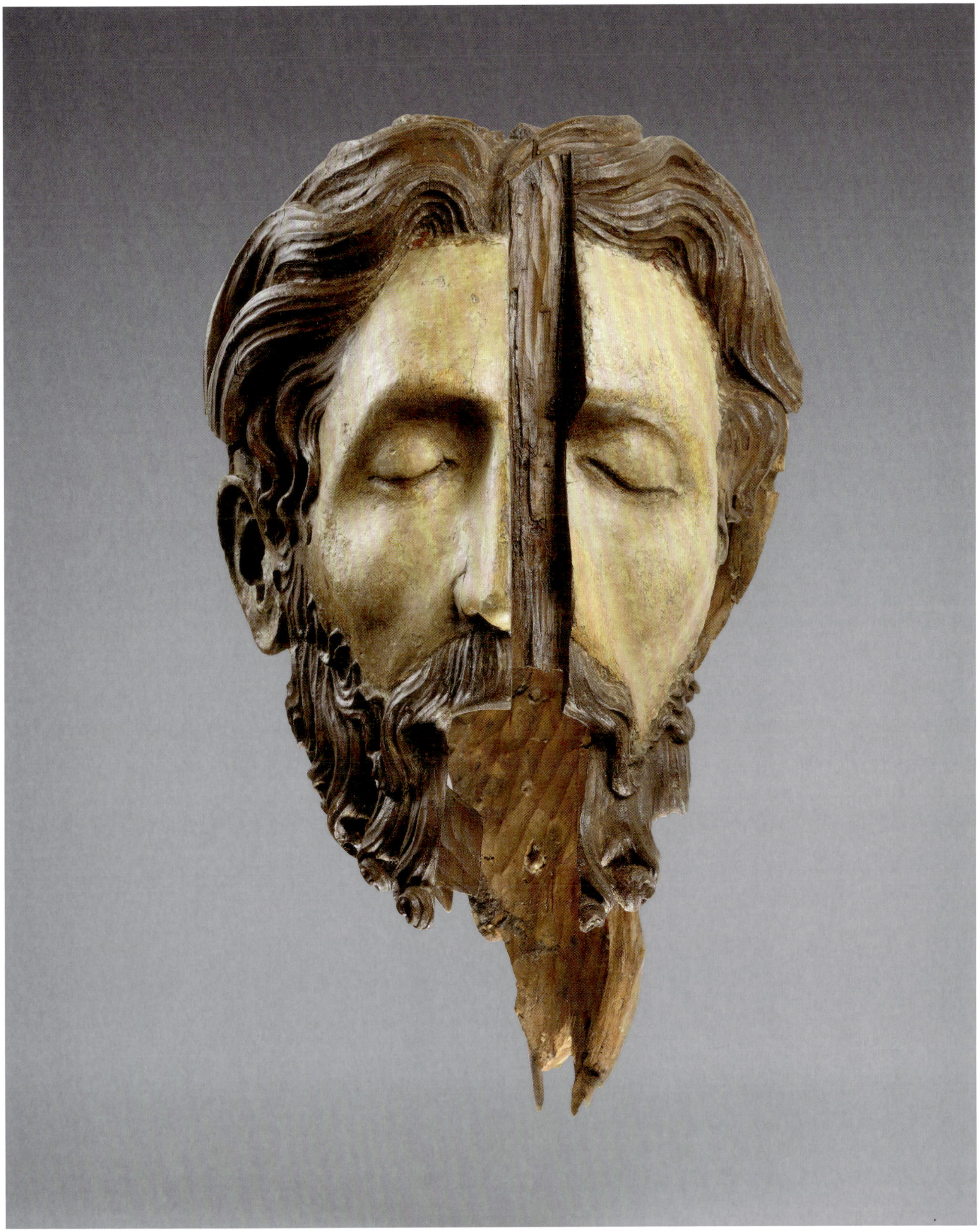

Lando di Pietro, *Head of Christ*, 1338, painted walnut wood
Museo Aurelio Castelli, Basilica dell'Osservanza,
Siena / Arcidiocesi di Siena—Colle di Val d'Elsa—Montalcino
Cat. 47

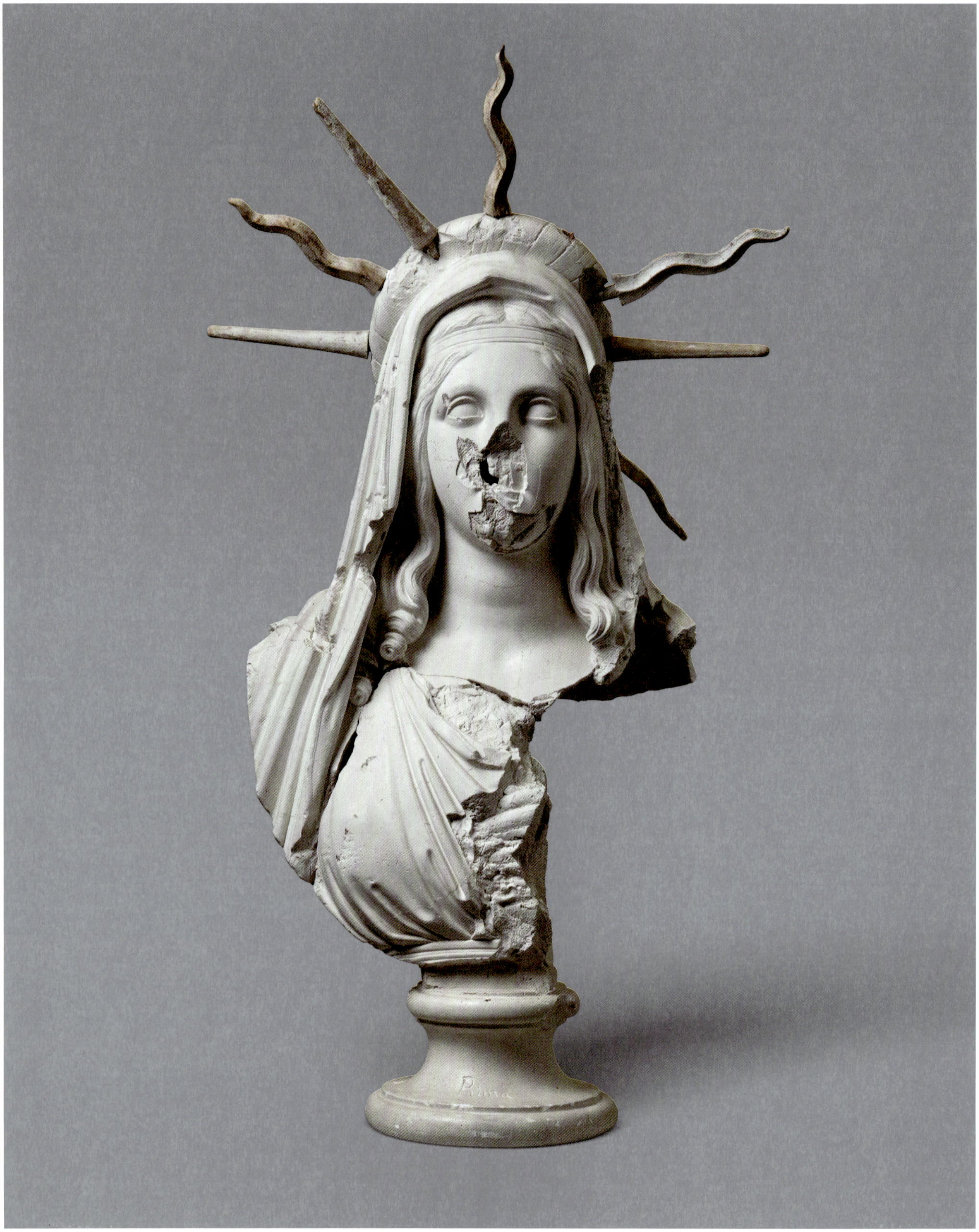

Antonio Canova, *Bust of Religion*, 1815, plaster
Museo Gypsotheca Antonio Canova, Possagno, 338
Cat. 64

40 French (Lavaudieu), *Torso of Christ*, late 1100s
poplar, gesso, paint, and metal leaf, 109.2 × 34.9 × 24.1 cm (43 × 13 ¾ × 9 ½ in.)
Lent by The Metropolitan Museum of Art, The Cloisters Collection, 1925 (25.120.221)

Selected references: Jean-René Gaborit, entry in Danielle Gaborit-Chopin, ed., *La France romane au temps premiers Capétiens (987–1152)* (Paris: Musée du Louvre, 2005), 386–387; Lucretia Goddard Kargère, "La sculpture romane polychrome sur bois en Auvergne et Bourgogne: Étude technique de quatre sculptures du Metropolitan Museum de New York," *Les Cahiers de Saint-Michel de Cuxa* 43 (2012): 111–121; Francesca Girelli, "Local Traditions and Itinerant Artists? The Crucifixes of Auvergne and Wooden Sculpture in France During the late Romanesque Period," *Convivium* 4, no. 2 (2017): 62–63, 66, 71; Lucretia Goddard Kargère, "The Lavaudieu Corpus at The Cloisters," in *Christ on the Cross: The Boston Crucifix and the Rise of Monumental Wood Sculpture, 970–1200*, ed. Shirin Fozi and Gerhard Lutz (Turnhout: Brepols, 2020), 282–301.

41 Workshop of Jean de Chelles?, *Head of a Magus*, 1250–1258
lutetian limestone with traces of pigment, 41 × 30 × 23 cm (16 ⅛ × 11 13⁄16 × 9 1⁄16 in.)
Musée de Cluny–Musée National du Moyen Âge, Paris, Cl. 23127

Originally decorating one of the doorjambs of the north-transept portal at Notre-Dame of Paris; mutilated and removed in 1793 during the French Revolution and later repurposed as foundation material for the Hôtel Moreau.

Selected references: Xavier Dectot, *Sculptures des XIe–XIIIe siècles: Collections du Musée de Cluny* (Paris: Éditions de la Réunion des Musées Nationaux, 2010), online catalog: http://www.sculpturesmedievales-cluny.fr, consulted January 6, 2026; Damien Berné, "Les statues du portrail nord du transept," in *Faire parler les pierres: Sculptures médiévales de Notre-Dame*, ed. Damien Berné (Paris: Musée de Cluny, 2024), 223–227.

42 Arnolfo di Cambio, *Head of Bishop Andrea de' Mozzi*, c. 1296–1300
pietra serena with traces of pigment, height: 39 cm (15 ⅜ in.)
Private collection

Sawed off the tomb effigy of Bishop Andrea de' Mozzi, located in the former church of San Gregorio della Pace in Florence, after 1880, when the property sold to the art collector and dealer Stefano Bardini.

Selected references: Silvia Colucci, "Un sepolcro vescovile del Museo Bardini e qualche ipotesi sull'origine di una tipologia funeria tardo-duecentesca," *Prospettiva*, no. 134–135 (2009): 76–90; G. Fattorini, "Nella Firenze di Dante e di Arnolfo: La testa del *gisant* del vescovo Andrea de' Mozzi," *Paragone Arte* 183, no. 907 (2025): 3–30.

43 Byzantine, *Arm Reliquary of Saint Anna*, 1300s
gilded silver, gold, gems, and semiprecious stones, 45 × 13 × 6 cm (17 11⁄16 × 5 ⅛ × 2 ⅜ in.)
Museo del Tesoro di San Lorenzo, Genoa
Florence only

Selected references: Caterina Marcenaro, *Il museo del tesoro della cattedrale a Genova* (Milan: Silvana Editorial d'Arte, 1970), pls. 3–4; Gianluca Ameri, "Nuove considerazioni sul Reliquiario del braccio di sant'Anna nel Tesoro del Duomo di Genova," *Mitteilungen des Kunsthistorischen Institutes in Florenz* 53, no. 2–3 (2009): 169–196.

44 Giovanni Pisano, *Fragments of the Funerary Monument of Margaret of Brabant (Elevatio animae)*, c. 1312–1314
Apuan marble, 78 × 118.2 × 33.8 cm (30 11⁄16 × 46 9⁄16 × 13 5⁄16 in.)
Museo di Sant'Agostino, Genoa, MSA 258
Florence only

Originally erected in the church of San Francesco di Castelletto in Genoa; partially destroyed between 1798 and 1810 with the church, which was converted into a residential building.

Selected references: Maria Falcone, "Sul monumento funebre di Margherita di Brabante, sulla Tomba del doge Tommaso Campogregoso e su altre opere liguri del Quattrocento," *Prospettiva*, no. 169–171 (2018): 47–89.

45 Mexica (Tenochtitlan [Mexico City]), *Statue of Chalchiuhtlicue*, c. 1325–1521
diorite, 80 × 37.5 × 27.5 cm (31 ½ × 14 ¾ × 10 13⁄16 in.)
Museo Nacional de Antropología, Mexico City, Secretaría de Cultura—Instituto Nacional de Antropología e Historia, 10-82215

Possibly damaged by the Mexica during some kind of renewal campaign such as the New Fire ceremony. More likely attacked and mutilated by the Spanish sometime after their arrival in 1519.

Selected references: Leonardo López Luján, *El capitán Guillermo Dupaix y su album arqueológico de 1794* (Mexico City: Instituto Nacional de Antropología e Historia, 2015), 158–169; Alison Caplan in Joanne Pillsbury, Timothy Potts, and Kim N. Richter, *Golden Kingdoms: Luxury Arts in the Ancient Americas* (Los Angeles: J. Paul Getty Museum and the Getty Research Institute, 2017), 258.

46 Pays de Vaud Workshop? (Romainmôtier), *Kneeling Cluniac Prior (Guillaume de Montricher?)*, c. 1330–1336
molasse sandstone and pigment, 84 × 36 × 62 cm (33 1⁄16 × 14 3⁄16 × 24 7⁄16 in.)
Collection of the Musée Cantonal d'Archéologie et d'Histoire, Lausanne, RO86/17279

Originally part of a monumental tomb in the Cluniac Abbey of Romainmôtier; broken in 1537 by a group of Protestant reformers from Bern.

Selected references: Brigitte Pradervand, Nicolas Schätti, and Jacques Bujard, "Les tombeaux monumentaux en Suisse romande à la fin du Moyen Âge," in *Le marbre et la poussière: Le patrimoine funéraire de la Suisse romande, XIVe–XVIIIe siècles*, Cahiers d'archéologie romande 143, ed. Dave Lüthi (Lausanne: Cahiers d'archéologie romande, 2013): 41–45; Brigitte Pradervand and Nicolas Schätti, "Inhumations et fondations funéraires dans l'église prieurale (XIe–début du XVIe siècle)," in *Romainmotier restaurée 1991–2001: L'église et son décor (XIe–XXe siècle)*, Cahiers d'archéologie romande 145, ed. Brigitte Pradervand and Nicolas Schätti (Lausanne: Cahiers d'archéologie romande, 2014): 87–88; Peter Eggenberger, "Synthèse des résultats des recherches archéologiques: L'évolution architecturale de Romainmôtier de la période gallo-romaine à la sécularisation du prieuré après la Réforme, en 1537," in *Romainmôtier: Mille ans de monachisme; résultats des recherces archéologiques entre 1971 et 2006*, Cahiers d'archéologie romande 183, ed. Peter Eggenberger (Lausanne: Cahiers d'archéologie romande, 2020): 156–158.

47 Lando di Pietro, *Head of Christ*, 1338
painted walnut wood, 31 × 22 × 18 cm (12 3⁄16 × 8 11⁄16 × 7 1⁄16 in.)
Museo Aurelio Castelli, Basilica dell'Osservanza, Siena / Arcidiocesi di Siena—Colle di Val d'Elsa—Montalcino
Florence only

Damaged when the church of the Osservanza in Siena was hit with an Allied bomb on January 23, 1944.

Selected references: Alessandro Bagnoli, entry in Alessandro Bagnoli, ed., *Scultura dipinta: Maestri di legname e pittori a Siena, 1250–1450* (Florence: Centro Di, 1987), 65–68; Roberto Bartalini, ed., *Scultura gotica senese, 1260–1350* (Turin: Fondazione Monte dei Paschi di Siena, 2011), 310.

48 Mexica (Tenochtitlan [Mexico City]), *Chacmool*, c. 1350–1450
volcanic rock and stucco, 48 × 47.5 × 94 cm (18 7⁄8 × 18 11⁄16 × 37 in.)
Museo del Templo Mayor, Mexico City, Secretaría de Cultura—Instituto Nacional de Antropología e Historia, 10-262479

Probably decapitated and buried by the Mexica as a dedicatory offering to fortify new construction at the Templo Mayor.

Selected references: Alfredo López Austin and Leonardo López Luján, "El *chacmool* Mexica," *Caravelle* 76–77 (2001): 68; Alfredo López Austin and Leonardo López Luján, "Los Mexicas y el *Chacmool*," *Arqueología Mexicana* 9, no. 49 (2001): 72–73.

49 Prague (Baden bei Wien), *Heads of Mary and Christ from a Pietà*, c. 1380–1400
limestone, Mary: 27.5 × 23.3 × 16 cm (10 13⁄16 × 9 3⁄16 × 6 5⁄16 in.); Christ: 16.5 × 17 × 12 cm (6 1⁄2 × 6 11⁄16 × 4 3⁄4 in.)
Skulpturensammlung und Museum für Byzantinische Kunst, Staatliche Museen zu Berlin, inv. 2743

Probably subjected to two fires, the first in 1812 in the Augustinian Cloister of Baden bei Wien, the second in May 1945 in the Friedrichshain Flak Tower in Berlin (a storage site for art during World War II). The figures' bodies were lost either in the bunker fire or when the sculpture was transported to the Soviet Union after the war.

Selected references: Julien Chapuis and Stephan Kemperdick, eds., *The Lost Museum: The Berlin Painting and Sculpture Collections 70 Years After World War II* (Berlin: Skulpturensammlung und Museum für Byzantinische Kunst, Staatliche Museen zu Berlin, 2015), 29–33; Dieter Köcher, entry in Tobias Kunz, ed., *Bildwerke nördlich der Alpen und im Alpenraum, 1380–1440: Kritischer Bestandskatalog* (Berlin: Staatliche Museen zu Berlin, Preußischer Kulturbesitz, 2019), 62–73.

50 Tuscan, *Christ Carrying the Cross*, late 14th–early 15th century
poplar wood with traces of pigment and gilding, 165 × 65 × 55 cm (64 15⁄16 × 25 9⁄16 × 21 5⁄8 in.)
Museo di San Marco, Florence

Recovered after the torrential floods that swept through Florence in 1966; original location remains unknown.

Selected references: Magnolia Scudieri, Maria Grazia Vaccari, and Francesca Fiorelli Malesci, *Piccoli grandi tesori alluvionati: Un patrimonio da non dimenticare* (Florence: Firenze Musei, 2006), no. 9.

51 Mexica (Tenochtitlan [Mexico City]), *Fragment of a Serpent Skirt of Coatlicue*, c. 1400–1500
basalt, 111 × 96 × 66 cm (43 11⁄16 × 37 13⁄16 × 26 in.)
Museo Nacional de Antropología, Mexico City, Secretaría de Cultura—Instituto Nacional de Antropología e Historia, 10-393493

Most likely attacked by the Spanish sometime after 1519.

Selected references: Elizabeth H. Boone, "The 'Coatlicues' at the Templo Mayor," *Ancient Mesoamerica* 10, no. 2 (1999): 192–193; Cecelia F. Klein, "A New Interpretation of the Aztec Statue called Coatlicue, 'Snakes-Her-Skirt,'" *Ethnohistory* 55, no. 2 (2008): 233–236; Eduardo Matos Moctezuma and Leonardo López Luján, *Escultura monumental Mexica* (Mexico City: Fundación Conmemoraciones, Fondo de Cultura Económica, 2012), 220–223.

52 German (Braunschweig), *Arm Reliquary of Saint Babylas*, 1467
silver, gilded silver, enamel, glass paste stones, rock crystals, and one amethyst on an oak core, 47.3 × 14.9 × 9.8 cm (18 5⁄8 × 5 7⁄8 × 3 7⁄8 in.)
Philadelphia Museum of Art, Purchased with Museum funds, 1951, 1951-12-1
Washington only

Selected references: Otto von Falke, Robert Schmidt, and Georg Swarzenski, eds., *The Guelph Treasure: The Sacred Relics of Brunswick Cathedral Formerly in the Possession of the Ducal House of Brunswick-Lüneburg*, trans. Silvia M. Welsh (Frankfurt am Main: Frankfurter Verlags-Anstalt, 1930), 86, 91, 215, pl. 105; Patrick M. de Winter, *Der Welfenschatz: Zeugnis sakraler Kunst des Deutschen Mittelalters* (Hannover: Touristbuch Hannover, 1986), 37–38, 125; Dean Walker and Jack Hinton, entry in Sarah Noreika, ed., *Philadelphia Museum of Art: Handbook* (Philadelphia: Philadelphia Museum of Art, 2014), 102–103.

53 Master of the Soest Altarpiece, *Soldier from Christ Carrying the Cross*, c. 1475–1500
oak with traces of pigment and gilding, 47 × 17.5 × 14 cm (18 1⁄2 × 6 7⁄8 × 5 1⁄2 in.)
Loan from the Rijksmuseum, BK-NM-12006-15-B

Originally part of an altarpiece that was dismantled and hidden in the tower of the Oude Kerk in Soest to safeguard it from one of the waves of Protestant iconoclasm that swept the region in 1566 and 1580; subsequently forgotten and rediscovered in its current state in 1905.

Selected references: Klara Broekhuijsen-Kruijer, "Het Passieretabel uit Soest," *Bulletin van het Rijksmuseum* 32, no. 1 (1984): 5–7; Bas Nederveen, "Het passieretabel van Soest: Kanttekeningen bij een reconstructie," *Bulletin van het Rijksmuseum* 52, no. 3–4 (2004): 272–274; Bram van den Hoven van Genderen, entry in Micha Leeflang and Kees van Schooten, eds., *Middeleeuwse beelden uit Utrecht, 1430–1530* (Utrecht: Museum Catharijneconvent, 2012), 218–223.

54 French (Nevers), *Head of a Female Saint*, c. 1500–1515
stone with traces of pigment, 28 × 25 × 25 cm (11 × 9 13⁄16 × 9 13⁄16 in.)
Musée du Louvre, Département des Sculptures, Paris, RF 882

Selected references: Françoise Baron, "Sculptures nivernaises du Moyen Age et de la Renaissance au Musée du Louvre," *Bulletin de la Société nivernaise des lettres, sciences et arts* 45 (1996): 179–181; Musée du Louvre, *Sculpture française*, vol. 2, *Renaissance et temps modernes*, pt. 2, *Goujon-Warin et anonymes*, ed. Jean-René Gaborit (Paris: Éditions de la Réunion des Musées Nationaux, 1998), 641.

55 Michelangelo Buonarroti, *Model of a Nude Woman*, c. 1533
terracotta, height: 35 cm (13 3⁄4 in.)
Casa Buonarroti, Florence, 193

Selected references: Jeannine O'Grody, "'Un semplice modello': Michelangelo and His Three-Dimensional Preparatory Works" (PhD diss., Case Western Reserve University, 1999), 262–266.

56 Italian, *Restored Right Arm of the Laocoön*, 1540s or 1600s (before 1722)
marble, 45 × 76.5 × 32 cm (17 11⁄16 × 30 1⁄8 × 12 5⁄8 in.)
Musei Vaticani, Vatican City, inv. 1067

Selected references: Paolo Liverani, entry in Francesco Buranelli, Paolo Liverani, and Arnold Nesselrath, *Laocoonte: Alle origini dei Musei Vaticani* (Rome: L'Erma di Bretschneider, 2006), 180–181; Ludovico Rebaudo, *Il braccio mancante: I restauri del Laocoonte (1506–1957)* (Trieste: Editreg, 2007), 30–42; Gabriella Capecchi, "Superare l'antico: Il Laocoonte 'perfetto,'" in *Baccio Bandinelli: Scultore e maestro (1493–1560)*, ed. Detlef Heikamp and Betrice Paolozzi Strozzi (Florence: Firenze Musei and Giunti, 2014), 129–155; Alan Chong, "Copies, Restorations, and Caricatures: Montorsoli at the Vatican," in *The Sculpture of Giovan Angelo Montorsoli and His Circle: Myth and Faith in Renaissance Florence*, ed. Alan Chong and Lorenzo Principi (Manchester, NH: Currier Museum of Art, 2018), 51; Francis Haskell and Nicholas Penny, *Taste and the Antique: The Lure of Classical Sculpture, 1500–1900* (Turnhout: Harvey Miller, 2024), 1:378.

57 Italian, *Restored Head and Right Arm of Sleeping Ariadne*, 1540s–1580s
Docimian marble, 43 × 67 × 38 cm (16 15⁄16 × 26 3⁄8 × 14 15⁄16 in.)
Museo Archeologico Nazionale di Firenze, 13727

Selected references: Antonella Romualdi, *I marmi antichi conservati nella Villa Corsini a Castello*, vol. 1, *Le statue* (Livorno: Sillabe, 2004), 191–192.

58 Adriaen de Vries, *Satyr*, c. 1580–1585
terracotta, height: 52 cm (20 1⁄2 in.)
Private collection, courtesy of McClain Gallery
Washington only

Selected references: Frits Scholten, *The Modeller: Adriaen de Vries in Search of the* Viva Figura, trans. Pierre Bouvier, Studies in Netherlandish Art and Cultural History 19 (Leiden: Brill, 2025), 69.

59 Jarai (Central Highlands, Vietnam), *Figure Wearing a Mask*, late 1600s–1700s
wood, 152 × 35 × 33 cm (59 13⁄16 × 13 3⁄4 × 13 in.)
Yale University Art Gallery, promised gift of Thomas Jaffe, B.A. 1971

60 Ngaju (Borneo), *Ancestor Figure (Hampatong)*, late 1600s–1800s
wood, 35 × 17 × 18 cm (13 3⁄4 × 6 11⁄16 × 7 1⁄16 in.)
Yale University Art Gallery, promised gift of Thomas Jaffe, B.A. 1971

Selected references: Jerome Feldman, *The Eloquent Dead: Ancestral Sculpture of Indonesia and Southeast Asia* (Los Angeles: Fowler Museum at UCLA, 1985), 23.

61 François Girardon (designer) and Jean Balthazar Keller (caster), *Left Foot from the Equestrian Statue of King Louis XIV*, 1692–1694 (cast and finished)
bronze, 40 × 71.5 × 29.5 cm (15 3⁄4 × 28 1⁄8 × 11 5⁄8 in.)
Musée du Louvre, Département des Sculptures, Paris, MR3448. On long-term loan to the Musée Carnavalet—Histoire de Paris

The statue, which originally stood on the Place Vendôme in Paris, was destroyed on August 12, 1792, as part of the French Revolution.

Selected references: Michel Martin, *Les monuments équestres de Louis XIV: Une grande entreprise de propaganda monarchique* (Paris: Picard, 1986), 92–117; Françoise de La Moureyre, entry in Geneviève Bresc-Bautier and Guilhem Scherf, eds., *Cast in Bronze: French Sculpture from Renaissance to Revolution* (Paris: Musée du Louvre and Somogy Art Publishers, 2009), 326–327; Alexandre Maral, *François Girardon (1628–1715): Le sculpteur de Louis XIV* (Paris: Arthena, 2015), 203–223.

62 Edme Bouchardon, *Right Hand from the Equestrian Statue of King Louis XV*, 1758 (cast)
bronze, 24 × 22 × 32 cm (9 7⁄16 × 8 11⁄16 × 12 5⁄8 in.)
Musée du Louvre, Département des Sculptures, Paris, RF94. On long-term loan to the Musée Carnavalet—Histoire de Paris

The statue, which originally stood on today's Place de la Concorde in Paris, was destroyed on August 10, 1792, as part of the French Revolution.

Selected references: Andrew McClellan, "The Life and Death of a Royal Monument: Bouchardon's Louis XV," *Oxford Art Journal* 23, no. 2 (2000): 25; Anne-Lise Desmas, entry in Anne-Lise Desmas, Édouard Kopp, Guilhem Scherf, and Juliette Trey, *Bouchardon: Royal Artist of the Enlightenment* (Los Angeles: J. Paul Getty Museum, 2016), 402; Yves Carlier and Hélène Delalex, eds., *Louis XV: Passions d'un roi, 1710–1774* (Versailles: Château de Versailles, 2022), 317.

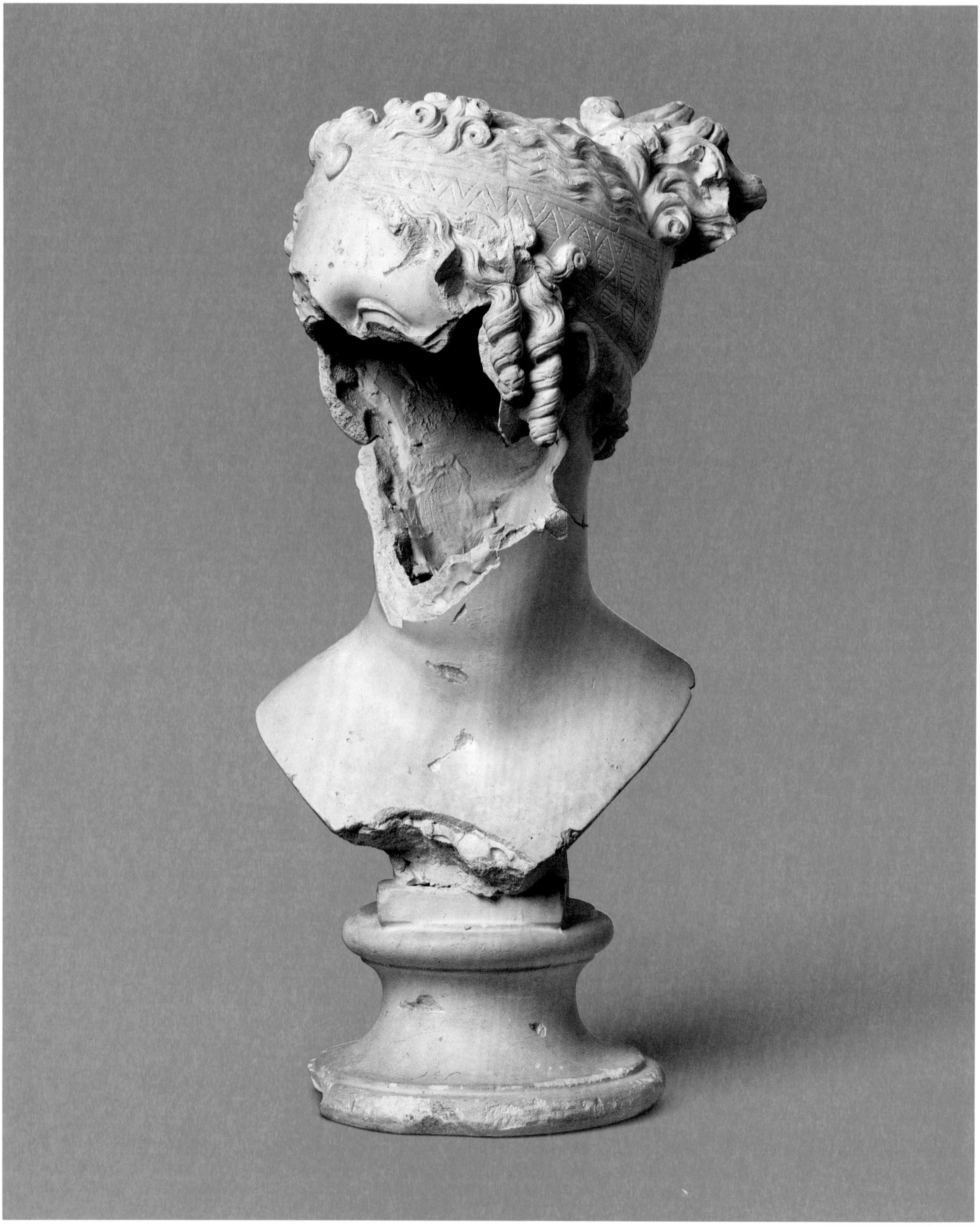

Antonio Canova, *Bust of Terpsichore*, 1817, plaster
Museo Gypsotheca Antonio Canova, Possagno, 316
Cat. 65

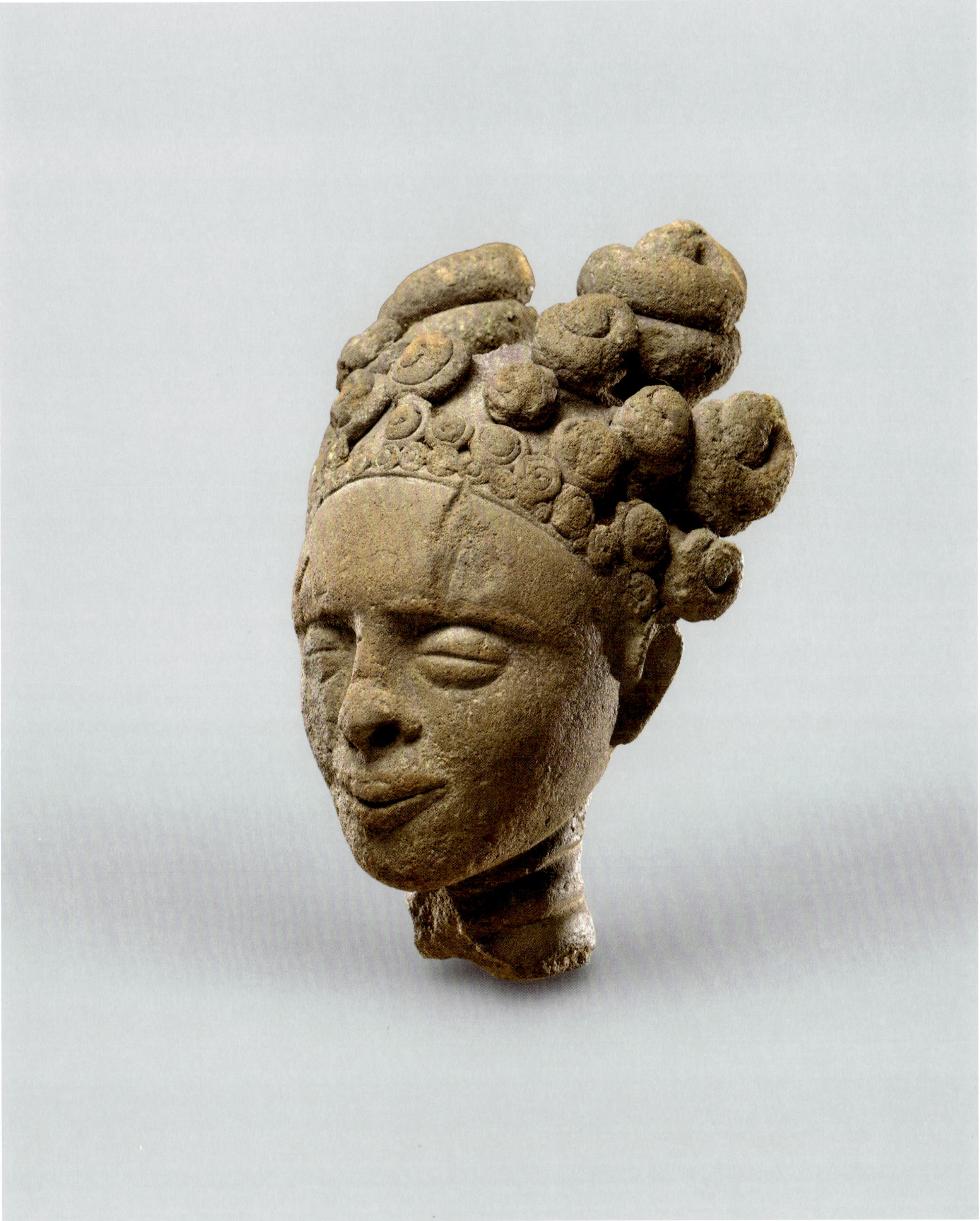

Akan (Ghana), *Commemorative Portrait Head*, c. 1900, terracotta with traces of pigment
Virginia Museum of Fine Arts, Richmond, Arthur and Margaret Glasgow Fund, 88.42
Cat. 68

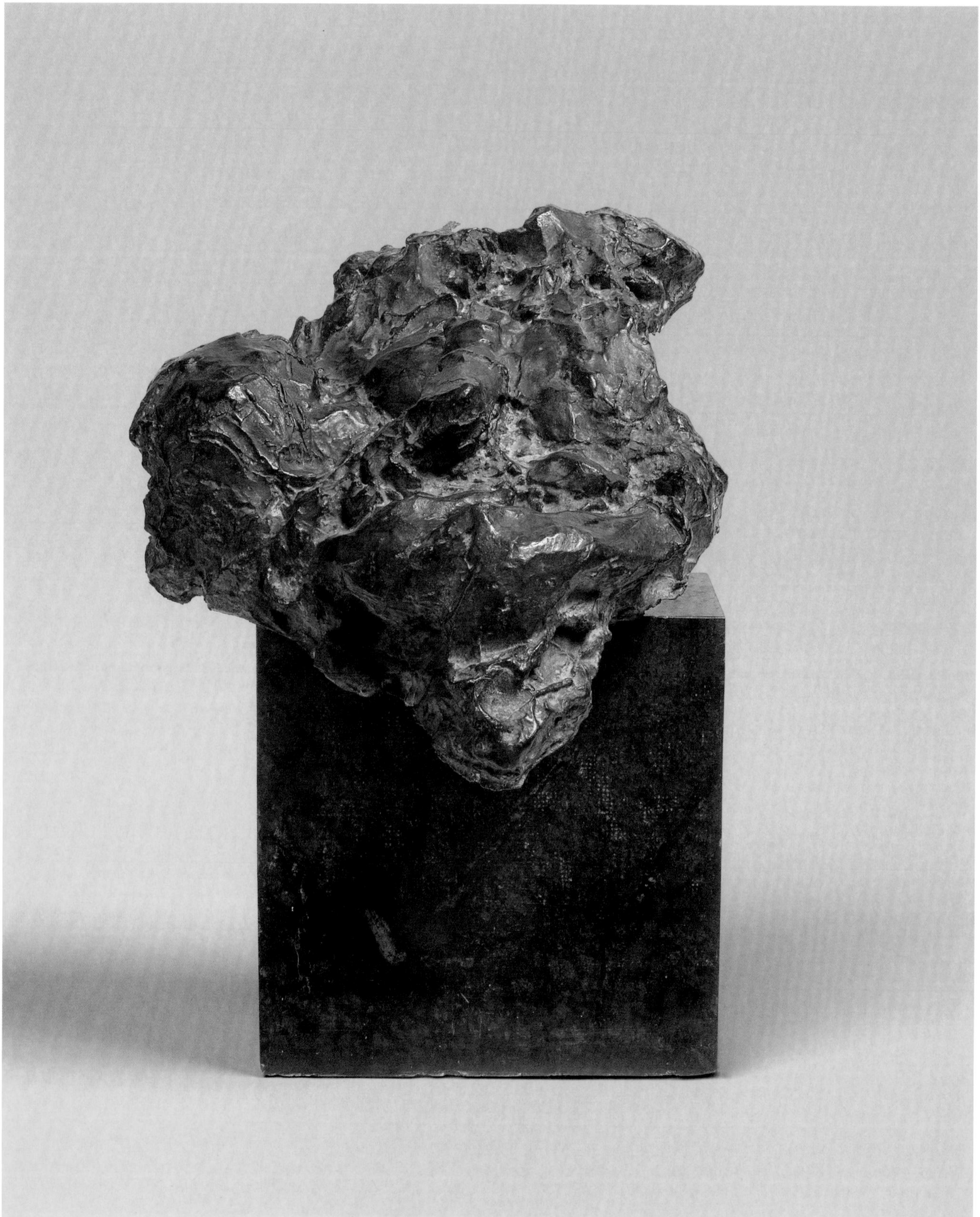

Medardo Rosso, *Enfant au sein (Nursing Child)*, 1889 (model); c. 1910–1914 (cast), bronze
Museo Medardo Rosso, Barzio, I.22e
Cat. 71

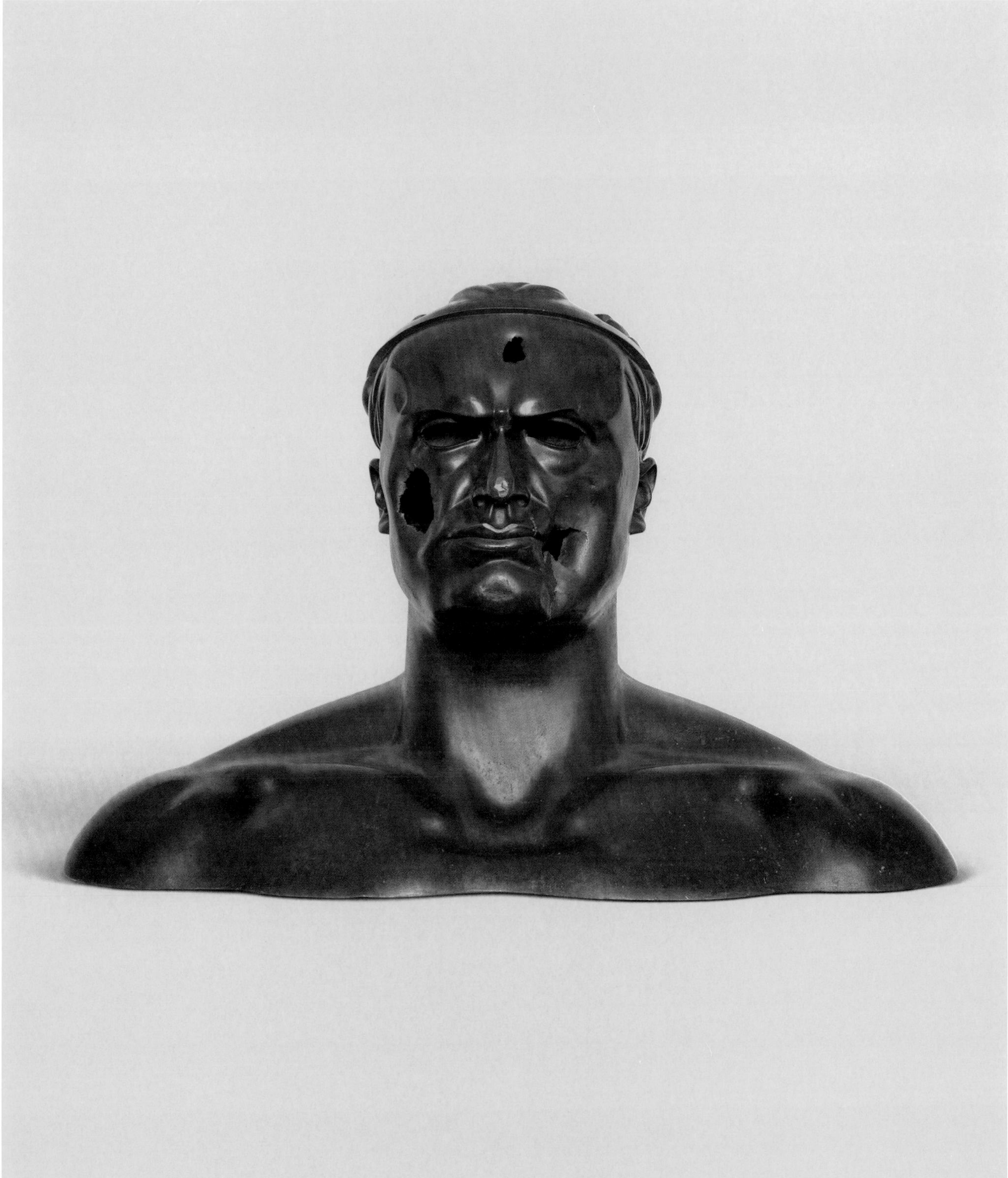

Adolfo Wildt, *Dux*, 1923, bronze
Collezione Carlo Eleuteri
Cat. 73

63 Joseph Wilton, *Tail from the Equestrian Statue of King George III*, 1770–1776
gilded lead, 20.3 × 15.2 × 72.4 cm (8 × 6 × 28 ½ in.)
The New York Historical, Purchase, 1878.6
Washington only

Attacked and destroyed on July 9, 1776, after a crowd (including Continental soldiers) had assembled around the statue, which stood on Bowling Green in Lower Manhattan, New York City.

Selected references: A. J. Wall, "The Statues of King George III and the Honorable William Pitt Erected in New York City, 1770," *New York Historical Society Quarterly Bulletin* 4, no. 2 (1920): 54; Wendy Bellion, *Iconoclasm in New York: Revolution to Reenactment* (University Park: Pennsylvania State University Press, 2019), 77–82, 97–99, 109–110, 114–122.

64 Antonio Canova, *Bust of Religion*, 1815
plaster, without rays: 81 × 43 × 35 cm (31 ⅞ × 16 15⁄16 × 13 ¾ in.)
Museo Gypsotheca Antonio Canova, Possagno, 338
Florence only

Damaged on December 25, 1917, when an Austro-Hungarian shell struck the museum during World War I.

Selected references: Mario Guderzo and Alberto Prandi, eds., *Antonio Canova: L'arte violata nella Grande Guerra / Art Ravaged in the Great War* (Milan: Silvana Editoriale, 2015), 168; Fernando Mazzocca and Gregorio Taccola, *La Grande Guerra: I luoghi e l'arte feriti* (Milan: Silvana Editoriale, 2015), 42.

65 Antonio Canova, *Bust of Terpsichore*, 1817
plaster, 52 × 27 × 23 cm (20 ½ × 10 ⅝ × 9 1⁄16 in.)
Museo Gypsotheca Antonio Canova, Possagno, 316
Florence only

Damaged on December 25, 1917, when an Austro-Hungarian shell struck the museum during World War I.

Selected references: Mario Guderzo and Alberto Prandi, eds., *Antonio Canova: L'arte violata nella Grande Guerra / Art Ravaged in the Great War* (Milan: Silvana Editoriale, 2015), 168; Fernando Mazzocca and Gregorio Taccola, eds., *La Grande Guerra: I luoghi e l'arte feriti* (Milan: Silvana Editoriale, 2015), 43.

66 Bamiléké (Bana, Cameroon), *Crest Mask (Tsesah)*, late 1800s
wood, 77 × 53 × 27.4 cm (30 5⁄16 × 20 ⅞ × 10 13⁄16 in.)
National Museum of African Art, Smithsonian Institution, Gift of Walt Disney World Co., a subsidiary of The Walt Disney Company, 2005-6-5
Washington only

Selected references: Pierre Harter, "Les masques dit 'Batcham,'" *Arts d'Afrique noir* 3 (1972): 35; Pierre Harter, entry in Susan Vogel, ed., *For Spirits and Kings: African Art from the Tishman Collection* (New York: Metropolitan Museum of Art, 1981), 182–183; Bryna Freyer and Christine Mullen Kreamer, entry in Christine Mullen Kreamer, Bryna Freyer, and Andrea Nicholls, *African Vision: The Walt Disney-Tishman African Art Collection* (Washington, DC: National Museum of African Art, Smithsonian Institution, 2007), 178–179; Yaëlle Biro, "The Canon and Its Consequences: The Reception of the Bamileke *Tsesah* Crests," *Tribal Art Magazine* 22, no. 2 (2018): 121, 124.

67 Auguste Rodin, *Group of* Abattis *(Body Parts)*, 1880–1917
plaster, dimensions range from 10.5 × 3.5 × 3.6 cm (4 ⅛ × 1 ⅜ × 1 7⁄16 in.) to 20 × 11.5 × 7.1 cm (7 ⅞ × 4 ½ × 2 13⁄16 in.)
Musée Rodin, Paris, S.01266, S.01286, S.04527, S.04983, S.05074, S.05088, S.05108–110, S.05275, S.05284, S.05500, S.05523, S.05527, S.05538, S.05553, S.05569, S.06178, S.06200, S.06260, S.06374

Selected references: Sophie Biass-Fabiani, entry in Nathalie Bondil, ed., *Metamorphoses in Rodin's Studio* (Montreal: Montreal Museum of Fine Arts; Paris: Musée Rodin, 2015), 62–63; Véronique Mattiussi, ed., *Kiefer–Rodin* (Paris: Musée Rodin; Philadelphia: Barnes Foundation, 2017), 74, 157.

68 Akan (Ghana), *Commemorative Portrait Head*, c. 1900
terracotta with traces of pigment, 30.5 × 20.3 × 14 cm (12 × 8 × 5 ½ in.)
Virginia Museum of Fine Arts, Richmond, Arthur and Margaret Glasgow Fund, 88.42

Selected references: David Bindman, Suzanne Preston Blier, and Henry Louis Gates Jr., eds., *The Image of the Black in African and Asian Art* (Cambridge, MA: Harvard University Press, 2017), 30; Richard B. Woodward, entry in Richard B. Woodward et al., *The Arts of Africa: Studying and Conserving the Collection: Virginia Museum of Fine Arts* (Richmond: Virginia Museum of Fine Arts, 2020), 96–97.

69 Baule (Lacs, N'zi Comoe, or Valle du Bandama region, Côte d'Ivoire), *Male Figure (Waka Sran)*, c. 1900
wood, 27.9 × 9 × 10.8 cm (11 × 3 9⁄16 × 4 ¼ in.)
Brooklyn Museum, Frank L. Babbott Fund, 61.3

Selected references: Susan Mullin Vogel, *African Art, Western Eyes* (New Haven, CT: Yale University Press, 1997), 8; William C. Siegmann, entry in in William C. Siegmann, ed., *African Art: A Century at the Brooklyn Museum* (New York: Prestel, 2009), 96–97; Z. S. Strother, "Les iconoclasmes en Afrique: Émergence d'un sujet d'étude," *Perspective* 2 (2018): 232.

70 Auguste Rodin, *The Walking Man (L'Homme qui marche)*, c. 1878–1900 (model); probably 1903 (cast)
bronze, 85.1 × 59.8 × 26.5 cm (33 ½ × 23 9⁄16 × 10 7⁄16 in.)
National Gallery of Art, Washington, Gift of Mrs. John W. Simpson, 1942.5.11

Selected references: Ruth Butler and Suzanne Lindsay, *European Sculpture of the Nineteenth Century* (Washington, DC: National Gallery of Art; New York: Oxford University Press, 2000), 317–320.

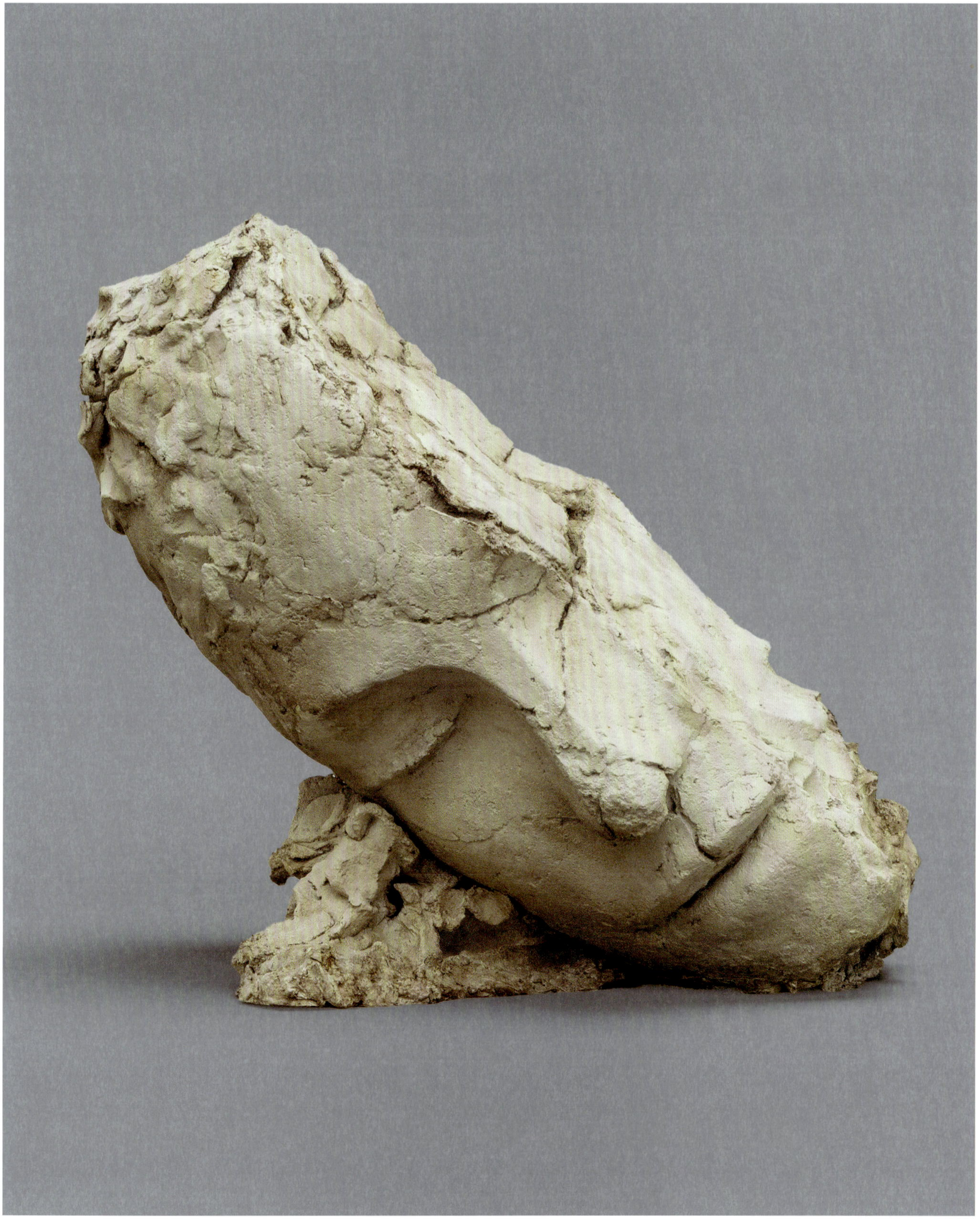

Mark Manders, *Tilted Head*, 2015–2026, painted acrylic resin and bronze, fiberglass, aluminum frame, and paper
Mark Manders Studio, Ronse
Cat. 82

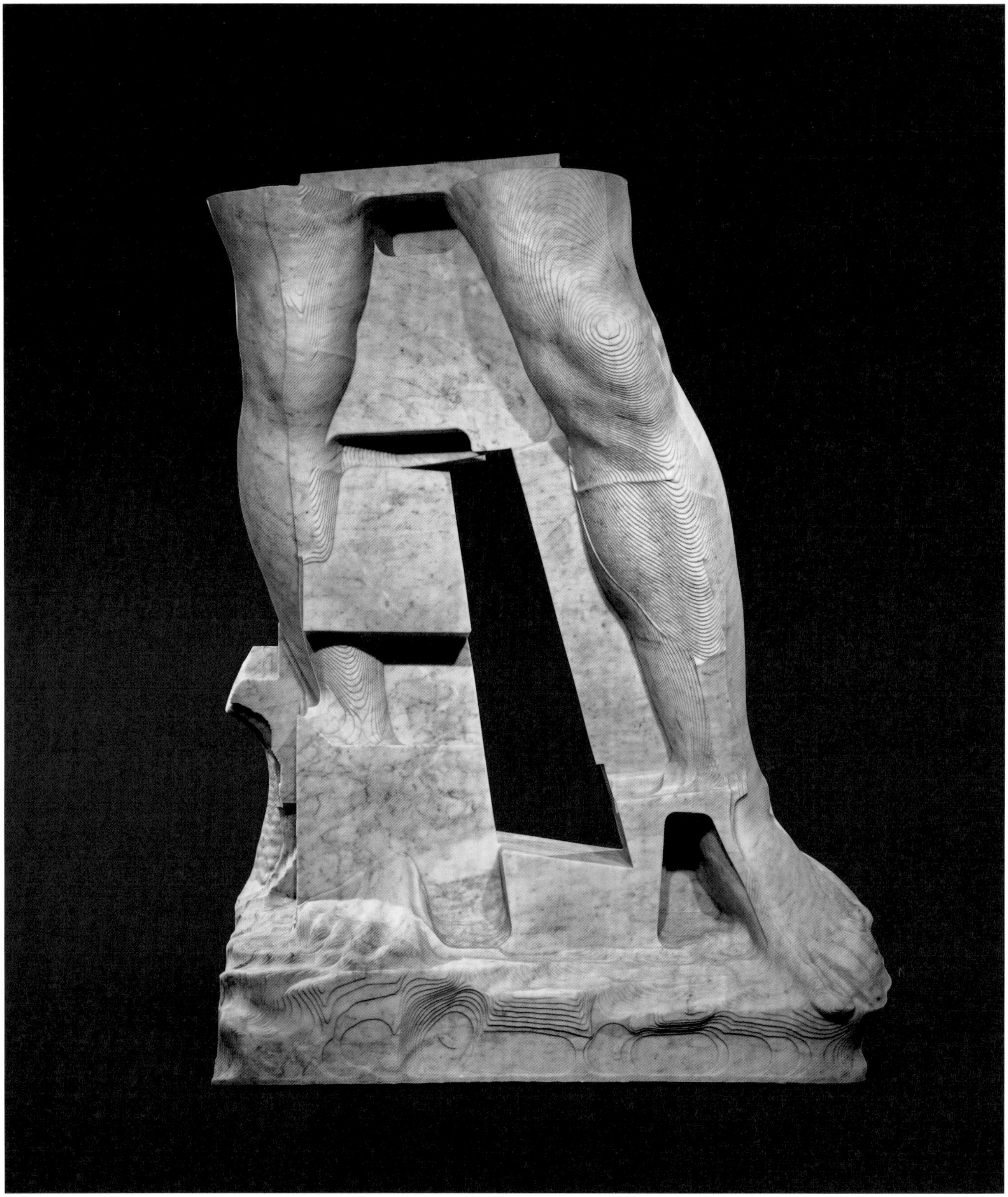

Adrián Villar Rojas, *Untitled (From the Series The Theater of Disappearance)*, 2019, interrupted robotic CNC milling reconstruction of the lower section of *David* by Michelangelo in Carrara marble
Courtesy of the artist and kurimanzutto, Mexico City / New York
Cat. 84

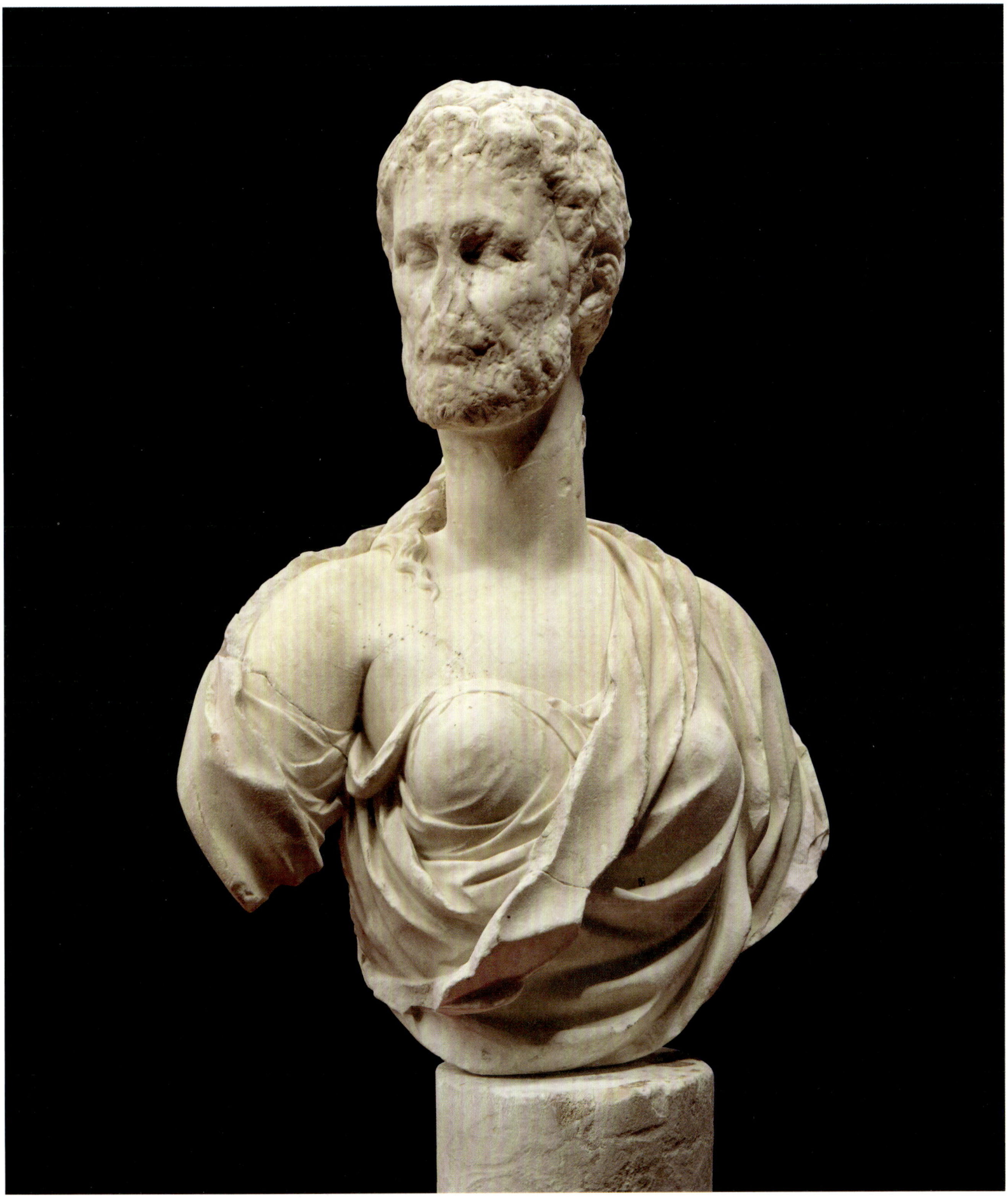

Francesco Vezzoli, *The Swan (Portrait of Marcus Aurelius with a Female Bust)*, 2023,
Roman marble head (c. 150 CE), Italian fragmentary bust (late 16th or early 17th century),
marble column, chalk, and acrylic paint
Courtesy of the artist and Galleria Franco Noero
Cat. 89

71 Medardo Rosso, *Enfant au sein (Nursing Child)*, 1889 (model); c. 1910–1914 (cast)
bronze, 50 × 45 × 20 cm (19 11/16 × 17 11/16 × 7 7/8 in.)
Museo Medardo Rosso, Barzio, I.22e
Florence only

Selected references: Paola Mola and Fabio Vittucci, eds., *Medardo Rosso: Catalogo ragionato della scultura* (Milan: Skira, 2009), 114, 272–273; Birgit Brunk, entry in Heike Eipeldauer, ed., *Medardo Rosso: Inventing Modern Sculpture* (Cologne: Verlag der Buchhandlung Walter und Franz König; Vienna: MUMOK; Basel: Kunstmuseum Basel, 2025), 333–340.

72 Camille Claudel, *Torso of a Crouching Woman*, c. 1884–1885 (model); c. 1913 (cast)
bronze, 35 × 27 × 26 cm (13 3/4 × 10 5/8 × 10 1/4 in.)
The J. Paul Getty Museum, Los Angeles, 2018.32
Washington only

Selected references: Anne Rivìere, Bruno Gaudichon, and Danielle Ghanassia, *Camille Claudel: Catalogue raisonné* (Paris: Adam Biro, 2001), 70–73; Clarisse Fava-Piz, "In Rodin's Studio," in *Camille Claudel*, ed. Emerson Bowyer and Anne-Lise Desmas (Los Angeles: J. Paul Getty Museum; Chicago: Art Institute of Chicago, 2023), 122–123.

73 Adolfo Wildt, *Dux*, 1923
bronze, 95 × 140 × 60 cm (37 3/8 × 55 1/8 × 23 5/8 in.)
Collezione Carlo Eleuteri
Florence only

Originally displayed at the Fascist headquarters in Milan (the Casa del Fascio), where it was shot three times at close range on Liberation Day (April 25, 1945).

Selected references: Fernando Mazzocca and Paola Mola, eds., *Wildt: L'anima e le forme* (Milan: Silvana Editoriale, 2012), 212, 214; Beatrice Avanzi and Daniela Ferrari, eds., *Arte e fascismo* (Rome: L'Erma di Bretschnieder, 2024), 551.

74 Constantin Brâncuși, *Torso of a Young Man*, 1924
brass, limestone, and wood, 148.6 × 29.2 × 29.2 cm (58 1/2 × 11 1/2 × 11 1/2 in.)
Hirshhorn Museum and Sculpture Garden, Smithsonian Institution, Washington DC, Gift of Joseph H. Hirshhorn, 1966, 66.611
Washington only

Selected references: Sidney Geist, *Brancusi: A Study of the Sculpture* (New York: Grossman, 1968), 59, 222; Sidney Geist, *Brancusi: The Sculpture and Drawings* (New York: Harry N. Abrams, 1975), 168, no. 159.

75 Alberto Giacometti, *La Jambe (The Leg)*, 1958
plaster with pigment, 223 × 30.3 × 46.1 cm (87 13/16 × 11 15/16 × 18 1/8 in.)
Fondation Giacometti, 1994-0347

Selected references: Véronique Wiesinger et al., *L'atelier d'Alberto Giacometti* (Paris: Centre Pompidou; Fondation Alberto et Annette Giacometti, 2007), 37, 366; Cecilia Braschi, entry in Véronique Wiesinger and Patrick Ramade, eds., *En perspective, Giacometti* (Paris: Fondation Annette et Alberto Giacometti; Lyon: Fage, 2008), 133.

76 Alina Szapocznikow, *Filozof (Philosopher)*, 1965
plaster, 137 × 25 × 31 cm (53 15/16 × 9 13/16 × 12 3/16 in.)
Courtesy The Estate of Alina Szapocznikow | Galerie Loevenbruck, Paris | Hauser & Wirth

Selected references: Allegra Pesenti, "Traces of Passage: The Drawings of Alina Szapocznikow," in *Alina Szapocznikow: Sculpture Undone, 1955–1972*, ed. Elena Filipovic and Joanna Mytkowska (New York: Museum of Modern Art; Brussels: Mercaterfonds, 2011), 100–101; Margo Norton and Pavel S. Pyś, *To Exalt the Ephemeral: Alina Szapocznikow, 1962–1972* (New York: Hauser & Wirth, 2019), 52–53; Julia Kloss-Weber, "Ponderation," in *Alina Szapocznikow: Körpersprachen/Body Languages*, ed. Ursula Ströbele and Ute Stuffer (Vienna: Verlag für moderne Kunst, 2025), 160, 164–168.

77 Paul Thek, *Untitled (Meat Cable)*, 1969
wax, paint, steel cable, and turnbuckles, dimensions variable
Tate: Presented as part of the D. Daskalopoulos Collection Gift 2023, T16080

Selected references: Irini Pari, *Contemplations of a Collector: Irini Pari in Conversation with Dimitris Daskalopoulos* (Paris: Cahiers d'Art, 2024), 280, 290–291.

78 El Anatsui, *Chambers of Memory*, 1977
ceramic and manganese, 40.6 × 27.9 × 26.7 cm (16 × 11 × 10 1/2 in.)
Courtesy of the artist and Jack Shainman Gallery, New York

Selected references: Olu Oguibe, "El Anatsui: Beyond Death and Nothingness," *African Arts* 31, no. 1 (1998): 54–55; Elizabeth Péri-Willis, "Chambers of Memory," in *El Anatsui: A Sculpted History of Africa*, ed. John Picton (London: October Gallery, 1998), 79–88; Z. S. Strother, "Iconoclasms in Africa: Implications for the Debate on Restitution of Cultural Heritage," *HAU: Journal of Ethnographic Theory* 10, no. 3 (2020): 943–944; Okwui Enwezor and Chika Okeke-Agulu, *El Anatsui: The Reinvention of Sculpture* (Bologna: Damiani, 2022), 101–102.

79 Robert Gober, *Untitled*, 1991
wax, cloth, wood, leather, and human hair, 31.3 × 26 × 95.3 cm (12 5/16 × 10 1/4 × 37 1/2 in.)
Whitney Museum of American Art, New York; Purchase, with funds from Robert W. Wilson 92.6

Selected references: Theodora Vischer, ed., *Robert Gober: Sculptures and Installations, 1979–2007* (Basel: Schaulager; Göttingen: Steidl, 2007), 284–285.

80 Fred Wilson, *Inside Story*, 1995
glazed ceramic found objects, 20.3 × 30.5 × 20.3 cm (8 × 12 × 8 in.)
Courtesy of the artist and Pace Gallery

81 Louise Bourgeois, *Foot*, 1997
fabric, metal, and plastic, 20.3 × 78.7 × 25.4 cm (8 × 31 × 10 in.)
Private collection, New York

Selected references: Marie Bernadac, Louise Neri, and Paulo Herkenhoff, *Louise Bourgeois: Oeuvres récentes* (Bordeaux: CAPC Musée d'Art Contemporain de Bordeaux; London: Serpentine Gallery, 1998), 60; Robert Storr, *Intimate Geometries: The Art and Life of Louise Bourgeois* (New York: Monacelli Press, 2016), 615.

82 Mark Manders, *Tilted Head*, 2015–2026
painted acrylic resin and bronze, fiberglass, aluminium frame, and paper, 340 × 421 × 332 cm (133 7⁄8 × 165 3⁄4 × 130 11⁄16 in.)
Mark Manders Studio, Ronse
Florence only

83 Paul Pfeiffer, *Incarnator*, 2018–present
mixed media, variable dimensions
Courtesy of the artist, carlier | gebauer, Paula Cooper Gallery, Perrotin, Thomas Dane Gallery

Selected references: Clara Kim and Paula Kroll, "Paul Pfeiffer: Prologue to the Story of the Birth of Freedom," in *Paul Pfeiffer: Prologue to the Story of the Birth of Freedom*, ed. Clara Kim (Los Angeles: Museum of Contemporary Art and MACK, 2024), 82–83.

84 Adrián Villar Rojas, *Untitled (From the Series The Theater of Disappearance)*, 2019
interrupted robotic CNC milling reconstruction of the lower section of *David* by Michelangelo in Carrara marble, 195.6 × 150 × 104 cm (77 × 59 1⁄16 × 40 15⁄16 in.)
Courtesy of the artist and kurimanzutto, Mexico City / New York
Florence only

Selected references: Thomas D. Trummer, ed., *Adrián Villar Rojas: The Theater of Disappearance* (Bregenz: Kunsthaus Bregenz, 2018).

85 Cannupa Hanska Luger, *Emergent*, 2021
ceramic, 61 × 213.4 × 152.4 cm (24 × 84 × 60 in.)
Courtesy of the artist and Garth Greenan Gallery, New York
Washington only

86 Danh Vo, *meat cables*, 2021
cupid (16th century), Roman marble (1st–2nd century CE), and Rimowa luggage, 71 × 39 × 50 cm (27 15⁄16 × 15 3⁄8 × 19 11⁄16 in.)
Courtesy of the artist and Xavier Hufkens, Brussels
ProWinko ProArt Collection

87 Danh Vo, *meat cables*, 2021
cupid (16th century), Roman marble (1st–2nd century CE), and construction wood, variable dimensions
Courtesy of the artist and Xavier Hufkens, Brussels
Florence only

88 Danh Vo, *meat cables*, 2021
cupid and column (16th century), Roman marble (1st–2nd century CE), and construction wood, 23.5 × 25 × 33.5 cm (9 1⁄4 × 9 13⁄16 × 13 3⁄16 in.)
Courtesy of the artist and Xavier Hufkens, Brussels
Private collection
Florence only

89 Francesco Vezzoli, *The Swan (Portrait of Marcus Aurelius with a Female Bust)*, 2023
Roman marble head (c. 150 CE), Italian fragmentary bust (late 16th or early 17th century), marble column, chalk, and acrylic paint, 193 × 70 × 38 cm (76 × 27 9⁄16 × 14 15⁄16 in.)
Courtesy of the artist and Galleria Franco Noero
Florence only

Selected references: Francesco Vezzoli and Stéphane Verger, eds., *Vita Dulcis* (Rome: Quodlibet, 2023), 136–137, no. 7.

90 Julius von Bismarck, *The Elephant in the Room (Otto von Bismarck)*, 2023
mixed media, 380 × 150 × 318 cm (149 5⁄8 × 59 1⁄16 × 125 3⁄16 in.)
Studio Julius von Bismarck, Berlin, alexander levy, Berlin, Sies + Höke, Düsseldorf, Max Levai, New York
Florence only

91 Huma Bhabha, *Untamed*, 2024 (edition of 3, and 1 artist's proof)
cast iron and concrete (pedestal), 139.7 × 55.9 × 55.9 cm (55 × 22 × 22 in.)
Courtesy the artist and David Zwirner

Selected references: Peter Eleey and Tausif Noor, *Huma Bhabha: Welcome . . . to the one who came* (New York: Zwirner Books, 2025), 24–29, 99–100.

92 Geumhyung Jeong, *Removed Parts: Restored*, 2027
mixed media, variable dimensions
Courtesy of the artist
Washington only

Selected references: Ruba Katrib, Annie Godfrey Larmon, Sheldon Gooch, and Serena Moscardelli, eds., *The Gatherers* (Long Island City, NY: MoMA PS1, 2025), 4, 43.

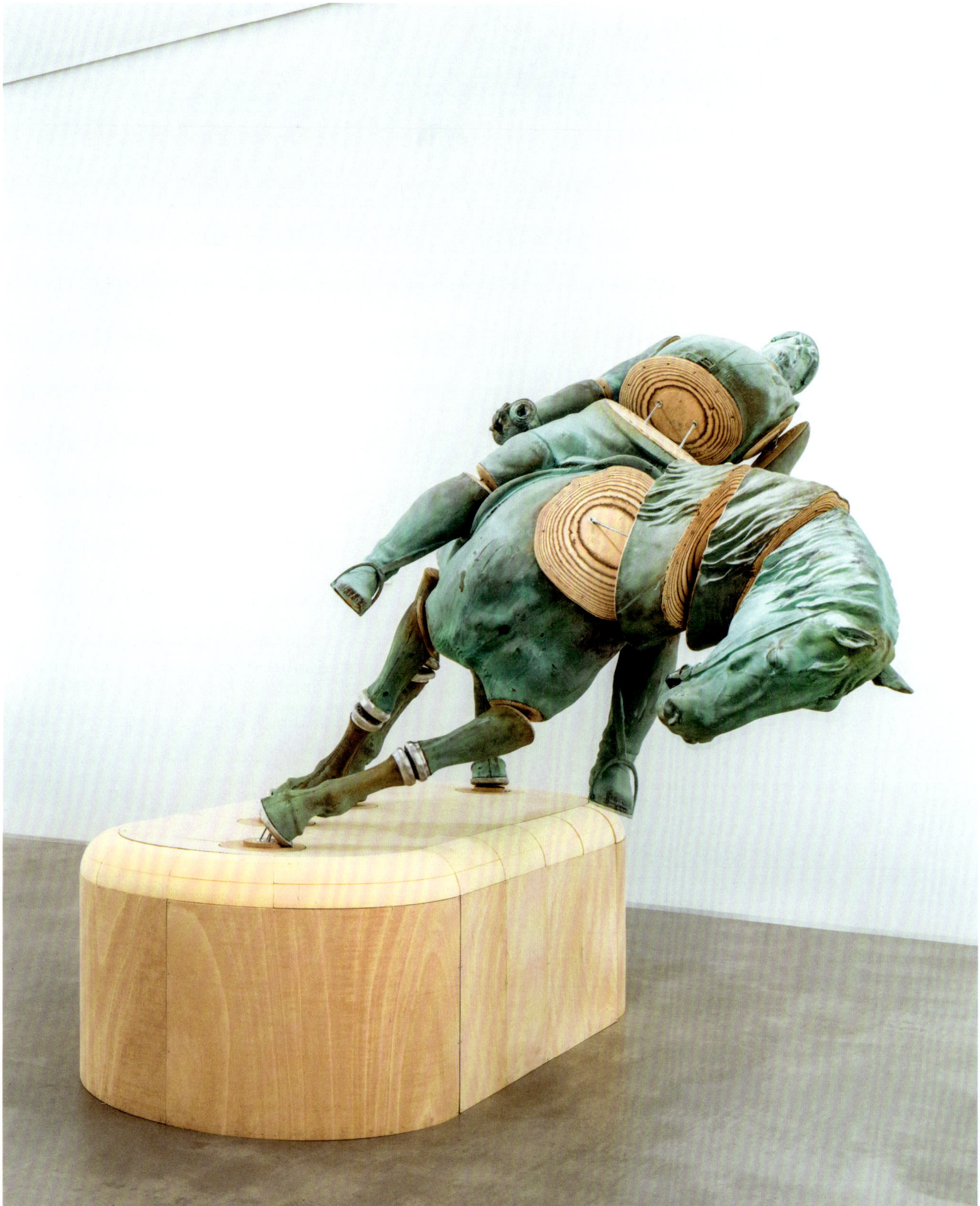

Julius von Bismarck, *The Elephant in the Room (Otto von Bismarck)*, 2023, mixed media
Studio Julius von Bismarck, Berlin, alexander levy, Berlin, Sies + Höke, Düsseldorf, Max Levai, New York
Cat. 90

SELECTED BIBLIOGRAPHY

Abe, Stanley K. *Imagining Sculpture: A Short Conjectural History*. Munich: Hirmer, 2022.

Ammaniti, Massimo, and Vittorio Gallese. *The Birth of Intersubjectivity: Psychodynamics, Neurobiology, and the Self.* New York: W. W. Norton, 2014.

Bagnoli, Martina, Holger A. Klein, C. Griffith Mann, and James Robinson, eds. *Treasures of Heaven: Saints, Relics, and Devotion in Medieval Europe*. Cleveland: Cleveland Museum of Art; Baltimore: Walters Art Museum; London: British Museum, 2010.

Bahrani, Zainab. *Rituals of War: The Body and Violence in Mesopotamia*. New York: Zone Books, 2008.

Barkan, Leonard. *Unearthing the Past: Archaeology and Aesthetics in the Making of Renaissance Culture*. New Haven, CT: Yale University Press, 1999.

Bellion, Wendy. *Iconoclasm in New York: Revolution to Reenactment*. University Park: Pennsylvania State University Press, 2019.

Bickford Berzock, Kathleen, ed. *Caravans of Gold, Fragments in Time: Art, Culture, and Exchange Across Medieval Saharan Africa*. Evanston, IL: Block Museum of Art, Northwestern University in association with Princeton University Press, 2019.

Biernoff, Suzannah. *Portraits of Violence: War and the Aesthetics of Disfigurement*. Ann Arbor: University of Michigan Press, 2017.

Bleiberg, Edward, and Stephanie Weissberg. *Striking Power: Iconoclasm in Ancient Egypt*. New York: Brooklyn Museum; St. Louis: Pulitzer Arts Foundation, 2019).

Boone, Elizabeth Hill, ed. *The Aztec Templo Mayor*. Washington, DC: Dumbarton Oaks Research Library and Collection, 1987.

Chapman, John. *Fragmentation in Archaeology: People, Places and Broken Objects in the Prehistory of South Eastern Europe*. London: Routledge, 2000.

Chapman, John, and Bisserka Gaydarska. *Parts and Wholes: Fragmentation in Prehistoric Context*. Oxford: Oxbow Books, 2006.

Chapuis, Julien, and Stephan Kemperdick, eds. *The Lost Museum: The Berlin Painting and Sculpture Collections 70 Years After World War II*. Berlin: Skulpturensammlung und Museum für Byzantinische Kunst, Staatliche Museen zu Berlin; Petersberg: Michael Imhof Verlag, 2015.

Cholidis, Nadja, and Lutz Martin, eds. *Tell Halaf V: Im Krieg zerstörte Denkmäler und ihre Restaurierung*. Berlin: De Gruyter, 2010.

Christian, Kathleen. *Empire Without End: Antiquities Collections in Renaissance Rome, c. 1350–1527.* New Haven, CT: Yale University Press, 2010.

Diagne, Souleymane Bachir, and Jean-Loup Amselle. *In Search of Africa(s): Universalism and Decolonial Thought*, translated by Andrew Brown. Cambridge, UK: Polity, 2020.

Elsen, Albert E. *The Partial Figure in Modern Sculpture from Rodin to 1969*. Baltimore: Baltimore Museum of Art, 1969.

Elsner, Jaś, ed. *Comparativism in Art History*. London: Routledge, 2017.

Feher, Michel, Ramona Naddaff, and Nadia Tazi, eds. *Fragments for a History of the Human Body*. 3 vols. New York: Zone Books, 1989.

Fiduccia, Joanna. *Figures of Crisis: Alberto Giacometti and the Myths of Nationalism*. New Haven, CT: Yale University Press, 2026.

Foster, Hal. *Prosthetic Gods*. Cambridge, MA: MIT Press, 2004.

Freedberg, David. *Iconoclasm*. Chicago: University of Chicago Press, 2021.

Gamboni, Dario. *The Destruction of Art: Iconoclasm and Vandalism Since the French Revolution*. New Haven, CT: Yale University Press, 1997.

Garland-Thomson, Rosemarie. *Extraordinary Bodies: Figuring Physical Disability in American Culture and Literature*. New York: Columbia University Press, 1997.

González Zarandona, José Antonio, Emma Cunliffe, and Melathi Saldin, eds. *The Routledge Handbook of Heritage Destruction*. Abingdon: Routledge, 2024.

Haskell, Francis, and Nicholas Penny. *Taste and the Antique: The Lure of Classical Sculpture, 1500–1900*. 3 vols. Turnhout: Harvey Miller, 2024.

Hauser-Schäublin, Brigitta, and Lyndel V. Prott, eds. *Cultural Property and Contested Ownership: The Trafficking of Artefacts and the Quest for Restitution*. London: Routledge, 2016.

Hicks, Dan. *Every Monument Will Fall: A Story of Remembering and Forgetting*. London: Hutchinson Heinemann, 2025.

Hui, Andrew. *The Poetics of Ruins in Renaissance Literature*. New York: Fordham University Press, 2016.

Kaltsas, Nikolaos, Elena Vlachogianni, and Polyxeni Bouyia, eds. *The Antikythera Shipwreck: The Ship, the Treasures, and the Mechanism*. Athens: Kapon Editions, 2012.

Klaus, Haagen D., and J. Marla Toyne, eds. *Ritual Violence in the Ancient Andes: Reconstructing Sacrifice on the North Coast of Peru*. Austin: University of Texas Press, 2016.

Kousser, Rachel. *The Afterlives of Greek Sculpture: Interaction, Transformation, and Destruction*. New York: Cambridge University Press, 2017.

Krauss, Rosalind E. *The Originality of the Avant-Garde and Other Modernist Myths*. Cambridge, MA: MIT Press, 1985.

Latour, Bruno, and Peter Weibel, eds. *Iconoclash: Beyond the Image Wars in Science, Religion, and Art*. Cambridge, MA: MIT Press, 2002.

López Austin, Alfredo, and Leonardo López Luján. *Monte Sagrado-Templo Mayor: El cerro y la pirámide en la tradición religiosa mesoamericana*. Mexico City: Universidad Nacional Autónoma de México and Instituto de Investigaciones Antropológicas, 2009.

López Luján, Leonardo, Laura Filloy Nadal, Barbara W. Fash, William F. Fash, and Pilar Hernández. "The Destruction of Images in Teotihuacan: Anthropomorphic Sculpture, Elite Cults, and the End of a Civilization." *Res: Anthropology and Aesthetics* 49/50 (2006): 13–39.

Millett-Gallant, Ann, and Elizabeth Howie, eds. *Disability and Art History from Antiquity to the Twenty-First Century*. New York: Routledge, 2022.

Morton, Timothy. *Being Ecological: With a New Preface by the Author*. Cambridge, MA: MIT Press, 2025.

Mundy, Barbara E. "Extirpation of Idolatry and Sensory Experience in Sixteenth-Century Mexico." In *Sensational Religion: Sensory Cultures in Material Practice*, edited by Sally M. Promey, 515–535. New Haven, CT: Yale University Press, 2014.

Murphy, Stephen A., Naomi Wang, and Alexandra Green, eds. *Raffles in Southeast Asia: Revisiting the Scholar and Statesman*. Singapore: Asian Civilisations Museum, 2019.

Nativ, Assaf, and Gavin Lucas, eds. *Shadow Archaeologies: In the Shadow of Antiquity or For Other Modes of Archaeological Worldmaking*. London: Routledge, 2025.

Nickel, Lukas, ed. *Return of the Buddha: The Qingzhou Discoveries*. London: Royal Academy of Arts, 2002.

Nochlin, Linda. *The Body in Pieces: The Fragment as a Metaphor of Modernity*. London: Thames & Hudson, 1994.

Parisi Presicce, Claudio. "Constantino come Giove: Proposta di ricostruzione grafica del colosso acrolitico dalla Basilica Costantiniana." *Bullettino della Commissione Archeological Comunale di Roma* 107 (2006): 127–161.

Pingeot, Anne, ed. *Le corps en morceaux*. Paris: Réunion des Musées Nationaux, 1990.

Rambelli, Fabio, and Eric Reinders. *Buddhism and Iconoclasm in East Asia: A History*. London: Bloomsbury, 2012.

Reudenbach, Bruno, and Gia Toussaint, eds. *Reliquiare im Mittelalter*. Berlin: Akademie Verlag, 2011.

Rizzolatti, Giacomo, and Corrado Sinigaglia. *Mirroring Brains: How We Understand Others from the Inside*, translated by Frances Anderson. New York: Oxford University Press, 2023.

Savoy, Bénédicte. *Who Owns Beauty?*, translated by Andrew Brown. Hoboken, NJ: Wiley, 2025.

Settis, Salvatore, ed. *Recycling Beauty*. Milan: Fondazione Prada, 2022.

Siebers, Tobin Anthony. *Disability Aesthetics*. Ann Arbor: University of Michigan Press, 2008.

Sörman, Astrid A. Noterman, and Markus Fjellström, eds. *Broken Bodies, Places and Objects: New Perspectives on Fragmentation in Archaeology*. London: Routledge, 2023.

Stewart, Susan. *The Ruins Lesson: Meaning and Material in Western Culture*. Chicago: University of Chicago Press, 2020.

Strother, Z. S. "Les iconoclasmes en Afrique: Émergence d'un sujet d'étude." *Perspective* 2 (2018): 219–246.

Summers, David. *Real Spaces: World Art History and the Rise of Western Modernism*. New York: Phaidon, 2003.

Thomson, Erin. *Possession: The Curious History of Private Collectors from Antiquity to the Present*. New Haven, CT: Yale University Press, 2016.

Tiffin, Sarah. *Southeast Asia in Ruins: Art and Empire in the Early 19th Century*. Singapore: NUS Press, 2016.

Tronzo, William, ed. *The Fragment: An Incomplete History*. Los Angeles: Getty Research Institute, 2009.

Tsiang, Katherine R. *Echoes of the Past: The Buddhist Cave Temples of Xiantangshan*. Chicago: Smart Museum of Art, University of Chicago Press, 2010

Tythacott, Louise, and Panggah Ardiyansyah, eds. *Returning Southeast Asia's Past: Objects, Museums, and Restitution*. Singapore: NUS Press, 2021.

von Oswald, Margareta, and Jonas Tinius, eds. *Across Anthropology: Troubling Colonial Legacies, Museums, and the Curatorial*. Leuven: Leuven University Press, 2020.

ACKNOWLEDGMENTS

The idea for *Broken: The Power of the Fragment in Sculpture* was seeded in 2018 during a trip to Rome with Mark Leithauser, former senior curator and chief of design at the National Gallery of Art, who had for years been keeping a list of the fragments he would love to see put into an exhibition. The pandemic provided time for research and consideration of the form an exhibition about fragments might actually take. National Gallery of Art director Kaywin Feldman has advocated strongly for the exhibition since its inception, and we are indebted to her and her fellow executives Kate Haw, Eric L. Motley, and E. Carmen Ramos for their unfailing support. Once the exhibition was approved, discussions began with the Palazzo Strozzi about partnering, and we cannot be more grateful to their director, Arturo Galansino, for championing the project from the onset. He and his team have shaped the exhibition in numerous, meaningful ways, and we are thankful for the opportunity to have worked with them—most especially with Ludovica Sebregondi, Francesca Calabretta, Linda Pacifici, and Letizia Rossello, who have been tireless in their pursuit of loans while always offering good cheer.

The exhibition would not have been possible without the public and private lenders who have generously shared works from their collections. The following curators, directors, and officials deserve our most profound thanks: Nikolaos Stampolidis and Anna Vlachaki, Acropolis Museum, Athens; Amin Jaffer, The Al Thani Collection; James Rondeau and Constantine Petridis, The Art Institute of Chicago; Soyoung Lee and Robert Mintz, Asian Art Museum of San Francisco; Nicholas Cullinan, Alexandra Green, and Thorsten Opper, The British Museum, London; Anne Pasternak, Yekaterina Barbash, Annissa Malvoisin, and Ernestine White-Mifetu, Brooklyn Museum; Cristina Acidini and Alessandro Cecchi, Casa Buonarroti, Florence; Carlotta Paola Brovadan, Direzione regionale Musei nazionali Toscana; Thomas B. F. Cummins and Juan

Antonio Murro, Dumbarton Oaks Research Library and Collection, Washington, DC; Catherine Grenier and Emilie Bouvard, Fondation Giacometti, Paris; Anthony Muroni, Fondazione Mont'e Prama—Museo G. Marongiu, Cabras; Yannick Lintz and Pierre Baptiste, Guimet—Musée National des Arts Asiatiques, Paris; Konstantinos Nikolentzos, Christina Avronidaki, Chrysanthi Tsouli, and Katerina Voutsa, Hellenic National Archeological Museum, Athens; Melissa Chiu and Anne Reeve, Hirshhorn Museum and Sculpture Garden, Smithsonian Institution, Washington, DC; Timothy Potts, Anne-Lise Desmas, and Kenneth Lapatin, The J. Paul Getty Museum, Los Angeles; Davide Quadrio, MAO Museo d'Arte Orientale, Turin; Christopher Freiherr von Oppenheim, Max Freiherr von Oppenheim Foundation, Cologne; Max Hollein, C. Griffith Mann, Diana Craig Patch, Julia Perratore, Lucretia Kargère, and Quincy Houghton, The Metropolitan Museum of Art, New York; Lionel Pernet and Sabine Utz, Musée Cantonal d'Archéologie et d'Histoire, Lausanne; Valérie Guillaume, Emmanuelle Bas, and Juliette Tanré-Szewczyk, Musée Carnavalet—Histoire de Paris, Paris; Séverine Lepape and Damien Berné, Musée de Cluny—Musée National du Moyen Âge, Paris; Laurence des Cars, Sophie Jugie, and Valérie Carpentier, Musée du Louvre, Paris; Amélie Simier, Isabelle Collet, and Chloé Ariot, Musée Rodin, Paris; Claudio Parisi Presicce and Daniela Tabò, Musei Capitolini, Rome; Barbara Jatta, Claudia Valeri, and Clara di Fazio, Musei Vaticani, Vatican City; Francesco Muscolino, Musei Nazionali di Cagliari; Daniele Federico Maras, Museo Archeologico Nazionale di Firenze; Don Enrico Grassini, Museo Aurelio Castelli, Basilica dell'Osservanza, Siena / Arcidiocesi di Siena—Colle di Val d'Elsa—Montalcino; Patricia Ledesma Bouchan and Judith Alva Sánchez, Museo del Templo Mayor, Mexico City; Mons. Marco Doldi and Maria Grazia Di Natale, Museo del Tesoro di San Lorenzo, Genova / Arcidiocesi di Genova; Marco Mozzo, Museo di San Marco, Florence; Simonetta Barboni and Paolo Persano, Museo di Sant'Agostino, Genoa; Moira Mascotto, Museo Gypsotheca Antonio Canova, Possagno; Danila Marsure Rosso and Guendalina Giannini Mochi, Museo Medardo Rosso, Barzio; Antonio Saborit, Laura del Olmo Frese, Bertina Olmedo Vera, Edgar Ariel Rosales de la Rosa, Cora María Antonieta Falero Ruiz, Gliserio Castañeda García, and Jonathan Tonatiúh Silva Pérez, Museo Nacional de Antropología, Mexico City; Luana Toniolo and Maria Paola Guidobaldi, Museo Nazionale Etrusco di Villa Giulia, Rome; Federica Rinaldi and Sara Colantonio, Museo Nazionale Romano, Rome; Pierre Terjanian and Phoebe Segal, Museum of Fine Arts, Boston; John Papadopoulos and Eirini Dimitriadou, The Museum of the Ancient Agora, Athens; John K. Lapiana and Kevin D. Dumouchelle, National Museum of African Art, Washington, DC; Chhay Visoth, Muong Chanraksmey, and Seang Sokha, National Museum of Cambodia, Phnom Penh; Rane

Willerslev, Ann Andersson, and Anne Haslund Hansen, The National Museum of Denmark, Copenhagen; Louise Mirrer and Wendy Ikemoto, The New York Historical; Gertrud Hvidberg-Hansen and Cecilie Brøns, Ny Carlsberg Glyptotek, Copenhagen; Francesco Sirano and Federica Colaiacomo, Parco Archeologico di Ercolano; Daniel Weiss and Jack Hinton, Philadelphia Museum of Art; Taco Dibbits and Frits Scholten, Rijksmuseum, Amsterdam; Andreas Scholl, Martin Maischberger, and Agnes Schwarzmaier, Staatliche Museen zu Berlin, Antikensammlung; Antje Scherner, Paul Hofmann, and Tobias Kunz, Staatliche Museen zu Berlin, Skulpturensammlung und Museum für Byzantinische Kunst; Barbara Helwing, Nadja Cholidis, and Lutz Martin, Staatliche Museen zu Berlin, Vorderasiatisches Museum; Maria Balshaw, Tate, London; Alex Nyerges and Ndubuisi (Endy) Ezeluomba, Virginia Museum of Fine Arts, Richmond; Scott Rothkopf, Kim Conaty, and Jennie Goldstein, Whitney Museum of American Art, New York; Stephanie Wiles, Ruth Barnes, and Arielle Winnik, Yale University Art Gallery, New Haven; Imelda Aguirre Mendoza, Hugo Cotonieto Santeliz, Manuel Axel Hermosillo Ramírez, and Estela Martínez Mora, Zona Arqueológica de Tamtoc, San Luis Potosí. We are also grateful to the cultural ministries of Mexico and Greece for their assistance with loans, with our special thanks going to Juan Manuel Garibay López, Miguel Ángel Trinidad Meléndez, Itzia Villicaña Gerónimo, and Josimar Fuentes of the Instituto Nacional de Antropología e Historia in Mexico and Ioanna Adamopoulou of the Ministry of Culture in Greece.

Among the private individuals who lent, we are to be able to praise several publicly: Carlo Eleuteri, John C. Weber, and ProWinko ProArt Collection. The exhibition was also granted generous loans by artists through their galleries and studios. Our thanks to alexander levy, Berlin, Sies + Höke, Düsseldorf, Max Levai, New York; carlier | gebauer, Paula Cooper Gallery, Perrotin, Thomas Dane Gallery; Lily Harants at David Zwirner; Galleria Franco Noero; Hugh O'Rourke and Julian Corbett at Garth Greenan Gallery; Emily Fayet at Hauser & Wirth (representing the Estate of Alina Szapocznikow); Tamsen Greene and Dylan Farley at Jack Shainman Gallery; Martha Reta and Natalie Espinosa Selde at kurimanzutto; Amanda Kopp-Ulanoff at Pace Gallery; Francesca Frediani and Grace Lockwood at Xavier Hufkens Gallery; Malena Cocca and Noelia Ferretti at the studio of Adrián Villar Rojas; Ginger Dunnill at the studio of Cannupa Hanska Luger; Marta Lusena at the studio of Danh Vo; Luca Corbetta at the studio of Francesco Vezzoli; Clara Stratmann at the studio of Julius von Bismarck; Simon Bultynck at the studio of Mark Manders; and Candela Bado, Angela Mewes, Kevin Reuning, and Julian Zehnder at the studio of Paul Pfeiffer. We would like to especially thank the following artists, whose insights and site visits greatly informed exhibition content and layout: Julius von Bismarck, Geumhyung Jeong, Cannupa Hanska Luger, Mark Manders, Paul Pfeiffer, Francesco Vezzoli, Adrián Villar Rojas, and Danh Vo.

Many individuals offered their assistance and insight during various stages of this project. We are deeply indebted to Salima Appiah-Duffell, Glen Adamson, Tommaso Astarita, Martin Bader, Jess Bailey, Mary Beard, Angélica Becerra, Alexis Belis, Maggie Bell, Kathleen Bickford Berzock, Monica Bincsik, Marc Bormond, Adriano Boschetti, Christine Brennan, Tamira Brennan, Peter Breunig, Dominic Bütschi, Andrew Butterfield, John Carpenter, Sarah Cash, Alban Chaine, Jacqueline Chao, Julien Chapuis, Blair Fowlkes Childs, Caitlin Clerkin, Carlyle Coash, Rachel Asbury Cole, Paul Collins, Lynne Cooke, Harry Cooper, Patrick Crowley, Lloyd de Beer, Louis de Strycker, Katie Dabin, Benjamin Diebold, Eirini Dimitriadou, Molly Donovan, Margaret Doyle, Hélène Duret, Adam Eaker, Susanne Ebbinghaus, Tae Edell, Beth Edelstein, Dylan Farley, Charlotte Ferra, Davide Ferri, Christina Fiorentzi, Kanitra Fletcher, Lola Fondbertasse, Alan Francisco, Beate Fricke, Frédérique Goerig-Hergott, Tamara Golan, Andrew Griebeler, John Guy, John Hagood, Shinji Hata, Mike Hearn, Elizabeth Honig, Ruth Horry, Anita Hosseini, Sylvia Houghteling, Meg Hughes, Aaron Hyman, Max Itzikovitz, Anna-Vasiliki Karapanagiotou, Grace Kuipers, Jessica Krauss, Alisa LaGamma, Kenneth Lapatin, Philip Larratt-Smith, David Lee, Rebecca Levitan, Alexandra Libby, Wei-Cheng Lin, Flora Lippuner, Yuri Long, Leonardo López Luján, Alison Luchs, Sonya Rhie Mace, Judith Mann, Susan Marti, Bill Martin, Rodrick McElveen, Julia Meech, Chikako Narita, Jennifer Nelson, Steven Nelson, Robert McClain, Mark McDonald, James Meyer, Simon Meynen, Iris Moon, Kerri Morgan, Nicole Myers, Megan O'Neil, Alison Oscar, Fabrizio Paolucci, Rachel Patt, Thomas Pauli-Gabi, Emily Pegues, Chloe Pelletier, James Pilgrim, Joanne Pillsbury, John Papadopoulos, Christine Quach, Fabio Rambelli, Ilona Regulski, Xavier Rey, Carolyn Riccardelli, Matthew Robb, Sasha Rossman, Neville Rowley, Caitlin Ryan, Symone Salib, Guilhem Scherf, Christine Sciacca, Jon Seydl, Hugo Shakeshaft, Alan Shapiro, Anthony Sigel, Julia Silverman, Sabine Söll-Tauchert, Emma Stein, Carol Thompson, Jean-David Touchais, Emiko Usui, Lindsey Vance, Stéphane Verger, Christina Vida, Natalia Vieyra, Ella Weiner, Bonna Wescoat, Betsy Wieseman, Aaron Wile, Sandy Williams, Keith Wilson, Maggie Wright, Beth Ziebarth, and Kathy Zurek-Doule. We would also like to thank the following chairpersons and tribal historic preservation officers for their guidance in representing Cahokian contributions to the history of fragmentation: Gail Cheatham, Kickapoo Tribe in Kansas; Lakota Hobia, Match-E-Be-Nash-She-Wish Band of Pottawatomi; Logan York, Miami Tribe of Oklahoma; Andrea Hunter, Osage Nation; Burgundy Fletcher, Peoria Tribe of Indians of Oklahoma;

and Liana "Staci" Hesler, Ponca Tribe of Indians of Oklahoma. To Isaidy Medina, who invaluably contributed as both a research assistant and thought partner throughout the planning and writing process, we are sincerely grateful. John Hobson, curatorial associate, deserves special thanks, having played no small part in helping to shape different sections of the exhibition and managing innumerable relationships. Finally, we are grateful for the help provided by the Embassy of the United States in Phnom Penh, with our special thanks to Katherine M. Diop, counselor for public affairs, and the Embassy of Italy in Washington, where Joel Melchiori, head of cultural affairs, has been pivotal on numerous fronts.

At the National Gallery of Art, the exhibition could not have happened without the enthusiasm and supreme organizational skills of Lawrence Hyman, Elizabeth Dent, and Jennifer Cipriano within the exhibitions department headed by Steven Mann. The captivating installation was created by Michael Lapthorn, chief of design, with Benjamin Butler, Jane Grigg, Donna Kirk, Jaime Lowe, Madeline Rikhoff, and Drew Watt. We are grateful to chief registrar Michelle Fondas and Melissa Stegeman, registrar for exhibitions, for managing the complex shipping logistics, and to their team of art handlers for their careful installation of the works. Conservators James Gleason and Antonia Mappin-Kasirer provided expert guidance for object care. Rachel Trinkley, Cassandra Anderson, and Mark Levitch developed the interpretative program, which includes digital in-gallery kiosks conceived and researched by Isabela Kellogg and an exhibition video produced by Scott Keiner, working with Karla Carnewal, Brian Dooda, Adam Enatsky, David Friedman, Goto McCagg, Sydni Myers, Chris Murphy, Memo Saenz, Sarah Turner, and Eileen Willis. Molli Kuenstner curated a wonderful companion exhibition for the National Gallery of Art Library drawn from its special collections. Also invaluable were contributions from several additional colleagues: Laurie Tylec, publicist; Isabelle Raval, associate general counsel, and Jessica Krauss, assistant general counsel; Paula Lynn, head of planning and evaluation, and Carolyn Bevans, audience research associate; Nick Sharp, chief digital officer; and Christina Paluvai, managing editor, brand. Thank you to our development office, led by Leslie Miller, for their support: McGowin Anderson, Giselle Obermeier, Crystal Padley, Arlene Williams, and Justina Yee.

We also wish to acknowledge the expertise and dedication of the staff of the Fondazione Palazzo Strozzi, who supported every phase of the project and were responsible not only for coordinating the Italian loans for the Florence presentation, but also for managing the loans destined for Washington. Our thanks go to President Luigi De Siervo, Honorary President Leonardo Ferragamo, and to the members of the Board of Trustees for their continued guidance and support. Our deepest thanks also go to Executive Director Antonella Loiero for her leadership. We wish to acknowledge the work of the exhibition team, whose precision and commitment ensured the successful realization of the project, particularly the contribution of Cristina Camaiti. We are equally grateful to the promotion and development team lead by Riccardo Lami, with Lavinia Rinaldi, Matthias Favarato, Alice Dainese, and Valeria Croce, for their strategic work in communication and audience engagement. Our thanks also extend to the education team, Martino Margheri and Irene Balzani, for their thoughtful and inclusive programs.

This book is the result of the devotion and hard work of many people. We thank the contributors for their passion, thoroughness, care, and guidance on working on such an interdisciplinary project. The volume was championed by Peggy Martin, chief content officer and publisher, who guided our peerless publishing team: Tracy Kompelien, Jasmine Lee, Lisa Shea, Christina Wiginton, and Emily Zoss. Manuela Bersotti, Emily Koller-Apelskog, and Barbara Wood realized an ambitious illustration program by securing images and reproductions rights. Matthew Rezac proved a magician with his design for the book, delivering a sumptuous product. We were blessed to have been assigned an extraordinary editor, Michelle Piranio, in whose debt we will remain for her good judgment and close attention to detail.

A final word is owed to our family and friends. C. D. Dickerson thanks his wife, Elyse, and children, Simon and Amelia, for their boundless support. Andrew Sears is greatly indebted to his husband, Felix, for his exacting advice and endless patience, and to his parents, Jeanie and Don.

CONTRIBUTORS

Stanley Abe is associate professor of art and art history at Duke University.

C. D. Dickerson III is dean of the Center for Advanced Study in the Visual Arts at the National Gallery of Art, Washington.

Kaywin Feldman is director of the National Gallery of Art, Washington.

Joanna Fiduccia is assistant professor of the history of art at Yale University.

David Freedberg is senior advisor to the provost, Pierre Matisse Professor Emeritus of Art History, and director emeritus of the Italian Academy for Advanced Study in America, Columbia University.

Rosemarie Garland-Thomson is professor emerita of English and bioethics at Emory University.

Dakota Hoska (Oglála Lakȟota, Pine Ridge, Wounded Knee Community) is curator of Native American and global Indigenous art at the National Gallery of Art, Washington.

Cannupa Hanska Luger (enrolled member of the Three Affiliated Tribes of Fort Berthold [Mandan, Hidatsa, Arikara] and Lakota) is an artist and cultural innovator based in Glorieta, New Mexico.

Timothy Morton is Rita Shea Guffey Professor of English and Creative Writing at Rice University.

Miriam K. Said is assistant professor of ancient art at Tufts University.

Andrew Sears is associate curator of northern European paintings at the National Gallery of Art, Washington.

A. E. Stallings is Oxford Professor of Poetry at the University of Oxford.

George Wheeler is senior scientist at Highbridge Materials Consulting in Pleasantville, NY.

LENDERS

Acropolis Museum, Athens
Adrián Villar Rojas, courtesy of kurimanzutto, Mexico City / New York
The Al Thani Collection
The Art Institute of Chicago
Asian Art Museum of San Francisco
The British Museum
Brooklyn Museum
Cannupa Hanska Luger, courtesy of Garth Greenan Gallery, New York
Casa Buonarroti, Florence
Collezione Carlo Eleuteri
Danh Vo, courtesy of Xavier Hufkens, Brussels
Direzione regionale Musei nazionali Toscana
Dumbarton Oaks Research Library and Collection, Washington, DC
El Anatsui, courtesy of Jack Shainman Gallery, New York
The Estate of Alina Szapocznikow | Galerie Loevenbruck, Paris | Hauser & Wirth
Fondation Giacometti
Fondazione Mont'e Prama—Museo G. Marongiu, Cabras
Francesco Vezzoli, courtesy of Galleria Franco Noero
Fred Wilson, courtesy of Pace Gallery
Geumhyung Jeong
Guimet—Musée National des Arts Asiatiques, Paris
Hellenic National Archeological Museum, Athens
Hirshhorn Museum and Sculpture Garden, Smithsonian Institution, Washington, DC
Huma Bhabha, courtesy of David Zwirner
The J. Paul Getty Museum
John C. Weber Collection
MAO Museo d'Arte Orientale, Turin
Mark Manders Studio, Ronse
Max Freiherr von Oppenheim Foundation, Cologne
The Metropolitan Museum of Art
Musée Cantonal d'Archéologie et d'Histoire, Lausanne
Musée Carnavalet—Histoire de Paris
Musée de Cluny—Musée National du Moyen Âge, Paris
Musée du Louvre, Paris
Musée Rodin, Paris
Musei Nazionali di Cagliari—MIC
Musei Vaticani, Vatican City
Museo Archeologico Nazionale di Firenze
Museo Aurelio Castelli, Basilica dell'Osservanza, Siena / Arcidiocesi di Siena—Colle di Val d'Elsa—Montalcino
Museo del Templo Mayor, Mexico City, Secretaría de Cultura, Instituto Nacional de Antropología e Historia
Museo del Tesoro di San Lorenzo, Genoa
Museo di San Marco, Florence
Museo di Sant'Agostino, Genoa
Museo Gypsotheca Antonio Canova, Possagno
Museo Medardo Rosso, Barzio
Museo Nacional de Antropología, Mexico City, Secretaría de Cultura, Instituto Nacional de Antropología e Historia
Museo Nazionale Etrusco di Villa Giulia, Rome
Museo Nazionale Romano, Rome
Museum of Fine Arts, Boston
The Museum of the Ancient Agora, Athens
National Gallery of Art, Washington
National Museum of African Art, Smithsonian Institution, Washington, DC
The New York Historical
Ny Carlsberg Glyptotek, Copenhagen
Parco Archeologico di Ercolano
Paul Pfeiffer, courtesy of carlier | gebauer, Paula Cooper Gallery, Perrotin, Thomas Dane Gallery
Philadelphia Museum of Art
Private collections
Private collection, courtesy of McClain Gallery
ProWinko ProArt Collection
Rijksmuseum
Royal Government of Cambodia, National Museum of Cambodia, Phnom Penh
Sovrintendenza Capitolina ai Beni Culturali, Musei Capitolini, Rome
Staatliche Museen zu Berlin, Antikensammlung
Staatliche Museen zu Berlin, Skulpturensammlung und Museum für Byzantinische Kunst
Staatliche Museen zu Berlin, Vorderasiatisches Museum
Studio Julius von Bismarck, Berlin, alexander levy, Berlin, Sies + Höke, Düsseldorf, Max Levai, New York
Tate
Virginia Museum of Fine Arts, Richmond
Whitney Museum of American Art, New York
Yale University Art Gallery
Zona Arqueológica de Tamtoc, San Luis Potosí, Secretaría de Cultura, Instituto Nacional de Antropología e Historia

INDEX

Page numbers in **boldface** refer to illustrations.

CREDITS

BROKEN HEAD OF A WOMAN

Photo: Acropolis Museum / Socratis Mavrommatis

FRAMING THE FRAGMENT

Fig. 1: Archivio Fondazione Mont'e Prama. Photo: Nicola Castangia; fig. 2: © Vanni Archive / Art Resource, NY; figs. 3, 6–7, 14: © Governorate of the Vatican City State—Directorate of the Vatican Museum. All rights reserved; fig. 4: The Master and Fellows of Trinity College, Cambridge; fig. 5: Archivio Fotografico, Fondazione Casa Buonarroti. © Foto Giusti Claudio Firenze; figs. 8–9: Courtesy Ministero della Cultura—Direzione regionale Musei nazionali Toscana—Museo Archeologico Nazionale di Firenze. © Foto Antonio Quattrone; fig. 10: R. Michelotti, 2006. © Castello del Buonconsiglio, Trento, Italy; fig. 11: Photograph by Franko Khoury; fig. 12: bpk Bildagentur / Antikensammlung / Staatliche Museen zu Berlin / Ingrid Geske / Art Resource, NY; fig. 13: © Hellenic Ministry of Culture—Hellenic Organization of Cultural Resources Development (H.O.C.RE.D.). Photo: K. Xenikakis; fig. 15: Photo: Brooklyn Museum; figs. 17–18 © Yale University Art Gallery

ENERGIES OF THE FRAGMENT

Figs. 1, 10: Image copyright © The Metropolitan Museum of Art. Image source: Art Resource, NY; fig. 2: © RMN-Grand Palais / Art Resource, NY; fig. 3: © 2026 Artists Rights Society (ARS), New York / SIAE, Rome. Image: The Solomon R. Guggenheim Foundation / Art Resource, NY; fig. 4: © The Trustees of the British Museum. All rights reserved; fig. 5: © archivio dell'arte | pedicini fotografi; fig. 6: Maggie Nimkin; fig. 7: By concession of the Ministry of Culture—Museo Nazionale Romano; fig. 8: © Musée des Beaux-Arts de Dijon / François Jay

DISMEMBERING AND REMEMBERING BODIES

Fig. 1: Human Origins Program, Dept. of Anthropology, NMNH. Photographer Chip Clark, NMNH; fig. 2: GDKE, LA-Speyer, F. Haack; fig. 3: photo by Robert Rosenswig, courtesy of Tomás Barrientos; fig. 4: Arnold Mikkelsen / The National Museum of Denmark; fig. 6: Shakado Museum of Jōmon Culture / Photographer: Akeo Tsukahara; fig. 7: © Acropolis Museum / Yiannis Koulelis; fig. 8: © Robert Gober, Courtesy Matthew Marks Gallery. Digital image © Whitney Museum of American Art / Licensed by Scala; fig. 9: © Geumhyung Jeong. Photo © Dohee Han (Studio Earlyspring)

WHAT THE FRAGMENT WANTS

Fig. 1: Staatliche Museen zu Berlin, Skulpturensammlung und Museum für Byzantinische Kunst / Mika Wißkirchen; CC BY-SA 4.0; fig. 2: Staatliche Museen zu Berlin, Skulpturensammlung und Museum für Byzantinische Kunst / Antje Voigt; CC BY-SA 4.0; fig. 3: Manuel Cohen / Art Resource, NY; fig. 4: © Sam Jinks. Image: Richard Harney; fig. 5: © Marc Quinn. Courtesy Marc Quinn Studio

PATTERNS OF DESTRUCTION

Fig. 1: © The Trustees of the British Museum. All rights reserved; figs. 2, 20: bpk Bildagentur / Vorderasiatisches Museum / Olaf M. Teßmer / Art Resource, NY; fig. 3: Photo: Brooklyn Museum; fig. 4: © Ralph Feiner; figs. 5–6 © Secretaría de Cultura—Instituto Nacional de Antropología e Historia—Archivo Digital de las Colecciones del Museo Nacional de Antropología; fig. 7: Photograph © 2026 Museum of Fine Arts, Boston; fig. 8: Image copyright © The Metropolitan Museum of Art. Image source: Art Resource, NY; figs. 9–11: © Hellenic Ministry of Culture / Organization of Cultural Resources Development (H.O.C.RE.D.); fig. 13: © Musée du Louvre, Dist. RMN-Grand Palais / Pierre Philibert / Art Resource, NY; figs. 14–15: © RMN-Grand Palais / Art Resource, NY;

fig. 16: © Musée des Beaux-Arts de Dijon / François Jay; fig. 17: CC0 Paris Musées / Musée Carnavalet—Histoire de Paris; fig. 19: Photography © The New York Historical; fig. 21: Photo: Chanraksmey Muong

FROM FRAGMENT TO FRAGMENT

Figs. 1, 3–5: Image copyright © The Metropolitan Museum of Art. Image source: Art Resource, NY; fig. 2: Image courtesy of The Metropolitan Museum of Art, New York

FRAGMENTS AND POWER

Fig. 1: Museum City of Qingzhou; fig. 2: © Askaen; fig. 3: © Fabrice Finotti; fig. 4: © The Trustees of the British Museum. All rights reserved; fig. 5: Photo courtesy of Eskenazi Ltd; fig. 6: Photograph © Asian Art Museum of San Francisco; fig. 7: © RMN-Grand Palais / Art Resource, NY

WEATHERING PAGANISM

Fig. 1: Ny Carlsberg Glyptotek, Copenhagen / Anders Sune Berg; fig. 2: By permission of the Ministry of Culture, Regional Directorate of Museums of Tuscany, Museo di San Marco. © Foto Giusti Claudio Firenze

BROKEN TO COMPLETION

Fig. 1: © Secretaría de Cultura—Instituto Nacional de Antropología e Historia—Museo del Templo Mayor—Jonathan Tonatiúh Silva Pérez; fig. 2: © Secretaría de Cultura—Instituto Nacional de Antropología e Historia—Museo del Templo Mayor—Gliserio Castañeda García; fig. 3: The Art Institute of Chicago / Art Resource, NY; fig. 4: © Secretaría de Cultura—Instituto Nacional de Antropología e Historia—Archivo Digital de las Colecciones del Museo Nacional de Antropología; figs. 5, 9: By concession of the Ministry of Culture—Museo Nazionale Romano; fig. 6: © The Al Thani Collection, 2021. All rights reserved. Photography by Matt Pia; fig. 7: Image copyright © The Metropolitan Museum of Art. Image source: Art Resource, NY; figs. 8, 11–12: © Dumbarton Oaks, Pre-Columbian Collection, Washington, DC; fig. 13: Photo: Brooklyn Museum; fig. 14: Courtesy of The Museum of Contemporary Art (MOCA). Photo by Zak Kelley

SCULPTING THE FRAGMENT

Figs. 1–3: Photo: Nick Ash; fig. 4: © The Estate of Paul Thek, courtesy Pace Gallery. Photo © Tate; fig. 6: © agence photographique du Musée Rodin, Jérome Manoukian; fig. 7: © Musée Camille Claudel / Marco Illuminati; fig. 9: © Succession Brancusi—All rights reserved (ADAGP) 2025. Rick Coulby. Hirshhorn Museum and Sculpture Garden; fig. 10: © ADAGP, Paris. Courtesy The Estate of Alina Szapocznikow | Galerie Loevenbruck, Paris | Hauser & Wirth. Photo: Thomas Barrat; fig. 11: © Succession Alberto Giacometti / Artists Rights Society (ARS), NY 2025. Courtesy Fondation Giacometti; fig. 12: © Musée Fabre de Montpellier Méditerranée Métropole / photographie Frédéric Jaulmes. Reproduction without authorization prohibited; fig. 13: © Estate of Claude Cahun. Image: The Art Institute of Chicago / Art Resource, NY; fig. 14: © The Easton Foundation / VAGA at Artists Rights Society (ARS), NY, 2026. Photo: Christopher Burke; fig. 15: © Fred Wilson, courtesy Pace Gallery. Photo: Kyle Knodell, courtesy Pace Gallery; fig. 16: © El Anatsui. Courtesy of the artist and Jack Shainman Gallery, New York; fig. 17: © Huma Bhabha. Courtesy the artist and David Zwirner. Photographer: Kerry McFate; fig. 18: Photograph by David Heald © Solomon R. Guggenheim Foundation, New York

DESTRUCTION AS CREATIVE PROCESS

Figs. 1, 5: © Cannupa Hanska Luger. Courtesy of the artist and Garth Greenan Gallery, New York; fig. 2: Photographic Archive of the Hellenic National Archeological Museum, Athens. © Hellenic Ministry of Culture—Hellenic Organization of Cultural Resources Development (H.O.C.RE.D.) / Photo: K. Xenikakis; fig. 3: © Secretaría de Cultura—Instituto Nacional de Antropología e Historia—Archivo Digital de las Colecciones del Museo Nacional de Antropología. INAH; fig. 4: Courtesy of the artist and Garth Greenan Gallery, New York

pp. 237–239: By concession of the Ministry of Culture—Museo Nazionale Romano. Photo © Azienda Speciale Palaexpo / Daniele Molajoli; p. 240: By concession of the Fondazione Torino Musei. Photo: Studio Fotografico Gonella 2026; p. 243: Photo: Luigino Visconti, Genova; p. 244: Foto Scala, Firenze; p. 245: Courtesy of the Archdiocese of Siena—Colle di Val d'Elsa—Montalcino. Photo by Bruno Bruchi; pp. 246, 250: Foto Lino Zanesco; p. 251: Photo: Travis Fullerton. © Virginia Museum of Fine Arts; p. 252: Courtesy Archivio Medardo Rosso; p. 255: © Mark Manders. Photo: © Hugard & Vanoverschelde; p. 256: © Adrián Villar Rojas. Courtesy of the artist and kurimanzutto, Mexico City / New York. Photo: Daniel Terna; p. 257: © Francesco Vezzoli, by SIAE. Photo Daniele Molajoli / Azienda Speciale Palaexpo; p. 260: Courtesy Julius von Bismarck; alexander levy, Berlin; Sies + Höke, Düsseldorf; Max Levai, New York.© Julius von Bismarck; VG Bild-Kunst, Bonn 2026. Photo: Roman März

The exhibition is organized by the National Gallery of Art, Washington, and the Fondazione Palazzo Strozzi, Florence.

Exhibition dates
Fondazione Palazzo Strozzi, Florence
September 25, 2026–January 24, 2027

National Gallery of Art, Washington
March 13, 2027–June 27, 2027

Produced by the National Gallery of Art
nga.gov

Editing by Michelle Piranio and Lisa Shea
Design by Matthew Rezac
Proofreading and indexing by Jane Friedman
Rights clearance by Emily Koller-Apelskog, Barbara Wood, and Manuela Bersotti

Chief Brand Officer and Publisher: Peggy Martin
Managing Editor: Emily Zoss
Project Editor: Lisa Shea
Art Director: Tracy Kompelien
Production Manager: Christina Wiginton
Production Associate: Jasmine Lee
Production Coordinator: Mariah Shay

Typeset in Mercure (Abyme)
Printed on Magno Volume by Conti Tipocolor, Italy

Copublished by The University of Chicago Press, Chicago and London
press.uchicago.edu

Library of Congress Control Number: 2026936956

ISBN-13: 978-0-226-85245-4 (hardcover)
ISBN-13: 978-0-226-85246-1 (ebook)
DOI: https://doi.org/10.7208/chicago/9780226852461.001.0001

Authorized Representative for EU General Product Safety Regulation (GPSR) queries: Easy Access System Europe—Mustamäe tee 50, 10621 Tallinn, Estonia
gpsr.requests@easproject.com
Any other queries:
https://press.uchicago.edu/press/contact.html

Illustration details
Cover: Roman, *Head of a Youth (Ephebe)* (p. 32)
Front endpapers: Greek (Athens), *Head of a Kouros* (p. 107); Alina Szapocznikow, *Filozof (Philosopher)* (p. 190)
Back endpapers: French (Nevers), *Head of a Female Saint* (p. 42); Camille Claudel, *Torso of a Crouching Woman* (p. 187)

10 9 8 7 6 5 4 3 2 1

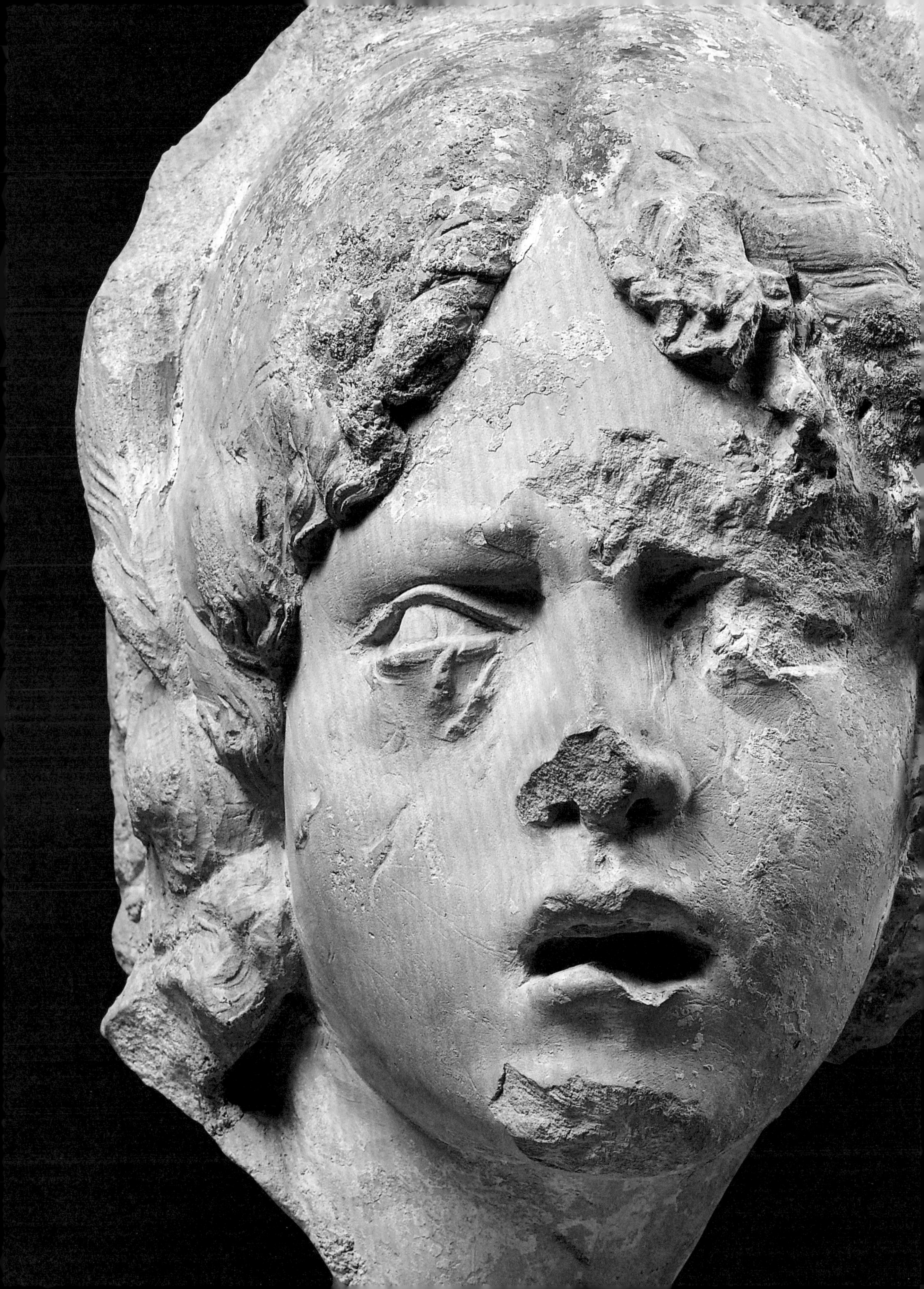

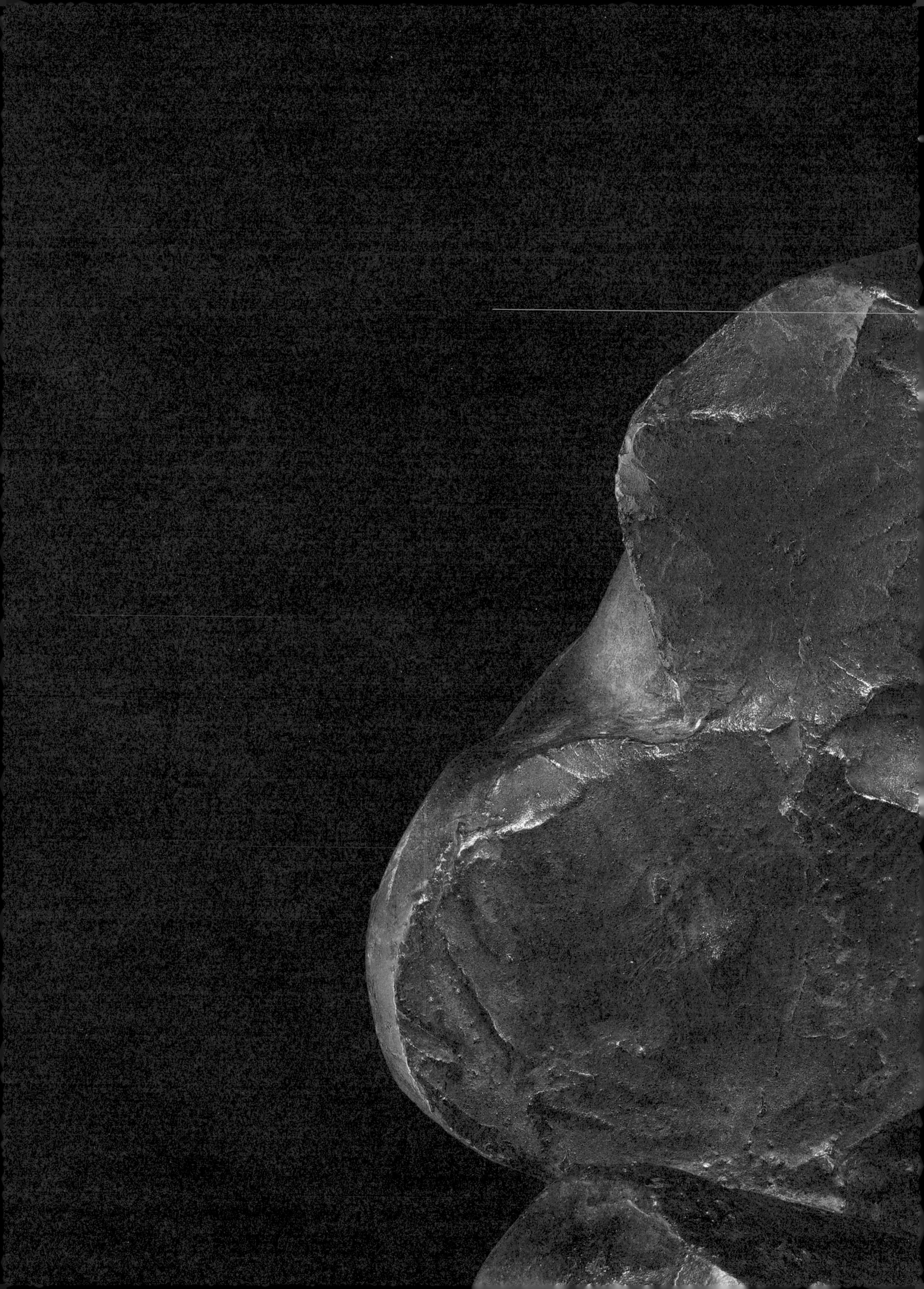